W9-CEF-409

NORTH CAROLINA

THROUGH

FOUR CENTURIES

NORTH CAROLINA

THROUGH

FOUR CENTURIES

WILLIAM S. POWELL

THE UNIVERSITY OF
NORTH CAROLINA PRESS
Chapel Hill and London

Library of Congress Cataloging-in-Publication Data
Powell, William Stevens, 1919–
North Carolina through four centuries /
by William S. Powell.
p. cm.
Bibliography: p.
Includes index.
ISBN 0-8078-1846-1 (alk. paper).
ISBN 0-8078-1850-x (text ed. : alk. paper)
1. North Carolina—History. 2. North Carolina—
Politics and government. I. Title.
F254.P63 1989   88-7691
975.6—DC19   CIP

The paper in this book meets the guidelines for permanence
and durability of the Committee on Production Guidelines
for Book Longevity of the Council on Library Resources.

Printed in the United States of America
93 92 91 90 89 5 4 3 2 1

For
Stephanie Lind Powell
James Keegan Powell
Caitlin Waldrop Powell
Charles Stevens Powell V
David Nathanael Feild

in expectation that their
lives in North Carolina
in the twenty-first century
will be as happy as their
grandfather's has been
in the twentieth

CONTENTS

Contents

Contents

21.
A Fresh Start, *404*

22.
A Time of Readjustment, *422*

23.
Great Anticipations for the Twentieth Century, *443*

24.
Down But Not Out: The State
Survives the Great Depression, *474*

PREFACE

NORTH CAROLINA has been fortunate in the twentieth century in having many good survey histories. Samuel A. Ashe in 1908, soon after the appearance of the final volumes of the *Colonial* and *State Records of North Carolina*, published the first volume of his *History of North Carolina* through the end of the American Revolution; it was followed in 1925 by a second volume bringing the account down to his own day. Ashe, a native of New Hanover County, an alumnus of the United States Naval Academy, a Confederate officer, and then a Raleigh newspaper editor, organized his history chronologically yet dealt with the government, people, society, war, religion, education, and a host of other topics. Succeeding historians of the state have generally followed the pattern set by Ashe.

A three-volume cooperative *History of North Carolina*, written by professional historians, was published in 1919. R. D. W. Connor was responsible for the volume recounting the colonial and revolutionary periods. William K. Boyd wrote on the federal and antebellum periods, while J. G. de Roulhac Hamilton covered North Carolina after 1860. This work became the standard source for information about the state's past for many years. Without actually supplanting the Connor-Boyd-Hamilton series, Connor in 1929 was the author of a two-volume work, *North Carolina: Rebuilding an Ancient Commonwealth*. Containing more detailed information yet written in a graceful style, Connor's work contributed to an even better understanding of the state's history.

In 1941 Archibald Henderson's *North Carolina: The Old North State and the New* appeared in two volumes. A mathematician rather then a historian, although he was certainly a student of history, Henderson prepared a readable account of the state that contained a great deal of new information particularly on social history. Published on the eve of World War II, this work never received the attention it might have otherwise. Because Professor Henderson strongly supported certain aspects of the state's history that others questioned, and because his work was neither annotated nor had a bibliography, it was viewed with skepticism by many professional historians.

Widely acclaimed as "Mr. North Carolina" and beloved by his students at North Carolina State College and at the University of North Carolina, Hugh T. Lefler was the author of several textbooks and survey histories of North Carolina. Read by untold thousands, Lefler's books were frequently cited to settle questions on points of state history. With his Chapel Hill colleague, Albert Ray Newsome, Lefler was coauthor of *North Carolina: The History of a Southern State* published in 1954. Revised with the addition of more current material in 1963 and 1973, it became both the standard textbook for advanced courses in North Carolina history and the reference book on the subject in homes across the state. In 1956 a two-volume version by Lefler alone, based largely on the 1954 work but with additional material in some places, appeared in a small edition.

North Carolina: The History of a Southern State was written in the late 1940s and early 1950s; its second author, Newsome, died in 1951. Although each of the three editions was reprinted many times, the heart of the work in its final 1987 printing was virtually unchanged from that issued almost thirty-five years earlier. The pressing needs of instructors and students, as well as the general reader, for a new work became more urgent as time passed. The increasing availability of new source materials in the flourishing archives and manuscript collections of the state, the constant appearance of significant articles in scholarly journals, the large number of theses and dissertations on North Carolina subjects, and above all the new specialized books on all aspects of the state's history shed new light on North Carolina's past. The contemporary scene also changed dramatically in the last quarter of the twentieth century with the growth of industry, a new relationship between the state and federal governments, the influx of "outsiders," and altered race relations. It was widely recognized that the time had come for a totally new history of the state.

In accordance with Lefler's wish expressed some years before his death, the University of North Carolina Press, publisher of the Lefler-Newsome book since its inception, asked me to undertake such an assignment. This provided an opportunity to review what I had said in my own North Carolina history classes since 1964, to reconsider notes I had made and filed away over many years, and to undertake some fresh research and reading. Most importantly, it led me to think more about the immediate past and to attempt in my own mind to account for certain things about the state today. While much that has been written about our history since the days of Ashe, Connor, and other authors remains valid, it has now become possible to understand more clearly the consequences of some of the turns the state took many years ago. We now know more about when and why decisions were made, who the responsible people were, and sometimes even what lay behind their actions. These fresh interpretations as well as modern methods of computing statistics reveal much of interest about our past that is new. *North Carolina through Four Centuries* may serve to explain to Tar Heels, old-timers as well as newcomers, what has brought us to our present state.

In preparing to write this new book, my first step was to seek the advice of a number of my colleagues across the state who have taught North Carolina history at the college level. I requested their guidance both as to what changes were desirable in the topics covered in the Lefler-Newsome volume and what entirely new topics should be included. I asked what they felt should be stressed and what omitted. They also were consulted as to organization and length of the book. Each of them responded in considerable detail, and I attempted to comply with their counsel as fully as I could. This book, I hope, meets the basic needs that they defined. To each of them I have expressed my gratitude; but on the chance that one or more of them might not be entirely pleased with what I have produced, they shall remain anonymous for the present. I am, however, indebted to Lindley S. Butler, Jerry C. Cashion, and Robert F. Durden for their careful reading of the entire manuscript and for their valuable suggestions. In the North Carolina Collection at the University of North Carolina, H. G. Jones, Alice Cotten, and Jeffrey Hicks provided advice and sources to help answer my questions, as did William S. Price and George Stevenson at the State Archives. At the University of North Carolina Press, David Perry went beyond the call of duty as an editor and helped me to see portions of my work that needed expanding. Also at the Press, Stevie Champion's skill as copy editor improved my manuscript greatly; her penetrating questions often sent me back to the sources. My wife, Virginia Waldrop Powell, gave me the benefit of her trained eye in discovering unclear passages in my prose. To one and all go my thanks for their help and interest and a blanket pardon to each from any share of the criticism that may be leveled at this work.

William S. Powell
Chapel Hill, North Carolina

NORTH CAROLINA

THROUGH

FOUR CENTURIES

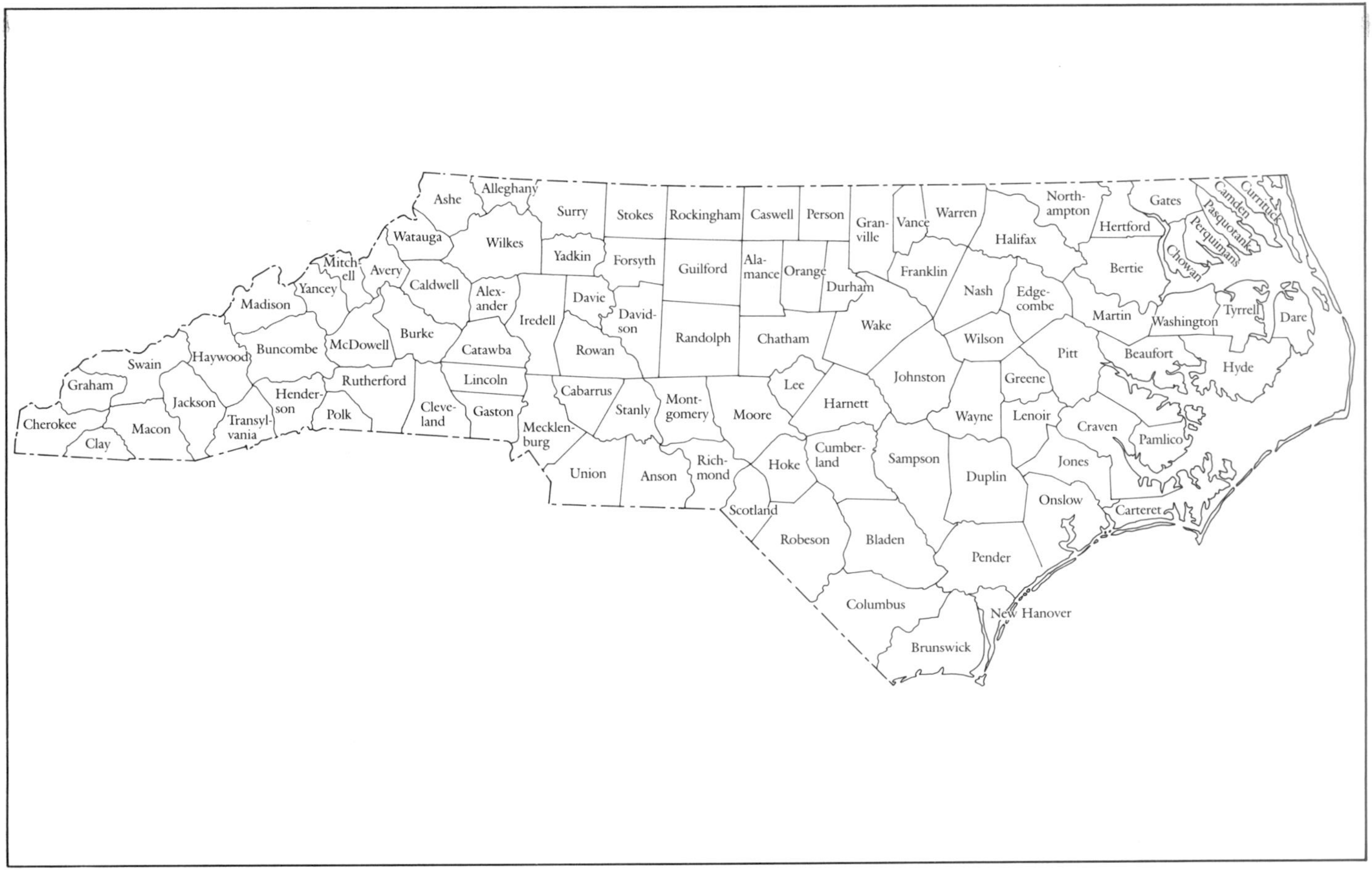

Map 1. North Carolina Counties

I

NATURAL FEATURES
AND NATIVE PEOPLES

THE VARIED features of the land in North Carolina have had a pronounced effect on its development. The state is usually described as being composed of three regions: the Coastal Plain, the Piedmont Plateau, and the Mountains. Each of these has a distinct history, and only in recent years have social and economic factors created a unifying force sufficient to overcome the differences and divisions long attributed to geographic influences.

One of the South Atlantic states, North Carolina is bounded on the north by Virginia, on the west by Tennessee, on the south by Georgia and South Carolina, and on the east by the Atlantic Ocean. It contains 52,712 square miles of which 49,067 are land and 3,645 are water, and ranks twenty-eighth in size among the states. From east to west North Carolina is slightly more than 500 miles, while at its widest point it is 188 miles from north to south. In elevation the range is from sea level on the Outer Banks at the Atlantic Ocean to 6,684 feet at Mount Mitchell, the highest peak east of the Mississippi River. It lies between latitudes 33°27'37"N and 36°34'25"N, and longitudes 75°27'W and 84°20'W.

The Coastal Plain

The broad, flat region of eastern North Carolina extends inland from the ocean for 100 to 150 miles and covers nearly 21,000 square miles. It is part of the vast coastal plain extending from New York southward down the Atlantic coast and around the Gulf of Mexico. The eastern limit of this region in North Carolina is the chain of long, narrow, sandy islands called the Outer Banks, extending from the Virginia state line to Bogue Inlet at the mouth of White Oak River on the Carteret-Onslow county line. The Outer Banks are separated from the mainland by several wide but shallow sounds. At Cape Hatteras, a little south of the midpoint of the Outer Banks, the land juts farther east into the Atlantic than at any other point on the North American continent south of Delaware Bay. The warm currents of the Gulf Stream in the Atlantic give Cape Hatteras and other

This early twentieth-century view of the North Carolina coast made by Bayard Wootten probably differs little from the isolated scene that greeted the earliest explorers of the region. (North Carolina Collection, University of North Carolina at Chapel Hill)

portions of these Outer Banks a milder winter climate than they otherwise would have.

The Outer Banks are more than 175 miles long, and until the twentieth century, when bridges and paved highways were built, they were accessible from the mainland only by boat. Inlets through which water from some of the state's rivers enters the ocean are frequently changed by storms. From north to south the most important inlets are Oregon and Hatteras, both opened by a hurricane on 7 September 1846, and Ocracoke which has been known since the days of the earliest explorers, although its exact location has shifted slightly with passing storms.

Of the sounds, Pamlico is the largest of the bodies of water between the Outer Banks and the mainland. It is approximately 80 miles long and ranges in width from 15 to 30 miles. It is the largest sound on the eastern coast of the United States, while Albemarle Sound is approximately 52 miles long and 5 to 14 miles wide. Other sounds in this section are Bogue, Core, Croatan, Currituck, and Roanoke.

The mainland of eastern North Carolina is level, marked by numerous swamps and lakes, and drained by many rivers and small streams. The soil is generally fertile black loam, moderately easy to farm and relatively productive.

The swamps and cypress trees on the shore of Albemarle Sound were typical of much of eastern North Carolina and suggest the difficulty of passage from one part of the colony to another. (North Carolina Collection, University of North Carolina at Chapel Hill)

Much of this region is less than 20 feet above sea level, but along its western limits it may rise to 500 feet. The strip of eastern counties where the altitude seldom exceeds 30 feet above sea level is sometimes referred to as the Tidewater Region.

Along the South Carolina border an area of the Coastal Plain is somewhat higher than the adjacent section. It is called the Sandhills and covers most of Richmond, Moore, and Hoke as well as portions of Cumberland, Harnett, Montgomery, Scotland, and Lee counties, reaching an elevation of around 300 feet. In this area the pleasant winter climate has contributed to the development of Southern Pines, Pinehurst, Aberdeen, and other communities as winter resorts.

The Coastal Plain is drained by several important rivers. Flowing into the sounds are the Chowan, Roanoke, Tar-Pamlico, and Neuse rivers. The short White Oak and New rivers flow directly into the Atlantic. The Cape Fear River, formed in the Piedmont by the junction of the Deep and Haw rivers, flows through southeastern North Carolina into the Atlantic. A well-traveled waterway since the early eighteenth century, this is the state's busiest river.

Natural lakes abound in this section of the state. In the northeast are Lake Phelps and Lake Mattamuskeet, the latter being the largest in the state with an area of 30,000 acres. Great Lake in the central east and Lake Waccamaw, White Lake, and Black Lake in the southeast are among the largest. The last three lie in an area marked by numerous smaller lakes as well as peat beds that once were lakes. Known as the Carolina Bays and particularly impressive when seen from the air, these elliptical-shaped features are believed to have been formed in prehistoric times by a shower of meteorites that pushed up a rim of sand along their southeastern rim. They are unique to this area along both sides of the line between the two Carolinas.

Eastern North Carolina, the earliest settled portion of the colony, was the scene of considerable growth as settlement pushed from north to south. After the Revolutionary War, however, the backcountry began to surpass the Coastal Plain in population and industry.

The Piedmont Plateau

The Piedmont section of North Carolina covers about 22,000 square miles. It is marked on the east by gently rolling hills with an elevation of around 500 feet and extends west to the foothills of the Blue Ridge Mountains with an elevation of around 1,500 feet. It is part of a broad belt extending from southern New York to northern Georgia. The soil of the Piedmont is frequently a sticky red clay when wet or hard and sometimes powdery dust when dry. Rocks of varying size, even up to large immovable boulders, are common here. Farmers have found the soil in the Piedmont to be more difficult to work and usually less fertile than that of the east; as a result, farms traditionally have been smaller here.

Rivers and other streams of the Piedmont often flow through deep cuts made in the clay soil. Their steep banks sometimes fill rapidly during heavy rains when excess water drains off the surrounding countryside. The chief rivers of this section are the Catawba and the Yadkin–Pee Dee, both of which rise in the mountains and flow southeast into South Carolina. Many smaller streams, swift and shallow, have been dammed to produce waterpower to operate mills. Numerous gristmills sprang up in the Piedmont soon after settlers arrived, and the first cotton mill south of the Potomac River was erected in Lincoln County on the banks of a small stream which provided ample power.

Dams erected on the rivers and streams of the Piedmont in the twentieth century impounded waters that made large lakes of considerable importance for recreation, flood control, or the production of hydroelectric power. Among them are Lake Gaston, Kerr Lake, Lake Hickory, Lake James, and Lake Norman. The face of the Piedmont has been changed from a country of small farms to a growing industrial region. The Piedmont Crescent extending from Wake County on the east through the cities of Raleigh and Durham and across Orange,

Alamance, Guilford, Randolph, Forsyth, Davidson, Rowan, Cabarrus, Mecklenburg, Gaston, and Lincoln counties is an almost continuous strip of industrial activity through the heart of the Piedmont.

The Piedmont also is marked by some unusual features. The Uwharrie Mountains extending northeast-southwest across Montgomery, Randolph, and Stanly counties have peaks rising to nearly 1,800 feet above sea level. Kings Mountain in Cleveland and Gaston counties extends down into South Carolina, but its highest point, The Pinnacle, at the northern end, has an altitude of 1,705 feet. A few miles away in Burke, Cleveland, and Rutherford counties are the South Mountains with several impressive peaks, the tallest of which is High Peak with an altitude of 2,720 feet. In the Sauratown Mountains of Stokes County, Moore's Knob is 2,579 feet. Pilot Mountain in southeastern Surry County, an isolated peak standing alone in generally flat country, is 2,700 feet above sea level, but it stands 1,500 feet above the countryside, serving as a landmark, a "pilot," visible from a great distance away.

While North Carolina was still its colony, England recognized the Piedmont as a potential source of profit. In 1767 an English writer described it as being more fruitful and healthy than the east; once "peopled and secured," he predicted, it would become a significant part of the "British dominions" and of "service to the nation." From this region, he believed, would come people to settle up the Mississippi and across the continent to "the territories of the Ohio." Time proved him correct, but only after independence was achieved.

The Mountains

The mountainous region of western North Carolina covers approximately 6,000 square miles and ranges in elevation from around 1,500 feet on the east to 6,684 feet a few miles northeast of Asheville at Mount Mitchell. In North Carolina this region is about 200 miles long and ranges in width from 15 to 50 miles. The mountains here are a part of the Appalachian system, which extends from Canada into northern Alabama but attains its greatest height and mass in North Carolina. The eastern limit of the section is marked by the Blue Ridge, the eastern continental divide, while the Great Smoky Mountains mark the division between North Carolina and Tennessee on the west. The average elevation of the Blue Ridge is 4,000 feet, but there are passes that sink as low as 2,000 feet above the level of the Piedmont. There are 49 peaks in the state's mountains with an elevation in excess of 6,000 feet, and 174 exceed 5,000 feet; hundreds are between 4,000 and 5,000 feet. In many areas this is extremely rugged country marked both by the main ridge running northeast-southwest and by lesser spurs shooting off to the east and west from them. On the streams of the mountains occur

A view in the mountains of western North Carolina with an unimproved variety of corn in the foreground, an old-fashioned apple tree on the right, and some wildflowers in the lower right corner. This photograph was made in the early twentieth century by Bayard Wootten, noted North Carolina artist-with-a-camera. (North Carolina Collection, University of North Carolina at Chapel Hill)

numerous waterfalls, many of which have intriguing names such as Bear Wallow, Raven Cliff, Bridal Veil, Whitewater, Soco, and Cullasaja. In some cases the water of these falls plunges into a deep pool over 1,300 feet below, while others tempt the visitor to slide down the smooth rock over which the water glides.

Rainfall on the eastern slopes of the Blue Ridge drains into the Atlantic Ocean through streams which rise in that region. Most of them then flow through the Piedmont and across South Carolina where they enter the Atlantic Ocean. On the western slopes water drains into the Gulf of Mexico through tributaries of the Mississippi River that rise in the mountains of western North Carolina. Chief among these are the Hiwassee, Little Tennessee, French Broad, Nolichucky, Pigeon, Elk, and Watauga rivers. The New River, however, formed

With Mount Pisgah in the distance on the Buncombe-Haywood county line, gently sloping grassland on the right, and a field on the left enclosed by a rail fence, this nineteenth-century view was intended to suggest that western North Carolina was a region of great beauty. (North Carolina Collection, University of North Carolina at Chapel Hill)

on the Ashe-Alleghany county line, flows north; it is said to be the only large river in the United States to flow in this direction.

Many valleys formed by the mountain streams are deep and narrow, and of the numerous waterfalls many are high and spectacular. The narrow defile through which Linville River flows in northwestern Burke County has been acclaimed the wildest gorge in the eastern United States. The New River, so called because it was discovered comparatively recently, is also in a wild and isolated section in the northwestern corner of the state. It is considered to be the second oldest river in the world, next after the Nile. In its waters and along its banks live fish and plants not known elsewhere.

With the creation of the Tennessee Valley Authority in 1933, many rivers of the North Carolina mountains were harnessed for the production of electricity. Among the lakes formed by dams are Chatuge, Fontana, and Hiwassee. Numerous smaller ones, some formed prior to 1933, also dot the region. In addition to power, these waters provide the means of flood control, recreation, and excellent fishing, and are sources of municipal water.

Many of the peaks in the Great Smoky Mountains are marked by balds. These are areas without trees, sometimes several thousand acres in size, usually above the 5,000-foot mark, and covered with thick native grass. The soil is black and deep, and almost invariably small springs may be found near the edges. No satisfactory explanation of the origin of the balds has been presented, but often landslides, fires, storms, and the direction of the prevailing winds have been credited with their formation.

The mountains were first explored by Europeans when a Spanish expedition under Hernando de Soto arrived in 1540. He reported the area to be pleasant and spent a month resting his horses and enjoying the hospitality of the natives. The region has been a popular resort since it first became accessible by road and rail. Many visitors enjoy the mild summer climate, long climbing expeditions, and the search for wildflowers and gemstones. The Appalachian Trail, a noted hiking route, passes through the region and brings many visitors as does the lure of ski slopes and some noted caves, particularly Linville Caverns and Bat Cave.

The Influence of Geography

A North Carolina historian, Christopher Crittenden, once wrote: "When Nature came to design the topography of eastern North Carolina, she almost persuaded herself to create a great maritime center." But this she did not do. The inlets and sounds along the coast are shallow and shifting. Nature intended instead that North Carolina should be first an agricultural region—soil and climate dictated this. Sources of power spurred the later development of industry in the backcountry, settled about a century later.

The lack of good harbors meant that few settlers would come directly to North Carolina from abroad. Many made their way to the Carolina frontier from Charles Town,[1] Norfolk, or Philadelphia, if they were recent arrivals from England or the Continent. Most, however, had been born and spent a part of their life in one of the other colonies (or states).

The course of the rivers in the Piedmont channeled traffic, which used their waters or the roads along their level banks, not to the towns of the Coastal Plain but into South Carolina. The Dan River carried trade into Virginia. The lack of deepwater ports along the coast forced the delivery of much produce to the markets of Virginia and South Carolina. Isolation and sectionalism played important roles in the development of North Carolina. Sectional conflicts occurred in the colony several times. Hardly a movement or an event can be described without reference to geographic factors.

Geology

The state consists of only two basic geologic regions. The eastern region coincides with the Coastal Plain where the soil is composed of sand and a black clay varying in thickness from ten to forty feet in belts ten to fifteen miles wide.

1. This important center of commerce, government, and culture on the Atlantic coast of South Carolina continued to use this form of its name until 1793, when it was incorporated as Charleston.

Examination of the subsurface reveals "marine terraces" underlying the region. Seven of these terraces exist in the state. Each was once the coastline. Evidence of these terraces can be seen in the steep banks of the Cape Fear River near Fayetteville, the Neuse River between Goldsboro and Kinston, and the Roanoke River east of Scotland Neck. These terraces began to be formed around 125 million years ago.

As the sea retreated, pockets of water remained and to these marine life retreated. The water finally evaporated or seeped into the earth, leaving shells and bones to form marl beds. Such beds exist in at least twenty-five Coastal Plain counties, and they have long been a source of lime for farms in the region. For generations, children in many parts of eastern North Carolina have delighted in finding sharks' teeth along the banks of many streams after heavy rains washed away the topsoil.

The Piedmont and Mountain regions comprise the second geologic region. Mountains once covered much of the Piedmont and their worn-down remains are known as the Uwharrie, Kings, and Pilot mountains. Some of the mountains that once existed in the Piedmont were formed by volcanic action. Many hills in Orange, Caswell, and Granville counties were formed in this manner. The Piedmont and Mountain sections, as they now exist, are the result of some 500 million years of evolution.

In addition to the shells and bones and the sharks' teeth, other fossils have been found throughout the state; these reveal much about the region in ancient times. Among the very oldest fossils discovered in North Carolina are a few teeth and bones, including jaws, of mammal-like reptiles from the Triassic period, 180 million years ago, in the Dan River and the Deep River basins. By the Cretaceous period, which began around 125 million years ago, magnolia, sassafras, poplar, and fig trees were growing here. These are among the oldest plant fossils found in the state. By the end of this period, 60 million years ago, the area was covered with the hardwoods commonly known today. There also were evergreens, as well as sedges and grasses.

In 1967, near Gulf in Chatham County, remains were discovered of at least four prehistoric animals from an era that began 180 million years ago. One was a crocodile-like reptile; another resembled an ox but with a turtle-like beak and three eyes. The third was an armored lizard with spikes similar to cow horns down its back, and the fourth was a dinosaur about twenty-five feet long.

Highly specialized dinosaurs and duckbills existed here, in addition to various flying and marine reptiles and marsupials, one of which was remarkably similar to modern opossums. Mastodons and mammoths roamed the swamps and woods of eastern North Carolina, while whales, porpoises, and dolphins, still swimming in the coastal waters off the state, were there at least 25 million years ago.

Soil

Heat, cold, rain, and wind operating on the geologic material and organisms, mainly plant life, have produced the covering soil of North Carolina. Geologic differences between the Coastal Plain and the Piedmont-Mountain sections account for the differences in the soil. Basically the latter two have similar soils, but the cool and moist climate of the mountains has had some influence on the type of soil found there.

The Coastal Plain, evolving in more recent geologic times, was never a mountainous region, and overlying the basic rock core is a sedimentary soil left as the sea retreated and as rivers and rains washed pulverized particles from the interior over it. The soil here is fine, often containing much sand mixed with clay. Drainage in many places has been poor and decaying plant life has been added to the soil. This has given a gray to dark gray color to much of the soil of eastern North Carolina. Some of it, however, is tinged red with iron oxide or, in well-drained areas, bleached white. The surface soil in this section is between ten and thirty-six inches deep, overlying the subsoil of sandy clay.

Most of the surface soil in the Piedmont is more than thirty-six inches deep over a bed of rock. It is composed of clay with a red, reddish-yellow, or yellow color in most areas, but in sections where drainage is not good it may have a gray color.

The Mountain soil is similar to that of the Piedmont, but it is usually less than thirty-six inches deep. The colors generally are brown to reddish brown. In both the Mountain and Piedmont sections the surface is frequently marked by numerous rocks.

Minerals

More than three hundred kinds of rocks and minerals are known to exist in North Carolina. This represents a large potential mineral wealth and is probably the greatest number found in any state. More than seventy of these have economic value and about fifty have been produced in commercial quantities.

The Coastal Plain is a source of clay, sand, gravel, and phosphate rock, and to a lesser extent of sandstone, greensand, shell limestone, marl, peat, and ilmenite sand. The Piedmont contains clay, shale, slate, granite, kaolin, mica, quartz, pyrophyllite, and soapstone. It also contains ores of gold, copper, iron, manganese, chromium, titanium, and tungsten. In the Mountain region the chief minerals are feldspar, mica, kaolin, and quartz. Granite, marble, limestone, talc, and ores of iron, manganese, titanium, copper, and gold are present.

Small quantities of other metallic minerals have been produced, and a few of them continue to be mined in some areas. Among these are lead, zinc, silver, molybdenum, nickel, pyrite, tin, and tungsten. The latter, from a mine in Vance County, was especially important during World War II when sources from abroad were cut off or difficult to obtain. This mine has been worked intermittently since the end of that war.

North Carolina has substantial deposits of nonmetallic minerals and rocks, and its production of feldspar, mica, kaolin, and pyrophyllite is significant. Sizable quantities of talc, marble, granite, and slate are also produced commercially. Grindstones for sharpening and shaping metal objects and millstones for grinding grain have been made in the state since the eighteenth century. Pottery clay and fine clay for china have been valued for just as long. Large numbers of bricks are also produced, while sand and gravel for highways, railroad beds, and the construction of buildings are found from one end of the state to the other. Quartz from the Chestnut Flats mine near Spruce Pine was used in making the world's largest telescope lens, two hundred inches in diameter, on Palomar Mountain in California.

Interest in gemstones is high. Rubies, beryls, emeralds, garnets, and other stones have been located. Diamonds have been found in four different counties.

The only mineral fuel found to date is a poor-quality coal in Chatham, Rockingham, and Stokes counties, but recent studies have suggested that between 70 and 100 million tons of recoverable coal is available. Serious faulting in the fields, however, has thwarted mining efforts.

Tests for oil and gas made between 1925 and the 1960s in the Coastal Plain were unproductive. Nevertheless, it has been reported that "the thickness and character of the sedimentary beds found along the coast makes the area interesting for further search."

Both the variety and the quantity of minerals found are perhaps the basis for a slogan sometimes applied to the state: "Nature's sample case."

Climate and Weather

In 1524 the earliest European explorer to visit the North Carolina coast commented on the "good and wholesome ayre, temperate, betweene hot and colde, [where] no vehement windes do blowe." Sixty years later explorers sent by Sir Walter Raleigh also recorded their observations of sun, wind, and weather. In the seventeenth century authors of promotional tracts, determined to persuade Europeans to immigrate to Carolina, pointed out that the colony lay in the same latitude as the Mediterranean Sea and the Near East from which many spices and fruits came. By implication Carolina enjoyed the same climate. Many trees and herbs that did not grow in England would thrive in Carolina, they believed.

Only gradually did the transplanted English come to realize that climates

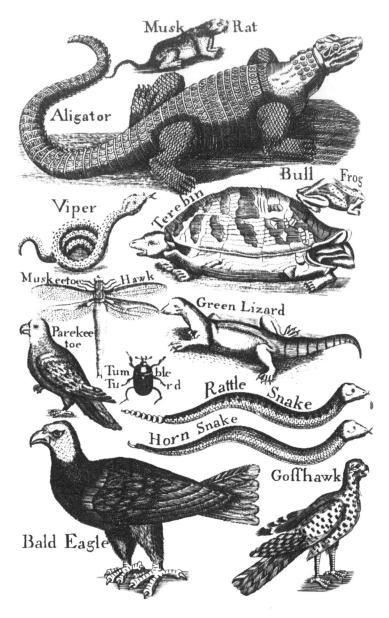

Dr. John Brickell's book, *The Natural History of North Carolina*, published in Dublin in 1737, attempted to suggest the variety of wildlife of the region. It contains other illustrations of this nature. (North Carolina Collection, University of North Carolina at Chapel Hill)

around the world, even in the same latitude, could be quite different. Climate is determined by the various daily weather conditions through the year. Weather, of course, differs from day to day and from place to place within a geographic area. Weather has been described as "the momentary state of the atmosphere." Temperature and precipitation are the main elements of climate and weather, although wind and air pressure must also be considered in establishing a broad definition. These elements of climate are affected by geography; not only the latitude and longitude but also the relation of the land mass to the ocean and mountains are significant. All of these factors must be considered in any description and explanation of the climate of North Carolina.

Lying wholly within the warmer part of the temperate zone, the state is near enough to the equator to have a moderate temperature. The length of the winter day provides enough sunshine to warm the surface of the earth and the surrounding air so that cold periods are of short duration. Yet the greatest variations in temperature occur during the winter, when low-pressure storms push farther south. These storms may be followed by warm southerly winds, which produce springlike days even in January and February. By March and April, when the northerly movement of the sun warms the land to the north, few masses of cold air from the arctic region and Canada ever push as far south as North Carolina. Warm spells and cool periods characterize the weather, and the precipitation changes from the more regular steady rains of winter to spring showers.

Toward the end of May most rainfall begins to come as thunderstorms, and these can be expected throughout the summer. Warm moist air from the Gulf of Mexico or from the tropical Atlantic Ocean produces warm, humid weather. Fall is often considered to be the dry season in North Carolina. It is the harvest time, with pleasantly warm days and cool nights which often last into November. December through February are the cold, damp winter months. Since temperature affects the rate of evaporation, the ground is almost always wet during this period.

The average year-round temperature for the state is 59°. For the Coastal Plain it is 62°, for the Piedmont 60°, and for the Mountains 55°. The record low for the state is −26°, recorded at Grandfather Mountain in Avery County on 30 January 1966. A maximum temperature of 110° was recorded at Fayetteville on 22 August 1983. The earliest reported killing frost in the fall occurred on 28 September 1947 in Ashe County. On the other hand, Hatteras in Dare County often passes the entire fall and through December without frost. The last killing frost in the spring has occurred as early as 20 January in Dare County and as late as 1 June on Mount Mitchell and at Banner Elk. The frost-free season in the state ranges from an average of 280 days in the east to 170 in the west.

In 1858 Silas McDowell of Franklin, Macon County, originated the "thermal belt" concept which became widely disseminated and spread to other states. It was modified by scientists and by residents of the area to suit their understanding of the theory. A thermal belt is generally recognized simply as a zone or belt on a mountainside where frost or freezing temperatures are less likely to occur than at higher or lower elevations. Although these temperature inversions may develop at any time, they are important in the early spring when the likelihood of damage to tender vegetation is greatest. When cold air drains down a slope into a valley in clear weather, it loses heat by radiation to space and is further cooled. Temperatures below freezing occur in the lower valley while temperatures in the thermal belt, farther up the slope, remain above freezing because of the heat lost by the circulating air. Higher up the slope frost will develop naturally as the temperature decreases with altitude.

Thermal belts have been described in Polk and Rutherford counties and elsewhere in western North Carolina. In reality they differ from time to time and from place to place, seldom following the exact pattern that popular tradition in the area assigns to them with positive limits and special characteristics. The term has come to be applied not only to the lower slopes of the mountains but also to a whole region. Much publicity has been given to this rather unusual occurrence in nature, and in many instances its benefits have been exaggerated.

Moisture in the form of rain or snow is fairly evenly distributed over the state throughout the year. The largest amount of rain usually falls in July and August and the least in October and November. Even so, most areas recognize no special rainy or excessively dry seasons. The Coastal Plain and the Mountain sections, however, generally receive more rain than does the Piedmont. Thunderstorms occur frequently during the hot months but more often in the mountains and along the southern coast than elsewhere. A hailstorm can be expected in most sections once or twice a year, but damage to growing crops is generally limited to small areas during any particular storm.

The southern coast is generally free of snow and sleet all winter, but the northern coastal counties sometimes have up to four inches annually. This amount may increase in the Piedmont to about seven inches. In the mountains some southern valleys may have about eight inches a year, whereas thirty inches or more may fall during a winter on the higher peaks. Except in some parts of the Mountain region, snow seldom lies on the ground for more than a day or two.

Hardly a summer passes without reports of dry areas within the state. In some years crops have suffered from the scarcity of rain. Such droughts occurred, for example, in 1911, 1925, 1953, 1954, 1968, 1983, 1986, and 1988. Topsoil and cultivated fields dry out rapidly through the top level; however, it is difficult for moisture to rise to the surface from deeper layers through a top dry crust. This fact has preserved many deep-rooted plants through a dry season.

The prevailing wind over North Carolina is from the southwest except in September and October when it is from the northeast. The speed of the wind varies greatly, but as a rule it is about thirteen miles per hour on the Outer Banks, about ten miles per hour in the eastern Coastal Plain, and about eight miles per hour elsewhere in the interior. Wind speed is reduced at night; it begins to increase about sunrise and reaches its maximum by the mid-afternoon. Storms, of course, considerably alter this pattern.

Wind has been recognized as both a positive and a negative force in North Carolina. Numerous windmills to grind grain were erected on the Outer Banks from the eighteenth century and used into the twentieth. Windmills for pumping water were more common across the state before the advent of cheap electricity, but they can still be seen occasionally. In 1978 the United States Department of Energy and the Blue Ridge Electric Membership Corporation, at a cost of approximately $30 million, erected the world's largest windmill atop Howard's Knob at Boone. Designed by the National Aeronautics and Space Administration to produce inexpensive electricity, the windmill stood 140 feet high with 100-foot propeller blades. A test machine, it was also the world's first wind-driven megawatt electrical generator. The energy produced was more expensive than anticipated; the turning propellers made an unbearable noise, and they rattled windows and disrupted television signals. The giant windmill was turned off in 1981 and torn down in 1983.

Coastal winds move the loose and shifting sands along the beaches. Wind erosion is as serious a problem in some spots as water erosion, and unstable sand dunes have been known to engulf beach cottages. Isolated trees have been buried in sand, while thickets of stunted trees, many of them misshapen by the steady ocean breezes, have been invaded by blowing sand. Picket fences and various kinds of grasses sometimes anchor these shifting dunes, and many of them have been stabilized.

Native Americans

The first report by a European of the coast of the United States was made in July 1524 by Giovanni da Verrazano, a Florentine navigator in the service of Francis I of France. During a brief visit at the mouth of the Cape Fear River and on Bogue Banks in the spring he saw a large number of native people who first fled at the sight of Europeans, but after being "assured with signes that we made them" they returned and proved to be quite friendly. The account describes them as being of a russet color with thick black hair tied behind and worn "like a little taile." Their clothing was of animals' skins and they wore "garlands of byrdes feathers." The natives were further described as well built, strong armed, broad breasted, and somewhat taller than Europeans.

The first English encounter with the natives came when the expedition

This engraving made in 1590 by Theodor de Bry of a John White watercolor depicts the Indians' method of making a boat. A controlled fire of moss and wood chips at the base of a tree caused it to fall, and a fire was then built along the top of the log. After the wood was charred, shell scrapers were used to hollow it out. Further fires and scraping followed until it was completed. (North Carolina Collection, University of North Carolina at Chapel Hill)

under Philip Amadas and Arthur Barlowe, sent by Walter Raleigh, arrived off the Outer Banks in July 1584. The Indians on Hatteras Island were friendly and curious to know more about their visitors. Barlowe's report to Raleigh described them as handsome, well-built people. "They are of colour yellowish, and their haire blacke for the most, and yet we sawe children that had very fine auburne, and chestnut colour haire," he continued. The Indians presented gifts to the Englishmen and received gifts in return.

Leaving the Hatteras area after a brief stay, the expedition made its way into the sound and up to Roanoke Island where further friendly demonstrations were exchanged between natives and explorers. The English were keen enough in their observations to realize that they had encountered two different Indian tribes; they also learned that there were others to the north on the mainland. They recorded the names of some of the tribes and of the "kings," and they acquired a little knowledge of the surrounding country both from brief expedi-

Painted by John White probably in 1584, this Indian wears a fringed deerskin apron and a necklace of beads or pearls holding a metal gorget. His hair is thin at the side with a roach down the middle and tied up at the back. White labeled this picture "A cheife Herowan" but the engraving by Theodor de Bry is marked "A cheiff Lorde of Roanoac." David B. Quinn, the English scholar who has studied the White drawings, suggests that this might be Manteo. (British Museum, London)

tions and from some kind of conversation with the Indians—probably by gestures and maps drawn in the sand with sticks.

In 1585 Raleigh sent a colony of men to occupy the region, and under Ralph Lane's leadership they ranged farther afield from their base on Roanoke Island. Visiting numerous towns and discovering more tribes, they attempted to use the names given them by the Indians. Thomas Harriot, an outstanding scientist, and John White, an artist, were members of the colony. Harriot seems to have learned to speak some Algonquian, the language of the local tribe, and he recorded much of what he saw and could learn from them. White painted water-color pictures of them, recording a large amount of detail not otherwise known.

Most Indian settlements contained ten or twelve houses, a few had twenty, while the largest seen had thirty. Some settlements were palisaded with poles stuck upright into the ground close together but others were open. The houses were made of poles for their sides with a rounded arch roof, all covered with bark or mats made of long rushes. A chief in some cases controlled only one town, but in other instances he might have as many as eighteen. The chief who commanded eighteen towns was able to raise between seven and eight hundred fighting men, Harriot believed. "The language of every government is different from any other, and the further they are distant the greater is the difference," he observed.

In wars, Harriot learned, their chief strategy was a sudden, unexpected attack carried out either at sunrise, by moonlight, or by ambush in daylight. "Set battles are very rare, except it fall out where there are many trees, where eyther part may have some hope of defence, after the deliverie of every arrowe, in leaping behind some or other." Scattered experience suggested that in an engagement with the English, Indians recognized that their best defense was to flee.

Harriot realized that two cultures had met. The English, of course, he regarded as superior, yet he wrote with admiration for the Indians and in hope that they might adopt English ways. Even without the tools and crafts of the English, the Indians were "very ingenious" and displayed "excellencie of wit." He further noted: "by howe much they upon due consideration shall finde our manner of knowledges and craftes to exceede theirs in perfection, and speed for doing or execution, by so much the more is it probable that they shoulde desire our friendship & love, and have the greater respect for pleasing and obeying us. Whereby may bee hoped if meanes of good government bee used, that they may in short time be brought to civilities, and the imbracing of true religion."

It was the invading English who broke the peace. Ralph Lane and his men were responsible for seizing an Indian chief, his son, and several others as well as for killing a number of Indians. Some of the natives ceased to assist the English or to provide food. Soon after the arrival of the John White colony in 1587, one of his colonists was slain, yet many of the Indians, particularly those in the Hatteras area, remained friendly. When White returned to England, contact with native Americans in the area was broken; it was not resumed until 1622, when John Pory from Virginia made an expedition to the Chowan River. Pory was well received by "the great King" who was "desirous to make a league with us."

Settlers from Virginia who moved into the North Carolina area in the second half of the seventeenth century purchased land from the Indians. The earliest surviving document concerning a transfer of land was dated 24 September 1660 and recorded in the deeds of Norfolk County, Virginia. It indicates that

Restored ceremonial mound at the Town Creek Indian Mound State Historic Site in Montgomery County. It was built by Creek Indians who migrated here about A.D. 1500. (North Carolina Division of Archives and History, Raleigh)

Nathaniel Batts acquired land from "Kiscutanewh Kinge of Yausapin."

Only after the publication in London of John Lawson's *A New Voyage to Carolina* in 1709 was a considerable body of information on the Indians of North Carolina available. His general description of them was similar to that of Verrazano. Lawson, however, lived so intimately with the Indians that he was able to understand, sympathize with, and even love them. He was as concerned as Harriot had been nearly a century and a quarter before with the welfare of these native Americans. Whites, he thought, ought to encourage the "Savages" to adopt English customs.[2] In brief, "every Englishman ought to do them Justice, and not defraud them of their Land, which has been allotted them formerly by the Government; for if we do not shew them Examples of Justice and Vertue, we can never bring them to believe us to be a worthier Race of Men than themselves."

2. The term "savage" was picked up by the English from some earlier French explorers who used the word "sauvage," meaning simply "native." It is unfortunate that it has such a different meaning in English.

According to Lawson, the native Americans were somewhat larger than Europeans and had good eyesight; they were quite dexterous with both hands and feet and unafraid of high places, readily helping to build houses for the English and showing no hesitancy in walking on roofs while thatching them or laying shingles; they were capable of running long distances or dancing vigorously with no sign of exhaustion; and they composed and sang long songs while accompanying themselves with drums and rattles. Young men were said to "labour stoutly" in planting corn and peas as well as in hunting to provide for their families. In their pole houses, they slept on benches covered with skins or rush mats. Lawson also reported on their marriage customs, on warfare, on community government, and on other aspects of their life. "Husquenawing" he considered a "most abominable Custom" by which young men approaching maturity were subjected to almost unbelievably harsh treatment from which they sometimes died. These traits, both good and bad, Lawson ascribed to the Indians he encountered all over the colony. He was well aware that they spoke different dialects, and that one tribe, or "Nation" as he called them, might be at war with another. Nearly all of the Indians lived in settled villages, engaged in agriculture, fished, and hunted; the men also went on long trading expeditions or fought distant tribes.

Lawson cataloged nineteen "Nations of Indians that are our Neighbours" and mentioned three others that he encountered while traveling across the colony's interior. His primary list, composed of Coastal Plain and neighboring Indians, included those whom he called Bear River Indians, the Chowanoc, Coree, Hatteras, Keyauwee, Machapunga, Meherrin, Neusiok, Nottoway, Occaneechee, Pamlico, Pasquotank, Potoskeet, Saponi, Shakori, Tutelo, Tuscarora, Woccon, and Jaupim or Weapemoc. Farther inland were the Eno, Esaw or Catawba, and the Sissipahaw. On his way from Charles Town to North Carolina he saw Congarees, Santees, Sewees, Sugarees, Waterees, and Waxhaws, some of whom could also be found within the bounds of North Carolina. In reporting on twenty-two tribes in the colony, Lawson missed only one important group—the Cherokees. In all, thirty-four tribes have been identified as having lived in North Carolina at one time or another. Today several additional small groups, which ethnologists apparently have never studied or classified, still make their homes in the state.

Ethnologists classify American Indians according to the root language they used, although it was not unusual for tribes belonging to the same general group to find it impossible to understand each other. Three basic groups—Algonquian, Iroquoian, and Siouan—were present in North Carolina, and each of these was part of a much larger group that flourished elsewhere in North America.

Only five of the many tribes in North Carolina played significant roles in the European settlement of the colony. Except for the Cherokees, most native Americans fell victim to white men's diseases, to their guns, or to their treachery before the mid-eighteenth century. The tribes with which the colonists were involved, in order of their initial contact, were the Hatteras, the Chowanoc, the Tuscarora, the Catawba, and the Cherokee.

Indian Tribes

The Hatteras (or Croatoan) Indians (Algonquian) greeted the earliest English explorers along the North American coast from their home near Cape Hatteras; they also frequently visited Roanoke Island. Manteo, who befriended the earliest English explorers and settlers on the North Carolina coast, was of this tribe. Many of these people stood by the English for more than 175 years. When Lawson talked with some of the Hatteras Indians before 1709, they told him that "several of their Ancestors were white People, and could talk in a Book as we do; the Truth of which is confirm'd by gray eyes being found frequently amongst these Indians, and no others. They value themselves extremely for their Affinity to the English, and are ready to do them all friendly offices." At that time they occupied only one town on the Outer Banks and had fifteen warriors, representing perhaps a total population of just under ninety.

During the Tuscarora Indian War between 1711 and 1715 the Hatteras supported the English, but apparently many of the tribe were captured. On escaping they appealed to the royal governor's Council for "Some Small reliefe from ye Country for their services being reduced to great poverty." The Council responded by giving them sixteen bushels of corn from the public store. According to Governor George Burrington, the Hatteras still lived in the colony in 1731 but they had fewer than twenty families. In 1761 and 1763 an Anglican missionary found the remaining Hatteras Indians living contentedly with the last of the Roanokes and a few others at Lake Mattamuskeet in Hyde County. In 1790 at the time of the first United States census, thirty-seven free, nonwhite persons living in that county may have been Hatteras or other Indians.

The Chowanoc Indians (Algonquian) lived primarily on the west side of Chowan River in the present Bertie-Hertford county region. A recent archaeological investigation at the site of one of their towns near the river suggests that it was a very large settlement and had been occupied for more than a thousand years. Both the Amadas and Barlowe expedition of 1584 and the Ralph Lane colony the following year (see Chapter 2) found these Indians to be friendly and well established. There were seven hundred warriors among them. In the midst of these Indians the first permanent white settlers of North Carolina built their houses. The Chowanocs adopted the ways and attire of the English; and when their white neighbors were busy growing tobacco or engaged in whaling, the

Chowanocs grew vegetables and furnished milk, butter, and cheese to sell. In 1675 some Indians in Virginia, at war with white settlers there, persuaded the Chowanocs to violate their 1663 treaty of friendship with the whites in Albemarle by attempting to drive them out of the county. People living on isolated farms were in constant fear of attack as the natives were said to "haunt" the woods. Travel in the area was hazardous. With limited means to protect themselves, the white residents engaged in a war that lasted until the arrival of arms and ammunition enabled them to defeat the Chowanocs in 1677.

By then, John Lawson noted, the natives occupied only one town and had only 15 fighting men. In 1713 it was reported that a mere 240 Chowanocs survived. Some of them joined the Tuscarora Indians in attacking white settlements; afterward they were confined to a reservation, which came to be known as Indian Woods, in Bertie County. By 1752 only a few families remained, and a few years later the Chowanocs reportedly consisted of just 2 men and 5 women. In 1820 they were said to be extinct.

The Tuscarora Indians (Iroquoian), when first encountered by the English in 1650 and until early in the eighteenth century, lived in the region between the Neuse and Pamlico rivers. They also claimed and hunted in a vast portion of the Coastal Plain from the Cape Fear River to near the modern Virginia line, some of which was also occupied by smaller tribes. In 1654 Francis Yeardley from Virginia reported that he had heard that these Indians had a Spaniard "who had been seven years with them, a man very rich, having about thirty in family, seven whereof are negroes; and he had one more negro, leiger with a great nation called the Newxes [Neuse?].[3] He is sometimes, they say, gone from thence a pretty while."[4]

In 1701 along the Eno River near modern Hillsborough Lawson met two Tuscaroras who had brought wooden bowls and ladles to trade for skins; according to him, they resented the presence of white men who might compete with them for the skins and furs in the area. As surveyor-general of the colony Lawson was frequently in Tuscarora territory. Although he was sympathetic toward these Indians, they must secretly have blamed him for the loss of their lands. They cruelly murdered him at the beginning of their war against the whites in 1711. Between then and 1715 the Tuscaroras waged a bitter and brutal war against white intruders on their land. Their attacks almost destroyed the white settlements between the Pamlico and Neuse rivers, while the English elsewhere in the colony felt the brunt of their blows through reduced trade, higher taxes, and a rapidly inflating paper currency which was first issued to help meet the expenses of this

3. "Leiger" is an old English term meaning agent, representative, or ambassador.
4. It is tempting to speculate that this may be evidence that Spain had stationed a spy here to observe the progress of English settlement.

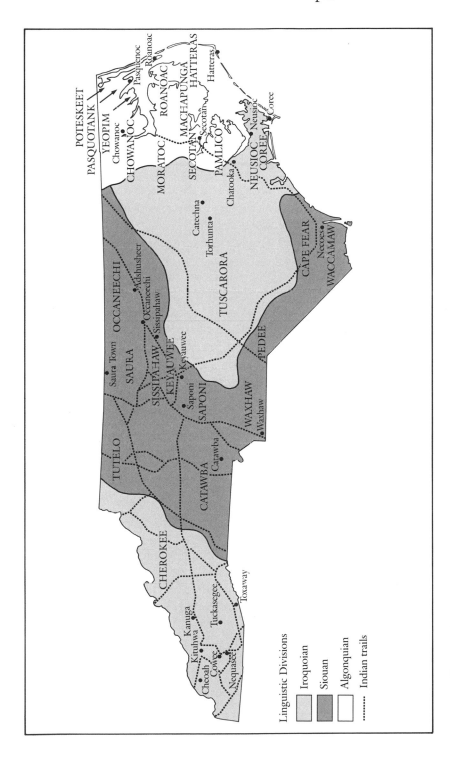

Map 2. Indian Populations at the Time of European Settlement

war. With the aid of troops from South Carolina, surviving whites dealt the Tuscaroras a sound but not fatal defeat. A portion of them living along the northern limits of their range remained neutral during the war and were considered friends of the whites. Under their chief, Tom Blunt or Blount, they received preferential treatment after peace was restored. By a series of treaties the Tuscaroras and their allies were confined to limited areas. Many of these Indians then left North Carolina to join Iroquoian relatives in the colony of New York.

By 1754 it was reported that there were 301 Tuscaroras in North Carolina, of whom more than 200 were women and children. During the French and Indian War some of these people performed guard duty for the colony while others joined Major Hugh Waddell for service on the frontier. And in 1760, about 50 took part in a campaign to stop raiding parties of Cherokees encouraged by the French along the western frontier of the southern colonies. Six years later some of their tribe from New York arrived to encourage their North Carolina relatives to join them. Selling most of their land, a majority of the Tuscaroras left for New York; 50 or 60 elderly men and women refused to go, however. In 1801 a group of Tuscaroras from New York called on North Carolina Governor Benjamin Williams about disposing of remaining lands in the state to which their tribe held title. Hearings were held and the General Assembly first leased and then sold the land with the proceeds going to the Tuscaroras.

The Catawba Indians (Siouan) once lived in the southern Piedmont, largely in the present Mecklenburg-Union county area; this was the northern limit of their territory, most of the tribe living in South Carolina and Georgia. A long and well-known Trading Path extended from Virginia across North Carolina to these people. Later highways, notably Interstate 85, followed much of this route. The Catawbas, like other Indians, suffered greatly from smallpox and other diseases contracted from whites; they had no natural immunity to these "foreign" diseases. The Catawbas, like the Hatteras and the Chowanocs, were friendly to whites. They joined in the war against the Tuscaroras and helped the English in the French and Indian War. Their last great chief, King Haigler, was killed and scalped by marauding Shawnees in 1763. These invaders, together with the Senecas, often raided both Indian and white settlements.

A reservation was set aside for the Catawbas in 1763; when the boundary between the two Carolinas was run, it was directed that it should be surveyed so as to leave the Catawba reservation entirely in the southern colony. This accounts for the unusual turns in the state boundary line between Union and Mecklenburg counties and South Carolina. Estimates of the number of Catawbas mentioned 4,600 in 1682, but by 1728 the number was reduced to 1,400. In 1761 there probably were only about 1,000. The census of 1910 counted 124—99 in South Carolina and 6 in North Carolina, with the remainder living in Virginia and Pennsylvania. In the early 1960s all pretense of reservation living was abandoned, and soon most of the remaining Catawba Indians were living in Greenville and Spartanburg, South Carolina.

A visitor to the Catawbas in 1784 found them to be friendly and helpful. The chief spoke no English, but a young member of the tribe who had attended the College of William and Mary served as interpreter. The visitor was served an excellent meal and was received so hospitably that he said a Parisian lady could have been no more cordial.

The Cherokee Indians (Iroquoian) are the largest group of Indians in the southeastern United States today. They once occupied the high mountains from Virginia through North Carolina, Tennessee, and South Carolina, and into northern Georgia and Alabama. They also claimed large segments of present Kentucky. Now they are concentrated on a reservation in southwestern North Carolina.

In 1540 a Spanish expedition under Hernando de Soto visited these people and found them to be most hospitable. The earliest English contact dates from 1674, when some Cherokees were found on the Savannah River. Ten years later officials from Charles Town made a treaty with the tribe and soon regular trading expeditions began. Over the years and well into the next century further treaties were made and trade flourished. The French, from their headquarters in Quebec, also engaged in trade with these people and came to encourage attacks on English settlements.[5] During the French and Indian War the Cherokees were the victims of English attacks made in an effort to halt their raids on white settlements. In 1760, they were decisively defeated and lost much of the land they had previously occupied.

During the American Revolution many Cherokees remained loyal to the British, who had had an agent stationed among them for a number of years. Directives from London had been aimed at protecting the Indians from white encroachment, so their loyalty is not surprising. During the war the Americans sent several military expeditions to halt Indian raids in support of the British. In the spring of 1777, the first in a series of treaties was drawn up; by these agreements, which continued into the next century, the Cherokees gradually lost their land. Finally, in 1838–39, the United States sent troops to round up the Cherokees. The major part of their relocation across the Mississippi River to the "Indian Territory" was contracted to Chief John Ross and other Cherokee officials. In 1848 Congress grudgingly permitted a small group of Cherokees who had escaped the roundup, as well as a large number who already held land under the 1819 treaty, to remain on the land their people had occupied for hundreds of years.

---

5. Surviving evidence of this can be seen in the name of East Laport, a community in northern Jackson County. Here in the eighteenth century the French had a trading post which they regarded as the eastern gate or door (*la porte*) to the Cherokee country.

Cherokee Indians have long been good citizens of North Carolina although their land is held in common as a reservation under federal supervision. They have taken part in the country's wars since the War with Mexico in 1846–48. During the Civil War, a Confederate officer reported, the young men of the Cherokee country were "loyal to us to an intense degree." Nearly four hundred served the Confederacy, whereas only a few joined the Union forces. Apparently the last real war dance of the Cherokees was held in Sylva during this time, when another ancient custom was also last practiced: they scalped Yankees in Tennessee. Sixty fought against the Germans in 1918 and one was killed, while thirty-five, including some women, saw service in World War II.

The number of Cherokee Indians has been variously estimated from time to time. There may have been as many as 22,000 in 1650 but in 1715 an official report listed 11,210. In 1835, on the eve of relocation, there were 16,542, of whom 2,528 lived in North Carolina. In 1895 it was estimated that there were 1,479 full-blooded Cherokees, but by 1900 this number had declined to 1,376. In 1980, however, 5,717 Cherokees were living on the reservation in portions of Cherokee, Graham, Jackson, and Swain counties; none were living on the part of the reservation in Haywood County.

The largest body of Indians presently residing in North Carolina are those who, for the most part, call themselves Lumbees because they live along the Lumber River. Some of them say they are descendants of the Tuscaroras. Largely of mixed ancestry, these people have no tradition of an Indian language; therefore, their tribal affiliation cannot be determined. They have been known by a number of names through the years. Hamilton MacMillan in 1885, perhaps as a result of the publicity that year of the three-hundredth anniversary of the Ralph Lane colony on Roanoke Island, theorized that these people were the descendants of Outer Banks Indians with whom the Roanoke colonists may have taken refuge. This has become a fixed belief among many people but is, of course, impossible to prove.

It is regrettable that the hopes of Thomas Harriot and John Lawson, among others, were not realized. These Englishmen recognized that the culture of the native Americans, though different from their own, met the needs of the people living in the "wilderness." Harriot particularly hoped that the Indians might accept the features of European civilization that would be advantageous to them. However, those who "invaded" America over the next two centuries had no such ideas. To supplant the original holders of the land was their primary goal. This became easy for two reasons. First, the Indians had no understanding that land could be owned. To the native American, land existed for the use and benefit of those who temporarily lived on it; when they died or moved on, the land remained for whoever followed. The European concept of perpetual ownership and passing it on to descendants was beyond their imagination. Thus, the exchange of a handful of trinkets for land was misunderstood. Indians believed these were merely gifts that permitted the Europeans to occupy the land for a time; in the European understanding, they were buying it forever.

A second common way for white settlers to acquire Indian land was by treaty. Representatives of the tribe would be called to a gathering of whites, who provided lots of good food; bundles of cloth and cups, perhaps, or mirrors and iron pots or other gifts; and kegs of brandy and rum. After several days of eating and drinking, the Indians would be presented a ready-made treaty to sign. Soon afterward settlers with new deeds would arrive to displace the Indians, if, indeed, they had not already been driven away by the nearest militia unit.

The native Americans welcomed the first European visitors, yet Ralph Lane in 1585 set the pattern for a policy in the English colonies that almost resulted in their extirpation. His violent, revengeful attack on a mainland settlement was the first step toward their decline. Diseases previously unknown to them and to which they had no natural immunity further contributed to the extinction of many tribes. Greed and envy, a feeling of racial superiority, and an indifference to human suffering were rampant among the whites. The late twentieth-century concern for "endangered species" probably never occurred to more than a handful of them. Unfortunately, too few people had the understanding of Thomas Harriot.

2

EXPLORATION AND
EARLY SETTLEMENT

W HEN CHRISTOPHER COLUMBUS, sailing under the auspices of King Ferdinand and Queen Isabella of Aragon and Castile, made his dramatic voyage to Samana Cay in the Bahamas in 1492, thirty-five-year-old King Henry VII had reigned uneasily for seven years in England. Discontent in many parts of his kingdom and suspicion in London kept his attention on domestic affairs. In France the twenty-two-year-old Charles VIII, on the throne for only a year, also faced trouble at home as well as abroad. In Portugal, King John II, forty-seven, had had eleven years to establish himself. Secure at home, he sent out explorers who discovered the mouth of the Congo River and the Cape of Good Hope. Ferdinand, forty, and Isabella, forty-one, had united their crowns at their marriage in 1469, and afterward they defeated the Moors and drove out the Jews. Spain as a world power was in the ascendancy.

John of Portugal suspected that some of Columbus's discoveries were in the region his own explorers had already visited, and he protested Spain's claim to them. The question was submitted to the newly installed Pope Alexander VI, a Spaniard incidentally, who decreed in 1493 that Spain should have all rights to land west of a line from pole to pole and passing 100 leagues west and south of the Azores and Cape Verde. John was not satisfied and a treaty the next year moved the line of demarcation 370 leagues west of the islands, giving Portugal a clear claim to Brazil. This may have prompted certain merchants in Bristol, England, to consider their own interests; engaged in shipping and trading abroad, between 1481 and 1483 they apparently had touched the coast of Brazil, or the Isle of Brasil as they called it. Bartholomew Columbus, brother of Christopher, had been in England in 1489–90 to discuss his brother's plans with King Henry and, perhaps, to gather what information he could about English discoveries. News of Columbus's second voyage in 1493, when he visited a number of Caribbean islands, must have concerned the Bristol merchants. Early in 1497 at their own expense, although under a charter from Henry VII, they sent Giovanni Caboto (or John Cabot), a native of Genoa who had settled in Bristol in 1490, to look for a northern route to the East.

Columbus, it was believed, had found a southern route to the riches of the Orient, and English merchants might well profit by a northern one. Cabot and his three sons, Lewis, Sebastian, and Santius, were authorized by King Henry—in clear violation of the pope's decree—"to saile to all parts, countreys, and seas of the East, of the West, and of the North, under our banners and ensignes." Departing Bristol on 2 May 1497, the Cabots passed along the coast of New-foundland and up and down the coast of Labrador. Sir Humphrey Gilbert in 1583 said that John and Sebastian Cabot "made discovery also of the rest from Florida northwards, to the behoofe of England," but this either was an error or was said simply to support England's intentions at that time to establish a colony farther south than Newfoundland. Cabot's voyage, nevertheless, was the basis of England's claim to much of North America.

French Interest

The circumnavigation of the globe in 1519–22 by Ferdinand Magellan's expedition for Spain demonstrated what most learned people of the day knew—that the world was round. This created new interest in exploration. Francis I of France, at age thirty, was suddenly inspired to know more of the New World. A group of expatriate Florentine and Portuguese merchants in Lyons obtained his support in sending Giovanni da Verrazano, a Florentine-born resident of France, in search of a new route to the Orient and of new lands between those already discovered by Spain and England.

In a report made on 8 July 1524 after his return, Verrazano said that he had sailed south past Spain before heading west into the open Atlantic near the Madeira Islands. He sighted land in 34°N latitude, near modern Cape Fear, on 21 March 1524, the first European to see what is now a part of the United States. Following the coast to the south for about 150 miles, Verrazano failed to find a suitable harbor and returned to his first landfall. Here a party landed and drew up a detailed description of the country, mentioning specific trees and animals. Moving up the coast, the expedition anchored in what appears now to have been Bogue Banks on Onslow Bay; an attempt was made to send a boat ashore with twenty-five men, but high waves prevented their landing. At that point some natives appeared on shore and directed the sailors to a safe cove, although only one sailor ventured to swim to land. From a safe distance he tossed sheets of paper, small mirrors, little bells, and other "trifles" onto the beach and then turned around to return to the boat. High waves soon knocked him over and he was washed ashore, battered, bruised, and unconscious. The natives picked him up and were carrying him away when he came to, grew frightened, and began to cry out "pitiously." Seeing his reaction, the Indians also began to cry. They put him down "at the foote of a little hill against the sunne, [and] beganne to beholde him with great admiration, marveiling at the whitenesse of his fleshe, and putting off his clothes, they made him warme at a great fire, not without our great feare which remained in the boate that they would have roasted him at that fire and have eaten him."[1] Instead, the natives proved to be "very courteous and gentle." When the mariner indicated by signs that he wanted to return to the boat, they gave him his clothes which they had dried by the fire, and "with great love clapping him fast about with many embracings, accompanying him unto the sea, and to put him in more assurance, leaving him alone, they went unto a high grounde and stoode there, beholding him, until he was entered into the boate." Such assurances of friendly natives were observed by later European explorers as well.

In sailing up the North Carolina coast along the Outer Banks Verrazano saw Pamlico and Albemarle sounds, but he did not see the mainland west of them. He mistook the large body of water behind the narrow sand banks for the Pacific Ocean. On a map of the New World drawn in 1529 by his brother, Girolama da Verrazano, an isthmus here joins the region known as Florida on the south with the remainder of the continent on the north. For a century and a half afterward, mapmakers and explorers thought that the Pacific Ocean or "South Sea" was not far to the west of the North Carolina coast.

France soon was bogged down in a long series of wars, and King Francis was captured and held for about a year by his enemies. Verrazano seems to have turned to England since he gave Henry VIII a parchment map of his discoveries and may even have made a second voyage under Henry's auspices. But the king was too busy establishing England's independence, creating a modern English society, and perfecting the Reformation. He generally ignored the New World while Spain and Portugal annexed vast unexplored regions. Nevertheless, King Henry VIII laid the foundations that enabled his daughter, Queen Elizabeth I, to expand England's dominion to America.

Spanish Interest

At almost exactly the same time France became interested, Spanish officials already in the New World began to expand their field of control. On the island of Hispaniola a civil official, Lucas Vásques de Ayllón, a native of Toledo, educated as a lawyer, wealthy, and "virtuous," became curious about North America. Between 1520 and 1525, at his own expense, he sent three expeditions to find sites

---

1. Four years later Verrazano was captured and eaten by Carib Indians on an island off the coast of South America. Cannibals seem to have believed that by eating someone they acquired the person's knowledge and ability.

for a colony. They explored a place the Indians called Chicora; it lay between the Cape Fear and the Santee rivers. On a Sunday, 30 June 1521, it was formally claimed for Spain when crosses were cut on trees to indicate Spanish occupancy. The king of Spain issued a patent to Ayllón in 1523 and named him lifetime governor of the region. In mid-July 1526 a fleet of six ships and a tender sailed from a Spanish base in the West Indies with five hundred men and women. Among them were three monks and some Negroes, the first slaves within the limits of the United States. There also were twenty-nine horses aboard the ships. It was recorded that the explorers landed at the mouth of a river they called Rio Jordan, which, from their account of it, was the modern Cape Fear River. On entering the mouth, one of the ships and all her provisions were lost but the crew was rescued. Immediately members of the expedition began constructing a replacement; they soon completed a small ship as well as a second one that could be rowed with oars or could be moved under sail—useful for exploring up the river. These were the earliest known European ships built on the North American coast.

Ayllón sent responsible men to explore the interior while others sailed up and down the coast, perhaps even discovering Chesapeake Bay. Scouts returned with reports of a more promising location farther down the coast and the colony abandoned the Rio Jordan site for one near the mouth of the Waccamaw River. Soon, however, even that location was deserted after illness reduced the colony to just 150.

Not until 1539 did Spain renew its interest in the Carolina region. In that year Hernando de Soto secured permission to conquer "Florida," as the vast, unknown southeastern part of the present United States was then called. Sailing from Havana in the spring with nine ships bearing more than five hundred men and two hundred horses, some mules, bloodhounds, and more than three hundred pigs, the expedition moved slowly north up the western coast of Florida. Swamps and swift streams delayed the expedition, which spent the winter of 1539–40 at an Indian town near modern Tallahassee. From this base scouting parties went out, and, when the Spanish broke camp early in March, they moved north and northeast across the pine barrens of modern Georgia and South Carolina. De Soto had learned of the "Chalaque" or Cherokee and in the South Carolina area he turned northwest, advancing parallel to the Savannah River to the mountains of North Carolina. The Cherokee Indians here seemed to be very rich and generous; they gave the intruders whatever they asked for, allowed their horses to graze in their meadows, and for a month provided the daily needs of the Spanish while they sought gold in the area. Finding none, they resumed their march, taking with them baskets offered by the Cherokees to carry their possessions. It was reported that the Indians also gave them some dogs. When members of de Soto's expedition crossed the Little Tennessee River, near the site of modern Franklin in Macon County, they were the first Europeans to discover a tributary of the Mississippi River; the next year, on 18 June, de Soto discovered the great river itself. Information based on de Soto's journey began to appear on maps a few years later, but the mountains were exaggerated and shown too near the Gulf of Mexico. Mapmakers as well as later colonists were confused by the reports; exploration and settlement were delayed because of the discouraging and erroneous accounts.

The Spanish treasure fleet, beginning in the early 1560s, assembled at Havana and sailed for Spain through the Florida Channel and up the Gulf Stream, sometimes as far as 36°N latitude at present Kill Devil Hills, before turning east. During the summer hurricane season it sometimes littered the shore with broken ships, scattered treasure, and stranded sailors. Arthur Barlowe in 1584 was told by Indians about one such wreck that occurred in 1558. When the ship was cast on the beach, some of the crew were still alive so the Indians "preserved" them. They were white people, the natives said but gave Barlowe no further information, at least none that he could understand. On another occasion Barlowe found Indians with iron tools. When he asked how they came to have them, he was told that twenty years before, in 1564, "out of a wracke which happened upon their coast of some Christian shippe, being beaten that way by some storme, and outragious weather, whereof none of the people were saved, but onely the shippe, or some part of her, being cast upon the sande, out of whose sides they drewe the nailes, and spikes, and those they made their best instruments." Indians in the South Carolina area found in one coastal shipwreck large lumps of gold and silver stamped with the mark of the Spanish mint.

Believing that they held the region along the Atlantic coast, the Spanish proceeded to establish forts and mission stations. In the summer of 1566 a group of twenty men, including Dominican priests, set out under one Domingo Fernández to install a mission station in the Chesapeake Bay. Sailing up the coast, they were delayed near 36°N latitude by a stiff wind that lasted four days; finally able to land after passing through an inlet a few miles north of modern Roanoke Island, the expedition sailed up the sound to what is now Currituck peninsula. One of the leaders, Pedro de Coronas, erected a wooden cross on the shore and led an exploring party through the area. A boat trip through some twenty miles of the area's waters followed, but no Indians were sighted. After the expedition returned to the open sea, the storm picked up and the plans for a mission were abandoned. Nevertheless, Currituck had been discovered, the region had been claimed for Spain, and a pilot named Fernández had gained knowledge of the area.

To further their scheme to restrict the French, Spain in November 1566 sent Captain Juan Pardo, Sergeant Hernando Boyano, and twenty-five soldiers into the Carolina region. Landing at St. Helena they marched north and west, often following the route of de Soto. Somewhere in the foothills of the Blue Ridge Mountains they built a fort where Boyano and some of the soldiers spent the winter. Pardo and the others turned east to the coast. Messengers passed back and forth during the winter, and in 1567 Pardo returned to the fort. The Spanish then passed through modern Macon, Clay, and Cherokee counties where they were well received by the Cherokee Indians. Along the way attempts were made to establish friendly relations with the natives and to tell them something of the Spaniards' religion. At some places small forts were built and a few men were left in them. It has even been suggested that one soldier was accompanied by his wife and daughter and that they remained in one of these outposts, but nothing further is known of them. The remaining members of this expedition made their way back to the coast along a great arc through what is now Tennessee, Alabama, Georgia, and South Carolina, opening a trail that the soldiers thought might be useful in resisting the French.

English Interest

In February 1562 a colony of French Protestants called Huguenots sailed under the command of Jean Ribaut; they intended to settle near the mouth of the Rio Jordan but through poor navigation landed at Port Royal instead. After depositing his colonists, Ribaut returned to France for reinforcements and supplies. However, because his country was involved in a religious war, help was not forthcoming. Turning to England, he found a cordial welcome and while there in 1563 published a book about his American experiences: *The Whole and True Discouerye of Terra Florida*. This was the first account of America written in English by someone who had just returned. Very likely one of those who read this little book was the boy Walter Raleigh.

With the support of Queen Elizabeth I, it was proposed that a fleet of five vessels go to the aid of Ribaut's colony under the command of Thomas Stukely. Although Stukely was not the most honorable man in England (he had betrayed state confidences, had served the king of Spain, and had been arrested by Queen Elizabeth for attacks on the ships of friends and enemies alike), he was the brother-in-law of Sir Richard Grenville. It was reported that Ribaut agreed to turn over to Stukely the American fort and its small garrison. Ribaut, however, was suspected of duplicity, and he was seized and imprisoned. Stukely sailed anyway but instead of accomplishing his mission he spent two years as a pirate, attacking the ships of many nations. The French colonists, in despair of receiving supplies, finally built a small ship and sailed for home. Their unseaworthy vessel was found by an English ship just before she sank, and the colonists were rescued.

Queen Elizabeth I (1533–1603), patron of Sir Walter Raleigh, who encouraged the exploration and settlement of the region that became North Carolina. (National Portrait Gallery, London)

England's interest in the New World had its first flowering during the great Elizabethan Age, which saw many important discoveries abroad as well as at home. William Shakespeare, Ben Jonson, John Donne, and Sir Philip Sidney graced the literary scene. Philosophers and scientists gave people new subjects to ponder. Historians became interested in England's past, while explorers brought back tales of the wonders of the world. When Queen Elizabeth I ascended the throne in 1558, only a little over a quarter of a century had passed since Peter Martyr, the geographer, had published a book declaring that America was a new world and that Columbus had not actually discovered a western route to China.

Elizabeth's subjects were envious of the wealth Spain drew from its colonies. The two countries, indeed, were rivals in many ways. Spain's source of wealth gave it an advantage that potentially could result in Elizabeth's downfall; it also threatened the Protestant religion of England and the nation's commercial independence. Many Englishmen were aware of this, and such great sea dogs as John Hawkins, Francis Drake, Richard Grenville, and Thomas Cavendish set out to capture Spanish treasure ships and to burn and spoil their enemy's American outposts. In words of the day, they "clipped the wings of Spain" and in so doing they also "singed the beard of the King of Spain." The gold, silver, jewels, spices, lumber, and other desirable goods brought home by these men excited everyone from the queen down to the lowest London servant. All wanted to know and see more of the treasures of America and to share in them. The actions required to do this were apparent to many, but none knew better than Walter Raleigh just what was necessary.

Raleigh realized that to destroy Spain's power England must build up its own, and that the first move in that direction required the establishment of English colonies in the New World as bases of operation. These colonies also would enlarge England's commercial operations by producing raw materials and other forms of wealth while at the same time creating new markets and extending the British Empire. To the accomplishment of this splendid hope for England, Raleigh devoted his life and fortune.

Some of young Raleigh's ideas he owed to his half brother, Sir Humphrey Gilbert, but Gilbert died before their plans bore fruit. In November 1577, when Gilbert was about thirty-eight and Raleigh about twenty-five, someone (the best evidence suggests that it was Gilbert) presented the queen a document marked "A discourse how Her Majesty may annoy the Kinge of Spaine by fitting out a fleet of shippes of war under pretence of Letters Patent, to discover and inhabit strange places." Under the provisions of a charter issued according to this plan, the queen would not openly authorize an attempt to seize Spanish possessions; rather, this would be a private understanding between her and the recipient of the charter. If things went awry, the queen could cite this charter and deny any role in the fiasco. With an official document from the queen merely authorizing him

This engraving of Sir Walter Raleigh (1552?–1618) is the only one published during his lifetime. (North Carolina Collection, University of North Carolina at Chapel Hill)

"to discover and inhabit strange places," the writer proposed to set out entirely on his own initiative to destroy the great Spanish fleets that went annually to the banks of Newfoundland to fish. "If you will let us first do this we will next take the West Indies from Spain," Elizabeth was promised. "You will have the gold and silver mines and the profit of the soil. You will be monarch of the seas and out of danger from everyone. I will do it if you will allow me; only you must resolve and not delay or dally—the wings of man's life are plumed with the feathers of death."

By early June 1578, the queen's mind was made up. On the eleventh she issued a formal document authorizing Gilbert "to discover, search, find out, and view such remote heathen and barbarous lands, Countries, and territories, not actually possessed of any Christian Prince or people, as to him . . . shall seem good." It was Gilbert's prerogative to govern any colonies he established in any manner he saw fit so long as their laws conformed to those of England. Citizens of the new land were to have all the rights and privileges of citizens and natives of England just as if they were still living there. So that the people residing in some foreign land might "live together in Christian Peace and Civil quietness," provisions were made for the maintenance of good order. Elizabeth directed that nothing be done "against the true Christian faith or religion, now professed in the Church of England" or "to withdraw any of the subjects or people of those lands or places from the allegiance of us, our heirs or successors, as their immediate sovereigns under God."

After several false starts Gilbert became concerned that his charter would soon expire. In the summer of 1582 a number of prominent Englishmen encouraged him to try again. Sir Francis Walsingham, Sir George Peckham, Captain Christopher Carlisle, and others engaged in some historical research. They read the reports of Verrazano and Jacques Cartier among others, and they interviewed an English mariner, David Ingram, who claimed to have spent eleven months in America walking from the mouth of the Tampico River north to Cape Breton. Gilbert himself interviewed three other men who knew the American coast.

All agreed that another expedition was in order, and final preparations were made. A document was drawn up by a number of people, including several merchants from Bristol, consenting to contribute to the expenses. Captain Carlisle drafted "A discourse upon the intended voyage to the hithermoste parts of America" which said that a hundred men should be sent to stay for a year so there would be a better understanding of the country and its "commodities." Carlisle was even prepared to explain the terms on which colonists would be accepted if any persons indicated an interest.

On 11 June 1583, Gilbert sailed for Newfoundland with six ships. He landed on 4 August and took possession in the name of the queen, intending to establish England's first American colony. But finding the land bleak and inhospitable, Gilbert lost his ambition before the end of the month and sailed for home. He was aboard the smallest of the ships when, on 8 September, she sank in a storm, taking Gilbert to his death.

Amadas and Barlowe Expedition

Raleigh picked up his half brother's interest in the original charter and, since it was soon to expire, he secured the support of several other men including another half brother, Adrian Gilbert, as well as Dr. John Dee, John Davis, and William Sanderson. The queen granted Raleigh a charter in his own name on 25 March 1584, New Year's Day under the calendar then used in England.[2] The new document contained the same provisions as those in Sir Humphrey Gilbert's grant with respect to religion, citizenship, and loyalty to the Crown.

Raleigh lost no time in readying a small exploratory expedition. He selected young Philip Amadas, about nineteen, of Plymouth, to command the reconnaissance voyage, perhaps on the *Raleigh* which had survived from Gilbert's last voyage. Arthur Barlowe was captain of the second small ship while Simon Fernándes, a Portuguese from Terceira, Azores, who had become a Protestant and married in England, was pilot. He may have been related to or, indeed, the same person as Domingo Fernández who led the Spanish expedition to the Currituck region in 1566. An artist, John White, went along, too. The ships seem to have been prepared in the Thames River at London before sailing from Plymouth on 27 April 1584. Going by way of the Canaries, southwest across the Atlantic and into the Caribbean, the little fleet apparently stopped at the southwestern tip of Puerto Rico before finding the Florida Channel. By 2 July it was near enough to Florida for those aboard to smell so sweet and strong a fragrance "as if we had bene in the midst of some delicate garden, abounding with all kind of odoriferous flowers." On the fourth land was sighted and identified as the "firme lande" of the continent. Between then and the thirteenth the ships coasted slowly up the Atlantic until members of the crew found the entrance they were seeking about midway between Cape Hatteras and Cape Lookout. After brief "thankes given to God for our safe arrivall thither," Barlowe recorded, "we manned our boates, and went to viewe the lande next adjoyning, and to take possession of the same, in the right of the Queenes most excellent Majestie, as rightfull Queene, and Princesse of the same."

For two days the small band of explorers examined the adjacent land, marveling at the tall red cedars and the abundance of wild grapes growing everywhere, even trailing down to the edge of the water. The "goodly woods" contained deer, rabbits, and birds. No native people were seen until the third day when a boat with three Indians rowed across the sound. Going ashore, the three were soon joined by Amadas, Barlowe, and Fernándes. Both groups spoke but neither understood the other. The English, nevertheless, persuaded the Indians to join them aboard ship, where the Indians gratefully received a number of gifts,

2. In 1582 Pope Gregory XIII introduced a new calendar to correct errors in the old Julian calendar of Julius Caesar's time. The new Gregorian calendar was rejected by England until 1752, when eleven days in September were dropped. This accounts for Old Christmas, still observed on the Outer Banks; the fact that George Washington was born on 11—not 22—February 1732; and many other curiosities about dates. Under the Julian calendar the new year began on 25 March, but under the Gregorian calendar it begins on 1 January.

including a shirt and hat as well as sips of wine and tastes of meat, all of which they "liked very well," Barlowe noted. After returning to their boat, the Indians began fishing, soon filled her, and then divided their catch between the two ships. The next day other Indians, including some of high rank, arrived and in a friendly manner attempted to exchange information. Following this amicable reception, Amadas and Barlowe made their headquarters on nearby Roanoke Island.

In his report to Raleigh, Barlowe commented on the deer and buffalo skins that were received in trade with the natives; on the meat, fish, corn, peas, pumpkins, melons, and grapes that the natives ate; on their methods of farming and the near-miracle of growing three crops of corn in one season; on the kind of shelter they had and the weapons they used; on how they made boats; on their religion and entertainments; on the awe and respect shown by the Indians for their leaders; and something about the relations between tribes. He mentioned having seen metal, but could not determine whether it was copper or gold; pearls also were plentiful, and the explorers gave Raleigh a little bracelet made from them. After a stay of six weeks on and around Roanoke Island, the expedition made a speedy voyage home, arriving by the middle of September. They took samples of the products of the country, as well as two of the native people: Manteo and Wanchese. John White's maps and watercolor drawings of the wonders of the region supplemented Barlowe's written report to Raleigh.

Raleigh was already at work on a second expedition before the first one returned. Amadas and Barlowe, to say nothing of the native Americans, were the objects of great interest and brought considerable publicity to Raleigh's plan. On Twelfth Day (Epiphany), the final day of medieval Christmas celebrations, Queen Elizabeth named the new country "Virginia" for herself, the Virgin Queen. Virginia was not too different from Wingina, the name of the chief of the Roanoke Indians, a fact that may not have escaped her notice. It was also later pointed out that the whole country "still seemed to retain the virgin purity and plenty of the first creation, and the people their innocency of life and manners." On the same day, 6 January 1585, at Greenwich, Raleigh was knighted. But the queen had even better Christmas presents for her favorite courtier. She permitted Raleigh to obtain valuable supplies of gunpowder from the Tower of London, and she placed one of her own ships, the *Tiger*, at his disposal. She also recalled Lieutenant Ralph Lane from his post in the government of Ireland (but continued his pay and allowances) so that he might serve Raleigh.

The Ralph Lane Colony

A fleet to go to America was in the making. Sir Richard Grenville was selected to command the expedition which got underway on 9 April 1585 with

Theodor de Bry's 1590 engraving of John White's map of the vicinity of Roanoke Island. (North Carolina Collection, University of North Carolina at Chapel Hill)

seven ships. Fernándes again was the pilot and Amadas also returned, this time with the title "Admiral of Virginia." Thomas Cavendish, destined to circumnavigate the globe the following year, was high marshall. Lane would be commander of the colony once it landed. Barlowe may have made the journey, but the records are not clear that he did. Artist John White was joined by Thomas Harriot, an outstanding scientist, and together they were responsible for preparing illustrations, maps, and detailed reports. Manteo and Wanchese, from whom Harriot and perhaps others had learned some Algonquian, also returned.

The fleet made good time to the West Indies, where several stops were made to get fresh water and salt and to build a small pinnace to be used in exploring the sounds around Roanoke Island. Although Grenville probably had horses aboard, he wanted to trade with the Spanish in the islands for more horses as well as for hogs, young cattle, bulls, and sheep. On 20 June the mainland was sighted, and on the twenty-third the fleet apparently arrived at Cape Lookout. Three days later it sailed with difficulty through an inlet at Wococon (modern Portsmouth Island) into the sound behind the Outer Banks. One of the ships, the *Tiger*, was damaged on the shallow bar and was beached with many of her sup-

One of the ships, probably the *Tiger*, that brought the Roanoke colonists to America. It appears anchored off the coast of North Carolina in one of the John White watercolors. (British Museum, London)

plies either lost or spoiled by seawater. After repairs were completed, the fleet continued north, passing Cape Hatteras on 21 July and soon afterward reaching the northern end of Roanoke Island. Here Lane constructed "the new Fort in Virginia" as Raleigh had directed.

Grenville and the fleet returned to England in late August, leaving Lane with a colony of 107 men. In addition to the English among them, there seem also to have been Irish, Welsh, German, and Dutch as well as one Jew, a native of Prague. Although Grenville would inform Raleigh of the need for additional supplies, Lane had adequate equipment for the moment. He also had men with special skills to carry out the assignment Raleigh had given him. Exploration, mapping, and the painting of pictures got underway promptly. The men under Lane's command were organized into three military units. One left for the Chesapeake Bay in the fall, established a camp, and spent considerable time searching the waterways for a suitable harbor for forays against the Spanish. The mainland west of Roanoke Island was also explored and declared "to bee the goodliest soile under the cope of heaven."

Lane himself led a second group into the interior by way of the sounds and the Chowan and Roanoke rivers. The third, remaining on or in the vicinity of Roanoke Island, explored such places as Port Ferdinando on the Outer Banks near modern Oregon Inlet and Croatoan at present-day Cape Hatteras. Lane's colony arrived too late to plant crops or gardens, and the poor growing season that year left the natives with little or nothing to share. Lane became violent toward the natives at the slightest provocation. On one occasion he led a raid on a native village on the mainland, inflicting numerous casualties. On another, when the Indians planned to attack the colony, only the warning of a friendly Indian enabled Lane to avert the conflict.

Relief from home was expected daily—by Christmas, by Easter, or at any moment. In the spring of 1586 corn was planted with hopes for an early harvest of roasting ears. Sir Francis Drake had been in the West Indies in the winter and early spring of 1585–86 looting and attacking the Spanish. Among the prisoners taken were galley slaves, mostly Moors but including some Europeans, Negro slaves, and about three hundred South American Indians. Now heading home, Drake stopped by Roanoke Island just to look in on the colony. Discovering the needy conditions there, he offered to leave a limited quantity of food, supplies, and several ships with crews and weapons. Lane was inclined to accept when suddenly a fierce storm blew up, dispersing and damaging the fleet. He decided to return to England with Drake. In loading the colony's goods in the storm which almost swamped their boat, sailors impatiently pitched overboard books, maps, and papers as well as valuable specimens gathered over nearly a year. On 19 June the fort on Roanoke Island was abandoned and so were three of Lane's men who were away on an expedition. The South American Indians and the Negroes may also have been left at the site as there is no further mention of them. If, indeed, they were abandoned, they must have fled the area, for they were not referred to by later expeditions. The Moorish prisoners, however, were eventually sent back to Turkey as a gesture of goodwill from Queen Elizabeth—perhaps to curry favor with leaders there along the trade route to the Orient.

Just a few days after Drake's departure, the first of several ships bringing the long-anticipated relief from home arrived; soon after that, Grenville and others dropped anchor off the coast. After searching for the colonists over a very large area, Grenville learned from some natives that they had left with Drake. With ample supplies and as many as four hundred men under his command, Grenville made the rather strange decision to leave only fifteen of them with supplies for two years to hold the region for England. By then it was late August and Grenville sailed away undoubtedly hoping to capture more Spanish treasure on the way back to England.

Later inquiry revealed that soon afterward about a dozen of the men left on Roanoke Island had been called out of their houses by Indians for what appeared to be a friendly meeting when they were suddenly attacked, probably in retaliation for Lane's harsh treatment. One of Grenville's men was killed. Those who escaped fought their way to the shore as the Indians burned their houses; others were picked up along the shore. The Englishmen rowed away in a small boat toward the Outer Banks and were never seen again. Later, however, a skeleton was found near the fort on Roanoke Island.

Three extremely valuable products of Lane's expedition arrived in England on 28 July 1586 with 97 survivors out of a colony of 107. These were the written reports of Thomas Harriot, the watercolor drawings of John White, and several excellent maps. A small book by Harriot, *A brief and true report of the new found land of Virginia*, was printed in London in 1588. One of its purposes was to discount rumors spread by malcontents among the returned colonists who, "after gold and silver was not so soone found, as it was by them looked for, had little or no care of any other thing but to pamper their bellies; or of that many which had little understanding, lesse discretion, and more tongue then was needfull or requisite." At the same time Harriot wanted to encourage future settlers, so he included generally accurate and encouraging accounts of the commodities found in America or capable of being produced there. Among them were flax and hemp; pitch, tar, rosin, and turpentine; sassafras, cedar, oak, walnut, and other trees; alum, iron, copper, and other minerals; various kinds of furs and skins including otter, deer, and skunk—buffalo skins had been received in trade from the natives, although Harriot apparently saw no buffalo; and various dyes and gums. Food would be no problem, he suggested, as several kinds of beans and peas, wheat, maize or corn, pumpkins, melons, herbs, grapes, strawberries, and other edible plants grew well in the fertile soil. Some prospective colonists would be pleased to know that from the Indian maize "wee made . . . some mault, where was brewed as good Ale as was to bee desired." Fish, fowl, and various kinds of animals for meat were plentiful. Finally, the reader found a good introduction to the native inhabitants, "the nature and manners of the people," as Harriot headed one section of his book.

White's paintings not only complement Harriot's text but also supply a great deal of new information. Pictures of birds, fish, and a few turtles and insects survive among others, but any pictures of animals that he painted must have been lost when sailors threw overboard some of the baggage being loaded from Lane's colony during the storm in 1586. From his paintings of Indians we have much information that is not otherwise available from early writings or archaeological excavations. Clothing, body decorations and ornaments, ceremonies, methods of cooking, fishing, farming, and many other aspects of daily life were depicted in a very realistic style which entitles White to a special place in the history of English painting.

White and Harriot collaborated closely in mapping the region they visited, and their work has been called "an impressive testimony of the first English attempt to survey an overseas territory—the most thorough topographical survey of an extensive tract of North America made during the sixteenth century." Surviving are a rough sketch-map attributed to White, a contemporary engraving, two manuscript maps by him, and an engraving based on one of the manuscripts. In addition, there are perspective drawings of two Indian villages on the North Carolina mainland.

In 1590 Theodor de Bry published Harriot's text and engraved many of White's paintings as illustrations. Printed in Frankfurt, Germany, in Latin, German, English, and French editions, this work made it possible for nearly every literate person in Europe to read of the wonders of the New World. A second edition in Latin and German appeared in 1608.

The John White Colony

Raleigh's plans called for a larger colony to follow Lane's but this time to be established on Chesapeake Bay, where a good deepwater port would better serve English ships. The beachhead on Roanoke Island commanded by Lane had been maintained as a military base, and his men apparently were paid regular wages for their services. The next colony was planned differently. It would be composed of men, women, and children and would have a civil government. The colonists would be investors in the undertaking and would receive grants of land. John White, whose enthusiasm for the prospects of an English colony in America must have pleased Raleigh, was appointed governor. On 7 January 1587 a corporate body was formed under the title "Governor and Assistants of the Cittie of Ralegh in Virginia," and a coat of arms was issued. Among the 12 assistants was Simon Fernándes, but he did not remain in the colony nor did 3 others who probably stayed in England to attend to colony affairs at home. The list of colonists contains 117 names including those of 17 women and 9 boys.[3]

The small fleet bearing this colony cleared England on 8 May, sailed south and west through the West Indies with several stops for food, water, and salt, and arrived at Roanoke Island on 22 July, intending to leave Manteo and another Indian named Towaye who had returned to England with Lane or Grenville and to pick up the men left by Grenville. At sea White and Fernándes had disagreed a number of times: the governor felt that the pilot took undue risks in Spanish

3. There is evidence to suggest that a number of the Roanoke colonists probably came from London. Because of overpopulation in the countryside, many people had recently moved to London in search of work and food. To discourage this (because of fear of fire, disease, violence, and unrest) a proclamation in the summer of 1580 prohibited the building of new houses. This may have prompted some people to join Raleigh's colonizing venture.

waters; he also declined to pause along the way when White thought it essential do so. Finally, on arriving off the coast near Roanoke Island, Fernándes refused to take the colony to the Chesapeake. Claiming that "the Summer was farre spent," he probably intended to try his luck at capturing some Spanish gold before returning to England.

A small party sent to the site of Lane's colony found the two-story houses to be in rather good condition, and, when the rest of the colonists arrived, the men set to work making repairs and building other structures. They had brought some brick and roofing tiles with them and were equipped to establish themselves permanently. George Howe, one of the assistants in the government and recently widowed, strayed two miles away while crabbing and was slaughtered by mainland Indians who came over to the island. But Manteo and other members of his tribe, the Croatoans, remained friendly. On 13 August 1587, Manteo was christened and—as ordered by Raleigh in recognition of his loyalty and service—made Lord of Roanoke and of Dasemunkepeuc, an Indian village. Another significant event soon followed. On 18 August Eleanor White Dare, the nineteen-year-old daughter of the governor and wife of Ananias Dare, one of the assistants, gave birth to a daughter who, on the following Sunday, was christened "Virginia" "because this childe was the first Christian borne in Virginia," her grandfather recorded in his journal. On the twenty-seventh a child was born to Dionyse and Margery Harvie, but White did not record its Christian name.

By this time the ships had about finished unloading supplies and equipment, and had begun to take on wood and fresh water for the voyage home. The colonists were completing their letters and getting souvenirs ready to send friends and relatives in England.

Like Lane's, this colony arrived too late to plant gardens and crops, and it was apparent that little or nothing could be expected from their Indian neighbors. Some discussion arose—"controversies," White said—between the governor and his assistants as to who should go back to England for supplies. At first Christopher Cooper agreed to go, "but the next day, through the perswaision of divers of his familiar friendes, he changed his minde." The journal continues: "The next day, the 22. of August, the whole companie, both of Assistants, and planters, came to the Governour, and with one voice requested him to returne himself into England, for the better and sooner obtaining of supplies, and other necessaries for them." White was reluctant to leave lest he be criticized at home for deserting his post. "Also he alleaged, that seing they intended to remove 50. miles further up in to the maine presently, he being then absent his stuffe and goods, might be spoiled." On the following day he was approached again by both the men and the women of the colony. A document was drawn up ensuring White against the loss of his possessions while he was away, "so that if any part thereof were spoiled, or lost, they would see it restored to him." Signed and sealed by "all their handes," this bond is described as "the first formal document to survive which originated in any English settlement on the mainland of North America."

White had just half a day to prepare for the crossing. On 27 August he took a small boat across the sound to board ship. After a stormy voyage when food became scarce and the water kegs leaked, White arrived off the western coast of Ireland on 15 October. Further mishaps delayed his meeting with Raleigh until 20 November, but on that occasion plans were made to send relief to the colony at once, to be followed by a fleet under the command of Sir Richard Grenville. At this point, in the face of threatened invasion by Spain, Queen Elizabeth ordered that no ships leave England. Although Grenville was then ready to sail, most of his ships and supplies were used to reinforce Drake's fleet in defense of the country.

Searches for the "Lost Colony"

White's persistent pleas must have been heard by a sympathetic person with considerable authority, for in the spring of 1588 he was allowed two small vessels which sailed from Bideford on 22 April with a cargo of biscuits, meal, vegetables, and perhaps other supplies for the colonists. One of the ships also carried seven men and four women while the other had four or five additional colonists who expected to join those already in America. The captains, unfortunately, were more interested in this rare opportunity to line their own pockets than in delivering the much needed supplies to their fellow countrymen in the New World. Sailing into the Atlantic together, each of them soon seized a couple of cargo ships at sea. They then parted company. As it headed for America, White's ship was captured by French pirates. Many seamen were killed and White and three colonists were injured. All of the supplies were taken, and there was nothing to do but return to Bideford. Shortly afterward the other ship also arrived.

The long-expected Spanish Armada approached England late in July but before the end of August it had been soundly defeated, partly by stout English ships and partly by a severe storm which blew Spanish ships into the North Sea and around to the western coast of Ireland where they broke up on the rocks. Raleigh, Drake, and Grenville were all involved in the defense of England both before and after the central drama of the Armada.

Raleigh had not been home long when a three-part agreement, designed to relieve the Roanoke colonists, was signed. Raleigh held the grant from the queen and formed one-third of an organization established to invest further in the colony and to share any profits. Thomas Smythe, William Sanderson, and others, mostly London merchants, but including the historian Richard Hakluyt, formed the second party to the agreement. The third unit consisted of John

White and the "Assistants of the Cittie of Ralegh." All parties agreed to contribute money, merchandise, shipping, munitions, food, and other commodities. This agreement was reached in March 1589, too late to get an effective relief expedition underway before the hurricane season. The unwillingness of the new investors to contribute heavily until they had further assurance of profit to themselves may also have been partly responsible for the delay. White was silent on these matters.

John Watts, another London merchant, made plans during the final months of 1589 for a great privateering expedition to America. Three ships were ready to sail in January 1590, when shipping was stopped again because of the threat of a renewed attack by the Spanish. White suggested to Raleigh that Queen Elizabeth might let Watts's ships sail if he agreed to take supplies, some additional settlers, and equipment to Roanoke Island. An understanding was reached, apparently through the efforts of William Sanderson. When the vessels were ready to leave near the end of February, however, Watts's crew refused to take any settlers or supplies except some artillery, and only reluctantly agreed to take White. He was permitted to sail on the *Hopewell*, which cleared Plymouth on 20 March. Two other ships that sailed about the same time were independent of Watts's fleet, as was a third, the *Moonlight*, owned by Sanderson and of which Edward Spicer, who had been with White in 1587, was captain. They all intended to call at Roanoke Island.

After capturing Spanish treasure at sea, the ships rendezvoused in July, but in August the *Moonlight* and the *Hopewell* broke away and headed for the North American mainland. Reaching Port Ferdinando on 16 August 1590, they sighted smoke in the direction of Fort Raleigh but darkness prevented a landing. The next morning, in high seas and a strong tide, one of the boats making for shore was swamped and overturned, and seven men drowned. Saddened by this accident and delayed by the forces of nature, White and a small number of men made their way up Roanoke Sound. As darkness began to blur their view, they saw a fire through the woods on the northern end of Roanoke Island. From the boats, White noted, "wee . . . sounded with a trumpet a Call, & afterwards many familiar English tunes of Songs, and called to them friendly; but we had no answere." The next morning, Virginia Dare's third birthday, the search party landed but found only dead grass and rotten trees afire, probably from lightning. There were fresh footprints left in the night by Indians, while carved on a tree were the letters *CRO*, "which letters presently we knew to signify the place, where I should find the planters seated, according to a secret token agreed upon between them & me at my last departure from them . . . in Anno 1587 I willed them, that if they should happen to be distressed in any of those places, that then they should carve over the letters or name, a Crosse ✚ in this forme, but we found no such signe of distresse."

A further search disclosed that the houses had been pulled down and "a high palisade of great trees . . . very Fort-like, and one of the chiefe trees or postes at the right side of the entrance had the barke taken off, and 5. foote from the ground in fayre Capitall letters was graven CROATOAN without any crosse or signe of distresse." Scattered inside the fort were iron bars, pieces of lead, four guns, some shot, and other heavy things almost overgrown with grass and weeds. Going to the waterside in search of the colonists' boats and the small ship that had been left with them, White and his party could find no clue. As they turned to leave, some sailors came up to report that they had just discovered some chests that had been hidden in the sand but later dug up and broken open. Three were White's and in them he found his books torn from their covers; his frames, pictures, and maps rotten and spoiled from the rain; and his armor almost eaten through with rust. By this time night was approaching and a storm was rising. The men headed for the ships as fast as they could. It was a foul and stormy night, and the sailors feared that the cables and anchors might not hold. The intensity of the storm increased, and it was decided the next day to abandon the search, go to the West Indies for the winter, and return in the spring. At sea conditions grew so fierce and the damage to the ships was so extensive that there was little choice but to let the wind drive them toward England. White, aboard the *Hopewell*, arrived in Plymouth on 24 October. Sometime afterward he settled on one of Raleigh's estates at Newtown, Kilmore, in County Cork, Ireland. From there, on 4 February 1593, he wrote a letter to Richard Hakluyt that contained his last known reference to the "Lost Colony" of 1587. After relating events of the investigation in 1590, he expressed regret at not being able to continue the search and hope that the colonists somehow had survived.

So long as no one could prove the contrary, it was assumed that Raleigh's colonists were still in America. This meant that his charter was still valid. And as long as the queen lived he was not likely to lose his claim. A ruling by an obscure local court that might have affected Raleigh's interests, however, apparently caused no concern. Under the common law of England an unaccounted for absence of seven years was necessary for a ruling of presumed death. In 1594, seven years after English men, women, and boys had sailed for America, the relatives of a youth, John Dare, natural son of Ananias Dare of the Parish of St. Bride's, Fleet Street, London, petitioned that he be awarded his father's property. The petition on behalf of young Dare was granted in 1597.

Queen Elizabeth died on 24 March 1602—the last day of the year—and Sir Walter Raleigh almost immediately fell under the suspicion of her successor, King James I. The new king was convinced that Raleigh had conspired with Spain to prevent his ascension to the throne of England. In November 1603, just eight months after the death of his patron and queen, Raleigh was found guilty. With the loss of his freedom and his position also went all his claims to Virginia. For most of the rest of his life, Raleigh was confined to the Tower of London; he was beheaded in 1618.

Results of Raleigh's Efforts

King James now held all the rights, privileges, and honors that Raleigh had enjoyed in the New World, costly though they had been, since New Year's Day, 1584. James was also free to make new grants in the area. When approached by some men seeking a royal grant for an American colony, James hesitated, for he was reluctant to see national resources wasted on useless projects. However, after calling in nearly a dozen of Raleigh's supporters for advice and receiving their assurances that further efforts were justified, he issued a charter in April 1606 to a private corporation called the Virginia Company. It was authorized to colonize the region from latitudes 34°N to 45°N—between Cape Fear in the south to what is now Bangor, Maine, in the north. In 1607 the members of this company planted a colony called Jamestown on Chesapeake Bay, where Raleigh had intended that his 1587 colony be established. This time the settlement lasted, built upon the experience of the Roanoke planters.

Because of Raleigh's persistence, England was able to establish colonies in North America. As a consequence, the United States today enjoys a heritage of freedom in government and religion. The English language, now the almost universal language, is also a part of that heritage as is much of our culture, literature particularly.

From time to time for a quarter of a century following the settlement at Jamestown, people in varying numbers visited the region to the south. Several attempts were made to locate the Roanoke colonists, but no positive evidence of their survival or of their fate could be discovered. In the spring of 1620 the Virginia Company became interested in the unexplored portion of their grant and employed Marmaduke Rayner to explore "to the Southward to Roanocke." A report from him was read before the company in London in July 1621, but no copy has survived. The first visit from Jamestown of which we have more than passing reference was made in 1622 by John Pory, former English newsletter writer and member of Parliament and more recently secretary of the Virginia colony and speaker of the first legislature in America. Pory explored along the Chowan River and described the very fruitful land with enormous forests of pine trees suitable for the production of tar and pitch for the English navy. The natives, anxious to engage in trade, gave Pory a piece of copper mined not far away which he sent to London to be tested. Soon residents along the James River and Chesapeake Bay began to distinguish between their Virginia and "Ould Virginia" which they later called "South Virginia" or, after the area began to attract settlers, the "Southern Plantation."

The colonists on the James River could have profited from the experience of the Roanoke colonists. As the Jamestown settlement took root further efforts to contact them ceased, but the fate of Raleigh's colonists has intrigued future generations. The only factual information about them is contained in the records left by the contemporary historian, Richard Hakluyt, and by the participants Thomas Harriot, John White, Ralph Lane, and a few others. Enlarging upon the clues provided in these documents, however, historians and others have advanced a variety of theories as to the fate of the "Lost Colony." One guess is as good as another at the present; perhaps some archaeological evidence will be found in the future or some presently unknown documentary source will be discovered. The most likely conclusion seems to be that the colonists went first to Croatoan (modern Cape Hatteras) as indicated by the sign they left at the fort. Afterward they may have attempted to make their way into the "interior," as White reported they intended to do. This is assumed to mean that they set out for the Chesapeake Bay area according to Raleigh's plan. Captain John Smith, of the Jamestown colony, reported that local Indians gave him to understand that the English colonists from Roanoke had been "slaughtered" during a conflict between two warring bands of natives in the vicinity of Jamestown shortly before the 1607 colonists arrived.

The Carolana Grant

Dissatisfied with the way the Virginia Company was being managed, the king invalidated its charter in 1624, leaving himself once more free to grant the land anew. James died the next year, however, and was succeeded by his son, Charles I. On 30 October 1629 Charles granted to his attorney general, Sir Robert Heath, the territory between latitudes 31°N and 36°N and named it "Carolana" in honor of himself. This vast region, which lay from about thirty miles north of the modern Florida state line to the southern shores of Albemarle Sound in North Carolina and from the Atlantic Ocean to the "South Sea," included none of the land already explored from Virginia except Roanoke Island.

Heath's charter included the significant Bishop of Durham Clause. Durham County lay on the Scottish border, and the bishop was the feudal lord who was expected to protect England from invasion from the north. The sole new proprietor of Carolana was given all the powers that the bishop of Durham had then or had ever had. This meant, among other things, that he could raise and maintain an army, collect taxes, create towns, and exercise almost regal power. Nevertheless, King Charles was the monarch of Carolana, and Heath was instructed to have on hand a 20-ounce gold crown inscribed *Deus Suum Opus* (God Crowns His Work) to be worn by the king if he should ever visit the region.

Sir Robert Heath (1575–1649), attorney general during a part of the reign of King Charles I, who in 1629 was granted a vast tract of land in America called "Carolana." His charter was the model for later charters with unusual grants of liberty to colonists. (Alexander Brown, *Genesis of the United States,* 1890)

Despite Heath's careful plans to send French Huguenots and other Protestants to his colony, they came to naught, as the Privy Council forbade anyone to settle in Carolana who did not acknowledge the Church of England. At this point Heath recruited forty persons in England and got them as far as Virginia, but transportation from there to Carolana was not available. Disappointed and busy with other matters, Heath transferred his proprietary rights to Henry Frederick Howard, Lord Maltravers, in 1638. The grandson of the duke of Norfolk, Maltravers persuaded officials in Virginia to lay out a county in Carolana which he named Norfolk, but he was no more successful than Heath in settling it. Civil war in England, revolution, and the execution of King Charles contributed to the failure. Nevertheless, many Royalists found refuge in Virginia, and in time news of the vast and fertile land lying south of Virginia created a new interest in the region.

By the early 1650s officials in Virginia were granting land beyond the southern limits of their own territory. Merchants and Indian traders as well as hunters and trappers began to appear in Carolana; farmers in search of better land as well as restless explorers seeking adventure were in touch with the friendly native Americans there. By 1655 Nathaniel Batts, the first known permanent settler in the region, had a house along Salmon Creek at the western end of Albemarle Sound from which he engaged in trade with the Indians. His house, twenty feet square with a very large chimney, was not promptly paid for and the workmen who went down from Virginia to build it had to sue Batts. Other settlers soon followed, and by 1663 more than five hundred people were probably living between Albemarle Sound and the limits of Virginia. There were so many, in fact, and they were so far from the center of settlement in Virginia that the Virginia Council, in October 1662, commissioned Captain Samuel Stephens to be commander of the Southern Plantation and empowered him to appoint a sheriff. Order, if necessary, would now be maintained, and these distant people could no longer escape the tax collector. This was the situation in what would eventually become North Carolina during the period following the beheading of King Charles I in 1649 and the restoration of the monarchy in 1660 when Charles II ascended the throne.

3

A PROPRIETARY COLONY,

1663–1729

A FTER THE BEHEADING of Charles I in 1649, Parliament and the Cromwells held sway in London. The return of the prince of Wales in 1660 as Charles II was not achieved without great personal sacrifice. This happy occasion for England was the result of much planning, secret negotiating, concealed motives, and the collaboration of hundreds under the leadership of a few. The debt of King Charles II to his friends who had remained in England during the eleven-year interregnum, as well as to those who had fled the country or who upheld the royal cause in the colonies where they had lived since 1649, was great indeed. The king repaid this debt in many ways. Titles, positions, estates in England, and land abroad were among the rewards.

The Carolina Charter of 1663

Eight men who contributed to Charles's return were rewarded in an unusual way. In 1663, at their own request, they were granted a vast tract of American land of which they were "the true and absolute Lords and Proprietaries." It lay between latitudes 31°N and 36°N and stretched from the Atlantic Ocean to the "West in a direct Line as far as the South Seas." This was from the Albemarle Sound, as this body of water came to be known, down to St. Marys River at the present Georgia-Florida boundary, and all the way west to the Pacific Ocean.

The Lords Proprietors soon discovered that their grant did not include the region on the Virginia frontier that was already settled, so they went back to the king and asked for more land. In 1665 their charter was amended to extend their holdings one-half degree north to the present North Carolina–Virginia line and two degrees south to a point about thirty miles north of Cape Canaveral, Florida, which was well below the Spanish town of St. Augustine. England was warning Spain of its intentions to occupy North America.

Based on the grant to Sir Robert Heath, the charter of the Lords Proprietors was issued on 24 March 1662/3, the last day of the year under the old Julian calendar then used in England, perhaps suggesting the end of an era. The name "Carolana" was dropped and "Carolina" adopted, this time in honor of the new King Charles. The charter contained the Bishop of Durham Clause as well as provisions for the enforcement of extensive feudal powers by the Proprietors. They could exercise martial law; establish counties, towns, and other civil units; construct forts and castles; levy taxes and collect duties; appoint officials; and grant pardons. They had other privileges as well—the right to certain fish and minerals, for example. On the other hand, colonists in Carolina also had important rights, demonstrating the new idea that private citizens might be protected in their rights by a formal document. Laws for the colony should be enacted "with the advice, assent, and approbation of the Freemen" or by their representatives in an Assembly. Although the Church of England was to be the established church in Carolina, the Proprietors were to permit freedom of worship to those who could not conform to the ritual and beliefs of that church so long as they did not interfere with it and paid their required tithes toward its support. For himself, King Charles demanded "Faith, Allegiance, and Sovereign Dominion" from all his subjects residing in Carolina. Colonists, in brief, were to have the same rights and obligations as if they had remained in England, and a century later they reminded Charles's successor of this fact.

The eight Lords Proprietors included several prominent officials as well as two people who had some knowledge of America. Ranking first was Edward Hyde, earl of Clarendon, a lawyer, member of Parliament, and close adviser to both Charles I and Charles II as well as lord high chancellor of England. George Monck, duke of Albemarle, was next; a general in Oliver Cromwell's army, he had switched allegiance at a critical time to assist in making it possible for the monarchy to be reestablished. William Craven, earl of Craven, an army officer and friend of the royal family, served on England's permanent council of war. John Lord Berkeley, after fighting valiantly for the royal cause at the beginning of the civil war, joined the royal family in exile. Anthony Ashley Cooper, afterward earl of Shaftesbury, was chancellor of the exchequer, but he remained in England in the service of Parliament until, at a propitious time, he took subtle steps to bring about the return of the monarchy. Sir George Carteret lived on the Isle of Jersey off the coast of France where he opened his home to members of royalty while they were in exile; a naval officer, he rendered good service to the king's cause. Sir William Berkeley was governor of Virginia at various times between 1641 and 1677, and he welcomed supporters of the Crown who were obliged to flee England for a time. His knowledge of the land south of Virginia made him a valuable member of the Proprietary body, and he may have suggested to his more influential colleagues that they seek a grant from the king. The last-named Proprietor was Sir John Colleton of Barbados, a loyal subject of the Crown who also was familiar with the Carolina region. A planter in the West Indies, he had been seeking a suitable place to move as land on Barbados fell into the hands of large sugar planters. He, too, may have suggested the desirability of a Carolina grant, for there is some evidence that he had visited the region.

Beginning Government

Initially the other Proprietors relied on Sir William Berkeley in Virginia to get things moving. Since his appointment in October 1662, Samuel Stephens had been "commander of the southern plantation," and two years passed before William Drummond, a Lowland Scot living in Virginia, was commissioned by the Proprietary board to be "governor and commander in chief" of the new "Countie of Albemarle." Almost at once, however, Berkeley began authorizing grants for land, and soon the Proprietors sent over instructions for the creation of three counties: Albemarle, Clarendon, and Craven. Since for them land represented wealth, early settlement was important. One of the Proprietors, Sir John Colleton, took out a grant for himself in Roanoke Sound; the site is now known as Colington Island. Sir William Berkeley tried to secure in his own name the region north of Albemarle Sound that had already been settled, but he was not successful. Nevertheless, for many years Virginia tried to claim this region, in part because it never acknowledged the loss of the land that it had called the Southern Plantation, which was given to the Proprietors in 1665 when their grant was enlarged.

The Proprietors established a land tax called a quitrent. It acquired this name because it "quit" the landowner from certain feudal obligations to which the Proprietors were entitled under the provisions of their charter. The quitrent varied from time to time from a farthing ($\frac{1}{4}$ *d.*) to a half-penny ($\frac{1}{2}$ *d.*) and was levied by the acre without regard to the location, productivity, or value of the land. This tax, which was continued throughout the colonial period, was the source of much dissension. To entice settlers, collection of the quitrent was delayed for several years. Land was granted on a headright basis,[1] with one hundred acres for each undertaker,[2] fifty acres for each manservant capable of bearing arms and equipped to do so, and thirty acres for each woman servant. Indentured servants, men and women, were to be given ten and six acres respectively on completion of their term of service. From quitrent revenue would come the costs of administering the government of the colony.

With the appointment of a governor of Albemarle, Sir William Berkeley was also instructed to select six persons to serve as a Council. The governor and Council jointly would elect both civil and military officers as necessary with the

---

1. A grant to the person who met certain conditions.
2. The person who arranged to acquire land and become a permanent settler.

exception of the secretary and the surveyor, both of whom were to be named by the Proprietors. Delegates to an Assembly were to be elected by the freeholders and they, together with the governor and Council, were to pass laws and ordinances for the sound government of the colony. All laws were to be sent home to the Proprietors within a year for their approval, but in the meantime the laws would be in force. New settlers began to arrive, joining those who had moved down from Virginia in search of land on the fringes of the area extending from the Jamestown center.

While settlers from Virginia were pushing south overland in search of better farms and opportunities to trade, others from New England arrived at Cape Fear by ship. Leaving Charlestown, Massachusetts, on 14 August 1662, they explored around the mouth of the Cape Fear River which they called Charles River. Finding fertile land, excellent climate, assorted valuable trees, and abundant wildlife, they purchased land from the natives. News of this country spread in New England and soon afterward a colony of men arrived. By early April 1663, however, the colonists left suddenly, abandoning their livestock and posting a note in the vicinity greatly disparaging the area.

Four months later, in August 1663, an expedition from Barbados sailed for the same region, which the visitors found to be most inviting. The Lords Proprietors encouraged them to settle, and in May of the following year a colony arrived and the county of Clarendon was established under the leadership of John Vassall. A third county envisioned by the Proprietors, to be named Craven, did not materialize until 1670 when a settlement to the south was begun; this became the nucleus of South Carolina.

Eager to promote the settlement of their new counties, the Proprietors made some "proposals" to prospective settlers. One of the most remarkable documents issued by them was the "Concessions and Agreement" drafted in January 1665 in consultation with Sir John Yeamans. Yeamans was then named governor of Clarendon County; also appointed were a deputy governor, a surveyor, a secretary, and other officers as well as an Assembly. The Concessions and Agreement implemented many provisions of the charter of 1663. It called for the creation of a legislature which could pass all necessary laws, the creation of courts, the erection of forts, the passage of naturalization laws, and the collection of taxes. It provided for the granting of land, and it also noted that no person was to be in any way "molested punished disquieted or called in question for any differences in opinion or practice in matters of religious concernment."

Charles Town, created as a trading center on the western bank of the Cape Fear River in Clarendon County, flourished for a time under the governorship of Yeamans. The county's population, according to a pamphlet published in 1666, grew to around eight hundred. Neglect from London and difficulty with the local Indians soon led to its decline. People began to drift away, some returning to Barbados and others going to Albemarle, Virginia, and New England. A few leaders tried to persuade some of the colonists to remain; but when the number dwindled to just half a dozen by the late summer of 1667, the site was abandoned. Houses in the village of Charles Town as well as those on surrounding farms, together with their gardens and fields, were left to the Indians. Some natives from as far away as the Cherokee country, who regularly passed this way en route to the seaside to gather yaupon leaves for a favorite tea they used in ceremonies, took whatever they found in the empty town and deserted houses that pleased their fancy. They even carried off bricks from the chimneys. It was reported that a young apple orchard was dug up and moved to a mountain village.

The Proprietors were unhappy about some of the provisions of the Concessions and Agreement, and they were disappointed by the fate of Clarendon and the slow growth of Albemarle. In another attempt to promote settlement as well as to protect property rights, a new document was prepared for the government of Carolina. This was "The Fundamental Constitutions of Carolina," supposedly written by philosopher John Locke, Ashley Cooper's protégé, who served for a time as secretary to the Proprietors. Dated 21 July 1669, it was intended "for the better settlement of the Government of the said Place, and establishing the interest of the Lords Proprietors with Equality, and without confusion; and that the Government of this Province may be made most agreeable into the Monarchy under which we live, and of which this province is a part; and that we may avoid erecting a numerous Democracy."

The Fundamental Constitutions provided for a feudal system in which Carolina would be divided into counties and other divisions maintained by a colonial nobility with such titles as palatine, cacique, and landgrave. The Proprietors and this nobility were to hold two-thirds of the land, and the rest was to be granted to settlers. Manors, owned by the nobility and worked by "leet men," whose status was perpetual, would be organized on a feudal pattern. Government would be controlled by the Proprietors, whose meetings were to be presided over by the oldest Proprietor, known as the palatine. A "parliament," consisting of Proprietors, nobility, and representatives of the people, would be established. Such a cumbersome and complex system might have worked in feudal Europe, but it clearly was not suitable for the wilderness of America. In spite of the fact that the document was declared to be "perpetual and unalterable," it went through five editions consisting of a maximum of 125 sections and finally a mere 41. Eventually, of course, it was abandoned.

Only a few portions of the Fundamental Constitutions were implemented. The Palatine Court became an important agency in setting policy, yet because the Proprietors were far removed from Carolina and knew so little about it, many of their plans were unrealistic. South Carolina had twenty-six landgraves and thirteen caciques, but North Carolina had only a handful. Among the landgraves were Sir John Colleton, Robert Daniel, Charles Eden, Christoph von Graffenried, and Sir John Yeamans, while John Gibbs, who at one time claimed to be governor, was a cacique. Although most of the provisions were impractical, some had much to commend them and were far ahead of their time. These included the registration of births, marriages, deaths, and land titles; biennial legislative sessions; trial by jury; and religious toleration. After trying for thirty years to persuade the colonial Assembly to approve the document, the Proprietors eventually instructed the governors to "come as nigh the Constitutions" as they could. Even this did not work, and in 1693 the Proprietors declared that the Fundamental Constitutions "are now ceased." Yet five years later they reissued them in abbreviated form.

Although Carolina was legally headed by the eight Lords Proprietors, the actual government of Albemarle was vested in the **governor** and his Council, which was chosen by the Proprietors, in conjunction with the Assembly, which was elected by the freeholders. The governors of Albemarle County (1664–89) and of North Carolina (1689–1729) were commissioned by the Proprietors. Their terms of office were indefinite, though at first there seems to have been a general agreement on three years. Their salary was left to the local Assembly and was to be paid from the quitrents and from the sale of land, with fees providing an additional source of income. The governor had extensive executive, legislative, judicial, and administrative powers. He appointed the Council, and called and presided over its sessions. He appointed all judicial and administrative officers, including most of the local officials; administered oaths of office and allegiance; and issued and revoked military commissions. He could remove officials without the Council's consent, and could grant pardons and reprieves. He had the power to summon, prorogue, and dissolve the Assembly, and the right to veto any law. With the advice and consent of the Council, he issued writs for the election of delegates to the Assembly. The governor also issued warrants for land grants; probated wills; conducted relations with other colonies, with Indian tribes, and with the mother country; headed the military and naval forces of the province; and exerted his authority in church affairs.

The **Council** assisted the governor in executive and administrative matters; in the early days, together with the elected members of the Assembly, they formed the legislative branch of the government. Sitting with the governor, the Council also constituted the highest court in the colony until the creation of a supreme court near the turn of the century. At first the Council had six members, then from six to twelve, and finally ten.

The **Assembly** was the popular or elective branch of the legislature. According to tradition a legislative Assembly of all the freeholders in Albemarle was held in 1664, but there are no records of such a meeting. Representative government actually began under the Concessions and Agreement of 1665, which provided that twelve men be chosen annually to sit with the governor and Council as a legislature. This system prevailed until 1670, when Albemarle was divided into four precincts: Chowan, Pasquotank, Perquimans, and Currituck, with each being allowed five delegates in the lower house.

Until some time around 1695–97, the elected representatives sat with the governor and Council as a unicameral body presided over by the governor or his deputy. After the adoption of the bicameral system, the lower house elected its own speaker and other officers, adopted its own rules of procedure, and exercised many "parliamentary privileges" similar to those of the British House of Commons, such as the right to expel members, enforce their attendance, decide contested elections, and initiate money measures. The house could meet only on the call of the governor and at a place designated by him, since there was no fixed seat of government. In fact, the legislature was convened biennially, or more often, because the governor depended on it for his salary. The house was jealous of its "power of the purse" and largely through this weapon increased its prestige and influence at the expense of the governor and Council.

Controversies between the lower house, led by the speaker, who was the highest elected official in the government, and the "prerogative party," usually led by the governor, who represented the Proprietors and later the royal prerogative, ran through the history of colonial North Carolina right up to the beginning of the American Revolution. The province, in fact, earned the reputation of being perhaps the most rebellious and unruly of England's American colonies. There were long and bitter quarrels over the governor's salary, quitrents, land patents, rent rolls, taxes, paper currency, defense, the selection of officials, the location of the capital, and numerous other matters. The "popular party" won many of these contests, and the lower house had a reputation for independence. In 1717 an Anglican missionary, the Reverend John Urmston, commented that "this Lawless people will allow of no power or authority in either Church or state save what is derived from them." Governor George Burrington declared in 1731 that "The Assembly of this Province have always usurped more power than they ought to be allowed." On another occasion, perhaps boasting, he wrote: "All the governors that ever lived in this Province lived in fear of the People (except myself) and Dreaded their Assemblyes."

At the head of the system of **courts**, both of Albemarle County and later of North Carolina, was the General Court, which at first consisted of the governor and Council and was the appellate court of the colony. In 1685 the Proprietors instructed the governor to appoint "four able discreet men" as justices for Albemarle, but as late as 1695 the governor and Council still acted as the highest court in the province. Sometime between then and 1702 the old court was reorganized, however, and in 1712 Christopher Gale was commissioned chief justice by the Proprietors.

There also was a court of chancery, made up of the governor and Council, which sat without a jury and probated wills, received and examined accounts of administrators and executors, tried public officials for malfeasance, and perhaps performed other judicial duties.

Each precinct (later called a county) had a court administered by justices of the peace who were appointed by the governor. This Court of Pleas and Quarter Sessions set the stage for what remained the basic form of county government until 1768. The justices not only had limited civil jurisdiction—cases valued up to £50—and criminal jurisdiction, but they also exercised many administrative powers such as the creation of road districts; the care of roads, bridges, and ferries; and the location of millsites. The apportionment of taxes was another duty of the county court. The executive officer of the precinct or county court was the provost marshal, an appointee of the governor. In 1738 the title of this office was changed to **sheriff**. There were also clerks of the precinct courts who kept a record of the marks or brands of livestock and did other clerical work.

When Clarendon County was abandoned in 1667, Albemarle County was the only organized government in the North Carolina region. For the next two decades, the history of Albemarle as a separate colony is a story of unrest, confusion, slow growth, and armed rebellion. There were numerous reasons for this unhappy state of affairs. Many settlers had been there before the Proprietors acquired their interest in the region and they resented the interference. Albemarle was an isolated settlement, largely out of touch with the outside world. Communication by land was almost impossible except with Virginia, and even this was difficult because of forests, swamps, and rivers which made travel hazardous. The inlets, sounds, and rivers in Albemarle were shallow and only small vessels could use them. After the founding of Craven County in 1670 and the settlement of Charles Town on the Ashley and Cooper rivers, the Proprietors turned their attention to that newly settled southern part of Carolina. Colonists moved there with the full knowledge that the Lords Proprietors had authority over them. Insofar as Albemarle was concerned, the Proprietors blamed the residents for their failure to expand, and they complained to the Albemarle Assembly about its "people that neither understood your own nor regarded our Interests."

Concerns over Land

Problems pertaining to land were most troublesome in the colony. The Proprietors tried to develop a land policy and on several occasions instructed the governor and Council about what to do. Some maps were prepared but the Proprietors seem never to have understood them, probably because their territory was so large. They were accustomed to a small country—England was about the same size as present-day North Carolina. The Proprietors also had some promotional tracts published in an attempt to counteract the unfavorable things being said about Albemarle. In 1666 *A Brief Description of the Province of Carolina*, written by a man who had never seen the place, described Carolina in glowing terms, stressing the fertile soil, the good weather, the healthy location, and so on—not unlike a modern chamber of commerce publication. It also offered new settlers a period of seven years' freedom from paying customs duties on certain articles, hundred-acre grants of land, a welcome opportunity to participate in making laws, and other advantages.

Still people did not move to Albemarle in large numbers. This was due in part to the confusion and uncertainty about the terms of landholding. The first legislature of Albemarle petitioned the Proprietors that its residents might hold land on the same terms that prevailed in Virginia. Quitrents there were just a farthing an acre, whereas in Albemarle the rate was twice that—a half-penny. In Virginia this tax could be paid in produce, but in Albemarle it had to be paid in coin. The Proprietors were told that many people in Virginia wanted to move to Albemarle but were discouraged by this discrimination.

Responding favorably to the legislature's request, the Proprietors on 1 May 1668 signed and sent to their new governor, Samuel Stephens, a document that came to be called the "Great Deed of Grant." It gave the settlers of Albemarle the same terms as those that prevailed in Virginia.

To implement this more attractive land policy, the Albemarle Assembly in 1669 passed several laws intended to stimulate immigration and to promote the colony's welfare. Newcomers were exempted from taxes for a year; they were also to be free for five years from lawsuits because of debt or from prosecution for crimes committed outside Albemarle. A new law prohibited the ownership of more than 660 acres in one tract, except by those who received grants directly from the Proprietors. There may have been several reasons for this law—to permit more people to acquire land fronting on the sound or river, to democratize landholding, and perhaps to check speculation. People who did not live in the colony were also prohibited from trading with the Indians. And since Carolina had no clergymen, civil officials were permitted to perform marriages and marriage was made a civil contract.

Some of these laws, especially that preventing lawsuits for five years, the marriage act, and the Indian trade law provoked Virginia officials. They began to make disparaging remarks about Albemarle, calling it a "Rogue's Harbor" and other unflattering names. They conveniently forgot that the Albemarle laws were copied—word for word—from those passed in Virginia in 1642, when conditions there were very much like those in Albemarle at this time.

Neither the Proprietors' action nor the laws of the Assembly had the desired

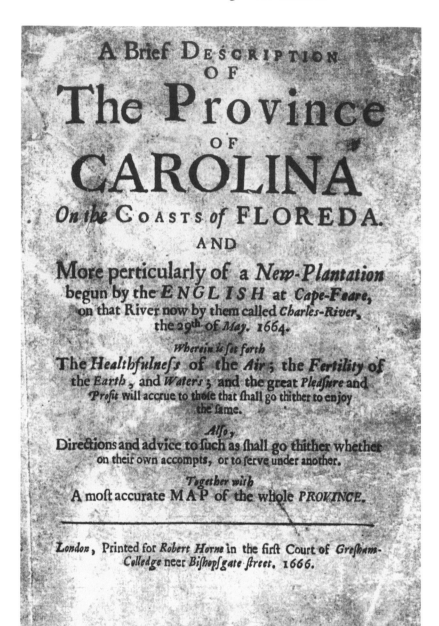

A Brief DESCRIPTION
OF
The Province
OF
CAROLINA
On the COASTS of FLOREDA.
AND
More perticularly of a *New-Plantation*
begun by the *ENGLISH* at *Cape-Feare*,
on that River now by them called *Charles-River*,
the 29th of *May*. 1664.

Wherein is set forth
The *Healthfulness* of the *Air*; the *Fertility* of
the *Earth*, and *Waters*; and the great *Pleasure* and
Profit will accrue to those that shall go thither to enjoy
the same.

Also,
Directions and advice to such as shall go thither whether
on their own accompts, or to serve under another.

Together with
A most accurate MAP of the whole *PROVINCE*.

London, Printed for *Robert Horne* in the first Court of *Gresham-
Colledge* neer *Bishopsgate street*. 1666.

Promotional tracts were frequently issued in England by individuals or groups of people interested in encouraging settlement in America. While this one pertained basically to the lower Cape Fear River section, it served to publicize the region acquired by the eight Lords Proprietors in 1663. (North Carolina Collection, University of North Carolina at Chapel Hill) effect. Moreover, the Proprietors instructed several governors to raise the quitrent rate higher than it had ever been; yet they continued to issue promotional tracts with glowing descriptions of their land and exaggerated promises to potential settlers. Opposition in Virginia grew, and at this time some of its leaders made an issue of the land north of Albemarle Sound. They wanted the region because, they said, it was being settled by idle debtors, thieves, pirates, and runaway servants. In 1679 Virginia prohibited the shipment of Albemarle tobacco through its ports, and it was suspected that officials in that colony were inciting Indians along the border to attack Albemarle settlers.

Culpeper's Rebellion

The failure of the Proprietors to establish a strong, stable, and efficient government was one of the greatest handicaps to the growth and progress of Albemarle. Some of its governors were weak and ineffective, some were unscrupulous, most were unsatisfactory. The Proprietors were forced to admit that it was difficult to get a worthy man to accept the position. The governors failed to preserve order, promote the welfare of the people, or defend the colony against Indians, pirates, and other enemies. Constant trouble marked their administrations. John Jenkins (1672–76) was deposed by a rival faction; Thomas Miller (1677) was overthrown and jailed by "armed rebels"; Thomas Eastchurch was forbidden to enter the colony; and finally Seth Sothel (1683–89) was accused by the Assembly of numerous crimes, tried, convicted, and banished.

Such a government was unable to protect its people during several small Indian uprisings. In 1675 the Chowanocs, spurred on by neighboring Indians to the north, attacked white settlements. It was said that colonists were afraid to venture far from home except in groups of three or four. The uprising was quelled "by God's assistance though not without loss of many men."

Following this outbreak, and while the people were still armed, there occurred in Carolina an uprising known as Culpeper's Rebellion. Its causes were deep-seated, going back almost to the beginning of the colony's history. The controversy involved two somewhat related factors: a factional fight between what might be called the Proprietary and anti-Proprietary factions; and the efforts of England to enforce the Navigation Acts, particularly the Plantation Duty Act of 1673.

Parliament, in attempting to carry out the policies of British mercantilism, passed Navigation Acts in 1651 and 1660. Their purpose was the promotion of direct trade between England and its colonies by limiting this commerce to British, Irish, and colonial vessels. In addition, certain "enumerated articles," including tobacco, could be shipped only to England. Open evasion of this legal requirement, such as the shipment of tobacco to New England labeled as "bait for New England fishermen," led to the passage of the Plantation Duty Act of 1673. This act permitted tobacco and certain other products to be shipped to other colonies provided a duty was paid. The duty on tobacco was a penny per pound. Tobacco was the chief source of income for the people in Albemarle, and most of it was exported in ships belonging to about half a dozen traders from Massachusetts and Rhode Island.

The Lords Proprietors had strong reasons to enforce the acts of Parliament. If they failed to do so, their charter might be withdrawn—particularly given the evidence of some sentiment in England against Proprietary colonies. They also believed that their colonists would benefit—by being able to buy goods directly from England at less cost and by getting a better price for their tobacco.

Such pre-1663 settlers as George Durant and John Jenkins, however, were opposed to the Navigation Acts since they denied them the benefits of a very profitable trade with New England merchants. In 1672 Governor Peter Carteret, at the request of the Assembly, went to England to discuss the colony's interests with the Proprietors.

At this point the two factions, Proprietary and anti-Proprietary, became even more active. In 1673 King Charles ordered all colonial governors to select officers who would enforce the trade laws, and two years later he repeated his orders. Since it appeared that Albemarle was not going to comply, the Treasury Board in England appointed both a collector and a surveyor for the colony, but these officers never showed up. Governor John Jenkins was then allowed to name two men, and he selected Valentine Bird as collector and Timothy Biggs as surveyor. Jenkins really had no intention of enforcing the Plantation Duty Act; in taking this position, he had the backing of Durant, Albemarle's most influential political leader, as well as of a newcomer, John Culpeper. Recently arrived from Charles Town in the southern part of Carolina, Culpeper had the reputation of a troublemaker who enjoyed a good fight. He had been "invited" to leave Charles Town and found the unstable conditions in Albemarle very much to his liking. A kind of coalition was formed by Durant, Culpeper, and Jenkins. Their opponents were Thomas Eastchurch, who happened to be Speaker of the Assembly, and Thomas Miller; both were relatively new to the colony and supported the Proprietary faction.

Jenkins, in an arbitrary effort to crush the opposition, had Miller arrested and jailed for "treasonable utterances," and he tried to prevent Eastchurch from appealing to England about the governor's failure to enforce the law and about the deplorable situation in Albemarle. When he ordered the dissolution of the Assembly, its members—under Speaker Eastchurch's firm control—refused to disband. Instead, the Assembly drew up a list of misdemeanors committed by Governor Jenkins, removed him from office, and put him in jail. Miller, in the meantime, had escaped from jail, and he and Eastchurch went to England to report to the Proprietors.

Their account must have been believed. In November 1676 Eastchurch was appointed governor and directed to halt the trade with New England. He was also instructed to establish three ports of entry where customs collectors would be stationed, to determine the depth of water at low tides through the inlets, and to do whatever was necessary to enforce the trade laws. At the same time, Miller was made secretary and collector of the customs.

On the voyage back to Albemarle their ship called at the island of Nevis in the West Indies. There Eastchurch met a wealthy widow and delayed his journey until he could court and marry her. He sent Miller on ahead with instructions to act as president of the Council and therefore also serve as acting governor. (This was improper as Eastchurch had not yet been installed as governor himself. After assuming office, however, it would have been his right to name a Council president.) Miller reached the colony and managed to install himself in most of his assorted offices. As customs collector he seized a large quantity of tobacco and other goods illegally imported, and he collected £8,000 in customs duties. As governor, however, he proved to be unacceptable. He interfered with precinct elections, imposed heavy fines, and arrested and imprisoned several prominent men. He also organized a "pipeing guard" which he said was for defense against Indians, but some suspected this was either for his personal protection or to glorify his position. His opponents charged him with corruption, vindictiveness, tyranny, and "many hanious maters." The Proprietors agreed that Miller "did many extravagant things" and soon "lost his reputation and interest among yᵉ people."

Smouldering resistance broke out into armed rebellion in December 1677, after Captain Zachariah Gillam arrived in the Pasquotank River with his usual shipload of goods (including guns and ammunition) to engage in trade. When Gillam went ashore, Miller personally arrested him for violating the Navigation Acts and held him under a heavy bond. Armed with a pair of pistols, Miller also arrested George Durant, who was aboard Gillam's ship, "as a Traytour." Gillam did not appreciate his reception and threatened to go elsewhere to trade, but the people, aroused to action by Durant and Culpeper, begged Gillam to stay and promised to support him against Miller.

After consulting with Durant, a group consisting of Culpeper, Bird, and others devised a plan to oust Miller. Assisted by about forty men from Pasquotank Precinct and armed with weapons supplied by Gillam, the insurgents surrounded Miller's house, captured and imprisoned him, seized the tobacco that he had collected, and took possession of the customs revenues and records. They then arrested other officials and issued a statement defending their actions and demanding that Albemarle have a "free parliament." For the latter purpose they called for an election of delegates to an assembly that would meet at Durant's house.

The response was favorable, and an assembly composed of eighteen delegates met and appointed five of their number to join with Richard Foster and one Proprietary deputy on their side as the council. The council then tried Miller and several other prisoners in an early instance of impeachment. Miller was imprisoned; the council declared that if Eastchurch attempted to take over the governorship, "they would serve him ye same sauce." To demonstrate the seriousness of its intentions, the council sent some armed men to the Virginia border to await Eastchurch's arrival. The Proprietary governor did reach Virginia, presumably with his new wife, and was promised the support of that colony's governor, but Eastchurch became ill—perhaps from a tropical disease—and died before he had an opportunity to test the intentions of the "rebels" in Albemarle.

Assuming the powers of government, the rebels conducted the government "by their owne authority & according to their own modell." The assembly appointed Culpeper customs collector. Some of the prisoners, including Miller, escaped from jail and went to England to present their case to the Lords Proprietors. The assembly then sent Culpeper to London to assure the Proprietors of its allegiance and to "insist very highly for right against Miller."

Crown officials ordered a full investigation of the so-called rebellion. The Proprietors were instructed to present an account of it, together with "an authentick Copy of their Charter." Fearful of losing their charter, the Proprietors minimized the uprising. Anthony Ashley Cooper, now the earl of Shaftesbury, who defended Culpeper in court, successfully demonstrated that there had been "no settled government" in the colony at the time and that those involved in the affair were guilty only "of riot." Culpeper was acquitted of the charges of rebellion. His presence in London for trial probably explains the use of the name "Culpeper's Rebellion" when others, Durant particularly, were more directly involved. Culpeper's Rebellion has been recognized as one of the first popular uprisings in the American colonies.

Seth Sothel's Excesses

Now aware of the existence and influence of factions in the colony, the Proprietors determined to improve conditions. Their next choice for governor had several qualifications: first, he was a Proprietor, having recently purchased the share granted in 1663 to Edward Hyde; he had been involved in the affairs of Carolina for fifteen years and was aware of the needs of the colony; and he was certainly not a member of either faction there. He was Seth Sothel, described as sober, moderate, and a man with the ability to "settle things well." After setting off for his new post, he was captured on the high seas by Turkish pirates and taken to Algiers. One report said that for a year in the dry heat of North Africa he was forced to haul brick on his back at a construction site.

Meanwhile, in Albemarle John Harvey, president of the Council, acted as governor and Robert Holden as collector. Both were "Quyetly and cherefully obeyed," but Harvey died within a year and the Council selected—and the Proprietors approved—John Jenkins as his successor. This was a clear victory for the Durant faction; "although Jenkins had the title, yet in fact Durant governed and used Jenkins as his property." Durant was the ablest leader in the province. Under his direction, order was restored, laws were enforced, customs duties were collected without difficulty, a tax was levied to make good the revenues seized "in the tyme of the disorders," and an act was passed pardoning the rebels. A few diehards of the opposing faction tried to make trouble, but it was reported in 1680 that "all things are in quyet."

Firm in their choice of Sothel for governor, the Proprietors again commissioned him in 1681. He arrived at his post in 1683. At this point conditions in the colony changed drastically. Sothel turned out not to be the man his colleagues on the Proprietary board thought him to be. Indeed, he quickly proved to be one of the most arbitrary and corrupt governors in any of the English colonies. It was charged that he imprisoned a large number of his opponents without trial; detained some on the false charge that they were pirates; illegally seized several estates; "detained" cattle, slaves, and even several yards of lace and seven pewter dishes belonging to others; and accepted bribes. When Thomas Pollock threatened to appeal to the Proprietors, Sothel had him jailed. Upon further protests from Pollock, the governor confiscated Pollock's entire estate for his own use.

By 1688 the people could no longer endure their Proprietary governor, and the following year he was tried by the Assembly. Sothel chose to be judged by the legislators rather than by his fellow Proprietors. He was found guilty on thirteen charges—for, among other things, oppression, tyranny, extortion, and bribery. By way of punishment he was banished from the colony for a year and declared to be forever ineligible to hold office in the government. Although he did not leave promptly, Sothel moved to South Carolina where he forced out the Proprietary governor, took over the post himself, and generally repeated his Albemarle behavior. After some delay the Proprietors succeeded in removing him from office; he then lived in South Carolina and apparently also in Virginia. He eventually returned to Albemarle, at least for a brief time, where he is said to have died at the home of John Porter.

Gibbs's Rebellion

Still intent on solving the problems of Albemarle, the Proprietors in December 1689 named Philip Ludwell governor. He assumed office the next year, probably in May, with instructions to see to the quiet and safety of the province and to deliver a letter to Sothel informing him of his dismissal. Ludwell was also told to select the three most honest and able men in the colony to "hear and determine all causes both Civill and Criminall according to Law." If he found anything deficient or inconvenient to the inhabitants, the Proprietors promised to provide a remedy.

The new governor hardly had time to unpack his trunk when he was faced with an unpleasant incident. Captain John Gibbs, a relative of the Proprietor George Monck, duke of Albemarle, and a cacique in the local nobility, claimed to be governor. He may have been so designated by Sothel when he was deposed, but more likely the claim was based on the fact that he expected to be the heir of the childless Monck and was also a cacique. Under the Fundamental Constitutions either fact would have made him eligible for the position. At any rate, on Ludwell's arrival Gibbs proclaimed himself governor and announced that he would defend his position. If anyone denied his rights, he said, he was prepared to "fight him in this Cause, as long as my Eyelids shall Wagg," quoting Shakespeare's *Hamlet*.

Although Gibbs and a handful of his supporters did break up a precinct court, taking two magistrates prisoner, they lacked adequate resources. Gibbs fled to Virginia, where he had lived before moving to Albemarle when Sothel was removed from office. At Ludwell's request the governor of Virginia "quieted these stirs" in some manner, but it was uncertain how long they would remain peaceful.

Probably at the suggestion of Governor Francis Nicholson of Virginia, Gibbs and Ludwell both went to England to present their claims to the Proprietors. There it was determined that Gibbs's claims were not valid. In Albemarle Thomas Jarvis was acting governor until November 1691, when Ludwell was named "Governor of Carolina." Largely ignoring the Fundamental Constitutions, the Proprietors instructed Ludwell to make the Carolina government conform to the charter from the Crown. As governor of the province, he was to reside in Charles Town and appoint a deputy for the northern part of the colony. There was to be a single "Parliament," but, because it was impractical for representatives to go there from Albemarle, this was never implemented. In addition, the five members of the Council previously elected by the Assembly were abolished.

Ludwell's administration inaugurated a new era in North Carolina history. For the next fifteen years the people enjoyed orderly, well-administered, peaceful government, a situation partially due to capable deputy governors and "acting governors"—Thomas Jarvis (1691–94), John Archdale (governor of both parts of Carolina, 1694–96), Thomas Harvey (1696–99), and Henderson Walker (1699–1704). Ludwell's clear understanding of the character and prejudices of the people, together with his good sense and sensitivity, enabled him to restore the peace. His recognition of the Great Deed of Grant pleased the colonists but annoyed the Proprietors to such an extent that they removed him from office.

Each of the subordinate governors residing in the northern part of Carolina was an old-timer. They were all men of good character and sound judgment. Some were well educated, and one was a lawyer and a sincere churchman. Henderson Walker in particular resented the "imputation of evil neighborhood" with which some Virginians tried to tag their southern neighbors.

Extended Settlement

About the time that Ludwell took office, settlers began to make their way across Albemarle Sound to occupy land along the Pamlico River. In 1694 the Proprietors, in an effort to encourage settlement, instructed Archdale to create as many counties as he deemed necessary for the better government of the colony. In compliance, Bath County was established in 1696; it embraced the entire region from Albemarle Sound to Cape Fear.

With improved conditions, settlers began moving into Carolina at a rapid rate. A great many came from Manakin Town, a French Huguenot settlement a few miles above the Falls of the James River near present-day Richmond. To escape persecution in France, the Huguenots had started this settlement in 1700 under the leadership of the Marquis de la Muce and Charles de Sailly, but the English had taken over most of the fertile land so that the French "were hemmed in on all Hands from providing more Land for themselves and their Children." In North Carolina they found the climate to be pleasant and the land cheap and abundant. These industrious people made a favorable impression on their neighbors and, according to John Lawson, set good examples of industry.

The movement of people from Virginia to this newly opened region grew so quickly that England's Board of Trade ordered an inquiry into the causes and possible means of preventing it. Virginia, after all, was a royal colony while Carolina belonged to the Proprietors; thus, the Board of Trade was concerned about the possible loss of a source of wealth. Governor Henderson Walker indignantly denied the charge that Virginia runaways were being harbored in his colony. He assured the board that after diligent inquiry he could find none, nor would he permit them to come if he could prevent it.

On a low bluff overlooking the Pamlico River, John Lawson, the surveyor general of the province, laid off a town; on 8 March 1706, through the efforts of Lawson, Joel Martin, and Simon Alderson, it was incorporated as Bath, the first town in North Carolina. Although Bath grew slowly and never became very populous, it was a place of considerable political and commercial importance for a number of decades. In 1715 Port Bath was created as the first official port of entry in the province and assigned a customs collector. The legislature met in the town in 1744 and 1752.

The Reverend William Gordon, an Anglican missionary who was in Bath in 1709, said it consisted of about a dozen houses. Although there was no church, the surveyors had laid out a glebe—a farm adjoining the town that was held for the benefit of the Church of England clergyman who might some day come to serve the people in the town. He also mentioned that a collection of books had been sent there from England by the Reverend Thomas Bray, of the new Society for the Propagation of the Gospel, for a public library. At the same time two additional collections of books were sent to other parts of the colony.

With the arrival of so many settlers from Virginia, the Council in 1706 observed that Bath County had "grown populous and daily increasing." As a result the Council divided it into three precincts: Archdale, Wickham, and Pamptecough (Pamlico). It was perhaps the very next year that a rather large group of Huguenots from Virginia passed through on their way to take up land along the Neuse and Trent rivers. John Lawson noted that nearly all of the French from Manakin Town had by then moved to the Trent River and that the few left were expected to arrive almost any day.

Most of the land from the Virginia border to the shores of Albemarle Sound had been occupied by 1710; people also had settled along the Roanoke, Pamlico, and Neuse rivers, sometimes in places extending thirty miles from the river. In 1675 the population of Albemarle was estimated to be around 4,000, whereas in 1715 the whole of Carolina (excluding, of course, the part that became South Carolina) contained approximately 11,000 people. Virginia officials regretted the loss of its colonists, reporting that "many of our poorer sort of Inhabitants daily removed themselves into our neighboring colonies, especially to North Carolina, which is the reason the number of our Inhabitants doth not increase proportionately to what might be expected . . . the chief cause of this Removal is want of land to plant and cultivate."

The largest and most significant settlement in the Neuse-Trent area was made in 1710 by a colony of Palatines from southwestern Germany, some Swiss, and a few English at a place selected and laid out by John Lawson. It occupied the site of a former Tuscarora village, Chattoka—a name the Indians took to the New York area when they moved north and there became Chautauqua. The 1710 colony was a result of the promotional activity of a Swiss land company, George Ritter and Company, headed by Baron Christoph von Graffenried and Franz

This map of Carolina was published in London in 1708. (North Carolina Collection, University of North Carolina at Chapel Hill)

Louis Michel. For some time the baron had been interested in planting a colony of persecuted Palatines and Swiss in America; he had made extensive inquiries about mines, agriculture, forest resources, and the best means of making a successful settlement. In London he talked with the duke of Albemarle, who impressed him with the advantages of Carolina. Parliament about the same time passed a naturalization law for foreign Protestants, and as a consequence approximately 13,000 Palatines arrived in England during the next two years. Most of these impoverished immigrants found their way to London, which was already burdened with its own poor and was in no position to cope with more.

Queen Anne, granddaughter of the original Proprietor, Edward Hyde, approved of Graffenried's plans for a colony. Her position coincided with that of a number of English capitalists, who supported the idea of colonization as a solution to the country's problem of overpopulation. The queen agreed to assume the £4,000 cost of transportation if Graffenried would take a hundred Palatine families to America. After conferring with John Lawson, then in London to arrange for the publication of his book, *A New Voyage to Carolina*, the baron decided to plant his colony in North Carolina. Ritter and Company purchased from the Proprietors nearly 19,000 acres of land on the Neuse and Trent rivers for £175. He also paid a substantial amount to the Indians who occupied this land.

The colonists, as well as tools, implements, and ships, were selected with great care. Graffenried recorded that he chose "young people, healthy, laborous and of all kinds of avocations and handicrafts in number about 650." His first contingent was sent ahead under the leadership of John Lawson and Christopher Gale while he remained in England to await the arrival of a group of Swiss from Bern.

The Palatines left England in January 1710, and after a disastrous and stormy voyage of thirteen weeks, during which about half of the settlers died, they arrived off the coast of Virginia. As they entered the James River, a French privateer plundered one of the vessels and took almost everything the passengers owned. Greatly reduced in number, the colonists traveled overland to the Chowan River where Thomas Pollock provided some provisions and transportation to take them to their destination. At the site of their settlement at the junction of the Neuse and Trent rivers they discovered that no preparations had been made for their arrival. In order to survive, they had to sell what little remained of their clothes and personal possessions to neighboring inhabitants.

Graffenried arrived in September with a hundred Swiss; finding his settlers in disarray, he began at once to organize the colony. Land was surveyed, forests cleared, houses built, and a gristmill erected. The town of New Bern, named for Bern, Switzerland, was well planned for growth. Laid out in the form of a cross, one arm extended from river to river while the street that crossed it stretched back into the wilderness. More cross streets could be built and the long one extended indefinitely. Within eighteen months the settlers were well established, happy, and prosperous. It was observed that these people made more progress in this short time than English colonists did in several years.

Some changes in the making throughout Carolina, however, were destined to interrupt the progress here as well as elsewhere. These pertained to—among other things—the establishment of the Church of England, the presence of dissenting Quakers, the crowding of Indians off their land, and an armed rebellion.

Religion in the Colony

Both charters granted by King Charles II had anticipated that the Anglican church would become the established, tax-supported church of Carolina. So had the Concessions and Agreement, the Fundamental Constitutions, and various instructions sent to the governors. Nevertheless, the Proprietors had done nothing about installing the Church of England; instead, they had permitted any Protestant group to worship as it pleased—these people were called "dissenters" because they dissented from the creed, beliefs, and rituals of the Anglican church.

An Anglican missionary in Albemarle in 1701 found that the colonists fell into four distinct categories with regard to their religious leanings. First and most numerous were the Quakers whom he regarded as enemies of "the Church." (Church, spelled with a capital letter, meant the established church.) The missionary, who undoubtedly had little sympathy for anyone who did not believe as he did, felt that these people did not really know what they believed. The next largest group, he observed, were those who seemed to have no religion but who would have been Quakers if they had been willing to behave themselves. The third category consisted of people "somewhat like Presbyterians, which sort is upheld by some idle fellows who have left their lawful employment, and preach and baptize through the country, without any manner of orders from any sect or pretended Church." These people, it has been suggested, may have been Baptists. Finally, the fourth and smallest group was composed of "the better sort of people, and would do very much for the settlement of the Church government there." The hopes of these Anglicans were stymied, however, by the three other groups which, although each was different, did all they could "to prevent any thing that will be chargeable to them, as they allege Church government will be, if once established by law."

Another Anglican missionary, surely not the most unbiased of observers, referred to the Quakers in Perquimans Precinct as "very numerous, extremely ignorant, insufferably proud, and consequently ungovernable." Those in Pasquotank he found to be "factious, mutinous, and domineering."

Under the governorship of John Archdale, a Proprietor with offices in Charles Town and a recent convert to the Quaker faith, Quakers held the balance of power in Albemarle. Their complete control of the government concerned Anglicans, who were anxious to see the established church assume what they regarded as its rightful role in the colony. Two events suggested that their hopes might be realized. First, Henderson Walker, an able and zealous Anglican churchman, became governor in 1699; he expressed concern that the colony had gone forty years "without priest or altar." By asking the bishop of London, whose jurisdiction included the American colonies, to send a missionary to the province, Walker was responsible for the second encouraging event—the arrival of the Reverend Daniel Brett in 1700. But because of his disorderly behavior, Brett was called "yᶜ Monster of yᶜ Age." Even Walker complained about him in a letter to the bishop: "It hath been a great trouble and grief to us who have a great veneration for the Church that the first minister who was sent to us should prove so ill as to give the Dissenters so much occasion to charge us with him."

Hope was not abandoned, for in 1701 Governor Walker, by "a great deal of care and management," secured the passage of the first church law in North Carolina. Referred to as a Vestry Act, it provided for the laying out of parishes, the organization of vestries, the erection of churches, and a poll tax on all tithables for the support of clergymen. Delighted members of the established church began at once to implement the law, creating Chowan parish (soon to be called St. Paul's Parish, Edenton) on 15 December 1701. Before long parishes were formed in Pasquotank and Perquimans as well. Quakers, Presbyterians, and even some Anglicans objected to the Vestry Act—on principle and because it increased taxes. They determined to have it repealed at the next Assembly, which would have a Quaker majority. The Quakers were relieved when the Proprietors rejected the law, not because of principle but because it gave too much authority to the local vestry and did not provide adequate salaries for the clergy.

In spite of Quaker strength in the Assembly, Walker got another bill through in 1703. It provided that all members of the Assembly must be communicants of the Church of England and also must take an oath of allegiance to Queen Anne. The latter requirement denied the right of affirmation, which Quakers had made previously because an oath was unacceptable to them. Governor Robert Daniel, who succeeded Walker in 1704, and some Anglican leaders contended that the oath had nothing to do with the question of the established church, but the Quakers maintained that it was aimed directly at them and denied their rights. Daniel's position was so unpopular with Presbyterians that they joined the Quakers in securing his removal from office in 1705.

Cary's Rebellion

Thomas Cary, a Charles Town merchant and son-in-law of John Archdale, succeeded Daniel. Cary had been considered friendly to dissenters, but his actions in North Carolina were even more offensive to Quakers than those of his two predecessors. Not only did Cary enforce the oath of allegiance and deprive Quakers of their seats in the legislature, but he also imposed a fine of £5 on any who entered an office without taking the oath. Further, he had the Assembly pass a law that voided the election of anyone who had "promoted his own candidacy."

Disturbed by these events, the Quakers sent John Porter to London to protest to the Proprietors. Through the influence of John Archdale, the Quaker Proprietor, Porter returned with an order to suspend all laws regarding oaths and to remove Cary from office. When Porter arrived, Cary was in Charles Town attending to business and serving in the legislature, and William Glover, president of the Council, was acting in his stead. At first Porter and the Quakers accepted Glover, but when he, too, refused to admit new members until they swore an oath, Porter's group formed an alliance with Cary to turn Glover out. Glover refused to step down and the two factions prepared for a confrontation.

The leaders of both groups agreed to submit their claims to the voters, and an election was held for members of the Assembly. In a bitter contest Cary's supporters had a few more delegates than Glover's; however, when the Assembly convened in October 1708, there were two sets of delegates from each county. Cary's faction, led by Edward Moseley, speaker of the house, prevailed, and Glover, still claiming to be governor, fled to Virginia. From 1708 until 1711 Cary served as governor by virtue of being president of the Council. All laws of the Glover administration were declared void, and Cary appointed a number of Quakers to office.

Unhappy over the chaotic conditions in their province, the Lords Proprietors decided on 7 December 1710 to appoint a governor of North Carolina "independent of the Governor of Carolina." They selected Edward Hyde, a distant relative of Queen Anne through the Proprietor of the same name. A year passed before his instructions were ready and the appointment was approved by the Crown. His commission was dated 24 January 1712. This marked the separation of Carolina into two parts—North Carolina and South Carolina. In the meantime Hyde had gone to the colony where he was acting as deputy governor when his first Assembly convened in March 1711. It passed laws for the punishment of sedition and libel against the government, levied a fine of £100 on officials who refused to qualify "according to the strictness of the laws of Great Britain now in force," provided that laws establishing the Church of England were in force, and nullified all of the laws of Cary's recent administration.

Edward Hyde (1667–1712), was governor of North Carolina in 1711–12, the first to hold that office after it was recognized that there were *two* Carolinas. (North Carolina Division of Archives and History, Raleigh)

Offended by this last action, Cary gathered his followers "with great Guns and other warlike stores" to defy Governor Hyde. While Hyde and his advisers, including Graffenried, were meeting in a house on the shore of Albemarle Sound, Cary, in a ship bearing six guns, approached and fired at the house. Cannonballs landed on the roof and rolled off into the garden. Investigating the commotion, some of Graffenried's servants, dressed in livery, went outside. Cary thought they were marines, and in his haste to retreat he trimmed his sails incorrectly. Instead of sailing off across the sound, his small ship was driven ashore. Then he and his companions jumped overboard and ran off through the woods.

When Governor Alexander Spotswood of Virginia sent a company of marines to assist Hyde, other supporters of Cary also fled. Cary was sent to England for trial but was released for lack of evidence, perhaps because there was no one to testify against him. Thus ended the episode known as Cary's Rebellion.

Tuscarora Indian War

For three years the colony had suffered from the conflict between Quakers and members of the Anglican church. The weather had been bad and crops had failed. People were divided and demoralized. The Tuscarora Indians living in the vicinity of Bath and New Bern and elsewhere in that part of the colony, but others as well, were victims of "sharp" and "irregular" practices by traders who cheated them at every opportunity. Indians witnessed the disagreements and confusion among their white neighbors and were aware of their great need during a long dry season when crops failed. Further, they resented losing their land. They had seen Surveyor General John Lawson go into the woods with his instruments and chain bearers to blaze trees. Soon new settlers arrived. They blamed Lawson for these intruders.

Other Indians also felt oppressed. In 1701 those who lived along the Pamlico River complained to Lawson that the English were "very wicked people and that they threatened the Indians for hunting near their plantations." Two years later the Corees staged a minor uprising but it was easily quelled. In 1706–7 Thomas Pollock marched against the Meherrins along the disputed Virginia-Carolina border, seized thirty-six Indians and imprisoned them for two days without food or water, wrecked their cabins, and threatened to destroy their crops if they did not surrender their land. When the North Carolina authorities appealed to Virginia for help in suppressing the Meherrins, Governor Spotswood and the Virginia legislature refused to act on the ground that the whites were the aggressors and that North Carolina was "the author of its own misery." In 1710 the Tuscaroras sent a petition to the governor of Pennsylvania protesting the seizure of their land and the enslavement of their people. A Pennsylvania law of 1705 against "the further importation of Indian slaves from Carolina" apparently had not been effective.

Quietly resolving to put an end to the causes of their trouble, the Tuscaroras seized Graffenried and Lawson in early September 1711 while they were exploring the Neuse River north of New Bern. Graffenried was soon released because the Indians thought he was the governor, but on the eleventh Lawson's body was stuck full of lightwood splinters and burned at the stake.

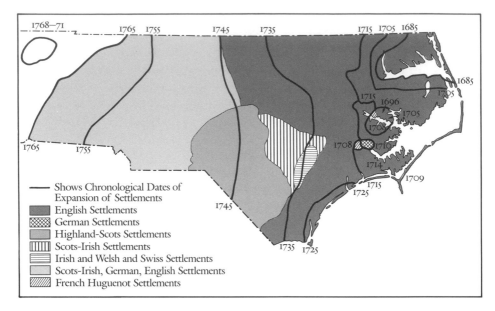

Legend:
— Shows Chronological Dates of Expansion of Settlements
English Settlements
German Settlements
Highland-Scots Settlements
Scots-Irish Settlements
Irish and Welsh and Swiss Settlements
Scots-Irish, German, English Settlements
French Huguenot Settlements

Map 3. The Pioneer People of North Carolina

Before Graffenried could return to New Bern, the Tuscarora Indians launched an all-out attack on white settlements along the Neuse and Pamlico rivers, including the town of Bath. Whites, suspecting nothing, had carried on as usual; some even entertained Indians overnight in their homes. But about dawn on 22 September hundreds of Indians in war paint and better armed than whites, thanks to white traders, rushed screaming and shouting out of the woods to murder, scalp, and burn. In one community they murdered more than 130 people in about two hours. Houses were plundered and then burned. Livestock was either slaughtered or driven away. Crops were destroyed. The bodies of whites were insulted and mutilated. A murdered man was laid atop his late wife's grave, the body of a woman was left kneeling before a chair as if at prayer, another woman was left with her skirts pulled up over her head, and unborn babies were ripped from their mothers' bodies and tossed into trees.

The whole region was described as "totally wasted and ruined," a scene of desolation, blood, and ashes. Houses had not been fortified in anticipation of attacks, supplies were low, and means of protection simply were unavailable. Only the Albemarle section was spared because the Tuscarora leader there, Tom Blunt, had remained neutral. As a token of their appreciation, white colonists reserved a large tract of land for his use. The records do not suggest that anyone saw the irony of whites giving land to Indians.

Governor Hyde faced a very difficult situation. In addition to the scarcity of food, the shortage of housing, and the lack of arms and ammunition, there was virtually no commercial activity and the Quakers refused to bear arms. Calling the legislature into session, he secured a law issuing £4,000 in paper money, the first of its kind in the colony's history. Also passed was a bill to draft all men between the ages of sixteen and sixty. Soon afterward the militia was reorganized and forts were built.

At the governor's request Virginia provided a modest amount of supplies—some blankets, a little money, and some cloth. Governor Spotswood sent troops to the border but would not let them cross into North Carolina unless the colony agreed to support his militia and until he received assurances that the area in dispute between the two provinces would be surrendered to Virginia. Governor Hyde refused to yield to this blackmail and turned instead to South Carolina.

The legislature in Charles Town responded promptly by voting to give North Carolina £4,000 and issuing orders that troops be sent without asking for any kind of support. With some 30 whites and about 500 friendly Indians, chiefly Yamasees, Colonel John Barnwell (known as "Tuscarora Jack") marched 300 miles through the wilderness and defeated the Indians in two battles near New Bern in January 1712. Reinforced by about 250 North Carolina militiamen, Barnwell then attacked the main stronghold of the Tuscaroras under King Hancock at a site now in Greene County. The Indians held out for ten days. Outside the fort the soldiers could hear the cries and lamentations of the prisoners within. When Barnwell shouted demands that the Indians surrender, a white woman, whose children were held in the fort, was sent out to deliver Hancock's ultimatum. The attack must end or Hancock would continue fighting until all in the fort were dead—both Indians and a large number of white prisoners. If Barnwell agreed to his terms, Hancock would release some prisoners then and others later, and he would abandon the land between the Neuse and Cape Fear rivers to the whites.

The North Carolina Assembly was critical of Barnwell for not entirely breaking the power of the Tuscaroras, and so refused the South Carolinian's request for a grant of land for his men and for the reimbursement of expenses, including five horses that had been lost. Barnwell became ill and returned directly home, leaving his men to follow. En route they discussed the way they had been treated by the Assembly. Deciding to have *something* for their trouble, they seized some Indians and sold them into slavery.

This violation of the terms of peace led to further Indian raids in the summer and fall of 1712. At the same time many colonists fell victim to a yellow fever epidemic which took about as many lives as the Indians did. Even Governor Hyde died of the fever; he was succeeded by the president of the Council, Thomas Pollock. The new acting governor had no choice but once again to call on his southern neighbors for help. This time Colonel James Moore, with thirty-three whites and around a thousand Indians, responded and in December 1712 soundly defeated the Tuscaroras. A report from Virginia noted that a number of captured Indians had been destroyed by "exquisite tortures" and that an unknown number had been sold into slavery at £10 each. Shortly afterward most of the surviving Tuscarora Indians left North Carolina to join their relatives in the colony of New York.

The war with the Tuscaroras left the colony in a particularly distressing condition. Deep in debt and left with rapidly depreciating paper money to redeem, the colony's finances were bleak indeed. In addition to the loss of human life, the destruction of houses and other buildings, and the depletion of livestock and crops, immigration had practically ceased.

On the other hand the separation from South Carolina, the defeat of the Tuscaroras, the virtual elimination of political factions under Pollock's effective leadership, and the increased authority of the government laid the foundations for a period of growth and progress. In the spring of 1714 Charles Eden assumed the reins of government.

Leaders of the province realized that North Carolina's troubles could be traced to (1) the weakness of the government, (2) inefficient and sometimes even corrupt officials, and (3) the general confusion resulting from the uncertainty as to what laws were in force. In 1715 Governor Eden called an Assembly to provide remedies, and this proved to be one of the most significant legislatures ever to meet in North Carolina. It revised "the ancient standing laws" and passed about sixty new ones designed to lay a sound and lasting foundation for the government. These laws provided severe punishment for anyone found guilty of spreading "false news" or "scurrilous Libels" against the government or participating in conspiracies, riots, and rebellions. The powers and duties of local officials were clearly defined, fees for services were set, details for holding elections were agreed upon, and provisions for biennial meetings of the Assembly were made. A new Vestry Act, firmly establishing the Church of England in the colony, was passed, and it remained in force until 1741. Another law permitted Quakers to make an affirmation instead of taking an oath of allegiance to the Crown, and all dissenters were given legal protection. Other laws were intended to encourage the establishment of sawmills and gristmills, the building of roads and bridges, and the maintenance of ferries. As a result of some of these provisions, a one-hundred-mile road was laid from the Neuse to the Cape Fear rivers. Finally, pilots operating in the sounds were directed to locate and mark the channels through which ships could pass.

To encourage the development of towns as centers of trade and culture, an act was passed giving all towns with sixty or more families the right to send a representative to the Assembly. These were called borough towns. Bath and New Bern already existed, and in 1722 the "Town on Queen Anne's Creek," established a few years earlier, was incorporated as Edenton. The legislature met here in 1722–37, 1740–41, and 1743. The town of Beaufort was started about 1715 and became a port of entry in 1722. Other ports of entry were also designated in an attempt to keep trade in legitimate channels.

With the establishment of sawmills the production of lumber increased and became an important export item. Tar, pitch, and turpentine also began to be shipped out. Now that channels had been cleared and marked, New England skippers returned to North Carolina, making their way into the sounds and up the rivers to the wharves of planters.

Piracy

Smuggling again developed in spite of modest efforts to prevent it. While cargoes of tobacco, corn, naval stores, and other produce were legally purchased from the producers, attempts were made to evade the payment of customs duties. This amounted to smuggling, as did the activities of acknowledged pirates. England had recently sent a new governor to its West Indies possessions to drive out the pirates who made their headquarters there. These robbers of the sea soon found a convenient refuge along the North Carolina coast. Geography was their ally. Their small ships could easily slip through the inlets and conceal themselves until a richly laden merchant vessel or a passenger ship sailed into view. Then it was simple enough to dash out and capture a valuable cargo for which a ready market could be found at many places along the coast or up the rivers. Numerous North Carolinians were glad of an opportunity to engage in such trade. After all, there were few merchants in the colony from whom goods could be bought, and ships like Captain Zachariah Gillam's came only at long intervals.

The most notorious Carolina pirate was Edward Teach, better known as "Blackbeard" for his long black beard and hair in which he twisted bits of smoldering rope to add to his fierce appearance when boarding a prize ship. Second to Blackbeard was Major Stede Bonnet, reputed once to have been a respected army officer, but whose shrill, nagging wife drove him to purchase a ship to transport merchandise to the colonies and thus out of the sound of her voice for months at a time. Eventually, the lure of more and faster profits turned him from legitimate trade to piracy.

Blackbeard made his headquarters at Bath briefly; Bonnet, on a fatal occasion, was at Cape Fear to careen his vessel. Together they ranged the Atlantic coast from Maine to Florida. In North Carolina it was apparent to many that they enjoyed the friendship and probably the encouragement of some high officials—perhaps even Governor Charles Eden but almost certainly Secretary Tobias Knight. Other officeholders, however, tried to put an end to the pirates' activities. Among them were Edward Moseley and Maurice Moore.

The pirate Blackbeard (ca. 1680–1718), who took refuge along the North Carolina coast in the early eighteenth century and contributed to its unfortunate reputation. He is shown with the bits of smoldering hemp rope that he twisted in his long black hair. It has been suggested, since hemp rope is made from the marijuana plant, that he acquired more than a terrifying appearance from this practice. (North Carolina Collection, University of North Carolina at Chapel Hill)

The blows that finally ended piracy in the waters of the province came from the two adjoining colonies. When the governor of South Carolina learned in September 1718 that a pirate had appeared off the coast, he sent an expedition under Colonel William Rhett to intercept him. Stede Bonnet was located up the Cape Fear River while removing barnacles from the hull of his ship. After a bloody battle Rhett captured Bonnet on 27 September, and took him to Charles Town where he was tried and convicted. He was hanged on 10 December and given a pirate's burial—at sea, underwater at low tide.

On 17 November, the governor of Virginia secretly fitted out two sloops with crews from a British warship stationed in the James River. Commanded by Lieutenant Robert Maynard, they set out in search of Blackbeard. On the twenty-second the pirate's ship was found near Ocracoke Inlet, attacked, and boarded. Maynard reportedly cut off Blackbeard's head with a slashing sweep of his sword. The head was hung high in the rigging of Maynard's ship when it sailed into Bath. There several local officials were confronted with evidence of their complicity in some of the pirates' evil deeds. There were many other pirates, including some females; during November and December 1718, forty-nine of them were hanged in Charles Town.

Expansion to the South

With the removal of the Indian threat, the suppression of piracy, and a period of moderately good government under governors Charles Eden, George Burrington, and Sir Richard Everard, another period of growth and improvement began in North Carolina. Immigration increased rapidly, settlements expanded to the west and to the south, and four new counties were created between 1722 and 1730: Bertie from that part of old Albemarle County on the western side of the Chowan River; Carteret from the eastern part of Bath County; Tyrrell from the northern end of Bath; and New Hanover in the southeastern corner of the province, on the Cape Fear River, in a region only recently opened to settlement.

New Hanover County included the site of the earlier Clarendon County and Charles Town, which had existed between 1664 and 1667. Colonel James Moore rediscovered the region when he and his troops were returning to South Carolina after helping put down the Tuscarora Indian uprising. Moore, his brother Maurice, and other members of his family, who were descendants of Sir John Yeamans, governor of Clarendon, acquired land and moved here.

About 1723 people began to take up land along the Cape Fear River, to clear fields, and to build houses in violation of directives from the Proprietors. When Governor Burrington realized that they were determined to do this without either acquiring titles or paying quitrents, he decided to take matters into his own hands by giving them deeds and collecting the rents due the Proprietors. He also ordered that a land office be opened. With titles assured, settlers were not long in arriving. The governor himself took out a grant for a tract that had been called "Stag Park" by some explorers from Barbados in 1663. The new one-hundred-mile road from the vicinity of New Bern lured whole families to this inviting region. They came from Albemarle as well as from South Carolina, Barbados and other islands in the West Indies, New England, Pennsylvania, Maryland, and Europe. Many of the family names most often found among the people of English descent in New Hanover County are also common in the city of Bristol, England. Evidently there was a close connection between the two places.

On the western bank of the Cape Fear, about fourteen miles above its mouth, Maurice Moore laid off a town in 1725 and named it Brunswick in honor of the reigning family of Great Britain. Although it was the home of several governors and the Assembly met there in 1761, the town did not flourish. With the establishment of Wilmington about 1733, sixteen miles farther up the Cape Fear River, Brunswick began to decline. After the American Revolution, the site was abandoned. Settlement of the lower Cape Fear gave the colony a direct outlet to the Atlantic Ocean and the commerce of the world. Wilmington became North Carolina's best harbor and by 1840 was its largest city, a distinction it held until the twentieth century.

The Proprietors Sell Their Shares

Because there was no marked boundary between North Carolina and Virginia, due in part to Virginia's continued unwillingness to accept the boundaries set by the 1665 Carolina charter, an almost constant dispute flourished between the two colonies. Questions concerning land grants, quitrents, Indian problems, and law enforcement often went unanswered. The Proprietors asked the Crown to authorize a survey, but the influence of Virginia partisans prevented it. Queen Anne once ordered a survey to be made, but Virginia refused to comply. On another occasion when the governors of the two colonies reached an agreement, some private individuals frustrated their plans.

Since at least 1689 various advisory agencies to the Crown had tried to obtain the release of the Proprietary colonies. By 1727, negotiations with the Proprietors of Carolina had reached the point where a survey of the northern limits of the colony was essential. King George II issued orders that finally were obeyed.

Four commissioners were appointed by the governor of North Carolina to work with those appointed for Virginia. William Byrd II of Virginia led the boundary line commission that set out on 5 March 1728 from Currituck Inlet surveying west. After six weeks, when the line had been run for 73 miles, work

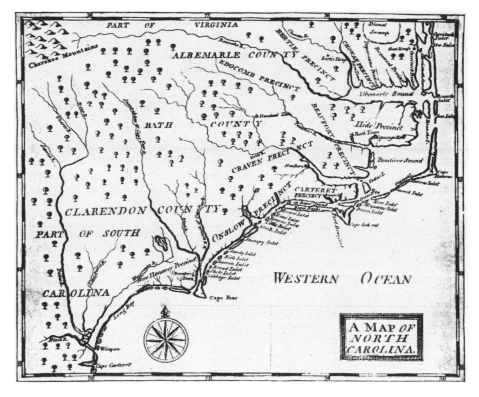

This map of North Carolina at the end of the Proprietary period was published in 1737 in Dr. John Brickell's *The Natural History of North Carolina*. (North Carolina Collection, University of North Carolina at Chapel Hill)

was halted until 20 September. By October 4 the surveyors had gone 50 miles beyond any known settlement, and the members of the North Carolina contingent left for home. They could not imagine that anyone would ever live that far inland. The Virginians, however, were a bit more confident and they continued the line for 72 more miles, ending it at what is now Stokes County, North Carolina. The boundary line had been run 161 miles across the sandy beach, waters of the sounds and rivers, and the Great Dismal Swamp as well as some fertile farmland.

The boundary line was honestly run and in keeping with the limits set in the 1665 charter; as a result of the survey, Virginia was obliged to give up its claim to land long occupied by North Carolinians. During his incursion into the backcountry, William Byrd kept careful notes. Some were intended for the public record and others were secret, for his own use. Many years later Byrd's journals of the running of the dividing line were published. His frank and full comments, intentionally humorous even though often derogatory of North Carolinians, are interesting and undoubtedly depict some of the people as they really were. Byrd's comments have found their way into countless anthologies of early American literature and probably contribute much to the general attitude of many Americans, often erroneous, toward North Carolinians today.

The Lords Proprietors had seen the handwriting on the wall, and, although they did not like what they read, they were wise enough to know what it meant. They got the best bargain they could when the pressure became too great to resist. South Carolina had become a royal colony in 1719, but North Carolina was left for the Proprietors to enjoy (or to suffer with) for ten more years. On 25 July 1729, papers were signed transferring seven of the eight shares in full to the Crown for £2,500 each plus £5,000 to make up for the quitrents still due the Proprietors. The share held by the descendant of Sir George Carteret, later to inherit the title Earl Granville, was not sold outright. He was, however, obliged to relinquish all voice in the government of the colony even though he retained ownership of one-eighth of the land in the original 1665 grant. This arrangement continued until the American Revolution, when the new state of North Carolina confiscated the Granville District as the property of an enemy alien.

4

ROYAL GOVERNMENT

WHEN NORTH CAROLINA was acquired by the Crown, the people saw no sudden or dramatic change in their government. The offices of governor, Council, Assembly, and courts, as well as other administrative agencies, remained as they had been. The Crown merely took the place of the Lords Proprietors as the immediate source of power. After a little while, however, North Carolinians began to detect a definite change in the efficiency and the spirit of government. A strong executive, capable of sustained policy, succeeded a weak, constantly changing executive and an uncertain policy. This made possible a stability of purpose and a strength of administration that had been impossible under the proprietorship.

The change also moved the province more fully into the stream of imperial affairs. Administration of the colony was under the direct supervision of the Crown (George II from 1727 to 1760, and George III from 1760 until the American Revolution) and various royal agencies such as the Privy Council and the Board of Trade. Although the board's role was only advisory, its advice was sought frequently and generally followed. The Board of Trade developed a firm colonial policy, and displayed consistency and tenacity in following it. In general, it tried to preserve and strengthen the political dependence of the colonies on the mother country and to bind them together into an economically self-sufficient empire. With these objectives in view, it sought (1) to reduce the colonial governments to a single administrative type; (2) to set aside, whenever possible, the colonial charters; (3) to make governors, judges, and other officials independent of colonial assemblies by providing fixed salaries for them; (4) to control the courts by commissioning judges to serve during the king's pleasure; (5) to restrict the growing power of colonial legislatures by a liberal use of the royal prerogative in determining a quorum, calling, proroguing, and dissolving the Assembly, and vetoing legislation; and (6) to amplify and strengthen the Navigation Acts and the powers of enforcement officials.

Imperial Conflicts

When efforts were made to implement these policies in North Carolina, officials met vigorous opposition. This was largely the result of different views as to the authority of the Crown on one hand and the rights of the people on the other. Imperial causes required the subordination of local interests. The Crown acted in the belief that its authority in colonial affairs rested in the royal prerogative, and it began to direct colonial affairs through long lists of detailed instructions that it maintained were binding on both the governor and the Assembly. Moreover, instructions were cumulative—those issued to one governor were considered applicable to all of his successors. They also were considered confidential between the governor and the Crown; he did not have to reveal them in advance of their application unless he chose to do so. These "rules" were not in line with the thinking of North Carolinians. They insisted, and sometimes with considerable energy, that the powers of the Crown were still restricted by the Carolina charter, and that the Crown was bound to administer the affairs of the colony in accord with the provisions of the charters issued to the Lords Proprietors. On occasion they even cited the charters as their "constitution" when demanding that their rights as Englishmen be recognized.

These opposing theories, together with clashing imperial and local interests, caused a lot of misunderstanding. The Crown, intent on the larger affairs of the empire, simply ignored the rights and concerns of the colony. The colony naturally put its own affairs first and never tried to understand or sympathize with the policies of the Crown. The result was inevitable. Controversies between the governor, in upholding the prerogative of the Crown, and the Assembly, in championing the rights and privileges of the people, marked the whole political history of North Carolina as a royal colony. Many of these differences were trivial in themselves, but behind all of them lay the important issue of whether the colonial Assembly was to be a truly legislative body, representing the will of the people, with the power of independent judgment and action, or whether it was to be simply a means of registering the royal will as expressed through instructions to the governor.

The men appointed by the king to govern his royal province of North Carolina from 1729 to 1776 were not so much favorites of the court as they were good, deserving Whig party members who supported the aims of the party to limit royal authority and promote that of the Parliament. A colonial governorship was one of the smaller plums that would scarcely tempt a really successful and influential person. The scheduled salary in North Carolina was about the same as that in the other colonies, but it was more difficult to collect, while the fringe benefits of the office and the opportunities to speculate, except perhaps in acquiring land, never brought notable wealth to any of the governors. Nevertheless, in this period of nearly half a century, Gabriel Johnston held office for eighteen years and his successor, Arthur Dobbs, governed for eleven. Three of the five royal governors—Johnston, Dobbs, and William Tryon—were colorful personalities who frequently opposed the groups and factions that tried to control provincial affairs. Even if they had been totally free of self-interest and had been great statesmen, they would still have aroused antagonism because of conditions resulting from the British colonial scheme.

Difficulties of the First Royal Governor

George Burrington received his commission as the first royal governor in January 1730 but did not reach the colony until February 1731 because he had to wait for his instructions to be issued. (The last Proprietary governor, Sir Richard Everard, remained in office until he arrived.) When the new governor appeared, he was given a suitable ceremonial reception. He was not a stranger in the colony, as he had been Proprietary governor in 1724 and 1725, when he sometimes allied himself with the popular party. The leaders of this group eagerly welcomed him, thinking, perhaps, that a friend had returned. It was not long, however, before they discovered to their dismay that Proprietary governor Burrington and royal governor Burrington were very different.

In Burrington's instructions the Crown offered, on two conditions, to remit to the people of both Carolinas the unpaid quitrents for which the Lords Proprietors had been allowed £5,000 as part of the purchase agreement. These conditions were (1) that the Assembly require the registration of all landholdings in the colony so as to provide an accurate "rent roll" or tax list to the Crown, and (2) that all quitrents and officers' fees, which until now had been payable in commodities at an understood value or in provincial currency, must henceforth be paid in proclamation money.

Proclamation money was not so much a definite kind of money as it was a practical though fluctuating value placed on various types of foreign coins circulating in the colonies. This might be considered a rate of exchange against the pound sterling. Its name came from the fact that the value was set by a proclamation after the governor and Council, and later involving the Assembly as well, reached an agreement. The term also applied to various commodities produced in the province that were in good, marketable condition, such as tobacco (100 pounds at 10 shillings), corn (1 shilling and 8 pence per bushel), or beaver and otter skins (2 shillings and 6 pence per pound). The latter were called "rated commodities" and they served as barter money. Provincial paper money also came to be included; although it had a face value printed on it, inflation robbed it of value and its worth came to be set by proclamation, too.

After Burrington explained the conditions under which the Crown would forgive the people their back taxes, the Assembly convened in April 1731. By executive order the governor had already set officers' fees in proclamation money, and he had a bill prepared for the Assembly dealing with quitrents. The members proved to be unexpectedly independent. They said that the unpaid quitrents were too small to be of any concern; they then resolved that all payments of quitrents would be made just as they had been in the past: "in some valuable commodities, or in the bills now current in the Province at proper rates." Further, they said, the Assembly alone had the power to regulate officers' fees.

Burrington told the defiant assemblymen that the king's instructions, giving the governor and Council the power to regulate and settle fees, had repealed all laws that fees should be received in other ways. This alarmed the legislators, who became concerned about their rights. They reminded the royal governor that the Carolina charter of 1663 had granted the people "all libertys, Franchises, and Privileges" enjoyed by the people of England; and they declared that among them was the guarantee "that they shall not be taxed or made lyable to pay any sum or sums of money or Fees other than such as are by law established." Therefore, they demanded that Burrington forbid the collection of fees in proclamation money "until such times as the Officers' Fees shall be regulated by Authority of Assembly."

The governor attributed all of this opposition to Edward Moseley who was not only speaker of the lower house but also public treasurer, there being no regulation about multiple officeholding in those days. He then set out to destroy Moseley politically. Burrington produced two other instructions issued by the Crown, one forbidding the expenditure of any public money except when authorized by the governor and the other directing that all commissions issued during the Proprietary period be withdrawn and that no public office be held except by a commission from the king. These he laid before the Assembly together with a declaration of his intention to appoint "a fitt person" to serve as public treasurer. The Assembly, resentful of this fresh attack, declared that no public money should be disbursed except as directed by the Assembly; moreover, it believed, the instruction about commissions did not apply to officers appointed by an act of the Assembly, as was the public treasurer, but only to those who held commissions from the Lords Proprietors. The legislators reminded the governor that a perfectly suitable treasurer, appointed by themselves, was then in office and that he need not bother to try to appoint another one.

Burrington promptly dismissed the Assembly and did not call a new one for two years. In the meantime, after receiving confirmation from London, he told the Assembly in July 1733 that the Crown was sticking by its original instructions.

He was especially forbidden to accept quitrents and fees in any other form than proclamation money.

The Assembly did not like his haughty manner any better than it liked his instructions. The members replied that they, too, had consulted the source of their power—the people—and had been advised not to burden the colony with any such payments in proclamation money. In the ensuing quarrel, neither side would yield. The governor called an Assembly three times, but the Assembly refused to pass a single bill. The representatives of the people openly refused to obey the king's instructions, while the representative of the Crown would accept nothing short of complete submission. Burrington on one occasion said: "If the King's Instructions are contrary to some Laws of the Province, the Governor must act in Obedience to the King's Commands, therefore you must not be surprized [if] whatever your law directs contrary to my Instructions is not taken notice of [by] me."

There followed several heated debates in which the governor was described as abusive, insolent, and dictatorial. The violence of his language was said to have passed all bounds of reason and decency. The dignity of the Assembly was at stake, and the house was determined to maintain its rights at all costs. Burrington's opponents complained about him to authorities in London. (Throughout the colonial period, many people in the colony seem to have had influential friends and even relatives in England whom they never hesitated to make use of when the situation called for it.) As a result of these complaints, together with clear indications of the governor's inadequacy in his reports to the Crown, Burrington was replaced in the summer of 1733. After returning to England he reported that three provincial officials had tried to assassinate him in his final months in office, but the charge was not investigated.

A Compromising Governor

His successor, Gabriel Johnston, assumed office at Brunswick in November 1734. A Scotsman of good birth and education, he was superior to Burrington in almost every way. He had taught at St. Andrews University and for the past seven years had been a member of the household of Spencer Compton, Lord Wilmington, in London. In North Carolina, Johnston proved to be a shrewd but honest politician whose administration was free of scandal. Although he showed just as little concern for the "rights" of the Assembly as Burrington had, he was willing to compromise and to try to work with the leaders of the popular faction.

The new governor not only maintained all of the positions taken by Burrington in the quitrent issue, but also insisted that the king had the right to fix the places of collection. He maintained that quitrents should be paid in gold or silver or in bills circulating at a rate of exchange fixed by the Council. In addition, he appointed a new collector—even though the one in South Carolina was supposed to serve both colonies—and instructed him to seize the property of anyone who refused to pay. The shock of this action produced wide compliance when the tax collector first appeared.

Soon, however, the opposition began to speak out and before long there were loud protests and threats of violence. Even Treasurer Moseley refused to pay his own quitrent the next time, and others followed his example. When a false report was spread that a man had been jailed in Edenton for not paying his taxes, five hundred men in Bertie and Edgecombe counties grabbed their guns and started for Edenton to release him. On the way a witness reported hearing them "cursing his Majesty and uttering a great many rebellious speeches." But word reached the angry marchers that the rumor was untrue, and they broke up before arriving in Edenton.

The Assembly received complaints that tax collectors were demanding £7 or £8 in local currency for every £1 sterling owed, to which they threatened to add extravagant charges if they had to seize property for payment. The legislators protested in vain. Then, taking their cue from the governor's actions, they ordered the tax collectors to be seized by their sergeant at arms.

At this point Governor Johnston displayed better tact than that shown by his predecessor. Using what he called "management" (today we might say he "played politics"), he worked out a compromise. He had recently been at odds with the Assembly over the validity of blank patents for land—that is, printed forms signed by the proper officials and containing the official wax seal, but with the date, name of the patentee, location of the land, number of acres, and amount of the purchase left blank. Officials had prepared these blank patents in large quantities so they would not have to be bothered every time someone required one. The forms had fallen into the hands of unscrupulous individuals who proceeded to find some unclaimed land and fill in a form themselves. This gave them a signed, sealed claim to the land, but because it was not registered they avoided paying taxes. It was estimated that as many as 500,000 acres had been acquired in this manner. Johnston maintained that the blank patents under which the land had been taken were worthless. What he wanted was a tax list, and he now came to an agreement with the Assembly.

Johnston consented to confirm titles held under blank patents. In return, the Assembly would prepare a tax list and limit the number of places at which quitrents should be paid. The governor also agreed to accept certain rated commodities or their equivalent value in provincial money. Thereafter, the Assembly would join the governor and Council in fixing the value of provincial currency. In 1739 these points were covered in a bill passed by the Assembly and signed by the governor.

From time to time Johnston played politics by getting the Albemarle and the Cape Fear sections to work against each other to his benefit. Each of the older counties elected five members to the Assembly and this gave them a majority. On one occasion the governor called a meeting of the Assembly in Wilmington to make it inconvenient for the members from Albemarle to attend. By disregarding their long-established rule of requiring the presence of a majority to transact business, the Assembly and the governor reached a compromise, to their mutual advantage, on several matters of dispute. This pattern was repeated several times, sometimes in reverse when Johnston needed the support of Albemarle delegates. The governor was also known to call an Assembly during a season of the year when many members were busy planting or harvesting and could not attend. In their absence, he would make concessions to those who were present in return for the passage of bills that served his own interests.

The Granville District

One cause of the quitrent dispute resulted from the requirement to give the heir of Lord Proprietor Sir George Carteret one-eighth of the quitrents collected in North Carolina, South Carolina, and Georgia, the three colonies developed from the original Carolina territory. To simplify the problem, King George II in 1742 ordered that Carteret's share be surveyed and identified. An equitable solution would have been to give him land in each of the three colonies. But for some reason—perhaps for the convenience of Carteret as well as for the surveyors—it was decided to use the North Carolina–Virginia line as the northern boundary and to survey just one line, the southern boundary. This put all of Carteret's land in the northern half of North Carolina. In 1744, the year in which Sir John Carteret became Earl Granville by inheritance at the death of his mother, the survey began at Cape Hatteras and went as far as Bath. In 1746 it continued, in stages, to the Haw River and then to Cold Water Creek in what soon became Rowan County. By September 1772 the survey had been extended to the Blue Ridge Mountains.

The Granville District, as this sixty-mile-wide strip came to be called, contained two-thirds of the people of the province and an even larger percentage of the wealth. It became a serious obstacle to North Carolina's development. Lord Granville's land office at Edenton was open only irregularly, and many of his officers were inefficient and corrupt. Squatters occupied much of his land, angry mobs resisted the collection of quitrents, friction and quarrels broke out, and the district was the scene of general unrest. The province was obliged to have two treasurers, one for the district and one for the rest of the colony. When the district's residents refused to pay taxes, people living elsewhere announced that

John Carteret, Earl Granville (1690–1763), inherited the Lords Proprietors' share in Carolina of his great-grandfather. He refused to sell his rights to the land in 1729 when the Crown purchased the remaining shares, and in 1744 an eighth of the original territory was assigned to him—all of it in the northern half of North Carolina. (North Carolina Collection, University of North Carolina at Chapel Hill)

they would not bear the total burden of operating the government. Soon two political factions appeared, one representing the northern portion of the colony and the other from the south. They quarreled about many things, not the least of which was the fact that the old counties formed in the Albemarle section each had five delegates in the Assembly while most of the new counties had only two.

The disruptive effects of the Granville District persisted until the beginning of the American Revolution, when the property was confiscated by the state. The last two royal governors failed to persuade the Crown to buy the Granville interests, and in 1773 the Assembly also submitted a petition to King George III to take over the district. After the Revolution the Granville heirs attempted to regain this property, but their suit was rejected in the United States District Court in Raleigh. An appeal to the Supreme Court was not perfected, probably for two reasons—the death of the Granville counsel and the succession of a young Earl Granville to the title. This turn of events probably was fortunate for North

Carolina, as Chief Justice John Marshall expressed the belief that the Treaty of Paris ending the Revolution prohibited a state from invalidating English titles to property.

North Carolina's concern with land during Gabriel Johnston's administration was not limited to the Granville property. A different type of controversy, but a cause of unrest, confusion, disorder, and even bloodshed, was the boundary dispute between the two Carolinas. Disagreements often developed over the enforcement of criminal laws, the execution of judicial papers, the collection of taxes, service in the militia, Indian affairs, and other matters. Private interests were also involved. Titles to land along the colonial lines depended on the right of the government under which they were claimed to issue grants, and conflicting claims often led to considerable discontent. This was especially true from 1753 to 1764. South Carolina surveyors were accused of marking off land to be granted north of the thirty-fifth parallel. The governor of South Carolina fined some men from North Carolina who ignored his summons to attend militia muster. Some North Carolinians seized and jailed a sheriff from South Carolina who was trying to collect taxes in Anson County.

Meeting several times after 1729, joint commissioners had agreed that the line between North Carolina and South Carolina should begin at the sea, thirty miles southwest of the mouth of the Cape Fear River, and run not closer than thirty miles to the river until it reached the thirty-fifth parallel. From there it would run directly west to the South Seas. If the surveyors encountered any Catawba or Cherokee Indians, they were to go around them so as to leave them in South Carolina.

Only about a hundred miles of the boundary—the straight northwestern line parallel to the river—was surveyed in 1735. Actually a mistake was made in locating the thirty-fifth parallel and the surveyors stopped too soon. In 1764, however, the line was continued from that point west until the surveyors met some Catawba Indians and once again suspended the work. Resuming the project in 1772, the surveyors went around the Catawba lands until they thought they were on the thirty-fifth parallel; in fact, they were about as far north of it as they had been south of it earlier! From what they thought was the proper line they traveled west to the Cherokee line of 1767. Not until 1813 were the errors discovered. At that time, when a strip of land ten or twelve miles wide and about seventy-five miles long was in dispute, it was concluded that, although the line was improperly marked, each state gained about as much of the other's territory as the other state had. Each had already established jurisdiction of what it thought was its territory, so they agreed to leave well enough alone. The true location of the elusive thirty-fifth parallel was not found until 1821 when the line between North Carolina and Georgia was marked.

Gabriel Johnston's long administration saw substantial improvements in

North Carolina. The colony's population rose from about 30,000 to more than 90,000, with settlements extending to the foot of the mountains. People moved into the colony not only from other colonies but also from abroad. Johnston's support of Wilmington virtually killed Brunswick. It was he who encouraged an extensive revisal of the laws and the establishment of a press to print them. He also did his best to develop new products in the province—especially wine, silk, indigo, hemp, and flax—and to increase the production of pork and corn.

After Johnston's death in 1752, first Nathaniel Rice and then Matthew Rowan, as presidents of the Council, administered the government. Johnston's appointed successor was Arthur Dobbs, head of an ancient Protestant family in Ireland. He had been sheriff of County Antrim, a member of the Irish Parliament, and surveyor-general of Ireland; he was a member of a syndicate that owned 60,000 acres of land in New Hanover County on which it proposed to settle Irish Protestants. With George Selwyn, Dobbs owned about 40,000 acres in Mecklenburg County; in 1748 he also had been one of the important shareholders in the Ohio Company of Virginia, which petitioned for 500,000 acres in what was then western Virginia. Dobbs supported the work of the Society for the Propagation of the Gospel in Foreign Parts, and he had been active in a search for the elusive Northwest Passage. These wide-ranging interests and investments made him perhaps the best informed governor of colonial North Carolina.

Dobbs was accompanied to North Carolina by his youngest son, Edward Brice, and by a nephew, Richard Spaight. He was sixty-five, a rather old age at that time, and actually had difficulty adapting to the colony. He had an exaggerated idea of the prerogative of the Crown and less tolerance for the constitutional claims of the Assembly than either of the two previous royal governors. Yet he arrived at a time when the people were anxious for peace and quiet. The French and Indian War was in progress, and imperial interests for the first time absorbed the attention of North Carolinians.

Colonial Wars

The struggle between Great Britain and France for control of North America began in 1689 and reached a climax in the "Great War for Empire" between 1754 and 1763. War emergencies, the need for men, money, and supplies from the colonies and more intercolonial collaboration forced England to grant many concessions as the price of cooperation. There was a degree of laxity in the enforcement of the Navigation Acts and other trade laws; on the other hand, a growing feeling of estrangement from England was felt within the colonies, though there was no evidence of a movement for independence.

For many years the American colonies had needed protection from three

Arthur Dobbs (1689–1765), governor of North Carolina during the important years of 1754–65 when settlement expanded and helpful relations with other colonies were established. At this time the colony began to take its place as a part of the empire. (North Carolina Collection, University of North Carolina at Chapel Hill)

sources of potential danger: the Spanish in Florida; the French who vied with the English for territory along the western frontier; and enemy Indians, who, in alliance with both the Spaniards and the French, were a constant threat. Out of these clashing interests came the century-long struggle between England and France for supremacy in North America. Four intercolonial wars marked the stages of this contest, although they did not always coincide exactly with those in Europe: King William's War (1689–97); Queen Anne's War (1702–13); King George's War (1744–48); and the French and Indian War (1754–63). North Carolina was only slightly involved in the first two conflicts, but in the last two it played a prominent role.

Until Georgia was chartered in 1732 and settled the next year, the Carolinas formed a buffer region between the English and the Spanish. The Georgia territory, of course, had been included in the Carolina charter of 1663. The first foreign attack on Carolina territory came in 1686 from the Spanish in Florida when a force from St. Augustine invaded South Carolina and destroyed Port Royal. England advised a slow response and that only after thorough preparation. Finally in 1702 South Carolina sent Robert Daniel, afterward deputy governor of North Carolina, to attack St. Augustine. Daniel sacked several villages nearby but failed in his main objective. Four years later a combined Spanish and French fleet attacked Charles Town but was repulsed.

In the second intercolonial war the French and Spanish frequently plundered the coast of North Carolina and, according to George Burrington, put the colony to great expense in equipping a force to repel them. Some of the Proprietors later said that it cost £20,000 to meet an attack by the French in 1707, and that neither Queen Anne nor her successors ever spent a penny to defend the colony.

North Carolina's contribution was far greater in the third intercolonial war. Now for the first time the colonies were called on to cooperate in a common cause, and they responded with enthusiasm. The British planned to attack Spanish colonies at some vital point, and in October 1740 they dispatched a strong fleet under Admiral Edward Vernon (whom Lawrence Washington, half brother of George, admired and for whom Mount Vernon was named) and an army to Jamaica. There they were to be joined by a colonial force of thirty-six companies of one hundred men each. When asked to recruit four companies, North Carolina gave generously of its human and financial resources. To equip the troops the Assembly appropriated £1,200 sterling, and the governor reported no trouble in recruiting men—in fact, he said he could easily have raised two more companies. Captain James Innes of the Cape Fear section, who spoke Spanish, was one of the commanders. The colonial force reached Jamaica in November 1740 and later took part in the disastrous expedition to Cartagena. A predawn attack was planned, but the troops were not landed until after sunrise. They quickly discovered that their ladders were too short to scale the fort, and large numbers were killed in the abortive attack. Others contracted tropical diseases. Almost all of the North Carolina troops died.

For eight years, Spanish and French privateers infested the colony's waters, captured merchant vessels, ravaged the coast, plundered towns, and levied tribute on the inhabitants almost at will. The Assembly ordered forts to be built at several places along the coast, but they were virtually useless. Fort Johnston, named for Governor Johnston, in what is now Southport, was among those constructed at this time; later it was of significant use during the Civil War.

The Spanish, finding little resistance ashore, attacked and plundered the town of Beaufort twice in 1747 and held it for about three days. On 3 September 1748 three Spanish privateers dropped anchor off Brunswick and opened fire on the ships in the harbor. Other Spaniards attacked the town from the land side, drove out all of the inhabitants, and occupied the site. They looted the houses and destroyed property with no fear of reprisal. In the end, however, their overconfidence was their undoing. The people of Brunswick recovered from their surprise, organized an armed force, and returned the attack. Catching the Spaniards off guard, they killed or captured a number of them and drove the rest to their ships. One of the Spanish ships, *The Fortuna*, fired on Brunswick, but was out of range of any guns the town had. Fire broke out aboard ship and *The Fortuna* blew up. Her commander, all of her officers, and most of her crew were drowned. The other ships hastily sailed down the river to Smith Island. Sending a flag of truce back to Brunswick, they sought an exchange of prisoners; as soon as this was accomplished, they disappeared at sea. One of the trophies of this engagement was an oil portrait of Christ wearing a crown of thorns, which now hangs in St. James's Episcopal Church, Wilmington.

The treaty in 1748 ending this war brought only a brief breathing spell. In 1754 the French and Indian War began when the French seized and fortified some strategic points on the Ohio River claimed by Virginia. When they refused to withdraw, the governor of the colony sent Major George Washington to drive them out, but he did not succeed. From Quebec to New Orleans all of New France responded to a single command. The English colonies, on the other hand, had thirteen separate governments, each relatively independent and disinclined to obey instructions from London. Not a soldier could be enlisted or a shilling appropriated for the common defense until thirteen popularly elected legislatures were persuaded that it was proper to do so. Moreover, thirteen colonial governors had varying ideas as to their appropriate role in the conflict. England began to recognize the need for cooperation and urged the colonies to take steps in this direction.

In September 1754 some of the colonies sent delegates to a congress at Albany, New York. North Carolina, however, was not one of the seven colonies invited by the Board of Trade to be represented. In Albany Benjamin Franklin proposed that a centralized form of government be established for all of the colonies. It would be presided over by a "president general" appointed by the Crown, and there would be a legislature made up of delegates selected by each colonial Assembly based on wealth and population. Yet, except among a few farsighted leaders, no real sentiment for a closer relationship existed in any of the colonies. Governor Dobbs presented Franklin's plan to the North Carolina Assembly and reported that King George hoped to see a happy union among the American colonies for their own general welfare and defense. The Assembly showed no enthusiasm but did order the plan to be printed, promising to consider it at the next session. But there is no evidence that it was ever thought of again.

The French had other advantages over the English. Their settlements were little more than military outposts, garrisoned by trained soldiers, fully equipped, and commanded by experienced officers. The English colonies, on the other hand, were commercial and agricultural communities, with almost no interest in anything military. There was not a single fort along the North Carolina frontier, although there were forts elsewhere; the militia was poorly organized and trained; and arms and ammunition were scarce until 1754, when the king sent a gift of a thousand stand of arms.

Immediately after the French victory over George Washington on the Ohio River in the spring of 1754, Virginia called on the other colonies for assistance. In North Carolina the Assembly unanimously voted to appropriate £12,000 to raise and equip a regiment of 750 men to aid its sister. Generous though the appropriation was, it proved to be sufficient to equip only 450 soldiers, who were ordered to the Virginia frontier under the command of Colonel James Innes. Extravagance and bad management forced the troops to return home before seeing action. Later, however, 100 soldiers were sent to assist Virginia and 50 more were recruited to keep the peace along the North Carolina frontier.

For three years the French occupied a fort recently built by Captain William Trente on the Virginia frontier. They renamed it Fort Duquesne and from there armed and encouraged Indians to raid English settlements in the area. Bands of Indians, largely Iroquois, roamed the backcountry of North Carolina destroying crops, slaughtering livestock, burning houses and barns, and murdering whites. Men working in the fields were killed, and women and children at home were killed or kidnapped.

The Moravians erected a stockade at Bethabara while palisades provided protection for others in the region. The assembly in 1755 ordered the erection of a fort in the backcountry where those along the frontier could take refuge. Major Hugh Waddell from the lower Cape Fear was in charge of Fort Dobbs, built near the Yadkin River north of the present site of the city of Statesville. It was intended to offer protection to friendly Cherokee allies from raids by "French"

Indians as well as to settlers whose homes more and more frequently were attacked by roaming bands of Indians.

In the winter of 1758 Waddell and about three hundred troops from North Carolina were ordered to Virginia to participate in a drive against Fort Duquesne. This was the first time that troops had been raised by a colony to serve outside its borders in a common cause and for mutual defense. Waddell and Sergeant John Rogers were on reconnaissance, disguised as Indians, when they captured an Indian who had recently been inside the fort. With the information they gained it was possible to threaten the fort so seriously that the French abandoned it. In English hands the fort was renamed Fort Pitt for William Pitt, the English leader who had devised a new and effective strategy for the war. The community that developed nearby was in time named Pittsburgh.

Continued Indian raids throughout much of the North Carolina frontier were of deep concern. For much of the French and Indian War, the Cherokees were British allies; however, after some Cherokee braves were killed by Virginia settlers, they ceased to be friendly. In the spring of 1760 an expedition of 1,600 Scottish Highlanders under the command of Colonel Archibald Montgomerie was sent into the Cherokee country to attack them. Taking little care for concealment, and marching along in good British army style, they were ambushed by the Cherokees near the site of the present town of Franklin in Macon County and soundly defeated. Atrocities inflicted on whites by Cherokees continued, and the next year a new campaign was mounted. This time another Scottish officer, Colonel James Grant, and an army of 2,250 men entered the Cherokee country. About two miles from the site of the defeat the previous year, they routed the Cherokees, drove them far up into the mountains, destroyed their towns, burned their stored grain, laid waste their fields, and cleared a strip of land that whites would soon settle.

The fall of Quebec to the English in 1759 decided the fate of the French in America, although the Treaty of Paris was not signed until 1763. It only remained for a treaty to establish peace with the Indians. King George instructed the governors of the four southern colonies to confer with the Indians of their colonies and elsewhere in the South. Governor Dobbs represented his colony at the meeting which opened on 7 November 1763 at Augusta, Georgia. John Stuart, British Indian agent for the Southern Department, was also present as were twenty-five chiefs and seven hundred warriors, including many from the Catawba and Cherokee nations. After six days of speechmaking, drinking, and feasting a treaty of "Perfect and Perpetual Peace and Friendship" was signed. It provided for the mutual forgiveness of all past offenses and injuries; the establishment of satisfactory trade relations; the punishment, by each party, of offenders of its own race for crimes against members of the other race; and the fixing of boundaries of a reservation for the Catawba Indians.

Grave marker at Thyatira Church, Rowan County: "In Memory of Richard King Kild by Indians Feb. Y 5. 1760, Aged 19 Years." The Wachovia Church Book for February 1760 contains some graphic accounts of whites killed by the Cherokees in the region west of that Moravian community. (Claude Pickett, Salisbury)

Aside from driving out the French and the Spanish and temporarily quieting the Indian question, other significant results of the war benefited English colonists. First, because people from different colonies had fought side by side, barriers of local prejudice began to crumble and North Carolina, at least, began to lose its sense of isolation. In this way, the colonies came to recognize their common interests and common destiny. Second, North Carolinians had fought under officers from other colonies as well as those from North Carolina, and their experience under fire would soon serve them well. Third, the western boundary of England's possessions was recognized as the Mississippi River rather than the South Seas or Pacific Ocean. Finally, the French defeat by England created a hope for revenge; this inspired France to assist the United States during the American Revolution.

Two additional developments during the administration of Governor Dobbs are worthy of note. As a royal colony North Carolina decided that it should have someone stationed in London to speak for it before the assorted administrative boards and officials whose decisions affected the colony. Such a person would be in a position to publicize the colony's needs and to represent private individuals in their dealings with the British government. Virginia and other older royal colonies had had representatives or agents in London for years. North Carolina now began to send either its own agent or to engage the services of Virginia's.

In 1755, during the early royal period, the fraternal society of Freemasons was established in North Carolina. A secret organization with an elaborate ritual and open only to men, it served as a social outlet and a source of mutual benefit. Among other things, it was concerned with the welfare of its members, financially, politically, and physically. A belief in God was essential, but otherwise it was not a religious organization. The Masons at various times are believed to have played an influential role in the life of the colony and state.

During the administrations of Johnston and Dobbs hints of a trend toward independence began to appear. The Assembly stood firm when its power to collect revenue and make appropriations was questioned. It also continued to appoint certain officials. The question of whether a majority of members constituted a quorum of the Assembly or whether a mere fifteen members were sufficient—as royal instructions maintained—was debated; like the British Parliament, the Assembly determined its own quorum as well as the qualifications for membership. Governor Dobbs once observed: "The Assembly think themselves entitled to all the Privileges of a British House of Commons and therefore ought not to submit to His Majesty's honorable Privy Council further than do the Commons in England, or submit to His Majesty's instructions to His Governor and Council here." In 1760, after a particularly trying encounter with the Assembly, Dobbs appealed to the king to strengthen his hand so that he could more effectively "oppose and suppress a republican spirit of Independency rising in this Colony."

While nearly all of the colonial governors of North Carolina were interesting men, one aspect of Governor Dobbs's life sets him apart from the others. Although he was considered an old man when he arrived in the colony, he may not have so regarded himself. In the fall of 1762, Dobbs, at age seventy-three, married fifteen-year-old Justina Davis in St. Philips Church, Brunswick. A few months later, while packing to return to Ireland, he suffered a stroke but lingered on for three years, most of the time in a wheelchair. He was buried in St. Philips Church.

Descendants of Arthur Dobbs still occupy Castle Dobbs, his home in Northern Ireland, and hold positions of importance in that country. Descendants of his nephew, Richard Spaight, who accompanied him to North Carolina, have long been prominent on this side of the Atlantic.

5

COLONIAL SOCIETY AND CULTURE, 1729–1776

A T THE BEGINNING of the royal period most people living in North Carolina were of English descent, but the majority of them were native-born. Few people looked to England as the mother country except in a political sense. Even the language began to change. Many Indian words were adopted by Americans while a number of Spanish and French words also crept into their vocabulary. On the other hand, Americans often kept older English words that had gone out of fashion in the British Isles—*fall* for which the English now use *autumn*, and *yard* which became *garden* in England, for example.

Growth and Expansion

The period of royal rule in North Carolina was one of remarkable progress and improvement among the colonists. An almost constant movement of immigrants into the backcountry took the frontier to the foot of the Blue Ridge, and the Indians were driven beyond the Appalachian barrier. Tremendous tracts of forest, never before cut even in the Coastal Plain, were cleared and the land put into cultivation. Mills were built, roads laid out, lighthouses erected along the coast, the channels of rivers and sounds cleared and marked, ferries established, towns incorporated, and trade expanded. People began to build better houses and to have better furniture. Parishes were laid out, churches erected, and schools established. By the beginning of the American Revolution North Carolina was the fourth most populous of the thirteen colonies.

The settlers of North Carolina, like those of some other colonies, passed through several phases. Gerald W. Johnson, a North Carolina–born journalist and historian, pointed this out in *Our English Heritage*. First were the "expendables," such as the Roanoke colonists, who led the way and conducted the initial exploration but were lost. (In Virginia, Jamestown went through a starving time when many colonists died.) Following them were the "indispensables" who cleared land, occupied the country, and demonstrated that Europeans could survive. Finally came the people who brought education, religion, industry, law, and government. This last group gave the country permanency and the characteristics that marked it as the inheritor of British culture.

The population of North Carolina in 1730 probably did not exceed 30,000 whites and 6,000 blacks, and was confined to the Coastal Plain; by 1775, more than 265,000 inhabitants were scattered from the Atlantic to the Blue Ridge. In the latter year Governor Josiah Martin estimated that there were close to 10,000 blacks in the colony. Much of the growth was due to natural increase; women married young and, as observed by an Irish physician, Dr. John Brickell, who was in North Carolina in 1729, most houses were full of babies and children. Yet immigration was responsible for most of the growth in numbers. North Carolina had permanent settlers at a later date than most of the other colonies, and it came to be regarded as a frontier region open to settlement by people from Virginia and South Carolina particularly, but also from Maryland, Pennsylvania, and New Jersey. Others arrived from the crowded cities of England and Northern Ireland, from the highlands and lowlands of Scotland, and from the valleys of the Rhine and the Danube rivers in central Europe. Thousands of hardy, enterprising pioneers poured into North Carolina, filling up the empty spaces in the older settlements; building along the banks of the Roanoke, the Neuse, and the Cape Fear; and spreading out over the hills and through the valleys of the Piedmont.

Explanation of this extraordinary movement may be found in a variety of causes, all of which acted and reacted upon each other. Land companies, exploiting the mildness of the climate, the fertility of the soil, and the cheapness of land, persuaded many to come. A spirit of adventure moved others, while a missionary zeal inspired a chosen few. Economic, religious, and political conditions in Scotland, Ireland, and Germany drove thousands to seek new homes on the Carolina frontier. To all of these causes might be added the promotional activities of royal governors, especially George Burrington, Gabriel Johnston, and Arthur Dobbs. Each of them took an interest in making the boundless resources of the New World known to the people of Europe.

The most striking development during this period occurred in the backcountry, but the Coastal Plain also filled up. By 1733 about twenty families had made their way to the head of navigation on the Tar River, and a hundred families had planted a thriving settlement on New River. Others, alone and in groups, settled up the Northeast Cape Fear River, and a small colony of Highland Scots soon made their homes on the upper Cape Fear. On his arrival in 1734, Governor Gabriel Johnston described some recent inhabitants of the lower Cape Fear as "a sober and industrious set of people." He observed that they had shown "an amazing progress in their improvement," making the Cape Fear the "place of the greatest trade in the whole province."

While most of the early settlers of the Coastal Plain were of English descent, several Lowland Scots were there before 1700. The first governor of Albemarle, William Drummond, and one of the early members of the council, Thomas Pollock, were both Lowlanders. By 1732 some Scottish Highlanders had arrived and settled in the Cape Fear River area. James Innes, Hugh Campbell, and William Forbes received grants of land in what was soon to be Bladen County. They were among the first wave of people who filled up that section in the next forty years.

Highland Scots

Gabriel Johnston has sometimes been given credit for encouraging Highlanders to settle in the province. He certainly promoted immigration every way he could. In 1740, following the landing of a group of 360 Highlanders, the governor supported a proposal exempting newly arrived foreign Protestants from local taxes for ten years. Sponsors of the bill said that it was designed to attract Highlanders to North Carolina, while Scots already in the colony often wrote back to Scotland urging their friends and acquaintances to join them.

In Scotland the defeat of the Highlanders at the Battle of Culloden in April 1746 and the harsh action of the British Parliament against the Scottish clans made life unbearable at home. Before this the people had been entirely dependent on farming for their livelihood, but now the countryside was taken over by English army officers and converted to grazing land for sheep. Native Scots were starving to death in their own country, and they had little choice but to leave. Liberal offers of land and favorable reports from friends brought thousands of Scots to North Carolina until the beginning of the American Revolution. Brunswick was the point of debarkation for a time, but after Wilmington was established it became the port of entry. Once landed, however, these people faced a difficult ninety-mile trip up the Cape Fear River to the Cross Creek section where present-day Fayetteville is located. In their new home they continued to speak Gaelic, to wear kilts, and as best they could to retain the clan system. There even was a printer who did work in Gaelic.

In 1754 the Scots were so numerous that it seemed reasonable to establish a county in the upper Cape Fear Valley. The Assembly met in February, after Governor Johnston's death; only fourteen out of twenty-one counties and two out of five borough towns were represented. This Assembly created the new county and named it "Cumberland" in honor of William, duke of Cumberland, English commander at the Battle of Culloden. The legislators, largely (if not entirely) of English descent, may thereby have displayed their disdain for the Scots. In 1784 an act was passed to rename the county "Fayette," but it was promptly repealed.

When the American Revolution erupted, the Highland Scots of North Car-

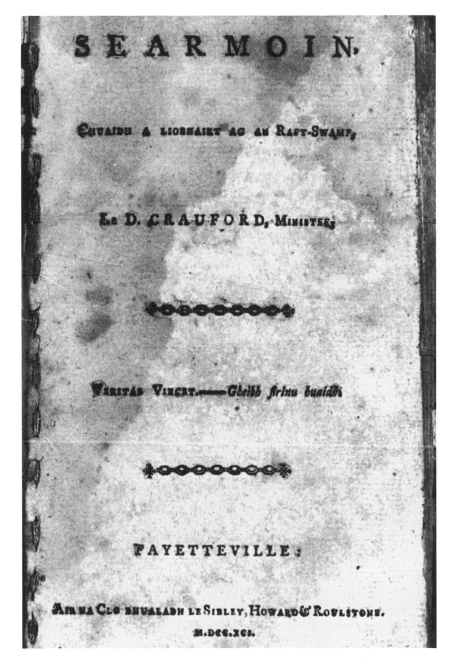

Title page of a sermon in Gaelic by the Reverend Le D. Crauford printed in Fayetteville in 1791. (First Presbyterian Church, Fayetteville)

olina generally remained loyal to Great Britain. Historians have never fully agreed as to the reasons, but certainly among them were the Scots' doubt as to an American victory; having once felt the fury of English vengeance in battle, they did not want to risk another defeat. Some had been required to take an oath of loyalty to England while they were still in Scotland, and as God-fearing Presbyterians they could not violate an oath. Perhaps a more practical reason was the bounty many of these people enjoyed from Parliament for the production of naval stores in the Cape Fear Valley; this would cease with American independence.

Scots-Irish

While the Highlanders were moving up the Cape Fear River, two other bands of people were entering the province. Though coming from the same place and along the same road, these two groups were quite different and, once settled, remained apart. One consisted of immigrants of Scottish-Irish descent while the other was made up of people of German origin. Both came almost exclusively from Pennsylvania and traveled down the Great Wagon Road through the Shenandoah Valley of Virginia. The people of both groups were mostly second- or third-generation "Americans." Their parents or grandparents had arrived in Pennsylvania to take up land or to follow a trade. These younger people found land there scarce just at the time North Carolina's backcountry was beginning to be opened to settlement.

The so-called Scots-Irish (the term they prefer rather than the more common Scotch-Irish), or Ulster Scots, were descendants of the Scots who had been sent by English monarchs to Northern Ireland in the early seventeenth century to "civilize" the country, to supplant the unruly Irish, and to industrialize that part of the empire. There these people drained swamps, cleared fields, grew crops including flax, and raised cattle and sheep. They were Presbyterians who displaced many Roman Catholics, thereby accomplishing another English objective—to make the country Protestant. They also developed a thriving linen and woolen industry that began to compete with English mills. They might be said to have succeeded too well, and after a century English policy changed—these people were encouraged to leave Ireland for America. Queen Anne, granddaughter of Lord Proprietor Edward Hyde, helped to provide transportation to Philadelphia for many Scots-Irish.

On the way to the Carolina backcountry some of these people stopped off in the Valley of Virginia, but larger numbers continued into Piedmont North Carolina as well as into upcountry South Carolina. A few also arrived by sea, sailing down the coast to Charles Town and from there traveling inland. With friends and relatives in other colonies as well as up and down the frontier, in time they came to play an important role in uniting the colonies in a sentiment for independence. They came by this sentiment naturally as dissenters to the Anglican church, as a people who had no love for the English, and especially because their democratic church government gave them experience in managing their own affairs. Their religion encouraged them to read and interpret the Bible, and it was largely for this reason that they supported education. They were highly literate— even many women could read and write, which was uncommon at that time.

The Scots-Irish were self-reliant, industrious, unemotional, opinionated, and often considered to be bigoted, reserved, and cold, but they were loyal to friends and family. They made ideal settlers of the backcountry. They cleared land, built barns and houses (often in that order), and soon afterward established churches and schools. The period 1735–75 saw the arrival of most of the colony's Scots-Irish settlers. They usually left their former homes in the fall as soon as crops were gathered and arrived in their new home, bringing food, livestock, equipment, and supplies, in time to acquire land, clear the trees, and be ready to plant with the coming of spring. Before long they also erected sawmills, gristmills, and tanneries.

During the American Revolution these people supplied large numbers of troops and a large proportion of high-ranking officers. Many also held office in the government as soon as English influence weakened.

Governor Arthur Dobbs, a Scots-Irishman himself, said that in one year 10,000 of his countrymen landed in Philadelphia; many of them traveled as far south as North Carolina before finding land to their liking and at a price they could afford. In a seven-year span, the legislature created five new counties to accommodate their numbers: Johnston and Granville (1746), Anson (1750), Orange (1752), and Rowan (1753). When Rowan was created, it already had at least 3,000 people; just ten years later Mecklenburg County was formed.

Germans

The other newcomers in the backcountry from Pennsylvania consisted of German Protestants, members of the Lutheran, German Reformed, and Moravian churches. They spoke German and many continued to do so until the 1840s, although the young people also spoke English. When asked by their English-speaking neighbors what kind of people they were, they replied "Deutsch" (German), and soon they were referred to as Pennsylvania Dutch, a term that their descendants revived during World War I when they wanted to deny their German background.

In central Europe several very cold winters and even some years "without a summer" killed vineyards and orchards, and drove farmers off the land. Many Germans went to Holland and eventually large numbers found their way to England. With Queen Anne's assistance, some sailed with Christoph von Graffenried's colonists to New Bern while others went to Pennsylvania. There the population increased and available land became scarce, so, like the Scots-Irish, young people of German descent took the Great Wagon Road for Carolina. The first wave reached what is now Rowan County by 1747. A few Lutherans also settled as far east as modern Alamance, Guilford, and Orange counties, although the majority found land to their liking in the area now encompassing Cabarrus, Rowan, Stanly, Union, Mecklenburg, Lincoln, Davie, Davidson, Catawba, and Burke counties. The members of the German Reformed and Lutheran congregations scattered across the backcountry.

Like the Scots-Irish the Germans arrived in the fall and were well settled by spring. Lacking German-speaking pastors, they built schoolhouses and in them held Sunday services. Unlike their neighbors whose British surnames were familiar to county officials, the Germans had names that were difficult to spell and even more difficult to pronounce. Sometimes they translated them into English themselves: Zimmerman to Carpenter, Schneider to Taylor, and Klein to Small, Little, or Short, as well as to Cline. At other times a county official simply wrote the name as he heard it: Eckel became Eagle and Durr became Dry. When these German-speaking people owned slaves, the slaves also spoke German, a peculiarity noted by outsiders passing through Salisbury. Even a printer in Salisbury offered pamphlets and almanacs in German.

During the American Revolution few people of German extraction held high positions in either civil or military affairs. The language barrier probably was a hindrance, but they certainly were not considered to be Loyalists. Perhaps the objectives of the war simply were not widely understood by this group.

Moravians

The largest body of Germans to settle as a close-knit group were the Moravians. From Pennsylvania Bishop August Gottlieb Spangenberg and a party of Moravians visited North Carolina and explored the northern half of the colony in search of a site for a settlement. They purchased 98,985 acres from Earl Granville and called the place Wachovia or Wachau-the-Aue (meadowland) because its streams and meadows bore some resemblance to a valley in Austria where some prominent Moravian leaders lived. The first contingent arrived at three o'clock on Saturday afternoon, 17 November 1753. As this precise time may suggest, these people kept very careful records, day by day, week by week, month by month, and finally, in yearly summaries. A dozen volumes of their journals were trans-

A view of Salem painted in 1787. (Courtesy of Old Salem, Inc.)

lated into English and published, while uncounted pages of equally interesting documents have been preserved in the Moravian Archives at Old Salem. Before settling in North Carolina, Moravian officials convinced Parliament to declare their church to be an "Episcopal" church and therefore entitled to the same privileges as the established church. As a result, St. Luke's Parish in Rowan County was divided and the northern portion, named Dobbs Parish, was assigned to the Moravians, as that was the center of their settlement.

The Moravian church held its property in trust for all of the people. Land for farms, mills, shops, and crafts as well as for homes was assigned by the church. In Moravian communities all people could buy and sell goods, obtain medical and dental attention, find accommodations at a comfortable tavern, hear good music on a variety of instruments including a pipe organ, and enjoy good food. During the Revolution the Moravians continued to pay their quitrent to Earl Granville, but they also honored their obligations to the new state government. In their effort to remain neutral in the conflict and because they opposed the use of force, they furnished supplies to all who came to buy without regard to loyalties. When the war was over, Salem was the first place in the state to stage a public observance of independence, perhaps the first celebration of the Fourth of July in the new nation.

Table 5-1. Estimated Number of Blacks in North Carolina, 1717–1767 (Various Years), with Totals from the 1790 Census

Year	Number
1717	1,000+
1720	3,000
1730	6,000
1754	15,000
1765	30,000
1767	39,000
1790	100,572 (slave)
1790	4,975 (free)

Welsh

Some people of Welsh origin also moved to North Carolina from Pennsylvania. Between 1730 and 1734 a number of individuals and families moved to the lower Cape Fear in what is now Pender County. There were enough of them to mark their community as "The Welsh Tract," which appears on at least one eighteenth-century map. One of the best known members of this community was a youth named Hinton James who became the first student at the University of North Carolina when it opened in 1795.

Blacks

Blacks also appeared early in the colony's history. It is likely that Sir Francis Drake, when he departed from Roanoke Island in 1586, left behind the black household slaves he had taken from the Spanish at Santo Domingo and Cartagena in order to make room for members of the Ralph Lane colony. The Concessions and Agreement of 1665 recognized slavery, while the Fundamental Constitutions of 1669 gave it a legal status. In 1694, 5 whites claimed rights to extra land for having brought 8 blacks into the colony. In 1709 211 blacks were living in Pasquotank Precinct and the next year 97 were in Currituck. By 1710 there were about 900 in the whole colony, although no firm figures seem to have been recorded before the first federal census in 1790. Estimates for succeeding years of the eighteenth century are provided in Table 5-1.

There were a few free blacks in North Carolina before 1715, but the number was never very large. Occasionally a litigant in court, suing for the payment of a debt, was identified as a Negro while others were identified as artisans. Black males qualified to vote by reason of their property holdings were, indeed, voters.

Orders of Society

During the colonial period social distinctions were carefully drawn. The highest social group was composed of "gentlemen" or the gentry class, consisting of planters, public officials, and professional men including the clergy. A few were connected by family ties with the gentry of England, Scotland, and Ireland, and here they tried to maintain some of the social distinctions that marked their class there. Evidence of social rank is seen in their use of the titles "gentleman," "esquire," and "planter." Some of them also used family crests and coats of arms, the latter especially on bookplates.

Land and slaves were the chief form of wealth of the gentry. Some members of that class owned between 5,000 and 10,000 acres, while a few owned up to 50,000. Governor Gabriel Johnston owned 24,000 acres and 103 slaves; Cullen Pollock owned 150 slaves in 1749, and the next year Roger Moore of Orton Plantation held 250.

Rivers offered the most desirable sites for plantations, as they provided the means for getting produce to market by water. Whenever possible, houses were built on bluffs overlooking the river. Many estates had names: Ashwood, Blew Water, Coneconara, Dogwood Ridge, Elbo, The Folly, Groveley, Haltons Lodge, The Image, Jacobs Wells, and so forth. Plantations had their own shops, mills, distilleries, tanneries, spinning wheels, and looms. Slaves were trained as blacksmiths, carpenters, millers, shoemakers, spinners and weavers, and for other jobs. Social distinctions were recognized by law as well as by custom. Guardians were required by law to educate their wards "according to their Rank & degree." The Carolina charter authorized the creation of a colonial peerage of sorts, while the Fundamental Constitutions actually supplied titles (cacique and landgrave) and an elaborate scheme of land distribution for their support. Nevertheless, few of these titles were ever granted. The rules of official and social precedence were carefully laid down; as late as 1771, Sir Nathaniel Duckenfield argued with the governor and Council over his right as a baronet to take precedence socially over councillors.

Below the gentry in social rank was the largest group in the colony, composed largely of small farmers. They also had a keen class consciousness and took pride in their titles: farmer, husbandman, yeoman. Their life, however, has been described as crude, with few luxuries. They worked hard, played hard, and lived hard. Dr. John Brickell observed that these people "equalize with the Negroes in hard Labour." The small farmers made the most lasting impression on visitors to

A selection of armorial bookplates used by colonial North Carolinians. These are from books that they owned. (North Carolina Collection, University of North Carolina at Chapel Hill)

the province. Their hard work, their honesty, and their love of independence suggested to many the same qualities displayed by the yeomen of England. R. D. W. Connor, a twentieth-century North Carolina historian, described them as strong, fearless, simple in tastes, crude in manners, provincial in outlook, democratic in social relations, tenacious of their rights, sensitive to encroachments on their personal liberties, and, when interested at all in religion, earnest, narrow, and dogmatic.

Following the small farmer class came the indentured servants who represented a variety of social classes and economic conditions. For some years, this group was the colony's main source of labor. Many indentured servants were "redemptioners," people who had voluntarily "bound" themselves to a master for a fixed period in order to "redeem" their passage across the Atlantic. Some, however, were political offenders; convicts sold into bondage in lieu of a jail term; military prisoners, particularly among the Scottish Highlanders; and women and children who had been kidnapped in London or other cities.

The term of service depended on the contract, but usually lasted from three to five years. Although the law varied from time to time, at the end of the term the servant was generally entitled to a supply of decent food and clothes and if a man, a serviceable gun. Until 1715, the colony also gave these people fifty acres of land. Many of the indentures or contracts provided that the servant be taught to read and write, and there were laws against cruel punishment.

Most of these "Christian servants," as they were often called, were energetic, industrious, thrifty, and ambitious and had simply taken this means of securing passage to the New World to share in its promise of a bright future and to improve their condition in life. Soon after the beginning of the eighteenth century, fewer indentured servants were brought to North Carolina. Yet in October 1776 Arthur Young wrote, in *Tour in Ireland, 1776–1779*: "Three years ago there was an emigration of indentured servants [from Carrick in Northern Ireland] to North Carolina of three hundred. . . . There had been something of this constantly, but not to that amount."

Many families from Virginia, after completing the terms of their indenture, chose to settle in North Carolina where good land was available. Leaving their servant status behind them, these people made a new start in the colony as small farmers or artisans. The ambitious and capable among them quickly became well established and some even rose up the social scale.

Similar to indentured servants were the numerous apprentices in North Carolina. Children were apprenticed to learn a trade, either with the consent of their parents or—if orphaned or illegitimate—by the court. In most cases they were also taught to read and write. Boys generally were apprenticed to mechanics, blacksmiths, carpenters, coopers, cord winders, weavers, tailors, joiners, mariners, wheelwrights, fishermen, silversmiths, ditchers, and barbers. Girls learned weaving, spinning, sewing, cooking, embroidery, and such "feminine accomplishments" as would make them good housewives or able to support themselves in case of necessity.

Blacks, both slave and free, were considered to be a separate social group. The laws of 1715 prohibited them from voting or marrying whites. Slaves gained their freedom in several ways. Some were freed under the terms of their master's will; others were freed by action of the General Assembly as a reward for bravery, such as saving someone from drowning or rescuing a person from a burning house. Sometimes a spouse or children were purchased and emancipated by free blacks. Many white fathers of children by a slave freed them. Since children took the status of their mother, the mulatto child of a white woman was free at birth.

Slaves were regarded as property and had numerous restrictions. Their freedom to move about the community was usually limited. As a rule they were not permitted to carry guns or to hunt game. Frequently they were forbidden to attend meetings with other slaves or to communicate at night. Harsh punishment was possible for violating these and other laws or customs.

The earliest slaves in the colonies were considered to be pagans, and masters were willing for them to remain so. It was widely believed that no Christian could be held in bondage, but in time this idea was abandoned. Missionaries and clergymen were permitted to visit and preach to slaves. In fact, some believed that if slaves became Christians they would be more docile and manageable. Some people in the colony opposed slavery, of course. Most notable among them were the Quakers and the Moravians; however, the latter never spoke out on the subject while the former began to express their views only in the late colonial period.

As the movement toward revolution got underway, local meetings were held to elect delegates to the Provincial Congress. On 8 August 1774 the freeholders of Rowan County resolved "that the African Trade is injurious to this Colony, obstructs the Population of it by freemen, prevents manufacturers, and other Useful Emigrants from Europe from settling among us, and occasions an annual increase of the Balance of Trade against the Colonies." About two weeks later the first Provincial Congress resolved "that we will not import any slave or slaves, nor purchase any slave or slaves imported or brought into this province by others from any part of the world after the first day of November next."

Housing

The dwellings occupied by colonial North Carolinians usually varied according to social class. While almost all classes lived in wooden houses, those of the gentry might be larger and in the most attractive setting. They were usually plain, unpainted buildings, lacking architectural grace, sacrificing beauty to comfort and convenience, and frequently without much landscaping. In the early days the less prosperous planters lived in one-story houses, often with a sleeping loft above. By the 1720s some story-and-a-half houses were being built. In Edenton, the first two-story Cupola house was erected about 1724. Soon afterward two-story structures began to appear elsewhere, sometimes with a wing and perhaps a small porch. Such elegant structures as the surviving Orton house on the lower Cape Fear River, Hayes house near Edenton, and John Wright Stanly house in New Bern were exceptional and came somewhat later. The Newbold-White house in Perquimans County, a small brick structure, possibly dates from the seventeenth century. A few more brick houses were built in the early eighteenth century; others were constructed by the end of the colonial period.

The usual plan for the "mansion house," as they were called, consisted of four rooms downstairs and four upstairs, each with a fireplace. Wainscoting and fine mantels were often included, but closets were rare and bathrooms nonexistent. There were numerous outbuildings—one or two privies, a laundry, a kitchen, perhaps an office, and sometimes a special building for a loom. Food was cooked in a large fireplace in the isolated kitchen, which was set apart to protect the main house from the possibility of fire. Still farther removed were the barn, stables, poultry houses, corncrib, smokehouse, and other structures. Houses for the slaves were often laid out along a "street."

Depending on the income and taste of the owner, the furniture was comfortable and ornate or less so and plain, homemade or imported from another colony or from abroad, ample or sparse. Inventories of estates indicate that planters owned such things as silver, tea and coffee services, china, glass, punch bowls, pewter, mirrors, musical instruments, games, telescopes, globes, books, and a great variety of beds, tables, chairs, chests, portraits, and pictures. Also mentioned are table linens, draperies, rugs, tapestries, featherbeds, quilts, and counterpanes, as well as rings, necklaces, bracelets, pins, cuff links, watches, and other jewelry.

The less affluent lived in smaller houses and had no such finery. Members of the small farmer class generally occupied a one- or two-room log or frame house, perhaps with a lean-to on the back. A single large fireplace was used for cooking and for heat. The furniture consisted of simple beds with corn shuck, straw, or feather mattresses, stools, benches, and a table. Dressers and chests were rare and seldom needed since there were few extra clothes or linens to store. Whatever was not worn was hung on pegs driven into the wall around the room.

The Shaw house at Southern Pines, dating from about the mid-eighteenth century. (North Carolina Division of Travel and Tourism, Raleigh)

Food

Almost every family, regardless of class, provided whatever food was needed. In season fresh fruits and vegetables were plentiful. Nearly all of the common garden produce of today was known in the colonial period. Beans, squash, potatoes, onions, rhubarb, lettuce, greens of various kinds, apples, peaches, assorted berries, figs, walnuts, pecans, and herbs were grown in abundance. Many of these could be dried in the sun or before a fire to be reconstituted and consumed in the winter. Beef, pork, mutton, turkeys, chicken, ducks, and wild game, including rabbits, squirrels, and deer, were found throughout the province. Rivers, lakes, the sounds, and the ocean offered a variety of fish as well as oysters and other seafood. Tea, coffee, and chocolate were imported and generally accessible only to the gentry. The "lesser sort of folks" might enjoy such rare treats on birthdays or holidays.

Alcoholic beverages were to be had by those who wanted them, and almost

This artist's drawing of a backcountry house suggests the kind of home that left an impression on visitors to the colony. Note the absence of windows—both because of the scarcity and expense of glass and the possibility that the family would have to take refuge inside from roaming bands of Indians. The stick chimney caulked with mud reflects the lack of bricks. Large families—five children are shown here—and pigs loose in the yard were also commented on by outsiders. (North Carolina Division of Archives and History, Raleigh)

everybody did. Wine, beer, rum, brandy, whiskey, and other liquors were common. Farms or plantations advertised for sale often were described as having large orchards of apple, pear, and peach trees, the implication being that they were available for making brandy.

Public Accommodations and Entertainment

Travelers through the province seldom found inns or taverns when darkness approached, so it was the custom to call at the closest house for accommodations. Nearly every family was delighted to offer its hospitality to strangers. People living in isolated areas welcomed the opportunity to talk to someone who could give them news of the outside world, tell some good stories, and share some new jokes. On these occasions the best a family had to offer would be brought out—silver and china, perhaps—and certainly a good meal would be provided. A French traveler in the colony reported with pleasure the fine venison and cider that he was served in a small backcountry house. Cakes and pies were remembered by some long after they had forgotten in which home they were enjoyed.

Those obliged to accept accommodations in the inns, or ordinaries as they were also called, often had cause for regret. Although there were good inns in some of the towns—Wilmington, New Bern, Edenton, Halifax, Hillsborough, and Salem, for example—most were poor indeed. Although by law an innkeeper was required to provide suitable lodgings, few did. Sometimes the owner and his family occupied the few beds available, while the traveler had to sleep on the floor before the fireplace in the "common entertaining room." In some cases strangers were expected to share a bed. There were no window screens, of course, and flies and mosquitoes were common menaces. Bedbugs were frequently found. Rowdy and noisy persons at the bar created disturbances, according to diaries kept by some of the travelers.

In many communities the inn was a gathering place for men who lived in the vicinity. Candidates for public office spoke from the porch during their campaigns. And often in the fall after harvest time, people "of the better sort" would go to a popular inn for a vacation, although they may not have used that word. Sometimes there was a racetrack nearby since horse racing was a popular pastime, as was cockfighting. People often placed bets on their favorite horse or game rooster, and on occasion large sums of money were won or lost. This practice, however, was widely condemned.

Dancing was popular, particularly among the gentry class, and dancing teachers traveled from place to place in the province offering lessons. Dr. Brickell observed that people danced whenever they could get someone to play a fiddle or a bagpipe. In fact, he said, "so attach'd are they to this darling Amusement, that if they can't procure Musick, they will sing for themselves."

Early and frequent marriages were common in the colony. Land was available, houses could be built quickly and simply furnished, and a man could easily make a living for his family. Moreover, it was lonely on the frontier. Women married young, sometimes as early as thirteen or fourteen. According to John Lawson, "she that stays single 'til 20 is reckoned a stale maid; which is a very indifferent character in that warm country." Large families were the rule; as Dr. Brickell commented, "women are very fruitful." Yet the hardships of pioneer life and the burdens of motherhood, especially in the absence of adequate medical treatment, wore women out early in life. The inscriptions on tombstones in colonial burying grounds are silent witnesses to this tragic fact. Women seldom had second or third husbands, but men, widowed once, married again and sometimes repeated the process a third or even fourth time. Colonial weddings usually were not important social functions, since before 1766 the marriage ceremony could be performed only by an Anglican clergyman or, in his absence, by a justice of the peace. Marriage licenses were required, for which a fee had to be paid, and sometimes it was necessary to travel a considerable distance to the courthouse to obtain the license and to find a justice. Often a prospective bride and groom simply set off alone to meet these legalities. But sometimes they did not bother, electing instead to have a common-law marriage.

Funerals, on the other hand, were usually public occasions. Private burials were prohibited, and planters were required by law to set aside a fenced burial place for interring all Christian persons, bond or free, who died on their plantation. This perhaps explains the existence of so many family cemeteries in North Carolina. To ensure that no foul play had occurred, a body had to be viewed by three or four neighbors; this resulted in publicity following a death. Sometimes an invitation to a wake or a funeral would be sent, and friends and acquaintances would come from a distance to attend. Food and lodging had to be provided, and it was the custom that no one be turned away. Frequently the rabble of a community would arrive simply to enjoy the food and drink provided for the "guests." Wine and whiskey were usually available at these gatherings—at a funeral in Mecklenburg County in 1767, seven gallons of whiskey were consumed and charged to the estate of the deceased.

At this time large numbers of people turned out for court days and militia muster. The county militia was required by law to hold four company musters and one regimental muster, for a total of five days of training each year. Early county maps often show a "muster field" or a "muster ground" at some convenient location. Since all white males between the ages of sixteen and sixty were required to serve, muster day was an important event. Families usually accompanied their men, and everyone had an opportunity to visit, to politic, to settle debts, to buy and sell, and perhaps to begin a courtship. To survive a hard day of training, liquid refreshment was needed, and by the end of the day few men felt any pain. Many, in fact, had energy left to engage in footraces, target shooting, wrestling matches, or other forms of physical contact. Sometimes serious fighting broke out and no rules of sportsmanship prevailed. On more than one occasion someone left the field with an eye gouged out, a nose slit, a tongue cut, a finger bitten off, or an ear twisted and pulled off. Since one of the punishments for counterfeiting and perjury was to have one's ears nailed to the pillory and then cut off, men who lost an ear in a friendly fight might later be suspected of having committed one of these offenses. Finally in 1754 the Assembly made it a felony to fight in this manner.

The use of tobacco, which was believed to have medicinal properties, was widespread in the colonial period. Men of all classes and women of the lower classes smoked pipes; many men chewed tobacco as well. Snuff was also used in the English fashion—a pinch of finely powdered tobacco was "snuffed" up the nose to inspire a hefty sneeze to "clear the vapours."

Religion and Churches

Colonial North Carolinians were not inclined to support any form of organized religion. Many years passed after the first white settlers arrived before ministers or missionaries appeared, and the first attempts by the government to encourage the establishment of the state church were resisted among people who danced, when dancing was considered by many to be sinful; who drank to excess; who engaged in cruel forms of combat or bet on horses and cockfights; who lived together outside of marriage; and who inflicted harsh punishment on those "beneath" them. Some outsiders cited such activities, which actually were common throughout the colonial South, as evidence that there was little interest in religion in North Carolina.

The colony's pioneer settlers probably had been members of the Anglican church in Virginia, but living on the fringes of settlement in the "Southern Plantation" and later in Carolina they were far removed from the influence of the church. Settlers had been in the area for more than twenty years before the first sermon was heard. When William Edmundson, an English Quaker, arrived in Albemarle in 1672, he found no evidence of religious concern. A few months later he was followed by George Fox, a Quaker missionary. Together they reported considerable success in converting people to their faith, and by 1678 the Society of Friends (Quakers) was well organized in the colony. Around 1689 Quakers from Pennsylvania started moving into Carolina, and, as they acquired political influence, their faith began to spread. During the first several decades of the eighteenth century as many as seventeen Quaker missionaries appeared.

About 1740 more Quakers from Pennsylvania arrived to settle in the area that is now Alamance, Chatham, Guilford, Randolph, and Surry counties. Here the New Garden Monthly Meeting was organized in 1754. For many years the Quakers played a significant role in the colony as an influence for good, particularly in the field of education and in their efforts to alleviate the harshness of slavery. During the American Revolution, however, their number declined. Their policy of pacifism could not be supported by some young Quaker men, who left the faith and joined the military forces fighting for independence. Few ever returned to or were accepted back into the Society of Friends. Also those who chose spouses out of the faith were disowned, thereby further reducing the roll of members.

The Anglican church followed the Quakers chronologically, although, as the state church of England, it had been authorized in the Carolina charters of 1663 and 1665 and in various documents prepared by the Lords Proprietors. In 1701 the Church of England began to conduct foreign missionary work through the Society for the Propagation of the Gospel in Foreign Parts (SPG). Almost at once it sent three extensive collections of books to Albemarle to serve as parish libraries. Among the books were contemporary religious works, of course, as well as volumes of general interest. One of these libraries was sent to St. Thomas Parish at Bath and another was intended for Albemarle, but the destination of the third is unknown. Between 1708 and 1783 the SPG sent thirty-three missionaries to the colony for service at twenty-two stations; another thirteen missionaries arrived without the society's assistance. Yet at times there were no Church of England priests in North Carolina. Governor Arthur Dobbs was a member of the SPG and a contributor of money; when he died in 1765, however, his funeral had to be conducted by a magistrate because no Anglican clergyman was within traveling distance.

Various acts passed by the Assembly made provision for the laying out of parishes, the collection of taxes to support the established church, and the construction of churches. Since this was a tax-supported, state church, its governing body, the vestry, was elected by the freeholders. In those counties where an active majority of dissenters existed, many vestries consisted of dissenters who prevented the church from being organized. But in most of the eastern counties and in a few of the backcountry counties, notably Orange and Rowan, it was possible for Anglican missionaries to work. Soon churches were erected in Wilmington, New Bern, Hillsborough, Halifax, Salisbury, and elsewhere. St. Thomas at Bath, begun in 1734, is now the oldest church in the state. The colonial church at Edenton, St. Paul's, also survives. St. John's at Williamsboro in Vance County, built in 1757, is the oldest wooden church in North Carolina.

The vestry, an official agency of the provincial government, had duties in addition to those pertaining to church affairs. The members were responsible for the care of the poor, orphans, and the unfortunate in general. In some parishes the vestry was in charge of a school. Around 1740 sets of weights and measures were sent from England to each county to be used in testing the weights and measures of local merchants. These were placed in the custody of the vestry, and presumably its members did the checking.

The Anglican church, as an agency of the British government, virtually disappeared with the Revolutionary War. Although the SPG continued to pay its missionaries until the end of the war, few of them remained in America. Except for around half a dozen parishes in eastern towns, not until 1817 was the Episcopal church organized in the state as successor to the old established church.

There were a few Presbyterians in the colony by 1708, but it was the Scottish

St. Thomas Church, Bath, built in 1734 for the Church of England parish, is the oldest church in North Carolina. (North Carolina Division of Archives and History, Raleigh)

Highlanders and the Scots-Irish who contributed most to the growth of the Presbyterian church in North Carolina. Although it was the "established church" in Scotland and was so recognized by the Act of Union in 1707 which unified the kingdoms of England and Scotland, it had no official standing in the colonies. Presbyterians settled in the Duplin and New Hanover County area as early as 1736, and from then until after the Revolution they continued to arrive in North Carolina. One of the Highlanders, who arrived in 1739, returned to Argyllshire in 1741 to request that church authorities send a minister who could speak Gaelic, but his trip was unsuccessful. Afterward a few missionaries passed through the colony, and in 1755–56 the Reverend Hugh McAden toured among the Presbyterians. In 1758, however, the Reverend James Campbell of Pennsylvania settled in the Cape Fear Valley and a little later that year the Reverend Alexander Craighead arrived in Mecklenburg County to serve congregations between the Yadkin and Catawba rivers. By the outbreak of the Revolution Presbyterians were scattered over almost the whole colony.

Baptists have a long history in North Carolina. Individual Baptists probably arrived as early as 1695, but their first congregation was not organized until 1727, when Shiloh Church was established in present Camden County. By 1755 there were sixteen congregations with a total of several thousand members. The arrival of Shubal Stearns from Connecticut in 1755 marked a period of growth for the denomination. Formerly a Congregationalist, he settled in what is now Guilford County and began spreading the Baptist doctrine. Sandy Creek Church, located northeast of modern Asheboro, sent out so many missionaries that it came to be known as "the mother of Southern Baptist churches." By 1769 two associations had been formed—Sandy Creek in the western part of the colony and Kehukee in the east. On the eve of the Revolution there was at least one Baptist church in each of the counties, and Baptists, who had had little or no opportunity to fill political offices in the colonial period, soon became officeholders.

One of the leading Baptists was the Reverend Henry Abbot. The son of the Reverend John Abbot, an official on the staff of St. Paul's Cathedral in London, he came to North Carolina as a young man to teach school. He was an Anglican, but in the colony it was said "he fell among the Baptists" and soon joined them. In due time he was ordained. He also was elected to the Provincial Congress which was destined to prepare the first constitution for the new state. Tradition credits Abbot with having presented Article 19 of the Bill of Rights, providing "that all men have a natural and inalienable right to worship Almighty God, according to the dictates of their own consciences." In addition, he seems to have played a leading role in the preparation of Article 34, which declared that "there shall be no Establishment of any one Religious Church in this State in preference to any other." Abbot's Anglican father did not live to learn that his son had played such a role in denying his church its favored position.

German settlers of the Reformed and Lutheran faiths, like the Presbyterians, were served by visiting pastors until they could persuade clergymen to settle among them. Moravians, however, perhaps because Parliament had recognized their church as being an "episcopal" church, brought a clergyman with them from Pennsylvania when they arrived in 1753, and others soon followed. In 1768 the Reverend Samuel Suther, a Reformed pastor, settled in Mecklenburg County, and in 1773 a Lutheran, the Reverend Adolphus Nussman, arrived. In August 1775, the first Lutheran ordination in North Carolina took place at Organ Church in Rowan County.

Many of the Reformed and Lutheran churches were union congregations, as their creeds were very much alike; their people intermarried and moved freely from one church to the other. In some respects the Lutheran and Anglican churches were similar, and in several communities they used the same church in turn. In what is now Lincoln County, the Reverend Robert Johnston Miller accepted Lutheran ordination because he could not afford to go to London for

Anglican ordination, but he served congregations of both churches. After the Revolution he was ordained as an Episcopal priest.

The last of the great Protestant denominations to seek a foothold before the Revolution was the Methodist church. The earliest Methodist missionaries represented a reform movement within the Church of England. In that capacity the Reverend George Whitefield in 1739 made the first of several visits to the colony. He noted that he was cordially received by the people, clergy, and government officials. In England in 1744 the denomination was created as a separate entity from the established church, but the first clergyman representing it did not appear in North Carolina until 1772. On 28 September the Reverend Joseph Pilmoor preached at Currituck Courthouse. Pilmoor was followed the next year by the Reverend John Williams, who organized the first Methodist Society in the colony. In 1774 Williams formed "a six weeks circuit" extending from Petersburg, Virginia, to a region south of the Roanoke River. This made services available on a regular basis. Methodist preachers began to appear in other parts of the colony, and in 1775 a revival swept over a large area, bringing new members to the denomination.

The Methodist church was not organized in America until after the Revolution when a conference met in Baltimore in 1784. The following year, the first annual conference of the church was held in the home of Green Hill at Louisburg, North Carolina. From that date the church enjoyed a steady growth. Many former Anglicans, now without their accustomed services, joined the Methodists as did former members of other denominations.

Dr. John Brickell in 1737 wrote that some Roman Catholics had settled along Pamlico Sound and that a priest lived among them. Since no further mention was made of these people, however, it is assumed that they either left or abandoned their faith. The next reference to members of this church was in 1811, when a Father Cleary died in New Bern where he had been visiting; he was buried in the town's Episcopal churchyard. In 1820 the Diocese of Charleston was created and a bishop named. Roman Catholics in North Carolina, previously under the Archdiocese of Baltimore, then fell within the jurisdiction of the South Carolina diocese.

Jewish historians have theorized that there may have been Jewish colonists on the Cape Fear River between 1664 and 1667, since a great many Jews were then living in Barbados where many of Sir John Yeamans's colonists originated. Better evidence of their presence appeared in 1702–3, when a formal protest was made that Jews, strangers, sailors, servants, Negroes, and others not qualified to vote had been allowed to cast ballots. In 1740 in Perquimans County a will was witnessed by Aaron Moses, presumed by his name to have been Jewish. In 1759 one Laney, described as a Jew, formed a business partnership in New Bern with a man named Haryon. There was no synagogue in the state, however, until 1875 when one was built in Wilmington.

Interest in religion and in education often ran a parallel course. Without clergymen people relied on laymen to conduct worship services. Without teachers, parents were obliged to train their own children. Early in the eighteenth century some people began to bequeath a portion of their estate for the establishment of schools—often another portion was designated to aid the poor in the community.

Schools and Education

Missionaries of the Church of England were the first to begin any real agitation for schools in North Carolina. To authorities in London they reported the lack of resources and stressed the need for education to impress upon the minds of youth the principles of religion and virtue that the church deemed essential. The problem was twofold: to get support and teachers from England, and to convince many adults in the colony that education was desirable. For most colonists, there were higher priorities. For one thing, children were needed to work in the fields.

The first known school in the colony was established in Pasquotank County in 1709 by Charles Griffin, a lay reader in the local Anglican church who had arrived from the West Indies in 1705. His school prospered. Even Quakers sent their children—in spite of the fact that religious training was required along with other studies. After three years Griffin moved to Edenton to teach, but his first school was continued by the Reverend James Adams. In Edenton Griffin became a Quaker and in 1711 moved a few miles north into Virginia to teach in an Indian school. Afterward he joined the faculty at the College of William and Mary.

By 1712 Edward Mashborne was conducting a school for white and Indian children at Sarum, now in western Gates County. A visitor reported that all of the students could read and write, and that they were well grounded in the principles of Christianity. The schools of Griffin, Adams, and Mashborne are the only ones known in the colony during the Proprietary period.

Many years passed after North Carolina became a royal colony before references to a school appeared in the records. In 1754 in Wilmington, Colonel James Innes's will left his plantation, £100 sterling, a large personal estate, and his library for the establishment of a school. As trustees Innes had named the colonel of the militia, the rector of the local church, and members of the vestry, but before the school could be organized some of the property was lost in a fire and the Revolution intervened. Innes Academy was not chartered until 1783, and it did not open until early in the next century.

In 1763 the Reverend Daniel Earl had a school in Edenton where Latin, Greek, English, and mathematics were taught. The schoolhouse that he probably used is still standing.

The idea of a significant academy to serve more than just a local community began to develop, and in 1764 the Assembly authorized the erection of a building on church property in New Bern for this purpose. It would receive financial support from both the church and a provincial tax; in return for the revenue provided by the tax, it would educate ten poor children free. The following year the New Bern Academy opened under the direction of Thomas Thomlinson with thirty pupils. Thomlinson was the son and grandson of schoolmasters from Cumberland County, England, where his family had operated schools for many years. With an able assistant, James McCartney, he provided a good education for young people, at least some of whom were from the Cape Fear section. Several years later when two of his charges required discipline, Thomlinson did not hesitate to apply it. Their father, who happened to be a trustee of the school, was offended, however, and was able to have the teacher dismissed. Thomlinson remained in New Bern where he became a wealthy merchant; the endowment he bequeathed to his family's schools in England still provides an income. In 1899, the New Bern Academy was incorporated into the public school system of the town. Thus, it may be considered the oldest educational institution in the state.

In 1766 the Reverend James Tate, a Presbyterian minister in Wilmington, opened Tate's School as the first classical school in the colony; it continued to prepare young men for college until the Revolution. In the same year Presbyterians also established Crowfield Academy in Rowan County. Still another Presbyterian school was opened in 1767 by the Reverend David Caldwell at a site now within the limits of Greensboro. Caldwell's school was described as "an academy, a college, and a theological seminary." Each year until it closed in 1822, it enrolled between twelve and twenty students. Many of Caldwell's graduates entered the junior class at Princeton or at the University of North Carolina.

One serious attempt was made to establish a degree-granting college in the province before the Revolution. In 1771 the Assembly chartered Queen's College in Charlotte (not related to the present school of the same name) and provided for a tax to support it. This action, approved by Governor William Tryon, was taken in part to show appreciation for the people's support in putting down the Regulator uprising. Clearly the institution would benefit dissenting Presbyterians, but royal approval could not be obtained unless the president was an Anglican. This limited association with the Anglican church did not work, however, and the charter was not approved. In the meantime the college had already been established, so the name was merely changed to Queen's Museum. It fell victim to the troubled times of the Revolution even though it was moved briefly to Salisbury and operated under the name Liberty Hall Academy.

Young men seeking higher education had very limited opportunities. Early records indicate that a few attended Yale, William and Mary, Brown, Harvard, Hampden-Sydney, and Princeton. Occasionally a graduate of Oxford or Cambridge appeared among the settlers of North Carolina, while a few young men left the colony to be educated at Eton College, the University of Glasgow, or some other school in Britain.

Many people, of course, were self-educated. While libraries to serve the public were limited to those sent by the Society for the Propagation of the Gospel and perhaps to a few subscription libraries, personal books were fairly plentiful. Wills and inventories of estates often listed books by name, and many volumes from colonial homes have survived. Popular writers of the day, classical works, and practical books of use to planters, housewives, lawyers, physicians, and others are represented. Bound files of *The Gentleman's Magazine*, *The London Magazine*, and *The Annual Register*, to which North Carolina readers subscribed, have been preserved. Newspapers of the day advertised the latest books as well as schoolbooks, and general merchants stocked assorted books, Bibles, prayer books, hymnals, and pamphlets.

Nine of the thirteen colonies already had printers at work before North Carolina did. In 1740 the colony's laws were printed in Williamsburg, Virginia, probably to let legislators see how they looked, but soon afterward a bill introduced to entice a printer to move to North Carolina was rejected. Royal governors pointed out to the Assembly "the shameful condition" of the provincial laws. After each session of the legislature handwritten copies of the new laws were made and sent around to the county offices, to lawyers, and to provincial officials who needed them. Often mistakes were made, words were left out, or new words were added. It was difficult to know what laws were in effect or whether the copy consulted was accurate. In 1746 a commission was named to collect, verify, and revise the laws, and to have them printed. When their work was done, the commissioners set about finding a printer. In Williamsburg they located James Davis, who was willing to move to New Bern as the provincial printer. A five-year contract was drawn up specifying that he print and distribute the laws, as well as journals, speeches, and other official publications. Davis might also print for the public as time permitted. He was to arrange to have official communications delivered around the province, and he might also deliver for the public. By late June 1749 Davis was settled in New Bern and the first product of his press was the journal of the 1749 legislature. In 1751 he printed the 350-page collection of laws that the commissioners had compiled. In the same year Davis began publishing *The North Carolina Gazette*, the first newspaper in the colony. He and later his son continued the *Gazette* until after the Revolution, except that no issues appeared for a few years during the war while young Davis was in the army.

Because the office of printer was tied in with politics, Davis sometimes failed to have his contract renewed. Andrew Steuart and Adam Boyd, both in Wilmington, were also colonial printers, and for a brief time Steuart was the official printer. Both also published newspapers as well as private pieces for the public.

6

COLONIAL ECONOMY: AGRICULTURE, TRADE, AND COMMUNICATION

L AND AND SLAVES, as has been indicated, were the chief forms of wealth in colonial and antebellum North Carolina. Towns grew slowly, and—as in all new and undeveloped countries—nearly everyone depended on agriculture in one way or another. In spite of the fact that for a long time land was plentiful and readily available, everything having to do with it was of great interest. Most people were concerned about the size of the grants they might obtain, the accuracy of surveys, the amount and manner of quitrent payments, and laws relating to the disposition of land. These were the subject of legislative debate for many years, and attempts were made both at home and from London to deal with them. Quitrents probably caused more problems than anything else. Rates went up from time to time and were not based on the value of the land or on the ability of the owner to pay.

Land was easy enough to acquire. One had only to find a plot not owned by someone else and secure an order from the governor or his representative in the land grant office to have it surveyed. A surveyor would prepare a plat of the land which would be returned to the office to be recorded. A patent, equivalent to a deed, would then be issued from the governor's office and delivered to the new owner. The cost usually was about £10 or less for 640 acres, and the annual quitrent in 1773 was 2s. 6d. per 100 acres. Surveyors were authorized a fee of £1 13s. 4d. for each 1,000 acres.

Agriculture

Early settlers attempted to produce some of the exotic fruits, herbs, and tropical plants that the promotional publications insisted could be grown in the colony's latitude. When those failed, they turned to such reliable crops as corn, beans, peas, and squash which they adopted from the native Americans. They also learned from the Indians some important secrets of farming. In England farmers simply broke the ground of a field and broadcast seed; hundreds of years had rid fields of many weeds and most insects, and the climate was conducive to growth. When they tried this in America, weeds quickly choked the sprouting seeds, and insects, birds, and wild animals devoured whatever survived. The Indians laughed at the whites, and began to teach them to plant their seeds in rows or hills, to chop out the weeds, and to tend the growing plants carefully.

Larger estates developed in the east than elsewhere and planters soon were exporting a large variety of products: grain of various kinds, salt pork and beef, tallow, barrel staves, naval stores, lumber, tobacco, and skins. These were often exchanged for rum, molasses, sugar, coffee, clothing, household goods, and other items.

In the backcountry farms were smaller, in part because the land was less fertile and the abundant hardwood trees were more difficult to remove than the pines so common in the east. Small industrial enterprises often developed on the swifter streams there, particularly among the Scots-Irish and Germans who were adept at building and operating gristmills and tanneries. In many isolated communities the weavers, carpenters, coopers, wheelwrights, wagon makers, tailors, blacksmiths, hatters, and rope makers—all of whom offered a necessary service—became the most prosperous.

Corn was grown throughout the colony. It was popular because it was relatively easy to grow, and it could be put to many uses. Sometimes after a crop of early corn was harvested, something else was planted in its place. Corn could also be grown on new ground before it was completely cleared. It was the practice of pioneer settlers simply to girdle a tree to kill it and leave the dead tree standing until it fell or until they found a more convenient time to remove it.

Among its assorted uses, corn could be eaten fresh as "roastin' ears," of course, or, when mature and dry, ground into meal to make cornbread, mush, or grits. It could also be treated with lye to make hominy. With no effort at all, whole ears could be fed to livestock. Thomas Ash, the author of a promotional tract in 1682, reported still another use. "At Carolina," he wrote, "they have lately invented a way of makeing with [corn] a good sound Beer; but it's strong and heady: By Maceration, when duly fermented, a strong Spirit like Brandy may be drawn off from it by the help of a [still]."

Well before the end of the seventeenth century, New Englanders were sending vessels to the Albemarle to pick up cargoes of corn and other surplus farm produce. This trade continued through the early decades of the next century. As the colony's population increased, the amount exported naturally showed a corresponding increase. In 1753, about 62,000 bushels of corn were shipped out; within fifteen years this had doubled, and in twenty years it had almost tripled.

The tract reporting the discovery of corn liquor also observed that some farmers had started growing wheat and that it did "exceeding well." By the early eighteenth century cargo inventories of ships sailing from Carolina listed hundreds of bushels of wheat, suggesting the special role of wheat in the colony's economy. It seems to have been grown *not* for bread to be eaten at home (corn was preferred for that) but raised almost exclusively as a commercial crop. A ready market existed, as the Reverend John Urmston implied in 1714, when he wrote that sloops from New England "sweep all our Provisions away—We have twice as many vessels this year as ever were wont to come, [and] there are above 7 now waiting like as many vultures waiting for our wheat & more [are] daily expected." In the interior, Cross Creek became a collecting point for wheat and flour produced in the backcountry. From there it was shipped down the Cape Fear River to Wilmington for export. All sections of the colony also produced large quantities of beans and peas for export.

In addition to food crops, others that could be readily sold for money were important. Tobacco was just such a crop. After John Rolfe at Jamestown introduced a variety from the West Indies that was more desirable than the species grown by the Indians, tobacco became a significant item of export. In 1666 concern over the quality of tobacco led to a pioneer instance of intercolonial cooperation. A meeting at St. Mary's, Maryland, attended by Governor William Drummond of Albemarle and the governors of Maryland and Virginia, was called to discuss ways of keeping poor quality tobacco off the market so the demand in England would remain high. It was decided that each year's production should be inspected and that of inferior quality destroyed.

As the population of the colony increased and new areas began to be settled, the production of tobacco increased. For export it was packed in 1,000-pound quantities in large wooden barrels called hogsheads through which an axle was inserted. The hogsheads were then rolled to market. As production expanded, the problem of maintaining high quality again arose, and once more a law was passed for the inspection of tobacco. In 1754 it was directed that warehouses be constructed at well-used crossroads or along navigable streams where tobacco would be inspected before it was approved for marketing. The activity generated by these warehouses attracted others—the merchant who opened a store nearby, the lawyer who built an office. Then a church would be organized. Before long it was recognized that a new town had come into being. It is likely that Kinston and Williamston had such an origin.

Scottish merchants played a significant role in the spread of tobacco production. One of these was John Hamilton and Co., whose main operation was in Halifax but which had branches as far away as Wilmington. This company and others lent money to planters to buy more land and slaves, and the loan would be repaid in tobacco at the end of the season. Such companies also offered an assortment of wares to tempt both the planter and his family and to encourage further

Both tobacco and cotton, labor-intensive crops, frequently required the attention of whole families. Their production contributed to the increase in the use of slave labor in those areas where they flourished. In this drawing of a tobacco harvest about 1750, note the wagon drawn by a pair of oxen. (North Carolina Division of Archives and History, Raleigh)

production of cash crops. The cured tobacco was shipped to Scotland, particularly to Glasgow, where it was manufactured into smoking tobacco and snuff.

Although corn, wheat, and tobacco were the most common agricultural products of North Carolina, others were exported from the colony. Rice and indigo were regularly produced, but usually in small quantities. Both were more difficult to grow than other crops and required a great deal of labor. Indigo, from which a popular blue dye was made, has long been supplanted by a chemical dye, but some rice continued to be grown in Brunswick and Hyde counties until the 1950s. Earlier it had been grown in Lenoir, Pitt, and Sampson counties as well. Other minor crops—fruits and vegetables—were mentioned in the records from time to time. Quakers in the Westfield Monthly Meeting (in Surry County) maintain that alfalfa was first grown in America in their community after a missionary named Jessup brought some seed from England. Another forage crop produced in the colony was timothy grass.

Livestock

Animals were important to the economy of rural North Carolina. Most livestock was allowed to "range" or roam at will instead of being confined in a fenced pasture. Domestic animals were kept on every farm, and most town lots also had room for a horse or two, a cow and a pig, and perhaps some chickens and other fowl. Horses, mules, and oxen were used in plowing and to pull wagons, carts, and other vehicles. Cattle, hogs, sheep, goats, chickens, turkeys, guinea hens, ducks, and geese in varying numbers and combinations were raised for market. Long drives to cities in Virginia, Maryland, Pennsylvania, New Jersey, and elsewhere were common. Although few farms produced large numbers of livestock or fowl, the total from individual farms was impressive. Colonists frequently banded together to conduct a drive to market, and along the way they found pens to confine their stock overnight. In 1728 Governor Sir Richard Everard reported that 30,000 hogs were driven to market in Virginia the previous year. Five years later Governor George Burrington said that 50,000 fat hogs were ready to be driven north.

Forest Products

Vast tracts of virgin forest offered opportunities for additional income. As early as 1622 John Pory from Virginia predicted that, when the pines of the North Carolina region were tapped, England would no longer have to depend on the Scandinavian countries for naval stores—tar, pitch, and turpentine. On both naval and merchant vessels these were essential for paint, caulking, and the preservation of wood and ropes. Intent on farming, however, the earliest colonists removed many of the trees, and naval stores production did not become important until the 1720s.

By 1768, 60 percent of the naval stores exported from the colonies originated in North Carolina. Of crucial importance in this industry was the longleaf pine for its high yield of rosin. The Cape Fear Valley became the center of production because so many of the trees grew there. Soon after Parliament offered a bounty in 1705 for the production of naval stores, it was settled by planters who held large tracts of land there and who owned many slaves who could work in the pine forests. Most naval stores could be produced at various seasons of the year, so slaves who were employed in the fields during the growing season could work in the woods at other times. The Cape Fear River, flowing through this region, offered another advantage—transportation. Barrels of naval stores could be floated downstream on barges or boats to Wilmington for shipment abroad.

The production of naval stores, for which Parliament offered a bounty, was an important industry in North Carolina for well over a century. This early nineteenth-century woodcut illustrates a kiln for producing pitch. Other forest products represented are lumber on the lower left and barrels and boats on the right. (North Carolina Collection, University of North Carolina at Chapel Hill)

The average annual value of naval stores exported from the province in the late colonial period was about £50,000, in addition to the bounty.

The naval stores industry flourished in North Carolina until the beginning of the Civil War, but afterward it declined for several reasons. In 1865 Union troops under General William T. Sherman burned many acres of turpentine forests, thereby decreasing the amount produced for a time; wooden sailing ships gave way to iron vessels, which reduced the demand for naval stores; and synthetic substitutes for turpentine as a paint thinner further cut the need. Nevertheless, so many North Carolinians worked in this industry and its production was so great that North Carolina came to be known as "the Tar Heel State." Tar that spilled on the ground where it was produced, or around turpentine stills, stuck to the feet of workers. But tradition is not consistent. One story says that the nickname came into use during the Revolutionary War. Another credits General Robert E. Lee with applying the name to North Carolina troops whom he commended for sticking to their posts during battle.

Many other kinds of forest products came from North Carolina. One of them suggests an early example of mass production. Since casks, barrels, and

Mule-drawn carts passing through swampy terrain on a corduroy road to collect shingles produced on the site. (North Carolina Collection, University of North Carolina at Chapel Hill)

hogsheads were widely used for shipping both liquid and dry goods, they were much in demand but could be quite bulky. Therefore, they came to be produced in parts—staves, headings, and hoops. Each of the pieces had to be very skillfully produced so they could be assembled to make tight containers wherever they were needed. Large numbers of planks were produced by sawmills in the colony; many of them were shipped to the West Indies, but some went to the northern colonies and to Great Britain. Since sawmills represented a considerable investment and were difficult to operate, their establishment was often a cooperative venture, especially among the Highland Scots in the upper Cape Fear Valley. Posts and rails for fences, oars and masts for boats, and even boats themselves were made in North Carolina. Wooden shingles became an important export, because they could be constructed at home at odd times. In the 1750s about a dozen families of shingle makers moved south from New Hampshire, where their source of white cedar had declined. In North Carolina they found that cypress trees made excellent shingles. This wood was easy to work, yet resistant to damage from frequent wetting and drying. From 1768 to 1772 the colony exported between 5.5 and 7.5 million shingles annually.

An unusual forest product produced almost exclusively in the Carolinas was oak bark—essential for the tanning industry in Great Britain. For a number of years this was the only region sending more than a token quantity, and in some years no other colony shipped any. Yet in 1765 almost 50,000 pounds were exported. Records do not indicate from what part of the colony it came, but it perhaps was from the backcountry where oak trees were abundant and where a great deal of land was being cleared by new settlers.

Transportation and Communication

Once people cleared their land and began to feel comfortable in their new surroundings, they began to pay some attention to means of getting their produce to market. With little understanding of the principles of engineering or experience in road building, they were able to do little more than clear a path through the wilderness. It was the custom to cut limbs from adjacent trees so that a person riding horseback would not be struck. A ditch along the road might provide some drainage in wet weather. Deep sand was a hindrance in the east, while large rocks and ruts in red clay made backcountry roads a challenge both to those on foot and those on horseback. A group of planters in Chowan County once recorded in a petition that the only outlet from their land was "but a blind path . . . surrounded with pocosins & lowgrounds so that it wearies our Oxen and breaks our carts." Governor Josiah Martin, on the other hand, said that the country west of Hillsborough was the most broken, difficult, and rough that he had ever seen.

The practice of killing trees and leaving them standing in the "fields" was responsible for another hazard. In time they rotted and fell, frequently blocking a road and sometimes striking passersby. A party of Moravians once had the misfortune to have a tree fall across their wagon just behind the horses. It broke the tongue of the wagon but luckily did no other damage. The ingenious Moravians got out their tools and converted the fallen tree into a new tongue and soon were on their way.

In 1774 from Brunswick, a missionary said the roads were "exceeding bad especially to Waccamaw, there being upwards of 12 swamps to cross, some of which are so deep that horses are frequently up to the saddle in crossing them." Other travelers commented on the loneliness and desolation of the roads. "Nothing can be more dreary, melancholy and uncomfortable," an Englishman wrote in 1775, "than the almost perpetual solitary dreary pines, sandy barrens, and dismal swamps, that are met with throughout the whole part of the country." A Scottish woman, Janet Schaw, arriving to visit relatives in the Cape Fear section around the same time, had to get out of her carriage and walk through the

For many years land was plentiful and readily available. Fields were fenced and crops planted among the tree stumps, while livestock was permitted to roam at large. (North Carolina Collection, University of North Carolina at Chapel Hill)

woods at night when fallen trees blocked the way. She caught her foot in a hole, perhaps where a tree had rotted, and became terrified, recalling tales she had heard of the wild animals that lived in the woods and swamps of the region. She said she would rather have been made "a feast for the fishes of the sea" than be devoured by some wild creature of Carolina.

The Assembly tried on many occasions to improve inland transportation by passing laws that authorized county courts to order the "laying out" of public roads, the building of bridges, and the locating of ferries. The courts were to designate annual overseers who would summon male taxables to build and repair the roads. These men would also be responsible for clearing the rivers and creeks. Signposts were to be placed wherever roads crossed and at forks, and mileposts erected. New roads would be located by a "jury" of twelve men and the chosen route cleared for a width of twenty feet with overhanging limbs removed. Bridges and causeways would be constructed over streams and through swamps. Keepers of ferries would be licensed by the court and a schedule of authorized fees established. Ferries were to be at least ten miles apart. As bad as the roads were in North Carolina, they had one advantage over those in England. Visitors, accustomed to highway robbers there, commented on the safety of travel in the colony, even for those traveling alone.

Fees could be charged—not just for ferries but also for bridges and roads when they were built and maintained by individuals or groups. Even so, specifications for their construction and operation were set by the county court. In counties divided by a river, it was ordered that tolls not be charged those crossing to the county seat for jury duty, for appearance as witnesses, or for other official business.

In an attempt to channel trade from the backcountry into the east rather then to Virginia and South Carolina, acts were passed to encourage the building of roads from such frontier counties as Mecklenburg, Rowan, and Guilford to the upper Cape Fear River. From there produce could be shipped south to Wilmington. In the northern part of the colony the Roanoke River served very much the same purpose—goods could be floated down to Albemarle Sound and from there to convenient markets.

A serious obstacle to travel in the backcountry was flooding. With so much new land being cleared, rain, instead of soaking into the ground, ran off and soon created floods. People fording streams might be caught by suddenly rising water. Lives and property were sometimes lost. Returning with the militia from the Battle of Alamance in the spring of 1771, Governor William Tryon had to wait three days for a swollen stream to return to its banks. Even then his men had to cut a tree, let it fall across the creek, and make their way over it "Indian file," one at a time, Tryon wrote. Josiah Quincy of Massachusetts, traveling in North Carolina to determine the sentiment of the people just before the American Revolution, had to crawl along a slippery log while a black man accompanying him swam with their horses across the creek he—not surprisingly—called "Buffalo River."

For travel by land a horse was almost indispensable. Most men owned at least one horse. In the east oxen were popular, not so much for personal transportation as for pulling heavy wagons over boggy or sandy roads and for plowing. A horse, of course, might be ridden, it might carry a pack, or it might be hitched to a variety of vehicles. Planters, lawyers, preachers, government officials, and almost everyone who traveled much regularly went on horseback. There were disadvantages, however. It was tiresome and uncomfortable, there was no protection from the weather, and very little food, clothing, or other baggage could be carried in a pair of saddlebags. All of these handicaps were compensated for by the fact that a horse and rider could pass through swamps, rivers, and other places where wheeled vehicles could not go.

A trip on horseback was also the fastest mode of travel. Early in 1779 Whitmel Hill rode from Philadelphia to his home in Martin County in just seven and one-half days, which was believed to have been a record. Fifty miles a day was usually considered extremely good, and thirty-five miles made an adequate day's journey.

Wagons and carts were used for transporting heavy goods. Sometimes men had to help the horses uphill or on bad roads. Brakes were not reliable, and occasionally when a wagon was going downhill a rope had to be looped around an axle and around a strong tree to keep it from running away. It once was reported that the average load of a wagon was two thousand pounds and of a cart one thousand. Two or four horses usually pulled a wagon, while a cart was pulled by one or two.

Other types of vehicles were much less common and usually belonged to the wealthier colonists. It was a mark of distinction to own some kind of carriage. They were usually light, had two wheels, and could travel almost as fast as a horse alone. Four-wheeled carriages and coaches were used for long trips; they offered protection from the weather but were hard to pull along the poor roads.

In the eighteenth century many people traveled on foot. Several times Moravians walked from Bethlehem, Pennsylvania, to Wachovia, a distance of about four hundred miles. Once such a trek took thirty days, but another time it took forty-one, perhaps by a different route or because of inclement weather. It was not unusual for someone to walk many miles on a local errand; pioneers in the Piedmont and mountainous regions were forced to walk because it was too difficult to ride a horse through the trackless forests. Footpaths in many communities led to the local gristmill, a crossroads store, or the church. North Carolina maps made between 1751 and 1771 show such paths as The Trading Path and Greens Path. At some time after the University of North Carolina opened in 1795, it was reported that a path to Raleigh was in use.

Until shortly before the Revolution the colonies south of Virginia had no formal postal service; in England, however, a postal system operated quite smoothly by 1750. The colonies between New Hampshire and Virginia also had one, though it was not particularly effective. Numerous substitutes were devised in North Carolina. Under a very crude, early scheme for dispatching official communications, private individuals were required to receive them and pass them along, in the proper direction, to their neighbor who would repeat the process. This farm-to-farm system undoubtedly was slow and cumbersome, and probably ineffective.

After 1749 James Davis, the printer, provided not only official but also private service for those near enough to take advantage of it. His riders went regularly—usually weekly—north, south, and west of New Bern, sometimes making connections with the post office in Virginia or delivering messages to Charles Town, South Carolina, from where they might be sent abroad by ship.

Individuals wishing to send a message might hire someone, usually referred to as an express rider, to take it to its destination. Sometimes people in a town (Halifax, Hillsborough, or Salisbury, for example) hired a rider to serve all of them by taking mail on a set route at intervals. Printers of newspapers in Wilmington and New Bern once planned to hire a rider to deliver papers to Halifax and elsewhere.

The Moravians were fortunate as far as communications of this sort were concerned. There was frequent passing between their towns in North Carolina and Moravian towns in Pennsylvania and elsewhere up the Great Wagon Road. Because their settlements in the colony provided such good service in so many areas and because the people there were interesting, numerous travelers made a point of visiting Bethabara or Salem. The Moravians discovered that by offering a "trinket" for the favor, most travelers would gladly take letters when they departed. These might be left with the post office in another colony or with a ship captain in port.

Gradually as the final quarter of the eighteenth century neared, the people of North Carolina came to have more contact with the outside world. Trade and transportation improved as did living standards and cultural opportunities in many areas.

7

SECTIONAL CONTROVERSIES
IN THE COLONY

O NE OF THE MOST important factors in the development of North Carolina has always been sectionalism. Many key events in the state's history came about because of rivalries and jealousies, first between the
northern and southern parts of the colony, next between east and west, and
more recently between urban and rural. Contributing to these have been geographic differences, the variety of national origins and religious elements, wide
social distinctions, and economic interests.

Sectionalism began to develop when the first settlers crossed the Albemarle
Sound and moved to the banks of the Pamlico River. The wide expanse of the
sound isolated the two parts of the colony, and, as people acquired land in the
Cape Fear region, there was a wilderness of swamps and sandy barrens to divide
them. The Neuse and Cape Fear sections were deeply interested in the issues
raised over blank patents, most of which were held in those sections. They were
quite willing to give the governor a tax list in exchange for his recognition of their
right to land held under them. Albemarle in many ways was still dependent
economically on Virginia, but the Cape Fear section had its own outlet to the
commerce of the world and was relatively independent. As a result, royal instructions or action by the Assembly that pleased one section might be considered
intolerable by the other.

Personal ambitions and local rivalries marked these differences. The
Albemarle counties enjoyed the right to send five delegates each to the Assembly, but the Neuse and Cape Fear counties were permitted only two each. This
grew out of the fact that old Albemarle County's assembly had consisted of
twenty members, and when the county was divided into four precincts each was
allowed five delegates. Perhaps to retain its majority in the Assembly the old
counties authorized only two assemblymen for newly created counties, with
two exceptions. Bertie and Tyrrell, created in 1722 and 1729, were initially allowed
five each; in 1746, however, their representation was reduced to three and four,
respectively. Thereafter, as long as possible, the Albemarle section used its political power to monopolize the speakership and other offices that the legislature

controlled. As other sections increased in importance, they naturally resented this political inequality. In time New Bern grew ambitious to become the capital, a goal supported by the Cape Fear.

The Albemarle versus the Cape Fear

These conditions prevailed when Governor Gabriel Johnston took up the quitrent fight about 1736. The southern counties were ready to revolt because of Albemarle's refusal to come to terms concerning the seat of government. They also were irritated by the apparent willingness of the northern counties to sacrifice all other interests to uphold their position in the quitrent controversy. In June 1746, when the Albemarle continued to defeat proposals to make New Bern the capital, the popular party, composed of longtime residents who felt no loyalty to the governor and his appointees, split into two factions. Johnston saw in this an opportunity to serve his own objectives.

Making common cause with the southern members, he prorogued the Assembly to meet in November at Wilmington. The Albemarle members declared that they would never attend a session there. Since they composed a majority of the Assembly, or House of Commons as the lower house was occasionally called,[1] they naturally expected that no session would convene. But they reasoned without consulting their Cape Fear hosts, because they could not believe that Samuel Swann, John Starkey, and other southern leaders, just for the sake of a petty sectional advantage (and at the urging of a royal governor), would surrender one of the fundamental principles of the popular party—that no number less than a majority should be considered a quorum of the house. Yet this is just what the southern faction did. On 18 November 1746, with only fifteen members attending out of a total of fifty-four, Speaker Swann declared a quorum present and notified the governor that the house was ready for business.

The business was cut and dried. Only two bills were considered. One combined two subjects: the first part made New Bern the capital, satisfying the southern members; and the second part regulated the General Court, satisfying the governor. The second bill probably pleased both the governor and the members present as it reduced the representation of the Albemarle counties from five to two delegates each. Johnston quickly sent these new laws off to London for approval without saying how he had managed to get them passed.

Legislators from the northern counties denounced the Wilmington Assembly as a fraud—even though royal instructions directed that fifteen members should constitute a quorum—and sent two local attorneys, Wyriott Ormond

---

1. The legislative branch was also called the House of Burgesses, but this name was not widely used.

and Thomas Barker, to London to protest its actions. After hearing representatives from both sides of the dispute, advisers to the Crown recommended that the Albemarle counties continue to have their five members just as they had for nearly a century. Precedent then, as now, was important in British government. On the other hand, the counselors ruled against the Albemarle in the matter of how many members constituted a quorum and upheld the royal prerogative to make a determination. But since the acts of the 1746 Assembly had been passed, they said, "by management, precipitation, and surprise," they advised the king to veto them.

This decision was not announced until 1754, and the eight years that elapsed had been a time of confusion, rebellion, and almost anarchy in the northern half of North Carolina. At the midpoint of the waiting period, in a letter to James Abercromby, the colony's agent in London, Governor Johnston wrote: "I have nothing more to trouble you with only to tell you how uneasy every body here is to have an account of the Determination of that tedious affair of the five Members which has now for four years compleat kept this Poor unhappy Province in inexpressible confusion; If it is not soon to be decided I don't see how we can long keep up the face of Government."

Moravian Bishop August Gottlieb Spangenberg stated that when he arrived in North Carolina in 1752 he found the colony in turmoil. The counties were in conflict with one another, the authority of the legislature and the magistrates was greatly weakened, and the northern counties would not obey any laws passed by the Assembly until the outcome of the representation controversy was known. "There is therefore in the older counties a perfect anarchy," he commented. "As a result, crimes are of frequent occurrence, such as murder, robbery, etc. But the criminals cannot be brought to justice. The citizens do not appear as jurors, and if court is held to decide such criminal matters no one is present. If anyone is imprisoned the prison is broken open and no justice administered. In short most matters are decided by blows."

The first election held under the questionable act of 1746 gave the governor an Assembly that suited his purposes, and he was determined to keep it as long as possible. After the election of 1747, it held fourteen sessions and was not dissolved until 1754. During all of those years the inhabitants of the Albemarle refused to send representatives to the Assembly, denied its authority, and refused to obey its laws; they even refused to use the currency that it issued. Further, the northern counties refused to pay fees and taxes, so the central and southern counties—having no intention of assuming the whole burden of government—also refused to pay.

Governor Gabriel Johnston never knew the king's pleasure as he died in the summer of 1752. Following acting governors Nathaniel Rice and Matthew Rowan, Governor Arthur Dobbs arrived in the fall of 1754. It was he who brought word of the Crown's decision about the number of representatives from the northern counties and how many members made up a quorum. Soon several additional towns—Brunswick, Halifax, and Salisbury—were recognized as borough towns, joining Edenton, Bath, New Bern, and Wilmington as members of the select group. A little later Campbellton and Hillsborough became eligible. Albemarle continued to have its superior delegation in the Assembly. Nevertheless, beginning with the Third Provincial Congress in the summer of 1775, most of the other counties also sent five representatives.

The Regulator Movement

During the time that north-south sectionalism occupied the attention of so many provincial leaders, the backcountry was filling up and foundations were being laid for an entirely new basis for further conflict. One of the primary causes of this new division originated in the east.

For nearly forty years after North Carolina became a royal colony there was no firmly established capital. The seat of government was considered to be wherever the governor lived, and he lived wherever he chose.[2] Members of the Council lived in various parts of the province. Sometimes the incumbent of a particular office would be from the Albemarle and sometimes from the Cape Fear. The Speaker of the House, however, was usually from the Albemarle but occasionally one from the Cape Fear managed to be elected. Official records of the colony were carted from place to place, and many of them were lost or badly damaged en route. One time when a cartload of records was being taken out of Edenton, some of the records blew off into the river while the cart was crossing a bridge. The attendant debated whether to jump in to rescue them but decided that the water was too cold.

The Assembly was meeting in Edenton when the Crown purchased the Lords Proprietors' shares; it continued to meet there until 1738 when it moved to New Bern. It returned to Edenton for several sessions but also met twice in Bath. The Assembly first convened in Wilmington under the unusual circumstances cited above, and thereafter until 1765 alternated between there and New Bern. From 1765 until 1778 it remained in New Bern.

Since the attempt in 1746 to make New Bern the capital was not approved, Governor Dobbs took steps of his own to find a spot for a permanent location. In 1758 he bought two tracts of land, totaling 850 acres, in what was then Johnston but is now Lenoir County near modern Kinston. The site was called Tower

2. The state constitution of 1776 vested sovereignty in the people to be exercised through their elected representatives in the General Assembly. Therefore, wherever the General Assembly met became the seat of government for the time being.

Hill because an observation tower had been erected there during the Tuscarora Indian War. Perhaps he thought that the name would appeal to officials in London, where there was also a Tower Hill; the name of Southwest Creek was changed to Canterbury Creek undoubtedly to add further to the illusion of civilization in that sparsely settled region.

Dobbs's advisers in London recommended that he first get the Assembly's endorsement of his proposal for a capital, then present it to the British government for final approval. Meeting in New Bern in 1758, the Assembly agreed with the plan and decided that the capital should be called "George City" in honor of King George II. It was to be laid out on 400 acres of the land purchased by Dobbs with the remaining 450 acres to serve as a town common. A home for the governor and a statehouse would be the first projects. A committee was appointed to plan the construction of the buildings and to lay off the streets in half-acre lots for sale to purchasers who agreed to erect houses of a specified size within five years. Further action was delayed until it was known whether Parliament intended to reimburse the colony for its expenses during the French and Indian War, but the undertaking was doomed for another reason. King George II died in 1760 before a decision was reached, and his successor, George III, took no action. Sectional differences in the province caused the plan to be dropped, and in 1762 actions were renewed to make New Bern the capital.

Because Dobbs had purchased the Tower Hill site himself, the property remained in his possession. At his death in 1765 it was left to his heirs, and after the Revolution it was simply taken over by the state as the property of a Tory.

The Assembly in 1766 passed "An Act for erecting a Convenient Building Within the Town of New Bern, for the Residence of the Governor or Commander in Chief." To construct this building, which came to be called "Tryon Palace" after Governor William Tryon who had succeeded Dobbs, the legislators appropriated £5,000 the first year and an additional £10,000 the next. The smaller sum was diverted from an earlier appropriation intended for schools. For the governor's residence, a tax was levied on imported wine, rum, and liquor, as well as rather heavy poll taxes imposed in two different years.

When Tryon came to North Carolina in 1764 as lieutenant governor to relieve Dobbs, who was authorized a period of leave for a visit home, he brought with him John Hawks, an experienced builder and architect. The building that Hawks designed and began constructing in 1767 was to be a home for the royal governor as well as a meeting place for the governor and Council; it also would provide an office for the provincial secretary. Governor Tryon wrote on 7 June 1770 that he had just moved into the palace although it would not be completed until the following Christmas. Built of brick and trimmed with marble, it was soon regarded as one of the most handsome public buildings in America. North Carolina now had a permanent capital, a place where public records could be found and consulted, and an office where provincial business might be transacted. These benefits had long been needed, yet they did not provide a meeting place for the Assembly. The legislative branch continued to meet in the courthouse, a church, or some other building large enough to accommodate it.

Nevertheless, the construction of this building burdened the people with a large debt that they could hardly afford. As a consequence, Governor Tryon drew severe criticism and open attack. The chief opposition to the building of Tryon Palace came from the backcountry, which had little connection with the east. In 1768 a resident of Mecklenburg County expressed the general feeling of his neighbors when he said that "not one in twenty of the four most populous counties will ever see this famous house when built, as their connections and trade do, and ever will, more naturally center in South Carolina." In other words, Charles Town, not New Bern, was their logical capital.

Opposition in the backcountry was due largely to the cost. The inhabitants were already deeply disturbed by abuses in the administration of their local affairs and especially by the inequities they saw in the system of taxation. They were in no mood for an additional burden. Their complaints were aimed chiefly at the method adopted for raising the money. A poll tax fell on rich and poor alike and was particularly burdensome in the back settlements where money was so scarce. They pointed out that "as the people in the lower counties are few in proportion to those in the back settlements, [a poll tax] more immediately affects the many, and operates to their prejudice; for . . . a man that is worth £10,000 pays no more than a poor back settler that has nothing but the labour of his hands to depend upon for his daily support." Citizens of Orange County, on 2 August 1768, told the sheriff: "We are determined not to pay the Tax for the next three years, for the Edifice or Governor's House. We want no such House, nor will we pay for it." Thus the erection of the "Governor's Palace" was closely connected with the most notable sectional controversy in the colonial history of North Carolina—the Regulator movement, so called because the people on the frontier wanted to regulate their own affairs.

Economic, social, and political differences between the east and the west created the atmosphere in which this movement thrived. By the mid-eighteenth century the eastern section of North Carolina had taken on many of the characteristics of an old, settled society. The west, however, was still in the pioneer stage. Some of the Regulators testified that there was not, among all of their acquaintances, a single person who could boast a cabin with a plank floor, or who possessed such a luxury as a feather bed, a carriage, or a sidesaddle. The east was dominated by a small group of wealthy planters and merchants who formed an aristocratic society based largely on slave labor. The west was more nearly a simple democracy of small farmers, living on isolated farms worked by their own labor. In many counties, however, some local offices were filled year after year by the same man or by representatives of the same family. All the political machinery of the provincial government was controlled in the east. From 1765 to 1771 all members of the Council lived in the east since the governor was expected to secure their advice and consent on important questions. In 1770 of the eighty-one members of the Assembly, only fifteen represented western counties which contained more that a third of the free white population.

One set of people in the backcountry copied the manners of the eastern aristocracy, and by their haughty attitude, selfishness, and total disregard of the sentiments—if not the rights—of the people brought down on themselves an almost universal dislike and even hatred. These were the public officials, who were sufficiently numerous and clannish to form a distinct class.

The people had little if any voice in selecting their officials and therefore had no control over them. Colonial government was highly centralized. Provincial affairs were administered by officials chosen by the Crown, whereas local affairs were generally administered by men named by the governor. With the recommendation of the assemblymen from each county, the governor in Council appointed the county justices who administered local government. These justices in turn nominated three landowners, usually from their own number, from whom the governor selected the sheriff. The governor also appointed the registrar and the officers of the militia. A clerk of the pleas farmed out the clerkships in the counties. In turn, these local officials controlled the Assembly. There was no prohibition against multiple officeholding, and as a rule the assemblymen were also clerks, justices, and militia officers. They composed the "courthouse ring." Where these rings consisted of men with local connections, as in most of the eastern counties, government was honestly administered. In the backcountry, however, most local officeholders had been sent into the county by the royal government. Sometimes they were inefficient or corrupt, and frequently they were oppressive.

Under this system of centralized government, the people were unable to obtain prompt and effective relief from their grievances. They complained of excessive taxes, dishonest officials, and extortionate fees. The scarcity of money in the backcountry also added to the hardships of the system, because it frequently gave brutal and corrupt sheriffs and their deputies an excuse to use force, to collect an extra fee in doing so, and to sell the unhappy taxpayer's property at less than its true value, often to some friend of the sheriff. Regulators charged that these officers and their friends made a regular business of such proceedings. Tax revenues, when collected, frequently were not turned over to the provincial treasurers, and royal governors often commented on the revenue long overdue from the tax collectors.

Sheriffs, clerks, registrars, and lawyers were supposed to charge fees fixed by acts of the Assembly. Such a schedule had first been drawn up in 1715, but these fees generally were unknown to the people who were obliged to accept the officers' word for the proper amount. Officials sometimes broke down a service for which a fee was specified into two or more functions and collected a fee for each. Perhaps popular rumors exaggerated or misrepresented the facts in some cases, and certainly contradictory fee schedules were in circulation. Nevertheless, there is no doubt that the people had serious grounds for complaint of fraud. A government responsive to popular sentiment would have speedily remedied matters.

Since the government did not respond to complaints from the backcountry, it only remained for someone to give voice and direction to the general discontent to set the whole countryside aflame. One of the first outbreaks occurred in January 1759, when considerable unrest in the Granville District over oppressive acts of the earl's agents led some men from Edgecombe County (of which present Halifax, Nash, and Wilson counties were then also a part) to seize Francis Corbin, Granville's chief agent, at one of his plantations near Edenton. After taking him to Enfield, their county seat, they forced him to post a high bond guaranteeing his return to the following spring term of court to restore fees that he had collected illegally. The attorney general reported that he heard some of the "rioters" say that they intended to "pull him by the nose and also to abuse the court" if their grievances were not resolved.

When the men reached Edgecombe County they learned that Corbin's assistant, John Haywood, had died suddenly after returning home from a trip. Many people, thinking his death was fabricated to protect Haywood from also being seized, dug into his grave. On finding that Haywood was really dead, they were deeply embarrassed and dispersed without further disturbance. After a brief time, a few of the rioters were arrested and jailed in Halifax, but the next day their friends went to the jail in broad daylight, broke down the doors, and released the prisoners.

In 1765 riots broke out in Mecklenburg County on land held by absentee landowner George Selwyn where many small farmers had settled without benefit of purchase. Henry Eustace McCulloh, who owned much land himself, was asked by Selwyn to survey the property and sell it to the squatters at a reasonable rate, giving those occupying it first opportunity to buy. Unable to come to terms, the settlers, led by Thomas Polk, with blackened faces and other disguises, attacked and severely beat McCulloh's surveyors, John Frohock and three Alexander brothers. One of the surveyors, hit over the head with a board, wrote that he had daylight let into his skull, while another said he was stripped as if he were before a draft board. This outbreak, referred to as the War on Sugar Creek, came to an end after Lieutenant Governor Tryon issued a proclamation seeking to identify those who were guilty. These rioters retreated peacefully and they seem not to have taken part in later disorders.

The next demonstration against the oppression of local officialdom occurred in Granville County in June 1765. George Sims, schoolmaster and laborer, was arrested for not paying a small debt. In the trial that followed he gained firsthand experience with the type of justice that so many poor people bore quietly. Sims, however, was not quiet. In his "Address to the People of Granville County," he reviewed the wrongs he and others were suffering and concluded by calling on "all honest men" to oppose them. The enemies he cited included lawyers, court clerks, and sheriffs, and he mentioned specific examples of the unlawful fees they charged. A poor debtor, he pointed out, sued for a debt of £5, would have to pay double that amount when the fees for collecting it were added. If he were unable to pay, he would have to work at a very low daily wage or perhaps have his horses, cattle, furniture, or even his land sold to settle the debt. Sims was especially careful to observe that his address was directed only against the county officers and not against the king or even the "Worshipful members of the Bench." He stated: "It is not our *mode* or *form* of government, nor yet the body of our laws, that we are quarreling with, but with the malpractices of the Officers of our County Court." The schoolmaster called on the people to meet for a discussion of their grievances, but the only result of his appeal was a petition to the Assembly which was ignored. County officials continued their abuses as before.

The names most prominently associated with the agitation that led to the formal organization of the Regulators are Herman Husband, Rednap Howell, and James Hunter. Husband, whose education and gift for expression enabled him to write pamphlets, became the chief spokesman of the movement. Howell was a schoolmaster who wrote songs making fun of local officials. It was said that his "ambling epics and jingling ballads" inspired the whole countryside to laugh and sing at the expense of his victims. Hunter was regarded as the man of action because he urged using force; he was called the "general of the Regulation."

On the other side, opposing the Regulators, William Tryon was most prominent because of his position. There is little evidence that the rebels held him personally responsible for the problems of the backcountry, but as governor he was obliged to try to maintain order. Most hated by the Regulators was Edmund Fanning, a typical product of the political system of the day. He was settled in Orange County a few years before the arrival of Governor Tryon, and there he became a member of the Assembly, registrar of deeds, judge of the superior court, and colonel of the militia. A graduate of Yale College, he was clearly a man of culture who enjoyed the finer things of life—lace and gold buttons on his clothes, good books, a comfortable house, compatible friends, and high position. To his equals (or his "betters") he was kind, hospitable, and considerate. To his inferiors, and he regarded most of the residents of Hillsborough and the surrounding area in that category, he was cruel and domineering. He despised the common people, and they willingly returned the sentiment. Fanning was a

Edmund Fanning (1737–1818), a native of Long Island, New York, was settled by 1760 in the community that became Hillsborough. A graduate of Yale with a master's degree from Harvard, he became a land speculator as well as the holder of numerous local and provincial offices. His haughty attitude, his ostentatious style of living, and his mistreatment of many people who had to do business with him at the courthouse earned him the enmity of a host of backcountry settlers. (North Carolina Collection, University of North Carolina at Chapel Hill)

native of New York who found a source of wealth in North Carolina politics—a forerunner of a later group known as carpetbaggers.

The first attempt to organize to obtain relief from the oppressive office-holders took place in Orange County in 1766. A mass meeting was called to try to determine "whether the free men of this county labor under any abuses of power or not." It resulted in the demand for a public accounting from local officials, but public officers in 1766 acknowledged no obligation to the people. They not only refused to attend the meeting but also ignored the call for an explanation of their recent actions in office. Even so, this meeting was well organized and enabled the participants to develop a clear statement of what was expected from the officials. Since additional documents grew out of future meetings, this one came to be recognized as "Regulator Advertisement Number 1." To continue the organization it was suggested that neighborhood meetings be held at which delegates would be chosen to attend a countywide meeting.

Such activity continued and finally reached a climax in 1768. In that year the sheriff called for payment of the special tax levied to build the "Governor's Palace" in New Bern. This led to the organization of an association of concerned citizens called "The Regulators." In due course, the members issued a formal statement setting forth their intentions (1) to pay no more taxes until they were satisfied that such assessments were according to law and lawfully applied; (2) to pay no fees greater than provided by law; (3) to attend meetings of the Regulators as often as possible; (4) to contribute, according to each person's ability, to the expenses of the organization; and (5) in all matters to abide by the will of the majority. Having done this, they sent a note to the county officers demanding a strict accounting and warned them that "as the nature of an officer is a servant of the publick, we are determined to have the officers of this county under a better and honester regulation than they have been for some time past." Such an ambitious directive was considered insulting to the appointed officials of the county, who were indignant that the rabble of the county should be so bold.

Orange County officials either did not realize how determined their less fortunate neighbors were, or else they wanted to test the determination of the Regulators. With conditions in an explosive state, the sheriff seized a Regulator's horse, saddle, and bridle and sold them for taxes. This raised a storm of popular fury. The Regulators rode into Hillsborough, overawed the officials, rescued their friend's property, and, as evidence of their temper, fired several shots into Edmund Fanning's house.

Now aware of the seriousness of the situation, county officers consented to meet with the Regulators and attempt to resolve their differences. Fanning, however, protested and tried to prevent the meeting. While the Regulators were preparing to go to the gathering, Fanning collected some friends who armed themselves and rode off to the Sandy Creek neighborhood where they arrested two leaders of the Regulators, William Butler and Herman Husband. Both were charged with inciting the people to riot and taken to Hillsborough. At this high-handed act, 700 citizens, many of whom were not Regulators, got their guns and set out for Hillsborough to rescue Fanning's prisoners. Word of this turn of events thoroughly alarmed county officials, who rushed to open the doors to the jail while urging Butler and Husband to meet the mob and turn it back.

Governor Tryon, too, was concerned about conditions in the backcountry which might mar his record. By proclamation he insisted that the Regulators disband, and he issued a public statement of the poll taxes that were due. At the same time he warned public officials against taking illegal fees and directed the attorney general of the province to prosecute any officer charged with extortion.

On receiving word of the governor's warning, the Regulators charged Fanning with extortion. His case was set for trial in Hillsborough at the September 1768 term of court, at which Butler and Husband were to be tried for riot. To protect the court against possible violence, Tryon called out a force of nearly 1,500 militiamen and led them to Hillsborough himself. By the time of the governor's arrival, 3,700 Regulators had gathered nearby; however, on seeing the militia they made no attempt to interfere with the proceedings.

Husband was tried and acquitted. Butler and two other Regulators were convicted but—on Tryon's advice—pardoned by the king. Fanning was convicted of extortion, yet the court was convinced by the evidence that he had not intended to violate the law. Judgment was reserved and no further action was ever taken in the case. Nevertheless, Fanning promptly resigned his office as registrar. Regulators complained that although Fanning was found guilty, he was not punished, a fact, they observed, which justified their distrust of the courts.

Earlier, in an address to the Assembly on 7 December 1767, Tryon had called attention to the need for further restrictions in the control of county officers. The Assembly in its formal reply to the governor observed that the "abuses in the Sheriffs' office cry aloud for and shall receive the strictest attention and correction, nor shall the embezzlement and irregularities commited by other collectors of the public revenues escape the most exact inquiry." The legislators then passed laws to regulate the fees of local court clerks and to correct other abuses in their offices. They also passed new laws about appointing sheriffs and regulating their duties in office. Tryon thought that this would eliminate the temptations that had led former sheriffs to fraud and embezzlement.

Concluding that the courts had failed them, the Regulators turned to the Assembly. In the summer of 1769 the governor dissolved the old Assembly and called for a new election. In Orange, Anson, Granville, and Halifax counties every member elected was a Regulator. Thus, when the Assembly convened, several petitions were presented stating the grievances of the Regulators as well as their suggestions for reform. The Assembly showed signs of sympathy; but, because the governor found some other resolutions (the Non-Importation Association, for example) offensive, it was suddenly dissolved before it could take up the measures necessary to relieve the complaints of the Regulators. Just before dissolution, however, it resolved "that if any public officer shall exact illegal fees, or otherwise under colour of his office unduly oppress the people, such officer so acting shall on conviction thereof receive the highest censure and punishment this House can inflict upon him."

This purports to be a portrait of Governor William Tryon painted in New York in 1767 by John Wollaston, according to the inscription on the reverse. Although its provenance is known, this attribution has been questioned because the uniform does not appear to be that of Tryon's regiment. Nevertheless, Tryon may well have been in New York during that year as his very regular correspondence from North Carolina breaks off in July and was not renewed until the following September. (Courtesy of Tryon Palace, New Bern)

If the Regulators had been willing to wait for the long, slow process of law to take effect, legal remedies surely would have been forthcoming. In many quarters, from the governor on down, it was recognized that changes were needed. But at the time, both the governor and the Assembly were distracted by the conflict between the colonies and Parliament over the question of taxation. Distressed by what they considered to be the indifference of all branches of the colonial government to their concerns and by the continued harsh actions of many local officials, the Regulators adopted a course that no government could think of condoning. This compelled the king's governor and the people's representatives to look less to the relief of grievances than to the suppression of anarchy.

When the superior court, with Judge Richard Henderson presiding, met at Hillsborough in September 1770, a mob of 150 Regulators, armed with sticks and switches, broke into the courthouse, drove the judge from the bench, and contemptuously set up a mock court. They filled the minutes of the court with statements of their own, including profanity. They dragged unoffending attorneys from the courtroom and through the streets at the peril of their lives, and carelessly assaulted peaceful citizens who refused to join in the lawlessness. One report said that they grabbed Edmund Fanning by the heels and pulled him down the stairs, banging his head on every step. Before riding out of town, they broke into his house, burned his library, destroyed his furniture, and generally demolished his house. To end the day, they gave Fanning a brutal whipping and then rode around smashing windows of other private homes and terrorizing the inhabitants.

As would be expected, these outrages threw colonial officials into a panic. Orange County officers demanded a special session of the General Assembly. The governor hastily summoned the Council, which urged him to call out the militia immediately. Rumors flew. It was reported that arsonists had burned Judge Henderson's home and stables in Granville County. Another account claimed that the Regulators were gathering in force to march on New Bern and overwhelm the Assembly. In the midst of such reports the legislature met on 5 December 1770. Regulator leader Herman Husband was a member, but he was not permitted to take his seat. Born in terror, this Assembly, it was said, passed away in blood. Several bills to placate the Regulators were promptly introduced. While they were being considered, word reached New Bern that the Regulators had assembled at Cross Creek to begin the march on the capital.

Reform measures were hastily laid aside and punitive measures taken up. In short order a proposal made by Samuel Johnston was adopted. Known as the Johnston Act or "The Bloody Riot Act," it empowered the attorney general to move cases involving charges of riot from the county in which the offense occurred to any county in the province. It proclaimed to be outlaws all persons who avoided the summons of the court for sixty days, and it allowed such outlaws to be killed with impunity. The governor was authorized to call out the militia to enforce the Johnston Act. Like most laws passed in passion and fear, its harshness largely defeated its purpose, but the Assembly felt, as James Iredell expressed it, that "desperate diseases must have desperate remedies."

The Regulators responded to the Assembly's desperate remedy with defiance. Public meetings were held in various parts of the province to discuss it. The reaction of the Freeholders in Rowan County was typical. Denouncing the

Governor William Tryon addresses a group of backcountry farmers at the time of the Regulator movement in this sketch made many years later. (Bruce Cotten Collection, North Carolina Collection, University of North Carolina at Chapel Hill)

Assembly for its "riotous act," they swore that they would pay no more taxes. They declared Fanning to be an outlaw to be killed on sight, and threatened all clerks and lawyers with the same fate. In their county, they said, there would be no more courts.

When Governor Tryon ordered that a special term of court be held in Hillsborough in 1771, the judges naturally protested, so the Council urged that the militia be called out for protection as well as to suppress the Regulators. Tryon lost no time in taking this advice. He raised a force of 1,452 men, of whom 1,068 came from the east, and on 14 May camped on Great Alamance Creek west of Hillsborough at a site now in Alamance County. Here he was met by about 2,000 Regulators. With the southern militia, Brigadier General Hugh Waddell was sent to Salisbury to try to outflank the rebels, but he was delayed by a band of Regulators from the Mecklenburg County area.

On 16 May 1771 the Regulators sent Tryon a petition requesting an audience. He replied that he would not confer with them as long as they were under arms against the government; if they would disperse and lay down their arms, he would hear them. He gave them one hour to respond. Infuriated, the Regulators

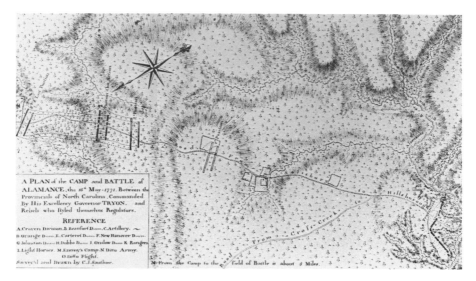

A PLAN of the CAMP and BATTLE of ALAMANCE, the 16ᵗ May 1771. Between the Provincials of North Carolina, Commanded By His Excellency Governor TRYON, and Rebels who ſtyled themselves Regulators.

REFERENCE
A.Craven Diviſion. B.Beaufort D—. C.Artillery. D.Orange D—. E.Carteret D—. F.New Hanover D—. G Johnſton D—. H.Dobbs D—. I. Onslow D—. K Rangers. L Light Horses. M.Enemy's Camp. N Ditto Army. O Ditto Flight. Surveyed and Drawn by C.J.Sauthier.

N° From the Camp to the Field of Battle is about 5 Miles.

Governor William Tryon brought Claude Joseph Sauthier, a Swiss military surveyor, to North Carolina, and between the fall of 1768 and the spring of 1770 Sauthier prepared handsome, detailed maps of Bath, Beaufort, Brunswick, Cross Creek, Edenton, Halifax, Hillsborough, New Bern, Salisbury, and Wilmington. These maps are now in the British Museum. Sauthier also prepared several maps depicting the Battle of Alamance in the spring of 1771; the one shown here is in the State Archives in Raleigh. (North Carolina Division of Archives and History, Raleigh)

failed to comply. At the end of the hour, Tryon sent an officer to say that unless they broke up he would fire on them. Their reply was "Fire and be damned." Accordingly the governor gave the order, the militia fired, and the Regulators returned it.

Organization and discipline, of course, carried the day. After two hours of fighting, the disorderly mob was driven from the field. Casualties among the militia amounted to nine killed and sixty-one wounded. The losses among the Regulators are unknown; they fought from behind trees and large rocks, and removed their casualties as they retired. The militia took a few prisoners, one of whom, according to Tryon, his victorious troops demanded be executed. So, without even the show of a military court, James Few, a Regulator from the Hillsborough vicinity, was hanged. Although the execution is often said to have occurred on the battlefield, Tryon reported that it took place at Great Alamance Camp on the morning of 17 May, the day after the battle.

Following his victory, Tryon's actions were marked by good judgment and leniency. Fourteen Regulators captured in battle were tried at a special term of the superior court. A dozen of them were convicted of treason and sentenced to death. Altogether six Regulators were hanged, but the others, on the governor's recommendation, were pardoned by the king. The day after the battle, Tryon issued a proclamation offering to pardon anyone (with a few exceptions) who would submit to the government and swear an oath of allegiance. The Regulators generally took advantage of this offer, and within six weeks 6,409 had complied with its terms. Tryon actually was more favorably inclined toward the Regulators than was the legislature. When the British government suggested that the Assembly pass a general amnesty act, the two houses could not agree on its terms and the proposed act failed to pass.

The Battle of Alamance was the climax of Tryon's career in North Carolina, for he had already received notice of his appointment as governor of New York. A few days after the victory at Alamance, he made a farewell address to his army and set out for New Bern to prepare to move. He took with him the good wishes of many members of the popular party in North Carolina.

The Regulation itself was at an end, its leaders either dead, in exile, or in hiding. Its members were scattered and disheartened, and the cause for which they had fought was temporarily lost. Most of the former Regulators returned to their homes, settled down quietly, and accepted their fate. Others left North Carolina. A few years later the *Virginia Gazette* reported that a settlement of Regulators on the banks of the Mississippi River (near the present site of Memphis) discovered that some of Edmund Fanning's former servants were living a short distance to the north. When the Regulators prepared to set out in pursuit of their neighbors, the former servants quickly moved away.

In the first great sectional struggle, the east—with the aid of some westerners—triumphed over the west and confirmed its grip on the government for the next three-quarters of a century. Yet the contest was not ended but merely laid aside. The Battle of Alamance was an internal matter and had nothing to do with the growing differences with the mother country; it was a struggle for political rights and individual liberty denied by provincial and local governments. No other colony experienced such an expression of concern.

In 1775 the men who had fought with Tryon at Alamance were themselves organizing committees, congresses, and armies for rebellion. Men of the back-country actually joined them, but afterward they renewed their struggle against sectional political domination and poor administration in local government, and for a stronger voice in their own affairs. Victory was a long time in coming, but it did eventually arrive.

8

A DECADE OF DISPUTE

I F THE ADVISERS to King George III had been alert, they would have anticipated the American Revolution. North Carolina might have served as a
model from which to learn a valuable lesson. Culpeper's and Cary's rebellions and the Regulator uprising all demonstrated that people in the colony
would go to great lengths to support a cause they believed in, especially when
they were convinced that they had been wronged. Several governors tried to
warn the royal advisers. In 1760 Governor Arthur Dobbs mentioned a "rising
spirit of independency" in his colony. The Assembly of North Carolina, it was
pointed out, thought itself a little English House of Commons, not to be dictated to by royal authority. Instructions to the governor, coming directly from
His Majesty, were ignored. One governor was impeached, another driven away,
another threatened with force if he tried to enter the colony, and finally the last
royal governor, fearful for his life, fled. Several received no salary for many years
because they displeased the people. Throughout much of the colonial period, for
a century and a quarter, North Carolina was as rebellious as any of the American
colonies, and because of the *number* of insurrections (Culpeper's, Gibbs's,
Cary's, and the Regulators') it had the reputation of being a place of considerable
unrest. In retrospect, their aims were as commendable as those of Nathaniel
Bacon's in Virginia (1676) and more so than Jacob Leisler's in New York (1689).

England regarded the American colonies as a business investment. "Mercantilism" was the governing policy, and North Carolina was simply a part of the far-
flung British commercial system. Nevertheless, it was affected by the economic
theories on which that system was built. A series of Navigation Acts, passed from
the middle to the end of the seventeenth century and later strengthened from
time to time, was intended to implement that system. One act provided that
colonial trade should be carried only in British ships or in ships owned by British
colonials. It was also decreed that Great Britain must be the agent through which
all European goods intended for the colonies passed. And finally, certain goods
could be exported from the colonies only to ports within the empire. Although
all of the acts applied to North Carolina, they were poorly enforced there before
1763. At that time the French and Indian War was over, England had to defend

more territory, and there was a large public debt to be paid. England, therefore, proclaimed a "New Colonial Policy."

The Royal Proclamation of 1763

One of the first steps taken to implement this new policy was the signing of the Royal Proclamation of 1763. Among other things, the king directed that no warrants to survey or patents to settle land were to be issued beyond the crest of the mountains. Showing unaccustomed concern for the welfare of the native Americans, King George III pointed out that it was "just and reasonable" that Indians living in British territory, and therefore under British protection, should not be disturbed unless they chose to sell or cede their land. Governor Dobbs some years earlier had been aware of the need to improve relations between his colonists and their Indian neighbors, so he offered "a Premium" of extra land to any white who married an Indian. Aware of society in the Spanish and Portuguese colonies, Dobbs pointed out that intermarriage would create "an integral society." Dobbs's policy was never a matter of real concern nor was the royal proclamation. In the latter case, this was true because in 1763 there were no settlements as far west as the crest of the mountains.

Parliamentary Acts of 1764 and 1765

The following year Parliament decided that the colonies should be taxed to help provide support for military forces to defend the colonies as well as to help reform the colonial system. The Sugar Act of 1764 placed duties on such colonial imports as sugar, molasses, indigo, coffee, wine, silk, and other kinds of cloth. The money raised would be sent to England and used to safeguard the colonies. Relatively little was heard of this act in poor North Carolina, where only a small quantity of wine, silk, and other items on the list was imported, but in the New England colonies there was violent opposition.

Parliament did not push this new program and let another year pass before taking the next step. In 1765 a Quartering Act required that provisions be made to house British troops stationed in the colonies. If regular barracks were not available, the soldiers could be put up in inns, livery stables, retail liquor shops, or other buildings. Also, under this act, certain other expenses of the troops were to be paid from colonial funds. Like the Sugar Act, this one had little impact in North Carolina since no troops were regularly assigned there. Only once was the Quartering Act put into effect—in June 1771 a recruiting party under the command of Lieutenant William Cotton of the Thirty-first (Huntingdonshire) Regiment arrived from South Carolina and asked for accommodations. Governor William Tryon directed John Hawks to rent an unoccupied house and provide food, utensils, and other necessities for his troops. While a few people may have muttered that this act of Parliament was unfair, it met with no outspoken opposition.

The Stamp Act Resisted

Shortly before the Sugar Act was passed in 1764, Prime Minister George Grenville announced in Parliament that at the next session he intended to introduce a stamp measure for use in the American colonies. After consulting some of the colonial agents residing in London, he explained, he had determined that this would be a legitimate means of raising revenue, in keeping with the benefits the colonies received from being a part of the empire. He also said that he was not sold on the stamp idea and was willing to listen to the colonial legislatures if they had better suggestions for raising the necessary funds. When Grenville's intentions were reported to the legislatures in the colonies, the protest was immediate and loud. The right of Parliament to levy such a tax was denied, although no other plan was proposed. Parliament was swamped with petitions from America, but, because of the time it took to prepare and deliver them, they arrived too late. A rule of Parliament prohibited the receipt of petitions concerning money measures once debate had begun.

The Stamp Act passed by a wide majority in March 1765, to become effective the following November. There was little opposition to the bill in Parliament, and even Benjamin Franklin, then in London, did not anticipate opposition in America. Its supporters pointed out that it was a tax on property and easily administered. Such a tax had been in force in England for seventy-five years and in America for a brief period. Some things that were taxed in England were exempted in America; thus, the tax would be much less burdensome in the colonies than at home.

This was more than three-quarters of a century before there were gummed stamps. Instead, taxed paper had a device like a stamp printed on the side of one of the margins. This would have to be bought for printing a variety of legal papers, bills of lading, clearance papers for ships, licenses for retailing liquor, bonds, warrants for surveying land, deeds, mortgages, appointments to public office, leases, contracts, playing cards, pamphlets, newspapers, and other paper products. Marriage certificates, pardons, and promissory notes were taxed in England but not in America; religious works and schoolbooks were also exempted in the colonies.

The Stamp Act would be administered by commissioners in England, and the funds collected, less the cost of administration, would be held in the Treasury in London. The law stipulated that this money was to be used to cover the cost of "defending, protecting, and securing" the colonies. Violations of the act would be prosecuted "in any court of record, or in any court of admiralty" in the province in which the offense was committed.

Because the Stamp Act did not become effective for more than seven months after it was passed, there was ample time for those who objected to organize. In general, the opposition took three forms: (1) arguments as to the measure's validity on constitutional grounds, (2) mob action, and (3) economic pressure through nonimportation agreements. North Carolinians had previously made their position known on the question of Parliamentary taxation. In the fall of 1764, on hearing about the Sugar Act, the Assembly informed Governor Dobbs that it regarded those "new Taxes and impositions laid on us without our Privity and Consent" as a violation of "our Inherent right and exclusive privilege of imposing our own Taxes." With another such tax about to be levied, the colony was ready to demonstrate its opposition. This was a tax that struck home. Lawyers were affected, and they were vocal.

The act had been under discussion in the province for several months when William Tryon arrived in October 1764 to relieve Governor Dobbs. After the old governor's unexpected death the following March, Tryon became governor in the midst of the turmoil over Parliament's plan to tax the colonies. Assembly speaker John Ashe warned Tryon that the Stamp Act would be resisted to the death. Public demonstrations broke out in Cross Creek, Edenton, New Bern, and Wilmington to confirm his prediction. When the citizens of Wilmington heard that the act had passed, they organized as "Sons of Liberty," drank toasts to "Liberty, Property, and no Stamp Duty," hanged Lord Bute (a former prime minister and advocate of the Stamp Act) in effigy, and forced the stamp agent, Dr. William Houston, to resign.

The most violent reaction was in the Cape Fear section because the new governor was then living on the outskirts of Brunswick. Also in this region an entrenched merchant oligarchy held sway. In Wilmington Andrew Steuart, the public printer, was warned that he had better print the *North Carolina Gazette* on unstamped paper. Governor Tryon became alarmed and called together a group of leading merchants for consultation. By exceedingly liberal and attractive offers—even suggesting that he himself would pay the tax on the paper used in the colony—he tried to persuade them to obey the law. But the merchants were unyielding, telling Tryon that this act of Parliament violated their rights as British subjects and that they were determined to resist it to the utmost of their power.

There was no way to test their intentions until 28 November 1765, when the ship *Diligence* arrived in Brunswick after having recently delivered stamped paper in Norfolk. Since not much printing was done in North Carolina, she probably had only a token amount to deliver—perhaps no more than could be contained in a modern box of typing paper.[1] The shipment was referred to as a "parcel" of "Stamp'd Parchment & Paper." News of the ship's arrival spread rapidly, and armed men from the surrounding countryside hurried to Brunswick to prevent the paper from being landed. In any event, there was no agent to receive it, as the residents of Wilmington had already forced him to resign.

In January 1766, two ships sailed into the harbor without stamped clearance papers from their previous port and were promptly seized by Captain Jacob Lobb of the British cruiser *Viper*, stationed at the mouth of the Cape Fear River. This so angered the people that they gathered in large crowds at Wilmington. There they signed an agreement to resist enforcement of the hated act and to refuse to furnish supplies to the king's ships. When some British sailors came into town for provisions, they were jailed.

When some of the protesters marched south toward Brunswick, Captain John Dalrymple, commander at Fort Johnston near the mouth of the Cape Fear River below Brunswick, spiked his guns. They compelled Captain Lobb to release the two ships he was holding and required public officials to take an oath that they would not—directly or indirectly—attempt to sell stamped paper in North Carolina. The day after Christmas 1765, Governor Tryon had written that the paper carried by the *Diligence* was still on board ship; on 1 February 1766 he repeated the statement in another letter. It must have been humiliating for the royal governor to have to send his correspondence out of the colony on a ship that sailed with unstamped clearance papers. The men of Cape Fear thus had prevented the Stamp Act from being enforced in their province—eight years before the more famous Boston Tea Party which supported the same principle. The stamped paper sent to North Carolina was never landed. Eventually, it was transferred to the *Hazard* and returned to England.

There probably has never been a mob more "unmoblike" in its composition and conduct. Even the governor never spoke of "the mob," but always of "the inhabitants in arms." As he noted, among the protesters were the mayor and governing body of Wilmington and most of the gentlemen and planters of the surrounding counties. Their leaders included Hugh Waddell, the most distinguished soldier in the colony; John Ashe, Speaker of the Assembly; and Cornelius Harnett and James Moore, members of the Assembly. None of them made any attempt to conceal their identity or their purpose; they committed no disorder or destroyed any property, and there was never any suggestion of drunkenness. They were simply determined to prevent the governor from enforcing an improper law, but they were careful to see that he suffered no indignity or insult.

---

1. If the paper had been landed and the demand for it had existed, more would have been provided.

They went so far as to offer him a guard, which he emphatically declined. He was acquainted with them all and knew he had nothing to fear.

It is interesting to note that Tryon's approach to dealing with rebellion in the colony was consistent. He declined to confer with the "gentlemen and planters" who composed the Cape Fear Sons of Liberty in 1765, just as he did with the backwoodsmen who composed the Regulators in 1771, unless they first laid down their arms. Tryon believed that the colonists had the right to petition for remedy of their grievances, but rebellion removed the guarantees of the British constitution.

Tryon quite likely understood the reasons behind the opposition to the Stamp Act and sympathized with the colonists. Both sides were greatly relieved with the arrival of word that Parliament had repealed the obnoxious law on 17 March 1766. The news was celebrated with great joy around the colony, and the gentlemen of Wilmington, who had so recently been in arms, rushed to exchange hearty congratulations with the governor.

The early struggle over the Stamp Act gave a firm push to sentiment for a union of the colonies. This feeling found expression in the Stamp Act Congress which met in New York on 7 October 1765. North Carolina agreed with the purpose and the work of this gathering but was not represented because Governor Tryon refused to convene the Assembly in time for the election of delegates. When the Assembly finally met in November 1766, it offered some rather caustic comments on the governor's action.

Three other colonies—New Hampshire, Virginia, and Georgia—were not represented at the Stamp Act Congress, but the delegates present spoke for all. They drew up a series of resolutions expressing a sense of affection and duty for the king and his government as well as presenting a concise statement of what they regarded as American rights. It was recognized that the colonists owed the Crown the same allegiance as subjects born in Great Britain, while at the same time they were entitled to "all the inherent rights and privileges" of such subjects. This was the "civil compact" by which they owed the king loyalty and he owed them protection.

The resolutions of the Congress further stated that the freedom of the people and their rights as Englishmen required that no taxes be imposed except by consent given personally or through their representatives. Owing to the nature of things, they continued, the colonists were not then and could not be represented in the House of Commons in London. Only through their own provincial legislatures could they be taxed. These very able resolutions were drawn up by a body that assembled without any guidance from the Crown. The action of Parliament was uniting the colonies, and the Crown showed no signs of assisting them in their struggle to resist Parliament.

Perhaps as a face-saving measure, the statute repealing the Stamp Act carried with it a Declaratory Act. This proclaimed the right of Parliament to legislate for the colonies "in all cases whatsoever." In a series of four acts passed in June and July 1767, Parliament undertook to put this law into effect. One of these placed an import duty on certain goods—including paper, glass, painters' colors, and tea—that even previously could be obtained legally only from Britain. The revenue collected from this tax was intended to pay the salaries of governors, judges, and other Crown officials in the colonies in order to make them independent of local legislatures. In the past the colonial Assembly, by controlling the purse, had been able to exercise some authority over royal officers. Now these officials would be beyond local control. Many Americans concluded that the home Ministry was about to exercise despotic control over the thirteen colonial governments. This gave them still another shove toward union. Massachusetts led the way by sending a "Circular Letter of 1768" to the other colonies, inviting them to join in measures to resist.

When the Assembly met in New Bern in 1768, Speaker John Harvey introduced the Massachusetts letter, but much to his disgust the House declined to take any formal action. It merely suggested verbally that Harvey reply himself. The house then resolved to send King George "an humble, dutiful and loyal address" seeking repeal of the latest tax laws of Parliament. Even so, it cited the American doctrine of "no taxation without representation." The document was forwarded to the colony's agent, Henry Eustace McCulloh, and reportedly gave "great satisfaction to the King." But King George reacted prematurely; he had not heard the whole story.

Meanwhile, Speaker Harvey and other members of the Assembly responded to the invitation of Massachusetts on behalf of their province. North Carolina's assemblymen would, indeed, "ever be ready, firmly to unite with their sister colonies, in pursuing every constitutional measure for relief of the grievances so justly complained of."

The Non-Importation Association

It was now Parliament's turn to strike the next blow. Massachusetts must be punished. When freedoms guaranteed in the province's charter were restricted, the other colonies realized that they might well be next. The cause of Massachusetts became the cause of all. Once again Parliament had pushed the colonies closer together. Virginia was the first to come to the beleaguered colony's aid, not only by denouncing the attack on Massachusetts but also by drafting and circulating among the colonies its proposal for a Non-Importation Association.

On 2 November 1769 Harvey laid the resolutions from Virginia before the royal Assembly. Without a dissenting voice the house moved to adopt them exactly as submitted. It also agreed on dispatching another protest to King George and instructed the colony's agent to have it printed in the British press after he had presented it to the king. On hearing what the Assembly had done, Tryon immediately sent for members of the house and gave them a piece of his mind. Their action in approving the Non-Importation Association, he said, had "sapped the foundations of confidence and gratitude." They had made it his "indispensible duty to put an end to this session," the same one that was considering some relief for the Regulators.

This sudden turn of events caught the Assembly unprepared for dissolution. Much important business remained unfinished—especially final approval of the Non-Importation Association. The leaders had no intention of going home until they had taken the necessary action to bring North Carolina into line with the Continental movement. As soon as the house disbanded, Harvey called the members together in a "convention," as he called it, to "take measures for preserving the true and essential interests of the province." Of the seventy-seven members who had attended the Assembly, sixty-four gathered in the courthouse and reorganized as a convention, independent of the governor. Harvey was unanimously chosen moderator. Two days later, the convention adopted a complete Non-Importation Association; the document was signed by the sixty-four "late representatives of the people" and afterward widely circulated in the colony. This was the first such legislative body in any of the colonies, and it was basically for this reason that the state of North Carolina used the slogan, "First in Freedom,"[2] on its automobile license plates during the celebration of the Bicentennial of the American Revolution.

The Last Royal Governor

Governor Tryon left North Carolina for his new post in New York soon after the Battle of Alamance. His successor, Josiah Martin, qualified on 12 August 1771. Probably no worse choice could have been made in such a crisis. Martin was honest, but that was perhaps his only qualification. He was stubborn, tactless, and intolerant. Even his own father was critical of him, saying on one occasion that Josiah was good at only two things—setting a good table and keeping his wife pregnant. Like Edmund Fanning, Martin bowed and scraped to anybody in authority over him, but was overbearing to those whom he regarded as his inferiors. In North Carolina he suddenly found himself in a position that required almost every intellectual quality that he lacked. The people were in no

2. Some historians believe that this slogan might refer to the Halifax Resolves of 12 April 1776, which authorized North Carolina's delegates to the Continental Congress to join with other delegates in declaring independence.

mood to put up with the petty tyrannies of a provincial governor, and Martin's personality became one of the chief factors that drove the colony headlong into rebellion and revolution.

Martin had a more exalted idea of the royal prerogative than any of his predecessors. He insisted that his instructions from the Crown took precedence over acts of the Assembly and were binding on both Assembly and governor. His attitude on this question presented the people's representatives with a serious dilemma. Should they allow the Assembly to degenerate into a simple machine through which the will of the king could be registered, or should they maintain it as a free, deliberative, law-making body, responsible for its own actions only to the people? Crucial to the history of North Carolina was the fact that the Assembly had the insight to recognize the importance of the issue and the courage to meet it. The legislators concluded as follows:

> Appointed by the people to watch over their rights and priviledges, and to guard them from every encroachment of a private and public nature it becomes our duty and will be our constant endeavour to preserve them secure and inviolate to the present age, and to transmit them unimpaired to posterity. . . . The rules of right and wrong, the limits of the prerogative of the Crown and of the priviledges of the people are in the present refined age well known and ascertained; to exceed either of them is highly unjustifiable.

In the meantime, similar controversies involving the question of government by prerogative were being waged in other colonies. Leaders everywhere were busy with plans for united resistance. The most notable plan was developed in 1773 by the Assembly of Virginia. It suggested the organization of a system of intercolonial committees to carry on with each other a "continental correspondence." Visiting Wilmington in March 1773, Josiah Quincy of Boston found the North Carolina leaders heartily in favor of this strategy. When the Assembly met in December, it named a Committee of Correspondence consisting of John Harvey, Robert Howe, Cornelius Harnett, William Hooper, Richard Caswell, Edward Vail, John Ashe, Joseph Hewes, and Samuel Johnston. Its instructions were "to obtain the most early and authentic intelligence of all such Acts and resolutions of the British Parliament, or proceedings of Administration as may relate to or affect the British Colonies and to keep up and maintain a correspondence and communication with our Sister Colonies respecting these important considerations." Having done this, the members were to report their proceedings to the Assembly. National in outlook, the committee's work soon became essential to the success of the American Revolution.

During this time open rebellion occurred in Massachusetts with the notorious Boston Tea Party. On the night of 16 December 1773, local patriots disguised as Indians threw overboard in the harbor 342 chests of tea belonging to the East India Company. This was to prevent its owners from paying a tax on the tea and Parliament from establishing the right to raise a colonial revenue by means of port duties.

Edenton Tea Party

Less than a year later, a different sort of "tea party" was held in North Carolina, although the word "tea" apparently was not mentioned. On 25 October 1774, fifty-one "patriotic ladies" gathered in Edenton to discuss the present political crisis; Mrs. Penelope Barker, wife of Thomas Barker who was then the colony's agent in London, presided. The participants solemnly declared that they could not be indifferent to whatever affected the "peace and happiness" of the colonies; anxious to prove their patriotism, they signed an agreement to do everything they could to support the American cause. This was an early instance of political activity by American women, and it attracted considerable attention.

An account of the Edenton Tea Party appeared in the London press and a magazine published a caricature with the faces of some prominent British politicians instead of the women's. James Iredell, Edenton resident and customs collector, received a letter from his brother, Arthur, in London after he had read about the tea party. "Pray are you become patriotic?" he asked sarcastically. The letter continued:

> I see by the newspapers the Edenton ladies have signalized themselves by their protest against tea-drinking. The name of Johnston [the maiden name of Mrs. Iredell] I see among others; are any of my sister's relations patriotic heroines? Is there a female Congress at Edenton too? I hope not for we Englishmen are afraid of the male Congress, but if the ladies, who have ever since the Amazonian Era, been esteemed the most formidable enemies, if they, I say, should attack us, the most fatal consequence is to be dreaded. So dexterous in the handling of a dart, each wound they give is mortal; whilst we, so unhappily formed by nature, the more we strive to conquer them, the more are conquered! The Edenton ladies, conscious, I suppose, of this superiority on their side, by former experience, are willing, I imagine, to crush us into atoms, by their omnipotency; the only security on our side, to prevent the impending ruin, that I can perceive, is the probability that there are but few places in America which possess so much female artillery as Edenton.

After the Boston Tea Party Parliament was even more determined to punish Massachusetts, passing a series of acts designed to reinforce the royal authority there as well as to restrict the people's liberty. These acts aroused the whole conti-

A caricature of the Edenton Tea Party published in a London magazine. The faces of the "ladies" resemble those of some of the leading English politicians of the time. The three women standing on the left hold tea caddies; two additional tea caddies appear in the lower right of the drawing. (North Carolina Division of Archives and History, Raleigh)

nent, and led to a call for a Continental Congress. Support for the idea was instantaneous. It was intended that delegates would be chosen by the colonial assemblies, but in North Carolina Governor Martin was determined not to convene an Assembly until it was too late to elect delegates. When Martin's secretary announced this decision, Speaker Harvey, it was said, flew into a rage and declared that in that case the people would hold a convention independent of the governor. What he proposed to do on his own initiative was treasonous, and his friends convinced him to make the call for a convention appear to come directly from the people rather than himself.

First Provincial Congress

The movement was launched at Wilmington on 21 July 1774 by a great mass meeting presided over by William Hooper and attended by colonists from all of the Cape Fear counties. There it was determined to be "highly expedient" that a Provincial Congress be held independent of the governor. At the invitation to send delegates, thirty counties and four towns promptly held local meetings to elect their representatives. Initially, it was planned that the congress would convene on 25 August at the Johnston County courthouse many miles up the Neuse River west of New Bern. Between the time delegates were elected and the twenty-fifth, however, provincial leaders decided to meet in New Bern under the very nose of the royal governor.

On the designated day, seventy-one delegates answered the roll call at the first such congress held in any of the colonies. Among those present were former speakers of the Assembly as well as many destined to become future governors, judges, and other officials of the state. The congress unanimously elected John Harvey moderator.

The First Provincial Congress remained in session only three days, but it fully launched North Carolina into the Revolutionary movement. It denounced Parliament's new laws to persecute Massachusetts, declaring that the people of that colony had "distinguished themselves in a manly support of the rights of America in general." The congress also endorsed the proposal for a Continental Congress and elected William Hooper, Joseph Hewes, and Richard Caswell as delegates. Having no other resources at their disposal, the delegates pledged the honor of the province in support of whatever the Continental Congress recommended. Finally, Harvey was empowered to call another Provincial Congress when he thought it necessary.

In addition to these matters of immediate concern, the delegates considered a number of other topics including their "Charter rights," the Magna Charta, and criminal justice. Regarding the slave trade, they agreed "that we will not import any slave or slaves, nor purchase any slave or slaves imported or brought into this province by others from any part of the world after the first day of November next."

The people of North Carolina were learning a valuable lesson. They could manage their own affairs without the intervention of a royal governor. The free-holders of Pitt County expressed this very well at one of their meetings: "As the Constitutional Assembly of this Colony are prevented from exercising their right of providing for the security of the liberties of the people, that right again reverts to the people as the foundation from whence all power and legislation flow."

The First Continental Congress met in Philadelphia from 5 September to 26 October 1774; although its official name was just "The Congress," "Continental" was added to distinguish it from the congresses being held by the provinces (or states, as they would soon be known). The Congress was called to consider what should be done to recover the colonial rights and liberties that were being lost. To accomplish this, a Declaration of Rights was adopted on 14 October. Further, six days later an agreement was reached by which the colonies would bind themselves into a Non-Importation and Non-Exportation Association; it would be enforced by Committees of Safety in each colony. This amounted to an economic declaration of war against Great Britain.

By its action the Congress completed the union of the colonies and, in fact, used the term "The United Colonies." Before adjourning the delegates agreed that, unless their grievances were relieved in the meantime, they would meet again on 10 May 1775. All of this activity was of a traitorous nature, so the proceedings were carried on in great secrecy. Reacting to the Second Continental Congress, King George III on 23 August 1775 issued a proclamation directing all British officials to suppress the rebellion in the American colonies.

The functions performed by the various delegates is not clear, but at a later time John Adams of Massachusetts suggested in a letter to Judge William Gaston that Richard Caswell played a leading role. "We always looked to Richard Caswell of North Carolina," Adams remembered. "He was a model man and true patriot."

Second Provincial Congress

Governor Josiah Martin, thwarted in his efforts to keep his province from being represented in the Continental Congress, was determined to make the best of a bad situation, so he summoned the Assembly to meet him in New Bern on 4 April 1775. John Harvey immediately called the Second Provincial Congress to assemble at the same place on the third. Leaders of the popular party (soon to be called Whigs, advocates of American independence) intended that the same

A miniature handed down in the family of Richard Caswell (1729–89) is believed to be of that colonial leader and first governor of the new state of North Carolina. (North Carolina Division of Archives and History, Raleigh)

men would compose both bodies, and with few exceptions that was the case. Martin was furious and denounced Harvey in two different proclamations. The Provincial Congress showed its contempt for the governor by electing Harvey moderator; and when the Assembly convened the next day, he was elected speaker. Both groups met in the same hall, the congress at nine o'clock for an hour of business; at ten o'clock, almost as if by magic, it became the royal Assembly. Both acted under a gavel administered by the same man.

Neither body accomplished much. The Provincial Congress declared it to be the right of the people, or their representatives, to assemble and petition the Crown for relief from their grievances. It also approved the Continental Association drawn up by the Continental Congress and authorized John Harvey—or in the event he was incapacitated, Samuel Johnston—to call another congress whenever he thought it advisable.

The Assembly only had time to organize and to exchange the customary formal messages with the governor before it was ended abruptly by Martin. Its initial offense was the election of Harvey as speaker. Then, on the second day, it offended the governor again by inviting the few delegates to the Provincial Congress who were not also legislators to remain in their places and to participate in legislative discussions. Martin issued a proclamation forbidding this intrusion on legislative business, but, he admitted, "not a man obeyed it." As if deliberately trying to provoke the governor, on the fourth day the Assembly adopted resolutions approving the Continental Association, thanking the delegates to the Continental Congress for their service, and endorsing their reelection. This, of course, was more than Martin could stand. His anger boiled over, and on 8 April 1775 he dissolved the last Assembly ever to meet in North Carolina at the call of a royal governor. Although he later called for a meeting on 23 June, things had gotten out of his control by then and the session was never held. The April Assembly was also the last one attended by John Harvey whose health had long been delicate. Wasted by disease, he said farewell to his associates who had given him such positive evidence of their esteem and confidence, and who, under his guidance, had entered on the course that led to the independence of North Carolina. About mid-May he died in a fall from his horse.

Rapidly converting their thinking from a restoration of their rights as English subjects to thoughts of independence, Americans awaited only some dramatic incident to spark the explosion. That occurred in Massachusetts on 19 April 1775, when General Thomas Gage of the British army attempted to seize military stores gathered by the Whigs. This led to the battles of Lexington and Concord—the famous "shot heard 'round the world." In a southerly direction sound traveled slowly. On 8 May, after nearly three weeks, a rumor reached North Carolina that there had been bloodshed in New England, but letters confirming the hostilities did not arrive until the middle of the month. Newspapers received from London about the same time reported that Parliament had declared Massachusetts to be in a state of rebellion.

North Carolina had some preparation for the events that followed. Committees of Correspondence and Committees of Safety had been at work organizing, drilling, and equipping troops; they also were aware of the need to prepare the minds of the people for war. Initial support for the move toward independence came from the eastern counties where people of English descent, often trained in English institutions and acquainted with English ideals of government, resented the treatment lately meted out by Parliament. Support also came from the counties with inhabitants of Scots-Irish descent who also understood democratic ideals and institutions, and who had experience through their churches in managing their own affairs.

On the other hand, many of English descent wanted no break with En-

ADVERTISEMENT.

NEWBERN, *January* 27, 1775.

PUBLIC Notice is hereby given, that Mr. *John Green* and Mr. *John Wright Stanly*, Merchants in *Newbern*, have agreed with, and are appointed by, the Committee of *Craven* County, to receive the Subfcriptions which is now, or may hereafter be raifed in the faid County, for the Relief of the diftreffed Inhabitants of *Bofton*, and to fhip the fame to the Port of *Salem* as foon as the feveral Subfcriptions are received. Proper Stores are provided by the faid Gentlemen for the Reception of Corn, Peafe, Pork, and fuch Articles as the Subfcribers may choofe to pay their Subfcriptions in.

Thofe Gentlemen therefore who have taken in Subfcriptions, either in Money or Effects, are defired to direct the fame to be paid or delivered to the above named Meff. *Green* and *Stanly*, on or before the Middle of *March* next; and to fend, as foon as poffible, an Account of the Subfcriptions which are or may be taken, by which they may be governed in receiving.

R. COGDELL, Chairman.

North Carolinians understood that the punishment meted out to Boston for opposing taxation by Parliament might well be applied to others. Supplies and money were collected in Craven County "for the Relief of the Distressed Inhabitants of Boston." (North Carolina Division of Archives and History, Raleigh)

gland—merchants, most of the Anglican clergy, many officeholders, and some of the wealthy planters and shippers. The Highland Scots also remained loyal to Great Britain for a variety of reasons that have already been mentioned (see Chapter 5). In almost every community, no matter what the ancestry of a majority of its people, there were Loyalists or Torys. The American Revolution in North Carolina had many of the aspects of a civil war because of this division.

Although documentary evidence is lacking—and one would not expect to find it—it has been claimed that at this time many prominent leaders of North Carolina, eager for a break with England, were afraid this was not the wish of a majority of the people. There was a real possibility that North Carolina would not support the Revolutionary movement, a concern substantiated by the numerous petitions expressing loyalty to King George. Members of the secret fraternal society of Freemasons, among whom were most of the Revolutionary leaders, are said to have organized a "shadow government" that was ready to take over by force if the Revolutionary ideal were rejected. This, of course, did not prove to be necessary.

Uncertainty over North Carolina's stance also led the Continental Congress in December 1775 to send two Presbyterian ministers from New Jersey, the Reverend Alexander MacWhorter and the Reverend Elihu Spencer, avid Patriots, to spend three months visiting in communities where support for the American cause seemed less than enthusiastic. They were to explain the causes of the differences with Great Britain and seek their cooperation. Loyalists in the state, however, were far from cordial in the reception given these visitors.

Governor Martin clearly was encouraged by the evidence of loyalty to the Crown that he recognized in his colony, and in March 1775 he applied to General Thomas Gage in Boston for arms and ammunition with which to equip a company of Loyalists. Rumors soon spread that he intended to use them against the people; it was even whispered that he might arm the slaves and encourage a revolt. Patriots began to observe the palace in New Bern very closely. Fearing for the safety of his family, the governor sent his pregnant wife and their children to New York. On the night of 31 May 1775, Martin himself secretly left to take refuge under the protection of the guns at Fort Johnston near the mouth of the Cape Fear River. From there he continued his Loyalist activities to such an extent that the Cape Fear Whigs resolved to drive him out of the fort. Learning of their plans to attack, Martin escaped in the nick of time to a British sloop of war in the river. Three days later, on 18 July 1775, five hundred local minutemen, under John Ashe and Cornelius Harnett, burned down the buildings inside the fort. This was the first overt act of war in the colony.

Mecklenburg Resolves

Although they could not have known it, on the same day that Governor Martin abandoned the palace, members of the Mecklenburg County Committee of Safety met and drew up a set of resolves expressing their reaction to recent events. They had just learned that Parliament had declared one of the colonies to be in rebellion. The patriots concluded that all laws and commissions confirmed by or derived from royal authority were no longer valid. That being the case, the committee agreed "for the better preservation of good order, to form certain rules and regulations for the internal government of this county until laws shall be provided for us by the Congress." It was then provided that nine military companies should be formed, two citizens designated to settle matters in dispute, and eighteen "selectmen" found to manage the county government, including the collection of taxes and the expenditure of funds. These and other provisions were to remain in force until the Provincial Congress made other arrangements or "the legislative body of Great Britain resign[ed] its unjust and arbitrary pretensions with respect to America." *The North Carolina Gazette* in New Bern published these resolutions on 16 June 1775.[3]

Third Provincial Congress

Following Martin's flight, events moved rapidly toward war, and during the summer of 1775 both sides did their best to get ready for the coming conflict. After Harvey's death in May, Samuel Johnston became the person most responsible for preparations in North Carolina. By mid-summer the situation seemed to require another session of the Provincial Congress, so Johnston issued a call for it to meet in Hillsborough on 20 August. This site was chosen perhaps to inform former Regulators of conditions and to seek their support. When the Third Provincial Congress convened, almost a year had elapsed since the first congress met in New Bern. At that gathering seventy-one delegates were present, but there were no representatives from five counties and three borough towns. Now every county and every town was represented. Samuel Johnston was elected "president," and once again "the common cause of America" was frequently cited from the floor.

Two critical issues were addressed and resolved by the delegates, for the time had come to create an army and to provide a government for North Carolina. Turning to the first challenge, the congress ordered that two regiments be raised, manned, and equipped to the same standard as the Continental army so that they could serve with the national army if needed. Colonel James Moore was appointed to command the first regiment and Colonel Robert Howe the second. It was also directed that six regiments of six hundred minutemen each be raised, one from each of the six military districts into which the province had long been divided. The minutemen would be enlisted for six months and when called into active service would be under the same discipline as Continental troops. Plans were also made for organizing the militia more effectively and for raising and organizing independent companies.

3. The Provincial Congress soon provided for local government and the Mecklenburg Resolves were forgotten. On 30 April 1819 the *Raleigh Register* published the recollections of some elderly Mecklenburg residents of a "Declaration of Independence" purported to have been drawn up in Charlotte on 20 May 1775. The original, they maintained, had been lost in a house fire in 1800, but they recalled that only one meeting had been held that May. The words of the so-called declaration are suggestive of portions of the resolves that have been confused with the national Declaration of Independence of 4 July 1776. Since no contemporary documentary evidence for a declaration survives, whereas the resolves are fully documented, the former is considered by most objective investigators to be a "spurious document." The confusion in text perhaps results from faulty memories, while the two dates may be accounted for by the eleven days' difference in the old-style and new-style calendars.

As funds to support this military force were required, a committee was named to seek an accounting from the provincial treasury. The committee discovered that the records of the provincial treasury were unavailable, but that large amounts of money were due from various sheriffs. Since there was little hope of recovering such debts, the Provincial Congress had to resort to the old policy of issuing paper money. It was somehow decided that $125,000 in bills of credit would be issued and the faith of the province pledged for their redemption. At this time the slow process of switching from the pound sterling to the dollar began, but it would, indeed, take many years. In North Carolina some county financial records were still being noted in pounds, shillings, and pence forty years later. The congress set a rate of exchange between the new dollars and the old pounds; inflation played havoc with the rate and it was changed from time to time.

Severe penalties were set for those who refused to use the paper money or who violated the approved rate of exchange. Those found guilty of counterfeiting, altering or erasing the face value of bills, or knowingly passing counterfeited or altered bills were to "suffer Death, without Benefit of Clergy." Benefit of clergy was an ancient provision of English law carried over into the colonies, and North Carolina in the nineteenth century was one of the last states to abandon it. It was originally intended to prevent members of the clergy from being tried in common courts of law where the jury, and perhaps even the judge, might be only semiliterate at best. In such a court where prejudice might exist against the clergy, the clergyman could invoke this provision and have the case moved to a higher court. In practice over a long period of time, it became possible for anyone who could read and write to plead "benefit of clergy" and prevent the possibility of a verdict being reached by biased jurors.

The second task before this Provincial Congress was to prepare a plan of government to serve during the "absence" of Governor Martin. A committee worked from 24 August until 9 September to develop an acceptable plan. The Provincial Congress would remain the main agency, while executive and judicial authority would be vested in a Provincial Council, six district Committees of Safety, and local Committees of Safety.

The Provincial Congress was the supreme power in the province and would meet annually at a time and place designated by the Provincial Council. Delegates would be elected each October, with each county entitled to five and the borough towns to one each. Voting was limited to landowners. Members of the congress would qualify by taking an oath, in the presence of three members of the council, acknowledging allegiance to the Crown but denying the right of Parliament to levy internal taxes in the colonies; they also would agree to obey the acts and resolutions of both the Provincial and the Continental congresses.

There was no limit to the authority of the Provincial Congress and it could review the acts of the Provincial Council.

Local government was vested in the Committees of Safety, but their actions were to be reviewed by district committees with the right to appeal to the Provincial Council. Although they could make whatever rules and regulations they thought necessary to enforce their authority, they could not inflict corporal punishment except by imprisonment. The local committees were charged with enforcing the orders of both the district committees and the congress; in doing so, they could arrest and examine suspected persons and, if advisable, hold them for trial by a higher court. Committeemen would be elected annually.

The Provincial Council was the chief executive authority and was composed of thirteen members—two from each of the six military districts and one from the province at large. Initially it met every three months, and a majority of the members constituted a quorum. It could call out the militia when needed and was to enforce existing laws concerning the militia. The council's real power, however, lay in a "general welfare" provision that empowered its members "to do and Transact all such matters and things as they may judge expedient to strengthen, secure and defend the Colony." This authority existed only during the recess of the congress; when in session, the Provincial Congress could review and pass on the proceedings of the council.

The ability and interests of the men chosen to administer this government, of course, would determine its effectiveness. As it turned out, they were well qualified. Samuel Johnston was chosen the at-large representative of the council, and selected from the districts were Cornelius Harnett, Samuel Ashe, Abner Nash, Thomas Person, Willie Jones, Thomas Eaton, Samuel Spencer, and Waightstill Avery. At least two of them had been members of the Regulators or sympathetic toward them. On 18 October the council held its first session at the Johnston County courthouse and elected Cornelius Harnett president.

The members of the Provincial Council, in directing the movement of the province toward revolution, were obliged to work under the most unfavorable circumstances. To succeed they had to rely on public opinion which, to a large degree, they had to create themselves, handicapped by limited newspaper coverage and poor postal service. People lived in isolation with limited means of communication. British ships were stationed in the mouth of the Cape Fear River while loyal Highland Scots controlled the head of navigation of that crucial river. North Carolina had no significant commercial center, no mills or factories, and few means of exploiting the area's natural resources.

In the face of these obstacles, the council had to deal with a number of difficult problems. It had to organize an army among a people divided in sentiment and unmilitaristic in nature; to equip its new army with no local source of clothing, arms, or ammunition; to train the army with few experienced officers; to maintain it without money; and, finally, to direct its movements against an enemy superior in numbers, equipment, and experience.

Created as a war measure, the council found its principal task to be the conduct of military affairs. North Carolina was threatened from the east by Governor Martin, who was organizing the Highland Scots and a few former Regulators to help him return to power. In Virginia, the royal governor was encouraging an insurrection of slaves in the Albemarle region. In South Carolina a band of Tories, called Scovelites, was overrunning the upcountry and threatening the southern frontier of North Carolina. On the western frontier Cherokee Indians, influenced by British agents, were becoming restless.

Battle of Moore's Creek Bridge

The Provincial Council drew upon every conceivable resource to deal with these threats. Although their efforts failed to meet all their needs, they did manage to send 760 men to South Carolina in December 1775 to join local troops in the "Snow Campaign" that crushed the Loyalists. Colonel Robert Howe and the Second North Carolina Continentals, as they were known by then, were sent to Virginia to help drive the royal governor, Lord Dunmore, out of Norfolk. And most encouraging of all, Colonel James Moore with the First North Carolina Continentals, supported by Colonel Richard Caswell and the militia from the New Bern district and Colonel Alexander Lillington with the Wilmington district militia, won an important victory over Scottish Loyalists at Moore's Creek Bridge early in 1776.

The Battle of Moore's Creek Bridge on 27 February 1776 has been called "the Lexington and Concord" of the South, and its significance certainly justifies the comparison. This battle undoubtedly kept the British from occupying the South at the very beginning of the war. From his shipboard cabin in the lower Cape Fear River, Josiah Martin never ceased his frantic scheme to restore royal authority in North Carolina. In the fall of 1775 he had sent a plan to London for the subjugation of the southern colonies. Royal advisers heartily approved his proposal and issued orders that it be implemented. Martin was to raise a force of Loyalists in the colony. Lord Charles Cornwallis with seven regiments of regulars would sail from Cork, Ireland, escorted by a powerful fleet under Sir Peter Parker; and Sir Henry Clinton, with two thousand more regulars, would sail from Boston to take command of the combined forces. A rendezvous was arranged to take place at Wilmington about mid-February 1776. This was an excellent plan, but it failed because the Loyalists were too eager and Cornwallis and Clinton were not eager enough.

On 3 January 1776 dispatches arrived advising Martin that his plan had been approved, that Cornwallis and Clinton had received their orders, and that he should proceed with his part of the scheme. At his command, therefore, 1,600 Highlanders, led by General Donald Macdonald, a veteran of the Battle of Culloden, marched out of Cross Creek on 18 February toward Wilmington. In the meantime, Colonel James Moore was fully informed of every move of the Loyalists, thanks to intercepted communications. He directed the maneuvers that, early on the morning of 27 February, brought colonels Caswell and Lillington, with 1,100 minutemen, face-to-face with Macdonald's 1,600 Highlanders at the Widow Moore's Creek Bridge. Patriots had removed the planks from the bridge that the Loyalists would have to cross, and the sleepers had been greased.

At sunrise the Highlanders attacked and tried to walk across the narrow, greased logs over the creek. They met a well-directed fire, and many who were not shot fell into the deep, cold water. With 30 of their best advance troops killed, the remainder lost heart, turned, and fled. The Whigs lost only 1 man killed and 1 wounded, whereas at least 50 Highlanders were killed or wounded and 850, including General Macdonald, were taken prisoner. It was a total victory for the Whigs, who also captured some desperately needed equipment: 35 guns, 150 swords and dirks, 1,500 excellent rifles, a large quantity of medicine and surgical supplies, and 13 wagons. Pursuing the Highlanders into Cross Creek, the patriot forces encountered a local black man who told them that he had seen the Highlanders conceal a box in a stable before beginning their march. At the site he indicated, they found that the box contained £15,000, an amount that the council would surely put to good use.

The victory at Moore's Creek Bridge was the crowning achievement of the Provincial Council, and it aroused the enthusiasm of the people to a new pitch.

While the misled Highlanders were marching unknowingly to their doom, Sir Henry Clinton was leisurely sailing down the Atlantic from Boston, pausing at New York for a word with Governor Tryon and at Chesapeake Bay for a chat with Governor Dunmore. Sir Peter Parker and Cornwallis were still in Ireland. When Clinton finally arrived at Cape Fear in March and Cornwallis in May, they discovered that they were too late. Americans in large numbers were now armed and prepared to meet them. Clinton landed briefly on Smith Island at the mouth of the Cape Fear but soon sailed away to Charles Town to batter unsuccessfully at the walls of Fort Moultrie. Accompanying him was Josiah Martin, the last royal governor of North Carolina. Meanwhile, on 12 April 1776, the Fourth North Carolina Provincial Congress, in the historic Halifax Resolves, empowered its delegates to the Continental Congress to "concur" with the representatives from the twelve other colonies in "declaring Independency." Royal rule was at end in North Carolina.

9

ATTAINING
INDEPENDENCE

THE BATTLE OF LEXINGTON on 19 April 1775 and the Battle of Moore's Creek Bridge on 27 February 1776 inspired those who yearned for independence from Great Britain. Until then the Whigs had indignantly denied that they were actually seeking to break all ties with the mother country.[1] It took something like these military engagements to demonstrate the absurdity of their position. Before 1775 with every expression of opposition to taxation by Parliament, they added a protestation of loyalty to "the best of Kings." *After* Moore's Creek Bridge the Whigs could scarcely continue to express loyalty to a sovereign who had ordered troops sent against them. Even then, however, they took the final step reluctantly and sadly. In North Carolina, resolutions favoring independence were received with much less rejoicing and excitement in 1776 than was the ordinance of secession from the Union in 1861.

Nevertheless, in North Carolina, as elsewhere in America, prophecies of independence had been more or less common for several years before the outbreak of the Revolution. In 1774 William Hooper observed that the colonies were "striding fast to independence," while a few months later Samuel Johnston saw the controversy as a "dispute between different countries" and predicted a complete separation unless England yielded.

Not everyone felt this way, however. As late as 1775 the average person, whatever he might have thought about Parliament's actions, expressed genuine sentiments of loyalty to the king. This was reflected in a resolution adopted at New Bern in August 1774 by the First Provincial Congress, which proclaimed that body's intention "to maintain and defend the succession of the House of Hano-

---

1. Members of the Whig faction generally had a negative attitude toward government, particularly as reflected in royal governors. Convinced that power fostered corruption, they favored a system of controls and checks in government through the people's representatives. They held that the ballot, exercised by those who were not dependent on anyone or any faction, was the best safeguard against corruption. They were *localists*, convinced that government for a small territorial area was best. They saw politics as a continuing struggle between power and liberty.

ver as by law established" and its "inviolable and unshaken fidelity" to King George III.

The First Call for Independence

A change gradually began to take place in the popular mind when it became apparent that the king was not going to take any action to stop Parliament's efforts to tax the American colonies. For many years the relationship between people and king, most believed, had rested in the civil compact. If either party violated this compact, it would cease to exist. Thus, when it was learned that the king had called on Parliament for troops to use in America, that he was hiring professional soldiers in Germany, and that he had proclaimed the colonies to be in rebellion and no longer under his protection, they concluded that the king himself, not they, had violated this unwritten understanding.

Fourth Provincial Congress Adopts Halifax Resolves

By the time the Fourth Provincial Congress met at Halifax on 4 April 1776, sentiment among the Whigs, or Patriots, was nearly unanimous for independence. "All our people here are up for Independence," Samuel Johnston wrote the next day. Robert Howe said: "Independence seems to be the word; I know not one dissenting voice." William Hooper and John Penn came home from the Continental Congress reporting very much the same view in Philadelphia. In some North Carolina counties, it was said, not a single person was willing to speak a good word for Britain.

On 8 April Cornelius Harnett, Allen Jones, Thomas Burke, and Abner Nash, among others, were appointed to a committee "to take into consideration the usurpations and violences attempted and committed by the King and Parliament of Britain against America, and the further measures to be taken for frustrating the same and for the better defense of this Province." After four days of deliberation, the committee on 12 April 1776 submitted a very important document—the Halifax Resolves. It directed that the delegates from North Carolina to the Continental Congress "be empowered to concur with the delegates of the other Colonies in declaring Independency, and forming foreign alliances, reserving to this Colony the sole and exclusive rights of forming a Constitution and laws for this Colony, and of appointing delegates from time to time (under the direction of a general representation thereof), to meet the delegates of the other Colonies for such purposes as shall be hereafter pointed out."

This was a bold move. It was the first call for independence, recommending that not only North Carolina but also all of the "Colonies" join in making such a declaration. The Halifax Resolves were well received. After they were read at the Continental Congress in Philadelphia, delegates from other colonies sent copies home and urged their constituents to "follow this laudable example." Virginia was the first to do so, and on 27 May the North Carolina and Virginia delegates delivered their instructions to the Congress. On 7 June Richard Henry Lee of Virginia moved "that these United Colonies are and of right ought to be free and independent States." Reaction to the motion was favorable, and on 4 July the final draft of the Declaration of Independence was laid before the delegates and approved. Signing it on behalf of North Carolina were William Hooper, Joseph Hewes, and John Penn.

The Halifax Congress then turned its attention to the drafting of a constitution but failed to agree on its provisions. James Iredell wrote: "The great difficulty in our way is how to establish a Check on the Representatives of the people to prevent their assuming more power than would be consistent with the Liberties of the People." After some bitter debate, the Congress adopted "a temporary form of government until the end of the next Congress." A few insignificant changes were made in the plan already in effect; district Committees of Safety were abolished and the name of the Provincial Council was changed to Council of Safety. Unlike the old council, which met every three months, the new Council of Safety would sit continuously and exercise greater authority. It could now grant letters of marque and reprisal,[2] establish courts, name judges of admiralty, and appoint commissioners to enforce trade regulations.

Efforts to secure the neutrality of the Indians had been frustrated by John Stuart, British superintendent of Indian affairs for the Southern Department, and his agents. Rumors circulated that the Indians were going to attack. In the spring of 1776, the Creeks and the Cherokees took up arms and laid waste the borders of the four southern colonies. As a consequence Virginia, North Carolina, South Carolina, and Georgia united to strike a blow that would subdue them at least temporarily. In the summer four expeditions were launched simultaneously from different quarters. General Griffith Rutherford led 2,400 troops from North Carolina against Cherokees along the Tuckasegee, Oconaluftee, Little Tennessee, and Hiwassee rivers. He destroyed thirty-six of their towns and devastated a vast area of country. Troops from other states achieved the same results, and on 20 May 1777 the Indians signed a treaty ceding all of their land east of the Blue Ridge.

Meanwhile, the Council of Safety faced a strong and energetic enemy in the heart of the state. Loyalist leaders, particularly among the Highland Scots, were

2. These were documents authorizing the owner of a private vessel to sail against the enemy and engage in warfare. The ship thereby became a privateer.

The home in Granville County of John Penn (1740–88), one of North Carolina's three Signers of the Declaration of Independence. (North Carolina Collection, University of North Carolina at Chapel Hill)

charged with such vague activities as denouncing the council, speaking out against the cause of liberty, trying to turn others against recent American action, and using their influence to prevent others from "associating in the common cause." More specifically, they were accused of refusing to use Continental currency and of corresponding with the British. In dealing with individual cases, the council generally allowed all Loyalists who accepted the Revolutionary government to remain at home unmolested. It "naturalized" prisoners taken in battle who demonstrated a willingness to take an oath of allegiance, and admitted them to citizenship. Persons merely suspected of disaffection, but who had not committed any overt act against the state, were required to post bond for good behavior. Those regarded as dangerous were taken from their homes and paroled within prescribed limits, while outspoken leaders were imprisoned—some in the state, some in Virginia, and others as far away as Philadelphia.

Fifth Provincial Congress Draws Up a Constitution

News of the adoption of the Declaration of Independence was received on 22 July, and it then became necessary for the state to adopt a constitution as soon as possible. An election was set for 15 October 1776 to choose delegates to the Fifth Provincial Congress at Halifax in November. Without loss of time both radical and conservative factions began a campaign to control the congress. Radicals defeated several conservative leaders, Samuel Johnston among them, but they did not succeed in electing a clear majority of their own followers. The radical representatives included Willie Jones, Thomas Person, and Griffith Rutherford; they were backcountry or western men, with at least moderate wealth, whose point of view differed from that of eastern officeholders of long standing. When the delegates assembled, they elected a moderate, Richard Caswell, as president, and for the moment partisan feelings were laid aside. Instead of voting by counties and towns as in the past, it was decided that a majority should govern. An eighteen-member committee was appointed to prepare a "Bill of Rights and Form a Constitution."

At least some if not all of the members of this committee were familiar with the English Declaration of Rights of 1689, and they used it as a source for North Carolina's Declaration of Rights. For the state constitution, they drew upon the constitutions already adopted by Virginia, Pennsylvania, Delaware, and New Jersey. They also wrote John Adams of Massachusetts for advice, and portions of the North Carolina constitution were based on his recommendations. North Carolina was less aristocratic and more radical (or democratic) than some of the other states; it was less influenced by a commercial class. The Church of England, with its aristocratic tendencies, was poorly established and had no noticeable influence on the delegates although some of them, including Richard Caswell, were members. Specific instructions from Halifax, Mecklenburg, and Rowan counties were kept in mind by those who drafted the constitution.

On 18 December the Provincial Congress approved the constitution, simply declaring it to be in force and not referring it to the people. Delegates may have been uncertain that the voters would approve it. It was a short and simple document, providing only the most meager framework of government and leaving the details to some future legislature as needs arose. Under its provisions the government resembled that of the colonial period—a governor, a two-house legislature, and courts. But while similar in form, the new government was different in spirit. The strong royal governor had made an adverse impression in North Carolina, so henceforth the state's governor would be weak. Elected by the legislature for a one-year term, he would not have the power to veto legislative acts. If he maintained good relations with the General Assembly, he might be elected to two additional terms but could serve no more than three out of six successive years. The governor actually had very little power at all, as he was required to seek the advice and consent of his Council regarding any matter of importance.

Each county was authorized to elect two members of the House of Commons and one senator. Free men who paid taxes, and this included blacks, could vote for members of the lower house, but only those who owned at least fifty acres of land could vote for senators. To serve in the House of Commons one had to own at least one hundred acres of land, while a senator had to own a minimum of three hundred acres. Governors were required to own land and property worth at least £1,000. Active clergymen could not serve in the legislature, nor could Roman Catholics, Jews, or atheists be officeholders at the state level. Not only the governor but also other officers, including councillors and judges, were elected by the legislature, and judges held office for life. The governor no longer had any control over when elections would be held, when and where the legislature would meet, or the power to dissolve or prorogue it. By joint ballot of the General Assembly, the state's delegates to the Continental Congress would be chosen annually and might serve three successive terms.

Among the constitution's other provisions, the officeholder was required to believe in "the Truth of the Protestant Religion." From the constitution of Pennsylvania came the section providing "that a School or Schools shall be established by the Legislature for the convenient instruction of Youth, with such Salaries to the Masters paid by the Public, as may enable them to instruct at low Prices, and all useful Learning shall be duly encouraged and promoted in one or more Universities." Under this document, local government continued very much as before but with the election, tenure, and duties of officials fixed by legislative enactment.

After adopting the constitution the Provincial Congress passed a series of ordinances providing for the government of the state until the meeting of the first General Assembly. Richard Caswell was named the first *state* governor of North Carolina. On 16 January 1777 the temporary officials took the oath of office at Tryon Palace, now serving as the state capitol. The first legislature met at New Bern on 7 April and organized itself, with Samuel Ashe as Speaker of the Senate and Abner Nash as Speaker of the House of Commons. On the eighteenth the legislators reelected Caswell and most of the other appointed officials, but judges were not designated until December when Samuel Ashe, Samuel Spencer, and James Iredell were appointed to the superior court. Also in December, Waightstill Avery became attorney general.

As all of the ordinances of the Provincial Congresses would expire at the end of the April session, it fell to this Assembly to enact all of the legislation necessary to put the new government into full operation. The first act of the first state legislature was a bill to establish a militia, self-preservation being first on its list of priorities. It also determined which portions of the English common law and which old provincial laws would be retained. It extended the definition of the law of treason to check the activities of Loyalists, and it made the counterfeiting of state or Continental currency a capital offense. Still other acts provided for the collection of import duties, a general property assessment, and the levying of an *ad valorem* tax on land, slaves, and other property. This new plan of taxing property according to its value was a departure from the old quitrent method under which value was disregarded.

Once all of this important work had been accomplished, many people felt that there was little left to be done. There was no military activity in evidence. Royal officials were gone, and an elected government replaced them. Independence seemed to have been achieved. Many then lost interest, and support of the Revolutionary cause became erratic and forced. Among the reasons for this relaxed attitude were the weakness of the governor under the new constitution, politics, the activities of Loyalists, and the absolute breakdown of the financial system of both the state and the nation.

Weak State Government

Governor Caswell had not been in office a year before he complained about his lack of authority when urged to take steps to fill up the state's regiments. In a classic example of hindsight being better than foresight, he blamed the last Provincial Congress, conveniently forgetting that he had presided over that body. Attempting to remedy this weakness, the Assembly in 1780–81, when faced with invasion by the British, created first a three-man board of war and then a council extraordinary, in turn giving them the powers that the chief executive should have had. They were instructed to do whatever was necessary to secure, defend, and preserve the state. It was said that this merely divided the executive power among three men, and that the people, not knowing whom to obey, obeyed no one. In any event, the state somehow muddled through and made significant contributions to victory.

Under the constitution many people began to participate in government who previously had been content to remain passive. Factions developed among the electorate, and members of the small farmer class, most of whom were radicals or "localists," began to win election to office. Some conservatives or "cosmopolitans" withdrew from public life. It was said that Democracy was in the saddle, and politics ceased to be a game played exclusively by eastern gentlemen. Nevertheless the legislature, perhaps still mindful of the deference previously paid to a ruling class, named experienced men to such posts as attorney general, the bench, the Council, and even to the office of governor. A few years later, when the federal constitution was presented to the people, the factions became political parties, although in the meantime the loyalties of some had shifted.

Loyalist Activities

One of the most urgent and persistent questions facing the state concerned the Loyalists—largely the Highland Scots of the upper Cape Fear Valley, although there were others in almost every community. In fact, there were so many of them that in North Carolina the American Revolution has sometimes been compared to a civil war. Initially the Whigs were inclined to be conciliatory, but the Assembly in 1777 set a sterner policy. It adopted an oath that offered the simple choice of allegiance or banishment. Most of the staunch Loyalists left the state, some returning to Great Britain and others emigrating to Canada, Florida, or the West Indies. Scottish Highlanders left in large numbers; their exodus from North Carolina has been compared to their exodus from Scotland after the Battle of Culloden. A few remained quietly at home accommodating themselves to the situation as best they could, serving neither side. Others, however, assisted each side in turn as the particular circumstances demanded.

As invasion became more imminent, it was necessary to restrict Loyalist opportunities to aid the British. The state adopted a series of confiscation measures under which the property of Loyalists was seized and sold, forcing still more to leave the state. Unlike similar policies in England and elsewhere, there were no provisions for a hearing in such cases. A mere rumor or suspicion that someone was a Loyalist was deemed sufficient to warrant the seizure of his property. Commissioners of confiscated property were accused of unfairly judging those under suspicion, of selling property to friends or acquiring it themselves, of selling it for less than its true value, and of failing to turn over to state authorities the money received. Individuals sometimes submitted fictitious claims against an estate and received payment, or they seized the property of some hapless Highlander even before the confiscation commissioners arrived. The operation soon was completely out of control, and the legislature tried without success to amend it. Many years passed before the descendants of some Highland colonists felt secure in North Carolina.

State Finances

When the war began North Carolina faced the immediate problem of financing an army with an empty treasury, without credit, with no commerce as a basis of credit, and with demands for resources beyond anything known in the colonial period. That the state was able to meet its needs is almost miraculous. It attempted to provide resources in several ways: (1) paper money, (2) taxation, (3) loans, and (4) the sale of confiscated property. Between 1775 and 1783 the Provincial Congress and the General Assembly issued a total of $8 million in paper currency and adopted numerous schemes to sustain its value. Laws were passed making it legal tender, and severe penalties were provided for those who counterfeited it, altered its face value, refused to use it, or in any way attempted to cause its depreciation. Yet neither appeals to patriotism nor threats of punishment were totally effective. Extensive depreciation set in, and not until the early years of the next century was the state able to remove the old money from circulation.

Members of the Assembly reluctantly and timidly approached the problem of taxation. Quite early an *ad valorem* tax was adopted. As the war progressed and needs grew, inflation increased, so the tax rate rose. Yet this method produced only a small portion of what was needed. The state finally resorted to a tax in kind, under which usable goods and supplies were accepted in lieu of money. Corn, wheat, and other grains, foodstuffs of all kinds, cured meat, cloth, arms and ammunition, equipment, and almost anything else that could be used by the army were acceptable. Commissary and quartermaster units were formed to receive, store, and distribute these supplies.

Finally, the legislature resorted to borrowing. Tax-exempt certificates bearing 5 percent interest were issued. A tax was levied for the purpose of redeeming these certificates when they came due; but because of the unsettled conditions of the time, inflation, and the uncertainty of tax revenues, it is likely that most purchasers of these certificates considered their investment a gift.

From the earliest days of settlement the inhospitable coast of North Carolina was a deterrent to commerce, yet during the American Revolution it proved to be an advantage. Whereas British naval vessels blockaded many ports elsewhere, they found it impossible to patrol the whole coast of North Carolina. The few inlets through which vessels could pass were far removed from a source of supplies and the ocean off them was treacherous. Small, locally owned vessels continued to engage in coastal trade, while those sailing to the West Indies were able to bring in supplies from foreign sources that were essential for the American cause.

North Carolina armed merchant ships, giving their owners letters of marque and urging them to prey on enemy shipping. These privateers contributed significantly to the American victory as well as to the wealth of the owners and crew. North Carolina also outfitted several ships as a state navy and joined with Virginia in operating still others. North Carolina agents, stationed abroad, sought out essential supplies and purchased them—usually with tobacco—for shipment home.

Military Concerns

From 1775 until the end of the Revolutionary War, the state was preoccupied with military affairs. The chief problems during those years concerned the raising, organizing, and equipping of troops; their maintenance in camps; and their operations in the field.

The first line of defense, according to Whig theory, was the militia. The right to bear defensive arms was one of the fundamental prerogatives cited in the Declaration of Rights, and the first state legislature's first law was entitled "An Act to Establish a Militia in this State." It provided that all free white males in the state between the ages of sixteen and fifty were obligated to serve—by either volunteering or being drafted. No accurate muster rolls of the militia were kept during the war, and the records of its service are very meager. In 1782 Governor Alexander Martin reported the total militia of the state at 26,822, but it is impossible to say how many of these saw active service.[3] While sometimes held in contempt by members of the Continental Line, militiamen frequently demonstrated qualities that might well have aroused the envy of regulars. No troops, it has been suggested, ever fought better than Colonel Henry ("Hal") Dixon's North Carolina militia at Camden; and, of course, it was the militia of this state and of Virginia that struck the blow at Kings Mountain to turn the tide of the war and ensure the final victory at Yorktown.

In addition to the regular militia, other military organizations were created from time to time. On 9 April 1776 three companies of Light Horse were formed, and a little later five independent companies were recruited, followed soon afterward by an artillery battery. The state legislature created military units at will and regulated their composition in detail without reference to any other sovereign body. All were paid, armed, and maintained by the state.

In 1775, when the Continental Congress began to raise a Continental army, North Carolina's quota was nine regiments. The Provincial Congress had already raised two regiments of five hundred men each, commanded by colonels James Moore and Robert Howe. These became the First and Second North Carolina Continentals. In April 1776 four additional regiments were recruited and placed under the command of Jethro Sumner, Thomas Polk, Edward Buncombe, and Alexander Lillington. The Seventh, Eighth, and Ninth regiments, under James Hogun, James Armstrong, and John Williams, were authorized in November. Having met with such success in filling its quota, the General Assembly the next April authorized a Tenth Regiment under the command of Colonel Abraham Sheppard. Moore and Howe were soon promoted to brigadier general and succeeded in command of their regiments by colonels Francis Nash and Alexander Martin.

Although Continental troops were supported by money advanced by the Continental Congress, only the state could order them into active service. Con-

---

3. In 1790 the first federal census revealed that there were 69,988 white males over sixteen in North Carolina.

gress, in properly phrased words, asked North Carolina to send its Continental troops to New York on one occasion and again to South Carolina, but state officials, feeling that they were needed to defend the state, simply ignored the communication. Finally when a request arrived that they be sent to join General George Washington, Governor Caswell, recognizing the need, issued the appropriate orders.

Troops from North Carolina saw their first service elsewhere in December 1775, when Howe led the Second Regiment to help Virginia drive Governor Dunmore out of Norfolk. In the spring of 1776 they went to Charles Town to aid in repulsing the British, who turned to that city after learning that the Highlanders had been defeated at Moore's Creek Bridge. After joining General Washington in Pennsylvania in January 1777, North Carolina Continentals participated in the maneuvers leading to the Battle of Brandywine in September and a few actually were involved in the battle. The first action in which they served as a unit, however, was the Battle of Germantown on 4 October. Their heavy losses, including the death of their commander, General Francis Nash, testified to their gallantry under fire. During the winter they were at Valley Forge, and in the summer of 1778 they formed a part of Washington's army which chased General Sir Henry Clinton across New Jersey. They also performed creditable service at the Battle of Monmouth in New Jersey on 29 June 1778.

The War Moves South

From 1776 to 1778 the southern states were free of the enemy. During this time the royal governors of North Carolina, South Carolina, and Georgia routinely assured their superiors in London that the majority of the people in their colonies were Loyalists at heart and would welcome the restoration of royal authority. Since their salaries continued to be paid, they could hardly say otherwise. This assurance may have misled the British government. Its commander in chief in America, Sir Henry Clinton, was not doing well in the middle states, so in 1778 it decided to transfer the war to the South. The implementation of this decision was left up to Clinton, however. The first blow fell on Georgia, the youngest and weakest of the states. The defense of Georgia was entrusted to a North Carolinian, now promoted to major general and the highest ranking officer from the state, Robert Howe. In December 1778 a force under Colonel Archibald Campbell landed at Savannah, defeated Howe, and captured the city. Within six weeks all of Georgia had fallen and royal government was restored.

Congress was not yet ready to give up Georgia, and in January 1779 Howe was recalled and succeeded by General Benjamin Lincoln. The new commander soon had an army of 7,000 men, a third of whom were North Carolina mili-

A representation of Robert Howe (1732–86), a major general of militia, North Carolina's highest ranking officer in the American Revolution. (North Carolina Division of Archives and History, Raleigh)

tiamen under General John Ashe and North Carolina Continentals under General Jethro Sumner. In the meantime General Augustine Prevost reached Savannah with 2,000 British regulars and took command. Lincoln, feeling strong enough to take the offensive, sent Ashe to capture Augusta, but Ashe was surprised and defeated en route. Lincoln himself also suffered a defeat at Stono Ferry on 20 June. In September and October a combination of Lincoln's forces by land and the French fleet approaching Savannah from the Atlantic was turned back with serious losses. In all of this action, of course, North Carolina troops were involved. In one thrust at Savannah North Carolina Continentals under Colonel Gideon Lamb faced the North Carolina Loyal Legion under Colonel John Hamilton, formerly a prominent merchant in the colony.

After his defeat at Savannah, Lincoln abandoned Georgia and sought safety behind the defenses of Charles Town. In this movement, Clinton, still in New York but well informed of conditions in the South, saw an opportunity to wipe out the disgrace of his defeat at Charles Town in 1776. At the same time he felt he might strike a decisive blow. Acting with more than his usual vigor, Clinton sailed from New York the day after Christmas 1779 and soon approached Charles Town with a powerful fleet and an army of 13,000 men. Lincoln attempted to defend the city by strengthening the fortifications and gathering every available soldier behind them. Among his forces were two brigades of Continental troops commanded by Jethro Sumner and James Hogun and about 1,000 militiamen, all from North Carolina. In the face of great odds, Lincoln would have been well advised to abandon Charles Town, but instead he unfortunately yielded to the pleas of civil authorities that the city be defended. As a result, on 12 May 1780 both Charles Town and the army capitulated. Seven generals, nearly 300 other officers, and more than 5,000 soldiers surrendered. Among the North Carolina captives were about 600 militiamen and 815 officers and men of the Continental Line including General Hogun.

The fall of its capital stripped South Carolina of all organized defenders and cleared the way for the conquest of the whole state. In short order all of the strategic points along the coast of South Carolina, like those of Georgia, were under British control. Soon afterward, many important places in the interior were seized and the restoration of royal authority throughout South Carolina was proclaimed. Lord Charles Cornwallis, who had arrived in Charles Town with the invaders, reported that upcountry South Carolina was "easily possessed, fortified, and garrisoned; all the immediate country was submissive, and protestations of loyalty resounded in every quarter."

Confident that Georgia and South Carolina were subjugated beyond recovery by the Americans, Clinton sailed for New York early in June, leaving Cornwallis with 8,345 men to hold the two southern states and plan the conquest of North Carolina. Neither of these officers doubted the ability of the British army to accomplish this in good order. Perhaps a lightninglike strike into North Carolina would have succeeded, but the summer of 1780 in the South was hot and humid, not the kind of weather to which Englishmen were accustomed. Besides, the British soldiers needed a rest and supplies were short. Cornwallis decided to spend the summer in Charles Town and move on to his next objective in the autumn. After all, royal governor Josiah Martin, who was with him, had confidence in the loyalty of his colony. Martin was in communication with assorted Loyalists who were anxious to see the old government restored. They accepted his suggestion that they work hard for the cause during the summer, collect provisions, and be ready to welcome the British army in August or September.

It was the completeness of the victory in South Carolina that led to Cornwallis's downfall. Supported by Martin's exaggerated claims, he became overcon-

Charles, Lord Cornwallis (1738–1805), British commander in America, whose frequent delays in following up clear advantages that his troops gained in the Carolinas contributed significantly to his nation's loss of its American colonies. (North Carolina Division of Archives and History, Raleigh)

fident. The delay was critical for North Carolina. During this period, the state gathered its scattered forces and prepared for resistance. Richard Caswell, as commander of the militia with the rank of major general, gathered men from the east at Cross Creek to intimidate the Highlanders in that region. In the west Griffith Rutherford, William R. Davie, William Lee Davidson, and Francis Locke joined other aggressive partisan leaders to muster the Scots-Irishmen of Mecklenburg, Rowan, and neighboring counties. By mid-June 1,300 men had been assembled—900 under Rutherford at Charlotte and 400 under Locke and other officers at Ramsour's Mill in Lincoln County, created in 1779 when Tryon County was divided and the name dropped; the new county was named for General Benjamin Lincoln soon after he was assigned to command the southern army.

These partisan bands were too weak in numbers, too poorly trained, and too short of equipment for complicated campaigns, but they were ideal for the quick advances and rapid retreats of guerrilla warfare, and they worked well with similar groups from South Carolina such as the one commanded by the "Swamp Fox," Francis Marion. In most cases these men were defending their home communities, which made them especially effective.

One of the most significant partisan strikes occurred on 20 June 1780 at Ramsour's Mill near the modern town of Lincolnton. A Tory, Lieutenant Colonel John Moore, who had just returned to his father's home from fighting with the British in South Carolina, called a meeting of his like-minded friends to tell them of Cornwallis's plans to march to Charlotte in a few months. Approximately 1,300 men arrived and camped atop a wooded hill; about a fourth of them were unarmed. When word of this encampment spread through nearby counties, Colonel Francis Locke of Rowan and Major Robert Wilson of Mecklenburg rounded up about 400 militiamen. At dawn on the twentieth, the Patriots advanced on the Tories. To identify themselves, since neither side had uniforms, at first the Patriots wore a piece of white paper in their hats and the Tories wore a sprig of green; but as these identifications attracted enemy fire, they were soon abandoned. After half an hour the Tories retreated, with each side sustaining about the same number of killed and wounded. This was another instance where neighbors and relatives fought on opposing sides.

Moore and thirty of his followers escaped to the British at Camden, where Moore was threatened with court-martial for having led the Loyalists into action before the appointed time. Cornwallis also was concerned that word of his future plans might have reached the Americans. But even more significant was the effect of the Tory defeat at Ramsour's Mill on hundreds of Loyalists who would have welcomed the British. Disheartened, they were nowhere to be seen when Cornwallis did arrive.

The hit-and-run raids of the militia and partisan bands continued throughout the summer and beyond. On 2 July Davie captured a foraging party, and on the twenty-first Davidson defeated and scattered a band of 250 Tories at Colson's Mill on the Pee Dee River. On the thirty-first he destroyed another group on its way to reinforce a British outpost, and still other engagements followed in August. Though not always successful, these raids were a constant annoyance and threat to the British, and such activity and daring escapades kept the spirit of resistance alive among the Patriots.

Both General Washington and the Continental Congress had been aware of the critical situation in the South. Early in the summer Washington ordered 2,000 excellent Delaware and Maryland troops from his own army under Baron Johann de Kalb to reinforce the southern army. Arriving in Hillsborough on 20 June, de Kalb found a complete lack of preparation and complained bitterly that his army subsisted only through his own efforts. Nevertheless, the presence of these troops encouraged Whig leaders of the state. Caswell and his eastern militia joined them as did some 400 Virginia Continentals—after all, if North Carolina fell Virginia was surely next on Cornwallis's list. As plans were being made to advance into South Carolina de Kalb was replaced by General Horatio Gates. Gates was impatient and rashly ordered an early march toward the British at Camden. His men were in no condition to fight, few had proper equipment, and there was practically no food to sustain them on the march. Passing fields of green corn and orchards of unripe peaches, the men were tempted, ate, and quickly became very ill. Food was so scarce that some of the officers thickened their gruel with the powder they ordinarily used to whiten their hair, after the fashion of the day. It was, therefore, a sick, hungry, and complaining army that marched south from Hillsborough.

Gates resolved to slip into Camden under cover of darkness, knowing that Cornwallis was aware of his arrival. By coincidence, the British decided to march out the same night. Generals Gates and Cornwallis stumbled into each other along a narrow stretch of causeway between two swamps. A few shots were exchanged in the dark, then both armies drew back to await the dawn.

As the sun rose on 16 August 1789 the battle lines of redcoats began to advance on the Americans. Firing one volley after another, they made an impressive and frightening sight. Some of Gates's men held their ground, but others began to fall back. Some Virginia troops who had never been in battle before threw down their loaded guns, turned, and fled. North Carolina troops followed. Fear was contagious, and soon most of the American army was running from the field. A few brave regulars stood fast, such as the militiamen under Colonel Hal Dixon who, when surrounded, cut their way out in a bayonet attack, and General Johann de Kalb who remained with his division after receiving eleven wounds from which he died a few days later. Gates and General Richard Caswell were among those who fled, leaving nearly 800 dead, half of whom were North Carolinians, and around 1,000 captured, including General Griffith Rutherford. Most of Gates's equipment, arms, and ammunition also was lost.

Steps to Victory

Once more North Carolina lay open to invasion and Cornwallis had only to advance to reap the fruits of his victory. But again he let the opportunity pass. His delay gave Americans time to rally their broken forces, and they took full advantage of it. Caswell rounded up the militia at Hillsborough, Salisbury, and Charlotte. The Maryland Continentals were also at Hillsborough, and from Virginia 300 more militiamen and 500 Continentals arrived. By mid-September it

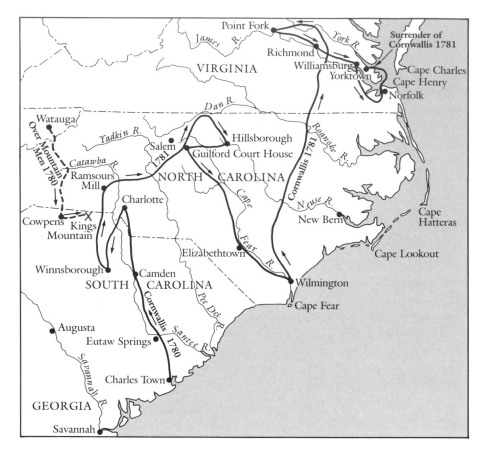

Map 4. Significant Campaigns and Battles, 1780–1781

seemed that enough men were on hand to repel the expected invasion, but they were not well organized, equipped, or led. They did, however, have guns. Many of the soldiers were reported to be almost naked while some were barefooted. When asked for assistance, Governor Abner Nash said that he lacked the authority to provide it. At this time, however, the legislature created the Board of War and gave it all the authority it needed to get the job done. The governor resented this action and declined to let his name be considered for reelection. The legislature also offended Caswell by naming General William Smallwood of Maryland to command the state's troops. Smallwood was the only officer to escape from the Battle of Camden with an untarnished reputation. Caswell resigned his commission and retired to his home at Kinston.

Meanwhile, Cornwallis was completing his plans. On 8 September he broke camp at Camden and, accompanied by Governor Martin, set off on the road to

Charlotte. His march was far from being the triumphant procession his friends had led him to expect. Partisan bands hung on his flanks and so harassed his movements that he did not reach Charlotte until 25 September. It took him seventeen days to cover seventy miles—or four miles per day! In Charlotte on 3 October, the governor announced that royal government had been restored. However seriously Martin took his own premature proclamation, Cornwallis must have thought it rather foolish, for in less than a week it was apparent that he was in what he called the "Hornet's Nest" of the Revolution. Charlotte, he said, was "an agreeable village but in a damned rebellious country." In this hotbed of Scots-Irish Presbyterians he found people with long memories of the ill treatment their families had received at the hands of the English.

Around Charlotte, the British reported, they were troubled by the "close attention" paid to them by William Lee Davidson and William R. Davie. These energetic young officers and their tireless bands patrolled the countryside day and night, watching every move of the enemy. They broke up its foraging parties, captured its scouts, and cut off its messengers so effectively that nearly a week passed after the decisive Battle of Kings Mountain before Cornwallis—who was anxiously awaiting news of Colonel Patrick Ferguson's activities to the west—heard of Ferguson's defeat and death.

When Cornwallis had begun his slow trek from Camden into North Carolina, he sent Ferguson, one of his best and most trusted officers, into the Ninety-Six District to stir the Tories into action and to protect his left flank from attack by some bands of "Over-Mountain men" from far western North Carolina over the Appalachians. Led by Joseph and Charles McDowell, Isaac Shelby, and John Sevier, these bold Patriots were showing signs of activity in the backcountry. Ferguson pursued the mountain men as far as Gilbert Town in Rutherford County. From there he sent a contemptuous message that unless they dispersed immediately and ceased further resistance, he would cross the mountains, hang their leaders, and lay waste to their settlements by fire and sword.

Shelby and Sevier answered this challenge by calling more of their friends to join them. At a rendezvous on the Watauga River on 25 September, Shelby and Sevier each had 240 men from Sullivan and Washington counties (both created by the North Carolina legislature in what is now Tennessee); they were joined by 400 Virginians under William Campbell and 350 men from Wilkes and Surry counties under Benjamin Cleaveland and Joseph Winston. Because of some personal rivalry among the North Carolina colonels, they consented to let Campbell of Virginia take command. As this little army made its way over the mountains, its numbers were increased by more than 1,000 more men from both Carolinas.

Ferguson laughed at this ragtag band, which he pretended to despise—he called it "a set of mongrels." Yet when he learned that the Americans were getting close, he rushed off a messenger to Cornwallis for reinforcements. With his own force, composed largely of Loyalists, he took refuge on the southern slopes of Kings Mountain, a ridge about sixteen miles long, running from a point in what is now Cleveland County, North Carolina, southwest into York County, South Carolina. From what he considered to be a secure spot he boasted that all the rebels out of hell could not drive him away. He must have forgotten, if he ever knew, that he was dealing with real mountain men who were used to climbing real mountains. To them Kings Mountain was no mountain at all, merely a hill.

The Over-Mountain men reached the foot of Kings Mountain about three o'clock in the afternoon of 7 October 1780, organized in three columns, and prepared for an assault. Campbell's men ascended the most difficult part of the ridge to open the attack. Ferguson advanced to meet them, and near the summit turned them back with a bayonet assault. But before the Loyalists could return to their position, Shelby's force had moved up the other side of the mountain to attack from the rear. Turning on his new assailants, Ferguson drove them back, but while he was thus engaged Campbell returned to the attack and Cleaveland's men entered the action from a third direction. No sooner did Ferguson turn to attack one force than another approached. To rally his men, Ferguson blew a silver whistle, but the sound drew enemy fire and he was shot through the heart. His second in command, Captain Abraham De Peyster, seeing how hopeless the situation was, raised the white flag.

The battle lasted about an hour. The victory was complete. Ferguson's entire corps was wiped out. He and 119 of his men were killed, 123 were wounded, and 664 were captured. This remarkable achievement cost the Americans only 28 killed and 62 wounded. It was acclaimed as the first ray of light to pierce the general gloom which had enveloped the country since the fall of Charles Town. Patriots everywhere hailed the victory as the turning point of the struggle. It spurred rebellion against royal authority in South Carolina and disheartened Tories everywhere. Lord Cornwallis felt deserted by his friends and threatened by fresh swarms of enemies; his thoughts of capturing North Carolina shifted to thoughts of flight. After just seventeen days in the state, the British abandoned Charlotte on 12 October and fled in some disorder to Winnsboro, South Carolina. They were closely followed by Davidson, Davie, and General Daniel Morgan, who continually annoyed them.

There was proof that many people had the spirit to defend their states. What was needed was competent leadership. Since the Continental Congress had tried its favorites—Robert Howe, Benjamin Lincoln, and Horatio Gates—without success, George Washington was asked to select an officer to command the Southern Department. He promptly chose Nathanael Greene, who hurried to Charlotte to take his new post. Arriving on 2 December, Greene quickly realized what a discouraging situation he faced. He reported finding only the shadow of an army. Although it numbered 2,307 men, half were untrained militiamen, 300 had no arms, and 1,000 were inadequately clothed. Yet they were eager to defeat the enemy. Greene soon was joined by a group of brilliant subordinates: Thaddeus Kosciusko, an experienced Polish engineer; William Smallwood, of Maryland, who had enhanced his reputation in the rout at Camden; Daniel Morgan, a great partisan fighter; William Washington, kinsman of George in blood and spirit; and "Light Horse Harry" Lee. Also there were partisan leaders from both Carolinas—Sumner, Davidson, Davie, Pickens, Sumter, and Marion. Nearly all of these men worked well together.

Because his army was too small to confront Cornwallis in the battlefield, Greene divided the force into two strong partisan bands to operate against the smaller British posts in the interior. One segment of 1,100 men under General Isaac Huger, which Greene himself accompanied, was sent to Cheraw to operate in the eastern part of the two Carolinas and to threaten Lord Rawdon at Camden. The other portion, composed of some 1,000 soldiers under Morgan, went to the Ninety-Six District to operate in the western area. In order to cover as much territory as possible, Morgan camped on the Pacolet River near the North Carolina border. The two detachments were 140 miles apart, with Cornwallis at Winnsboro between them. Cornwallis had a total of 11,000 men widely scattered across South Carolina, but never more than about 4,000 at any one place under his immediate command.

Greene was aware that he was playing a most hazardous game, as Cornwallis might easily turn on either segment of Americans and destroy them before the other could go to their assistance. Greene had studied his enemy, however, and believed that this would require quick thinking and aggressive action on the part of Cornwallis, abilities that Cornwallis lacked. Events proved that Greene had understood his lordship correctly.

Following Greene's example, Cornwallis divided his own army. General Alexander Leslie was ordered to reinforce Rawdon at Camden, and Lieutenant Colonel Banastre Tarleton was sent to pursue General Morgan in the west. Meanwhile Cornwallis kept his main army idle at Winnsboro. Learning of Tarleton's movements, Morgan took up a position at Cowpens and waited for Tarleton's attack. With the Broad River some five miles to the rear, a fence to the left, and a hill to the right, he placed his militia in the front rank with orders to fire and drop back to reload. The force was somewhat penned in and could not easily abandon the field. The British reached Cowpens early in the morning of 17 January 1781 expecting to drive the Americans head over heels into the river, so they took no precautions but rushed into battle. They met surprisingly stubborn resistance. The American militia poured a destructive fire into British ranks. A bayonet charge by the Continentals threw them into confusion, whereupon Washington's dragoons, sweeping down on their left flank, turned disorder into panic. Many of the British threw down their arms and surrendered. The rest,

A Rhode Island native, Quaker-born Nathanael Greene (1742–86) became a major general in the American Revolution. When North Carolina anticipated invasion by the British in 1780, he was sent to Charlotte by General George Washington. There Greene rallied North Carolina soldiers who were joined by troops from other states. The campaign that followed reached a climax at the Battle of Guilford Court House, resulting in serious losses to the British and contributing to their surrender at Yorktown in October 1781. (North Carolina Collection, University of North Carolina at Chapel Hill)

imitating Tarleton himself, turned around and fled, closely pursued by the American cavalry. Only 270 of Tarleton's men found their way back to Cornwallis's camp; 300 were killed or wounded and 600 were captured. The loss of another excellent corps, so soon after Ferguson's defeat at Kings Mountain, was a blow from which the British in the South never recovered.

Stung into unaccustomed activity, Cornwallis broke camp at Winnsboro and set out in pursuit of Morgan who lost no time celebrating his victory. With Cornwallis just 25 miles away commanding a force four times the size of his own, Morgan first secured his prisoners and began an escape from the danger zone. Even before his cavalry returned, Morgan was retreating into North Carolina in order to put the Catawba River between himself and the British. After a week's march of nearly 90 miles, he crossed the Catawba at Sherrill's Ford on 24 January. The next day Cornwallis, in pursuit, reached Ramsour's Mill still 25 miles behind. Here Cornwallis stripped his army of heavy baggage, wagons, tents, extra clothing, and all supplies that were not considered absolutely essential.

At almost exactly the same time, Greene learned what had happened and in the development he saw a chance to strike Cornwallis a critical blow. Greene laid careful plans for what was to follow. Accordingly, while Huger moved rapidly up the Yadkin to the vicinity of Salisbury, Greene struck out across country to intercept Morgan. Crossing the intervening distance of 125 miles from Cheraw in just three days, Greene joined Morgan at Sherrill's Ford. Cornwallis was then on the opposite bank of the Catawba River, but it was swollen and he could not cross. Almost in sight of the enemy the Americans finalized their strategy. Greene and Morgan would draw Cornwallis as far as possible from his base of supplies in South Carolina and, uniting the two segments of the American army, would turn on him and destroy him. On 31 January they began their retreat toward the Yadkin River.

Greene's management of this retreat entitles him to a high rank among the greatest soldiers of the time. No detail of routes, marches, supplies, or camps escaped him. He used every means possible of moving his own army and of delaying the enemy. He participated in the dangers and hardships just as his men did. All suffered and endured the cold, rain, and mud of the winter with little protection. After retreating continuously for twenty-two days, Greene and Morgan finally joined forces with Huger at Guilford Court House. The British then were at Salem, 25 miles away. On 13 February Greene crossed the Dan River into Virginia and there let his men rest in safety. He had saved his own army and led the British into a trap.

Cornwallis was 230 miles from his source of supplies, in the heart of his enemy's territory, and with a hostile militia in his rear. He had lost many men on his march across North Carolina. Some of the German mercenaries, when they passed through settlements where the people spoke German, deserted and settled down. Some English soldiers, probably tired of the struggle and perhaps even sympathetic with the American cause, also found a welcome and deserted, intending to spend the rest of their lives in the state. Altogether Cornwallis lost 250 men during the march.

Cheated out of his prey, Cornwallis abandoned his pursuit and retired to Hillsborough to rest his army, to try to gather provisions, and to seek Tory sup-

One of the earliest surviving Stars and Stripes, this flag was carried at the Battle of Guilford Court House on 15 March 1781. It is now in the North Carolina Museum of History in Raleigh. (North Carolina Division of Archives and History, Raleigh)

port. With a printing press that he apparently had picked up along the way, he published a proclamation announcing his intention to rescue His Majesty's loyal subjects of North Carolina "from the cruel tyranny under which they have groaned for several years" and inviting "all such faithful and loyal subjects to repair, without loss of time, with their arms and ten days' provisions, to the Royal Standard now erected in Hillsborough." His appeal fell on deaf ears. The people clearly understood his predicament, and they lost their enthusiasm for the royal cause. Cornwallis was forced to admit that he found himself "among timid friends." As a result, when he marched out of Hillsborough late in February to meet Greene at Guilford Court House, his army was numerically weaker than it had been when he set out from Ramsour's Mill in pursuit of Morgan.

On the other hand, Greene was stronger. He had inspired confidence in his leadership and troops poured into his camp. When he went into Virginia, he had 1,400 exhausted troops; three weeks later, when he recrossed the Dan into North Carolina, he had an army of some 4,000, of whom 1,715 were Continentals.

Both generals were eager for battle. For Cornwallis a victory was a necessity, but Greene would be satisfied merely to inflict further losses upon the British. The two armies met at Guilford Court House on 15 March 1781. Fighting was intense on both sides, particularly between the British regulars and the Continentals. Twice the British were turned back with heavy losses, but they were recalled by Cornwallis in person. After the second time he brought up fresh troops and prepared for a final assault, but Greene, satisfied with the damage he had inflicted on the enemy and determined to preserve his own army at all

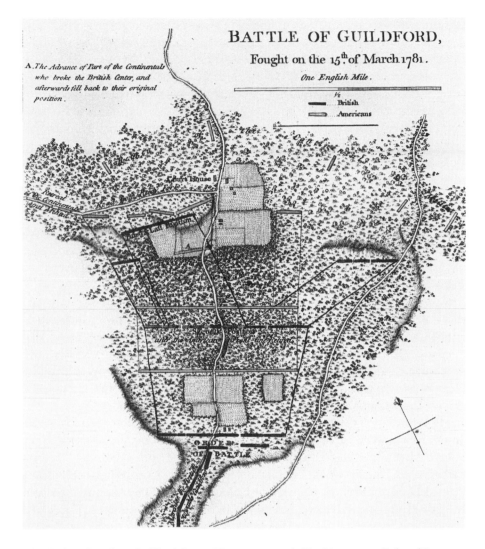

The Order of Battle at Guilford Court House as recorded by Lieutenant Colonel Banastre Tarleton of Lord Cornwallis's staff. (North Carolina Collection, University of North Carolina at Chapel Hill)

costs, withdrew, leaving Cornwallis in possession of the field.

Cornwallis rightly claimed the victory, but he paid dearly for it. Greene lost 1,046 militiamen, most of whom were declared missing but they later returned; he also lost 78 killed and 183 wounded. The British lost 93 dead and 439 wounded or missing. This was more than 25 percent of their total strength, a loss that could not be replaced.

In announcing his triumph Cornwallis called on all loyal subjects to come forward to "take an active part in restoring good order and government." The response to this invitation was reflected in a report that he made: "Many of the Inhabitants rode into Camp, shook me by the hand, said they were glad to see us, and to hear that we had beat Greene, and then rode home again; for I could not get 100 men in all the Regulator's Country to stay with us, even as Militia." His predicament was clear. He was too weak to take the offensive, and his position grew weaker every day. It was too precarious to permit him to follow his usual course of sitting still and doing nothing. He decided to march down to Wilmington through friendly Scottish Highlanders' country. Wilmington was then held by a British force under Major James H. Craig. There he could get in touch with the British fleet and perhaps repair some of the damage suffered by his badly shattered army. On 18 March, abandoning his wounded to the care of kindly Quakers in the vicinity of Guilford Court House (who, when recovered, were granted safe passage through the state to join their comrades), Cornwallis made his way to the Cape Fear country. He arrived in Wilmington on 7 April and stayed until the twenty-fifth.

Cornwallis was harmless in Wilmington. As soon as Greene was sure that that was where he was going, he dismissed him from further concern and went to South Carolina. Cornwallis is said to have been offended when he learned that Greene did not consider him worth pursuing. In South Carolina Greene began a series of remarkable movements in which he finally forced the enemy to abandon every important post in the interior, but British forces remained in Charles Town as well as in Savannah.

In Wilmington Cornwallis considered his options. If he returned to Charles Town, he would be admitting that all was not well with the British cause in the South. After all, he could claim that he had captured both Carolinas. The best move, he concluded, would be to take Virginia next. Cornwallis then began a slow, deliberate march through eastern North Carolina, terrorizing the countryside. Houses were burned and personal property appropriated. Tories and camp followers were responsible for much of the damage inflicted along the way.

The weakened British army took up a position at Yorktown, Virginia, from which it soon discovered it could not escape. The surrender there on 18 October 1781 was certainly no surprise to North Carolinians who had witnessed the low state of the once mighty redcoats during the previous spring.

IO

A FREE STATE

THE DEPARTURE of the armies of Nathanael Greene and Lord Charles Cornwallis left North Carolina at the mercy of many loosely organized, undisciplined bands of armed men. For more than a year they carried on a relentless civil war, and the state was the victim of as much or more pillage, murder, and general disorder as came during Reconstruction after the Civil War. Each side was guilty of abuses and crimes that often served as excuses for merciless retaliation. Gangs of robbers, masquerading as Whigs or Tories, as suited their purposes at the moment, robbed people, burned houses, murdered men, and attacked women indiscriminately. These midnight raids and neighborhood battles were all the more criminal, whether committed by Whigs or Tories, as they could not by any possible means affect the outcome of the war.

The most notorious of the Tory raiders was David Fanning, who held a commission as colonel of the loyal militia issued by Major James H. Craig, the British commander in Wilmington. A native of Amelia County, Virginia, Fanning grew up in Johnston County, North Carolina, where he served an apprenticeship. He ran away to Orange County, it has been said, because of harsh treatment. As a partisan leader he was unexcelled on either side in the Carolinas. During the war Fanning led bands of Tories on raids, terrorizing large areas of both states, and sometimes marched with Cornwallis or other British leaders. In July 1781 he dashed into Pittsboro, where a court-martial of several Loyalists was about to begin, and seized more than fifty prisoners—among them several militiamen and Continental officers and three members of the General Assembly. On 12 September during a raid on Hillsborough he took around two hundred prisoners, including Governor Thomas Burke. These captives were sent to the British at Wilmington; later the governor was transferred to Charles Town where he was regarded as a hostage for the safety of Fanning, kept in close confinement, and denied the right of exchange.[1] After Great Britain and the American states signed

1. After protesting his treatment, Burke was transferred from a prison compound on one island to another where he was closely watched. On one occasion his room was fired into. He escaped in mid-January 1782, violating an oath not to do so. On returning to North Carolina he was criticized for this violation and soon withdrew from public service in considerable disgrace; he died at age thirty-six.

the terms of peace, Fanning sought a pardon, but his petition was turned down. He then moved to Nova Scotia where many Highland Scots and other Loyalists from North Carolina already lived. Before his death in 1825 he was tried for serious crimes committed in the Canadian province.

Along with Fanning, Major Craig (later prominent in Africa and India, and governor of Canada) was responsible for unsettled conditions in North Carolina. Craig and his force of 450 regulars led raids throughout the eastern part of the state, causing extensive damage. They also furnished and encouraged Tories to engage in hostile acts. Among Craig's prisoners were John Ashe and Cornelius Harnett; held under unhealthy conditions, both men became ill and died within a few days after their release.

Griffith Rutherford's militia forced the evacuation of Wilmington by Craig on 18 November 1781, bringing to an end the American Revolution in North Carolina, but not until Fanning left in May 1782 did conditions begin to approach normalcy. On 19 April 1783 Governor Alexander Martin informed the General Assembly that Great Britain had acknowledged American independence. While encouraging the people of the state "to enjoy the fruits of uninterrupted Constitutional Freedom," he urged them to remember the sacrifices made by the soldiers. He also recommended that the Loyalists, who "through ignorance and delusion" had also suffered, be forgiven. These people, he stressed, "have fresh claims to your Clemency on this happy occasion." Thousands of cultured, intelligent people left the state during the Revolution and, with the passage of an "Act of Pardon and Oblivion," many returned. Their former neighbors, some of whom had acquired abandoned or confiscated property, did not always welcome them and the former Loyalists had to make the best of a difficult situation, move elsewhere in the state, or go back to their recent place of refuge. Many, of course, returned to their former homes and had no serious problems with their neighbors.

Unsettled Conditions

Between the end of the Revolution and 1789 North Carolina and the other American states were in a precarious situation. England and Spain particularly, but France and other nations as well, watched with great interest to see what would happen. If the states disagreed among themselves, some or all of these nations were eager to move in and take over. The numerous problems that the states faced both individually and collectively were critical, and on their solution depended the future of much of North America.

There were around 350,000 people in North Carolina, but they were without economic, racial, social, or political unity. Roughly a quarter of the people were held in bondage. Planters of English descent controlled the eastern counties while small farmers, largely Scots-Irish though numerous German descendants were thickly settled in some sections, occupied the backcountry. During the Revolution about a third of the white people in the state had remained loyal to Great Britain, many vigorously expressing it. In the interest of military victory, it was necessary for the state to levy heavy taxes and, in the case of reluctant owners, even to seize property useful to the military. Paper money became virtually worthless and there was little profit to be made in agriculture that produced more than was needed for home consumption. Commerce all but stopped. Hundreds of families were reduced from ease and comfort to poverty and misery.

Intellectual, moral, and social institutions also fell into ruins. Most of the schools and academies closed. No newspaper was published in the state after 1778. Except for essential official dispatches, the postal service was discontinued. Religious conditions reflected a similar decline. With the separation of the colony from England, the Church of England collapsed, and the other Protestant denominations, Baptists and Presbyterians particularly, were little better. In 1780 the Methodist leader, Francis Asbury, described the people of North Carolina as "gospel slighters." One of the most important social institutions in the state, the Grand Lodge of Masons, which had been established at Wilmington in 1735, ceased to exist after 1776.

Factionalism

Political conditions in the state were chaotic. Old alignments of colonial days broke up, and new alignments were slow to take form. Between 1776 and 1789 political questions were resolved chiefly in terms of sectional, local, and personal interests, and political strife became intense and bitter. The claim of soldiers to political preference over civilians, a claim that would recur after every future war, produced fierce contests. Colonial distrust and hatred of both lawyers and merchants remained alive after the war. All of these factors—national origin, economic status, religious preference, place of residence, and veterans' status—contributed to the rise of factions. Those who wanted a return to as many prewar ideals or conditions as possible, such as a renewal of trade with England, stable government, a sound currency, a safe home and countryside, and the like, were called **conservatives**. They consisted of the professional class, lawyers and merchants, planters, and the wealthy. On the other hand, a numerous and determined group of people—called **radicals**—wanted as few governmental restrictions as possible, low taxes, no sympathy or consideration for the former Loyalists, and no obligation to pay prewar debts to British merchants. Each

James Iredell (1751–99) contributed much to the understanding by North Carolinians of the philosophy of the American Revolution. He also was influential in securing the adoption of the federal Constitution by North Carolina. As a United States Supreme Court justice, however, he expressed a states' rights point of view which contributed to the adoption of the Eleventh Amendment. (North Carolina Collection, University of North Carolina at Chapel Hill)

group rallied its forces for the coming struggle that both anticipated between government and liberty.

About this time James Iredell, one of the most effective conservative leaders, compiled a telling eleven-point "Creed of a Rioter." In the piece, he satirically observed that the radicals, whom conservatives sometimes referred to as "rioters," blamed *gentlemen* for all of the state's difficulties. They believed that they had the right to take another person's property if they wanted it, that they were always right, that they should take care of their own needs themselves, and that they should have no concern for the future.

Small farmers and underprivileged people in prewar North Carolina had enjoyed virtually no voice in government. In political affairs they usually meekly followed the lead of the gentry, voting as the prominent men in the community did. This has been called "deference democracy." After the war they began to reject this kind of leadership and to make their wishes known. Many conservatives retired from the political arena.

Members of the General Assembly wisely ignored some of the problems most likely to split the state still further, and instead prepared an agenda of important matters on which nearly all could agree. First, they would look after the veterans who had helped to win the war. Second, they would work to secure the release of prisoners still held by the British. Third, they would adopt a policy with respect to the former Loyalists.

In 1780, when invasion was imminent, large tracts of land beyond the mountains had been set aside as a bounty to encourage the enlistment or reenlistment of men. The legislature now ordered that this land be surveyed and granted to those eligible to receive it. A resolution was passed asking Governor Alexander Martin to open negotiations with General Alexander Leslie, the British commander at Charles Town, for an exchange of prisoners. After long and tedious negotiations, the governor was able to report that through the able assistance of General Nathanael Greene the exchange had taken place.

Treatment of Loyalists

The Loyalist question was not quite so simple. According to the Act of Pardon and Oblivion, offenses would be pardoned and forgotten except for Loyalists who fell in one or more of five categories: (1) those who had accepted commissions and served as officers in the British army, (2) those who had been cited by name in the confiscation acts, (3) those who had left the state with the British armies and not returned within twelve months prior to the passage of this law, (4) those accused of serious political crimes—namely, Peter Mallet, Samuel Andrews, and David Fanning, and (5) those guilty of deliberate house burning, murder, and rape. Mallet was later determined to have been falsely suspected and his name was removed from the act.

Only time, not an act of the legislature, could heal the rupture that occurred in North Carolina during the American Revolution and only after several generations were old wounds healed. During the War of 1812 recruiting officers reported that young men from former Loyalist neighborhoods enlisted in large numbers in an attempt to demonstrate that "good red American blood" flowed in their veins.

Creating a New State Capital

Some of the confusion and inefficiency in government resulted from the continued reluctance of the legislature to designate a fixed seat of government.

New Bern, the colonial capital, was no longer centrally located and was open to invasion from the sea. Tarboro, Fayetteville, and Hillsborough were ambitious to take its place. At almost every session from 1777 to 1790 the Assembly tried without success to make a choice. Politics and sectional rivalries caused difficulties. In 1782 Hillsborough was selected, but the next year the Cape Fear members, who preferred Fayetteville, traded votes with western members to elect Alexander Martin of Guilford County as governor and to repeal the Hillsborough bill. The next year Tarboro came within three votes and Hillsborough within two of victory. No town could get enough votes to win and any two could defeat the third. For nearly two decades after independence, governors and other state officials administered public affairs from their own homes and the legislature migrated from town to town. Between 1777 and 1794, seven towns, none of them adequate for the purpose, enjoyed the honor and reaped the profits of legislative sessions.

In 1787 the situation became so intolerable that the legislature was forced into a humiliating confession of its own weakness. It could not solve the problem and had to refer it to a convention that it called to consider the proposed new federal constitution. This convention, which met in Hillsborough in the summer, adopted an ordinance that the capital be located within ten miles of Isaac Hunter's tavern in Wake County, but it left the exact site within that great circle to the legislature.[2] Even so, 119 delegates objected to the recommendation, predicting that a site in the wilderness far removed from a commercial center would never be more than a village. Those who still wanted Fayetteville to be the capital did not give in easily, preventing the legislative sessions of 1788, 1789, and 1790 from taking any action on the convention's decision. Finally in 1791 advocates of the Wake County site succeeded in getting enough support to name a commission to locate the capital, and on 2 April 1792 it purchased a thousand acres of the Joel Lane plantation for £1,378.

North Carolina's interest in history and tradition may be demonstrated by the fact that the capital was named "Raleigh," reminiscent of the Cittie of Ralegh ordered by Sir Walter Raleigh to be established as the capital of his 1587 colony. Further tradition was followed by William Christmas, the surveyor who laid out the town. His plans followed precisely those drawn up in 1758 for George City as a colonial capital during Governor Arthur Dobbs's administration. Union Square in the center was reserved for the statehouse, and four main streets, each 99 feet wide, led off in the four directions. All other streets were 66 feet wide, and a 4-acre square was reserved in each of the four quarters of the new city—an

---

2. Isaac Hunter is reported to have served the patrons of his tavern a particularly popular rum punch. The convention members felt that locating the state capital in the vicinity would surely please legislators.

A new capital named for Sir Walter Raleigh was surveyed in the woods of Wake County in 1792. This contemporary oil painting of the statehouse erected there is in the North Carolina Museum of History in Raleigh. (North Carolina Division of Archives and History, Raleigh)

excellent example of city planning, be it 1758 or 1792. The remaining 276 acres were marked off in 1-acre lots to be sold to individuals and the income used to erect the capitol and other public buildings.

Commissioners were also named to oversee the building of the capitol, and they retained the services of an architect from Massachusetts, Rhody Atkins. The cornerstone of the brick building was laid in 1792, and the structure was completed in two years. In 1819 a committee was named to sell the remaining city lots and to use the money to remodel the statehouse. Finished in 1822, the work included the addition of porticoes. A coat of stucco, marked in squares to resemble building blocks of stone, was applied to cover the plain brick of the building. On the advice of Thomas Jefferson, the committee engaged a noted Italian sculptor, Antonio Canova, to construct a marble statue of George Washington which was placed in the rotunda of the building.[3] Before long this statue was acclaimed to be "the most precious work of art in the country," and travelers to North Carolina made a point of visiting the capitol to see it. The committee also had a portrait of George Washington painted for the building.

3. When the capitol burned in June 1831, the statue was so badly damaged that it could not be restored. In 1970 a replacement, following Canova's original model which survives in the Canova Museum in Italy, was installed in the present capitol.

This handsome marble statue of George Washington was made by the Italian sculptor, Antonio Canova. When the Marquis de Lafayette visited Raleigh early in 1825 he visited the rotunda of the capitol with young Elizabeth (Betsy) Haywood and George West. The general pronounced the likeness to be quite good. (North Carolina Division of Archives and History, Raleigh)

Foundations for the Future

Despite the squabbling among politicians, the people of North Carolina confidently repaired the wastes of war. In readjusting their intellectual, social, and economic life and laying the foundations on which the future greatness of the state was built, they undertook many new initiatives. At New Bern in 1783

Late in November 1818 this portrait of George Washington, painted by Thomas Sully after one by Gilbert Stuart, arrived in Raleigh to adorn the state capitol. It was rescued in June 1831 when the capitol burned and was hung in the house chamber of the new capitol after it was completed in 1840. (North Carolina Division of Archives and History, Raleigh)

Robert Keith opened a printshop and in August began publishing a new newspaper, *The North Carolina Gazette, or Impartial Intelligencer, and Weekly Advertiser*. By the end of the century papers also served Wilmington, Halifax, Salisbury, Fayetteville, Edenton, Hillsborough, and the new capital city, Raleigh. These newspapers, along with many unusual and interesting questions growing out of independence, stimulated political discussion. They also created a group of pamphlet writers (or pamphleteers) who produced a large body of material, mostly under pseudonyms such as Atticus, Sylvius, Sully, Tiberius Graccus, and True Citizen. Sermons, biographies, poetry, and pamphlets on such practical subjects as agriculture and livestock appeared as well. In 1785 the General Assembly passed a copyright act "to encourage genius, to promote useful discoveries and to the general extension of arts and commerce."

Other evidence of renewed intellectual activity could be seen in the formation of circulating libraries and debating societies, and in the appearance of both local dramatic groups and "strolling players" in some of the towns. As a part of their stock-in-trade merchants began to advertise books, and book salesmen frequently appeared at residents' doors. Among the latter was Mason Locke Weems, better known as "Parson" Weems—the man who made up the tale of George Washington and the cherry tree. More people bought John Marshall's five-volume *Life of George Washington* from him than any other book offered by salesmen.

The need for education was not forgotten even as people were involved in the war. Severing ties with England, leaders realized, would remove church support for schools. The 1776 constitution contained a section requiring the legislature to establish schools with at least some public support as well as one or more universities. As a result of this provision, before 1800 more than forty academies were chartered by the legislature and granted exemption from taxes. Their charters frequently stipulated that a number of poor children be admitted free of tuition. Such schools might be offered the vague hope of a state subsidy when conditions permitted it, and they often were authorized to raise funds through a lottery.

People often spoke of the "experiment in democracy" in which they were engaged, and they recognized the need for an educated citizenry to make it effective. Means of higher education would also be necessary, as the Provincial Congress in Halifax recognized in November and December 1776. The former Queen's College (or Queen's Museum) in Charlotte, which the king had disallowed, was rechartered in 1777 by the first state legislature as Liberty Hall Academy.

At the beginning of the American Revolution there were only nine colleges in all of the colonies. Within a decade of the British surrender at Yorktown, the number doubled. In 1784 a bill—based on the constitutional mandate—was introduced in the General Assembly to charter the first state university in America. Political differences prevented its approval until 11 December 1789, when the University of North Carolina was chartered, largely through the leadership of William R. Davie, a few days after the state had approved the federal constitution. A week later the trustees met and began plans that culminated in 1795 with the admission of Hinton James as the first student. The university graduated seven classes before the second state university opened in Georgia. North Carolina alumni soon began to provide leadership for the state, as well as to hold high positions both in other states and in the national government.

In an attempt to stabilize economic conditions in the state, the General Assembly suspended the statute of limitations to give people time to carry out certain legal requirements that had been delayed by the war. Titles to property could be clarified, for example, or debts settled. A stay law was passed for one year to delay legal action until those concerned could come to terms. A scale of depreciation for the troublesome paper currency was adopted, and equity jurisdiction was granted to superior court judges, previously restricted to criminal cases. Land offices were opened to dispose of vast tracts of land acquired by the state from former owners who were British subjects. The state abolished the custom of entails by which property owners could restrict the inheritance of their estate in perpetuity to a certain class—always the oldest son, for example. Other acts called for the opening of inlets, the clearing and marking of channels, the erection of lighthouses, the building of roads and bridges, and the inspection of exports. This period also saw an increase in land speculation, and between 1783 and 1789 the legislature incorporated twenty-nine new towns.

Concern over property precipitated a significant legal case in North Carolina. Mrs. Elizabeth Bayard, the daughter of Samuel Cornell, a Loyalist merchant, sued to recover her father's confiscated property which had been purchased by Spyers Singleton. Although the state constitution guaranteed a jury trial "in all Controversies at Law respecting property," a state law of 1785 prohibited courts from hearing suits for the recovery of property when title to the property was derived from the confiscation laws. A battery of distinguished lawyers appeared: Samuel Johnston, William R. Davie, and James Iredell represented Mrs. Bayard, while Abner Nash and Alfred Moore represented Singleton. His lawyers argued that, in view of the state law prohibiting such cases, the suit should be dismissed. Her lawyers, however, citing the constitutional provision, maintained that the trial should continue. A landmark decision was rendered in *Bayard v. Singleton* when it was determined that the act of the legislature was unconstitutional—the first such ruling in American jurisprudence. The judges were Samuel Ashe, Samuel Spencer, and John Williams. The case was heard, but Mrs. Bayard failed to regain her property.

Plans for a National Union

Several times before hostilities broke out with England, it was suggested that there should be some means for expressing positions on issues of concern to all the colonies. As early as 1754, at a congress in Albany, New York, a plan of union proposed by Benjamin Franklin contained the basic ingredients of the ultimate

American union. The Stamp Act Congress of 1765, the nonimportation agreement in 1768, and the organization of the Committees of Correspondence each contained elements that contributed to sentiments of union. With the signing of the Declaration of Independence, however, the question became more immediate. Richard Henry Lee of Virginia included with the motion for such a declaration the additional provision that the Continental Congress also prepare a plan of confederation to be submitted to the states for their consideration. To draft such a plan, one delegate from each state was appointed. Representing North Carolina was Joseph Hewes.

The Articles of Confederation were reported out of committee in July 1776, but not finally approved by the Congress until November 1777. They did not take effect until 1781—at the end of the war—when the thirteenth state finally ratified the document. The Articles provided for "a perpetual union" or "firm league of friendship" among the states, yet each remained sovereign and independent. They retained every right not expressly ceded by the document to the general government. A single agency of government, the Congress, was established. Although the number of delegates per state varied, each state had only one vote. The states were to supply money to operate the government and to fill quotas of troops when called upon. The Congress was expected to manage foreign affairs, to deal with matters pertaining to war, and to provide postal service. It might also borrow money, issue bills of credit, and determine the value of coins. It appointed naval officers and superior military officers, and it controlled Indian affairs. Three important powers that the Congress lacked were the authority to raise money directly, to enlist troops directly, or to regulate commerce. States also were forbidden to do certain things. They could not enter into treaties, confederations, or alliances; meddle in foreign affairs; or wage war without congressional consent unless invaded. On the other hand, every state was required to give free inhabitants of the other states all the privileges and immunities of their own citizens.

Most of the states ignored the opportunity to ratify this document. The small states feared they would be overwhelmed on the floor of the Congress by the large states. The larger states did not want to be restricted in any way, and they disregarded requests that they release unoccupied western land to the central government. Virginia in January 1781 broke the deadlock by agreeing to surrender its western territory northwest of the Ohio River. A few weeks later Maryland's ratification brought the Articles into force even though Virginia's offer was not made effective until 1784.

The Congress in 1780 recommended that Virginia, North Carolina, and Georgia surrender their western land. After considerable debate in the legislature as well as extensive public discussion, North Carolina, in October 1782, began to consider following Virginia's lead on several conditions advantageous to the state. One of these was that if a new state were formed in the released territory, a portion of the state's debt should be transferred to it. Both Virginia and North Carolina arranged to reserve western land to pay veterans' bonuses. Virginia took formal action in March 1784 to release its land, and North Carolina followed in April with certain "strings" attached. The ceded land was to be considered as a common source of benefit for all of the states, any state formed in the territory was to be "a distinct republican state" with the same rights and powers of other states in the union, and the offer terminated in a year if Congress did not accept its terms. In the meantime, North Carolina retained control of the land. Many state leaders protested that nothing was said about reducing the state's debt, so when the Assembly met in October (before the year granted Congress to make a decision had expired) this offer was repealed. North Carolina was criticized for withdrawing the option prematurely.

The State of Franklin

In the interval of about six months between the passage of the act of cession and its repeal, preliminary steps were taken in the western territory to organize the state of Franklin. This was one of a number of separatist movements among backcountry people that soon changed the character of the original confederation from a corporation of thirteen states into a flexible union capable of indefinite expansion. In that early process North Carolina contributed much in men and ideas.

Between 1769 and 1775, in direct violation of the Royal Proclamation of 1763, Daniel Boone led many groups of hunters and settlers on long expeditions through what became Tennessee and into Kentucky. Good land was the primary incentive. These new settlers were a great distance from the center of government in North Carolina and, of course, beyond any political control of the state. There was even some question as to whether they were within the bounds of North Carolina or Virginia territory. Talk of separation began and grew strong. By 1783 settlements on the Watauga and Holston rivers had expanded over the counties of Washington, Greene, and Sullivan, and even farther afield to Davidson County, all created by the North Carolina legislature between 1777 and 1783. This region was the home of the Over-Mountain Men who were so effective at the Battle of Kings Mountain. The cession act of April 1784 seemed to be virtually an invitation to form an independent government, and people beyond the mountains welcomed the prospect of being on an equal footing with their parent state. About the time news of North Carolina's action reached them, the settlers also learned that Congress had adopted an ordinance drawn up by Thomas Jefferson for creating new western states.

In August 1784 some citizens of Washington, Greene, and Sullivan counties laid the foundations for a new state by calling for the election of delegates to a convention. In December the convention met in Jonesboro, after North Carolina had repealed the offer to cede the territory, and decided to pursue their dream in spite of the state's action. Delegates from all four counties were heartily in favor of creating the state of Franklin and adopted a constitution virtually identical to North Carolina's. An early election was held, an assembly gathered, and in March 1785 John Sevier was chosen governor.

Meanwhile Governor Alexander Martin of North Carolina dispatched an influential negotiator to the region, but the people rejected his overtures for a peaceful redirection of their loyalty to North Carolina. The residents of Franklin cited offensive names that their former legislature had called them—"offscourings of the earth" and "fugitives from Justice"—virtually identical to those that Virginians had applied to the residents of Albemarle more than a century before.

Martin threatened to use force, though he probably was not certain that his militia would be willing to engage in battle with the sharpshooters across the mountains. Besides, North Carolina was bankrupt and could not afford the expense of a military expedition. Diplomacy was the governor's best weapon, and both he and his successor tried that device. When a special messenger from Franklin to the Congress could not obtain the support of Benjamin Franklin or other delegates, people in the region began to feel discouraged, and this played into the hands of the leaders of North Carolina. Although the Congress was sympathetic and, in fact, wanted the large states to release their land, there was nothing that could be done to force North Carolina to grant independence to the western counties. In January 1787 the Assembly in Fayetteville made overtures of peace, but they were rejected. The new governor, Richard Caswell, shrewdly offered Sevier's friend and ally, Evan Shelby, an appointment as brigadier general of the western district; he was tempted and accepted, thus starting a split among officials of Franklin.

Many people there had not supported the break anyway. There remained two sheriffs in each of the four counties, and one often broke up court sessions of the other. When North Carolina offered a remission of overdue taxes, Franklin had no choice but to make an identical offer, thereby denying itself tax revenues. Without revenue the western state could not long survive, and in the summer of 1787 North Carolina offered to forgive the rebellious leaders on its frontier. By then there was good evidence that a new federal government was in the making, so the western leaders were more willing to bide their time. On 3 March 1788 Sevier's term as governor expired and there was no legislature to elect a successor. The state of Franklin collapsed and the following year Sevier was elected to the North Carolina Senate in which he willingly served. It surely was with a sense of satisfaction that he saw the legislature the following year cede its western land to the new United States. In 1796 the state of Tennessee, much larger than the old state of Franklin but including all of its territory, was admitted to the Union.

The experience of North Carolina with the state of Franklin was watched with interest throughout the country. It contributed to the understanding of how the limited nation of thirteen states might expand. The county of Kentucky was agitating for separation from Virginia, as was the county of Vermont from New Hampshire. The early allegiance of Franklin to the Congress prompted other regions, ambitious for independence, to look to the Congress for assistance.

A New National Government

Weaknesses in the old Articles of Confederation were evident even before they were ratified, and the course of events under this loose government convinced leaders all the more that the powers of the central government had to be increased. Once again, Virginia took the lead and called a convention to meet in Annapolis, Maryland, in September 1786. Since it was expected to discuss trade and North Carolina enjoyed only limited trade, the state was not represented. Of the five delegates named by Governor Caswell only Dr. Hugh Williamson made an effort to attend, and he arrived after the convention had adjourned. From Annapolis, however, a call was issued for another convention to meet in Philadelphia the following May to review the general condition of the country and to take whatever steps might be necessary to make the Articles better serve the needs of the states. The actions of this new body were to be reported to the Congress and, if approved, to be submitted to the legislatures of the states for their reaction. With the approval of the states, the changes would take effect.

In North Carolina the legislature of 1786–87 reluctantly endorsed the proposal to revise the Articles, and on the final day of the session, 6 January 1787, it appointed Richard Caswell, Willie Jones, Alexander Martin, Richard Dobbs Spaight, and William R. Davie as delegates to the Philadelphia convention. Jones was opposed to the idea and declined to serve. Caswell was not well and stayed at home. Acting under the authority conferred on him by the Assembly, Caswell then named Hugh Williamson and William Blount to the vacancies.

Except for Martin, all of these delegates were strongly Federalistic; that is, they favored a strong central government. Williamson proved to be the most active member of the convention, speaking most frequently and serving on more committees. Williamson and Spaight were present from the time they reached Philadelphia until the convention adjourned, but Davie and Martin left early. Blount was present at the end but had been absent a great deal because he was also a member of the Congress in session in New York.

Willie (pronounced *Wiley*) Jones (1741–1801) held several colonial offices before represent-ing his county in the legislature during and after the American Revolution. He also served in the Continental Congress but refused appointment to the state's constitutional con-vention. An ardent believer in states' rights, he opposed ratification of the federal Con-stitution. (North Carolina Division of Archives and History, Raleigh)

Because of their social backgrounds and experience in public affairs, all five of the state's "founding fathers" in the Constitutional Convention were persuaded that the country required a stable government with power to enforce the rela-tions between one state and another and between the states and the central gov-ernment. They also recognized that there must be a government capable of defending the country from outside enemies.

With delegates from seven states present, the convention was organized on 25 May 1787. State legislatures chose sixty-five delegates but ten did not attend, and Rhode Island was never represented. By adjournment on 17 September, only thirty-nine had signed the document produced by the convention.

After the members settled down to business, Edmund Randolph of Virginia introduced some resolutions that were a surprise. Instead of suggesting revisions for the old Articles of Confederation, he presented a new plan for the delegates to work on. It contained provisions for legislative, executive, and judicial departments. The legislative branch would consist of two bodies: a House of Representatives (lower house), elected by the people; and a Senate (upper house), chosen by the lower house. The chief executive and members of the judicial branch—to consist of supreme and inferior courts—would be named by the legislative branch. Judges would serve during good behavior.[4]

Randolph's recommendations were discussed from late May until late June with the debate turning on the question of nationalization, which was favored by the large states but opposed by the small ones. North Carolina delegates sided with the large states. When Alexander Hamilton of New York moved that representation in the legislative branch be based on population, Richard Dobbs Spaight seconded the motion. Spaight also first suggested that members of the upper house be elected by the state legislatures, and as a result the convention rejected the election of the upper house by the House of Representatives.[5] North Carolina delegates were opposed to granting the president the power of veto, but when their wishes did not prevail Williamson suggested that all legislation be passed by a two-thirds vote. Williamson also was against permitting the legislative branch any power that would restrict the internal police power of the states.

The small states grew increasingly unhappy over the threat that the large states would be strong enough to force their will on the small ones. They opposed what was called the nationalizing process and made the question of representation in the upper house a test of strength, demanding equality of representation. A vote on the question resulted in a tie. North Carolina voted against equality. A committee of one delegate from each state was appointed to reach an agreement, with Davie representing his state. The committee reported in favor of equality and of counting blacks as three-fifths of a person in apportioning representation in the lower house.

The Constitutional Convention now faced a serious crisis. Several issues were

4. "Good behavior" in this context had nothing to do with the appointee's morals, character, or personal behavior. Rather, it applied to the soundness of his professional activity.

5. United States senators continued to be named by the General Assembly until the Seventeenth Amendment (1913) provided for the popular election of senators. Beginning in 1900 a Democratic primary was held to select nominees of that party in North Carolina, and the winners were "elected" by the legislature. The first popular election under the new amendment was held in 1914.

involved, but the main one was the equality of the states in the Senate versus representation based on population. Williamson objected to the committee's report favoring equality and held out in support of the interests of the large states. Nevertheless, when the question was put to a vote, North Carolina generously supported the compromise; Virginia and South Carolina were opposed and Georgia was divided. North Carolina's vote contributed toward keeping the convention in session, as the small states' delegates might have left if their cause had been lost.

An equally difficult question concerned the basis of representation in the lower house. A committee recommended a member for each 40,000 people, but commercial interests secured an amendment incorporating wealth in the formula. Williamson bitterly opposed this, and he was instrumental in its ultimate rejection by moving that the census, by which the apportionment would be made, should be limited to the free and slave populations. Although the antislavery interests were opposed to including slaves at all, South Carolina and Georgia demanded that blacks be counted equal to whites for this purpose. The three-fifths compromise by which five blacks were counted as equal to three whites, as suggested by a committee, was defended by Davie. Again North Carolina's vote in favor of this compromise was generous, for it would have been to the state's advantage to count every black in determining representation.

North Carolina favored a long term of office for the president, and, when the four-year term was finally adopted, it cast the only dissenting vote. The idea of impeachment was first suggested by Williamson, who moved—seconded by Davie—that the executive be removable by impeachment and conviction of malpractice or neglect of duty. (Many years later, the only president ever to be impeached was a native of North Carolina—Andrew Johnson—although he was not convicted.) Williamson also fixed the majority necessary to override the president's veto at two-thirds.

When the convention's work was finished, the new United States Constitution was signed on their state's behalf by William Blount, Richard Dobbs Spaight, and Hugh Williamson. As required by the legislation permitting the convention, its work was submitted to Congress where it was approved. The Constitution was then presented to the state legislatures for ratification or rejection.

Even before the convention adjourned many North Carolinians were aware of the main features of the new government. Small farmers and the poorer people generally distrusted a government with the power that this one obviously would have. Most eastern counties, however, favored it. After undergoing some readjustment in membership and redefining their objectives, the old factions came to be recognized as political parties. Many former conservatives came to be called Federalists; they liked the Constitution and believed that a strong, efficient federal government would protect property rights, stimulate trade, stabilize currency, and put the national credit on a sound basis. Their former concern for the whole continent made this change appropriate. The radicals, now called Anti-Federalists, opposed almost everything their opponents favored. They were strong believers in states' rights and wanted larger issues of paper money and more punishment for the Tories. Their former concern with local matters was in keeping with this approach.

Leaders of the Federalists were Davie, Williamson, Spaight, and James Iredell. Among the Anti-Federalists Willie Jones, Thomas Person, David Caldwell, Lemuel Burkitt, Samuel Spencer, and Timothy Bloodworth were most active. From Philadelphia Williamson wrote a friend at home urging him to do his best to see that men sympathetic to the Constitution were elected to the next General Assembly. The radicals also worked on behalf of their cause and, in fact, won the day. When the legislature met in November it called for the election of delegates to a convention that would decide the fate of the Constitution in North Carolina. This convention would meet in Hillsborough on 21 July 1788; and, to permit delegates to understand the new government, copies of the Constitution were ordered to be printed for public distribution.

The Federal Constitution Rejected

A vigorous campaign followed for the election of delegates to the Hillsborough convention. Among the candidates were the most able political leaders in the state. James Iredell presented the case for the Federalists and published several pamphlets in support of the Constitution. The Anti-Federalists found Willie Jones to be an effective leader. Although an aristocrat himself, he was an ultrademocrat and a believer in individualism. He was convinced that the new Constitution would ruin the poor through heavy federal taxes; moreover, he saw no security under the document for freedom of conscience. David Caldwell, the Presbyterian minister and teacher, and Thomas Person, another aristocrat but one who had sympathized with the Regulators, were also outspoken in their opposition. Lemuel Burkitt, a Baptist minister, preached sermons opposing a strong central government.

The Anti-Federalists were victorious statewide. They went to Hillsborough with 184 delegates, whereas the Federalists had only 84. When it organized, the convention selected Governor Samuel Johnston, a moderate Federalist, as president, but the sentiment of the majority was clear. Willie Jones promptly moved that a vote be taken; he saw no need to keep so many men away from their work when everyone already knew what the outcome would be. After Federalist James Iredell asked that the delegates remain to examine the document carefully and discuss it, Jones withdrew his suggestion.

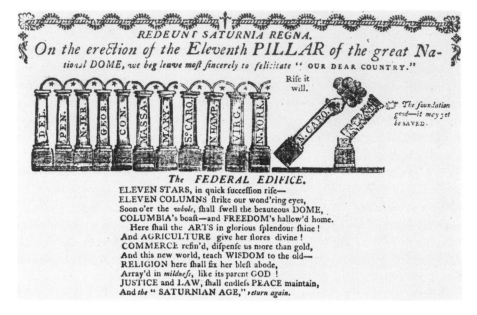

REDEUNT SATURNIA REGNA.

On the erection of the Eleventh PILLAR of the great National DOME, we beg leave most sincerely to felicitate " OUR DEAR COUNTRY."

Rise it will.

The foundation good—it may yet be SAVED.

The FEDERAL EDIFICE.

ELEVEN STARS, in quick fucceffion rife—
ELEVEN COLUMNS ftrike our wond'ring eyes,
Soon o'er the *whole*, fhall fwell the beauteous DOME,
COLUMBIA's boaft—and FREEDOM's hallow'd home.
  Here fhall the ARTS in glorious fplendour fhine!
And AGRICULTURE give her ftores divine!
COMMERCE refin'd, difpenfe us more than gold,
And this new world, teach WISDOM to the old—
RELIGION here fhall fix her bleft abode,
Array'd in *mildnefs*, like its parent GOD!
JUSTICE and LAW, fhall endlefs PEACE maintain,
And *the* " SATURNIAN AGE," *return again.*

North Carolina's hesitation in ratifying the Constitution prompted this cartoon in the Massachusetts *Centinel* of 2 August 1788. Not until November 1789 did North Carolina become the twelfth state to join the Union. Rhode Island, represented by the broken column, did not join until 29 May 1790. (Courtesy of The New-York Historical Society, New York City)

The strategy of the Anti-Federalists was to ask troublesome questions; to offer short, pointed criticisms; and to throw the burden of the discussion on the Federalists. Samuel Spencer on one side and James Iredell on the other were the main spokesmen. The Anti-Federalists objected to the establishment of a consolidated rather than a federal union; they objected to the implications of "We the People," and wanted to know why that phrase had been used instead of "We the States." They pointed out that the Treaty of Paris ending the American Revolution had cited each of the thirteen states separately, not the United States. In addition, they opposed the power of Congress to levy direct taxes, and they feared the power of what they foresaw as a host of federal officials far removed from any control by the electorate. They suspected future problems from the control of Congress over the election of federal officials, and they scented danger to the liberties of the people in a system of federal courts. And they wondered whether the impeachment clause would be applied to state as well as federal officials.

Their second fundamental objection was that, unlike their state constitution with its Declaration of Rights, this new document had no guarantees of personal and property rights—for example, a jury trial in federal courts was not guaranteed. In brief, they pointed out, there was no bill of rights.

The Federalists discussed all of these objections with considerable understanding and sympathy. They admitted that the Constitution might need amending, but they felt it would be best to adopt it first and amend it afterward. Despite the ability of the Federalists in debate, however, it appeared that Willie Jones was right when he said that their arguments changed not a single vote.

In the end, ratification was defeated by a vote of 184 to 84. By the same vote, the convention also resolved that a declaration of rights and certain amendments should be proposed and considered by Congress and the states before ratification by North Carolina. A recommended Bill of Rights and twenty-six amendments were then submitted to Congress and the other states. After a session of almost two weeks, the convention adjourned on 4 August leaving North Carolina out of the federal Union.

II

A JEFFERSONIAN
REPUBLIC

OR MORE THAN a year after its refusal to ratify the United States Constitution at Hillsborough, North Carolina remained outside the Union. Only the tiny state of Rhode Island had chosen the same course. Insofar as possible, however, North Carolina complied with the regulations of the national government. Movement of the citizens of other states into North Carolina was not hampered, for example, and customs duties were collected according to the federal schedule. The state, in fact, quite early anticipated becoming a member of the new nation.

By the end of July 1788 eleven states had ratified the Constitution, and the Congress resolved that steps be taken to implement it early the next year. Following elections, the first Congress under the new document would convene on the first Wednesday in March. Federalists in North Carolina lost no time in launching a vigorous campaign of education to reverse the decision of the Hillsborough convention. When the General Assembly met in November, members were deluged by a flood of petitions urging that a new convention be called to reconsider the decision not to ratify. Anti-Federalists were unable to slow the demand, and both houses, by large majorities, passed resolutions calling for a second convention to meet in Fayetteville on 16 November 1789.

In May 1789 the United States Congress began to consider amendments to the Constitution, and in June James Iredell and William R. Davie, at their own expense, published the debates of the Hillsborough convention. They had had the foresight to employ a reporter to take down its proceedings. In August, delegates were chosen to the Fayetteville convention. The Federalists won an easy victory, electing 195 out of 272 members.

The Federal Constitution Accepted

North Carolina's second constitutional convention organized in Fayetteville and, like its predecessor, elected Governor Samuel Johnston president. The debates of this convention were not published, as the thoroughness of the discussion in Hillsborough precluded the need for another report. Delegates had had ample opportunity to reflect upon what had already been said, and to make up their minds. On 21 November 1789, after a session of just six days (much of the time being spent on unrelated matters), the Constitution was ratified on behalf of North Carolina by a vote of 195 to 77.

It has been said that the state rejected the Constitution because it had no Bill of Rights, and that its final acceptance came only after the first ten amendments were added. This is not entirely correct, but it is possible that North Carolina's refusal to ratify was a kind of sacrificial offering to secure a Bill of Rights. The Anti-Federalists may have recognized that only a dramatic step such as this would draw attention in an effective way to so serious a defect.

When North Carolina called for a second convention in November 1788, the amendments had not even been proposed in Congress. Not until May 1789 did they come under discussion and not until September were they submitted to the states for ratification. When North Carolina consented to the Constitution in November 1789, not a single state had ratified the Bill of Rights. Although there was no doubt in the minds of most delegates that their former objections would soon be met, recommendations made by the Hillsborough convention for still further amendments were rejected by Congress. Because of its delay in joining the Union, North Carolina had no voice in selecting George Washington as the first president of the United States. The penultimate state to join, it was the last to withdraw from the Union in 1861.

For president, George Washington was the unanimous choice. A good general, though not a brilliant one, he was a poor speaker and knew little of the principles of government. Yet he was honest, fair-minded, dignified, and faithful to the liberty of America. He could command obedience, and both Federalists and Anti-Federalists trusted him. As president he could control the factions and his authority would be respected. People everywhere spoke of the "experiment" in government that was under way, and the personal character of the president was an important factor in its success. On 30 April 1789, in New York, he took the oath of office.

The new government faced countless problems. It had to address the needs not covered by the Articles of Confederation—a revenue law, for example. Many officers had to be appointed and federal courts created. The Revolutionary War debt had to be paid, commerce regulated, and some portions of the Treaty of Paris implemented. Foreign relations had to be defined by treaties and a site selected for a national capital.

North Carolina and Washington's Administration

Once North Carolina joined the Union, its citizens became eligible for appointment to federal offices. The first presidential appointee from the state was James Iredell, who was named to the Supreme Court by President Washington; he was confirmed by the Senate in February 1790. In those days members of the Court also rode the circuit, and Iredell wore himself out performing both duties. For a brief time his circuit lay in the small New England and central states, but afterward he served in the South where he had to ride farther, through more sparsely settled country and in places where public accommodations were rare. During his nine years of service, however, he maintained contact with family, friends, and colleagues through correspondence. Iredell's letters, which have been published, throw interesting light on events during this important period in American history.

The early phases of Washington's administration were marked by a decline in partisanship. All factions cooperated to make the experiment work. Two members of the president's cabinet, however, were at opposite poles in their views of the power and role of the new national government. Alexander Hamilton of New York, secretary of the treasury, believed in a strong, powerful central government in order to maintain the public credit, to hold the states and individuals together, and to gain respect abroad. He advocated government by "the rich and the well-born," somewhat on the order of the "deference democracy" that had existed in North Carolina at different times. Hamilton is said to have believed that government *for* the people was desirable, but government *by* the people would lead to weakness, insecurity, and anarchy. He felt that by loosely following the Constitution, a better government would result. Hamilton was a Federalist spokesman.

Thomas Jefferson of Virginia, secretary of state, held opposing views. In a true democracy, he maintained, self-government was the best government. Any mistakes the people made could be corrected, certainly more easily than those made by a dominant minority. A central government to Jefferson's liking would be one that safeguarded state and individual rights. He said that "the way to have a good and safe government is not to trust all to one, but to divide it among the many." War and peace, foreign relations, and matters affecting the nation as a whole should be the concerns of the federal government. Unlike Hamilton, he believed in a strict interpretation of the Constitution, under which the powers not turned over to the central government by the states would be reserved to the states. William Gaston of North Carolina, although he was a Federalist, later expressed the same views: "I owe no allegiance to any man or set of men on earth save only to the State of North Carolina, and, so far as she has parted with her sovereignty, to the United States of America." Jefferson's views were those of the

Anti-Federalists who soon came to be called Republicans. In time they became Democratic-Republicans and still later, Democrats.

Many Federalists in North Carolina—among them William R. Davie and Samuel Johnston—rejected the views of Hamilton and expressed opposition to the growing strength of the federal government. This was evident in 1790 when the North Carolina House of Commons refused to take an oath to support the federal Constitution. About the same time it also gave a vote of thanks to a state court of equity for refusing to obey a writ of the federal district court ordering the removal of a case from state to federal jurisdiction. And because the legislature chose the state's senators, it also frequently told them what actions to take and what bills to support—to oppose taxes, to repeal "monstrous salaries" paid to federal officeholders, and to report to the legislature when it was in session and to the governor at other times. The General Assembly clearly distrusted, feared, and perhaps even was jealous of the new government.

In 1793 Supreme Court Justice James Iredell had an opportunity to put in a good word for states' rights. In *Chisholm v. Georgia*, the heirs of Alexander Chisholm of South Carolina wanted to sue the state of Georgia for certain claims that Georgia refused to acknowledge. A majority of the Court ruled that a citizen of one state had the right to sue another state in federal court, but Iredell issued a dissenting opinion. Maintaining that the Constitution contained no such provision, Iredell held that states retained all powers that they had not specifically delegated to the federal government; he described the nature of the Constitution as a compact between sovereign states, referred to as the states' rights theory. This opinion was widely hailed by members of the Republican party and soon led to the adoption of the Eleventh Amendment, which deprived federal courts of jurisdiction in cases against one state by citizens of another.

On many occasions when they faced uncertain situations or detected strong opposition in Republican circles, the Federalists called upon President Washington to change the focus of their opponents. In the spring of 1790, between sessions of Congress, the president took a long trip through the northern states, and in the spring of 1791 he set off on a southern tour accompanied by an aide, Major William Jackson, and several servants. The first stage of the second jaunt took Washington to the Potomac River where he selected the site of the new national capital, in the region where he had grown up and not far from Mount Vernon, his home. Crossing Virginia, he entered North Carolina and visited the town of Halifax, the home of both the Federalist William R. Davie and the Anti-Federalist Willie Jones. Although he was the dinner guest of a group of local citizens headed by Colonel John Baptista Ashe, the congressman from the district, his reception there appears to have been mixed. Jones reportedly said he would not greet Washington as president but that he would welcome him as a soldier and a man. Thomas Person was quoted as previously having denounced

Washington as "a damned rascal and traitor to his country for putting his hand to such an infamous paper as the new Constitution." These were exceptional comments, of course, for Washington was much admired elsewhere. Since he was the foremost Mason in the country, Freemasons were usually involved in welcoming ceremonies. Enthusiastic crowds gathered in the towns and often could be seen along the road as he passed in his white carriage, equipped with venetian blinds and glass windows and pulled by four horses. A white riding horse, given to him by Emperor Frederick the Great of Prussia, was led behind the carriage for the president's use wherever he stopped.

From Halifax the presidential party moved to Tarborough (as it was then spelled). With their single piece of artillery, the local militia fired often and noisily in salute. Twenty-five miles farther along the president passed through Greenville, and after fourteen more miles en route to New Bern he stopped overnight at the Crown Point Inn, a popular place with most travelers. Washington, however, found it to be a "very indifferent house without stabling"; for the first time on his tour, his horses had to stand in the open throughout the night. Whether he realized it or not, this far south livestock often was not put up at night.

Proceeding toward New Bern, he soon was joined by a local company of mounted troops who rode along beside him. Entertained at a banquet and ball in Tryon Palace, the state capitol, he observed that it was "a good brick building but now hastening to ruin." A few days later he reached Wilmington where he was greeted by three volleys from each of fifteen guns, a much more proper salute for the Federalist president than Tarborough had been able to manage. Several old friends called on Washington in Wilmington and he probably enjoyed himself. Sailing down the Cape Fear River on a revenue barge, he visited Benjamin Smith before moving on to South Carolina and Georgia.

Returning north through the backcountry, Washington ate dinner in Charlotte at the home of General Thomas Polk which Lord Cornwallis had used as his headquarters during a brief stay during the war. Pushing on, he had Sunday dinner on 29 May with Colonel John Smith, a veteran of the Revolution, and at suppertime he stopped at the home of another veteran, Major Martin Phifer, about three miles west of the present city of Concord. In Salisbury he was joined by numerous officials and politicians. Ladies of the town invited him to have tea with them and he accepted; but when asked to step onto the front porch of his hotel so that more people could see him, he complained of the bright western sun, then setting, which blinded him.

From Salisbury the presidential party moved on to Salem where they were accommodated in the Salem Tavern, dined, and were entertained graciously. The exchange of formal addresses, private meetings, and occasions when music was played were all carefully described in the formal diary of the Moravians. Wash-

The Tavern at Old Salem in Winston-Salem. President George Washington, who spent the nights of 31 May–1 June 1791 here, recorded in his journal that he was pleasantly entertained by the Moravians. (North Carolina Division of Travel and Tourism, Raleigh)

ington lingered here an extra day to wait for the arrival of Governor Alexander Martin, with whom he conferred. On 2 June the president visited the site of the Battle of Guilford Court House and displayed considerable interest in studying the field. Soon afterward he set out for Virginia, crossing a corner of Caswell County and stopping for breakfast the next morning at the Gatewood family home near the state line.

The Continental Congress in 1783 asked the states to take a census, and the General Assembly of North Carolina in November 1784 issued instructions to that effect. This census survives in apparently complete form for twenty-four counties—the records are incomplete for eight counties and do not exist for nineteen. The United States Constitution provided that a census should be taken every ten years to determine the basis of representation in the House of Representatives. In 1789 Congress directed that the first census begin in August 1790 and be completed within nine months. In North Carolina this task was carried out by the deputy marshals, but they were not always reliable. George Washington wrote that it was "very inaccurately & Shamefully taken." In some cases the marshals relied on militia officers for information, and in others people avoided being listed altogether for fear that the census might be another means of increasing taxes. Many citizens simply refused to appear when asked by the census taker to report. In spite of its shortcomings, the census revealed that North Carolina had so many more people than had been estimated earlier to determine how many congressmen should represent the state that the number was increased from five to ten.

It was found that North Carolina was the third most populous state, exceeded only by Virginia and Pennsylvania. In Maryland, Virginia, South Carolina, and Georgia there were two whites to every slave, whereas in North Carolina the proportion was nearly three to one. The 1790 census listed the name of the head of every family, but beyond that it recorded only the number of males below and above age sixteen, the number of females, the number of slaves, and the number of other free persons attached to each household.

Although Federalists controlled the national government for the first dozen years of its existence, this was not the case in North Carolina. Of the first five governors after 1789, only two were Federalists and one of those became a Republican. Washington's southern tour revived interest in his party for a time but it declined before he retired from office. In fact, when Congress drafted a reply to Washington's Farewell Address, four congressmen from North Carolina voted against its adoption because it was "too adulatory." After 1798 Federalism in the state declined rapidly. The people had opposed much of that party's program, as well as national policy under its leadership and certain acts of Congress. The threat of war between France and England, into which the United States might be drawn, was removed and no longer unified the people. There was opposition to John Jay's treaty with England, ratified in 1795, and the retirement or death of Federalist leaders in the state further hastened its demise. As president, Thomas Jefferson retained a few of the state's Federalists in appointive positions outside the state to prevent them from influencing local politics—John Steele, named comptroller general, was one of them; and Davie, sent on a diplomatic mission to France, was another.

Rise of Republicanism

It has been said that Federalism defeated itself in North Carolina because it favored a strong central government. It relied on the propertied class, disregarded public sentiment, and expressed contempt for the common people. Historian Hugh T. Lefler concluded that "the state was Republican when state rights were threatened by extreme centralization; it was Federalist when the Union was threatened by extreme state rights doctrine."

The end of Federalism and the rise of Republicanism in North Carolina was further hastened by the arrival of Joseph Gales in 1799. A printer and newspaper editor in England, he was obliged to flee to America because of his outspoken sympathy with the working class. First settling in Philadelphia, where Congress was in session, he obtained employment as a shorthand reporter and soon began publishing a newspaper. His articles criticizing many aspects of Federalism attracted the attention of North Carolina congressmen who, of course, shared his views. When the national capital was moved to Washington, D.C., he sold his Philadelphia paper; within a short time it, too, moved to Washington as the *National Intelligencer*. North Carolina Republicans, particularly Congressman Nathaniel Macon, persuaded Gales to establish a partisan newspaper in Raleigh, the new state capital. Macon, from Warren County, entered Congress in 1791 and served until 1815 when he was elected to the Senate; he was Speaker of the House in the period 1801–7. As a devout member of the Republican party, Macon typified conservative North Carolinians. He supported economy in government, strict construction of the Constitution in favor of the states, and the interests of the masses. For more than thirty years he was the dominant personality in Congress and dispensed Republican patronage in North Carolina.

Joseph Gales's newspaper, the *Raleigh Register*, began publication on 22 October 1799 and quickly became the leading paper in the state. Republican leaders, who subsidized Gales, sent bundles of his newspaper to post offices across North Carolina for free distribution to readers. With Republicans in firm control of the state, Gales secured the state contract for printing. In time he also acquired an interest in the *National Intelligencer* and Joseph Gales, Jr., joined its staff. Soon young Gales, by express rider, was sending his father a copy of the Washington paper as soon as it came off the press, enabling the *Raleigh Register* to extract news from it and publish it ahead of others. Gales's paper molded and influenced public opinion in North Carolina as few other papers have been able to do.

The remaining Federalists in the state tried to counteract the effect of the Gales paper by bringing William Boylan and his *North Carolina Minerva* from Fayetteville to Raleigh, but this was ineffective. Although a few elderly Federalists survived, their party ceased to be of any concern to the growing Republican party. By 1815 it had disappeared as an organized party in the state.

In these late years of the eighteenth century, an event that occurred outside North Carolina was destined to have considerable influence in the state as well as elsewhere in the South. Eli Whitney, a native of Massachusetts, who for several years had been employed in Savannah, Georgia, patented the cotton gin in 1794. This significantly reduced the amount of time needed to separate the seed from the fiber of cotton and almost immediately created an enormous demand for the product. Compared to other southern states, there were few slaves in North Carolina, but the growing market for cotton for mills in the North worked a

The first use of a primitive cotton gin which preceded the improved gin patented in 1794 by Eli Whitney is depicted here. This labor-saving device, called an "engine" at first, relieved labor from the time-consuming and tiresome process of removing the seed from the fiber. It thereby increased the demand for cotton by northern mills and led to greater production of this one crop in the southern states and their dependence on slave labor. (North Carolina Collection, University of North Carolina at Chapel Hill)

change. Because cotton production required a great deal of labor, the number of slaves increased. In 1790 no cotton was exported from the United States; in 1794 only 1.5 million pounds were exported, but in 1795 the amount jumped to 5 million pounds.

Until the demand for this staple proved to be overwhelming, it appeared that North Carolina might develop a balanced economy. Agricultural production grew apace with the expansion of areas of settlement, and home industries such as spinning and weaving and the making of hats flourished. About 1813 Michael Schenck built North Carolina's first cotton mill near Lincolnton; soon afterward more than 40,000 looms, widely scattered in the state, produced more than 7 million yards of cloth—exceeding that manufactured in Massachusetts.

In 1800 Thomas Jefferson was elected president, serving from 1801 until 1809. Thereafter, although nominally in power, the Republican party broke up into sectional factions rather than remaining a genuine, united party. Under its long leadership, however, there was a slow broadening of the suffrage, a growing democratizing of local life, a new interest in humanitarian reform, and, after the War of 1812, the appearance of a nationalistic spirit. With growing regional interest in such national questions as the tariff, the Second United States Bank, and internal improvements, a new and logical alignment within the Republican party began to occur. "National" and "Democratic" Republicans developed, and within a short time they evolved into the Whig and Democratic parties.

One of the last strongholds of Federalism in the state was the University of North Carolina. Its charter created a self-perpetuating board of trustees, and since like begets like that body changed little in political orientation over the years. Republicans charged that non-Federalists were dismissed from the faculty, that anti-Republican books were used, and that the young men of the state lost their Republican principles after a stay in Chapel Hill. President Joseph Caldwell denied these charges, but members of the General Assembly were unconvinced and eliminated two sources of income that had supported the institution. In 1789 the Assembly had allotted escheats (land, money, personal property, or other goods for which no legitimate owner could be found) to the university together with unsold confiscated land. The legislature of 1800 removed both of these, eliciting loud protests from Federalists. An attempt to reverse that decision at the next session failed, but the trustees were permitted to hold a lottery to raise funds for the university. This met with little success, and in 1804 another effort to regain escheats miscarried as did a bill to tax carriages for the institution's benefit.[1]

North Carolina's attack on its university was criticized around the country. Even the *National Intelligencer* expressed its regret and pointed out how much more generously South Carolina and Georgia supported their young colleges. One observer commented that "friends of science in other states regard the people of North Carolina as a sort of Semi-Barbarian." William R. Davie noted that in South Carolina "a professorship is more eagerly canvassed for than a Secretaryship in the Government of the United States."

The trustees were obliged to take the matter to court. In 1804, in the case of *University v. Foy* dealing with confiscated land, the court ruled that the creation of the university had been the result of action by the people assembled in a constitutional convention. A convention was superior to a legislature, and the legislature could not deprive the university of its support. The court pointed out that "the right to education," which the people secured in the convention, was beyond the control of the legislature. Escheats were restored to the university, but the legislature (like Parliament after the repeal of the Stamp Act) felt that it somehow had

---

1. This bill must have been introduced with a certain sense of humor, as carriages were associated with the wealthier class. A tax on such vehicles undoubtedly would have affected more Federalists than Republicans.

to demonstrate its authority. Accordingly, it altered the university's charter to make the governor, who was himself a creature of the legislature, chairman of the board of trustees, and to empower the legislature to fill vacancies on the board. At the same session of the General Assembly, fifteen additional trustees were elected. The university was now protected against "aristocracy." Perhaps still dissatisfied, legislators denied an appropriation to complete the main [South] building on the campus. As a result, the trustees made personal contributions for that purpose. In 1809 the legislature came to the aid of the struggling university by permitting the trustees to recover certain escheats together with all debts due the state from before 31 December 1799. Both proved to be productive, and, although the Republicans were not noted for their generosity to the university, the legislature ceased to penalize it.

In most respects the Republican legislature was very economical, demonstrating a reluctance to tax the people for any purpose. The governor's salary was set at £800 when he was first required to reside in Raleigh, and it was not changed for many years. The house provided for him was not properly maintained and became so nearly uninhabitable that Governor Benjamin Smith said it was not "fit for the family of a decent tradesman." He threatened to return home to New Hanover County, but in 1813 the erection of "a convenient and commodious dwelling house" was approved.

Money and Banking

A serious problem facing the state when it joined the Union was the large quantity of inflated currency still in circulation. Some had recently been redeemed through the sale of land certificates and by a property tax. Money received from these two sources was simply removed from circulation by the state. A more effective method over the long run was the use of dividends from bank stock. The first banks established in the state were the Bank of Cape Fear and the Bank of New Bern, both chartered in 1804 as private banks. Their combined capital was $450,000, and the state reserved the right to subscribe for 250 shares in each bank.

There was immediate evidence that these institutions had a beneficial effect on business and commerce. They paid promising dividends, and their notes, on paper with silk threads in it, were so well received that the state in 1807 subscribed for all the shares reserved for it. But when the banks yielded to temptation and began to recirculate old state currency, the state levied a tax on bank stock and restricted the amount in notes that the banks could issue. Violation of the latter might result in cancellation of their charter. In 1810, the state decided to go into the banking business itself and created the State Bank of North Carolina.

The central bank was in Raleigh, with branches in Edenton, New Bern, Wilmington, Fayetteville, Tarboro, Salisbury, and Milton. The result was two-fold: the state was able to remove the old currency from circulation by receiving dividends in that form, and the State Bank proved to be a boon to business in those areas that it served. The very profitability of bank stock, however, was unfortunate. It deterred the legislature from establishing a more secure tax base which, in turn, prevented the state from providing essential services for the people. In the long run, this contributed to the general decline of the state.

In addition to concern over old currency, the young state faced a problem on its frontier created by white encroachment on Indian land. This was further compounded by the presence of traders, Indian agents, and missionaries. After suffering a crippling defeat by American forces in the Revolutionary War, the Cherokee Indians were confined by treaties to a small area in the southern Appalachians. With reduced hunting grounds, the Indians began to change their life-style by living a more settled life on small farms. Traders and Indian agents helped to introduce them to many of the comforts enjoyed by whites. The legislature abandoned the directive of the Royal Proclamation of 1763 prohibiting settlement beyond the crest of the Blue Ridge—leading to bloodshed on both sides. In 1776 John ("One Eye") Davidson was killed west of the Cherokee boundary determined by Governor Tryon in 1767; and when, in the fall of the next year, pioneer settler Samuel Davidson constructed a cabin at the foot of Jones Mountain near the Swannanoa River, the Cherokees promptly murdered him.

Acting on behalf of North Carolina in November 1785, United States commissioners negotiated a treaty with the Cherokees to establish a new boundary between whites and Indians. The main valley of the French Broad was left to the Cherokees, but land along the Swannanoa nearly to the site of Asheville and in the Toe River country was opened to whites. This included all or most of present Yancey, Mitchell, Avery, Madison, and Buncombe counties. This process was repeated many times over the next half century, and the Indians gradually lost nearly all of their ancestral land.

On one occasion the question was raised as to whether land released through the offices of federal commissioners then belonged to the United States or to North Carolina. The courts ruled that the commissioners only acted on behalf of the state, and that the state was free to dispose of the land.

The "Walton War"

An interstate clash in 1804 on the poorly defined frontier between North Carolina and Georgia, but also involving South Carolina, precipitated the "Wal-

Table 11-1. Indian Land Released by Treaty

Year	Square Miles
1777	4,414
1785	550
1791	722
1798	587
1819	1,542
1835	1,112

ton War." The site lay in or at least adjacent to the land ceded to the national government by the three states. Each of the states had granted land there to settlers though none knew for certain where the state line was. In this "Orphan Strip" about twelve miles wide, settlers far removed from any state authority held community meetings for their own well-being. Thinking that they were in Georgia, the area's approximately 760 white and 40 black residents petitioned that state for protection. When the Georgia legislature created Walton County in 1803, officials in Buncombe County, North Carolina, objected. They denied the validity of Georgia land grants, demanded taxes and militia service of the residents, and protested the suspected presence of land speculators.

As a result of the dispute, there were instances of armed conflict, militia from the two states fought, houses were burned, and general "bandittey," as one resident wrote, prevailed. Appeals by Georgia for congressional intervention were unsuccessful. Meanwhile North Carolina strongly maintained that the thirty-fifth parallel of north latitude was the proper boundary between the two states, and the line was surveyed several times. Georgia was reluctant to accept the surveyors' findings until 1807, when commissioners from the two states came to an agreement. Not until 1810, however, after Georgia had conducted its own survey, did its protests cease. North Carolina's claims were sustained.

In 1835 it became federal policy to move the Indians from the eastern United States to a reservation across the Mississippi River. General Winfield Scott in 1838 was sent into the southern Appalachian Mountains with a contingent of troops to force the Indians' removal to the Oklahoma region. Thousands were rounded up and herded along "The Trail of Tears" in the winter of 1838–39. Nearly a fourth of them died, but a few led by Tsali (called "Charley" by whites) escaped. In return for Tsali's surrender, his followers were permitted to remain; Scott ordered him and his sons to be shot by captive Cherokees. This program of removal has been termed "one of the most infamous incidents" perpetrated by the United States against Indians.

War of 1812

In the early nineteenth century North Carolinians were aware of England's continued friendly relations with the Indians on the frontier. Outposts in Canada stocked guns and ammunition with which they supplied the Indians. England's provocation of America increased between 1793 and 1812 when England and France were at war. Both nations disregarded the rights of neutrals and stopped American ships on the high seas in search of their own nationals who might be evading military service. For example, in 1807 a British ship fired on an American ship, boarded her, and removed four sailors, three of whom were Americans. Attempts to negotiate these differences with England failed, but in time France ceased this practice. The Embargo Act of 1807 halting all but coastwise trade harmed the United States more than it did England or France, and it was repealed after two years. Subsequently a nonintercourse act prohibited trade with the offending nations, but it was generally ineffective. President James Madison finally recommended that preparations be made for war.

The War of 1812 had little effect on North Carolina except that people were divided in their support. Many said that the United States had withstood the insults of England and France for years, and that no new incidences had occurred; others agreed that the freedom of the seas should be defended. The North Carolina press also had divergent opinions, some newspapers endorsing the war and others condemning it. Some of the state's congressmen supported the president; others rejected his call for assistance. Recruiting teams found men of Scottish descent, as we have seen, eager to serve, while others held back. Nevertheless, the state contributed several important heroes to the war.

The president's wife, Dolley Payne Madison, was a native of North Carolina. In Washington, as the British were entering the city from the opposite direction, she delayed her departure from the Executive Mansion long enough to collect the presidential silver and executive papers, and to cut a portrait of George Washington from its frame. These she threw into the foot of the carriage in which she and the president escaped before the British burned the residence. Later the blackened walls were painted white and the mansion became known as the "White House."

Benjamin Forsyth of Stokes County was a lieutenant colonel in the army in 1814, when he distinguished himself along the northern border. He was killed at Odelltown in Canada and, like General Francis Nash in the American Revolution, he came to be regarded as a hero. The state presented a handsome sword to his eight-year-old son and awarded him $250 a year for seven years.

Otway Burns of Onslow County was a ship captain and a shipbuilder. During the conflict, as a licensed privateer operating up and down the Atlantic coast, he brought in large quantities of supplies useful in the war effort.

Dolley Payne Madison (1768–1849), a native of Guilford County and wife of President James Madison, became a national heroine during the War of 1812 by saving the presidential silver, papers from her husband's office, and a portrait of George Washington from almost certain destruction by the British. (North Carolina Division of Archives and History, Raleigh)

In recognition of the services and sacrifice made by Captain Johnston Blakeley (1781–1814) during the War of 1812, the North Carolina General Assembly gave his young daughter this silver tea service and provided funds for her education. After her early death the silver passed into the family of her husband, a Danish nobleman. In 1968, it was purchased by citizens of the state and given to the North Carolina Museum of Art in Raleigh. (North Carolina Division of Archives and History, Raleigh)

Captain Johnston Blakeley lived in Wilmington and in Pittsboro; after attending the University of North Carolina, he began a naval career. As the commander of several warships he sailed boldly around England capturing and destroying British shipping. On the last occasion, after seizing a valuable cargo and placing a prize crew aboard to take it to the United States, he sailed east. Soon smoke was seen on the horizon but the fate of Blakeley and his ship was never determined. The General Assembly gave his young daughter a handsome silver tea service and provided funds for her education. She later married a Danish nobleman but left no descendants. Eventually the tea service was offered for sale; it was bought by a group of North Carolinians and presented to the state.

A final Tar Heel hero was General Andrew Jackson, a native of the Waxhaw region along the North Carolina–South Carolina border. He read law in Salisbury and was licensed to practice in the state, living in Greensboro for a time before moving west to Tennessee. In the War of 1812 he became the hero of the Battle of New Orleans, where he won a great victory with few American losses. Because of the long time it took for messages to cross the Atlantic, this battle was fought after the terms of peace had been agreed upon. Ironically, a similar delay was responsible for the war itself: England withdrew its orders to search American ships before Congress declared war, but no one knew of the directive in time.

The War of 1812, which lasted more than three years, settled almost nothing. The British no longer stopped American ships, of course, but neither Canada nor Florida was taken by the United States as many people had anticipated. On the other hand, General Jackson's campaign in the South shattered England's standing among the Indians and opened large tracts of land in Georgia and Alabama to white settlement.

12

A STATE ASLEEP

D URING THE FIRST HALF of the nineteenth century North Carolina seemed unaware of much that was going on anywhere, even within its own boundaries. Most people in the eastern section of the state were satisfied with their social, economic, and political conditions. Their voice prevailed in the government, and they were content to do little or nothing for the improvement of the whole state. Citizens in the interior were even more isolated by the lack of roads and other means of communication. They were self-sufficient, producing only what was absolutely necessary and not missing luxuries they had never known. It seldom crossed their minds that the government might take steps to improve their lot in life. When people from other states became aware of conditions in North Carolina, they began to refer to it as the "Rip Van Winkle State."

The State's Dismal Outlook

In 1819 a North Carolina lawyer and legislator, Archibald DeBow Murphey, observed that throughout the nation the War of 1812 had brought "admittance to liberal ideas"; however, he asserted, this was certainly not true of his own state, for no state in the Union at that time was less receptive to liberal ideas than North Carolina. Earlier, in 1786, a traveler who journeyed from Edenton to Charlotte had said that no state had done as little as North Carolina to promote education, science, and the arts. The mass of people, he found, were "in a state of mental degradation." Murphey pointed out that in 1792 only three schools in the state offered the basic elements of a classical education that would prepare a student for higher education. In 1826, the semicentennial year of the Declaration of Independence, Governor Hutchins G. Burton told state lawmakers that many people believed it was more difficult to obtain a primary education in North Carolina then than it had been in 1776.

One reason for these inadequacies was the failure of the type of school the members of the Fifth Provincial Congress seem to have had in mind when they wrote the Forty-first Article of the state constitution (requiring that the legislature establish "a School or Schools") in 1776. They relied on local academies, 42 of which had been chartered by 1800. By 1835, 135 more had been added to the list with at least one in each county except Ashe, Columbus, and Person. The academy was primarily a boys' institution; of the 177 chartered before 1835, only 13 admitted girls. Few prospered because the legislature declined to extend state aid to enable the masters "to instruct at low Prices," as the constitution directed. An academy could be created only through local initiative, just as local interest was needed to maintain the building, employ a teacher, plan a program, and in many cases provide convenient accommodations for children who lived too far away to walk to daily classes. Although the charter might require free tuition for a limited number of poor scholars, many needy families were too proud to take advantage of this opportunity. The burden of tuition made the academy available only to those of at least moderate means.

In 1810 Thomas Henderson, editor of a Raleigh newspaper, *The Star*, adopted a new means of gathering data from a broad spectrum of people. He prepared an interesting questionnaire which he sent to leading citizens in each county, and from their replies he reported on conditions in the state. For example, before the University of North Carolina opened in Chapel Hill, he knew of no one who had left Edgecombe County to attend college or an academy. A third of the people in the county could not read, and only about half the men and a third of the women could write. Out of a population of over 8,000, only 108 subscribed to a newspaper. From Caswell County it was reported that fewer than half the people could "read, write and cypher," and "many of the inferior class of society appear more depraved than ever." There was only one academy in the county, where between 1805 and 1810 enrollment dropped from 65 to 38. Henderson's informant, Bartlett Yancey, admitted that his native county had never been distinguished for its great men, but he seemed to take perverse pride in the fact that it had a large number "entitled to the rank of mediocrity." He also found satisfaction in the fact that everyone then living in the county was a native, and that "we have no spreeing Irishmen, revolutionizing Frenchmen, or speculating Scotchmen among us." Yancey perhaps unwittingly put his finger on the greatest obstacle to the development of North Carolina up to that time: its contentment with the role of mediocrity.

Similar conditions prevailed in the state as a whole. In 1810 another correspondent of the *Star* said that he knew of only twenty academies and grammar schools in operation in the entire state. The University of North Carolina, after fifteen years of precarious existence, "deserted and frowned upon by the Legislature," attracted only sixty-five students. Six years later Archibald Murphey said that elementary education in the state, in large measure, was left to chance and that as a result thousands were growing up in total ignorance.

In 1838 the chairman of the state senate Committee on Education reported that "there is an average of nearly one-half in every family of the state who have received no education and who are as yet unprovided with the means of learning even to read and write." President Joseph Caldwell of the university had good cause to say, in 1832, that North Carolina was many, many years behind the other states in the education of its children. A careful estimate made in the same year placed the number of illiterate children in the state between ages five and fifteen at 120,000. The federal census of 1840 revealed the humiliating fact that, after more than sixty years of independence, one-third of the adult white population of North Carolina could neither read nor write.

From 1790 to 1802 not a single bill relating to public education was introduced in the General Assembly. In 1802 a plan for establishing a military school was rejected and the following year two bills for the creation of public academies were killed. From 1804 to 1814 the subject was not even mentioned in the legislature. Despite the fact that every governor except one between 1800 and 1825 urged legislators to establish schools, committees on education were not appointed until 1815. The following year Murphey began a period of agitation for the creation of an effective system of public education that belatedly bore fruit.

Causes of Backwardness

North Carolina was unprogressive in large measure because of the individualism that characterized most of its people. Isolation bred individualism, of course, and the people were conservative and provincial. Prejudice and superstition were widespread. Ignorance always tends to perpetuate itself, and so the attitude prevailed that "what was good enough for grandpa is good enough for us and our children." This certainly eliminated any pressure on the legislature for expensive public services, and those in control of that branch of the government, sensitive to their own pocketbooks, were reluctant to suggest any changes. Economy was the rule of the day.

Referring to public schools, President Caldwell commented that legislative habits were old ones and that providing for education had never become habit-forming. He recognized that the philosophy of individualism was strongly developed in North Carolina and that it was an obstacle to progress in every field. The people of the state, he pointed out, disliked any law that placed even the slightest restraint on them. A system of public schools would involve two compulsory measures: taxation and attendance. Both would regulate individual action, and that fact alone meant that such a system would be resisted.

Hand in hand with individualism went a narrow view of the proper function of government. It was considered at best to be a necessary evil, and its functions were extremely limited. Any government had done all it was supposed to do, most North Carolinians assumed, when it had (1) maintained order, (2) protected life, and (3) safeguarded the rights and interests of property. The eastern majority, tightly holding the reins of government, felt very much the same way—either through sincere conviction or for financial reasons. Education, to be sure, was a good example of something with which the government should not concern itself. This was a private matter. The state, it was widely believed, had no moral right to tax one person's property to educate another person's child. President Caldwell related that he had heard some express the belief that "Taxation is contrary to the genius [spirit] of a Republican Government." Those holding such views were confident that government had carried out its duties when it had preserved order, punished crime, and kept down the tax rate.

There also were significant economic reasons for North Carolina's backwardness. As an agricultural state, it had little industry, limited commerce, and inadequate banking. Most families were self-sustaining and had little available cash. With the smallest per-capita wealth of any state in the nation, North Carolina spokesmen insisted that the state was too poor to consider any progressive action. Forward-looking people, however, responded that the state was poor because the people were ignorant. They cited the vast natural resources at hand waiting to be developed under intelligent direction. Improvements in agriculture, the establishment of mills and factories, and the development of trade all awaited the education of the masses. It was such leaders as these who began to present a twofold program of education and internal improvements for the state.

A serious stumbling block to public education, or any other significant program for that matter, was the existence of Negro slavery. Slaveholders instinctively felt that public education and slavery were irreconcilable. They were more concerned about the "peculiar institution" of slavery than almost anything else. As a class they could see to the education of their own children, and on the whole they opposed the education of the masses. They definitely did not want their slaves taxed to provide revenue for public schools. Laws prohibiting the education of slaves encouraged the belief that laborers generally did not need an education. Education, someone said, would merely make the working class discontented with the state in life to which it had pleased God to call them. Another observer wondered, if everyone were educated, "who will do the *work* of the world?"

Some of the economic evils of slavery are obvious. It consumed capital that might otherwise have been used to develop industry and improve agriculture. Between 1815 and 1850, the value of slave property increased 157 percent, whereas the value of land increased only 12.5 percent. Because slaves were found to be most profitable in the production of cotton and tobacco, food crops were neglected. Millions of dollars were spent outside the state for foodstuffs as well as for all kinds of manufactured goods. At the railroad depot in Raleigh, Paul

Cameron of Orange County once saw hay imported from the North being unloaded for stock in town as well as for use in the country. He also commented that butter from Orange County, New York, was being sold in Orange County, North Carolina.

Slave labor was responsible for certain rural practices that made it more profitable to abandon an old field and clear a new area rather than to fertilize the old one. Much abandoned land quickly eroded and was useless for a long time. This procedure took a heavy toll of much good woodland, and the timber itself was often burned instead of being used or marketed. Loss of the West Indies trade after the American Revolution and heavy taxes levied in Great Britain on imports from the United States reduced the demand for lumber and other products.

Farm Conditions and Migration

In time farmers came face-to-face with a future so bleak that, in the words of one of them, they must either "move, improve, or starve." Sad to say, conditions never became quite bad enough to force any widespread corrective action. Many large slaveholders, however, sold their land and moved to the Old Southwest. This migration began in the late 1820s and reached a climax in the 1830s. Very few planters made any attempt to improve their land or to preserve its fertility. Although there is no record that any actually starved, many continued to eke out a bare existence on their constantly eroding land. Between 1815 and 1833 the assessed value of land dropped from an average of $2.04 per acre to $1.54.

Contributing to this bleak situation was the lack of adequate transportation and communication. Few of the rivers were suitable for boats or rafts, and roads were deficient and poorly maintained. Bridges were rare, fords were dangerous, and floods were common. Governor John Motley Morehead in 1842 told the General Assembly that it cost a farmer one-half of his crop to get the other half to market. As a result, few farmers grew more than was needed for their own use.

These conditions persuaded many families to leave North Carolina. Between 1815 and 1850 one-third of the people emigrated. Archibald Murphey estimated in 1815 that 200,000 natives of the state had moved to Tennessee, Alabama, and Ohio. He observed that "thousands of our wealthy and respectable citizens are annually moving to the West in quest of that wealth which a rich soil and commodious navigation never fail to create in a free state, while thousands of our poorer citizens follow them, being literally driven away by the prospect of poverty." Between 1830 and 1840, thirty-two of the sixty-eight counties lost population. The increase for the state as a whole was a mere 2.5 percent. The census of 1850, for the first time, gave statistics on interstate migration. It revealed the amazing fact that 31 percent of all native North Carolinians then living in the

United States resided in some other state. North Carolina's indifference to education, neglect of resources, resistance to taxation for *any* purpose, and general backwardness had driven away 405,161 people, two-thirds of whom were white. Of this number 58,000 moved to the free states of the Middle West, undoubtedly to escape the evils of slavery. Between 1816 and 1890, 163 natives of North Carolina served in the General Assembly of Indiana alone. Others were newspaper editors, state officials (treasurer and governor), lawyers, teachers, and railroad officials.

Economic Conditions and Sources of Revenue

North Carolina's declining economy was, of course, reflected in the state treasury, whose dire condition could be attributed to the widespread aversion to taxation. Taxes on land and a poll or head tax were the most stable sources of revenue, yet the land tax rarely yielded as much revenue as the poll tax; with the decline in population, revenue from the poll tax also declined. As the legislature continually sought new sources of revenue to relieve the land tax, it came to depend on a schedule of miscellaneous taxes on such things as licenses for peddlers, brokers, slave traders, shows, and the like; as well as taxes on stores, billiard tables, gates, carriage wheels, cotton gins, and bank stock. In 1830 these assorted taxes produced 41 percent of the total revenue of the state.

As long as bank stock was productive, the state's investment in banking provided income. For a time public land was also a source of revenue; however, because the state provided no public services, the demand—beyond salaries for legislators and public officials—was modest.

Political Conditions

A final flaw contributing to the decline of North Carolina can be explained by political conditions that developed after 1776. The state constitution placed political power in the least progressive section of the state and among its most conservative people. Once the Revolution was over and there ceased to be a reason for wholehearted cooperation between the sections and among people of diverse interests, differences began to appear. While the state government was a representative democracy in form, it was not so in practice. Representation in the General Assembly was not based on population since each county—regardless of size, wealth, or population—had two members in the House of Commons and one senator. Moreover, the colonial borough towns, most of which were in the east, still had their representatives.

Voting and officeholding were the privileges of property. No man could vote for a state senator unless he owned fifty acres of land. However, all free men, even blacks before 1835, who paid taxes were eligible to vote for members of the lower house. To serve in the House of Commons one had to own one hundred acres of land, while a senator had to own three hundred acres. Governors had to hold property valued at £1,000. All state officials before 1835, including the governor, were appointed, and the government was tightly controlled by the landowning interests. The strength of this class was in the east, and for more than fifty years this section dominated state politics.

Initially no inconsistency was envisioned in the machinery of government, and in the ordinary course of events there would have been none. In 1790 roughly 62 percent of the people in the state lived east of Wake County. Fifty years later only 49.5 percent did. The population of the east increased only 53 percent during that half century, but the west increased 156 percent. It was expected that, as the backcountry filled up, new counties would be created and entitled to representation in the Assembly. The east, however, early recognized this potential threat to its dominance and prevented the creation of new counties.

Frequently, in attempting to get new counties established, the west would propose that they be named after popular living eastern leaders in the hope of receiving support from their friends and admirers in the east. This is why *Ashe* County was named in honor of Samuel Ashe of New Hanover County; *Buncombe*, in honor of Colonel Edward Buncombe of Tyrrell; *Cabarrus*, in honor of Stephen Cabarrus of Chowan; *Haywood*, in honor of John Haywood formerly of Edgecombe but a resident of Wake when the county was formed; *Iredell*, in honor of James Iredell of Chowan; and *Macon*, in honor of Nathaniel Macon of Warren.

When the east was forced to yield, as it sometimes was, it tried to offset the effect of the new western county in the legislature by dividing an old eastern county. This is why there are so many small eastern counties. Occasionally when an eastern member of the legislature voted to create a western county, he was never again elected to the General Assembly because he had "betrayed" his section. On the other hand, when a legislator pleased his section he might expect to retain his seat for a very long time. Between 1777 and 1823 thirty-three new counties were created. Of these, eighteen were in the west and fifteen in the east. In spite of the fact that the west surpassed the east in population, the east retained its control over state government. In 1830, for instance, there were sixty-four counties in the state; thirty-six of these were east of Raleigh and contained only 41 percent of the voting population. Nevertheless, they elected 59 percent of the members of the General Assembly.

The voting population of the eastern counties was less than 10 percent of the *total* white population of the state, yet it elected a majority of the legislators by whom the laws were made and the governor and other state officials were chosen. Fifty-nine years passed from the inauguration of Richard Caswell in 1777 to the retirement of Richard Dobbs Spaight II in 1836, the last governor elected under the 1776 constitution. During that time, twenty-four men served as governor; only six of them were from western counties, and they served a total of only fifteen years. The eighteen governors from eastern counties served a total of forty-four years. The east thus controlled all the branches of state government.

This government was not only undemocratic in form; it was also undemocratic in spirit. Since all state officials were elected by the legislature, and since that branch of government was controlled by the landed aristocracy, *property* not people controlled the government. The most important kind of property was land and slaves, and the class that owned this property was ultraconservative. Living on their plantations supported largely by slave labor, satisfied with their easy, patriarchal existence, these planters and large farmers assumed a patronizing attitude toward the great mass of citizens whom they called "the common people." They encouraged the majority to look to them for leadership in another instance of "deference democracy." Those in charge strenuously opposed granting "the common people" any more political power, or giving state aid to improve their material, intellectual, or social well-being. Able to provide for their own needs in these areas, they could hardly be expected to release their hold on government.

In the west, conditions were quite the opposite. Most of the residents were farmers of small tracts of red clay land, which often was not very fertile, and who were far removed from a market for their produce. Social life in the west was more democratic than that in the east. Out of this democratic social system came the first demand for public schools. There the rivers were better suited to provide power for manufacturing and that required adequate transportation. Once again the need for education and internal improvements united and formed an important goal of westerners.

The sectional bias of eastern leaders became apparent when the legislature in 1813 rejected a bill calling for an *ad valorem* land tax. A tax based on the value of land, rather than—as in the case of the colonial quitrent—on a flat rate per acre which the recent "specific tax" provided, was favored by the west but opposed by the east. Even a modest increase per acre under the old scheme was rejected. Westerners began to unite in their concern over their treatment by the east. A bill they introduced in the House of Commons calling for a constitutional convention was defeated by a clear sectional vote. About the same time the people of the west became aware of the proposals being made by Archibald Murphey, a legislator from Orange County.

13

THE VISION OF
ARCHIBALD D. MURPHEY

A SMALL GROUP of North Carolinians who were deeply concerned about the unsavory reputation of their state across the nation between 1815 and 1840 not only eliminated its causes but also set the state on a totally new course. The leaders of this movement included Bartlett Yancey, Joseph Caldwell, Charles Fisher, David L. Swain, William Gaston, John Motley Morehead, and William A. Graham. But foremost was Archibald DeBow Murphey. As a representative of Orange County in the North Carolina Senate from 1812 until 1818, he championed a system of public education, internal improvements, and constitutional reform. Reflecting on events during his own public career, former governor William A. Graham in 1860 wrote that it was Murphey who "inaugurated a new era in the public policy of this State" and left to posterity "the noblest monuments of philosophic statesmanship to be found in our public archives since the days of the Revolution."

Murphey's Preparation for Leadership

Murphey was born in Caswell County about 1777 and attended David Caldwell's school at what is now Greensboro. He was graduated with distinction from the University of North Carolina in 1799 and remained in Chapel Hill for two years as a tutor and professor of ancient languages while also studying law in Hillsborough. In 1801 he qualified for the bar and soon began to practice law in Hillsborough. From 1818 to 1820 he was a superior court judge and frequently acted as a special justice of the supreme court when it heard cases in which one of the three regular justices had been counsel or on the lower bench during litigation leading to the appeal. He also edited three volumes of reports on cases heard between 1804 and 1819. Among his many additional occupations, Murphey became the owner of a gristmill and a country store in Orange County. He was a planter who owned 48 slaves in 1829 but only 7 in 1830. He frequently purchased adjoining or nearby land, often with borrowed money. He also acquired land in

Archibald DeBow Murphey (1777?–1832), teacher, attorney, planter, legislator, and judge, made his greatest contribution to his native state in none of these professions. In fact, even in his greatness he was unsuccessful. He was a planner, a dreamer, and a schemer—all for the benefit of North Carolina. In anticipation of improvement, he projected plans for good transportation, quality schools, more productive agriculture, the elimination of slavery, and the preparation of a state history. The state, however, had to await better times to implement his ideas, and he died before they came to fruition. (North Carolina Division of Archives and History, Raleigh)

various parts of the state adjacent to rivers marked for navigational improvement under the state's internal improvements program.

One of Murphey's ambitions was to write a history of the state. He collected materials, interviewed Revolutionary leaders, and petitioned the legislature for appropriations with which to copy documents in British archives. If the people of the state understood the origin and effect of past events in their part of the world, he believed, they would take more pride in North Carolina and its future. Only an excellent outline and an introductory chapter were ever completed.

Joseph Caldwell (1773–1835), president of the University of North Carolina, aided and abetted Archibald Murphey in his plans. Caldwell spoke frequently in support of a program of progress for North Carolina. He also wrote several popular pamphlets. One on education contained instructions for organizing schools, plans for schoolhouses, and a course of study. Another advocated the building of railroads, which were still in their infancy; these, he maintained, would open new markets for the state, provide a means of communication across the land, and enable many people to rise above the poverty level. (North Carolina Collection, University of North Carolina at Chapel Hill)

In politics he was a scholar and an idealist; his social concepts were quite advanced for his time, and in later years he was recognized as the prophet of a new era. Yet he was a poor business manager and suffered financially throughout most of his life; he even spent a brief time in jail because he could not pay his debts.

Although trained as a lawyer, Murphey did not consider law his primary interest. He was much more concerned with the improvement of economic and social conditions in North Carolina. Like many others of his time, he realized

William A. Graham (1804–75), like Archibald Murphey, anticipated progress for North Carolina. He entered the political scene in the 1830s as a legislator and delegate to the 1835 convention, then became successively a United States senator, the governor of North Carolina, a cabinet member, and a vice-presidential candidate. Throughout a long public career, Graham worked tirelessly for the advancement of both state and people. (North Carolina Collection, University of North Carolina at Chapel Hill)

that the changes he contemplated depended on the development of effective methods of transportation and communication and on the creation of a system of public education. The former were referred to as "internal improvements." Both programs must move along together, he maintained, with support for one engendering support for the other.

Murphey's unique role in the development of public schools in the state rested on his presentation of the democratic theory of popular education and the detailed reports through which he informed the public. Years after his death, when public schools were finally opened, they were based on plans first advanced in Murphey's reports. Legislators, having ignored the recommendations of many governors that they consider providing for public education, finally responded in 1815 when both houses created committees on "Seminaries of Learning." In 1816 Senator Murphey issued a report for his committee.

In that report, Murphey rejected the idea of charity as the fundamental basis of public education and instead advocated a policy that would "embrace in its view the rich and the poor, the dull and the sprightly." The system he proposed would "include a gradation of schools, regularly supporting each other, from the one in which the first rudiments of education are taught, to that in which the highest branches of the sciences are cultivated." Having submitted his forward-looking report, he recommended the appointment of a committee "to digest a general system of Public Instruction" for consideration at the next session of the General Assembly. Although his recommendation was adopted, there is no indication that such a committee was named.

At least some legislators must have paid attention to Murphey's ideas, however. In 1817 a representative from the previous session, John M. Walker of Warren County, who was not reelected, sent the speaker a report on teacher training in which he proposed that teachers be trained at public expense; in return, they would agree to teach for three years at a modest salary. When children were educated, Walker maintained, fewer people would depend on the public for support and crime would decline. It was ordered that his report be printed and a copy distributed to each member of the legislature; but like other ideas entailing the expenditure of public money, nothing came of his proposal.

Murphey contributed an even more detailed report in 1817 than he had the year before. This plan envisioned a complete system of public education, including primary schools, high schools, schools for "the deaf and dumb," and the university. Primary and high schools were to be supported in part by local taxation but with supplementary state appropriations. Certain funds would be set aside as a school fund and the income used as a part of the state aid. This fund would be managed by a state board, with the governor as president. The board would have the power to locate schools, fix teachers' salaries and qualifications, appoint local committeemen, prepare plans for the promotion of pupils from the primary school grades through the university, and generally supervise the whole system. In his report, Murphey also discussed courses of study, methods of instruction, discipline, and other related subjects, indicating that he was thoroughly familiar with educational programs in England and Switzerland. As had become the custom, the General Assembly ordered his report to be printed, but it did nothing else.

This thoughtful presentation set in motion a movement that could not be stopped, and that is all that Murphey expected. His reports were widely read and adopted by future leaders. Governor John Branch, in his annual message in 1818, referred to them as "luminous and impressive appeals" and told the lawmakers that it was their "imperious duty" to heed them. Legislators, however, were not ready to be pushed into anything of the kind, and between 1815 and 1825 they rejected every proposal to establish public schools.

The Literary Fund

Although Murphey was no longer a senator, his friends in the General Assembly continued to promote his recommendations and in 1825 won their first victory. A bill, drawn up by Speaker Bartlett Yancey, a former law student under Murphey, was passed to create a fund for the establishment of "common schools." Known as the Literary Fund, it consisted of bank stock, receipts from a retail liquor tax, and income from the sale of swampland owned by the state. Management of the fund was entrusted to a Literary Board composed of the governor, the chief justice, the speakers of both houses of the legislature, and the state treasurer. Authorized to invest its funds in certain specified securities, the board would eventually be expected to distribute the income to the counties in proportion to their free white population.

The Literary Fund grew very slowly and its history reflects the legislature's attitude toward education. In 1827 two bills were introduced to repeal the law creating the fund, but its friends saved it. In 1828 a committee, formed to inquire into the possibility of using a portion of the fund for the education of poor and indigent children, reported that it was "yet too small to justify the Legislature in entering upon an active and extensive system of education." The report concluded that the committee members could think of no method of "expelling from our country the moral and intellectual darkness which now broods over it" except to "unite in the prayer that a kind Providence will hasten the time when literary, moral and religious instruction shall pervade our country." Apparently believing, as Benjamin Franklin did, that "God helps those who help themselves," some members introduced bills in 1826, 1830, and 1831 to increase the Literary Fund. As they must have anticipated, all of these were rejected.

Other setbacks occurred as the Literary Fund came to be considered by the state, by private corporations, and by many individuals as a convenient source for borrowing when in need. Losses were sustained through dishonesty, poor investments, and bad faith on the part of the legislature. On the death of the state treasurer in 1827, it was revealed that he had misappropriated over $28,000, but four years later the money was recovered when the General Assembly made a direct appropriation to the fund. The decline in bank dividends also hurt the fund as did the practice of borrowing from it to pay legislative salaries. As late as 1839, when the first school law was passed, the president of the Literary Board reported that the $30,509 received in interest on loans during the year "would have been considerably increased, but for the necessity of the Public Treasurer's using a considerable amount of the funds to meet the current expenses of the Government, until the taxes of the present year were received."

Having created the Literary Fund, the legislature, it was said, rested from its labors. There followed "ten unfruitful years" during which politicians could point to the fund as holding hope for the future but probably as a means of delaying effective action as well. But this by no means enabled them to escape from constant reminders by the governors. Governor Hutchins G. Burton in 1826 urged that the work of the previous year be carried on; according to him, "if the beginning is not well sustained and pursued, the present generation may pass away, before anything effectual is accomplished." A few years later Governor John Owen felt compelled "to raise a protesting voice against a species of economy, which has so long kept the poor in ignorance, and the State in poverty."

One of the most avid supporters of public education was President Joseph Caldwell of the University of North Carolina. In a series of articles for the newspapers, which later were collected and published as a 102-page pamphlet entitled *Letters on Popular Education*, he offered practical suggestions regarding such topics as organizing local school committees, erecting a schoolhouse, a floor plan for a typical one-room school, daily schedules for classes, and estimates of costs. He also attempted to show some benefits of public schools to local communities, made plans for training teachers, and proposed the creation of demonstration schools. President Caldwell very slyly suggested that prospective teachers should not be trained at the university as they would be exposed to courses in other fields and might be lured away from becoming schoolteachers.

The few legislators who favored public schools were hailed by Caldwell, of course, but numerous clergymen and newspaper editors also spoke and wrote in their support. Together they succeeded in creating a public sentiment that was able to make itself heard after the constitutional reforms of 1835 broke the grip of eastern politicians on the state government.

Internal Improvements

Hand in hand with the movement for public education went the program for economic development. The problem was largely one of transportation. Although agricultural and industrial resources were ample for the production of great wealth, without means of transportation they could not be developed. The building of roads and the improvement of rivers and harbors, therefore, became of great interest to those who anticipated improvements for North Carolina.

The solution to the question of road building was difficult because it involved not only a change in methods of construction and upkeep but also a revolution in the political thinking of North Carolinians. The immense distances to be covered, the difficulties of construction through great stretches of wilderness, woods, and swamps, and the sparsity of population meant that this was beyond the skill and financial resources of almost every community. The only solution lay in construction by the state. Before this could be done people had to be convinced that road building was a proper function of the state, and, as in the case of public schools, this required a change in the popular idea of the nature of the state and its services to the people.

The rivers of the Piedmont were too shallow and rapid for navigation without extensive canals, and the mountain section was entirely dependent on turnpikes. Both of these were beyond the ability of individuals, or even of communities, to manage. The same was true with respect to keeping inlets open along the coast and widening and deepening river channels.

The friends of internal improvements began to look to the state for support. As early as 1791 Governor Alexander Martin had said: "The internal navigation of the State . . . requires legislative assistance, our sister States are [rivaling] each other in opening their rivers and cutting canals, while attempts of this kind are but feebly aided among us." In 1806 Governor Nathaniel Alexander recommended that liberal provisions be made for internal improvements, particularly for the establishment of good roads and the extension of inland navigation. Advocates of internal improvements from across the state presented memorials and petitions, senators and representatives introduced bills, and the history of the agitation for public schools was duplicated. Each followed a parallel course. Before 1815 private resources were expected to meet the needs of the people for both schools and transportation, often under state charters. Just as academies were chartered in those years, so were companies to operate toll roads, bridges, and canals.

The development of the steam engine prompted the chartering of several navigation companies between 1815 and 1825. The Roanoke Navigation Company and the Cape Fear Navigation Company both operated successfully for a time. By 1818 the Neuse River Navigation Company was operating a steamer between

New Bern and Elizabeth City; within a short time the Edenton and Plymouth Steamboat Company was also running a steamer between those two towns. In 1818 Captain Otway Burns built the first steamboat in the state, the *Prometheus*, which ran between Wilmington and Fayetteville, and soon others were involved in the same trade. The promoters of Fayetteville boasted that a cargo shipped from New York arrived by steamer before the bill of lading which had been sent overland by mail. Considerable enthusiasm for steam navigation was generated in 1819 when President James Monroe visited the state and toured the waterways of the east on board the *Prometheus*. His visit to Roanoke Island to view the remains of Ralph Lane's Fort Raleigh also spurred interest in the state's history.

Archibald D. Murphey in 1815 drew up the first well-rounded plan for internal improvements presented for state action. Taking advantage of a brief and rather timid reference to the subject in Governor William Miller's message, he offered a resolution in the Senate, "That it is expedient to provide more efficiently for the improvement of the inland navigation of the State." He then moved for the appointment of a joint committee to look into the matter. The committee was duly named, with Murphey as chairman. The general principles that he laid down in its report were later expanded in a series of reports in 1816, 1817, and 1818. They were summarized and further developed in his excellent *Memoir on Internal Improvements* of 1819. His enthusiasm, knowledge, and ability to express his ideas in a clear and forceful way made him the natural leader of the movement, and enabled him to project the subject into the thinking of the state as a live issue.

The chief features of his scheme were (1) to improve the methods of transportation, (2) to build up markets in the state by developing market towns at strategic points, and (3) to drain the swamplands of the east, reclaiming them for agricultural purposes while at the same time improving the health of the people who lived near them. Murphey had in mind the development of an integrated system of inland transportation that included deepening the inlets and sounds along the coast; clearing the river channels, building locks, and otherwise making the principal rivers and their tributaries navigable; and connecting these streams into three systems by means of canals and good roads. One such system was to be formed by improving the Roanoke River and its tributaries and giving them an outlet through Albemarle Sound; another, by connecting the waters of the Tar and Neuse rivers and giving them an outlet through Ocracoke Inlet; and the third, by connecting the Yadkin and Catawba rivers with the Cape Fear, thereby giving westerners an outlet to the Atlantic. Areas of the state not served by water routes would utilize a system of turnpikes.

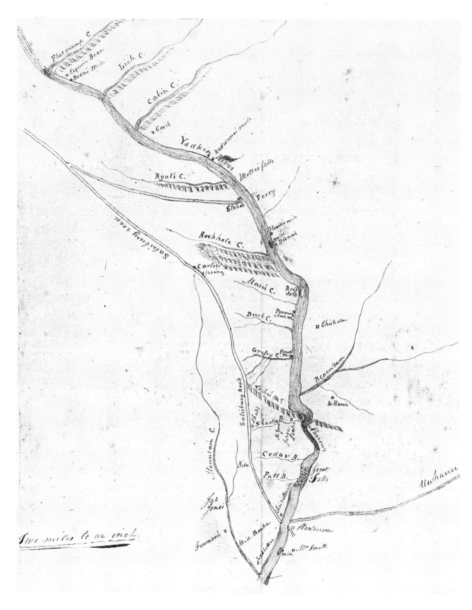

The Board of Internal Improvements created in 1819 employed surveyors and engineers to draw up specific plans in various parts of the state. One of these anticipated the development of water transportation on the Yadkin River, and the drawing shown here suggests the care with which this work was executed. (North Carolina Division of Archives and History, Raleigh)

The State Hires an Engineer

In 1817 the General Assembly named a commission, with Murphey as its chief member, to employ an engineer and direct his work. This proved to be a more difficult task than the legislators anticipated. The state now had to pay the price for its stingy policy toward education. The University of North Carolina, which had existed for nearly a quarter of a century, had clearly foreseen the need for competent engineers by emphasizing engineering courses in its curriculum, but the state's stingy policy toward the university limited the number of graduates.[1] The first student, Hinton James, became an engineer, however, and some of the stonework he laid along the waterfront at Wilmington is still in place. Unable to find an engineer in the state who could undertake the work, the commission searched elsewhere in the country but found that all were employed and unavailable. Peter Browne, chairman of the commission, was in England and there employed Hamilton Fulton at a salary of £1,200 in gold—a fee unheard of in economical North Carolina. Fulton arrived in July 1819 and immediately set to work in accordance with plans prepared by Murphey. Although he was well qualified for the project, Fulton's salary aroused the envy of politicians. As a result of their constant criticism, he finally resigned in 1825.

During his six years on the job, Fulton prepared some valuable reports which led to the creation of a fund for internal improvements and the organization of a Board of Internal Improvements. The fund was derived from two sources: the sale of approximately a million acres of Cherokee land in western North Carolina to which the Indians' title had been extinguished by treaties with the United States in 1819, and over a thousand shares of stock each in the Bank of New Bern and the Bank of Cape Fear. The Board of Internal Improvements was composed of the governor and six commissioners chosen by the legislature. In 1823, as part of the campaign to get rid of Fulton, the composition of the board was changed to include the governor and three directors elected by the legislature. After the last reorganization in 1831, it consisted of the governor, the state treasurer, and one elected member. The board's duties were described simply as administering the fund and supervising the work.

Creation of the fund and the board stimulated public interest in the subject. Shortly it became apparent that every community had its pet project—some stream to be cleared, a canal to be dug, or a turnpike to be built. Public meetings were held across the state to gain support for local projects, and internal improvement "conventions" became popular. Demands for larger and larger

1. The surveying instruments used by the boundary line commission under William Byrd in 1728 were given to the University of North Carolina soon after it opened. These instruments continued to be used in the training of surveyors until the Civil War, when they disappeared while the campus was occupied by federal troops.

expenditures were presented to the General Assembly. The board itself took the lead, recommending in 1821, 1825, and 1830 that the state borrow $500,000 for internal improvements. Finally in 1833, carried away by popular enthusiasm, the board recommended that the state borrow $6 million. That year a statewide internal improvements convention in Raleigh was attended by delegates from forty-eight of the sixty-five counties, but its request that $5 million be made available for various enterprises was rejected by the legislature.

The internal improvements fund was no more successful than the Literary Fund. It could never collect the notes due it from the sale of the Cherokee land, and it lost considerable sums through the decline and final suspension of dividends on the bank stock. It also lost over $29,000 through misappropriations of the state treasurer. Between 1819 and 1836 the fund invested over $291,000 in various internal improvement projects, but only three of them ever paid any dividends—and they were small and irregular. The other companies were complete failures. Further, the influence of local interests prevented the adoption of a systematic statewide scheme. This was a pitfall that Murphey had anticipated and cautioned against, but board members ignored his warning. Another serious defect was the lack of engineering experience and skill in the projects that were undertaken.

Most North Carolinians considered engineering to be "a lot of academic stuff" without practical value. The average farmer was confident that he could take a gang of laborers with spades, shovels, wagons, and drag pans, and dig a canal, channel a river, or construct a turnpike while the "professor fellows" were "figguring on it" and drawing a lot of useless plans. Many people were convinced that the engineers were stupid. For instance, while surveying the Neuse River in Johnston County, civil engineers met in the lowgrounds an old War of 1812 veteran who had served on a privateering vessel and considered himself to be something of a navigator and engineer. When they asked him what he thought of straightening some of the sharp bends so steamboats could navigate the river from New Bern to Smithfield, he replied that if they did that "every damn drop of water in the river will run straight out into Pamlico Sound." The old man must have been astonished a few years later to see the steamer *Neuse* pass by the very spot where he had made his prediction.

The final blow to the work of the Board of Internal Improvements came with the appearance of the locomotive engine. In 1827, two years after the first railroad was built in the United States, President Joseph Caldwell of the University of North Carolina published some newspaper essays over the pseudonym "Carlton" advocating this new form of transportation. When they were collected and published in 1828 in a pamphlet entitled *The Numbers of Carlton*, his ideas caught the public imagination. Around this time interest in inland navigation and canal companies slowly began to decline, but more rapidly after 1834 when the legislature chartered the first railroad company in the state.

Call for Constitutional Reform

Closely related to Murphey's programs of education and internal improvements was a program of constitutional reform. The democratic west wanted schools and transportation, but the east opposed both and the east controlled state government. Both of these desirable goals could be achieved by the west only after it waged and won a battle for constitutional reform. The chief issue was the basis of representation, which the west demanded be changed from county to population. Agitation for reform actually began in 1787 when a proposal was adopted by the senate but rejected by the house to refer the question to the convention the next year. A similar proposal in 1788 to refer it to the convention of 1789 met the same fate. Bills to call a constitutional convention were defeated in 1808 and 1811.

In 1816 a petition from Rutherford County seeking a convention was referred to a senate committee of which Murphey was chairman. Taking advantage of the opportunity, he prepared a masterful report giving the reform movement its first literary expression. His argument in favor of a convention rested on the fundamental principles of democracy. The constitution was "strictly conformable to the principles of Republican Government" in 1776 but in operation it had not remained so, he pointed out. The inequality of representation in the General Assembly was its main fault after so many years. "That a majority should govern," he wrote, was one of the first principles of a republican form of government, but as the system was then working "about one third of the White Population elect a Majority of the Members of the General Assembly."

To give North Carolinians an opportunity to remedy this and other weaknesses "of minor importance," Murphey recommended that the legislature refer to the people at the election of 1817 the question of calling a constitutional convention. He did not expect favorable action, of course, but only intended to attract general attention to the issue. Although he cited figures showing that the existing system discriminated against some eastern counties, a sectional vote in the house defeated Murphey's proposal and the senate simply postponed any consideration of it. This time even a motion to print his proposal was rejected. Clearly the east believed that wide dissemination of the facts would be too dangerous.

For the moment constitutional reform went the way of schools and internal improvements. Murphey's program was sacrificed to the interests of a selfish and short-sighted sectionalism. Time, however, was on his side. He was a prophet, not a builder. He dreamed dreams that others would convert to reality. He pointed the way to an intellectual awakening, a material prosperity, and a greatness that he foresaw very plainly in his mind but was destined never to see in reality. He devoted his life, it has been said, to the task of arousing the people of North Carolina from their indifference and ignorance, of pointing out to them their opportunities, of inspiring them with confidence in themselves and in their state, of kindling their pride and ambition. To this work he brought a thorough understanding of the natural and human resources of the state, a clearer awareness of its needs, a bolder and more philosophical grasp of the policies necessary for relief, and a more sincere belief in its future than any other man of his time.

Before his death in 1832, Murphey must have thought that his life had been a failure. Yet in the same year a new political party was born; with Murphey's program as its platform, it would inaugurate the era of progress that he had so clearly foreseen.

14

THE CONSTITUTIONAL
CONVENTION OF 1835

C ONSERVATIVE EASTERN members of the General Assembly were the predominant cause of the state's failure to move forward during the first three and a half decades of the nineteenth century. They determined the state's role in the national government as well, since United States senators were elected by the legislature. The prestige of Nathaniel Macon, a conservative Republican (Democrat) of Warren County, who was Speaker of the United States House of Representatives during most of the administration of President Thomas Jefferson and president pro tempore of the Senate in 1826 and 1827, also influenced political thinking in the state. North Carolina's leaders demonstrated more concern and participated more generally in matters pertaining to the nation than they did in those important to the state. Easterners dominated the Republican party in North Carolina; however, their support of a do-nothing program, together with a declining interest in national elections, led to a split in the state party.

National Issues and North Carolina Politics

A question related to the extension of slavery produced the first evidence of this split. In an effort to resolve the debate over the admission of new states to the Union and whether slavery should be permitted in the Louisiana Territory, the Missouri Compromise evolved. With an equal number of slave and free states in the Union in 1819, the question of admitting Missouri as a slave state was critical. Congress considered several versions of a bill involving compromise, but finally Maine was admitted as a free state and Missouri as a slave state on the condition that slavery be prohibited in the future north of 36°30′N latitude. During the debate of 1819–20 North Carolina's congressional delegation was evenly divided. Westerners favored excluding slavery while those from the east supported its extension.

The presidential election of 1824 further split the Republican party. Macon

Nathaniel Macon (1758–1837), a veteran of the American Revolution, was considered an old man in 1835. He made his last public appearance as a member of the convention following distinguished service in both houses of Congress and as Speaker of the House of Representatives. Although an aristocrat, educated at the College of New Jersey (now Princeton), and a wealthy planter, he lived a simple life and advocated the cause of the "common folks." He believed in strict economy in government, annual elections, and states' rights, and he did not approve all of the changes proposed for North Carolina in 1835. Nevertheless, he was highly respected and his policies were supported by a great many people. (North Carolina Division of Archives and History, Raleigh)

and a majority of the state's congressmen and other political leaders supported a Georgian, William H. Crawford, who believed in a strict interpretation of the Constitution, states' rights, and governmental economy. He was opposed to internal improvements utilizing federal funds and to a protective tariff; he also rejected the nationalistic program of the national Republican party. Crawford's positions would not benefit western North Carolina.

Opposing Crawford was John C. Calhoun of South Carolina. His support of internal improvements, including a new inlet to Albemarle Sound, an inland waterway from Boston to Savannah, and a road from Maine to Louisiana, appealed to both westerners and the people in the sound region. Nevertheless, by the customary legislative caucus North Carolina's support was thrown to Crawford and he became his party's nominee.

Led by Charles Fisher of Salisbury, Calhoun's friends secretly formed the "People's Ticket" as an opposition party. The members of this faction soon were aware of a growing public interest in Andrew Jackson, popularly known as "Old Hickory" and the hero of the Battle of New Orleans. By a compromise Jackson became their candidate for president and Calhoun for vice-president. Appeals to the common people generated support for Jackson. Crawford was called the "caucus" and the "Virginia" candidate, and eastern leaders were criticized for supporting him without testing public opinion. Although Archibald D. Murphey thought Crawford to be better qualified, he supported Jackson rather than have North Carolina follow Virginia's lead as it had done for so many years.

New campaign techniques were brought to North Carolina when numerous mass meetings were held. For a change, the "common people" were called upon to decide for themselves which candidate to support. It has been said that they were entertained and fired with the zeal of a holy crusade for the rights of the sovereign people. "It is very difficult to electioneer successfully against General Jackson," a Crawford supporter observed. "One cup of generous whiskey produces more military ardor than can be allayed by a month of reflection and reason." The People's ticket overwhelmed its opponent, carrying the west as well as several counties in the east. The election of 1824 was hailed as a victory for democracy and for the west, and as a demonstration of North Carolina's break with Virginia. The west and the Albemarle Sound region had made common cause and the solid Republican party was split.

Across the nation no candidate received a majority so the House of Representatives had the task of choosing from the three leading hopefuls. Henry Clay threw his support to John Quincy Adams, who was selected president and who named Clay his secretary of state. Jackson supporters claimed that their hero was clearly preferred by the people as he led in both popular and electoral votes, but a "corrupt bargain" cheated them out of victory. There was a growing interest in democracy, and they immediately began a campaign to ensure his election in 1828. The Republican party split into two factions—National Republicans, led by Adams and Clay, held forth in New England, the Middle States, and the Northwest, while the Democratic-Republicans flourished in the South and the West.

After 1824 North Carolina Republicans had little choice. They could support Jackson or they could support Adams, and even easterners chose Jackson as the lesser of two evils. Jackson's election to the presidency in 1828 was applauded by a united North Carolina; but once in office, he disappointed many North Carolinians when he opposed federal banks and internal improvements. The west and the Albemarle Sound region lost their enthusiasm for Jackson and in time this led to further resentment of eastern leadership. By 1834 the dissatisfied element in North Carolina was ready to switch its allegiance to a new opposition party, the Whig party, which grew out of the National Republican faction devoted to Henry Clay and his program of internal improvements, a protective tariff, and nationalism. A portion of the Whig support came from planters in the South who advocated a program of states' rights, but in North Carolina the Whigs were more nationalistic and supported internal improvements.

Jackson's supporters soon dropped the old names of their party and came to be known as Democrats. Two parties, Whigs and Democrats, began a twenty-year rivalry that contributed significantly to the progress of North Carolina.

Rise of the Whig Party

The young Whig party in North Carolina had little hope of support if it remained merely an opposition party. Jackson was still popular with many of the "common people" and the Whigs had to do more than attack the growing power of the presidency. The situation in state politics played right into their hands. In opposing banks Jackson alienated commercial interests in the east. Governor James Iredell, Jr., commented that the bank had certainly done no harm in the state. The new party gained the support of several North Carolinians with old Federalist inclinations—William Gaston of Craven County, Edward B. Dudley of New Hanover, Edward Stanly of Beaufort, and David Outlaw and Kenneth Rayner of Bertie. The state's western congressmen opposed Jackson and sympathized with the ambitions of their section for education, improved transportation, and equality of representation in the General Assembly. It was good politics for Whigs with commercial interests to join forces with westerners who wanted those improvements. In state politics, then, the Whig party adopted the program of Archibald D. Murphey as it became the champion of constitutional reform, public schools, and internal improvements, at the same time favoring a sound currency.

Heading the list as a necessary prelude to all of the others was constitutional reform. After the defeat of Murphey's early resolution in 1816 in favor of a convention, the contest became an open and clear struggle for sectional supremacy, and by 1834 many western leaders were publicly advocating revolution as the only possible means they saw to the end they sought. Convention bills introduced in the senate in 1819 and in the house in 1821 were killed by eastern votes. In 1822 the western members of the legislature decided to take their case straight to the people. At a meeting in Raleigh during the final days of the session, they adopted an address presenting the case for the west and calling on western counties to elect delegates to a state convention where public sentiment could be expressed; they distributed 10,000 copies of this address. The convention, attended by delegates from twenty-four western counties, met in Raleigh on 10 November 1823 and drew up some proposed amendments to the state constitution to be laid before the legislative session a week later. Unfortunately disputes over some minor questions on one or two amendments divided the convention and prevented unanimous action. This harmless division among the reformers provided eastern legislators an excuse to kill the convention bill.

The east maintained that if representation were determined solely by population, the rights and interests of property would be ignored. Western leaders, in an attempt to reach a compromise, proposed that representation be based on either (1) a combination of white population and taxes paid into the state treasury; (2) federal population, permitting eastern slave owners to count their slaves; or (3) North Carolina Senate districts created according to taxable property and a House of Commons elected by counties and population. The east would agree to none of these, and as time passed the inequities became more glaring.

Demands of the West

The social and economic interests of the west became increasingly tied to constitutional reform, and the movement ceased to be simply a contest between eastern and western politicians. In the west it grew into a truly popular movement. Newspaper support, mass meetings, and unofficial polls all gave clear evidence of the united public sentiment on the issue. The most notable expression of opinion was revealed at the general election of 1833 when an unofficial poll on the convention question was held in thirty-one western counties. The vote was 30,000 for a convention versus 1,000 against. These results were presented to the next legislature by Governor David L. Swain, and two bills were introduced to submit the question to the people. But eastern landowners still refused to support any measure that might shake their hold on state government.

This bold defiance of an indisputable popular desire for a convention was criticized even in the east, and some eastern newspapers took their representatives to task for their voting record. A great wave of indignation was said to have swept over the west. Revolution was actually discussed, and even conservatives did not shrink from the suggestion that for the west this might be the only solution. In Salisbury the *Carolina Watchman*, a newspaper widely read in the western part of the state, declared that, if the glaring weaknesses in the constitution were not recognized by some "formal mode" at the 1834 session of the General

Assembly, westerners were determined to initiate remedies without the help of the legislature. The editor admitted that it was a dangerous course; nevertheless, given their great resolve and the spirit of their Revolutionary fathers still fresh in their minds, he felt that they could solve the problem. And he set a deadline. The people of the west would begin to act as soon as the next session of the legislature adjourned. The threat of revolution was unmistakable.

The *Watchman* had not exaggerated. During the convention, which was held in due course, Governor Swain, one of the western delegates, again solemnly repeated the threat of revolution if his region's demands were not satisfied.

While the reformers were still agitating for action, two events brought them unexpected support. One was the burning of the state capitol; the other was the election of William Gaston by the General Assembly as an associate justice of the North Carolina Supreme Court.

The capitol burned on 21 June 1831 in a fire accidentally started by some workmen repairing the roof. Immediately people in Fayetteville and elsewhere began to try to have the seat of government moved there. Raleigh, they pointed out, was still a country village with less than two thousand inhabitants. Many felt that it was the state capital in name only, with no promise of ever becoming a real political or business center. The superior commercial advantages of Fayetteville, if combined with the political advantages of the state capital, would convert it into a real metropolis, something the state badly needed. Since the capital had been fixed by an ordinance of the Convention of 1788, another convention would be required to authorize its relocation. The supporters of Fayetteville, therefore, were quite willing to join the west in favor of a bill to call a convention.

The General Assembly of 1831 met in the "Government House," as the official residence of the governor was called. Because this house stood just outside the corporate limits of the capital city, doubts of the legality of sessions held there were said to have plagued the honest minds of a number of members. This uncertainty played an important part in the contest over where to rebuild the capitol.

Soon after the legislative session began, a senator from Wake County introduced a bill to appropriate $30,000 to rebuild the capitol in Raleigh. Fayetteville, of course, promptly rallied its supporters to oppose this bill. Debate in both houses ran high and covered a wide range of political, constitutional, financial, economic, and social concerns, some directly and others only remotely related to the issue. This debate again clearly demonstrated the complexity of sectional alignments in the legislature.

In the 1831 session the combined western and Fayetteville supporters mustered enough strength to defeat the bill to rebuild the capitol in Raleigh, but because of the defection of the lower Cape Fear counties they were unable to put through a bill to call a convention. So the issue was carried over into the session of 1832. Again there was a coalition between the forces of constitutional reform and relocation of the state capital, but the unsightly ruins of the old capitol building, the qualms of legislative conscience over holding sessions outside the corporate limits of the capital city, and the needs of the state were too strong a combination to be beaten. Fayetteville lost its fight, the capitol was rebuilt in Raleigh, and the eastern party once more succeeded in postponing the day of reform. However, the west gained some friends in the east whose votes later proved to be decisive in the contest over constitutional reform.

The election of William Gaston, a Roman Catholic, to the supreme court in 1833 brought to a head the growing sentiment against the clauses in the constitution of 1776 that imposed religious tests for officeholding. The Thirty-first Article said that no clergyman, "while he continues in the exercise of his pastoral Function," should serve as a member of the legislature or of the Council. The Thirty-second Article said that no person "who shall deny the being of God, or the Truth of the Protestant Religion, or the Divine Authority of either the Old or New Testaments, or who shall hold Religious Principles incompatible with the Freedom and Safety of the State, shall be capable of holding any Office, or Place of Trust or Profit in the Civil Department, within this State." This clause was popularly supposed to be aimed at atheists, Roman Catholics, Jews, and such religious bodies as Quakers, Moravians, and others who refused to bear arms in time of war.

The senate had enforced the Thirty-first Article on three occasions. In 1801 it had expelled John Culpepper and William Taylor, and in 1820 Josiah Crudup, because it was found that they were regularly ordained ministers "in the exercise of the pastoral Function." Culpepper and Crudup turned to federal politics and were elected to Congress.

Only one attempt was made to enforce the Thirty-second Article. Jacob Henry, a Jew, represented Carteret County in the House of Commons in 1808. He was reelected in 1809; but when he arrived to take his seat, a fellow member tried to exclude him under the provisions of this article. Henry spoke ably in his own defense and was warmly supported by Gaston, then a borough member from New Bern. The house declined to exclude Henry on the grounds that a seat in the General Assembly was not an office in the "Civil Department" of the state within the meaning of the constitution.

These cases brought the question of religious tests for state office to public notice, and opposition to them quickly arose. When the Western Convention met in Raleigh in 1823, a motion was made to include among the proposed amendments one repealing the Thirty-second Article as "hostile to the Principles of Religious freedom and unworthy of the liberality of the age." Although general agreement was expressed, the motion was withdrawn when it was pointed out that it was out of keeping with the purposes of the convention as a *western* convention.

In 1832 the advocates in the legislature of a constitutional convention included

William Gaston (1778–1844), lawyer and teacher of law, legislator, congressman, and judge, was one of the most highly regarded men in the state at the time of the 1835 convention. As a Roman Catholic he was uncomfortable with a provision in the state constitution that allowed only Protestants to hold certain offices. At the convention he delivered a moving address on this subject. (North Carolina Collection, University of North Carolina at Chapel Hill)

a modification of the Thirty-second Article among the suggested amendments, and in 1833 in their "Address to the People" on the convention question some legislators urged the striking out of this "odious restriction upon conscience."

Sentiment was growing for modification of the article when the election of William Gaston to the supreme court made immediate action imperative. Gaston himself raised the question as to whether a Roman Catholic was eligible for office. He had no doubt as to his qualifications otherwise, an opinion upheld by the best legal minds in and outside of the state. The article had always been ignored. Charles Fisher, without contradiction in the Convention of 1835, said that "we have seen every grade of office in the State, from Governor down to Constable, at one time or another, filled by men of the Catholic persuasion."[1] Nevertheless, many able North Carolinians of the time, though not actually guilty of religious bigotry, had no quarrel with the provision.

Gaston had not been an active candidate for the position and agreed to serve on the bench only because he could not refuse without seeming to be lax in his duty as a patriotic citizen. He was naturally anxious to see all doubts of his eligibility removed. He felt, too, that the article was a stigma on people of his faith and entirely without justification. Although he was an easterner, Gaston had advocated a constitutional convention long before there was any question of his own eligibility for office. No individual in the state was better fitted by training, character, and experience than he, and his election made clear the absurdity of a test law that, even by implication, might disqualify him. Since he was very popular in the east, many of his friends there were now willing to vote for a convention so that any question of his ineligibility could be dismissed.

A third factor that had become important to the convention question was the great democratic movement then being felt by many governments around the world. In England, this movement was reflected in the Catholic Emancipation Act and in the act abolishing slavery throughout the British Empire. In America it appeared in the creation of new states with democratic constitutions, in the extension of the suffrage in nearly all of the old states, in the election of Andrew Jackson to the presidency, and in the growth of a strong antislavery movement in some parts of the nation. It was impossible for North Carolina to resist the influence of this universal spread of democracy. All that was needed to bring the state into line was a leader with the ability, the tact, and the personal popularity to unite the various forces that were ready for change.

Out of the newly settled region beyond the Blue Ridge, this leader appeared in the person of David Lowry Swain. A young man in his early thirties, his outward appearance, it has been said, gave little promise of leadership. A descrip-

1. It was widely believed, although incorrectly so, that Governor Thomas Burke was a Roman Catholic.

tion of him, undoubtedly by an easterner who had occasion to dislike him, said he was "malformed in person, out of proportion in physical conformation, apparently thrown together in haste, and manufactured from the scattered debris of material that had been used in other work; gawky, lanky, with a nasal twang that proclaimed him an alien, and a pedal propulsion that often awakened derision." Swain was a native of Buncombe County, a recent member of both the House of Commons and the North Carolina Senate, and a judge, whose personal popularity and ability earned him election as governor in 1832 at age thirty-one even though he was a westerner.

Swain's program in office entitles him to high rank among the most progressive governors of North Carolina. For instance, he regularly expressed concern about coastal defenses, internal improvements, taxation and finances, education, and constitutional reform. His tact and popularity with the people statewide had much to do with the success of his policies. Archibald Murphey's plans were the source of many of his recommendations, but he supplied the political leadership that Murphey had lacked. Swain was fully aware that the state's development depended on constitutional reform and that became his chief aim. In his annual message to the legislature in 1834 he discussed the origin and history of the plan of representation in the 1776 constitution, the method by which it might be amended, the changes in the state that made amendment imperative, the discontent of the west, and the evils of the sectional controversies created by inequality. This message, the best ever presented on the subject, the other questions that now demanded reform, and the general democratic movement of the time overpowered the opposition and made it possible for the west to win the first victory for constitutional reform in North Carolina since 1776.

The Convention

A bill was introduced in 1834 to submit to the people the question of calling a convention to amend the constitution in certain specified ways. If called, the convention would be required by this bill to frame amendments establishing membership in the senate and the lower house in certain ways. The North Carolina Senate would consist of not less than 34 nor more than 50 members chosen by districts laid off in proportion to the amount in public taxes paid into the state treasury by the residents of that district. The House of Commons would have not fewer than 90 nor more than 120 members, excluding borough members, distributed to the counties "according to their federal population." In addition, the convention would be required to provide a method of amending the constitution in the future. The General Assembly also provided that the convention, if it chose, might abolish borough members, disfranchise free blacks, alter

David L. Swain (1801–68) from Buncombe County was governor in 1835 when he participated in the constitutional convention. In large measure, his skillful political maneuvering brought about the important changes that set North Carolina on a new and progressive course. (North Carolina Division of Archives and History, Raleigh)

the Thirty-second Article, provide for biennial sessions of the legislature, provide for the election of the governor by voters who were also qualified to vote for members of the House of Commons, and prescribe the term for which the governor should be elected and his eligibility for reelection. The Assembly specified other minor revisions that might be proposed, as well as several changes that the convention was specifically forbidden to consider: (1) in determining senatorial districts, no county could be divided so as to fall into two districts; (2) no county could be without at least one member of the House of Commons; and (3) no free man presently qualified to vote could be disfranchised by the revisions—except, of course, the convention might deny the vote to free persons of color.

In the house, thirteen easterners, including the members from Cumberland (who appreciated western support in trying to make Fayetteville the capital) and from Craven (who appreciated western support of William Gaston) joined the western members in passing the bill by a vote of 66 to 62. In the senate it passed by 31 to 30 with the help of the senators from the same two counties. When the people were polled as to whether they wanted a convention, the response was strictly sectional. Of the 27,550 votes for a convention, 24,849 came from western counties. The opposition cast 21,694 votes, of which 18,083 came from the east. For the first time ever, the people had had an opportunity to vote on an important issue affecting all of North Carolina.

The convention assembled in Raleigh on 4 June 1835 with 128 delegates present. Since the new capitol was not finished, the meeting was held in the Presbyterian church. Present were Governor Swain, 3 former and 2 future governors, 3 who had been or were destined to become United States senators, 6 judges, 11 who had previously presided over one house or the other of the General Assembly, 15 former or future congressmen, and 88 former members of the General Assembly. It was an able and impressive collection of men.

Nathaniel Macon, retired now at age seventy-seven after a long career in Congress, William Gaston of Craven County, and Governor Swain of Buncombe were the most conspicuous figures present. Macon was chosen president, but Emanuel Shober, a Moravian from Salem, usually presided. Some of the members objected to taking an oath that would require them to abide by the restrictions placed on them by the General Assembly's act authorizing the convention. When it was pointed out that any action taken by unsworn delegates would be ineffective, the reluctant ones took the oath and turned to the business of the day.

Amendments were approved providing for a senate of 50 members and a house of 120, the maximum number permitted in both cases. As directed by the legislature, the upper house would be chosen by districts created according to taxes paid to the state, while representation in the lower house would be determined by population, including slaves, thereby permitting easterners more members than a white-only basis would have allowed. Reapportionment for representation in the house would follow the censuses of 1840 and 1850, but, as a result of a compromise, thereafter it would occur only every twenty years.

Opposition to biennial sessions of the General Assembly came from Nathaniel Macon and others who believed that annual elections were fundamental in a democracy. People should have a frequent opportunity to review the work of their representatives in government. "Where annual elections end, tyranny begins," Macon said. When an amendment was a adopted for biennial sessions he observed sadly, "Democracy is dead in North Carolina."

Macon and Gaston were among the opponents of the proposal to provide for

John Motley Morehead (1796–1866) represented Guilford County in the 1835 convention and a few years later became governor of the state. His primary interests were the advancement of education, the establishment of cotton mills, and the construction of railroads. (University of North Carolina Photo Lab, Swain Hall, Chapel Hill)

popular election of the governor. To do so, they predicted, would result in "that vile machinery" by which political parties sought to carry elections. Nevertheless by a vote of 74 to 44 the delegates approved an amendment to provide for the election of the governor by all who were qualified to vote for members of the House of Commons.

Also producing a great deal of debate was the proposal to alter the Thirty-second Article having to do with religious qualifications for officeholding. Views ranged all the way from keeping the article as it was to Macon's position that there should be no religious test. Gaston felt much as Macon did, but when he saw that this view would not prevail he moved to substitute the word *Christian* for *Protestant*. After numerous speakers had expressed their belief that there should be no change, Gaston was said by one delegate to have risen slowly from his seat and "with great deliberation, and amid breathless silence, for two days riveted the attention of all present, by a speech, which is unequaled in our memory." It was described as a masterpiece of oratory, filled with eloquence, wit, humor, and logic, and displaying a wide and profound knowledge of history. The proposed amendment was adopted, 74 to 52, but voting with the minority were many who opposed any religious test whatsoever.

As it was permitted to do, the convention considered other changes. Among those approved were (1) by a vote of 66 to 61, to disfranchise free blacks; (2) to fix the term of office of the governor at two years and to limit the length of service to two successive terms; (3) to change the term of office of the attorney general from good behavior to a term of four years; (4) to fix the terms of the secretary of state and the treasurer at two years each; (5) to equalize the poll tax on all persons, bond and free, who were subject to such a tax; (6) to prohibit private legislation on, and provide by general laws for, divorce and alimony, the changing of names, the legitimization of children born out of wedlock, and the restoration of citizenship to persons convicted of infamous crimes; and (7) to provide for impeachment by the house and trial by the senate of public officials.

Finally, as required by the act permitting it to function at all, the convention studied ways to amend the constitution in the future. Although the legislature only required one method, the convention established two. By a two-thirds vote of each house, the General Assembly could call a constitutional convention. Or the constitution could be amended by a legislative process. A proposed amendment, if passed by three-fifths of the members of both houses at the session when it was introduced and by a two-thirds vote at the next session, would be submitted to the people for ratification at an election called for that purpose.

After one month and one week, the convention adjourned on 11 July and its work was submitted to a referendum. By a vote of 26,771 to 21,606 the proposed amendments were ratified. The vote, however, was overwhelmingly sectional. Of the affirmative votes, 23,491 were cast in counties west of Raleigh; of the negative votes, 19,279 came from the east. Sectionalism was still alive in the state; but with the western counties more equitably represented in the legislature and with a better opportunity to elect a westerner governor, the chances for significant change were improved.

Along with broader representation of the electorate, the two-party system began to take hold in North Carolina. Both the Whig and the Democratic parties were about evenly matched, and party platforms became important as leaders tried to appeal to a majority of the people. Although party machinery—even the "vile machinery" that Macon had feared—developed, each party tried to tempt its ablest leaders into becoming candidates. There also followed the spoils system whereby the faithful were rewarded. Enemies might expect to be punished and reputations made suspect through unfounded accusations. Newspapers took sides, frequently making personal attacks on candidates, as well as saying nothing but good about the party they supported and only bad things about the other. This was an era of greater democracy, and no longer would a handful of intelligent leaders claim the "deference" of the masses and run things to suit themselves.

Once an election was over and the "vile machinery" put away until next time, North Carolina benefited from the rivalry of the two-party system. The state flourished during a generation of honest, progressive, and enlightened government. Between 1835 and 1860 the good things that Archibald Murphey had predicted came to be, including public schools, internal improvements, sound banks and currency, and the promotion of industry. It was a period when capable people rose to positions of leadership in many fields, largely under the guidance of the Whig party. This new party found its greatest strength in the small farmers of the west, though there was sizable support from the Albemarle Sound region and, indeed, from others throughout the state. Sectionalism was quieted for a time as eastern and western wings of the Whig party cooperated.

The Democratic party until about 1850 merely opposed Whig programs; but having suffered a number of humiliating defeats, its leaders became more progressive. The Whig party, in power for so long, became complacent, opening the way for Democrats to step in with some popular issues and take over. The stage was set for a dramatic period of North Carolina history in two phases, the first under Whig leadership and the second under the Democratic party, but a period that ended in tragedy nevertheless.

15

THE WHIG ERA,

1835-1850

UNDER THE REVISED constitution the people of the west gained an effective voice in the affairs of the state, marking a quarter century of progress. The two-party system that appeared on the eve of the Constitutional Convention of 1835 created a healthy and fruitful competition. For the first fifteen years of this period the Whig party held sway, but in time it became overconfident of its support and the Democrats gained the upper hand. They, too, proved to be capable custodians of the state's flourishing reputation.

Many Prompt Improvements

A handsome new state capitol was completed in 1840 under the direction of architects Ithiel Town, A. J. Davis, and David Paton. Built of local stone carved by Scottish stonemasons and designed in the Grecian Doric style, it came to be considered one of the most perfect examples of its kind in the United States. During this period North Carolina rendered essential aid to the construction of railroads and to the opening of schools for the "deaf, dumb, and blind," and an asylum for the insane. A state system of "common schools" was developed, and by 1860 it ranked as the best in the South and one of the best in the nation. The basis of taxation was reformed, suffrage laws were broadened, criminal laws were liberalized, the legal status of women improved, enrollment at the University of North Carolina grew from eighty-nine in 1836 to well over four hundred by 1860, and many new academies and colleges were founded. As the literacy rate increased, more newspapers were established and more books and pamphlets published. Agriculture flourished and new factories were opened while wealth and commerce grew. The years before the tragic Civil War were the most progressive North Carolina had known since its first permanent settlers arrived more than two hundred years before.

These great changes were made possible as a result of new western strength in the political arena. The development of two competing political parties compelled the leadership of each to contend for support, and that produced ideas

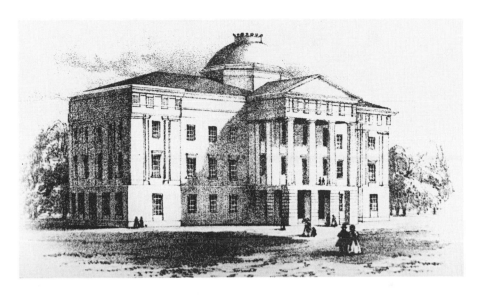

When the old capitol burned in June 1831, a struggle began immediately to move the state capital to Fayetteville, head of navigation on the Cape Fear River. Various political combinations, however, resulted in the rebuilding of the capitol in Raleigh, and this handsome new structure was occupied in 1840. (North Carolina Division of Archives and History, Raleigh)

and effective plans for the public good. The new Whig party initiated an appealing and constructive program based on ideas advanced by Archibald D. Murphey many years earlier. His proposals were well known and their implementation had been anticipated by progressive North Carolinians for a quarter of a century.

At the first election after the people approved the changes in the constitution, Edward Bishop Dudley, a Whig born in the eastern county of Onslow but now a resident of Wilmington, was elected governor. He had represented the Wilmington District in Congress from 1829 to 1831, but refused to run for another term, declaring that Congress was not a fit place for an honest person. An early advocate of constitutional reform and state support of internal improvements and education, he was a leader in the formation of the Whig party. In the popular election for governor, Dudley defeated the incumbent, Richard Dobbs Spaight, Jr., by slightly over 4,000 votes; when he ran for reelection two years later, opposed by former governor John Branch, he won by a large majority. In 1838 the Whigs also gained control of both houses of the General Assembly.

An outside event over which the Whigs had no control contributed in large

Pride in the state was raised by William Gaston's patriotic song, "The Old North State," published in 1844. (North Carolina Collection, University of North Carolina at Chapel Hill)

measure to the success of their program. During the presidential administration of Andrew Jackson all federal debts were paid, and a surplus mounted in the treasury through the sale of public land and the collection of a protective tariff. This proved to be embarrassing to the administration, as southerners would have been pleased to see the tariff abolished while northern manufacturers wanted it retained. When its opponents began to discuss ways to dispose of the money, a solution was found in an act of Congress of 1836 under which all funds in excess of $5 million would be distributed to the states in four installments on the basis of their representation in Congress. Although this was described as a "loan," there was no expectation that it would ever have to be repaid. North Carolina's share was $1,433,757.39, and how it might be used became the subject of political debate among the state's leaders. Democrats wanted to use the money to pay the state debt and to apply it toward the ordinary expenses of state government. Whigs, on the other hand, wanted to invest it in railroad construction and other internal improvements, and in public schools. The plan adopted by the General Assembly contained features of both proposals, but leaned more heavily toward the wishes of the Whigs. It reserved $100,000 to pay current expenses and earmarked the remainder for the purchase of bank stock and railroad securities, and to support internal improvements. Because income from the investments would benefit the Literary Fund, ultimately all of the state's receipts from the federal surplus, except $100,000, was used to support public schools.

Railroads

The proposal to aid railroads appealed to legislators, so this aspect of internal improvements received early attention. At the first meeting in the state to discuss the prospects of rail transportation, held on the farm of William Albright in Chatham County in 1828 and attended by about two hundred men—largely or totally farmers—of Orange, Chatham, and Guilford counties, it was concluded that a route through the middle of North Carolina would at last make it possible for farmers to get their produce to market. Unfortunately these men lacked both the resources and the political influence to go beyond the talking stage. In the same year, however, the first experimental railroad in the state was constructed. In Fayetteville convex wooden rails were laid up Person Street from the site of Campbellton on the Cape Fear River to St. James Square. On this crude line a wagonlike conveyance, with concave iron wheels and pulled by horses or mules, hauled goods from the steamer to a warehouse.

In 1833 a similar mile-long "experimental railroad" was laid in Raleigh from a quarry to the site of the new capitol. It was used to haul stone for the building, but on Sunday passengers were taken for pleasure rides. When the General

Assembly was in session, legislators also had an opportunity to try it as did delegates to two internal improvements conventions in 1833. As the state's leading commercial center, Wilmington began to think about the advantages of a "real" railroad with a steam locomotive and cars. Yet it was financially unable to follow the pattern of Norfolk, Petersburg, and other cities in Virginia and begin its own rail line. The North Carolina treasury was empty, the struggle of the west to gain strength had not been resolved, and almost everybody knew some story of bad investments in internal improvement companies. Even so, members of the Whig party, which was just beginning to be organized, showed interest.

The annual election of 1835, held before the constitutional convention adjourned, resulted in a Democratic majority in both houses of the legislature. A Democrat, Richard Dobbs Spaight, Jr., was elected governor, the last to be chosen by the General Assembly. In the same year the Democrats were responsible for chartering the first two railroads in the state. These lines had three promotional centers—Wilmington, the Roanoke River, and Raleigh. None of these would benefit the west, of course.

Citizens of Wilmington, having concluded that the future of their city depended on rail transportation, put forth extraordinary and self-sacrificing efforts to get it. In 1833 subscriptions totaling $400,000 were reported, and in 1834 the Wilmington & Raleigh Railroad was chartered. In 1835, after the citizens of Raleigh displayed no interest in this project, the charter was amended to allow the company to build a line to the Roanoke River instead. The company could also own and operate a line of steamboats from Wilmington to Charleston, South Carolina. Even before their charter was amended, the promoters decided that the route would pass nearly forty miles east of Raleigh and cross the Neuse River at Waynesboro, near the site of modern Goldsboro.

In March 1836 the company was formally organized in the home of one of Wilmington's wealthiest citizens, Edward B. Dudley, who was elected the first president. Soon afterward he accepted the informal Whig nomination for governor and was elected by the people. In October, two months after the state elections, a formal ceremony marked the beginning of construction on the Wilmington & Weldon Railroad, as it was now to be known under its revised charter. The honor of removing the first spadeful of dirt went to the line's president, governor-elect Dudley. Construction began in earnest from both directions in 1837. Weldon was made the northern terminus, as its location on the Roanoke River would enable it to receive produce from the Roanoke Valley in competition with a rail line from Virginia that already reached the northern banks of the river.

By November 1838 the road was operating out of Wilmington along the right bank of the Cape Fear River for a distance of sixty-four miles to Faison's Depot in Duplin County, the home of Elias Faison, a stockholder in the company. At the other end of the line, from Weldon south, twenty miles had been completed to Enfield. The road was completed on 7 March 1840.

A rival road was also under construction. When it was decided that the Wilmington road would go to the Roanoke River, citizens of Raleigh began negotiating with officials of the Petersburg, Virginia, railroad. As a result the North Carolina legislature granted two charters which, when put together, called for the construction of a railroad from the state capital north to join the Petersburg road. The first of these charters authorized a railroad to be known as the Greensville & Roanoke, to run from a point at Emporia in Greensville County, Virginia, to the Roanoke River at or near what was then Wilkins' Ferry in Northampton County, North Carolina. This line was soon completed and its southern terminal took the name of Gaston.

In December 1835 the legislature chartered the Raleigh & Gaston Railroad to run from Raleigh to Gaston. At a meeting in Raleigh early in January the citizens of Petersburg matched the local subscriptions, and later Richmond also subscribed for a block of stock. From the outset this was an interstate undertaking, although the charter required that the directors of the Raleigh & Gaston Railroad be North Carolinians. The first president was George W. Mordecai. Financial difficulties slowed construction work, but by May 1838 the section of ten miles from Gaston to Littleton was opened, and in September the first trains ran to Henderson.

As a result of this work Weldon became the chief railroad center in the state. The Wilmington & Weldon Railroad in April 1840 was 161½ miles long, then the longest railroad in the world. A traveler in 1849 reported that it took eleven hours to go from Weldon to Wilmington and that the fare was five dollars. "This railroad," he noted in his journal, "offers great facilities to farmers both to improve their land by lime and in transporting produce to market. Travellers who grumble at the bad condition of the road would not do so if they knew what difficulties the company have had to encounter, and how poorly as yet they have been paid." He further commented: "Passengers for Raleigh leave this train about midnight, right in the woods; and those for Wilmington have to change cars at Weldon at 2 or 3 o'clock, in the open air, which, although a serious inconvenience, is far better than the old mode of staging."

Some years later another traveler going north reached Raleigh by train "tired and dirty" yet happy to be "freed from the hot, suffocating cars, and lodged in a comfortable room." After leaving Raleigh, he said, the heat in the cars was excessive; and after changing at Weldon, "The cars were constantly filled with dust so that we could not see each other with any distinctness, and what rendered the ride more intolerable, I had no one to fret and fidget with me. . . . I had to wet a towel we had provided ourselves with, having had a foretaste of this when we went to Raleigh. I had to wet this towel whenever we stopped, and clear the dust from my eyes, in order to preserve any kind of vision." In the 1850s the trains moved through the state at the remarkable speed of 14½ miles an hour!

It was not long before farmers along the route of these two lines began to use them to transport cotton, corn, tobacco, and other produce to market and to obtain fertilizer and equipment from suppliers. Farmers, merchants, and manufacturers in western North Carolina also realized the benefits to be gained from such service. Governor John Motley Morehead in 1842 told the legislature that the state should construct a network of rail lines to make North Carolina economically independent of its neighbors to the north and the south. With some state aid, private investors would come forward to carry on the work. Specifically, he proposed that the state extend the Raleigh & Gaston Railroad to Charlotte and that branch lines be constructed to Goldsboro and Fayetteville.

The needs of rural North Carolinians recognized by Governor Morehead as well as by Archibald Murphey a generation earlier were still not being met, however. Late in 1845 the *Greensborough Patriot* observed that emigration from the state was still at "flood tide." "Never have we seen such a rush of our population for the great West. All manner of vehicles, and pack-horses, and foot travellers pass through town every day literally in crowds and caravans. It would not be too much to say that on yesterday, before noon, fifty vehicles passed, each with a family, amounting in aggregate numbers to 150 or 175 souls."

The North Carolina Railroad

Governor Morehead's recommendation was rejected because of opposition from Democrats and from those who had an interest in the route between Wilmington and Weldon. Rufus Barringer of Concord and John W. Ellis of Salisbury joined others in suggesting the incorporation of a company to build a railroad from Danville, Virginia, to Charlotte with a connection to Columbia, South Carolina. Easterners declared that any such line would permit Danville to "steal" trade from North Carolina and that the whole scheme was a "sell-out" to Virginia and South Carolina. Westerners were more interested in having almost any railroad than they were in the kinds of questions that were being raised by easterners, and they were willing to consider alternatives. This was the situation in the state when an eastern Democrat, W. S. Ashe of New Hanover County, introduced a bill in the General Assembly in 1849 to charter the North Carolina Railroad Company.

Its charter provided for a capital of $3 million, of which the state would subscribe $2 million, and the line would run from Goldsboro to Charlotte, passing through Raleigh. The vote on chartering the road was a tie in the senate and

Among the public works resulting from the changes that occurred in North Carolina after the mid-1830s were many useful canals. This one near the North Carolina-Virginia border attracted considerable patronage. (Courtesy of The Mariners Museum, Newport News, Virginia)

Speaker Calvin Graves, a Democrat, cast the deciding vote in favor. The line would serve the state well, but it would not pass through his home county of Caswell as the proposed Danville to Charlotte line would. By his magnanimous vote Graves ended his political career, since his party felt he had betrayed it.

The leading figure in the construction of the North Carolina Railroad was former governor John Motley Morehead. He became personally involved in the sale of stock to private investors, surveying the route, and road construction. The whole state was enthusiastic and watched the progress with great interest. At a meeting in Salisbury on 11 July 1850 the private stockholders met and organized the company, and on 21 August surveys got underway. In Greensboro on 11 July 1851 Calvin Graves participated in a ceremony laying the first rails, and on 29 January 1856 the road was ready to open from Goldsboro to Charlotte, a distance of 223 miles. This was one of the plans advocated by Joseph Caldwell in his *Numbers of Carlton*.

The new railroad made a great arc across the map of North Carolina, passing through Hillsborough, Salisbury, and Concord, the hometowns of William A.

Graham, John W. Ellis, and Rufus Barringer, respectively, all of whom had taken an interest in the development of this mode of transportation. Old freight rates by wagon were now halved, and new markets were available. The railroads united the people of the state, created a new pride and patriotism, and helped to stop the flow of people out of North Carolina to other states.

Common Schools Established

Another phase of the Whig program pertained to education, and party leaders turned their attention to it at the same time they were promoting railroads. Early in 1837 the distribution of the surplus federal revenue brought an unexpected addition to the Literary Fund, and late the next year the Literary Board prepared a plan for a system of public schools modeled on the 1817 proposals by Archibald Murphey.

In January 1839 the General Assembly passed the state's first public school law. It provided for the division of the state into school districts and the establishment of a primary school in each district through county tax supplements and by allocations from the Literary Fund. County and district school boards began to inaugurate the system in August in those counties that approved it. All but seven of the state's sixty-eight counties accepted the bill's provisions. On 20 January 1840 the first public school in North Carolina opened in Rockingham County, the year in which there were 632 primary schools of any kind in the state. A decade later there were 2,657 "common" or public schools.

The system established was far from perfect. It did not fix responsibility for the operation of schools, and the erection of schoolhouses was optional and usually required private resources. Frequently the county school board was composed of inefficient, sometimes even illiterate, men. If funds were adequate to maintain a minimum-level school, they were satisfied. Apparently it did not occur to them to seek additional tax revenues to lengthen the school term, to improve the schoolhouse, or to buy new equipment.

In 1841 the legislature made federal population instead of white population the basis of distributing the Literary Fund. This clearly discriminated against the west, which had few slaves, and gave a disproportionate share of the money to the east. About the same time, however, the legislature determined that free blacks would not be required to pay taxes to support schools since they were not permitted to attend.

Another flaw was that the school districts were too large to make the location of the schoolhouses convenient to everyone in the district. Farms were widely scattered and in order to get enough students to make it worthwhile to build, the district had to be large. In a typical case it was noted that early in a term there might be more than fifty pupils at a school, but before the end of the term there

Old-Field schools, so called because they usually sat in an abandoned and eroded field, were maintained by local communities in many parts of the state before public schools were established. (North Carolina Collection, University of North Carolina at Chapel Hill)

number would have fallen to around ten. One reason for this was that some families lived so far away that their children could not make the trip every day. Some parents refused to let their children attend because of the stigma they imagined was attached to attending public schools. Others would not permit their daughters to attend schools that were also attended by boys. And some felt the need for their children to work in the fields rather than to go off each day to sit in a schoolhouse. Finally, there was still competition from the "old-field schools" and academies that had been established years before.

The establishment of common schools in North Carolina was a significant achievement. Throughout the pre–Civil War period a majority of the people were indifferent to education. Many, in fact, small farmer and gentry alike, were actually opposed to the idea of public education. Yet a few farsighted individuals had always been in favor of general education for the masses and others were converted to the theory by the American Revolution. A few state leaders for years, through the pulpit, the press, and the halls of the legislature, advocated education. Converts were won slowly, but after 1840 the people began to boast of their common schools just as they did of their state university and as they had earlier of their handsome marble statue of George Washington. A small group of men, in their devotion to a worthy cause, had forced the state, ridiculed by its neighbors as backward and ignorant, into a step as progressive as any taken by its scorners.

This evidence of state pride may have prompted Warren County Senator Weldon N. Edwards in 1845 to introduce in the General Assembly an unusual bill. He pointed out that the state owned neither a national nor a state flag "by which she may be designated among her other sisters" of the nation. The governor, therefore, was authorized to purchase for the state "a National Banner, and also one bearing the arms of North Carolina." This is the earliest known reference to a North Carolina state flag. A little later, in the Mexican War, North Carolina troops carried a "banner" bearing the state seal.

War with Mexico

While the attention of most North Carolinians was focused on local affairs, as was usually the case, some took notice of or actually were involved in the War with Mexico between 1846 and 1848. The causes of this conflict were the annexation by the United States of Texas, to which many North Carolinians had recently moved, and claims for American losses in Mexican revolutions. Also influencing the war was the belief in the "manifest destiny" of the United States to expand westward to the Pacific. James K. Polk, a native of Mecklenburg County and an alumnus of the University of North Carolina, was then president of the United States, and under his leadership a vast new territory was acquired which included California and New Mexico. Altogether the United States enlarged its boundaries by half a million square miles at a cost of $100 million and the loss of 13,000 lives.

North Carolina was asked to raise a regiment of about a thousand men. At first enthusiasm was high and enlistments generous until the War Department delayed in calling the men into active service. When strict terms of enlistment were specified, interest declined. Some men from Edgecombe and Mecklenburg counties saw service while others were called up from Ashe, Buncombe, Cabarrus, Caswell, Cherokee, Cumberland, Davie, Lenoir, McDowell, Orange, Rockingham, Rowan, Surry, Wake, Wayne, and Yancey counties. Altogether thirty-two companies volunteered. The North Carolina troops suffered both battle casualties and deaths from disease, and some deserted. Nevertheless, the training and experience under arms received by many of the survivors stood them in good stead when they later served in the Confederate army.

Concern for the Unfortunate

A modest concern for humanitarian reforms developed under Whig domination of the state. In the colonial period the care of a community's unfortunate was often left to the vestry of the local parish just as it was in England. In North

James Knox Polk (1795–1849), a native of Mecklenburg County and a graduate of the University of North Carolina, was the eleventh president of the United States (1845–49). His attainment of this high office and his role in expanding the United States across the continent instilled a new sense of worth and pride in North Carolinians. (North Carolina Division of Archives and History, Raleigh)

Carolina, however, where the Anglican church was not widely established, this was not always an effective tool. More often than not concerned individuals provided the care and resources necessary. After the American Revolution a new system developed as an outgrowth of these two methods.

An agency of between two and seven men, called the Overseers or Wardens of the Poor, came into being, serving very much as the churchwardens had earlier. In 1817 county courts were authorized to levy a modest tax to provide resources for the relief of the poor and unfortunate in a county. This was frequently supplemented by private contributions or by bequests from the estates of deceased persons.

Legally the poor were defined as the unpropertied class, persons incapable, in the opinion of the Wardens, of earning a living by reason of physical or mental incapacity to work. Children were never classified as paupers, even in infancy, if it was possible to apprentice them to someone willing to maintain them in return for the labor rendered. As a rule, therefore, the legal poor were afflicted children, retarded or insane persons, invalids, and aged persons. When identified, fathers of illegitimate children were obliged to post a bond that the child would not become a public charge.

There were four general methods of caring for the poor in antebellum North Carolina: (1) allowances were given to the individual pauper; (2) someone was paid to keep him or her on a low-bid basis; (3) the state contracted with individuals to care for one or more such people; (4) care was provided in a poorhouse. The first three were commonly used early in the nineteenth century, but after 1831 when the General Assembly authorized counties to erect poorhouses that method was widely adopted. When they were able to do so, inmates were expected to help care for livestock and to raise crops to supply some of their needs in the county poorhouse. Surviving floor plans, as well as a few original buildings, suggest that housing was adequate and even comfortable. Small rooms, with a fireplace and a door on one side opening to the outdoors and on the other to a hall, typically accommodated single inmates or a couple. Meals were taken in a common room that also provided space for religious services and above which the caretaker and his family lived.

Dorothea Dix, a philanthropist and reformer of Boston and New York, in 1848 spent three months in North Carolina gathering information about jails and poorhouses and studying the treatment of the unfortunate. During visits to many parts of the state, she witnessed the distressing conditions under which the insane, deaf, mute, and blind were maintained. Particularly concerned about the care of the insane, she observed: "Short excursions, resort to the workshops, carpentering, joining, turning, [and] the use of a good library, are aids in advancing the cure of the patient." She was aware that Democrats in the legislature were opposed to providing funds for the treatment of these people. As an effective lobbyist and a skillful politician, she invited a handful of the most influential leaders of the party to her hotel where she handed them a copy of a "memorial" she had prepared citing examples of harsh treatment of many individuals. She did not meekly *request* but instead *told* John W. Ellis that she expected him to present the memorial to the General Assembly and to move to have it printed. He complied, and while she was still in the state a bill was introduced to provide some of the measures she advocated. The bill, however, did not attract much support.

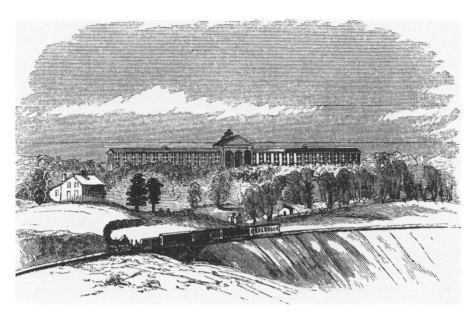

The state mental hospital erected on Dix Hill in Raleigh as well as an expanding system of railroads across the state were further benefits of the new understanding after 1835 of the function of state government. (North Carolina Collection, University of North Carolina at Chapel Hill)

In Raleigh Dorothea Dix made numerous calls on Mrs. James C. Dobbin, the incurably ill wife of a leading member of the House of Commons. These visits cheered Mrs. Dobbin; a few weeks later as she was dying, she obtained a promise from her husband that he would support the bill to establish an insane asylum so favored by Dorothea Dix. Soon afterward, in a very emotional speech, Dobbin united the Whigs and the Democrats on its behalf and the bill was passed. A special tax was levied and after it had accumulated for a few years, construction began in 1853 at a site in Raleigh that soon was called Dix Hill. In 1856 the legislature made its first direct appropriation to the hospital for the insane, which accommodated 150 patients.

Archibald Murphey's thoughtful report to the General Assembly in 1817 on education recommended the inclusion of the deaf in future planning. Ten years passed before a few leading citizens met in Raleigh to organize the North Carolina Institution for the Instruction of the Deaf and Dumb, but their action proved to be premature. These men did, however, draw attention to the need for such a school, and as members of the General Assembly they kept the subject alive. In 1842 Governor Morehead recommended that the legislature establish such a school, and in 1844 William D. Cooke, principal of the Virginia Institute for the Deaf and Dumb, arrived in Raleigh to try to found a private school. Encouraged by Governor Morehead, Cooke demonstrated his methods to members of the General Assembly. They were impressed and appropriated $5,000 to help him get started; they also authorized counties to levy a tax to provide pupils with financial assistance. Assuming complete responsibility for the school, Cooke opened it in the spring of 1845 and soon had twenty-three students between the ages of eight and thirty who attended his classes in reading, writing, arithmetic, history, geography, and domestic and industrial arts. Impressed with the results, legislators in 1852 incorporated the school as the North Carolina Institute for the Deaf, Dumb, and Blind.

Private philanthropy continued to assist many unfortunates in the state. Drought, flood, fire, hard times, illness, and other tragedies always found people ready and willing to help. Individual planters and farmers felt a keen responsibility toward their less fortunate neighbors during these periods. Often a small, unoccupied house would be offered to tide a family over, and sometimes a garden plot and even food and forage would be made available. Town dwellers collected money and goods to be given to victims. Young men in town might put on a dramatic performance or sponsor a dance or a party to raise money for a good cause. Doctors often attended the poor and other unfortunates with no thought of reimbursement, and women served as nurses where they were needed.

In seaport towns such as Wilmington, Beaufort, and New Bern concern was demonstrated for the welfare of sailors. In Wilmington a Seamen's Friend Society was formed "to improve the social, moral, and religious condition of seamen." Members opened an "economical, moral boarding house" for sailors which also served as "an asylum for shipwrecked and destitute seamen and a hospital for such sick seamen as are not provided for by the government." In 1854 the society's buildings were valued at $15,000; in the same year it cared for nearly five hundred sailors, eighty-six of whom were ill.

Women of North Carolina did a great deal to care for the "worthy poor." Their religious societies and nondenominational benevolent societies were spread across the state. A Newbern Female Charitable Society was incorporated in 1812, the Raleigh Female Benevolent Society by 1822, and the Fayetteville Female Society of Industry in 1830. Among their concerns were "destitute female children," but they also helped to provide work for women whose families depended on them for daily support. Handicrafts made by women, special collections taken up on public occasions, and fairs were all sources of income for the work of these organizations.

The good work undertaken by so many people did little to reform the harsh criminal code inherited from the common law of England. Imprisonment for debt was abolished for a brief period through the action of Archibald Murphey, but soon after its repeal he himself was one of its victims. Efforts to secure funds for a state prison and a program to rehabilitate criminals were unsuccessful, although reform advocates were able to get the number of capital offenses reduced from twenty-eight to seventeen and finally to a dozen: arson, bigamy, burglary, counterfeiting, dueling, forgery, horse stealing, housebreaking, inducing a slave to run away, murder, rape, and stealing a slave. During the antebellum period various forms of punishment, also inherited from England, continued to be accepted in the state—among them, branding, the ducking stool, fines, hanging, imprisonment, the pillory, stocks, and the whipping post. Women occupied a lower legal status than their husbands, but a law in 1848 made it illegal for a husband to sell or lease real estate owned by his wife at the time of their marriage without her consent.

North Carolina was less suited to the large-scale production of cotton than the Deep South states where it was the staple crop, and thus plantations with large numbers of slaves were rare. Before the early 1830s many citizens applauded the hopes of James Iredell and William Gaston that slavery might be ended. Antislavery societies were organized, and masters were encouraged to free their slaves. Formed in 1816, the North Carolina Manumission Society had twenty-eight branches by 1825 and more than a thousand members. The American Colonization Society, with up to forty branches in the state, reported the emancipation of around two thousand slaves between 1823 and 1826.

The so-called black code laws applying to slaves were subject to some changes during the period of Whig ascendancy, but as a rule only to strengthen them. When the importation of slaves from Africa ceased in 1808, the value of slave property began to increase. Fear of slave insurrections in North Carolina grew in the 1820s when word spread that eighty runaway slaves were hiding in the swamps of Onslow County; that fear became even more real after the Nat Turner insurrection in 1831 in Southampton County, Virginia, bordering Northampton County, North Carolina. The North Carolina Manumission Society held its last meeting in 1834. There was more unrest, however, when the "missionaries" of antislavery societies centered in the New England states began to appear in the South.

The strengthening of the "black code" further restricted the freedom of slaves to move about the community, associate with others, bear arms, trade, teach, preach, or be emancipated. Free blacks' loss of the ballot during the Constitutional Convention of 1835, although it was by a very close vote, was another reflection of uneasiness on the part of whites.

Yet at the same time several judicial decisions enlarged the security of slaves. In 1835 Judge William Gaston determined, in *State v. Will*, that slaves had a right to defend themselves against the unlawful attempt of their masters to kill them. This was in direct opposition to an 1829 decision rendered by Chief Justice

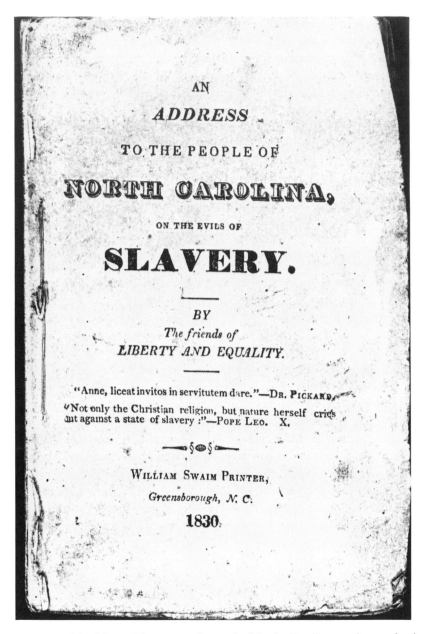

AN

ADDRESS

TO THE PEOPLE OF

NORTH CAROLINA,

ON THE EVILS OF

SLAVERY.

BY

The friends of
LIBERTY AND EQUALITY.

"Anne, liceat invitos in servitutem dare."—Dr. PICKARD.

"Not only the Christian religion, but nature herself cries out against a state of slavery :"—POPE LEO. X.

WILLIAM SWAIM PRINTER,
Greensborough, N. C.

1830.

There was considerable antislavery sentiment in North Carolina, and organizations opposed to slavery operated with few or no restrictions during the early nineteenth century. This pamphlet, issued under the auspices of the North Carolina Manumission Society, was both printed and distributed in the state. (North Carolina Collection, University of North Carolina at Chapel Hill)

Thomas Ruffin, in *State v. Mann*: "The power of the master must be absolute to render the submission of the slave perfect." Nevertheless, Ruffin had confessed his personal "sense of the harshness of this proposition" and felt that "as a principle of morale right every person . . . must repudiate it." In 1838, in *State v. Manuel*, Gaston held that a free black was a citizen and entitled to the guarantees of the constitution. Where the punishment of a slave was "barbarously immoderate . . . and denotes plainly that the master must have contemplated a fatal termination," the master would be guilty of murder.

The state's growing investment in railroads, schools, assorted humanitarian institutions, and other services to the people required larger revenues. To meet these demands the Whigs instituted a reassessment of property and a new determination of those who were obligated to pay a head or poll tax. They were reluctant, however, to raise the tax rate on these traditional sources high enough to make much difference in the state's revenue. As a result, in the late 1840s new taxes were levied on income, inheritances, licenses, and luxuries—sources that placed the heaviest burden on the wealthy and particularly on the professional and business community. Slaves, however, were subject only to a head (poll) tax and not according to their value. Even so, these changes almost doubled the state government's income—from $71,740 in 1835 to $141,610 in 1850.

During fifteen years of effective leadership the Whig party reversed the backward condition of North Carolina and directed it into a position of predominance. The first three governors, Dudley (from the East), Morehead (from the West), and Graham (from the center), were relatively young (aged forty-six, forty-five, and forty-one, respectively), progressive and active, with the ability and zeal to push their party's program. The last Whig governor in this series was fifty-four-year-old Charles Manly, whose interests were similar to those of his predecessors, but their impressive accomplishments apparently dimmed his enthusiasm. While at least rendering lip service to education, internal improvements, and the other good causes of his party, there seemed little left for him to suggest. He proposed that the General Assembly establish a geological survey and undertake a project to copy North Carolina colonial records from sources in London. When mumblings about secession from the Union began to be heard from other states, Manly rejected the idea. His administration did not impress the people very much. A report on the geology of the state had already appeared in the years between 1827 and 1829, and another one was not authorized until he had left office. The colonial records were not copied to any extent for well over a century, and in time North Carolina followed other southern states out of the Union. As soon will become evident, Manly played a critical role in the demise of the Whig party in North Carolina.

16

A CHANGE IN MIDSTREAM

EVEN THOUGH their leaders grew old and less progressive, the Whig party continued its hold on the government of North Carolina. That hold had never been a strong one, however, as the party often won by a close margin. Edward Bishop Dudley's first election (1836) was by just 4,043 votes. Between 1840 and 1842 John Motley Morehead dropped from a difference of 8,581 to 4,572 over his opponent. William A. Graham, on the other hand, gained in his second campaign, winning by 7,859 (1846) as opposed to 3,153 (1844). Charles Manly in 1848 won by a mere 854 votes. Whig candidates for president of the United States in 1840 and 1844 carried North Carolina by a somewhat larger margin than did the gubernatorial candidates, and in 1848 approximately the same number of Whigs voted for the Whig presidential candidate as usually did, but many abandoned the party when Manly ran for governor.

The Democrats Prevail on Suffrage Issue

Progressive young men began to join the Democrats and to change its program. In favor of greater support for both railroads and education, they hoped to find that party's platform to their liking. They also realized that the requirements for voting were still the same ones implemented by the Provincial Congress of December 1776 and that the state constitution was still restrictive in that respect. One of the most active and effective of these new leaders was William Woods Holden. In 1843, at age twenty-five, he became editor of the *North Carolina Standard*, a Raleigh newspaper. A brilliant journalist, Holden soon made it the leading paper in the state as well as one of the most attractive. He appears to have adopted some of his ideas for design and layout from publications using the printing techniques and new fonts of type developed at William D. Cooke's school for the deaf and dumb.

Coming from very humble origins in Orange County, Holden stood up for the "common people." As a means of taking control away from the Whig party, he urged the Democratic party to adopt a program that would appeal to a great many North Carolinians. Having been in power for fifteen years, Whigs were growing more inattentive to the needs and desires of the mass of people. The Democrats, however, had difficulty persuading able men to run for governor because the Whigs, it was assumed, would always win. In 1848 the Democratic convention nominated David S. Reid, an attorney, a militia officer, and a former member of the General Assembly; at the time, he was completing his second term in Congress. Holden and Robert P. Dick, a prominent leader of the party, urged Reid to run, but he—as others before him—proved to be a reluctant candidate. Holden was about to publish Reid's letter declining the nomination when some other party leaders asked him to delay a bit. In the meantime they set about to change Reid's mind.

Although the party's platform said nothing about broadening the suffrage, Reid brought it up. In replying to the request of party leaders that he reconsider his decision, he said: "Gentlemen, this nomination was not sought by me, and it has been my purpose for a long time if I should be a candidate for a state office before the people, to broach one issue, which I deem very important. What I mean is that the state constitution shall be so amended that all voters for a member of the House of Commons shall be allowed to vote for Senators." The party was far from unanimous on this question, but Reid had made this declaration for himself. At a political meeting in Beaufort when both Reid and Charles Manly, the Whig candidate, were on the platform, Reid again spoke out in favor of manhood suffrage. Manly hesitated to commit himself and asked for a day to think it over. The next day, before a political gathering in New Bern, Manly said that he was opposed to broadening the suffrage. His statement marked the beginning of the end of the Whig party. It divided the Whigs, and eventually the question of permitting slavery in new territories destroyed the party.

Throughout the campaign of 1848, Manly consistently belittled Reid's proposal, referring to it as "political claptrap" and nothing more than an attempt by an office-hungry party to seek votes. Merely changing the suffrage requirements for the senate, Manly pointed out, would have little effect so long as property qualifications remained for officeholding. Anything as serious as this ought to grow out of a nonpartisan movement and be kept above the dirt and grime of party politics.

Although Whig influence was still strong, Manly—as noted above—was elected by only 854 votes. This was in marked contrast to the election of 1846, when the Whigs had won by almost 8,000 votes. It was obvious that manhood suffrage had become a popular issue and one on which the Whigs could no longer appear indifferent, but they did try to hinder the means by which such a change could be accomplished. To broaden the suffrage, Democrats wanted the state constitution amended by the process of legislative enactment rather than by constitutional convention. In 1848 the General Assembly took up the matter, and the House of Commons passed a bill providing for equal suffrage. Whigs

David S. Reid (1813–91), as the Democratic candidate for governor in 1848, raised the issue of free manhood suffrage which precipitated a vigorous campaign. (North Carolina Division of Archives and History, Raleigh)

opposed it and attempted to get a bill through to call a convention. The senate, controlled by the land-owning interests, rejected this approach—undoubtedly as being too risky because a convention might consider some questions that would be detrimental to eastern landowners.

The issue was revived in the 1850 campaign, when Reid reluctantly consented to run again. The Whigs supported Manly for reelection. Democrats favored a suffrage amendment by the legislative method; Whigs either opposed the idea or halfheartedly advocated a convention, or at least a referendum to determine whether the people wanted a convention. This time Reid was elected governor and by nearly 3,000 votes. In a last address to the legislature Manly conceded that many North Carolinians obviously wished to have the constitution revised. He urged, however, that a referendum be held to be certain that the people desired a change and if so whether they preferred the convention method.

The 1850 legislature passed an amendment by the required three-fifths vote only after a great deal of debate, dissension, and difficulty. Many members wanted senate representation to be based on white population, but this frightened landowning easterners. The senate approved the house amendment only when it was suggested that a call for a convention might pass. To become effective, the proposed amendment next had to be passed by a two-thirds referendum

Charles Manly (1795–1871), the Whig candidate for governor in 1848, was taken aback on the campaign trail when his opponent turned to him in debate and asked how he felt about free manhood suffrage. Manly declined to answer immediately, but the next day spoke against broadening the suffrage. Although he won the election by a close vote, he was afterward defeated. Manly's rejection of this popular issue contributed to the disappearance of the Whig party in the state. (North Carolina Division of Archives and History, Raleigh)

at the 1852 session. Opposition quickly developed and that, together with an error in naming committee members which put opponents to the amendment on a critical committee, led to the amendment's very narrow defeat in 1852. Two years of legislative discussion and action were lost, and the manhood suffrage amendment had to start its course all over again.

In the 1854 campaign Thomas Bragg was the Democratic candidate for governor on a platform favoring free suffrage by legislative enactment but opposing any change in the basis of representation. The Whig platform was virtually identical except that it favored a convention. Bragg pointed out that there was no constitutional requirement that a convention submit its work to a vote of the people, but, by legislative enactment, an amendment would be offered to the people for approval.

When the legislature convened late in 1854 David S. Reid was still governor, and he continued to work for manhood suffrage. He noted that 50,000 men were denied the privilege of voting for members of the senate. Whigs still held

At an Election held at William N. Pearces for the
purpose of Electing three persons for to act as committee
men of common Schools in the 7th district
~~September~~ October 3rd 1846

William J Halley
George W Simpson
Mathew B. Simpson
John Churwell
Nathaniel Williams
William Bratten
William N Perel
William Williams
John Rush

We do hereby Certify that the above
Statement is trew given under our hand
October 3rd 1846

Wm Bratten
William J Halley

Until the General Assembly adopted the Australian or secret ballot in 1929, voting was generally conducted openly and in public. Voters appeared before election officials and stated their choice verbally; it was recorded on a tally sheet such as this one. (North Carolina Division of Archives and History, Raleigh)

out for a referendum to see whether the people even wanted the question to be considered.

Early in 1855 Thomas Bragg became governor and in his inaugural address urged the passage of the suffrage amendment. The senate soon did so with 5 more votes than the required three-fifths. In the face of Whig efforts to kill it, the bill also was passed by the house. At the 1857 session the proposed amendment passed the house by a vote of 109 to 4 and by a safe margin in the senate. This answer to a question first raised in 1843 and presented seriously by Reid in 1848 was in keeping with the pattern of change in North Carolina.

The Democratic party's support of suffrage gave it a new image and brought still more young men into its fold. The party's platform became more liberal as demonstrated in its support of railroads, plank roads, schools, and other state programs that it had opposed previously. For several years the state had been in the midst of a program to build plank roads as an inexpensive but effective means to open up regions not served by railroads. In January 1849 the Fayetteville and Western Plank Road Company was chartered and in good time completed a road from Fayetteville through Salem to Bethania, a distance of 129 miles and reputedly the longest such road ever built. Many other stock companies were also chartered, and numerous shorter roads were completed and operated as toll roads. Unfortunately, these roads—often referred to as "farmers' railroads"—deteriorated rapidly, and their maintenance was difficult and expensive. The expansion of railroads, followed soon by the Civil War, put an end to the building of plank roads.

Educational Progress

In the 1850–51 session of the General Assembly, Calvin H. Wiley of Greensboro introduced a bill to create the office of superintendent of common schools, but it was rejected. The next year, however, it was passed, requiring the superintendent to codify the educational laws of the state, to enforce the law, to see that school funds were properly spent, to obtain annual reports from county school boards, to collect full information concerning the condition and operation of schools in each county, to find reasons why schools grew or were retarded, to consult with and advise teachers, to instruct the examining committees as to the proper qualifications of teachers, to attend meetings of the Literary Board, to deliver educational addresses, to make an annual report to the governor on the progress of the public school system, and otherwise to promote the cause of education.

Only a very special kind of person could perform these varied tasks, but Wiley, who introduced the bill, was prepared to take on the job. Not only was he a member of the General Assembly and a man of political ability, but he also was a Presbyterian minister, a lawyer, and an author and editor. Wiley was enthusiastic about his work and had a genuine devotion to North Carolina. He wrote many books and pamphlets, including several novels, one of which was published in a pirated edition in England in the days when there were no copyright laws. One of his most popular and useful works was the *North-Carolina Reader*, which appeared in eight editions between 1851 and 1874. As superintendent he required every schoolroom to have a North Carolina map; he also provided a large poster with information about the state which could be displayed.

THE

NORTH-CAROLINA READER:

CONTAINING

A HISTORY AND DESCRIPTION OF NORTH-CAROLINA,

SELECTIONS IN PROSE AND VERSE,

MANY OF THEM BY EMINENT CITIZENS OF THE STATE,

HISTORICAL AND CHRONOLOGICAL TABLES,

AND A

VARIETY OF MISCELLANEOUS INFORMATION AND
STATISTICS.

By C. H. WILEY.

"My own green land for ever!
Land of the beautiful and brave—
The freeman's home—the martyr's grave."

Illustrated with Engrabings, and designed for Families and Schools.

PHILADELPHIA:

LIPPINCOTT, GRAMBO & CO.

NO. 14 NORTH FOURTH STREET,

*And for sale by Agents, Merchants, and Booksellers, in all the Counties of
North-Carolina.*

In 1851 Calvin H. Wiley, then a lawyer and legislator but soon to become superintendent of common schools, published the *North-Carolina Reader* for use in the schools of the state. He reasoned that young people while learning to read ought to have access to good material about their state, so he prepared this interesting anthology. (North Carolina Collection, University of North Carolina at Chapel Hill)

Wiley adhered to the earlier theory about education that had been voiced by Thomas Jefferson: popular education must form the basis on which rests a republican form of government. In his speeches, letters, and reports he constantly advanced the idea that a "system of common schools for a great and growing state is a vast and sublime moral obligation."

In 1853 when Wiley became state superintendent, he found the school system "obscured in darkness." After spending most of his first year in traveling around the state, visiting schools, inquiring into conditions, and sounding out public opinion, he noted in his first annual report: "I feel bound to say that money is not our greatest want. . . . We want more efficient management—a constant embodiment and expression of public opinion—a watchful supervision—a liberal course of legislation, good officers, and patience and energy in all having an official position in the system." During the dozen years that he headed the school system, he made the accomplishment of these goals the chief duty of the office.

Wiley had little, if any, difficulty in obtaining the cooperation of the legislature to improve schools. He also gradually won the support of the county and district committees, and in the end he made the public schools a credit to the state. In 1860 he could report without hesitation that "North-Carolina has the start of all her Southern sisters in educational matters." In that year he had been in office only seven years, yet he had revolutionized the public school system in the state. Between 1853 and 1860 the number of school districts increased by nearly 500, the number of schools from 2,500 to 3,082, and the number of pupils from 95,000 to 118,852. Licensed teachers increased from 800 to 2,752 and expenditures from $150,000 (1854) to $278,000 (1860). However, Wiley was unable to lengthen the school term, which remained at about four months until after the Civil War.

The decade of the 1850s was a prosperous period and the Democratic party, formerly the party of economy, raised taxes and increased appropriations especially to the school for the deaf, dumb, and blind, and for the insane asylum. Land and poll tax rates, unchanged since 1817, were doubled in 1854 from six to twelve cents on a hundred-dollar valuation on land and from twenty to forty cents on the poll. Both were increased still further in 1856 and in 1858.

17

THE ECONOMY AND
ANTEBELLUM SOCIETY

ORTH CAROLINA emerged from the dark years of its Rip Van Winkle
sleep, passed through a period of growing awareness of its potential,
and enjoyed a brief taste of prosperity and hope for the future before it
was led reluctantly into civil war. The changes that occurred in the state must
have astounded those who lived through them. Many had seen the coming of
steamboats and railroads, telegraph lines, cotton mills, tobacco factories, a few
furniture manufacturers, new newspapers whose presses also issued pamphlets
and occasionally published books, public schools, denominational colleges, hospitals, asylums, and orphanages serving the people in ways undreamed of by
previous generations. These contributed to the well-being and the expectations
of those fortunate enough to be in a position to appreciate them.

A segment of the population, of course, was hardly aware of this progress.
These were the many landless whites who moved from place to place seeking
employment where it could be found. Often referred to as "poor whites," they
worked for wages, were only semiliterate at best, and had no voice in government.

Blacks, who also composed a significant portion of the population of the
state, fell into two categories: free and slave. Free black men lost their right to
vote in 1835; during this period, as the historian John Hope Franklin has shown,
a number of free blacks, especially children, were seized, removed from their
home community, and sold into slavery. Most free blacks, however, were artisans
who performed essential services for wages or fees. They were blacksmiths, carpenters, cabinetmakers, mechanics, tailors, barbers, commercial fishermen, or
people who followed some other occupation. A notable example was Thomas
Day, of Milton, who made fine furniture for over thirty years; a member of the
local Presbyterian church, he owned extensive property (including slaves who
worked in his shop) and trained a number of apprentices and workmen, both
black and white. Several of the earliest cotton mills in the state also employed
slave as well as free black and white workers.

These years, however, saw the appearance of societies that supported the

Fishing was an important antebellum industry in North Carolina, particularly in some of the rivers of eastern North Carolina. Shad and herring fisheries on the Roanoke and Pamlico rivers in season were busy and thriving sites. Here a seine is being pulled ashore where the fish will be salted down or smoked, packed in hogsheads such as those under the shelter in the upper left, and shipped out. (North Carolina Collection, University of North Carolina at Chapel Hill)

abolition of slavery and sometimes advocated the resettlement of blacks in free states or territories or even in Africa. It also was a time of much agitation by members of such organizations from outside North Carolina. Blacks held in bondage continued to work just as they and most of their ancestors had done before. Their labor contributed to the completion of such public works as railroads, turnpikes, courthouses, jails, and post offices, as well as churches, academy buildings, and private homes, and to the development of agriculture and livestock production. Some worked in mines and a few in factories; others were employed in domestic service. But no matter what their occupation, most slaves made it possible for their owners to participate in government, to engage in creative activities, and in some cases to travel far from home.

Agriculture was the mainstay of the state, and it flourished in the antebellum period. In the farm journals that began to appear—several of which were published in North Carolina—contributors suggested new methods of farming as well as new crops. Farmers' almanacs had been published in the state since the

A street through the slave quarters of a plantation. A few slave houses still survive in North Carolina such as those at Stagville, the Cameron family plantation north of Durham. Other examples of slave quarters can be seen at Somerset Place in Washington County. (North Carolina Collection, University of North Carolina at Chapel Hill)

early nineteenth century, but now their popularity increased. Many farmers began to adopt scientific methods and to give some thought to maintaining the fertility of the soil. Fertilizers and mulches began to be used. Annual local fairs were planned. County and even community agricultural societies were organized. In 1852 the State Agricultural Society of North Carolina was formed, and in 1853 it sponsored the first state fair. Two years later a chair of applied chemistry to deal with agricultural matters was created at the University of North Carolina, followed soon afterward by the use of an experimental farm just south of Main Building (now South Building).

Tobacco

One rainy night in the late summer of 1839, a young slave named Stephen, who worked on the Slade family plantation in Caswell County, fell asleep while watching a barn of curing leaf tobacco. When he awoke he was distressed to find that the fire had almost gone out, so in desperation he grabbed the charred ends of some logs and threw them on the dying embers. The sudden burst of high heat drove the remaining moisture out of the curing leaves, producing a beautiful, unsplotched yellow leaf. His master, Abisha Slade, did not understand the cause of this remarkable accomplishment—the unexpected appearance of a whole barn full of bright yellow tobacco—but he began to experiment and before long understood what Stephen had discovered. Charcoal was the secret to curing the tobacco grown in the particular kind of soil in that part of the state. Soon "bright leaf" tobacco became very important to many North Carolina growers. Some years later Stephen Slade, as he came to be known, acquired a farm that had belonged to his former master and continued producing tobacco. On his death at about age ninety-three, he was buried on the land that he loved.

The Bright Leaf Belt was a strip on both sides of the North Carolina–Virginia state line and included along its southern edge the North Carolina counties from Halifax to Stokes. Granville and Warren were the most productive, but all of the counties in that region soon enjoyed "lush prosperity."

In many other counties, most in the east but some in the Piedmont and the foothills, cotton became an important crop. The number of 500-pound bales produced in the state grew dramatically: from 34,617 in 1840, to 73,845 in 1850, to 145,514 in 1860. While not so impressive as this increase, the production of other crops also rose, and by 1860 both the variety and the quantity must have amazed those who could remember the backward days of the 1820s and 1830s. On the eve of the Civil War North Carolina produced 8 million pounds of rice—all but 400,000 pounds from Brunswick County, a county, incidentally, that continued to produce at least a little rice until the 1950s. Wheat, grown largely in the Piedmont, more than doubled in the 1850s, but corn production grew only slightly despite its many and varied uses. Perhaps corn production was high enough all along to meet the demand. Among the other agricultural products of some significance were barley, beans, buckwheat, flax, fruit, hay, hops, Irish potatoes, oats, peas, rye, sweet potatoes, and vegetables of many kinds. Cane was raised to make molasses, and bees were kept to produce honey.

The Gold Boom and Iron

Gold, one of the most sought-after resources of the New World, lured both explorers and settlers, but it eluded them in North Carolina until the final years of the eighteenth century. Although occasionally found in small deposits, not until 1799 was a significant discovery made. Even then it was not recognized for what it was until a few years later. With a bow and arrow, young Conrad Reed and a younger brother and sister, the children of John Reed of Cabarrus County, were shooting fish in a creek when Conrad found a shining piece of rock and took it home. It weighed about seventeen pounds, and for three years it served as a doorstop. In 1802 the elder Reed took the rock to Fayetteville where a jeweler fluxed the gold and ran it into a bar about six inches long. Not knowing its value, Reed accepted the $3.50 that he was offered for it. Later, when he discovered its true worth, he sued and was awarded $1,000. (In the 1980s that quantity of gold would probably be worth more than $217,000.)

Reed soon began a search for more gold and within a year had found nuggets weighing up to 28 pounds. The excitement created by his finds was contagious and before long North Carolina was the object of a gold rush. As news spread that stream beds and mines elsewhere in Cabarrus County as well as in Anson, Mecklenburg, Montgomery, and other counties were producing, prospectors from around the nation and overseas arrived to try their luck. New mines were reported every week and sometimes every day. In Charlotte in 1831, a nest or bed of gold with several pieces weighing a total of 120 pounds was found and valued at $20,000. At one time it was estimated that 30,000 workers were employed in one phase or another of gold production. Gold mining companies were formed, and engineers were hired from abroad. Boom towns developed, and a report from one of them noted that the workers included natives of England, Wales, Scotland, Ireland, Spain, Sweden, Germany, Switzerland, Poland, Austria, Brazil, Turkey, Mexico, Hungary, Italy, and Portugal, as well as Jews, blacks, and Cornishmen. It was claimed that in one mine thirteen different languages were spoken.

Attempts to have a branch of the United States mint established in North Carolina failed, but in 1831 Christopher Bechtler, a native of Germany, opened a private mint at Rutherfordton. An accomplished and honest goldsmith, he won immediate acceptance and carried on the business until 1843, when two sons and a nephew succeeded him. Operations were continued until 1857. This mint made coins in denominations of $1.00, $2.50, and $5.00, which became the common medium of circulation in the region; it also refined gold and made it into bars valued at $500, $1,000, and $2,000. In 1840 Bechtler reported that he had coined $2,241,840.50 and fluxed an additional 1,729,988 pennyweights of gold. His coins were carefully made and contained slightly more gold than the indicated value. Whenever the United States mint got any of Bechtler's coins it melted them down and reissued them, making a little profit on the side from the extra gold. In addition, the firm sometimes made collar buttons, cuff links, necklaces, rings, stickpins, watch chains, and other gold objects.

After several attempts, southern congressmen succeeded in getting a bill passed to establish a branch mint at Charlotte, which opened on 4 December 1837. Large quantities of gold were taken there to be coined until 1861, when it was appropriated by the Confederate government. After the war it opened for assaying only; it finally closed in 1913. By 1860 the branch mint in Charlotte had coined just over $4.5 million in North Carolina gold whereas the Philadelphia mint had coined over $9 million. From the reports of the various mints, it appears that nearly $16 million in gold coins came from North Carolina.

Gold mining declined in the state for several reasons. Some unscrupulous companies sold stock in barren mines. People resented working under the direction of foreigners and declined to negotiate with them. Rich veins ran out, and deep mining was too expensive and dangerous. And finally the discovery of gold in California lured North Carolina miners, including native-born miners, to new fields there.

Nearly every mineral found anywhere in the United States has also been found in North Carolina, but seldom in sufficient quantities to be commercially important. While not particularly noteworthy, the production of iron served local and regional needs for a time. Hundreds of small deposits were worked, a few beginning in the colonial period. Small quantities of pig iron were shipped to England in the 1720s and 1730s, and the upper Cape Fear Valley produced some in the 1750s and 1760s. By 1771, two furnaces were operating in Orange County and it was anticipated that one soon would open near Salisbury. The need for cannon and cannonballs during the American Revolution spurred production along the Deep River in Chatham County where ruins of the Wilcox works can still be seen.

Lincoln County became the center of a flourishing iron industry after Peter Forney and some associates acquired a vast tract of land where hardly anything grew. For many years the site, which came to be known as the "Big Ore Bank," provided iron for furnaces in the neighborhood. Alexander Brevard, John Davidson, and Joseph Graham, related by marriage, and others produced skillets, pots, pans, ovens, washpots, and tools and implements of various kinds. They also made hinges, locks, and nails, as well as bars of iron for use by blacksmiths. In some ironworks skilled blacks were an integral part of the business. All of these men, and others as well, learned their trade by trial and error without previous experience to guide them. They took a great deal of pride in their work, which in some cases was continued by sons and grandsons of the original owners until after the Civil War. Usually these ironworks were operated when there was little or no work to be done in the fields, as the owners were also planters or farmers.

The lack of transportation facilities meant that the ironworks faced little competition for the sale of their products. They were too heavy to be moved very far in bulk, although some items were brought up the Catawba River from Charleston into upcountry South Carolina, a region also served by North Carolina foundries. Alexander Brevard employed his brother, Joseph, to act as his agent. A lawyer and judge, Joseph covered a large territory in that capacity and during his trips he took orders for ironware. The Brevards kept a stock of iron goods on hand for sale to customers who called at the foundry. Occasionally one of the manufacturers would also send a wagonload of pots and skillets and some hinges and tools over into Tennessee or down into South Carolina.

In Caswell County the Yarbrough family foundry, in addition to the customary pieces, made stoves both for heating and cooking, large vats for scalding hogs or washing clothes, corn shellers, wagon wheels, plows, hoes, small tools, doorstops in the shape of animals, and wheeled toys of various kinds including children's wagons. At the foundry the Yarbroughs also opened a wagon shop, a general store, a lawyer's office, and a post office. At first they relied on waterpower, but in time used a steam engine when the water was low. The shortage of labor during the Civil War forced them to close; afterward, when a flood washed away some of their buildings and damaged their machinery, they went out of business.

The small rural iron industry began to decline on the eve of the Civil War due to a scarcity of wood for fuel and the expense of limestone, essential in the manufacturing process. Moreover, improved transportation made available better quality iron products with which the more crudely made pieces could not compete. Several iron foundries, particularly those that produced sheet iron in Charlotte, were acquired by larger out-of-state interests and converted into machine shops. Nevertheless, in 1860 there were thirty ironworks in the state including eight in Lincoln County, five each in Cherokee and Cleveland, four in Surry, two each in Catawba and Caswell, and one in each of four other counties.

Several other minerals were produced in lesser quantities. Copper and silver mines were worked, and the coal fields along Deep River in Chatham County provided a poor quality fuel. During the Civil War some of the coal was used for blockade-runners, although because of its inferior quality it emitted a thick smoke that helped identify the ships to the enemy.

During the antebellum period the state produced other goods in quantities that met local needs but left little or none for sale outside the state. In this category were such things as hats, shoes, harnesses and other leather goods, guns, furniture, and whiskey. North Carolina was second in the South in the value of its commercial fishing, though that might also be classed as a minor business. There were thirty-two fisheries along the coast while others operated in the Albemarle Sound and on the Roanoke River. Some fish were sold fresh, but large quantities were either dried, smoked, or salted to preserve them.

As in the colonial period, most North Carolinians in the first quarter of the nineteenth century produced at home whatever they needed for their own use. Spinning wheels and looms furnished cloth. Tallow or beeswax made candles, the common source of light. With home-tanned leather, a family member or a neighborhood cobbler made shoes using a wooden form shaped to match the foot of the person who needed them. Hatmakers were at work around the state, a few of whom produced large numbers of fur hats for the market. Potters, tin-smiths, carpenters, and other skilled craftsmen who provided essential services could be found in many communities. Services or goods that one person could provide frequently were exchanged for services or goods that someone else offered.

Even with the improvements that changed the character of North Carolina, agriculture remained the leading occupation. In 1860 there were thousands of small farmers in the state, and 97.5 percent of the population was rural. Only four planters—one each in Bladen, Chowan, Orange, and Stokes counties—owned three hundred or more slaves, marking them as millionaires.

Manufacturing

The demand for cotton to supply the mills both of England and of New England induced farmers and planters to abandon diversification and to plant more and more cotton. This meant that rural people became less self-sufficient. It also meant that any spare capital was likely to be used to buy more land and slaves in order to grow more cotton.

Comparatively little capital was invested in industrial enterprises. Nevertheless, this was a field of growing interest particularly in the Piedmont where waterpower was available. Between 1850 and 1860 the number of manufacturing plants of all kinds grew from 2,663 to 3,689, while the capital invested increased from $7.5 to $9.7 million and the value of industrial products from $9.7 million (1850) to $16.7 million (1860). The foundation was thus firmly laid for the enormous growth that would follow the Civil War.

During these years five families accounted for most of the progress in the textile industry. Michael Schenck had led the way in 1813 when he built the first cotton mill in the state near Lincolnton, and three years later he was joined by Absalom Warlick; other mills in the vicinity were later established by Schenck's descendants. The state's second mill was built by Joel Battle in 1818 at the Falls of the Tar River where the town of Rocky Mount soon developed. It was burned in 1863 by Federal troops but rebuilt after the war and put to the torch once again "by an incendiary." Rebuilt in 1871 and remodeled and enlarged since, it is still in the hands of the Battle family. John Motley Morehead in 1828 built a cotton mill at Leaksville in Rockingham County; the site later became very significant in the industrial production of North Carolina. In 1836 Francis Fries began construction of the Salem Manufacturing Company. This cotton mill did so well that in 1839 he opened a wool spinning mill and was soon joined by other members of his family in an expanded manufacturing enterprise in which the family is still involved. In 1837 Edwin M. Holt built the Alamance Cotton Mill on Great Ala-

About 1813 Michael Schenck erected the state's first cotton mill on a small stream near Lincolnton. In time five generations of the family established or operated cotton mills. Not many years after these pioneer efforts 40,000 looms across the state produced 7 million yards of cloth annually. This pen-and-ink sketch of the state's first mill was made by a descendant of the founder as he remembered it. (Southern Historical Collection, University of North Carolina at Chapel Hill)

mance Creek not far from the site of the Battle of Alamance. It flourished and before long he was selling his fine cloth in Hillsborough and Fayetteville and as far away as Philadelphia. After the Civil War northern merchants were anxious to buy fabric from his mill again. In 1853 Holt began to produce cloth using colored thread; his famous "Alamance plaids" were the first colored fabrics produced in the South. By 1860 North Carolina had more textile mills than any other southern state, but its thirty-nine mills ranked third in the value of their production.

Turpentine was far and away the state's leading manufactured product in 1860, with most of it being produced in the longleaf pine forests of New Hanover, Bladen, Cumberland, and adjacent counties along the Cape Fear River. Valued at $5.3 million, it represented about two-thirds of that produced in the

United States. Ranking next below turpentine were the gristmill products, flour and meal; just before the Civil War nearly 640 mills in the state produced well over $4.3 million worth. Tobacco products were third with nearly 100 small factories producing snuff, pipe tobacco, and plug and twist tobacco for chewing valued at more than $1 million a year.

The census of North Carolina in 1860 found that its people were engaged in a variety of occupations, but, as shown in Table 17-1, these were largely related to agriculture. Nevertheless, the modest growth of industry spurred development in many of the towns. Wilmington, with its rail connections, and as a seaport near the mouth of the Cape Fear River, flourished as a center of trade and in the 1840s surpassed New Bern as the state's largest town. Fayetteville and Raleigh each had a population of more than 4,000 while Salisbury and Charlotte had about half that many. Seven towns had more than 1,000 residents, and twenty-five smaller places were recognized as towns for purposes of the federal census. Many new towns were incorporated. Frequently their boundaries were described simply as being so many feet from a landmark, such as the southeastern corner of the courthouse. In these cases, the town limits formed a circle, so North Carolina became a state with many "round towns." Indiana and Mississippi, where many North Carolinians relocated, also had a number of round towns. Some of the state's antebellum towns, however, were well planned with streets laid off in a regular pattern, and care was often taken to preserve trees. Travelers commented on the attractive appearance or setting, for example, of New Bern, Wilmington, and Raleigh in the east and Lincolnton and Morganton in the west.

Higher Education

Along with many other significant changes came an intellectual awakening, perhaps due in large measure to the public school system, that dissociated North Carolina still further from its unprogressive reputation of a few decades earlier. Under Calvin H. Wiley's leadership, the number of certified teachers grew and their quality was reflected in the better educated citizenry that they produced. Yet although there was a marked increase in the literacy rate between 1840 and 1860, almost 70,000 whites over age twenty in a population of nearly 630,000 still could not read and write in 1860. At the same time many private academies continued to serve those who could afford the cost, often operating on a longer schedule and providing courses not taught in the common (public) schools, such as Latin and Greek, rhetoric, logic, moral and natural philosophy, and astronomy. It was these institutions that prepared young men for higher education. The University of North Carolina operated a preparatory school adjacent to the

Table 17-1. Occupations of North Carolinians, 1860

Occupation	Number
Farmer	87,025
Laborer	63,481
Tradesman	27,263
Professional worker	7,436
Planter (owning 20+ slaves)	4,065
Merchant	3,479
Teacher	1,936
Clerk	1,626
Manufacturer	1,308

campus in order to help students overcome any deficiencies before admitting them to the university.

Those who sought special training to enter one of the professions could find opportunities in the state. Lawyers and judges accepted young men into their offices so they could read law and prepare themselves to be examined before the local court for licensing. A few prominent lawyers conducted law schools— among them, William H. Battle, Leonard Henderson, James Iredell, Jr., Archibald D. Murphey, Richmond M. Pearson, and John Louis Taylor. Very much the same system operated in the medical field, although a few North Carolinians went to the North or to England, Ireland, or Scotland for training. A doctor would take an apprentice or two and train them as he made his rounds of patients. It is not unusual to find youths in their late teens and early twenties listed as doctors in census returns of the antebellum period. Physicians also served as dentists at the time. There were military academies at Charlotte, Fayetteville, Hillsborough, Smithfield, and elsewhere. Itinerant teachers moved about the state, advertising in local or regional newspapers when they would be available. They offered in short order to create artists, musicians, bookkeepers, dancers, and experts in penmanship of anyone who took advantage of the opportunity.

For a time it was the practice to establish manual labor schools where students engaged in hard work for a part of each day to pay for at least a portion of their expenses. In 1834 some Baptists opened such an institution in Wake County; there the principal, the Reverend Samuel Wait, combined manual labor and literary studies. But the scheme soon proved to be unpopular, and enroll-

Wake Forest College in 1834 was the next major educational institution to be opened in North Carolina after the establishment of the state university. This view of the original building at Wake Forest illustrates a feature that all these institutions shared—a site in the middle of a forest. (North Carolina Division of Archives and History, Raleigh)

ment dropped from 142 in 1836 to 51 two years later. At that time the General Assembly chartered the school as Wake Forest College. Manual labor by students was abandoned, and the school was firmly established to serve not only members of the Baptist denomination but many others as well.

Presbyterians became interested in higher education in the 1770s and attempted to secure a charter for Queen's College in Charlotte. When the Crown rejected their request, they simply gave it a slightly different name, operating it first as Queen's Museum and then as Liberty Hall Academy until it fell victim to hard times at the end of the American Revolution. In 1837 members of the denomination established Davidson College on the manual labor principle. The next year they obtained a charter from the legislature, and in 1841 gave up the manual labor requirement. Their school, they announced, was now a classical college modeled after the Presbyterian institution at Princeton, New Jersey. By 1860 it employed 6 professors to instruct a student body of 112. With the handsome legacy of Maxwell Chambers from Salisbury, it had erected Chambers Hall, "the most imposing college building in the state."

Methodists in 1838 or 1839 opened a log school in the community of Trinity in

Randolph County. In 1841 it was chartered as Union Institute and the next year began to train Methodist ministers. It was rechartered as Normal College in 1851 and given the privilege of certifying teachers for the common schools. Falling on hard times, it was turned over to the Methodist Conference and in 1859 once again had its charter altered. This time it adopted the name Trinity College and by 1869 had a student body of almost two hundred.

Other denominational colleges as well as some schools that evolved into colleges were established before the Civil War. New Garden Boarding School, established by Quakers in 1835 as the state's first coeducational institution, became Guilford College. The German Reformed Church established Catawba College at Newton in 1851, and, with the assistance of the Methodist church, an earlier school at Louisburg became Louisburg College for females in 1857. The latter institution reflected the new and strong interest in higher education for women that developed in antebellum North Carolina, usually as a result of denominational influence. Salem Female Academy, opened in 1772 by the Moravians, added college courses many years later and won recognition as one of the best schools for women in the South. Greensboro Female College (Methodist, 1838), St. Mary's (Episcopal, 1842) in Raleigh, Chowan Baptist Female Institute (1848) in Murfreesboro, and two Presbyterian schools, Statesville Female College (1856) and Peace Female Institute (1857) in Raleigh, all served their students well, as they still do—some of them under different names. Several other schools for women no longer exist, most closing during or soon after the Civil War. In 1860 Governor John W. Ellis reported that 900 males and 1,500 females in North Carolina were attending college.

Reading, Writing, and Religion

In 1823 only a dozen newspapers were published in North Carolina, and only three of those were more than about twelve years old. The *Raleigh Register*, established in 1799 by Joseph Gales, a native of England, was the oldest and one of the most distinguished and influential. Dennis Heartt's *Hillsborough Recorder*, established in 1820 when he came to the state from Connecticut, was also highly regarded and widely read. In Salisbury, the *Western Carolinian*, under the management of Philo White, a native of New York, was a militant advocate of western rights. The *Fayetteville Observer*, the *Greensborough Patriot*, the *Tarborough Press*, the *North Carolina Standard* (Raleigh), and the *Carolina Watchman* (Salisbury) spoke effectively either for the whole state or for the interests of their region. Through each of them people were well informed on foreign affairs, since that was usually featured, but, as the 1840s and 1850s passed, the editors also alerted their readers to the significance of sectional problems developing in the nation.

During the first two decades of the nineteenth century these papers were small weeklies, usually appearing a day or two after the arrival of the customary northern mail gave the editors time to include extracts from out-of-state papers. The weekly pattern was broken briefly in 1804 when the *Register* appeared twice a week while the legislature was in session. In 1823 it became a semiweekly on a regular basis, and in 1846 the Wilmington *Commercial* began publishing three times a week. Soon afterward the Raleigh *Star* also became a triweekly. While the General Assembly was in session in the winter of 1850–51, the *Register* appeared daily. In September 1851, the editor of the newly established *Wilmington Daily Journal* observed that North Carolina was almost, if not actually, the only state in the Union without a daily newspaper. A few months later in Charlotte the *North Carolina Whig* began to appear daily. By 1860 there were eight dailies, two each in Wilmington, Fayetteville, and Charlotte, and one each in Raleigh and New Bern.

Here, as elsewhere in the United States, there was no uniformity in the makeup of an antebellum newspaper. The front page was no more important than any other page—a practice that would change during the Civil War. Editorials, which developed during the 1840s, were moved about from place to place in the paper. Nor were the names of newspapers sacred; during a single month the Raleigh *Star* changed its name three times. On one occasion some jokers got into the office of the *Halifax Compiler* after it was ready to be printed the next day, and they switched the type. Not until the paper had been printed did the editor discover the name had been changed to *Helfiar Compilax*. Headlines were also considered unimportant. Over and over publishers used the same headlines: "Read! Read!," "Important," "A Fact Worth Knowing," or "An Improbable Story." There were virtually no illustrations or cartoons to break up what has been described as the "dreary sea of type" found on every page.

When the Wilmington *Journal* became a daily, it began to publish classified "cards" in a section where the same notice might be run week after week; these were the forerunners of classified advertisements of a later time. As already mentioned, in 1810 the Raleigh *Star* pioneered in the use of a questionnaire to gather information from a wide area on related topics (see Chapter 12). The *Star* was also the first newspaper to feature state news over foreign or national news, as well as to use regular "departments"—that is, special places in the paper devoted to agriculture, medical reports, literary notes, biographical information, and the concerns of youth and women.

A number of magazines also began to appear from presses across the state. Among the earliest was the *Harbinger*, a literary magazine issued "under the supervision of the Professors of the University" between 1833 and 1835. During the same years Benjamin Swaim's *Man of Business*, a monthly, was published first in New Salem, Randolph County, and then in Greensboro "to render every man his own counsellor in matters of ordinary business." In Chapel Hill the *University of North Carolina Magazine* was established by the senior class in 1844, but it lasted only until the end of the year. Begun again in 1852 it has continued—with a few breaks and several changes of title—until the present time as a literary magazine. Several periodicals were devoted to the professions, including the *North Carolina Journal of Education*, founded in 1857 under the editorship of Calvin H. Wiley, and the *Medical Journal of North Carolina*, begun in 1858 and edited by Dr. Edward Warren. Among the religious publications were the Baptist *Biblical Recorder* (1835), the Methodist *North Carolina Christian Advocate* (1855), the *North Carolina Presbyterian* (1858), and the Episcopal *Church Intelligencer* (1860).

One of the most popular books by a North Carolinian was published first in 1851 and reprinted many times since, right up to the present. *Historical Sketches of North Carolina* by John H. Wheeler, former state treasurer, attempted to tell the story of the state from 1584 until its own time. Its appeal probably was in the brief sketches of each of the state's counties and the list of representatives in the General Assembly. Despite its factual errors and limited interpretation, the first edition of 10,000 copies sold within a year. Wheeler's work was followed in 1857 and 1858 by Francis L. Hawks's two-volume *History of North Carolina*, published in Fayetteville. Although it ended its account with the Proprietary period, it presented a great deal of social and economic material as well as information on war and politics.

Not surprisingly, some home-produced schoolbooks were also printed in the state. Elisha Mitchell, a professor at the University of North Carolina, was the author of *Elements of Geology, with an Outline of the Geology of North Carolina*, published in 1842 without an imprint. Brantley York, a teacher in Iredell County and later in Randolph County, published *English Grammar* at the Salisbury printshop of the *Watchman* in 1855 and *Common School Grammar* at a Raleigh printer's in 1860.

Demonstrating the range of interests of the state's native writers are titles such as *Farmer's Own Book: A Series of Essays on Agriculture and Rural Affairs* (1819), by George W. Jeffreys; *Fevers of Eastern North Carolina*, by Matthias E. Sawyer of Edenton, of which no copy apparently has survived so the date is unknown; *Journal of the Texian Expedition Against Mier* (1845), by Thomas Jefferson Green; *Cherokee Physician, or Indian Guide to Health* (1849), by James W. Mahoney; and *Mountain Scenery* (1859), by twenty-three-year-old Henry E. Colton, which contains a number of attractive illustrations.

Women also wrote and published. Winifred Gales was the author of a novel, *Matilda Berkely*, which appeared in 1804. Caroline Lee Hentz, the wife of a professor at the University of North Carolina, wrote poems and plays; one of her novels, *Lovel's Folly*, published in 1833, contains several characters drawn from her acquaintances in Chapel Hill. In the 1840s and 1850s Sarah J. C. Whittlesey, a native of Williamston, wrote a number of novels and won a short story contest sponsored by the *Greensboro Times.* Mary Mason in 1859 published a book for children, *A Wreath from the Woods of Carolina.*

North Carolina produced a large number of poets of varying abilities. Mary Bayard Clarke, a native of Raleigh, in 1854 edited a two-volume anthology containing more than 180 poems by sixty authors. Among them was Judge William Gaston's "The Old North State," later adopted as the state song. The editor herself contributed to the anthology an entry intended to persuade native writers to take up their pen:

> Come rouse you! ye poets of North Carolina,
> My State is my theme, and I seek not a finer,
> I sing in its praise, and I bid ye all follow,
> 'Till we wake up the echoes of "Old Sleepy Hollow."
>
> Come show to his scorners "Old Rip" is awakening,
> His sleep like the cloud of the morning is breaking;
> That the years of his slumber, at last have gone by,
> And the rainbow of promise illumines the sky.

A black poet of this period attracted considerable attention. George Moses Horton lived on his master's farm in Chatham County, not far from Chapel Hill. At the University of North Carolina, where he often went to sell vegetables, he became acquainted with students who discovered his talent for writing verse, especially acrostics. Writer Caroline Hentz encouraged young Horton in his literary endeavors, and in time he not only sold short love poems to students to send home to their sweethearts, but he also saw three volumes of his poems published: *The Hope of Liberty* (1837), *The Poetical Works of George Moses Horton* (1845), and *Naked Genius* (1865).

The type of writing most vitally touching the lives of the people was the casual literature that came from local presses, such as broadsides, almanacs, and pamphlets. Local poets, writers of ballads, and composers of "spiritual hymns" often resorted to the press. Political parties, religious societies, reform organizations, and private individuals with a cause to support issued broadsides and pamphlets. At least three newspaper editors, Joseph Gales, Thomas Henderson, and William Boylan, published almanacs for many years.

The use that Archibald D. Murphey and Joseph Caldwell made of the press has already been demonstrated (see Chapters 13 and 15), but there were many others. William Gaston's address urging the end of slavery, which he delivered before the literary societies at the University of North Carolina in 1832, had been issued in at least five editions by 1858. George Davis of Wilmington was a pioneer in local history and biography with his *Early Men and Times of the Cape Fear*. On the other hand, a great many worthwhile addresses, which might have been printed to the benefit of succeeding generations, were lost as soon as the speaker sat down. It has often been said that the oration was the highest type of literary effort developed in the antebellum South. Not a great many people read literary magazines or encouraged the publication of a book, but they would "travel many miles to be present at court and listen to the oratory of the lawyer and the wisdom of the judge." They would quickly drop whatever else they had to do and spend a day or two listening to a debate between political opponents. And it was not unusual for sermons to last several hours. Before the Civil War, a writer commented in the *University of North Carolina Magazine*: "Excepting [in] a few large cities, it is doubtful whether finer specimens of genuine, moving eloquence in sermons and in prayers have been uttered anywhere in America, than before the uneducated, unliterary audiences that have attended the Southern and Western Camp-meetings."

In the early nineteenth century camp meetings dominated the religious life of many North Carolinians. As a tremendous religious upheaval known as the Great Revival swept the country from Maine to Georgia, particularly among the Presbyterians, Baptists, and Methodists, such meetings were used in an attempt to evangelize the whole state.

Sites in various sections of the state were set aside for periodic camp meetings, and temporary shelters were built to house families for a week or longer during meeting time. On these occasions evangelical preachers would deliver long and emotional sermons, and many who attended would undergo both physical and mental strains—"exercises," they were called. People reacted in different ways. Some shouted, others danced, some fainted, some leapt about or whirled around and around, some talked in "strange tongues." Over time, the camp meeting came to be regarded by many as something of a vacation, taking place when crops were "laid by" and usually before harvest time. It offered the more seasoned adults an opportunity to renew old acquaintances, while young men and women met new people their own age; sometimes romance blossomed from a chance meeting. Critics described camp meetings as the scene of less-than-religious thought and behavior, of undue concern over fancy dress and fine food, and even of drinking and other "unwholesome" activity.

Many educated ministers and laymen were opposed to the camp meeting movement. It resulted in "light, frothy, and trifling conversation," some said. Captain Alexander Brevard of Lincoln County spoke of a revival as a "religious distemper." One ruling elder of the Alamance Presbyterian Church made it a rule not to attend a night meeting or to allow his family to attend. Scoffers often were present and sometimes heckled the preacher. Others, on the fringes of the site, brought goods to sell, including liquor. In Pitt County, in a house near the site of a camp meeting, "some rabble" had a ball "where considerable disorders took place," clearly intended to disturb the meeting.

During much of the late eighteenth and early nineteenth centuries many educated people in North Carolina scorned the idea of religion. Only a few of these skeptics admitted to membership in any church. Others, however, the "poor but pious" as they were called, highly valued their religion. In the 1850s the Protestant churches began to expand, more "common people" chose to join and attend a church, and even the better educated gentry class ceased to be so openly deistic.

Opposition to the Anglican church during the colonial period reflected adversely on its former members after the American Revolution and only a few congregations survived. In 1790, at a meeting in Tarboro, an unsuccessful attempt was made to organize the Protestant Episcopal church in the state as the successor to the old Church of England. The new church's Diocese of North Carolina was not established until 1817 and did not secure its first bishop until 1823. By 1830 eleven Episcopal clergymen served thirty-one congregations. In 1831 a new bishop, Levi Silliman Ives, succeeded the first one, John Stark Ravenscroft. But in 1853 Bishop Ives renounced his position and became a Roman Catholic, demoralizing the Episcopal church in North Carolina. His successor, Thomas Atkinson, however, in time was able to heal the dissension, and by 1860 the church was enjoying a period of quiet growth. Its members, as in the colonial period, came largely from the gentry class but consisted also of professional people, business leaders, and public officials. It was a church with influence far surpassing that suggested by its membership figures.

Baptists in the state constituted the largest denomination on the eve of the Civil War (see Table 17-2). It was a loosely organized church, lacking a central authority. The Baptists offered an emotional religion, were for many years unconcerned about educating their ministry, and appealed to the small farmer class. By 1830 they began to split into different groups. There were Calvinistic Regular (Primitive) Baptists and Separate (Missionary) Baptists. The latter organized a State Convention in 1830; as a progressive and evangelistic body, they helped found Wake Forest College as a means of acquiring an educated ministry.

Following its organization in Baltimore in 1784, the Methodist Episcopal church began to spread. Its early opposition to slavery was soon abandoned, and it began to grow in North Carolina. Pioneer clergymen Francis Asbury and Thomas Coke visited North Carolina several times, preaching, converting people to the Methodist faith, and helping to organize congregations. The effective organization of this church, inherited from its parent Anglican church but without that church's ritual, together with its persistent evangelism, its emphasis on prayer and education, and its general humanitarianism, appealed to a wide range of people. By 1860 the Methodist church was almost as popular in the state as the Baptist church.

Table 17-2. North Carolina Churches in 1860

Denomination	Number of Congregations	Number of Members
Baptist	780	65,000
Methodist	966	61,000
Presbyterian	182	15,053
Lutheran	38	3,942
Episcopal	53	3,036
Christian	44	3,000
Moravian	10	2,000
Quaker	22	2,000
German Reformed	15	1,633
Roman Catholic	7	350

Presbyterians appeared in North Carolina in the early eighteenth century, and with the arrival of the Highland Scots and the Scots-Irish they spread rapidly across the colony. They believed in an educated clergy and encouraged education among the people so that they could read and interpret the Bible for themselves. Presbyterians, who were largely from the gentry and middle class living in towns and in the Piedmont, frequently held public office and exercised considerable authority in the state.

The Society of Friends or Quakers was the earliest religious group in the colony, but beginning in the 1830s, when young Quaker men still refused to serve in the militia, they began to face hostility. Many Quakers left North Carolina and moved to Indiana, Ohio, and other midwestern states. Young people who resented being disowned for marrying someone who was not a Quaker often left the denomination, and the antislavery sentiment voiced by the Society also contributed significantly to its decline. Yet members were admired for their assistance to the poor, orphans, widows, and others, and for their interest in education.

The Disciples of Christ, a denomination that developed after the American Revolution, attracted dissatisfied elements of several other Protestant groups. Early leadership came from ordained Presbyterian ministers (one each from Iredell and Orange counties) and from a Methodist clergyman. Eventually the Disciples united with the Congregational church to form a democratic, loosely organized body which also drew members from the Baptists and other denominations.

Among the German-speaking people in the state the Lutheran, Moravian, and German Reformed churches flourished. German continued to be spoken until the 1840s. These churches required an educated ministry and established schools in their communities; because of the language barrier, however, they did not spread.

*　　*　　*

By 1860 North Carolina was much changed from the state Archibald D. Murphey had known just a generation earlier. On the surface it had become progressive, as demonstrated by its splendid system of public or common schools; its railroads, including one owned largely by the state; its newspapers; its natives holding high national office, among others a president, a vice-president, a cabinet member, and an ambassador; and, most important, its many new business enterprises. Yet the people had changed hardly at all. They were still largely rural and dependent on agriculture, very independent, ultraconservative, often superstitious, clannish, seldom aware of events outside their immediate neighborhood, and above all satisfied with these characteristics.

18

THE COMING OF
THE CIVIL WAR

IN 1860 the white population of North Carolina was 629,932. In that year more than 272,000 natives of the state were living elsewhere, whereas fewer than 24,000 people who lived in the state were born somewhere else. There were 361,522 blacks of whom 30,463 were free. Of all the Southern states, only Virginia had more free blacks. In the South as a whole there were 300 owners of 300 or more slaves, undoubtedly millionaires, but only 4 of them were North Carolinians. The census further showed that some 30,000 people were engaged in "commerce, trade, manufacturing, mechanic arts and mining" while about 19,000 were farm laborers. There were 85,000 farmers in the state, but less than 27,000 of them owned any slaves at all. Among slave owners in the Coastal Plain only about 1 in 20 had 20 or more slaves, and in the Piedmont only about 1 in 50 had that many. Ownership of 20 or more slaves marked one as a "planter," so it is clear that North Carolina was a state of farmers and not planters.

Slave owners in the state constituted a small minority and a special interest group, but with political influence completely out of proportion to its actual voting strength or the total valuation of its property. As members of a special interest group, slaveholders were alert even to such moderate recognition of political privileges as the free Negro suffrage, which was almost retained by the 1835 constitutional convention. They also were sensitive to the mild social and economic reforms suggested for the improvement of working conditions among both the free and the slave populations.

Although in the early colonial period a slave owner was considered to have absolute authority over this form of property, the law had changed greatly by 1860. It was then established that the master owned just the slave's labor and could not take his or her life with impunity. Slaves, nevertheless, were required to work, while the master was obliged to feed, clothe, and care for them. These were the terms of ownership, sometimes considered as an employer-employee relationship.

Southern defenders of slavery concluded that a similar relationship existed in other states where there was little or no slavery. In those states the employer

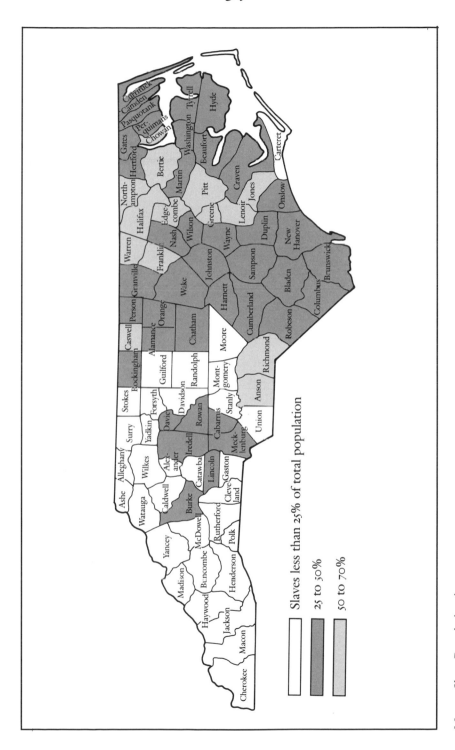

Currituck
Camden
Pasquotank
Per-
quimans
Chowan
Gates
Hertford
North-
ampton
Bertie
Tyrrell
Hyde
Washington
Beaufort
Martin
Pitt
Greene
Craven
Jones
Lenoir
Onslow
Carteret
Warren
Halifax
Edge-
combe
Nash
Wilson
Wayne
Duplin
New
Hanover
Brunswick
Franklin
Granville
Person
Caswell
Wake
Johnston
Harnett
Sampson
Bladen
Columbus
Cumberland
Robeson
Orange
Chatham
Moore
Richmond
Anson
Union
Rockingham
Alamance
Guilford
Randolph
Mont-
gomery
Stanly
Cabarrus
Meck-
lenburg
Stokes
Forsyth
Davidson
Davie
Rowan
Surry
Yadkin
Iredell
Alleghany
Wilkes
Alex-
ander
Catawba
Lincoln
Gaston
Cleve-
land
Ashe
Watauga
Caldwell
Burke
Rutherford
Polk
Yancey
McDowell
Madison
Buncombe
Henderson
Haywood
Jackson
Macon
Cherokee

Slaves less than 25% of total population

25 to 50%

50 to 70%

Map 5. Slave Population in 1860

bought not the person, of course, but the labor of the employee, paying wages by the hour, week, or month. In theory, the mutual obligations consisted of the payment of wages and the performance of labor. Terms might be by written contract or merely verbal, but in either case they were relatively simple. Legally, of course, employers had no authority over their employees outside of working hours, but slave owners did—or at least attempted to exercise it.

The Southern planter who was concerned about the welfare of his slaves had as his counterpart, it was pointed out, the Northern industrialist whose concern was reflected in the prosperity of the community where his business was located. The cruel and arrogant master in the South was also matched by the driving and despotic millowner whose wageworkers were bound to him by what Edmund Ruffin called "slavery to want." Apologists for slavery at the time maintained that the differences between the voluntary servitude of the masses of industrial workers and the involuntary servitude of the Southern blacks consisted in a larger degree of economic and social security for the black slaves. It has been suggested that slaves often had more physical comforts of life than Northern industrial workers. The privilege to move about, however, was not considered.

The immigration of workers from Germany, Holland, Scandinavia, and Ireland beginning in 1830 provided a ready source of labor for the mines, mills, and factories of the North. Because of the presence of an involuntary labor system, these immigrants rarely chose to settle in the South. There were a few in the coastal cities, including Wilmington, North Carolina, but few settled elsewhere.

In the late colonial period the Piedmont section of North Carolina was settled by people who came from a variety of places and largely from non-English backgrounds. With their own labor they cleared land and farmed it. A few eventually owned slaves, but for them slaves simply provided a somewhat easier style of living; they did not actually depend on slave labor. Basically the same kind of people lived in the interior from Pennsylvania down into Georgia. Many of them would later comprise the great flood of migrants who traveled west to settle the American frontier. By 1850 they had pushed far beyond the Mississippi River where they were joined by recent immigrants from abroad or their children. These people had no desire to compete with slave labor. They had, in fact, already cleared and settled large regions before planters with their slaves began to leave the South and settle in the territories and the new states west of the Mississippi.

Slavery also became a moral issue. Quakers were foremost in refusing to hold human beings in bondage; their opposition to slavery was as strong in North Carolina as it was in Pennsylvania where many of the North Carolina Quakers had previously lived. Quakers were the chief supporters of the manumission societies, and Quaker families such as the Coffins, who moved north to Ohio and Indiana from Randolph and Guilford counties, furnished some of the out-

Emigration to Liberia.

NOTICE.

THE *MANAGERS* of *the AMERICAN CO-LONIZATION SOCIETY* give NOTICE, that they are ready to receive applications for the conveyance of free people of colour to the Colony of Liberia.

In all cases. the age, sex and profession of the Applicants must be mentioned.

Application may be made,in Baltimore to *Hon. Judge Brice, Charles Howard, John H. B. Latrobe, Esq. or Charles C. Harper, Esq.* Agents of the Society.   **June 25.**

Attempts to find a solution to the problem of slavery grew more vigorous as the century passed its midpoint. This advertisement, perhaps intended to entice owners to free their slaves, appeared in state newspapers. It proposed to transport free blacks to Liberia. Many North Carolinians contributed to the work of the American Colonization Society. (North Carolina Division of Archives and History, Raleigh)

standing leaders in the Underground Railroad movement. The most systematic efforts to ease the plight of slaves took the form of encouraging and helping them to escape to the free states. The ultimate goal, of course, was the extinction of slavery.

The Balance of Power: Slave and Free States

Southern leaders were concerned about the intent of Northerners to end slavery, but so long as there was an equal number of slave and free states in the Union the abolitionists could do little through congressional action. Abolitionists, nevertheless, demanded that "the immoral, inhumane, and undemocratic institution" be ended immediately with neither compensation to the owner nor colonization of blacks either in Africa or in a free state. Although there were no slave insurrections in North Carolina, they did occur elsewhere, and they were blamed on the presence of abolitionists. Fear of an uprising, however, was very real and prompted the adoption of strict measures to control the movement of blacks.

The acquisition of new territory by the United States, especially that obtained from Mexico during the administration of President James K. Polk, a native of North Carolina, alarmed many Southerners. If the balance between slave and free states were broken, the existence of slavery would be endangered. This was not a new problem, but one that had been allayed for more than seventy years by the Northwest Ordinance of 1787 which prohibited the introduction of slaves into the area north and west of the Ohio River. The ordinance might have continued to maintain the status quo except for two things—the acquisition of new territory from which states would later be created, and the growing opposition to slavery both by humanitarian and reformist groups and by outspoken individuals.

The trouble really began after the United States in 1803 purchased from France the Louisiana Territory between the Mississippi River and the Rocky Mountains. In 1818 the new state of Missouri applied for admission to the Union as a slave state, but the United States House of Representatives would agree only on condition that the state, if admitted, undertake to end slavery. But the Southern senators were able to block this requirement. The Missouri Compromise of 1820 admitted the state with its slaves and Maine as a free state, thus maintaining the balance of power in the Senate. In the long run, however, this was no victory for slavery since Congress decreed that no slaves be permitted in the remainder of the Louisiana Territory north of the latitude of 36°30′ and reaffirmed its authority to determine whether slavery would be permitted in a territory or state. (As noted above, the Northwest Ordinance of 1787 had already excluded slavery in the territory north and west of the Ohio River.) Reason prevailed momentarily, however, as new states were admitted to the Union in pairs—one slave and one free.

Texas won its independence from Mexico in 1836 and was admitted to the Union as a slave state in 1845. Many Southerners, including a great many North Carolinians, moved to Texas even before it became a state. In 1848, after the War with Mexico, the United States acquired the area that became New Mexico and much of California. In the same year, Oregon was admitted as a free state and gold was discovered in California. California filled up rapidly and before the end of 1849 applied for admission as a free state. The South was in danger of losing control of its destiny, with the North more strongly opposed to slavery than ever.

When Congress appropriated money at the end of the Mexican War in connection with negotiating peace and acquiring new territory, Congressman David Wilmont of Pennsylvania attempted to insert a "proviso" that slavery be prohibited from any territory so acquired. Because of the Southern strength in the

Senate, this provision was rejected, thereby increasing sectional bitterness and starting angry debates in Congress. Many Southerners were convinced that the North wanted to control the Senate in order to pass legislation abolishing slavery everywhere.

Among the efforts at compromise was a proposal that those who lived in a territory applying for admission to the Union be given an opportunity to indicate by ballot whether they preferred to become a free state or a slave state. Since neither this plan nor others were acceptable, Congress finally attempted to resolve the issue by action that came to be called the Compromise of 1850. To please the North California was admitted as a free state and the slave trade was ended in the District of Columbia. To placate the South a stricter fugitive slave law was passed, intended to expedite the return of runaway slaves who either had been taken or had fled to free states or territories. New Mexico and Utah were then organized as territories, with the slavery question left to be settled later by their legislatures or by local courts. This so-called compromise, in reality, was a defeat for proslavery interests as the admission of California broke the balance of power in favor of the abolitionists.

In the interim, while Congress was debating the compromise, nine slave-holding states, but not including North Carolina, sent delegates to a convention in Nashville, Tennessee, to discuss the future prospects for the South and to consider the possibility of withdrawing from the Union. (Governor Charles Manly, a Whig, refused to call a special session of the legislature at which delegates might have been named.) The theory of secession was not new. It had been suggested in 1798 by Judge John L. Taylor of North Carolina as a possible response to undesirable Federalist legislation. In New England some Federalists in 1801 proposed secession in response to the election of Thomas Jefferson to the presidency; eleven years later it was raised again by New England shipping interests who opposed the War of 1812. Both Vermont and Kentucky also at one time considered withdrawing. South Carolina in 1832 indicated that it might secede over tariff acts that it opposed. Aware of these precedents, the delegates to the Nashville convention condemned the Compromise of 1850 but took no further action in expectation that the North would respect the guarantees of the Constitution concerning slavery.

For the South a significant section of the Compromise of 1850 was the Fugitive Slave Act. It provided that private citizens as well as officers of the law should assist in apprehending and returning runaway slaves. Although there were heavy penalties for failing to comply with this law, it was widely disregarded with impunity. The act was, therefore, generally ineffective. In addition to refusing to return escaped blacks into slavery, many officials and individuals in the Northern states began to take active roles in the operation of the Underground Railroad. Composed of abolitionists, largely under the leadership of Quakers, members of the Railroad secretly helped to move escaped slaves from one hiding place to another as they made their way to free states or territories. Levi Coffin, a native of Guilford County who moved to Indiana in 1826, became president of this movement.

With the adoption of the Compromise of 1850 things quieted down for four years. According to the Missouri Compromise of 1820, no slave states were to be created in the region north of latitude 36°30'. Yet the territories of Kansas and Nebraska were rapidly being settled north of that line. To forestall any possible dispute, Illinois Senator Stephen A. Douglas, convinced that slavery was not economically profitable in either territory, proposed "squatter sovereignty"— that is, allowing the settlers who lived there to decide the matter. Antislavery advocates promptly termed the plan a violation of the old geographic agreement—even though the admission of California as a free state had already violated the practice of admitting states in pairs of one slave and one free—and this sparked a new crisis. Although either territory might permit slavery, it was more likely that Kansas would since most of its settlers came from the slave state of Missouri.

Anxious to see Kansas settled by opponents of slavery, the New England Emigrant Aid Society assisted Free-Soilers who wanted to move there. At the same time, a secret proslavery group in Missouri organized what they called "Blue Lodges" and, together with the Sons of the South, prepared to move quickly into Kansas to help elect a government favorable to slavery. These opposing organizations resorted to violence and abuse. Physical attacks actually occurred on the floor of Congress by a member from one group against a member of the other. Bitter advocates of one section or the other, giving no thought to the ultimate consequences of their actions, made it impossible to settle the question sensibly and peacefully.

The Hedrick Affair

An incident at the University of North Carolina in the fall of 1856 revealed the limits to which partisan feelings could be carried. In the heat of the presidential race between Democrat James Buchanan and Republican John C. Frémont, a university professor, Benjamin S. Hedrick from Davidson County, said that he was opposed to the extension of slavery. He wished that he could vote for Frémont, but there was no Republican ticket in North Carolina. This new party, formed in Michigan in 1854, attracted those who opposed slavery and championed the small landowner; its partisans supported aid to railroads, free homesteads, the settlement of the West by free labor, and a protective tariff to assist manufacturers. A heated exchange of letters between Hedrick and William

Woods Holden, editor of the *North Carolina Standard* in Raleigh, brought the matter to public attention and precipitated a demand around the state that Hedrick be dismissed from the faculty.

University president David L. Swain pointed out that since the university was "patronized by all denominations and parties, nothing should be done calculated to disturb the harmonious intercourse of those who support and those who direct and govern it." Members of the faculty also regretted their colleague's "indiscretion." The executive committee of the trustees concluded that Hedrick's position "was well calculated to injure the prosperity and usefulness of the institution" and that the outspoken professor had "destroyed his power to be of further benefit to the University." It was hoped that he would resign, but when he did not his chair was declared vacant.

At this unhappy time, the United States Supreme Court in 1857 ruled that a slave, Dred Scott of Missouri, by virtue of his slave status was not a citizen of either the state or of the United States. For a while he had resided in free territory, but that did not make him free. Although the Court was not attempting to settle the question of slavery in the territories, it did lay down several principles: slaves could not be citizens, and they were a kind of property that was protected by the Constitution and that Congress could not abolish. Further, since slaves were a form of property protected by the Constitution, their presence could not be prohibited; hence the Missouri Compromise was unconstitutional. This decision certainly pleased the South, but was unacceptable to the North.

The Banning of a Book

As disputes between the two sections approached the breaking point, a native of Davie County, North Carolina, added fuel to the fire. Hinton Rowan Helper, who had been educated locally, left the state to join the California gold rush but recently had lived in New York. In 1857 his book, *The Impending Crisis of the South: How to Meet It*, caused an uproar throughout the South. The volume was condemned not only for its opposition to slavery but also because of the insulting terms it applied to Southern slaveholders. On the other hand, it was hailed in the North as a splendid document advocating the end of slavery. In fact, it was largely a book of statistics gathered from the federal census returns of 1790 and 1850 and very carelessly interpreted.

Helper's thesis was that slavery blighted the opportunities of free white laborers and was the cause of the South's lack of economic progress. He was unconcerned about the status of blacks and instead was making a plea for white supremacy and better treatment of poor whites. Nevertheless, *The Impending Crisis* became extremely popular in the North and was banned in the South. The

Hinton Rowan Helper (1829–1909), who grew up near Mocksville, was just twenty-eight when his book was published. Because of its reception he never returned to North Carolina. At his death, one newspaper observed: "The world had wrestled with him and thrown him. His mind was shattered and his heart broken. Friendless, penniless, and alone, he took his own life, and died at the age of eighty—this man who had shaken the Republic from center to circumference and who at a critical period had held and filled the center of the stage." (North Carolina Division of Archives and History, Raleigh)

Republican party adopted it as a campaign document, and it was issued in a condensed version. Helper, no longer welcome in his native state, spent the remainder of his life abroad or in the North.

In addition to the Dred Scott decision and the publication of Helper's book, a third event in 1857 was to have dire consequences for North Carolina. The Reverend Daniel Worth, a native of Guilford County and former Quaker, but more recently a Wesleyan Methodist living in Indiana, returned to North Carolina to serve churches of his denomination in and around Randolph County. Worth had long been an antislavery leader and had served in Ohio as pastor of a church composed of seventy former slaves. He was sixty-two years old, over six

THE

IMPENDING CRISIS

OF

THE SOUTH:

HOW TO MEET IT.

BY

HINTON ROWAN HELPER,

OF NORTH CAROLINA.

COUNTRYMEN! I sue for simple justice at your hands,
Naught else I ask, nor less will have ;
Act right, therefore, and yield my claim,
Or, by the great God that made all things,
I'll fight, till from my bones my flesh be hack'd !—*Shakspeare.*

The liberal deviseth liberal things,
And by liberal things shall he stand.—*Isaiah.*

FOURTH THOUSAND.

NEW-YORK:

BURDICK BROTHERS, 8 SPRUCE STREET.

1857.

This book by a native of the state was published in 1857 after he had sought unsuccessfully for well over a year to find a publisher. Although it created a national sensation, *The Impending Crisis* was banned in North Carolina. A condensed version became a Republican political tract. (North Carolina Collection, University of North Carolina at Chapel Hill) feet tall, and weighed 275 pounds. His friendly personality and his appealing speaking style won him friends among people of all classes. Before long he was preaching in ten churches as well as to groups of slaves in many communities. Several younger assistants joined him, and they began distributing antislavery tracts, selling subscriptions to the *New York Daily Tribune*, and circulating copies of Helper's book even though it had been condemned by the legislature. Worth reported that this abolitionist literature was "doing a work little inferior to a living preacher." For more than two years his actions met no opposition. Even slaveholders invited him to visit them and to spend the night.

As growing antislavery sentiment around the nation began to reach North Carolina, however, Worth's activities came to be questioned. It was whispered that he had been sent to the state by "incendiary abolitionists." An event outside North Carolina brought the matter to a head. On 16 October 1859 at Harpers Ferry, Virginia (now West Virginia), a violent and crusading abolitionist, John Brown, led a raid by a small band of white men plus five free blacks against the United States arsenal. They intended to seize some weapons to equip an uprising to end slavery, but they failed miserably. Contrary to their expectations, no slaves joined them, and some of the raiders were killed in the fighting with troops from Maryland and Virginia commanded by Colonel Robert E. Lee. The raid frightened Southerners and made them more defensive than ever.

A North Carolina newspaper, in response to news of John Brown's intentions, called upon the state to exterminate the "abolition vipers" in its midst. To his friends in the North, Worth reported that the area around him was in "tremendous ferment" and that his safety was threatened. Three days before Christmas, warrants were issued in Guilford, Alamance, Chatham, and Randolph counties for the clergyman's arrest. Since he had friends and relatives in Greensboro, he chose to surrender to Guilford County officers. At a preliminary hearing he was accused of distributing inflammatory literature "to cause slaves to become discontented with their bondage" and with arousing blacks to "a spirit of insurrection, conspiracy, or rebellion."

Needless to say, the grand jury found the charges to be true. Worth was tried in the early spring of 1860 and found guilty by a jury that contained four slaveholders. But the judge imposed a light sentence—a year in prison, omitting the flogging and standing in the pillory provided by law. Denied a new trial, Worth appealed to the state supreme court. Bond was posted by several of his friends, and Worth left at once for New York. There and elsewhere he conducted a speaking tour, addressing large audiences and collecting money with which he reimbursed the friends who had posted his bond. In time he returned to Indiana, where he was joined by his wife and a group of friends from North Carolina; he died in 1862.

Despite Worth's conviction and the state's opposition to his abolitionist

Daniel Worth (1795–1862), a native of Guilford County who moved to Indiana, returned to North Carolina in 1857 as a Wesleyan Methodist missionary and abolitionist. For two years he freely distributed antislavery publications, but fear of slave insurrections resulted in his prosecution for such activities. Following a trial and conviction, he fled the state. (North Carolina Collection, University of North Carolina at Chapel Hill)

activities, people did not resort to mob violence. The law took its course and the defendant's rights were carefully sustained.

Political Dissension in 1860

In North Carolina there was a lack of unity in sentiment and action among the people. Seldom did they rally as a body to any common cause. Diversity of national and geographic origins still was apparent, and sectional influences continued to prevail. Political inequities, though mended in large measure by the 1835 constitutional convention, left bitter east-west feelings that survived. The refusal of the General Assembly to adopt an *ad valorem* tax appeared to be another blow at the west. The political division that resulted served to slow the move toward secession.

Like the Whigs earlier, the Democrats now had a firm grip on state politics and they grew more conservative. A few leaders became increasingly powerful and were able to dictate party policy. Before 1848, when the party was out of power, it had been managed by aristocratic slaveholders from the eastern counties and by cotton and tobacco planters of the Piedmont. They shared their authority and were even guided by the young, forward-looking Reid-Holden faction during the free suffrage debate. This, they reasoned, was necessary to increase party strength and to gain control of the state. The ploy worked, but after a few years the old factions took over again. With little real concern for democracy and the ordinary people, they once more made the Democratic party the tool of the states' rights advocates and those concerned over the status of slavery and other Southern interests and of property. This switch became apparent to the people, and it soon divided the party and contributed to its loss of power.

At the state Democratic convention in 1858, the nominating committee selected superior court judge John Willis Ellis of Rowan County over William W. Holden as the party's gubernatorial candidate. He was a slaveholder of aristocratic birth and training. His ancestors had come to North Carolina from New Jersey about the middle of the eighteenth century and made their home in the "Jersey Settlement" along the Yadkin River in eastern Rowan County. After he was graduated from the University of North Carolina, Ellis studied law and practiced in Salisbury and then for ten years he was a judge.

Holden was better known and had contributed a great deal to the rise of the Democrats in North Carolina. He had made no secret of his interest in obtaining the nomination and had even conducted a preconvention campaign—the first in the state's history. Holden was popular among the small farmers and the working class, but had made enemies in his own party and, according to a contemporary, was "heartily despised by the other side." Aristocrats in the party did not want to have to associate with Holden as governor despite his reputation as a skilled politician. He was illegitimate (although recognized by his father and fully accepted into the Holden family), self-educated, and not noted for his polish. While useful, he still was an embarrassment to many, and party leaders were unwilling to see him in high office. Even though he was rebuffed, Holden was a loyal Democrat and worked for the election of Ellis as the party's candidate. Later in the year he was rejected again when Democratic leaders in the state senate elected Thomas Bragg to the United States Senate instead of Holden. A more sensitive man surely would have lost his political ambitions, but he was not like other men. Nevertheless, he and many others who shared his concern for the "common people" were thereafter only lukewarm Democrats.

To many at this time Holden appeared to be an opportunist who for political reasons championed the working man and the small farmer. Because of his own

John W. Ellis (1820–61), as governor on the eve of the Civil War, was an ardent supporter of secession. When the call came to raise men to force South Carolina's return to the Union, he informed President Lincoln's secretary of war that he would "get no troops from North Carolina." (North Carolina Collection, University of North Carolina at Chapel Hill)

humble origins, of course, he had a good claim to represent the interest of the "common man." On the other hand, his background as well as his willingness to switch party allegiance prevented his acceptance by the class of people who believed that it was they who were "born to rule."

While conducting his pioneering campaign to obtain the Democratic nomination for governor in 1858, Holden discovered that, although his party was composed of all classes, the dominant faction was the planter aristocracy. In the nominating convention, the slaveholding eastern counties had a majority and they rejected Holden's candidacy. Holden, because of this, probably held a grudge that during Reconstruction bore bitter fruit for the people of North Carolina as well as for Holden himself. In the election Ellis won by 56,429 votes to 40,036 for his opponent, Duncan K. McRae.

During Governor Ellis's first term in 1859, the *ad valorem* tax question arose and united the opposition. A nucleus of support for this tax came from the Raleigh Workingmen's Association, which emphasized as its first demand that slave owners be forced to share a more equitable burden of taxation. This issue revitalized the Whig party, which played a part in the state's reaction to secession. Whigs, of course, advocated this plan of taxation, but Democrats opposed it. Although Holden was a Democrat, he supported *ad valorem* taxation.

The idea of such a tax was widely discussed because there was a need for additional state revenues. To those who owned no slaves, it seemed to be a fair and equitable means of sharing the costs of government. Slaves worth approximately $113 million were not taxed because those under twelve or over fifty years old were exempted. Others, valued at about $140 million, were taxed after 1858 at only eighty cents each regardless of the individual's value. Slave property was worth more than land, but taxed at a much lower rate. Income and savings were heavily taxed, and many free workmen were required to obtain a license for five dollars in order to work. Yet a slave who did the same work was taxed at only eighty cents. As the present method clearly discriminated in favor of slave property, this new form of taxation had wide appeal. Attempts by Whigs in 1858 to implement it failed; nevertheless, some Democrats supported it.

While North Carolinians were preoccupied with this internal matter and paying relatively little attention to the secession crisis raging elsewhere in the country, President James Buchanan visited the state in June 1859 to deliver the university commencement address in Chapel Hill. In his remarks, the president made a powerful plea for the preservation of the Union under the Constitution. Earlier that year Governor Ellis had recommended a tolerant attitude toward the opinions of people in other states; at the same time, he insisted on the rights and safety of his own sovereign state. With the news of John Brown's raid in October, people began to talk of what lay behind it. For many, the raid at Harpers Ferry was the ultimate proof that Northern fanatics were willing to take the most extreme measures to end slavery. And with such proof it was no longer necessary for Southern radicals to hide their secessionist sentiments. Public opinion changed almost as rapidly in this situation as it did in 1776 when it became apparent that King George III did not intend to protect the colonists from the arbitrary acts of Parliament. A resolution of the Council of State echoed a resolution of the Provincial Congress: "If we cannot hold our slave property and at the same time enjoy repose and tranquility in the Union, we will be constrained, in justice to ourselves and our posterity, to establish new forms."

The Whig party in 1860 nominated John Pool of Pasquotank County for governor and endorsed an *ad valorem* amendment. The Democrats renominated Ellis and warned citizens of the danger of dividing over the tax issue—unity was necessary, they maintained, in the face of the abolition menace. Slaveholders realized that they were under fire not only from Northern abolitionists but also from a leveling democracy at home. Kenneth Rayner, a Whig and a slave owner, expressed disgust with his party for its stand on the tax issue and for potentially splitting the state. During the campaign party lines were often obliterated, and divisions occurred between east and west and between rich and poor. Democrats recalled that equalized poll taxes had resulted from a compromise in the Constitutional Convention of 1835 and described *ad valorem* taxation as an attack on slavery and therefore a comfort to abolitionists. By characterizing their party as the only safe custodian of Southern interests, they managed to win the gubernatorial election by just 6,093 votes, whereas in 1858 Ellis had garnered 16,393 more votes than his opponent.

Conditions outside North Carolina brought to a halt the constructive influence of two-party politics and led the state perilously close to destruction.

The election in November 1860 of Abraham Lincoln, a Republican from Illinois whose name was not on the ballot in North Carolina, alarmed many North Carolinians. The new president had received a minority of the total popular vote but a clear majority in the electoral college. Rayner wrote to Judge Thomas Ruffin urging him to consult with Governor Ellis and in the emergency to recommend cautious but firm action. Holden's newspaper advised the people to "Watch and Wait." Many states' rights Whigs, claiming that the right of revolution was one reserved to the states, still agreed with William A. Graham that "the necessity for revolution does not yet exist." In an address to the legislature on 16 November, the governor said that Lincoln's election did not yet pose a threat, but "an effort to employ the military power of the general Government against one of the southern states *would* present an emergency demanding prompt and decided action on our part. It can but be manifest that a blow thus aimed at one of the southern States would involve the whole country in civil war, the destructive consequences of which to us could only be controlled by our ability to resist those engaged in it."

An ardent secessionist himself, Ellis anticipated that force would be used to hold the Southern states in the Union. He advised that preparations be made to resist such force, but when he urged the calling of a state convention he was moving faster than public opinion justified. In November and December mass meetings were held in more than thirty counties, where the petitions adopted and the speeches delivered represented every shade of opinion. Views expressed at a series of meetings in one community might completely contradict those of another. The secession of South Carolina on 20 December 1860 produced an outburst of secessionist enthusiasm in many parts of North Carolina. But two days later when the General Assembly recessed for Christmas, there was no consensus on calling a convention.

So long as his state remained in the Union, Governor Ellis was careful to see that no hostile act was committed. Therefore he refused the request of Wilmington citizens to occupy Fort Caswell and Fort Johnston at the mouth of the Cape Fear River. In spite of the governor's orders, on 8 January 1861 state troops and local citizens seized the forts, but Ellis ordered them restored immediately to Federal control.

In New Bern Judge Matthias E. Manly thought that Lincoln's election afforded an opportunity for people to have "a better understanding with our northern neighbors." But, he continued, "if they insist upon regarding slaves at the south as a *moral taint* which it is *their* duty to eradicate, we must quit them." About the same time, Kenneth Rayner toured several eastern counties to sample public opinion of "the plain country people." Many nonslaveholders, he reported, said that they "would not lift a finger to protect rich men's negroes."

There really was nothing to do but to "watch and wait," as Holden had suggested. The legislature reassembled on 7 January 1861, and two days later word came that Mississippi had followed the example of South Carolina, with Florida and Alabama withdrawing from the Union on the tenth and eleventh, then Georgia on the nineteenth. The secession of Louisiana and Texas in the final week of January took all of the Deep South out of the Union. When representatives from these seven states assembled in Montgomery, Alabama, on 4 February and adopted a constitution for Confederate cooperation, the process of achieving a separate "nation of the South" was completed. This meant that along its southern limits North Carolina now bordered the Confederate States of America, and it was unlikely that a decision on whether to join its Southern neighbors could be avoided much longer.

Many people were convinced that the Republican president would find his program impossible to implement because there was a Democratic majority in the Senate. Yet as one state after another left the Union, the Republicans gained control of both houses of Congress. Consequently, the power, if not the desire, to take coercive measures was now in the hands of the North. Governor Ellis pointed out that the crisis would be reached when the Federal government attempted to use military force against one of the Southern states.

Those who were convinced of the correctness of the doctrine of states' rights concluded that South Carolina, in resuming its sovereignty, had also resumed its power of eminent domain. This justified the action taken by the state in demanding possession of the forts in Charleston harbor that were under Federal control. They would be returned to the state after fair and just compensation had been made, of course.

If time had been allowed for tempers to cool, and if the people—Northerners and Southerners alike—had been given an opportunity to express their real sentiments, some basis of reasonable settlement surely could have been found. The danger lay in giving popular conventions the power to make decisions that were not subject to review and approval by the people. Accordingly, when the General

Assembly of North Carolina on 24 January 1861 passed a bill providing for a referendum on the question of whether to call a convention, state senator Jonathan Worth (a cousin of Daniel Worth) of Randolph County, a planter, businessman, and lawyer who was anxious to preserve the Union, advised his constituents that, if they really wanted to save the Union, they should vote against holding a convention. At the same referendum, votes were to be cast for delegates on the chance that a convention was held. Worth further advised that voters be very careful for whom they voted.

W. W. Holden, a unionist, voted in favor of a convention and predicted that the majority of delegates would be Union men so that when they assembled secession would be prevented. The total vote was not quite 94,000, considerably lower than the vote in the November presidential election. By a majority of just 651 the convention proposal was defeated in February 1861, but had it carried the delegates chosen stood at 74 unionists and 46 secessionists.

The General Assembly near the end of January named two sets of commissioners—one to attend a conference in Washington of other commissioners from both North and South, and the other to confer with representatives of the seceded states in Montgomery. Each group was instructed to work for an adjustment "of all the difficulties that distract the country" and to consult "for our common peace, honor and safety." Three weeks of effort by the men gathered in Washington produced nothing that satisfied either side, and Congress gave no serious consideration to their report.

Those who went to Montgomery arrived in time to witness the organization of the provisional government of the Confederate States. Commissioner David L. Swain, who drew up the report for the North Carolina delegates, commented on the large number of North Carolina natives who played significant roles in the events they observed. These were described as men of wealth, intelligence, and respectability, whose positions in their adopted states marked them as leaders of the Confederacy. Swain reported that he had inquired but found little indication that anyone wanted to consider a return to the Union.

The Roots of Secession

After the inauguration of President Lincoln on 4 March 1861, the Senate remained in executive session, thus providing an opportunity for debate over the question of protecting Federal property in the seceded states. On 15 March Senator Stephen A. Douglas from Illinois offered a resolution calling for the withdrawal of United States troops from all of the forts in the seceded states except those at Key West and the Dry Tortugas, and Senator Thomas L. Clingman of North Carolina introduced a similar resolution. These proposals were tabled, but Lincoln did not deny reports circulating throughout the country that the forts, including Fort Sumter at Charleston, were to be evacuated.

On 6 March Lincoln had conferred with a number of his advisers and in a few days considered the military alternatives. Overwhelmingly he was advised to order the evacuation of Fort Sumter as a means of avoiding war. Even Gideon Welles, his secretary of war, commented: "I am not prepared to advise a course that will provoke hostilities." Yet the wavering continued and further meetings followed. Sometime between 28 March and 4 April, however, Lincoln made his own decision, and soon Federal ships and troops were en route to Charleston to reinforce Fort Sumter. When word reached South Carolina, Fort Sumter was attacked on 12 April by forces of the Provisional Confederate Government under General P. G. T. Beauregard and the fort's defenders surrendered to the Confederacy. Two days later Lincoln called on all of the governors of the states still in the Union to furnish a total of 75,000 militiamen to aid in restoring the Union. Southern conservatives who had been shocked by the attack on Fort Sumter were now bristling with sectional patriotism at this threat to uphold Federal authority by military force. The prospect of invasion by Federal troops welded the South into a unit of defense.

Governors of all the border states, still components of the United States, refused to comply with the president's request for troops. In his reply to the secretary of war, Governor John W. Ellis stated that he regarded the levy of troops "as in violation of the Constitution and as a gross usurpation of power," and concluded: "You can get no troops from North Carolina." On 17 April Virginia passed an ordinance of secession, and on 6 May Arkansas followed. The Tennessee legislature adopted an alliance with the Confederacy on 7 May and passed an ordinance of secession, which was ratified by a popular majority on 8 June.

On 17 April Governor Ellis called a special session of the General Assembly to meet on the first day of May. In the interim he directed the taking of the forts, arsenals, and other property of the Federal government located in North Carolina in the name of the state. Ellis's zeal for the secession cause prompted him, a week before the legislature assembled and nearly a month before the state formally broke its ties with the United States, to promise the Confederate secretary of war a regiment of volunteers for service in Virginia. Nevertheless, he said that he could not lawfully draw on the state treasury for funds to transport them.

The governor also consulted with Daniel Harvey Hill of the North Carolina Military Institute in Charlotte and with Charles C. Tew of the Hillsborough Military Academy and asked them to prepare a "shopping list" for the purchase of military supplies. He then sent Colonel Charles Lee to Richmond, Baltimore, Philadelphia, New York, New Haven, Springfield, Hartford, and elsewhere to place orders. Everywhere Lee found munitions makers anxious to fill the state's orders, although two of them said they could not guarantee delivery if the state seceded.

The people by this time were fully behind their governor. After Lincoln's call for troops, all of the newspapers in the state that previously had sympathized with the Union promptly changed their position in favor of states' rights. On 12 April, at Danbury in Stokes County, three prominent North Carolinians had presented the Union's point of view during a public debate. A few days later two other men planned to do the same thing in the town of Madison, but cancelled the debate after hearing on their arrival of the attack on Fort Sumter and the president's call for troops. Within a week all of these former unionists were out raising troops to fight for the South.

Ellis, of course, was aware of these and other incidents, and when the legislature convened on 1 May he asserted that "all party feuds [are] forgotten." The first act of this session was to set 13 May as the day for the election of delegates to assemble at a state convention on the twentieth. The convention met as scheduled and elected Weldon N. Edwards of Warren County as its presiding officer. The delegates considered but *rejected* a nine-paragraph ordinance setting forth both the specific reasons and the philosophical principles justifying secession, not so much as a constitutional right but in reaction against the "unconstitutional" and coercive policy of the Lincoln administration. Instead, the convention opted to pass an ordinance simply repealing the ordinance of 1789 by which North Carolina had joined the Union in the first place. It then asserted that North Carolina once more was a completely sovereign, free, and independent state. The delegates were unanimous in this decision. North Carolina had already chosen its place with the other Southern states on 15 April, and the ordinance of 20 May was a mere formality.

The comments of former unionist Jonathan Worth were prophetic. According to him, the ultimate result of secession would involve a series of sectional governments requiring "the cartridge box instead of the ballot box" to preserve them. Although he disliked the idea of secession, he found Lincoln's provocative action to be untenable. Lincoln, Worth said, "showed want of common sense in adopting the course he did" in attempting to reinforce Fort Sumter. Worth disapproved of extremists on both sides, but he could not now hesitate to support his own section. "Lincoln," he continued, "has made us a unit to resist until we repel our invaders or die." To a member of his family, however, he confessed that "I think the South is committing suicide, but my lot is cast with the South and being unable to manage the ship, I intend to face the breakers manfully and go down with my companions."

Worth believed that if Lincoln "had withdrawn the garrison of Fort Sumter on the principle of military necessity and in obedience to what seemed to be the will of Congress . . . this state and Tennessee and the other states which had not passed the ordinance of secession, would have stood up for the Union." Instead, at this critical hour, Lincoln sent the fleet to Charleston harbor. "All of us who had stood by the Union, felt that he had abandoned us and had surrendered us to the tender mercies of Democracy & the Devil," he wrote.

Governor Ellis, understanding that the majority of state leaders, as well as most other North Carolinians, had now swung to the secessionists' point of view, had no hesitation in recommending to the legislature that the convention of the people have "full and final powers." The General Assembly, then, did not limit the convention to a specific program or to any particular number of sessions. Nor was the ordinance of secession submitted to a popular referendum, but, as the governor had requested, it was "final" from the date of its adoption.

Delegates in the convention were chosen without restriction to represent the people as the ultimate authority, and they took upon themselves powers hardly contemplated when they were elected. The convention suspended an act of the legislature for raising troops, and when the General Assembly reassembled in August 1861 it attempted unsuccessfully to legislate the convention out of existence. The convention, however, considered itself to be supreme, and it held four sessions between 20 May 1861 and 13 May 1862. Among other things it amended the state constitution to provide for an *ad valorem* tax on slave property; it also provided another amendment eliminating the literal disqualification of Jews from holding office.

19

THE CIVIL WAR

LTHOUGH THE SENTIMENT for secession was far from unanimous in North Carolina, once a decision had been made it was either generally supported or tacitly accepted by the people as the policy of the state. About two dozen men in the lower Cape Fear acted prematurely. On 31 December 1860 some citizens of Wilmington wired Governor John W. Ellis seeking his permission to seize Fort Johnston and Fort Caswell, located on the west side of the Cape Fear River near its mouth on each side of the Elizabeth River. Each fort was occupied by a single United States ordnance sergeant who guarded a small store of military supplies. Permission was denied since North Carolina was still a part of the Union, but the next day a delegation arrived in Raleigh to make the same futile request in person. Returning home, they found secession meetings being held almost every night and young men wearing "rosettes made of small pine cones" to signify their allegiance to North Carolina. Under the local militia commander "Cape Fear Minute Men" were organized. On 8 January 1861 a rumor spread that an armed United States vessel was on its way to Fort Caswell. It was feared that a sizable contingent of troops might soon control the mouth of the Cape Fear River. The Minute Men, with their personal arms—mostly shotguns—and a week's supply of provisions, boarded a small schooner and sailed down the river. The next day at four o'clock in the morning, they went to the door of the quarters of Sergeant James Reilly (destined to become a major in the Tenth North Carolina Regiment) at Fort Johnston and demanded the keys to the magazine. Telling him how useless it would be for one man to resist the determination of twenty men, they persuaded him to comply with their demand. But he did so only after the contingent from Wilmington consented to give him a receipt for the supplies in his care. The same process was repeated across the Elizabeth River to obtain Sergeant Frederick Dardingkiller's cooperation at Fort Caswell.

When Governor Ellis learned of this he sent a regiment of state militia to restore the forts to Federal control. Where the sergeants had been in the meantime is not clear, but on 14 January Reilly reported: "They came back to both me and Sergeant Dardingkiller and asked us to take back the public property. I answered, yes; if there was none of it broken, or none of the ammunition expended. It was returned in good order."

The governor, in the interim between the forts' seizure on 9 January and their return on the fourteenth, kept President James Buchanan informed. Buchanan assured the governor that he had no intention of garrisoning the forts.

This rather comical episode, nevertheless, was serious in that it occurred during the time when additional states were seceding from the Union, and it contributed to the excitement in North Carolina. Following the taking of Fort Sumter in South Carolina on 14 April and the subsequent withdrawal from the Union by North Carolina, events moved rapidly to active warfare—the Civil War.

The conflict between North and South was called a civil war, but if the South had been victorious it would have been regarded as a revolution. Nevertheless, during the war it was sometimes referred to as a rebellion, and many Northerners spoke of the "War of the Rebellion." Southerners, on the other hand, called it the "War for Southern Independence," the "War Between the States," or even the "War of Northern Aggression."

Comparison of Resources and Aims

Neither side expected that the war would last very long. The first Union soldiers were recruited for just three months. North Carolina's first new troops were enlisted for six months. Recruiting officers predicted that they would be able to wipe up with a silk pocket handkerchief all the blood that would be shed. A Southerner, boasting of the military experience of his friends, their skill in hunting, their fondness for riding, and the active outdoor life they led, said Southerners could "whip the Yankees with cornstalks." Reminded of this after the war, he sheepishly observed: "But they wouldn't fight with cornstalks."

The two sides, in fact, were so unevenly matched that observers were amazed that the South held out for four years. Northern resources were clearly superior. With a government already in existence, the North had the nucleus of an army and navy, an established foreign trade, money and banking regulations, and other features contributing to stability. The new Confederate government, on the other hand, had none of these and had to create them. Whatever the Southern states might have paid in the immediate past to the Federal treasury, needless to say, would no longer benefit them. The differences, when laid out side by side, were staggering. There were twenty-four Northern states but only eleven in the Confederacy. The North had two and one-half times as many people. During the entire war there were approximately 850,000 soldiers in the various Confederate armed forces while the Union had around 2 million. Although the South used blacks largely for construction, the North enlisted about 186,000 to fight.

Table 19-1. Resources of North and South, 1860

	North	South
Population	22,700,000	9,000,000[a]
Railroads (miles)	21,700	9,000
Value of manufactures	$1.7 billion	$156 million
Corn (bushels per year)	717,000,000	316,000,000
Iron (tons per year)	480,000	31,000

[a]Including 3,500,000 slaves.

The strategy and the goals of the two sides also differed. As President Jefferson Davis said in his inaugural address in Montgomery, the South wanted only what the old Union had promised: "to establish justice, insure domestic tranquility, provide for the common defense, promote the general welfare, and secure the blessings of liberty to ourselves and posterity." The Federal government no longer rested "upon the consent of the governed," he pointed out, but had been "perverted from the purposes for which it was established." Many Southerners hoped to withdraw in peace and form their own government based on the ideals of the men who drew up the Constitution. Others, however, were anxious for a fight and a great many volunteered for military service before and at the time of secession. The South had no ambition to expand—each of its constituent states joined the Confederacy freely—and there were no plans to invade the North. "States' Rights" was the Southern goal, and after Lincoln's call for troops it became a sectional aim to repel the Northern invasion. Any war fought by the South, Confederate leaders anticipated, would be a defensive war only.

The initial goal of the North, a congressional resolution declared, was to preserve the Union, but after Lincoln's announced intention in September 1862 to issue an emancipation proclamation, the abolition of slavery became an avowed goal as well. To accomplish these objectives, it was necessary for Northern troops to invade the South, defeat its defenders, and destroy its resources. Theirs would be an aggressive war.

That the program implemented by the North would be so harsh clearly did not occur to Southern leaders in 1861. In the summer of that year capitalists in Europe offered to lend the Confederate government $600 million, to be secured with cotton, but President Davis thought that amount excessive and ordered that in no event should more than $15 million be accepted. During the same time, the South could have sold 100,000 bales of cotton to European consumers for $50 million and easily shipped them before the projected Federal blockade of

Southern ports took effect. The government, however, withheld it from the market in hopes of enticing those nations that needed cotton to recognize the Confederate States of America. But Confederate leaders did not anticipate the determination with which their former colleagues in the North would pursue their aims.

Troops and Supplies Raised

Immediately after informing Washington that no troops would be forthcoming from North Carolina, Governor Ellis ordered state troops to take Fort Macon on Bogue Sound, Fort Caswell, and Fort Johnston. All three surrendered quietly. On 20 April 1861 a company of the Charlotte Grays seized the United States Mint in that city, and two days later the captain in charge of the Federal arsenal at Fayetteville, together with a thousand or more troops, surrendered. From the arsenal the state acquired 37,000 muskets which skilled workmen soon converted into percussion weapons.

Although North Carolina did not secede until 20 May, the General Assembly on the first day of the month passed legislation to recruit ten new regiments for three years or the duration of the war. Soon afterward an adjutant general, a quartermaster general, and a commissary were appointed. Steps were taken at the same time to obtain supplies that might be needed to defend the state. Horses for the cavalry and transport service were purchased in Kentucky, which was then still neutral ground, and driven in droves through the mountains. Saddles and harnesses were bought by special agents in New Orleans and rushed to Raleigh by rail. Powder works and arsenals to manufacture and remodel arms were created. Arms and ammunition became available in quantity only after the first few Confederate victories in battle, when materiel thrown away by Northern troops in flight was carefully gathered.

In May 1861 the state established camps at various places, usually in rural settings beside a railroad, to provide basic training for soldiers. Some men gradually became skilled armorers under the supervision of the few residing in North Carolina. They made sabers, bayonets, and swords. Percussion caps were provided by a private firm in Raleigh, while factories to make shoes and uniforms were established at several places around the state. At foundries cannon for the artillery were made largely by melting down church and farm bells; this source was supplemented from time to time when mounted guns were captured from the enemy.

The state bought four steamships in 1862 and sent agents abroad to sell cotton and buy supplies for soldiers. North Carolina was the first state to do this, and were it not for this farsighted enterprise it is doubtful whether its citizens could have been fed and clothed as well as they were during the war. Privately owned vessels soon joined the fleet of blockade-runners, whose cargo reflected

General James G. Martin (1819–78), a native of Elizabeth City and a graduate of the United States Military Academy, was on duty at Fort Riley, Kansas, on the eve of the Civil War. He returned to North Carolina to prepare for organizing, equipping, and training the state's first ten regiments. Afterward he served as adjutant general of North Carolina before seeing active duty in the field. (North Carolina Collection, University of North Carolina at Chapel Hill)

READINGS
FROM
SHAKSPEARE ᴀɴᴅ OTHER POETS!

This evening, at 7 o'clock, in the COMMONS HALL,

MRS. HEAVLIN OF GRANVILLE,

Who has high testimonials of her skill and attainments, will read from Shakspeare and other authors. The audience may expect a treat of the highest order. Mrs. H's object is a benevolent one; it being her purpose to appropriate the proceeds of these readings to the benefit of our brave soldiers who are fighting our battles.

Tickets can be had at the Bookstores of Messrs. Turner and Pomeroy, and at Mr. Pescud's Drug store. Price 50 cents.

Raleigh, N. C., Nov. 20, 1861.

Various means were used to raise funds in support of the war effort. This handbill announced a program presented in Raleigh in November 1861 by Mrs. [Robert A. (Lizzie Strong)?] Heavlin. (North Carolina Collection, University of North Carolina at Chapel Hill)

the state's requirements for subsistence. Nearly $500,000 worth of ordnance stores were imported, as well as 60,000 pairs of hand cards. Cotton and wool cards were needed by women and young people to make cloth for clothing. But cloth was also imported for uniforms, overcoats, jackets, trousers, caps, sacks, skirts, and other uses. In addition, these ships brought in shoes, boots, oilcloth, oil, tape, thread, buttons, paper, calfskins, leather, medicine, dyes, belting, cobbler's awls, needles, bleaching powder, buckles, scythe blades, iron, copper, wire, anvils, and many other articles.

Even so, the success of the blockade-runners hardly made a dent in the requirements of the state. The operation of factories was hindered by a lack of parts and oil for the machinery. Iron for the railroads was critically short, and the price of necessities rose to unbelievable levels. The success of the blockade contributed significantly to the Northern victory. Eventually North Carolina was obliged to appropriate $6 million to provide relief for soldiers' families, to sell provisions at low prices, and to manufacture and distribute salt to preserve meat.

Most of the imported cloth was made into uniforms. The manufacturing establishment in Raleigh was presided over by quartermaster officers. Clothing was cut by expert tailors and then sent out to women to be sewed. Some was shipped to distant towns to be made up by clubs of women and returned to quartermaster warehouses for distribution to the troops. The state not only clothed its own troops but also sold many uniforms to the Confederate government.

Although nearly all of the medical supplies for the Southern army came into Wilmington on blockade-runners, a manufacturing laboratory was established near Lincolnton under the direction of Dr. A. S. Piggott. Here large quantities of medicine were prepared from native herbs and other sources.

The Ordnance Department was also diligent. Reportedly it had available and supplied to the army every conceivable article—from frying pans to cannon. The state constantly manufactured or remodeled arms and repaired captured ordnance. Individual soldiers often supplemented their equipment by a clean sweep of the battle site after the enemy had departed. Nitrate for gunpowder was obtained mostly by digging up the ground around smokehouses and leaching out the nitrate. Rifle factories were established at Jamestown and Greensboro, and a firm in Wilmington made sabers and bayonets. A boring machine was developed by which smoothbore muskets were turned into rifles, and thousands of privately owned antiquated muskets were converted from flint and steel to percussion locks.

Another source of supplies for the troops consisted of goods sent by the women of the state directly to husbands, sons, sweethearts, relatives, and friends in the army. During three months in 1864 it was reported that $325,000 worth of such supplies was sent from North Carolina through the post office in Richmond. Although this was a time of great hardship when goods were scarce at home as well as on the battlefront, women still shared generously.

The population of North Carolina in 1860 was close to one million, of which fully a third were black. Many blacks did their share in raising provisions on the farms to support soldiers as well as people at home. Thousands also were drafted at various times to build breastworks and forts, to mine coal, and to work on the waterfront or aboard ships. Many Confederate officers were attended throughout the war by young black men from home, whose acts of heroism and devotion are described in many accounts. Not a single attempt of insurrection or serious lawlessness by blacks was recorded during the four-year conflict. In fact, many white families managed to subsist through the help of black families while the head of the house was at war. Slaves in large measure, nevertheless, yearned for freedom and release from the oppression that many had endured for so long.

However, once a region was occupied by Federal troops blacks appeared to work for them. This was particularly true on Roanoke Island and in and around New Bern where they were employed in the construction of fortifications and elsewhere as laborers. Sometimes blacks also served as spies within the Confederate lines, and a unit known as the North Carolina Colored Troops, U.S.A., was recruited.

Troops

The proportion of soldiers furnished by North Carolina to the Confederate cause was nearly one in five of the total white population of the state. Of the troops of the eleven Confederate states, more than one-sixth were soldiers from North Carolina. The state also furnished fully one-fifth of the provisions and other supplies for the Confederate armies. According to the 1860 census of North Carolina, 128,889 men between the ages of twenty and sixty resided in the state; of that number, it has been estimated that 125,000 served in the Confederate armies. Only about 19,000 waited to be drafted—all the others volunteered. The 19,673 Tar Heel soldiers killed in battle represented more than one-fourth of all Confederate battle deaths, beginning with Henry Lawson Wyatt of Edgecombe County—the first Confederate soldier killed in action—who died at the Battle of Big Bethel in Virginia on 10 June 1861. In addition, 20,602 died of disease. North Carolina's total loss of 40,275 exceeded that of any other Southern state. Although North Carolina entered the war reluctantly, once committed, it was generous with both men and supplies.

In time troops became discouraged, however, and like troops in every war many deserted. Over the four-year period, around 23,000 enlisted men and 423 officers from the state took this course. Contributing to their action were such things as long absences from home, the suffering of their families, a feeling that the struggle was hopeless, illness, and pro-Union sentiment. At home many civilians were indifferent to deserters and sometimes helped to shield them. Yet of the deserters some 8,000 returned to duty.

Military Activity

Northern strategy for the war called for the invasion and conquest of Virginia; the taking of Richmond, the capital of the Confederacy; and splitting the South by gaining control of the Mississippi River. It also included a blockade of Southern ports to stop the importation of supplies from abroad. Initially Confederate forces halted the Northern invasion. The Battle of First Manassas, southwest of Washington, D.C., on 21 July 1861 turned the Union army back, while observers—members of Congress as well as some Washington matrons, all of whom had expected to witness the swift end of the Confederacy—were obliged to flee in haste and confusion. Because of a shortage of ammunition, however, the Confederate forces were unable to follow up their success with a drive on Washington. This initial victory made the South overconfident and at the same time spurred the North to renewed effort. For two years the South won brilliant victories over superior armies in the East, preventing the capture of Richmond and twice taking the war into Northern territory. In the West, on the other hand, Federal forces soon predominated, seizing strong points on the Tennessee and Cumberland rivers and finally capturing New Orleans at the mouth of the Mississippi River. Troops from North Carolina were involved in most of this action, and for their exemplary performance in Virginia they were highly praised. On one occasion, following a battle in which Virginia troops fled but North Carolinians stood fast, General Robert E. Lee is quoted as having said: "God bless the Tar Heel boys," giving rise to the nickname proudly accepted by the people of the state. Others, however, have claimed that he only said "God bless good old North Carolina."

After being defeated at Manassas, Virginia, Union leaders turned their attention to the Outer Banks of North Carolina. Along the isolated and treacherous coast, particularly at Hatteras, the state had stationed some steamers to harass enemy shipping. In a period of just six weeks one of them took at least sixteen prizes. Nevertheless, this large area was virtually impossible to defend. When North Carolina officials were unable to persuade the Confederate government to send troops to protect the exposed coast, the state had hastily constructed forts on the Outer Banks near Oregon, Ocracoke, and Hatteras inlets and elsewhere. On 29 August 1861 Fort Hatteras surrendered to Federal forces. The other forts in the vicinity were quickly abandoned, and shortly afterward the enemy began to occupy the coast of northeastern North Carolina.

The Methodist minister at Hatteras, Marble Nash Taylor, was reported to have aided Federal landing parties; he became the first islander to take the oath of allegiance to the Union. Taylor then tried to convince other residents of Hatteras to cooperate with the Federal forces. In the fall he and Charles Henry Foster, a native of Maine but recently living in Murfreesboro, took steps to create a unionist government. Through several local "conventions" and elections, a "provisional state government" was formed with Taylor as governor and Foster as congressman for the Hatteras district. The latter went to Washington but was ridiculed and gave up his pretensions. Federal officials seem to have paid no attention to Taylor's activities, and after February 1862 he abandoned his claims. He remained at Hatteras throughout the war, afterward was appointed to a minor post in Cumberland County, and ended his days selling fruit trees in the Sandhills.

After the fall of Fort Hatteras, a massive Union fleet under General Ambrose Burnside was sent to secure the beachhead. Between 3:00 P.M. and midnight of 7 February 1862, 7,500 troops landed on Roanoke Island, and in the early hours of the next morning 2,488 Confederates surrendered. The island was lost, and it

Union troops landed at Hatteras on 28 August 1861 under conditions not quite so peaceful as this wartime sketch suggests. Heavy seas swamped many of the iron-hulled surfboats and broke up the wooden fishing boats ferrying troops ashore from the large Federal fleet. Nevertheless, from this beachhead the troops spread out and soon occupied much of coastal North Carolina. (North Carolina Collection, University of North Carolina at Chapel Hill)

soon became a base from which much of eastern North Carolina was taken. An enemy fleet sailed up the sound and bombarded Elizabeth City, which on the tenth was pronounced a "dead town . . . dead as a graveyard." New Bern was occupied in March and made the headquarters of the Federal forces; Fort Macon was captured on 26 April. On 6 July Burnside was ordered to Virginia to participate in an attack on General Lee, and in New Bern General John G. Foster took command of the Union forces.

As each new community was threatened by the enemy some residents "refugeed" by moving inland. Raleigh, Chapel Hill, and Hillsborough were particularly popular destinations for people from the northeastern part of the state, while many from the southeast chose Pittsboro. Other easterners made their home temporarily as far west as Asheville. When it became apparent that Federal troops were about to expand the area they occupied, the state, insofar as possible, removed everything in their path that might be of use. Foodstuffs, forage, wagons, cotton, and other movable goods were acquired and reserved for the benefit of the Confederate army.

From their bases, but especially from New Bern, the entrenched forces conducted raids, frequently under General Foster's leadership, to destroy property or to occupy additional territory. Plymouth, Murfreesboro, Tarboro, Wash-

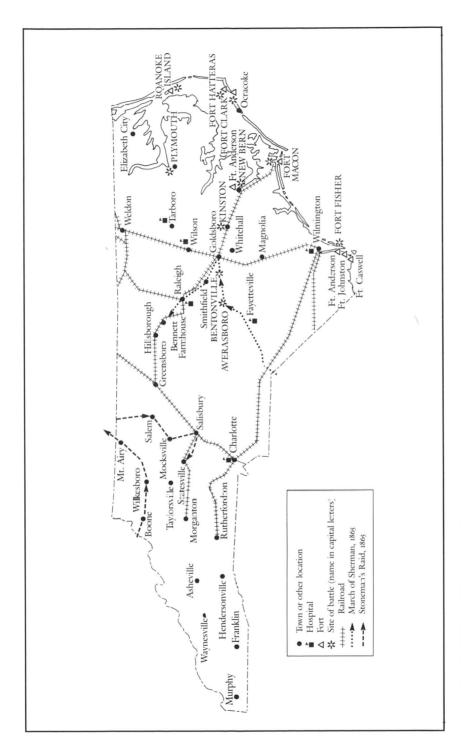

Map 6. The Civil War in North Carolina

ington, Kinston, Goldsboro, and Rocky Mount were such targets. Railroad bridges were burned and the rail line itself damaged. The Battle family's cotton mill at Rocky Mount was burned. Standing crops were trampled, fence rails used for firewood, livestock slaughtered, smokehouses raided, houses and barns set afire, coastal saltworks destroyed, and people frightened. Confederate forces were sent to resist many of these raids, and campaigns were mounted to retake some of the places. Plymouth, for example, changed hands several times. On one occasion the drive to retake New Bern nearly succeeded, but from early 1862 the enemy remained firmly in control of much of eastern North Carolina. Many people blamed the Confederate government both for the original loss and for not providing a force adequate to drive out the "Yankees" who held it. This was an important cause of the dissension that existed between the state and the Confederate governments.

Emancipation Plans

With a fairly large portion of eastern North Carolina under Union domination, the president of the United States, Abraham Lincoln, deemed it proper to inaugurate a plan to return the state to its prewar status. It was his hope that "a loyal government" might be established, so he named Edward Stanly governor. Stanly, a native of New Bern, was graduated from a school in Connecticut; he practiced law in Washington, North Carolina, before serving in the General Assembly and then as a Whig congressman. Since 1852, however, he had lived in San Francisco where he had been an unsuccessful candidate for governor. From there he had opposed secession, and during the war offered to return to his native state as a peace emissary. As "governor" Stanly arrived in New Bern on 26 May 1862 and soon discovered that he faced an impossible task. He was regarded by North Carolinians as a traitor, and he offended Northern abolitionists when he objected to the establishment of a school for blacks in New Bern. Such a school, he warned Lincoln, would do "infinite mischief" and in no way contribute to peaceful relations with the residents of the state. Stanly resigned on 15 January 1863. No successor was named, and presidential reconstruction in North Carolina was abandoned until after the war.

At the same time, Lincoln was considering a move to free the slaves in the seceded states. He discussed such a plan with his advisers on 22 July 1862, and they recommended that he withhold a public announcement until his troops improved their performance in the field. Following the Union victory at Sharpsburg (called Antietam by the North) on 16–17 September 1862, Lincoln announced on the twenty-second his intention to issue a proclamation on 1 January freeing the slaves in all states still "in rebellion against the United States." An election of members of Congress between September and the end of December would prove a state no longer to be "in rebellion." No Southern state, of course, did so, and on New Year's Day 1863 the preliminary proclamation was declared to be in effect. Exempt from its provisions were portions of certain states, named in the proclamation, which were already under Federal authority. None of North Carolina was exempt, however.

The emancipation proclamation did not accomplish its stated purpose because the United States was unable to exercise the necessary authority in the states to which it ostensibly applied. Nevertheless, it had other far-reaching effects. It became clear that the war was now intended not only to "save the Union," but also to free the slaves. It was perhaps because of this new objective that the North began to recruit black men in large numbers to serve in its army and navy. Moreover, from this time European nations ceased to give serious thought to recognizing the South because that would appear to support the institution of slavery.

So long as they were convinced that they were engaged in a struggle to gain freedom from an oppressive Federal government and to uphold states' rights, the mass of people in North Carolina, who were nonslaveholders, supported the war. A fight to maintain slavery, however, was another matter. Many soldiers began to grumble, not only because they might be fighting to preserve slavery but also because they were not adequately clothed, fed, and housed. Families at home were suffering, too. Goods were scarce, prices were high, and they needed help on their farms; further, they had lost loved ones both in battle and from disease. Thus, the emancipation proclamation proved to be a most effective document although not in the way a superficial reading of it might suggest.

The War in Eastern North Carolina

In 1863 and 1864 North Carolina troops were deeply involved in the hard fighting that occurred in Virginia. In 1863 General Lee took the war into the North, but at Gettysburg, Pennsylvania, his army suffered heavy losses in the three-day battle of July 1–3. During that engagement, the Twenty-sixth North Carolina Regiment under General James Johnston Pettigrew drove farther north in the face of heavy enemy fire than any other troops. Of the 15,301 Confederate soldiers killed or wounded, 4,033 were North Carolinians. Gettysburg was considered the high-water mark of the Confederacy as it signaled the beginning of the end of the war. The loss of Vicksburg on the Mississippi River on 4 July further contributed to the gloom that swept over the South in the summer of 1863. At this time, England and France—yielding to complaints from Washington but also undoubtedly looking to the future—ordered that work be discontinued on more than half a dozen naval vessels under construction for the Confederacy.

In a cornfield beside the Roanoke River in Halifax County, at about the same time as the Battle of Gettysburg, work began on a special kind of ship. She was to be an ironclad ram intended to surprise the enemy farther down the river. This ship, christened the *Albemarle*, was designed and built under the supervision of nineteen-year-old Gilbert Elliott, a native of Elizabeth City. Powered by an engine from a railway locomotive and with iron armor two inches thick, she had an eighteen-foot prow that could be used to ram less sturdy vessels. Since iron was scarce, the men working on the project had to scavenge for old pots, useless railroad rails, and even nuts and bolts. Some of this "junk" was sent to the Tredgar Iron Works in Richmond to be melted and rolled into iron plate; other materials were sent to Wilmington where the Clarendon Foundry made iron fittings. By March 1864 the unfinished ram was floated down the river to Hamilton to be completed where the water was deeper.

In 1864 the Confederate high command, responding to pleas from North Carolina, ordered the return of some state troops from Virginia to "drive out the invader." In January, while work was under way on the *Albemarle*, an attack was launched against New Bern. Although several units took a number of prisoners and a quantity of supplies, they could not penetrate the Union fortifications. A Confederate naval attack led by Commander John Taylor Wood, President Jefferson Davis's own aide, was more successful, however. Under cover of darkness a party of some 250 select seamen, 25 marines, and 35 officers in fourteen boats rowed down the Neuse River from Kinston. At daybreak the men concealed themselves on a grassy island opposite New Bern, and that night rowed over to and boarded a Federal steamer. In hand-to-hand combat they captured the ship, but much to their dismay they discovered that there was not enough steam in the boilers to get under way so they had to destroy her.

Unwilling to abandon the effort, Confederate leaders directed that another attempt be made against the enemy. A North Carolina general, Robert F. Hoke, who was placed in command, asked for the assistance of the *Albemarle*. Although she was not yet ready for battle, his request was granted. On 18 April 1864 General Hoke moved against Plymouth from the land side, attacking forts that had been erected around the town. The ram arrived late at night, with a small boat in tow bearing a portable forge. Workmen continued to scramble over her, putting on the touches necessary to make her even halfway serviceable. Young Elliott was aboard as a volunteer. On the way downriver, a part of the rudder broke and repairs had to be made as the ship drifted toward Plymouth.

The *Albemarle* was so strong that shots striking her iron hull, members of the crew reported, sounded like "pebbles against an empty barrel." They did not even bother to return the fire. Downstream ahead of the *Albemarle* two Federal steamers loomed in the dark. Lashed together with long wooden strips and chains, they intended to catch the *Albemarle* between them so she could be battered and sunk. The *Albemarle* crew, alert to the scheme, moved close to shore and, once alongside, turned and rammed one of the steamers. With a large hole in its side, the steamer *Southfield* promptly sank. The *Albemarle* then opened fire on the other steamer, and the Union captain was an early casualty. His second-in-command promptly turned around and fled down the river to safety, followed by several smaller ships that had not been involved in the encounter.

Infantry and artillery forces finished the work of taking Plymouth on 20 April. North Carolinians who helped the Union forces were called "Buffaloes," and it turned out that some of them were in Plymouth when General Hoke's men arrived. Fearing the treatment they might receive at the hands of the victorious Confederates, the Buffaloes took off across the river in canoes. A Federal officer reported that late in the day he heard rifle fire in the woods there and assumed that the Buffaloes had been captured and shot. With the fall of Plymouth, the Union forces holding Washington, North Carolina, also fled. Before leaving, however, troops pillaged the shops and other buildings and set fire to the town.

During the spring and summer of 1864 the *Albemarle* remained a threat to Federal control of the waters off eastern North Carolina and thus became an enemy target. Attacked by a large Union fleet, the Confederate ram was bombarded and rammed but put up a brave fight. At last, with her smokestack full of holes, she was unable to keep up enough steam to continue. Nevertheless, she escaped her tormenters and made her way back up the Roanoke River to Plymouth. Still determined to sink her, a Federal launch was sent up at full speed on 27 October with a torpedo attached to a spar which was run under the *Albemarle* and exploded. When the *Albemarle* sank, the launch became entangled in the boom and was captured. However, Lieutenant William B. Cushing, the officer who had planned and executed this bold maneuver, jumped into the river and escaped. Without the *Albemarle* to protect it, Plymouth was soon retaken. In the fall Confederate forces in Virginia, struggling against great odds to protect Richmond, were in such dire straits that General Hoke and his men were ordered to return to Virginia. Shortly northeastern North Carolina was again controlled by Federal forces.

Activity in Western North Carolina

Certain segments of the western part of the state were scenes of unrest. As early as November 1861, Governor Henry Clark expressed concern over raids from eastern Tennessee. The mountain region became a place of refuge for men who sought to evade military service with either side. They came from far and near, often concealing themselves during the day, and at night helping themselves to whatever they could find in order to survive. Many counties along the Tennessee border, as well as Yadkin and Wilkes counties, were centers of disaffection. In counties as far east as Forsyth and Guilford there also were reports of disloyalty, but Chatham, Davidson, Montgomery, Moore, and Randolph were particularly strong centers of opposition. The isolated high hills of Randolph offered especially secure hiding places for the "outliers," as draft evaders were called. Some were Quakers; others resented the exemption from military duty granted certain occupations and public officeholders. On occasion Confederate forces were sent into the Uwharrie Mountains to flush out deserters. At the beginning of the war, however, western counties had furnished more than their proportion of volunteers, and in some communities the Confederate conscription laws contributed to the unrest.

Madison County became an early refuge for deserters and Union sympathizers, many of whom had fled from Tennessee. They concealed themselves at the head of Laurel Creek from where they conducted raids to seize food, ammunition, and supplies; to threaten local residents; and to attack Southern men. Confederate attempts to halt their activities failed, and late in 1862 two hundred men under Colonel James A. Keith were sent into the area to restore peace. In scouring the region for the culprits, the troops were attacked from ambush, but in January 1863, it was reported, Keith's troops had killed thirteen and captured twenty more. Governor Zebulon Vance, himself a native of adjoining Buncombe County, heard "rumors and reports of a brutal mass murder of prisoners" and ordered an investigation. Keith maintained that his orders had been to take no prisoners, so he had had a dozen or more old men and boys shot after they were captured. Keith was permitted to resign on the grounds of incompetency, and he soon moved to Arkansas. Meanwhile, local militiamen continued the effort to restore order to the region.

Blockade-Running

During the heavy fighting in Virginia, Lee's army depended largely on North Carolina for supplies as well as for men. The port at Wilmington was never successfully blockaded because of the strength of Fort Fisher near the mouth of the Cape Fear River. Supplies from abroad continued to arrive, thanks to courageous and skillful sailors. The Wilmington & Weldon Railroad, which carried supplies from the port to Virginia, was called "the lifeline of the Confederacy," and North Carolina troops worked diligently to keep it open and to protect it from raiding parties sent out from New Bern.

Since supplies from abroad were essential to the South, the Confederate government encouraged blockade-running. Important sources of these goods were the warehouses in neutral harbors of the West Indies, particularly in the Bahamas and Bermuda, where overseas manufacturers shipped their products and where they were picked up by Confederate ships. Before the end of the first year of the war a number of low, fast, camouflaged ships were sailing on a tight schedule between these islands and Wilmington, Charleston, and Savannah. Running the blockade was a very profitable business; a cargo could be purchased cheaply abroad and sold at high prices in the South. Cotton from the South was much in demand in England and France, but since there was only a limited local market it could be purchased at a low price and sold at an enormous profit. After just a few successful round trips, ship owners, officers, and crew became wealthy. In some cases English naval officers offered their services to the South and pursued a lucrative new career. If their ship were captured by Federal forces, there was no great danger to them. The vessel would simply be taken to New York and confiscated along with the cargo; those of the crew who were not Americans would be released as subjects of a foreign nation.

Eluding the blockade below Wilmington was not regarded as particularly difficult. Starting out at the darkest time of night, the low-decked vessels, painted as near the color of the water as possible, sailed along the coast so as not to present a silhouette against the sky. Ten minutes of fast sailing usually took them beyond the range of Federal ships stationed around the mouth of the Cape Fear River. Approaching their destination in the West Indies, blockade-runners often found Federal ships waiting just outside the three-mile limit. Southern complaints that this was virtually a blockade of a neutral port were ignored. Skillful maneuvering of his vessel usually enabled the blockade-runner to escape, but sometimes a Federal ship might follow the Confederate ship into port and dock alongside her; then the officers of both would go into the hotel dining room to enjoy a friendly meal.

Captain John Newland Maffitt was one of the most skilled blockade-runners, and after the war he wrote about some of his escapades. Around dusk one evening early in 1862, he sailed from Nassau in the Bahamas, almost due south of Wilmington, headed for home. Late the next day, he was about seventy miles southeast of Wilmington and dashed off sixty miles at full speed, managing to pick his way cautiously through the blockaders for the other ten. As usual, the lights on shore had been extinguished so they would not aid the Federals in a night attack. "Success in making the destined harbor," he maintained, "depended on exact navigation, a knowledge of the coast, its surroundings and currents, a fearless approach, and the banishment of the subtle society of John Barleycorn." Calculations were carefully made, and as the ship was nearing shore the crew heard seven bells [11:30 P.M.] strike on a ship's clock just ahead. It was time for high tide on the bar, just as Maffitt had planned. Straining to see what lay ahead in the dark, he very dimly recognized two Federal men-of-war located on either side of the channel. He decided to dash through, hoping to escape detection, so he ordered full speed ahead. Then he heard a hissing sound, the noise of a rocket flare ascending; this told him that he had been discovered. Suddenly from a speaking trumpet that seemed to be directly overhead, he heard: "Heave to, or I will sink you."

"Ay, Ay, sir!" he responded. And in a very loud voice Maffitt ordered: "Stop the engines." All of his crew feared the worst—capture by the enemy. But Maffitt had no such thought because by this time the momentum of his ship had carried her beyond the two sentinels who were getting ready to send over a boarding party.

The gruff voice from the speaking trumpet sounded again, this time just behind the Confederate blockade-runner. "Back your engines, sir, and stand by to receive my boat."

In a very low voice to his engineer, Maffitt said: "Full speed ahead, sir, and open wide your throttle-valve!" In the darkness the Federal ships could not tell that the vessel was not really backing; and men having been sent out to board the "captive," Federal gunners were in no position to fire.

By just a few moments of quick thinking and skillful sailing, the blockade-runner escaped. And a good thing it was. The cargo consisted of nine hundred barrels of gunpowder which, if hit, could have blown the ship out of the water. Instead, the vessel was soon anchored under the friendly guns of Fort Fisher and Fort Anderson. The next morning the gunpowder was unloaded on the waterfront at Wilmington and soon on its way to General Albert S. Johnston for use at the Battle of Shiloh in Tennessee in the first week of April.

Soon after this action Maffitt was given command of a Confederate naval vessel, the cruiser *Florida*, and he remained at sea for eight months. During that time he destroyed about $10 million worth of enemy shipping. At the end of the war, failing to find a Southern port open for berthing, he sailed for England and turned his ship over to authorities in Liverpool. For two years he served as captain of a British merchant steamer plying to South America. Considering it safe to return home, he then settled in the country near Wilmington.

Split Loyalties

Not many months after the beginning of hostilities, the support initially demonstrated for the state's position began to split. The unanimous voice of the Secession Convention and the people's need to protect themselves from "Northern aggression" had created an unnatural bonding of opposing points of view.

Captain John Newland Maffitt (1819–86) was born at sea during his parents' voyage to America from Ireland and grew up near Fayetteville. At the beginning of the Civil War he was an officer in the United States Navy, but subsequently he became a Confederate naval officer and for a time commanded the ironclad *Albemarle*, built on the Roanoke River. His most noted contributions, however, came as a blockade-runner when he made numerous trips out of Wilmington and other Southern ports to bring in badly needed supplies. On one cruise that lasted eight months he destroyed enemy property valued at some $10 million. (North Carolina Division of Archives and History, Raleigh)

Thus, outside events had forced the majority, opposed to secession, into a coalition with the minority secessionists. North Carolina had long been a state with two active political parties, and it was traditional that a minority voice should be heard. Time, however, coupled with some Northern victories and a clearer picture of what the future surely held, brought changes as the Democratic party dissolved into two factions. The Confederate party, which flourished at the time of secession, was composed primarily of former Democrats who favored secession. But it also welcomed Whigs and members of the recent American (or

Know-Nothing) party. It considered a military victory critical for Southern independence, and it upheld the policies of President Jefferson Davis. Even though its members were strong advocates of states' rights, they were willing to lay those beliefs aside in the interest of a Confederate victory.

The Conservative party was made up mainly of Whigs and the Democrats who had been loyal to the Union. Opposed to secession until the beginning of the war, they counted among their members such prominent North Carolinians as William A. Graham, William Woods Holden, John Motley Morehead, Zebulon B. Vance, and Jonathan Worth. Although they blamed the present plight of the country on the abolitionists and on the hasty and sometimes irrational actions of the secessionists, they saw no option except to "fight to the finish" for a Confederate military victory and Southern independence. Nevertheless, while most Conservative party leaders had supported a strong national government under the old Constitution, they were now strong advocates of states' rights and frequently opposed a number of policies of the Confederate government that abridged rights guaranteed under the Constitution. They abhorred the limits placed on freedom of speech and freedom of the press, they objected to the idea of the supremacy of military authority over civilian authority, and they spoke out against sedition laws, test oaths, and the suspension of the writ of habeas corpus. Among additional causes for complaint were the failure of the Confederacy to prevent the capture of so much of eastern North Carolina, the large number of North Carolinians killed in battle in Virginia, the number of high ranking officers from other states placed in command of North Carolina troops, the fact that there were so few officers of general rank or members of the Confederate cabinet from the state, the Confederate Conscription Act of 1862, and tax laws. Holden's newspaper, the *North Carolina Standard*, the chief organ of the Conservatives, became a bitter critic of President Davis and the Confederate congress.

The Confederate party wanted to abandon plans for the gubernatorial election in 1862, but the Conservative party objected. Unable to persuade William A. Graham, a former Whig governor, United States senator, and cabinet member, to run, the Conservatives turned to Colonel Zebulon B. Vance, popular commander of the Twenty-sixth North Carolina Regiment. A former Whig congressman and a unionist, Vance reluctantly accepted the nomination after Holden insisted and offered the support of his newspaper. Neither Vance nor the Confederate candidate, William J. Johnston, a railroad official who lived in Charlotte, campaigned. Vance, who was only thirty-two, was criticized for his youth, for being a "pliant tool of Holden," for his known opposition to the Davis administration, and for being the "Yankee" candidate. Vance's response was that the South's only hope lay in continuing to resist the invader and attaining independence. In the balloting he carried all but eleven of the state's eighty-three counties—a vote of 55,282 to 20,813. In 1864 Vance was reelected by an even larger majority, 58,070 to 14,491, carrying all but three counties in a campaign against W. W. Holden.

As governor from 8 September 1862 until 29 May 1865, Vance became as popular with the people as he had been with the troops under his command. His pleasing personality, his charm as a public speaker and especially his stock of humorous stories, his concern for the welfare of North Carolinians, his struggle for independence, and his defense of the state against the central government all endeared him to the people. He gave voice to the numerous complaints that circulated about many of the actions of the Confederate government, including the Conscription Act of 1862 which implied that men would be recruited for the defense of the state but instead they were sent elsewhere. Also in 1862 the writ of habeas corpus was suspended under certain conditions, resulting in the arrest and imprisonment without trial of a number of North Carolinians suspected of disloyalty. Vance announced that it was his duty to protect the people of his state, and he directed state judges to issue writs of habeas corpus. On another occasion he threatened to remove North Carolina from the Confederacy if President Davis did not change his policies concerning the state. It was believed that North Carolina's reluctance to leave the Union led the Confederacy to distrust its patriotism and accounted for President Davis's hesitancy in naming North Carolinians to his cabinet or recommending them for promotion to high military rank.

Governor Vance also spoke out against the presence of Confederate purchasing agents in the state, in violation of an agreement by which North Carolina would clothe, feed, and equip its own troops. He was deeply disturbed by and effectively resisted a directive that each blockade-running ship, even though privately owned, was required to deliver one-half of its cargo "on Confederate account." Once when exhausted cavalry horses were sent into western North Carolina to graze on private land without permission, the governor threatened to send in troops to remove them. He vigorously supported states' rights, and he was almost equally as vocal in protesting apparent discrimination against the state's men in uniform with regard to promotion, command, and place of service.

The pall of gloom that descended on the state following the fall of Vicksburg and the failed invasion of Pennsylvania in July 1863 gave rise to a peace movement. At some one hundred public meetings in forty counties the conduct of the war was criticized; it was even suggested that the Confederate government should seek terms of peace. There was concern among officials both in Raleigh and in Richmond that some North Carolinians might organize a convention that would lead to the state's withdrawal from the Confederacy. Holden's newspaper, the *North Carolina Standard*, publicized these meetings and encouraged those who shared such feelings to speak out. While some people supported Holden's stand, others rejected it. A regiment from Georgia made its position clear when, in passing through Raleigh, it paused long enough to demolish the *Standard's* office. In retaliation a band of Holden supporters dealt a like fate to the office of the *State Journal*, which had expressed views opposing Holden's.

At a peace meeting on 10 February 1864, Holden received the Peace party's nomination for governor. Vance once again was the candidate of the Conservative party. In an effort to halt the peace movement Vance persuaded President Davis to name a North Carolinian, George Davis, attorney general in his cabinet. For the same purpose General Hoke was sent home at this time with orders to drive the enemy from eastern North Carolina. Vance, of course, was reelected by a large majority, ending the possibility that North Carolina might seek a separate peace and leave the Confederacy. While disagreeing with some of the policies of the Confederate government, Vance constantly urged North Carolinians to support it. It was his practice, it has been said, to "fight the Yankees and fuss with the Confederacy." There is no convincing evidence that Holden ever intended to lead the state out of the Confederacy; yet at the end of the war people distrusted him and he was rejected by the leadership of both the former Whig and Democratic parties. Political alignments for many years to come had their roots in the differences that developed during the Civil War.

Around-the-World Cruise of the *Shenandoah*

With so little to encourage them, it is regrettable that Southerners could not have known of the exploits of Captain James Iredell Waddell of the Confederate cruiser *Shenandoah* in 1864 and 1865. News of his adventures, however, had to await the end of the war. A native of Pittsboro, North Carolina, and the descendant of prominent colonial families, he was serving in China as an officer in the United States Navy when the Civil War began. At word of North Carolina's secession, he offered his resignation but it was refused. He was shipped to New York, arriving early in 1862, but he had not been paid since leaving Hong Kong many months earlier. Waddell refused tempting offers of exciting commands and chose instead, still without his pay, to go to his home in Annapolis, Maryland, where he had previously taught navigation at the Naval Academy. From there he made his way to Richmond, was commissioned in the Confederate navy, and assigned to sea duty. In October 1864 while in England he took command of a ship, whose name was changed at sea to *Shenandoah*, and set off on a long voyage.

One of Waddell's ambitions was to inflict enough damage on Federal shipping to compensate him for the pay he never received. At sea he began capturing enemy vessels from which he took supplies and enlisted sailors to help man the Confederate cruiser. On some of the ships he placed prize crews and sent them off

The *Shenandoah*, the only Confederate ship to sail around the world, was commanded by North Carolinian James Iredell Waddell. (North Carolina Collection, University of North Carolina at Chapel Hill)

to Southern ports, but others were burned after he had removed any cargo of value. One ship offered an adequate supply of coal, another meat and vegetables, and nearly all of them additional seamen. From one vessel Waddell carried off a captain and his wife, their six-year-old son, and the wife's maid. Whenever he took more prisoners than his own ship could accommodate, he placed them in boats that he towed behind until he captured another ship worth sending home with a prize crew. Often the captured sailors joined the prize crew so they would be taken home.

Sailing past the tip of Africa, the *Shenandoah* made for Australia where she underwent repairs. At sea again it was discovered that fourteen young Australians had stowed away in order to enjoy the excitement.

The Confederate steamer then set a course for the arctic region, where she encountered nearly a dozen old wooden New England whaling vessels, their sails hanging limp in the calm sea. Waddell picked them off one at time, burning most of them as they were not worth the trouble of a prize crew. Turning south, he made plans to dash into San Francisco and hold it for ransom. En route he boarded a British ship, recently in San Francisco, from which he hoped to learn details of the city's defenses. Instead, he found newspapers reporting that the

Civil War was over. Realizing that if captured he would be considered a pirate for everything he had done since the war ended, he ceased to plunder the ships of the "late enemy."

Avoiding contact with other vessels of any nation, the *Shenandoah* sailed down the Pacific Ocean, around Cape Horn, and into the South Atlantic. Still cautious, Waddell eluded possible capture and at daylight on 5 November 1865 reached Liverpool, England. There, in a moving ceremony, he lowered the tattered Confederate flag from his cruiser, the only Confederate ship to sail around the world. He had destroyed $1,172,223 worth of United States shipping, ample revenge for his unpaid salary of a few hundred dollars.

Sherman's Coming

While Waddell was taking his revenge on the far side of the world, Union General William T. Sherman was making his presence felt across the South. Sherman decided to use his military force against the civilian population as well as against the Confederate army in the belief that this would demoralize not only the noncombatants but also the men under arms wherever they were. In 1862 he had said that he wanted to make war so terrible that the South in the future would exhaust all peaceful remedies before ever again going to war.

Sherman began applying this policy in Mississippi and continued it across Georgia where he reached Savannah a few days before Christmas 1864. From there it was generally expected that he would quickly transfer his army of 60,000 veterans by rail to Virginia to assist Ulysses S. Grant in the final drive against Richmond. Instead, however, he decided to march his men north across the Carolinas, applying the policy of total war as he went. His strategy called for feigned attacks on Augusta and Charleston while actually moving directly to Columbia and from there into North Carolina. He would go by way of Fayetteville to Goldsboro where he expected to get supplies by rail from New Bern. Meanwhile, cutting himself off from a source of supplies, he intended to live off the land by foraging.

Attempts were made to control the foragers by organizing them in groups of between thirty and fifty men under the command of an officer. Although they were instructed not to enter occupied houses or to burn any buildings, their victims frequently related different stories. Many of them were reported to have become mounted bands of robbers, but apologists in recent years have concluded that much of the burning and pillaging was done by stragglers following the army. Some of the Union officers began to use the term "bummer," defined by a member of Sherman's staff as "a raider on his own account, a man who temporarily deserts his place in the ranks and starts upon an independent foraging mission." Reports at the time claimed that foragers committed every kind of outrage imaginable, often destroying what they could not use.

Toward the end of January 1865, Sherman began his march through the Carolinas. Only limited and scattered Confederate forces lay ahead. General Joe Wheeler's cavalry was closest, but farther along General Joseph E. Johnston was gathering scattered units in the hope of striking a blow against at least a segment of the Union force. Although he hoped to avoid it, Sherman realized when he left devastated Columbia and took the road to Fayetteville that the possibility of a battle existed.

Just before crossing the boundary into North Carolina, Sherman ordered his troops to stop their needless raids on the countryside. He knew that in 1860 and 1861 there had been many unionists in the state, and he hoped that they would now welcome his army. Sherman, however, was unaware of a tempting situation that his men would face and therefore gave no instructions concerning it. Once in North Carolina his soldiers found vast tracts of longleaf pine trees whose bark had been partially removed so that rosin could be collected for the turpentine industry. These scarred places were covered with flammable rosin and when touched by a lighted match they flared up in what one man called "fantastic splendor." Soldiers ran from tree to tree starting fires and creating a spectacle of flame and smoke that surpassed anything they had ever seen. Thick overhanging branches of the pine trees formed a canopy from which the smoke could not easily escape; and with the high, straight pine trees looking like giant columns, it was said that the scene suggested a cathedral with huge candles burning.

The state for the first time felt the full weight of this new invasion when the right wing of Sherman's army arrived on 8 March. One soldier's first impression was that North Carolina was "real Northern like. Small farms and nice white, tidy dwellings," he wrote. But later that day a heavy downpour changed the scene. Roads were turned into trails of mud and water, and they became almost impassable for troops and wagon trains. But an even greater obstacle lay in the way: the dark, churning waters of the Lumber River and the swamps on either side of it. Wagons and artillery carriages had to be dragged along by mules with the help of soldiers who pushed from behind, tugged at ropes in the front, or tried to turn the wheels with their hands. A soldier from Ohio wrote: "Such a wild scene of splashing and yelling and swearing and braying has rarely greeted mortal eyes and ears." The march continued long after dark, and along the way thousands of pine torches carried by the men added to the light of the blazing trees. Altogether this moving army presented an alarming spectacle to those who lived along its path.

Under General Judson Kilpatrick the cavalry crossed the Lumber River on the eighth and discovered that the Confederate cavalry under General Wade Hampton was only a few miles away moving fast to Fayetteville. Hoping to

This pen-and-ink sketch made at the time shows "bummers" from Sherman's army entering Fayetteville and "capturing" the courthouse on 12 March 1865. (North Carolina Collection, University of North Carolina at Chapel Hill)

intercept it, Kilpatrick set a trap only to have his own camp surprised and put to flight very early on the morning of 10 March by horsemen in gray. To make his escape, Kilpatrick, wearing only his underwear, had to jump from the warm bed of a "lady" traveling companion, mount the nearest barebacked horse, and disappear into a nearby swamp. Officially this was the Battle of Monroe's Crossroads, but Sherman's infantry always called it "Kilpatrick's Shirt-tail Skedaddle."

Hampton succeeded in opening the road to Fayetteville, and his cavalry proceeded there to join forces with General W. J. Hardee who had come from Charleston. On 11 March the Confederates left Fayetteville and, after crossing the bridge over the Cape Fear River, burned it. Sherman entered from the south and immediately destroyed the former Federal arsenal along with a number of other public buildings. The advance troops who entered the town did considerable plundering; but after his own arrival, Sherman ended such behavior. Here he also cleared his army of 20,000 to 30,000 refugees, white and black, and assorted camp followers. Sick, exhausted, and feeble horses and mules that had brought him this far were also released and replaced by animals taken from the surrounding countryside.

By mid-March the entire Union army had crossed the Cape Fear River and was en route to Goldsboro, as scheduled. Full of confidence, Sherman became careless and allowed his army to become strung out along the road. At Averasboro in Harnett County General Hardee engaged a portion of them, but it was little more than a delaying action.

Table 19-2. Casualties in the Battle of Bentonville

	Killed	Wounded	Missing
Confederate	239	1,694	673
Union	304	1,112	221
Total	543	2,806	894

Battle of Bentonville

At the small Johnston County community of Bentonville, General Joseph E. Johnston gathered all of the Confederate troops available and awaited the arrival of Sherman. On Sunday morning, 19 March, Union foragers encountered some of Hampton's cavalry. Throughout the day shots were exchanged and the Federal forces were pushed back. The battle continued on Monday with heavy losses on both sides. "The federals fought back," Dennis Rogers wrote in 1979 in a reflective account of the battle, "but something kept the rebels coming. Maybe they were tired of retreating, maybe they simply wanted revenge for Sherman's destruction of the heartland, but for whatever reason, veterans described it as some of the most furious fighting that happened in that bloody war." A Union officer who witnessed the battle commented that "it was a painful sight to see how close their battle flags were together, regiments being scarcely larger than companies and a division not much larger than a regiment should be." With between 85,000 and 90,000 troops involved, it was the bloodiest battle ever fought in North Carolina. The total killed, wounded, and missing was 4,243.

On Tuesday the remainder of Sherman's army arrived and the Confederates withdrew, moving into Smithfield and then on toward Raleigh. Sherman went to Goldsboro expecting to find supplies sent up by rail from New Bern. In this, however, he was disappointed as the railroad repairs had not been completed. Instead, he found waiting for him only some Federal troops who had marched up from Wilmington.

Fort Fisher

Fort Fisher near the mouth of the Cape Fear River, an enormous earthwork in the shape of the letter "L" with its angle toward the sea, had come to be called the "Gibraltar of the South." Largely designed by Colonel William Lamb and under his command since 4 July 1862, it protected shipping on the river throughout the war and kept the port of Wilmington open longer than any other

Confederate port. Under the guns of Fort Fisher essential supplies arrived on blockade-runners to support General Lee's troops in Virginia. The fort withstood numerous Federal attempts to take it. A strong Union fleet approached a few days before Christmas 1864, and on the evening of the twenty-third it exploded an old Federal warship packed with 185 tons of gunpowder just two hundred yards from the earthen fort in an attempt to cause its collapse. This was the largest fleet of combat vessels ever assembled up to that time under the United States flag, and it gave Fort Fisher "the most awful bombardment that was ever known for the time," wrote a witness from Fort Caswell. It was also ready to land soldiers to complete the capture, but the scheme failed. Although the fort was undamaged, Federal commanders were not deterred. On Christmas Eve 3,000 Federal troops landed in what proved to be still another exercise in futility. The men were said to have "scurried" about and engaged in brief skirmishing while their commanding general, Benjamin F. Butler, got a close look at the fort. Realizing the hopelessness of his situation, he gave the order to retreat.

This testing undoubtedly was not without benefit to Federal commanders, who promptly began assembling ships and men at Beaufort for an even greater assault. On 12 January 1865 Union ships in the Cape Fear River began a heavy bombardment of Fort Fisher. At one time it was estimated that one hundred shells a minute were bursting over and in the fort. At precisely three o'clock on the afternoon of the fifteenth, the shelling stopped. The silence was startling. Then every ship in the river sounded a shrill, ear-piercing blast and sailors and marines scrambled ashore, approaching the fort from various directions. The defenders inside were obliged to turn in first one direction and then another to try to drive them back. Finally a detachment of Federal soldiers broke through the defenses, and there followed fierce hand-to-hand combat with bayonets, knives, and gun butts. The Confederates were heavily outnumbered, as General Braxton Bragg had recently withdrawn five companies of the Thirty-sixth North Carolina Regiment and sent them to Georgia to oppose Sherman. By nightfall Federal forces occupied the entrance to the Confederacy's last open port.

The railroad to New Bern was opened by 25 March and Sherman concluded that his assignment was finished. A long, winding strip forty miles wide through the South—from Savannah, Georgia, to Goldsboro, North Carolina—lay in ruin. His army was united with other units of the Federal army and large stores of supplies were available once more. It now seemed to be time to consider joining Grant in Virginia to participate in the last maneuver to take the capital of the Confederacy. In the late afternoon of 25 March in Goldsboro, Sherman boarded a train for Grant's headquarters at City Point, Virginia. But the visit proved useless. Grant was not inclined to delay his own drive to fame (or perhaps to share it with Sherman). He would finish off Lee without additional help.

In five days Sherman was back in North Carolina to begin his march to

Raleigh. Confederate General Johnston at Smithfield, with his small command, set out on the same route, just ahead of Sherman. Word reached Sherman during the night of 11 April that General Lee had surrendered at Appomattox on the ninth. He announced the news to his men the following morning, and this put them in a happy frame of mind as they continued toward Raleigh. This news also prompted William A. Graham and David L. Swain to seek permission from Governor Vance to call on Sherman about a "suspension of hostilities" in the hope of saving Raleigh from the fate of Columbia, Atlanta, and other places. Vance, while not enthusiastic, granted their request. Aboard a locomotive engine Graham and Swain set out to intercept the Federal army, but all they could get from Sherman was the promise of protection for state and municipal officials in the capital.

The Surrender at the Bennett Farmhouse

In the meantime Governor Vance and the remaining Confederate forces evacuated Raleigh. State records and other valuables were put aboard a train for Greensboro. President Davis was in Greensboro, and General Johnston, having learned of Lee's surrender, advised Davis to seek a suspension of hostilities. Reluctantly, Davis authorized Johnston to do so. Sherman arrived in Raleigh on the morning of 13 April and set up headquarters in the governor's mansion at the foot of Fayetteville Street. The next day he received Johnston's communication requesting a meeting. Sherman consented and offered to start for Greensboro so that he and Johnston could confer somewhere along the way. Each with a small number of aides met at the farmhouse of James Bennett a few miles west of Durham Station. There on 17 and 18 April Sherman granted terms intended to return both North and South to the same relationship that had existed before the break, thus enabling the Southern states to resume their place in the nation by electing senators and representatives and otherwise assuming their normal functions.

While negotiations were under way, Sherman had the task of informing his army of Lincoln's death on 15 April. To prevent any serious outbreak of trouble, he delayed the announcement until precautionary measures could be taken to ensure the safety of Raleigh.

Sherman assumed that the terms he granted Johnston would be acceptable to the administration in Washington, and for a few days all went well. Federal soldiers were contented in Raleigh, found many of the people to be cordial, and commented on the city's trees, wide streets, and handsome public buildings. Confident that the war was over, Sherman was most distressed with news brought to him in person by General Grant. Arriving in Raleigh on 24 April,

The only major Confederate prison in North Carolina was at Salisbury. Occupying an abandoned cotton mill and some of the surrounding property, it held some 15,000 men; almost 4,000 died and were buried at the site, which is now a national cemetery. (North Carolina Collection, University of North Carolina at Chapel Hill)

Grant reported that the terms granted Johnston were not acceptable in Washington. Once again Sherman met with Johnston, but this time could offer only the same conditions that had been offered to General Lee—the fighting would stop. This meant that specific terms would be developed at some later time.

Having accomplished what he regarded as his mission, Sherman clearly was disappointed that the South would not promptly be accorded its prewar status. To ease the burden, however, he encouraged his men to release horses, mules, and other livestock, and whatever else was available to the people of North Carolina so that they could begin planting crops. On 28 April Sherman called his corps and army commanders to his headquarters to announce that he was leaving, and on the next day he boarded a train for Washington.

These belated attempts to assist North Carolina probably were not appreciated, especially in the light of events occurring in the western part of the state during the final days of the war. Union General George Stoneman on 28 March moved into the town of Boone from his base in Tennessee and destroyed public buildings preliminary to a rapid sweep that took him through Wilkesboro, while some of his men went to Blowing Rock and Lenoir. United again at Wilkesboro, they proceeded to Mount Airy and then into Virginia. Returning to North Carolina they moved on through Mocksville, Danbury, and Salisbury; in the latter place they destroyed military stores, railroad property, public buildings, and some of the buildings at the Confederate prison where as many as 15,000 men had been confined. From Salisbury Stoneman returned to Tennessee by way of Statesville and Taylorsville, but some of his men went off on side expeditions to Charlotte, Morganton, Marion, and Asheville. All along the route extensive damage was done to private as well as to public property. At Waynesville on 6 May 1865, General James G. Martin surrendered the army of western North Carolina, the last Confederate force in the state.

North Carolina, along with the other states in the South, was devastated. The loss of life left virtually no family untouched. Many potential leaders had been cut off in their prime. Enormous property damage was evident everywhere. The will to face the future was drained from countless numbers of people. Apathy prevailed. Defeated both in their hope for what they felt to be fair treatment under the old Constitution before the war and for the opportunity to set their own course through a new independence, they faced an uncertain future. Even the negotiations ending the fighting gave them no hint of their fate or hope for what lay ahead.

20

A STATE MADE NEW

WHEN William A. Graham and David L. Swain did not return from their call upon General Sherman by the time expected, Governor Vance on 12 April took a train to the west. He found that President Davis by that time was in Charlotte so he went there to confer with him. Afterward he returned to Greensboro where he announced the surrender of General Johnston at the Bennett farmhouse near Durham and then surrendered himself to a Union general. Informed that there were no orders for his arrest, Vance joined his family in Statesville where friends had provided safety. Two weeks later, on his thirty-fifth birthday, the governor was arrested and sent to a prison in Washington, D.C. In early July he was paroled without ever having been told why he had been detained, and in March 1867 he was granted a presidential pardon.

Presidential Plans to Restore the Union

Since the United States Congress was not in session at the end of the war, President Andrew Johnson alone was obliged to determine how the Southern states would be restored to the Union. As the Constitution did not provide for such an action, the president did what he thought proper. His plan, the one that Lincoln had tentatively designed, was to accept the states back into full fellowship as quickly and as easily as possible with only the most essential restrictions. The North had maintained all along that the right of secession did not exist, and that it was impossible for a state to withdraw from the United States. Logically, therefore, it should only have been necessary for the recently unruly states to take such steps as repealing the ordinance of secession and formally freeing the slaves—to demonstrate their change of heart—before resuming their former role in the nation. This was a simple policy of reconciliation. In the meantime the South was occupied by the military. General John McA. Schofield, who was in command of North Carolina, immediately issued proclamations declaring the war at an end and the slaves freed. He also placed General J. D. Cox in charge of the western part of the state, General A. H. Terry in the Piedmont, and General J. R. Hawley and General J. M. Palmer in the east.

President Johnson began the implementation of his program with North

On hearing that they were free, former slaves quickly left the plantation to seek a new life elsewhere. (North Carolina Division of Archives and History, Raleigh)

Carolina, his native state, appointing William Woods Holden provisional governor on 29 May 1865. Johnson and Holden were on friendly terms as Johnson was aware of Holden's unionist sympathies and his role in the wartime peace movement. Holden corresponded with and visited the president in Washington. In his new position, he was to have the cooperation of military authorities to restore order among the people, to enforce the laws, and to suppress guerrilla warfare. Having accomplished that, he was to call a convention to revise the state constitution, hold an election for state officials, and provide for the election of congressmen to be seated in December. Certain restrictions on voting and officeholding were laid down—those who had engaged in "rebellion" had to take an amnesty oath, and there were certain categories of offenses for which only a presidential pardon would qualify one to vote. Voters also had to be eligible under the provisions of the law as it existed before 20 May 1861.

Holden named Jonathan Worth as state treasurer and Charles R. Thomas as secretary of state, positions they had held under Vance. The treasury was exhausted, but Worth set about to collect taxes and otherwise to replenish it. Federal troops had seized large quantities of cotton in North Carolina and sent it to New York to be sold as "rebel" property. Worth succeeded in halting the sale and obtaining some revenue from this source to help meet the state's most pressing needs. Since local government had also collapsed, Holden found it necessary to appoint numerous county and municipal officials as well. He called upon his political friends around the state to submit the names of candidates for these positions, and from their lists he chose individuals to fill state and local offices. Altogether Holden named more than three thousand people, most of whom had never before held public office. He also determined which men should be pardoned for their activity during the war. In laying the foundations for his administration Holden demonstrated personal concern for the welfare of the state, and, had he not been the target of animosity leveled by those who had personal grievances against him, he might have served North Carolina well.

Reaction to a Constitution Rejected

As he was directed to do, Holden called a convention which met in October 1865 and in May-June 1866. Complying with the federal directive, delegates at the first session nullified the ordinance of secession, formally abolished slavery, and repudiated the Confederate debt. At the second session a state constitution was prepared; this was largely a restatement of the 1776 constitution, including the 1835 revisions, but with a few new features. It specified that only whites could be counted in determining representation in the General Assembly. A five-year residence requirement was inserted for legislators and the governor, and the office of lieutenant governor was created. In the future, instead of there being two ways to amend the constitution, amendments could be made only by a convention called by the General Assembly. Property qualifications for voting and office-holding remained in effect.

Some complained that the convention was illegal because it had not been called in accordance with provisions of the constitution in effect at the time. When submitted to a referendum in August 1866, relatively few men voted and the constitution was rejected by a vote of 21,770 to 19,880. Conservatives were still upset over the recent repudiation of wartime debts, declaring that the loss of slave property was costly enough without having this additional loss placed on them personally and on the state through the wiping out of investments, particularly those of the University of North Carolina and the Literary Fund. The more liberal element in the state was unhappy that blacks would not be able to vote and that the residence requirement for voting and officeholding was so long.

During the first session of the convention Holden was much in evidence as he attempted to lay the foundation for a gubernatorial campaign. His private secretary commented, "I believe that in everything he did, he kept constantly in view no object but his own political advancement." Before adjourning, more than fifty members of the convention petitioned Holden to become a candidate for governor. It was believed that he was President Johnson's choice and that opposition to Holden would impede the state's return to the Union. Nevertheless, a group of Conservative leaders persuaded Jonathan Worth to run. Neither man campaigned extensively, but Holden's followers maintained that his election would enable the state to return to the Union promptly while Worth was hostile to the president's plan. Even though Worth won by nearly 6,000 votes out of 57,616 cast, Holden's forces elected four of the seven congressmen. Northern newspapers immediately claimed that North Carolina was not yet ready for statehood.

The election gave Holden's supporters a majority in the General Assembly; when it met on 27 November 1865, he sent a message urging harmony in the interest of restoration to the Union. A step toward that end was taken on the second day when both houses approved ratification of the Thirteenth Amendment abolishing slavery. There was, however, strong opposition in the senate over the unlimited power it granted to Congress; under its provisions, it was said, freedmen might have the right to bear arms, testify in court, marry whites, and even vote. In other words, the South was being forced to take action that, under different circumstances, it would have resisted. The legislature also elected the state's two United States senators. This, however, proved to be an exercise in futility as Congress refused to seat either representatives or senators from North Carolina, in part, perhaps, because most of them were Democrats and the Congress was Republican.

On 15 December 1865, a few days before the regular session adjourned, Jonathan Worth was sworn in as governor. He was immediately faced with a great many problems. Among them was concern for the numerous freedmen in the state. While many blacks found employment in the communities where they had long lived—often now as tenants or on rented land—or worked under contracts usually negotiated with the assistance of the military, others gathered in towns. In some cases, with no means of support, they expected the government to provide for them. Somehow the expectation arose that each would be given "forty acres and a mule." A Federal agency, the Freedmen's Bureau, did, in fact, assist them. The bureau supervised the drafting of contracts and work arrangements of the freedmen, and before it was abolished in 1872 its agents registered black voters. Emergency food and shelter were provided, schools were established, and military courts heard their complaints. Former masters, as well, could present grievances to these courts.

In 1866 the adjourned session of the previous year's General Assembly convened and, following the lead of other Southern legislatures, enacted a series of laws designed to regulate the conduct of blacks. Called "Black Codes," the North Carolina version validated the marriages of former slaves, generally changed the law of apprenticeship to apply equally to both races, gave blacks the same rights and privileges as whites in courts of law and equity, made the criminal law applicable to both races alike with the single exception of rape, provided that blacks could testify in court, and granted blacks protection from fraud and ignorance in making contracts with whites. However, it did not guarantee full civil rights to blacks.

At this time the unconquered "rebels" among the students at the University of

North Carolina enjoyed one last bit of revenge. Without letting the faculty know what they were up to, the managers of the Commencement Ball on 7 June 1866 named former President Jefferson Davis and four Confederate generals, including Robert E. Lee, as "honorary managers." The names of these high officers in the Confederacy, bearing their late titles, were engraved on handsome invitations that were distributed before word of it got out. University president David L. Swain and the trustees were thrown into a panic at the thought of how Federal authorities might retaliate against the university, but they need not have been concerned. The action was ignored, undoubtedly recognized as a harmless student prank.

From the moment W. W. Holden completed his term as provisional governor, he began a new drive to attain the state's highest office for a full term. His plans began to take shape in the summer of 1866, when supporters led by Charles R. Thomas called for a meeting of "unmistakable loyal men" who were dissatisfied with Governor Worth. Under Holden's chairmanship, a convention of delegates from thirteen counties met in Raleigh and resolved that the state should ratify the Fourteenth Amendment granting both Federal and state citizenship to blacks. While the amendment guaranteed citizenship for all people, it denied public office to anyone who participated in insurrection or rebellion after having taken an oath to support the Constitution of the United States. This gathering further concluded that most North Carolinians wanted to cooperate with the president's plan for Reconstruction whereas Governor Worth was delaying its implementation.

Before his supporters went home in September Holden named a steering committee to promote the Union cause, and the members began to consider how to gain statewide support. A new political party, they were convinced, was necessary, and soon petitions were being sent to Washington. One, with some five thousand names, asked that a new state be created in the mountain region much as had been done in the case of West Virginia during the war; if that was not possible, the petition requested that the whole state be organized on a "Union basis." Finally, in December 1866 Holden himself led a delegation to the capital to consult with Radical Republicans about organizing a state Republican party, to try to get legislation introduced to dismiss Governor Worth from office, and to return the state to the Union promptly. A bill drafted by Holden and his friends was actually introduced in the General Assembly but did not call for the total enfranchisement of blacks.

Worth, in the meantime, took steps to return the state to the Union. In January and February 1867, with the help of President Johnson, a plan was drawn up to readmit Southern states without disqualifying those who supported the Confederacy. This plan contained a clause declaring the Union to be perpetual, and required a constitutional amendment in each state for equal suffrage but with certain property and educational restrictions. In rejecting this arrangement, which had the president's approval, Congress began a course of action that killed presidential Reconstruction and supplanted it with its own more radical plan.

It was in large measure to test the attitude of the Southern states—or more likely simply to confirm what the Radical Republicans already knew—that the Fourteenth Amendment was passed by Congress in June 1866 when none of the eleven Southern states were represented. It was promptly submitted to the states for ratification. Its acceptance would determine whether a Southern state could again be represented in Congress and thus returned to membership in the Union. When the amendment was rejected, Congress began to implement its own terms under which the states might be restored.[1]

On 2 March 1867 a bill entitled "An Act to Provide for the More Efficient Government of the Rebel States" became law over the president's veto. It was shortly supplemented by three additional acts that drastically altered the status of the Southern states. Congress divided the "unreconstructed" states into five military districts; directed that the president assign a general officer of the United States Army as commander of each district; instructed the commanders to maintain the peace and protect the personal and property rights of individuals in their district, using troops and military courts if necessary; said that the existing state governments were *provisional* in nature and subject to modification or even abolishment by the authority of the United States; and prescribed a program to be followed by each state in order to qualify its congressmen to be seated again. It was reported that the possibility existed that state boundaries might be erased and totally different states created.

Specifically, the new law required that a constitution consistent with the Constitution of the United States be formed by each state, acting through a convention elected by its male citizens, twenty-one years or older, of whatever race, color, or previous condition, who had been a resident of the state for at least a year, except those persons disfranchised for "rebellion" or for felony; and that the resulting state constitution extend the suffrage on the same basis as prescribed for the election of delegates to the constitutional convention.

In North Carolina Conservatives received the Reconstruction act with a mixture of despair and resignation. Faced with what they considered to be the twin disasters of Negro suffrage and military rule, people realized that active resistance to the demands of Congress would be useless. Although they were convinced that the act was unconstitutional, there was no hope that the United States Supreme Court would do anything about it. The only course was to accept the South's fate.

If Conservatives agreed that submission was necessary, they were certainly divided over whether active cooperation with congressional Reconstruction was wise or consistent with honor. One faction argued that cooperation was desirable

---

1. The Fourteenth Amendment was rejected by ten Southern states and by Delaware, Kentucky, and Maryland, and not acted upon by California. Tennessee accepted it and was readmitted.

The education of blacks of all ages became the concern of a large number of Northerners, formerly active abolitionists, who moved into the South behind the Federal army. (North Carolina Division of Archives and History, Raleigh)

and prudent, since it might enable Conservatives to control the approaching constitutional convention and prevent an unduly radical constitution. Another faction, however, insisted that cooperation with Congress would be an endorsement of the South's humiliation and, therefore, was dishonorable and unthinkable. The very existence of this faction gave the Radicals an opportunity to claim that Conservatives were trying to obstruct the progress of Reconstruction. Regardless of their differences over the question of cooperation, white North Carolinians anticipated military rule with considerable, and understandable, apprehension.

Military Rule

The district commander's personality and views, it was generally agreed, would have a great influence over the course of Reconstruction. The appointment of Major General Daniel E. Sickles to the Second Military District, composed of the two Carolinas, was not surprising as he had recently been military commander of South Carolina. He was a lawyer who had risen through Tammany Hall, New York's political fraternal organization, to serve in that state's legislature. A friend of President James Buchanan, he held pro-Southern views before the war and defended the right of states to secede. His political career ended suddenly in 1859, however, when he shot and killed his young wife's lover, Philip B. Key, son of

A State Made New

The Freedmen's Bureau and other agencies acted quickly to provide employment for blacks. This blacksmith and wheelwright shop took advantage of skills acquired in slavery to enable men to support their families. (North Carolina Collection, University of North Carolina at Chapel Hill)

Francis Scott Key. Acquitted on a plea of insanity, he organized a brigade of troops at the beginning of the war in which he served creditably until he lost a leg at Gettysburg. Even before the war ended he began to urge "magnanimity and justice and conciliation" toward the South. This view, plus his initial public address in Charleston advising blacks to seek honest employment and avoid anyone who might want to create racial tension, augured well for the future.

In the spring of 1867 President Johnson attended commencement exercises at the University of North Carolina, accompanied by Sickles and other officials. During their visit, the university administration recommended to the students that each of these guests be made an honorary member of one of the campus literary societies. Johnson was initiated into the Dialectic Society and all of the others except Sickles were acceptable to the Philanthropic Society. Sickles was rejected "by a small minority . . . in order to emphasize their hostility to the Reconstruction Acts." There is no indication that the general took offense at this youthful act.

President Johnson was welcomed by university president David L. Swain. In response, Johnson recalled that it had been forty-one years since he passed through Chapel Hill on his way west from Raleigh. On foot, weary and hungry, he had walked the streets of the little town looking for a place to spend the night. James Craig took him in and the next morning gave "the forlorn boy a bag full of bread and meat for his future needs" as he traveled across North Carolina to find a new home in Tennessee.

Holden and some of his friends made plans for the formal creation of the Republican party in North Carolina in the spring of 1867. They drew up a list of 156 carefully selected loyal unionist white men whom they invited to a meeting in the house chamber of the capitol in Raleigh on 27 March. Through the columns of the *North Carolina Standard* Holden also issued a general invitation to any interested blacks and assured them of a cordial welcome. When Ceburn L. Harris opened the convention, 101 whites and 46 blacks were present. Over the ineffective objection of a minority, which preferred the name "Union party," the Republican party was organized. Its platform, adopted at the convention, supported the congressional plan of Reconstruction and complete civil and political equality for blacks. Formation of the new party was hailed by the Northern press, and the *Nation* proclaimed that "in North Carolina we suppose nearly half of the vote of the State can be controlled by it." At home, however, the reaction was quite different. The *Raleigh Sentinel* said the convention was composed of "Old party hacks, broken down, spavined demagogues, mere seekers of office." A little more objective, a Greensboro paper observed that "part of its members were honest, genuine men, who were bamboozled into the affair to give it *eclat*. The remainder were shams, perfect political mushrooms." The *Wilmington Dispatch* called the delegates "Holden miscegenationists." In fact, there were some capable men, both Conservative and Republican, in the convention; otherwise the 1868 constitution, which served the state until 1971 (and in large measure is still reflected in the contemporary document) could not have been drawn up. Some of the carpetbaggers—S. S. Ashley and Albion W. Tourgée, for example— made important contributions both to this convention and to the state generally.

With the assistance of an executive committee Holden, who held no official post in the party hierarchy, began organizing the Republican party from the local level up. On the same day, an Independence Day celebration was observed in Raleigh by a parade of blacks and whites, many of them Union League members, and long orations by members of both races.[2] The national Republican

2. In North Carolina, as elsewhere in the South, many whites began to ignore the Fourth of July, which before the war had been the occasion of day-long celebrations with the firing of cannon, numerous toasts, picnics, and entertainment. Reasoning that by Northern domination they had lost their "independence," they transferred some portions of the old celebration—such as setting off firecrackers—to Christmas. (Shooting at Christmas had been a custom since colonial days.) In 1875 when the centennial of the Declaration of Independence was marked by an exposition in Philadelphia, North Carolina exhibited only a minimum interest even though a native of the state, expatriate Joseph R. Hawley, was chairman of the planning commission. The continued presence of a Federal army of occupation undoubtedly contributed to the lack of enthusiasm.

Andrew Johnson (1808–75), born in Raleigh, succeeded to the presidency on the death of Abraham Lincoln on 15 April 1865. He attempted to follow the lenient plans of his predecessor in accepting the seceded states back into the Union, but they were overthrown by Radicals in Congress who imposed harsh restrictions instead. (North Carolina Division of Archives and History, Raleigh)

executive committee sent large quantities of printed material together with seventy full-time speakers and organizers. It also gave the young party $20,000 in cash and provided free postage. The Republican party in North Carolina also received a large boost from the Union League, an organization founded in Illinois in 1862 to restore Northern morale after military and political losses; it later served to publicize Southern "outrages," and eventually its objective was to promote the policies of the Radical Republicans. From offices in North Carolina the League helped to recruit members for the new party.

Public attitude toward Major General Sickles began to change as it became apparent that he would play a political role in his district, and as he issued a series of General Orders. These, he directed, were to have the force of law; among other things, they ostensibly subordinated state law to military law, made military courts superior to civil courts—even Federal courts, and gave the military commander authority over local elections. On his own initiative Sickles declared some elections invalid; quarantined ports; and ordered that no grain be used for distilling alcoholic beverages, that no mortgages be foreclosed, and that no private debts incurred between the time South Carolina seceded and 15 May 1865 be collected. North Carolinians especially objected to the latter restriction, since for nearly five months of that period their state had remained in the Union.

Governor Worth and others sometimes requested explanations and further information from Sickles, but he refused to elaborate, merely indicating that he was carrying out the will of Congress. The question was raised whether a military commander could go beyond the specific, expressed directives of Congress. Worth began to suspect that Sickles intended to dismiss him, and he relayed his concerns to the president.

At Johnson's request, Henry Stanbery, the attorney general of the United States, issued an interpretation of the Reconstruction act. In it Stanbery challenged the right of Congress to delegate its full authority to the district commanders. This confirmed Worth's position that district commanders were limited to carrying out only the stated will of Congress and refuted the assumption of absolute power as reflected in some of Sickles's General Orders. After reading the attorney general's opinion, Sickles informed his superior in Washington, Secretary of War Ulysses S. Grant, that the power of removal and appointment was essential and asked that he either be replaced or be permitted to appear before a board of inquiry. When Johnson refused to honor either request, Congress reacted quickly to this challenge. At a special session in July 1867 a second supplement to the Reconstruction act was passed over the president's veto stressing that, according to the true intent and meaning of the act, the provisional governments were subject in all respects to the district commanders. Further, the supplement stated, the act *had* given the commanders the power of removal and appointment; it confirmed all past actions in that regard, and it provided that no district commander could be bound by an opinion of any civil official, even one of the United States. Radicals in Congress clearly intended to have their way in dealing with the South, and power was now consolidated in the hands of Congress.

About a month later a Wilmington military court, conducted by one of Sickles's subordinates, interposed one of the commander's General Orders to prevent the execution of a judgment of a Federal circuit court. President Johnson at this point instructed the attorney general that no military order could be issued and enforced in conflict with the rulings of a court of the United States.

Sickles upheld the action of his subordinate, and he refused to revoke or modify the General Order in question. An impasse had been reached. Because the president's sphere of effective action was severely limited by the dominance of Congress, Johnson decided to register his protest in the only way he could. On 26 August 1867 he relieved Sickles of his duty and named General E. R. S. Canby to replace him. As military commander, however, Canby proved to be equally as intent on carrying out the provisions of the Reconstruction act.

President Johnson and even many Northern Democrats were shocked at the harshness of the Radicals' demands, believing that conditions in the South in 1867 did not require such extreme steps. To return to the Union each state had to hold a constitutional convention to frame a new constitution that would grant suffrage to blacks. Blacks were to be permitted to register and vote for delegates to such a convention, but many prominent whites, consisting of about 10 percent of the white population in North Carolina, could neither vote nor serve as delegates as they had not yet been pardoned. An additional requirement for returning to the Union was ratification of the Fourteenth Amendment. Since Radicals had a two-thirds majority in each house of Congress, their will was supreme. With Canby in total control of the Second Military District, Governor Worth became just a symbol. The new military commander was even more insistent on having his own way than Sickles had been; he supervised blacks more closely and interfered more frequently in local and state government. He did many things to stir up racial and party strife.

Under both Sickles and Canby, W. W. Holden was an outspoken supporter of Radical reconstruction. In a letter to a Republican senator from Ohio, he wrote that he believed the state governments in the South were illegal and could "have no binding effect on the people." When President Johnson vetoed the Reconstruction acts of Congress, Holden said: "It is a sad reflection that a public man with so noble a Union record should have staked and lost himself for Rebels and Rebellion."

After the war, although most native whites probably were Conservatives, they did not forget the differences that separated them in the antebellum years. Secession Democrats and unionist Whigs of the early 1860s were still divided and could not unite against the new Republican party. Although thousands were disgusted with the Reconstruction program of Congress, they remained aloof. Many did not even bother to register although they could easily have done so, and others who registered did not vote. This was a serious mistake, and it left its mark on the state. In 1867 there were 179,653 registered voters, of whom 106,721 were white and 72,932 black. Nineteen counties had a black majority.

A New Constitution

At General Canby's direction, in compliance with the orders of Congress, an election was held in November to choose delegates to a constitutional convention. The vote for holding a convention was 93,006; it was opposed by 32,961, while 53,686 registered voters did not express themselves one way or the other.

Among those elected were 107 Republicans: 18 carpetbaggers, 15 blacks, and 74 native whites. The latter, who composed the majority, of course, included William B. Rodman and Holden's future son-in-law, Calvin J. Cowles. Cowles was chosen president. Among the active carpetbaggers were Albion W. Tourgée of Ohio, General Byron Laflin of Massachusetts and New York, General Joseph C. Abbott of New Hampshire, Major H. L. Grant of Rhode Island and Connecticut, John R. French of New Hampshire and Ohio, and the Reverend Samuel S. Ashley of Massachusetts. Active black delegates included Abraham H. Galloway, a native of Brunswick County, a former slave who had escaped to Ohio, returned, and represented New Hanover County; James H. Harris represented Wake County, and James W. Hood of Ohio represented Cumberland County. Among the Conservatives prominent during the proceedings were Captain Plato Durham and Major John W. Graham. Carpetbaggers were chairmen of most of the committees and therefore very influential in writing the constitution. Most of the members took their task seriously and devoted themselves to the work at hand.[3] At the time, however, they were subjected to harsh criticism by most of the state's newspaper editors and by many individuals because most of the delegates had little or no experience in making laws. It was also said that the carpetbaggers were drawing up a document better suited to their native states than to North Carolina. Nevertheless, the resulting constitution—prepared in the brief time between mid-January and mid-March 1868—served the state, with a few modifications, until 1971 when a number of changes were made. The present constitution is still heavily marked by portions drawn up in 1776 and 1868.

Congress decreed that certain provisions be included and they were. Section

---

3. The minutes of the convention reveal that for some reason—not explained—no business was conducted on a certain day. A local newspaper for that day, however, noted that a circus was in town.

4 declared that North Carolina would henceforth remain a member of the American nation with no right to secede. Section 5 said that a citizen's first allegiance was to the Constitution and the government of the United States. Section 6 made it clear that any debt "incurred in aid of insurrection or rebellion against the United States, or any claim for the loss or emancipation of any slave" would not be paid.

The constitution of Ohio, the home state of Albion Tourgée, was the model for some of the provisions in North Carolina's new constitution. The creation of townships, as a new and artificial unit of county government, for example, came from that source. Other more progressive provisions were based on the constitutions of various Northern states. Some of these changes came to be looked upon as "modern, progressive, liberal, and democratic." Slavery, of course, was specifically prohibited. Universal manhood suffrage, regardless of race, was guaranteed, and there were no religious or property qualifications either for voting or holding office, except that atheists could not hold public office. Henceforth state and county officials would be selected by popular vote. The governor and lieutenant governor would serve for four years instead of two. The name of the House of Commons was changed to "House of Representatives." A Board of Charities and Public Welfare was created, as was "a general and uniform system of Public Schools" to be operated at least four months each year for young people between the ages of six and twenty-one. The state university was declared to be a part of the free public school system, and the General Assembly was directed to "establish and maintain in connection with the University, a Department of Agriculture, of Mechanics, of Mining and of Normal Instruction." The Assembly also was required, "as soon as practicable," to establish one or more "orphan Houses, where destitute orphans may be cared for, educated and taught, some business or trade" and "to devise means for the education of idiots and inebriates." It was also directed that "all deaf mutes, the blind, and the insane of the State, shall be cared for at the charge of the State." The number of capital offenses was reduced to four (arson, burglary, murder, and rape). According to the new constitution, the punishment for other crimes was "not only to satisfy justice, but also to reform the offender, and thus prevent crime."

Many other new provisions were included, as well. Imprisonment for debt was abolished. The old system of county justices was abandoned and county commissioners were created as the governing body. Personal property owned by a woman before her marriage or acquired by her after marriage was made secure and could not be taken to pay any debt or other obligation of her husband. Anyone who fought a duel would be ineligible to hold office.

Since it was drafted by native Republicans and carpetbaggers, the constitution was widely attacked by Conservatives. Their objections were varied: they resented black suffrage, felt that representation in the Senate should be based on wealth rather than population, and opposed the election of judges for eight-year terms. The broadened suffrage was especially criticized, since hereafter, in addition to legislators, all important state executive officers would be elected, as would judges and county officials. Political control of the state would be diluted. The wealthier, land-owning element would lose control; many feared domination by the poor of both races, but particularly by blacks. Few blacks could read and write, and it was believed that those who could not do so were easily swayed. Their vote might be bought; and to enable them to cast the "right" ballot, ballots could be illustrated with a picture—a bale of cotton or some other familiar object—or printed on colored paper. Politicians for years had been accustomed to buying votes for a drink of liquor, but now this would not be so easy with a new party and a new race participating in elections. In brief, the new constitution introduced a more democratic element into all levels of government in North Carolina, and this rankled those who previously had had sole control of the state's affairs.

Many of the state's wartime leaders were still disfranchised, and this further galled them. Numerous newspaper articles deplored the fact that the convention had cost the state $100,000, and described in most uncomplimentary terms the celebration that occurred when the delegates completed their work.

Ku Klux Klan Appears

The constitution was submitted to a referendum of the people at the same time that an election was held for new state and county officials and congressmen. In the bitter campaign preceding these events both the Union League and the Ku Klux Klan participated, the latter making its first appearance in the state.

In the southern Tennessee town of Pulaski on the border of Alabama, probably in late May or early June 1866, six young Confederate veterans met in the law office of Thomas M. Jones, a native of Person County, North Carolina, and the father of one of the men. There they organized what they intended to be a secret social club (on the order of a college fraternity) to enliven the local scene. With that objective in mind, they chose a Greek name, *kuklos*, meaning "circle" or "band"; "klan" was added for its alliterative quality. Members devised fancy individual costumes and a ritual for initiation. They found a rundown old house on the outskirts of town for their headquarters or "den," as it came to be called, and played harmless pranks and held parades. By 1867 a number of politicians and vigilantes had infiltrated the group, its membership spread into other states, and, as the Ku Klux Klan, it came to have other goals. Some of the original members withdrew in regret that their "fun" organization had gotten out of hand, but others likely approved of the changed objectives.

The continued presence of a visible Federal army of occupation played a role in the campaign for ratification of the 1868 constitution. The national Republican party, it was claimed by opponents of the new constitution, sent "flocks" of black students to North Carolina from newly established Howard University in Washington, D.C., and spent $200,000 in preparation for the balloting. A new voter registration was required, and out of a total registration of 196,872 there were 79,444 blacks.[4]

Large numbers of registered voters, perhaps in disgust over contemporary conditions or unhappy that a document to which they had contributed nothing was being forced upon them, stayed away from the polls. Nearly 30,000 of them did not vote. The Republicans carried fifty-eight of the eighty-nine counties and elected W. W. Holden governor. The Conservatives elected only one judge, one solicitor, and one representative to Congress. In an election that took place over the three-day period, 21–23 April, the new constitution was approved by a vote of 93,084 to 74,015.

North Carolina Returns to the Union

Once again the military commander removed an elected governor early—this time, Zebulon B. Vance—to install Holden. He took office on 1 July 1868 and the General Assembly, which Holden had called on 29 June, convened on the same day. Tod R. Caldwell, Republican of Burke County, was the state's first lieutenant governor and presiding officer of the senate. Holden's twenty-four-year-old son, an alcoholic without legislative experience, was elected by the house as its speaker. Wasting no time, the Republican-dominated legislature ratified the Fourteenth Amendment on 4 July; it also elected two Republican senators—John Pool, a native of Pasquotank County, and Joseph C. Abbott, a carpetbagger from New Hampshire who had been made a brigadier general for his role in taking Fort Fisher. North Carolina's new congressmen and senators took their seats on 20 July 1868, and the state was back in the Union. But the occupying military force remained.

The Republican party, composed in large measure of carpetbaggers, blacks, and scalawags, had firm control of state and local government. Although they kept it for only two years (1868–70), some prewar leaders of the state accused them of providing a "bad government" and a time of "pillage and plunder."

4. At this time, in February and March 1868, the impeachment of President Johnson was taking place in Washington. Holden telegraphed several Northern newspapers urging his conviction and removal, saying: "The salvation of the South depends on the conviction of Andrew Johnson." Johnson, once a strong supporter of Holden and an advocate of moderate Reconstruction, was not convicted.

If members of the new General Assembly were familiar with the constitution, they quickly ignored one of its sections. This was the provision that read, in part: "the General Assembly shall have no power to give or lend the credit of the State in aid of any person, association or corporation, except to aid in the completion of such railroads as may be unfinished at the time of the adoption of this Constitution, or in which the State has a direct pecuniary interest, unless the subject be submitted to a direct vote of the people of the State, and be approved by a majority of those who shall vote thereon." In view of what happened, it almost seems that the drafters of the constitution had a premonition of what was going to happen. If so, however, their efforts to prevent it were futile.

Carpetbaggers, Scalawags, and the Klan

Many of the state's railroads were in serious disrepair at the end of the war, and even the Conservatives generally recognized the need for improvements. To provide money to overhaul them, the General Assembly began to issue bonds which were sold by railroad officials themselves. Income from the sale was intended for building and repairing railroads and nothing else. But certain politicians and some businessmen, working together, began to take advantage of the public's trust in them so as to make a personal profit.

The Convention of 1868 and the Republican legislatures of 1868 and 1869, as they had the authority to do, approved the issuing of $28 million in bonds. Most of this was for the Western North Carolina, the Chatham, and the Wilmington, Charlotte and Rutherford railroads. However, this was an excessive amount, more than the state was believed able to redeem, and the prices dropped. More bonds had to be issued to meet the railroads' needs. The difficulty was that it was unconstitutional for the state to sell bonds for less than would have to be paid the holder, unless a special tax was levied to cover the interest. Legislators also violated the law by chartering new railroads without obtaining the approval of the people in a special election.

Some members of the General Assembly, tempted by opportunities they saw to get rich, participated in fraudulent activities and sold their votes for large sums of money. Most deeply involved was a carpetbagger from New York, General Milton S. Littlefield. With funds he received from a North Carolina native, George W. Swepson, who had been named by Holden as president of the western division of the Western North Carolina Railroad, Littlefield bought votes and did numerous favors for legislators. Among the latter, a bar to serve alcoholic beverages reportedly was set up in one wing of the state capitol. About this time the Fifteenth Amendment was ratified on behalf of North Carolina. On 5 March 1869 the legislature approved this step guaranteeing the right to vote to all citizens regardless of race, color, or previous condition of servitude.

These scandals, bad enough as they were, were widely publicized by the Conservative press. Editor Josiah Turner, Jr., of the *Raleigh Sentinel*, for one, played up instances of fraud and bribery, citing the perpetrators by name and often giving them humorous but apt nicknames. No journalistic code of ethics inhibited writers from levying unfounded accusations, so whether some underhanded deed actually took place or not the Republican legislature was described as "a minstrel of ignorant Negroes and greedy carpetbaggers and scalawags." The presence of twenty black men as members of the General Assembly during the 1868–69 session, to say nothing of the large number of carpetbaggers, stirred many Conservative whites to seek ways to bring about changes in what they claimed was an oppressive, brutal, and corrupt government. The agency already at hand to help accomplish this, they believed, was the Ku Klux Klan.

By December 1867 some North Carolinians were members of the Klan; Colonel William L. Saunders, Conservative editor of the Wilmington *Journal*, probably was its head, but since it was a secret group very little is known about its organization. It seems to have consisted largely of local, independent bands with little central direction. Its total membership may have reached 40,000. The apparent rationale for its existence was the feeling by the conservative element, the prewar Democrats who had renamed themselves Conservatives during the war, that there was no hope of regaining control of government from the Republicans through ordinary political activity. The Klan, then, became the device by which they might return to power. Members of the Klan, in attempting to justify their existence, often cited the presence of various Northern organizations such as the Red Strings and the Heroes of America, but particularly the Union League, of which Holden was the first president. Members of these groups were *accused* of murder, rape, barn burning, and other crimes, but it is extremely unlikely that they would have mistreated their own members or sympathizers simply to place the blame on the Klan. Additionally, Union League leaders such as Wyatt Outlaw and Mayor William R. Albright of Graham clearly advised the membership to reject such activity. The League was largely a means of keeping blacks loyal to the Republican party whereas the Klan's goal was to prevent that. The Klan also resented blacks who demonstrated ambition or independence, or those who were "impudent" or who possessed firearms.

It was both the aims and the methods adopted to accomplish them that gave the Klan a bad name during the two years (1868–70) it flourished in North Carolina. Judge Richmond M. Pearson in 1868 wisely urged patience and moderation, however, saying, "When the storm is over, the Conservative party representing as it does, the property and intelligence of the State, will take the guidance of affairs, and all will be well." Usually wearing white (but sometimes colored) sheets or other elaborate costumes, tall conical hats, and masks, and riding horseback, heavily armed Klan members terrorized blacks as well as whites who helped blacks advance or otherwise associated with them, or who taught in black schools—particularly women from New England. Murder by various modes—shooting, hanging, drowning—was by no means rare. Such activity frequently was carried out in one county by Klansmen from an adjoining county; then, a few nights later, members from the county where they had struck would "return the favor."

The Klan generally did not operate in counties where there was a large majority of blacks; in such places it would have little chance of changing enough votes—or preventing enough people from voting—to make any difference, and blacks might unite to retaliate. Instead, it concentrated on counties where a slight drop in the Republican vote would be to its advantage. Nor did Klansmen usually vent their spleen on well-known or highly popular Republicans or blacks, as this would result in adverse publicity in the North. They chose, instead, to attack or frighten numerous "little" people in many communities, thereby spreading the terror around and preventing more people from voting.

Between the spring and fall elections of 1868, the strength of the Republican party declined in North Carolina as it lost control of thirteen counties. Only Alamance and Caswell counties were added to the party's roster. As the elections of 1870 neared, Klan terrorism thrived in these two counties. Late in 1869 a bill drawn up by United States Senator John Pool was introduced in the General Assembly by T. M. Shoffner, a senator from Alamance County who, it was rumored, was paid a substantial sum to sponsor the bill. It authorized the governor to suspend the writ of habeas corpus and to call out the militia to maintain order where Klan activity could not be controlled by local law enforcement officers. The Shoffner Act, as it became known, was passed and shortly was put to use by the governor.

Near midnight on 26 February 1870 in Graham, the county seat of Alamance, a large band of robed horsemen went to the home of the black Republican leader, Wyatt Outlaw. He was president of the local Union League, had helped found the Republican party in the state, and had been active in opening a school for blacks. Outlaw was abducted and taken to the town square, where he was hanged from a large oak tree within a hundred feet of the courthouse.

In nearby Caswell County the white Republican leader, a native of Guilford County, was John W. Stephens. A tobacco trader, he had been an agent of the Freedmen's Bureau and an active member of the Union League. In his work he associated freely with local blacks who outnumbered whites in the county. In 1868 Stephens was elected to the state senate over Bedford Brown, former United States senator and recognized prewar political leader of the county. Many people grew to dislike Stephens, and nothing said about him was too bad to be believed. He was socially ostracized and even expelled from the local Methodist church.

When his life was threatened, he insured his life, fortified his house, and began carrying two pistols.

Stephens actually was a political and racial moderate, but his affiliation with the Republican party and his association with blacks brought about his downfall. In May 1870, while observing a Conservative county convention in the Yanceyville courthouse, he was lured to a basement room by Frank Wiley, a prewar Democratic sheriff whom Stephens was urging to accept the Republican nomination for sheriff. By prearrangement, Wiley and a group of other Klansmen were waiting in a small basement room. They tied up Stephens, stabbed him, and left his body on a woodpile there. Riding out of town, the men threw the key to the locked room in a creek. Although Federal authorities questioned many people, including all of those involved in the deed, the murderer was never identified. The Klan members, sworn to secrecy, revealed nothing. The facts were not known for sixty-five years, until after the death of the last participant. He had been persuaded to write his recollections of the event and deposit the document, sealed during his lifetime, in the state archives in Raleigh.

The "Kirk-Holden War"

Governor Holden reacted swiftly to Stephens's murder. Not only was he concerned over the death of a loyal Republican leader, but he also feared losing yet another county. Calling out the militia, he placed Alamance and Caswell counties under martial law with Colonel George W. Kirk of Jonesboro, Tennessee, in command. During the war Kirk had deserted the Confederate army and become commander of a Union force, leading raids through western North Carolina. Now with a small "army" of untrained men ranging in age from fifteen to seventy, Kirk arrested a number of prominent men in Caswell County and detained them at his camp. In Hillsborough he also arrested Josiah Turner, Jr., the outspoken newspaper editor. No hearings were held, and at Holden's order the writ of habeas corpus was denied Kirk's prisoners. When Chief Justice Richmond Pearson directed that writs be issued, the governor ordered that they not be served. Pearson then said there was nothing further that he could do. To hold a person without due process of law violated the recently adopted Fourteenth Amendment, and a Federal judge in Salisbury ordered most of the prisoners released.

The "Kirk-Holden War," as this episode was called by the governor's opponents, came to a hasty end. An election in August demonstrated that the aims of the Ku Klux Klan had been accomplished—a majority of Conservatives were elected. The Klan had been active in ten of the fifteen recently Republican counties that voted Conservative in 1870. In September Holden disbanded the militia, and in November he declared that the insurrection in Alamance and Caswell counties was over.

Impeachment of the Governor

Conservatives began suggesting that Governor Holden be impeached for his actions in Alamance and Caswell counties. Petitions were submitted to the General Assembly, and on 9 December 1870 a representative from Orange County, Frederick N. Strudwick, formerly a member of the Klan, introduced a resolution for that purpose. On its approval, a house committee was appointed to appear before the senate on 15 December to impeach W. W. Holden because of his high crimes and misdemeanors in office. The house drew up eight articles of impeachment. Among other offenses, he was charged with declaring martial law, unlawfully raising troops, and illegally declaring counties to be in a state of insurrection; with unlawfully arresting eighteen citizens; with seizing, detaining, imprisoning, and depriving those citizens of their liberty and privileges as freemen; and with refusing to obey a writ of habeas corpus.

The trial got under way on 2 February 1871 and lasted until 22 March, a period of seven weeks. A separate vote was taken on each of the eight charges, and Holden was found guilty on six. Although Holden was the second American governor to be impeached, he was the first to be convicted.[5] By a vote of 36 to 13 the senate expelled him from his post and declared that he should never again be eligible for public office in the state. Thus culminated the long feud between Holden and his political opponents.

Holden was succeeded by Lieutenant Governor Tod R. Caldwell, also a Republican but virtually powerless. The General Assembly repealed the Shoffner Act and amended the militia law so that what Holden had done was not likely to occur again. Membership in secret political and military societies was also outlawed.

The Klan thereupon virtually disappeared in most parts of the state. In a few western counties, particularly in Cleveland and Rutherford, however, it remained active. Republicans in North Carolina, anxious to remove this blot from the state's reputation, sought the assistance of the Federal government. An investigation was conducted by the United States Senate, and the Klan's activity was denounced as violent and unlawful.

Soon a joint committee of both houses of the Congress examined witnesses from throughout the South and reached the same conclusion. Former presumed

5. Governor Charles Robinson of Kansas was impeached in 1862 but the charges against him were dismissed.

FACTS FOR THE PEOPLE

To Read, Ponder and Digest, if they can.

For the benefit of those who really desire information, and to show in proper light the Extravagance, Wastefulness, and utter disregard for the people's best interests, shown by the Radical party, we submit the following comparison of the expense of one year of Democratic rule, under Gov. Bragg in 1857 & '58 ; and one year ending Sept. 30th, 1869, under the Radical rule of William W. Holden :

	Expenditures 1857, '58.	Expenditures 1868, '69.
Adjutant General,	$ 200 00	$ 1965 56
Capitol Square,	1277 82	3687 78
Executive Department,	2550 00	7752 65
Treasury Department,	2750 00	6082 96
Keeper of Capitol,	266 00	1054 19
Auditor's Department,	1000 00	4010 54
Binding Laws,	1073 25	6596 96
Copying Laws,	348 50	1608 50
State Department,	800 00	5903 25
Public Printing,	5240 57	28,685 10
Judiciary,	28,165 15	54,130 50
General Assembly,	49,115 54	191,102 10
Fugitives from Justice,	572 75	6,834 00

Contingences for 1868, '69, $76,506 64

☞ Among the expenditures for 1868, '69, may be found such items as these :—

D. D. Colgrove, one copy of " How to Make the Farm pay,"	4 50	Douglass Bell, for Toilet Soap,	6 00
L. D. Wilkie, Holden's detective,	1042 90	Geo. W. Nason, jr., Drawer locks, Chairs and Water Coolers,	130 20
L. H. Mowers, "	949 75	Phil. Thiem, 6 Baskets, 1 Corkscrew,	9 00
State Militia, (to outrage Jones County,)	1864 91	Half doz. ostrich feathers, water bucket and dipper,	16 75
Newbern Republican, for adv. duties S. C. C.,	250 00		
Newbern Times, printing Badges for Militia,	18 80		

OTHER FACTS FOR THE CITIZENS OF CRAVEN COUNTY ESPECIALLY.

The entire tax for this County levied for all purposes in 1867, under a Democratic State Government was $18,000. This, deducting the tax on Polls, was only 3-4 of one per cent on the assessed value of property.

The tax for this year, under Radical rule, will reach $47,000. Deduct the Poll tax and the tax levied on real and personal property as assessed, will reach 2 1-2 per cent.

Citizens of Craven, how like you this picture of increase in the short space of two years ? Again—It is a fact worthy of note, that the principal officials, County Commissioners, Legal Adviser of the Board, (R. F. Lehman, Esq., $500,) have all been paid dollar for dollar of their claims, while the jurors, witnesses, &c., have their tickets on hand, or have been subjected to a shave of seventy per cent. to get the money for them.

☞ This is Radical justice—Radical love and care for the poor white and colored man, with a vengeance !

☞ Next week we will show you other iniquities of the party in power.☜

In an attempt to discredit the Radical control of state and local government, this comparison of expenditures and taxes collected in 1857–58 and in 1868–69 was circulated by the Conservative (or Democratic) party. (Rare Book Room, Duke University Library, Durham)

head of the Klan, William L. Saunders, became a hero of the Conservatives when he answered every question: "I decline to answer." His was a pioneer use of the Fifth Amendment, a response that has been widely employed in such cases since the 1950s. Numerous other witnesses, who were willing to testify, provided enough information to warrant further intervention by the Federal government in the local affairs of Southern states. In 1870 and 1871 Federal laws were passed levying fines or imprisonment, or both, on anyone guilty of certain specified acts such as those committed by the Klan. Potential jurors in future trials involving a suspected Klan member were required to swear that they had never belonged to the Klan or any similar organization. Another provision gave the president power to use Federal marshals or military force to restore law and order. The president was also authorized to suspend the writ of habeas corpus. An earlier law pro-

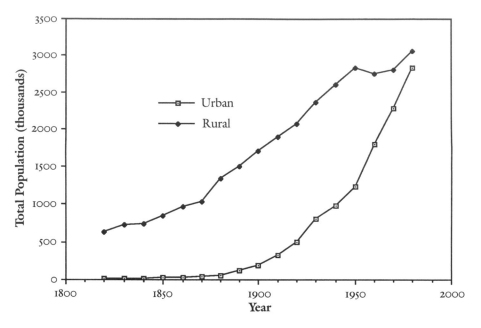

Rural and Urban Populations, 1820–1980

vided for Federal control of elections in the South and made it a punishable offense to deprive a citizen of the rights guaranteed under the Fourteenth and Fifteenth amendments.

Following the passage of these acts Federal troops concentrated in the regions of the most recent Klan activity. Hundreds of arrests were made and some 1,400 indictments were issued. Trials were held in Federal court in Raleigh in late 1871 and early 1872. A great many of those arrested were freed, but about thirty were convicted and sentenced to serve prison terms in Albany, New York. The most severe penalty was meted out to Randolph A. Shotwell. A native of Virginia, educated in Pennsylvania, and from the age of fourteen a resident of North Carolina where his father moved in 1858, Shotwell was a Confederate military officer and after the war a newspaper editor in the western part of the state. He was never a member of the Klan but instead tried to act as a moderating influence on some of its activities. This, however, provided an excuse for Radicals to have him arrested on 5 July 1871. Tried before a partisan judge and a carefully selected jury, he was convicted and received a sentence of six years in prison and a fine of $5,000. He was immediately offered a pardon if he would reveal the names of prominent Conservatives connected with the Klan. This Shotwell refused to do, and he was sent to the Federal penitentiary. Late the following year President Ulysses S. Grant issued him an unconditional pardon.

Many people believed that the Federal government acted only after the Klan had virtually ceased to exist, and that it did so as an excuse for increasing the number of troops posted in the South. Troops and the presence of Federal marshals would help to ensure a Republican victory in the 1872 election, they reasoned. The Conservatives hoped to elect Augustus Merrimon governor, but the Republicans wanted to retain at least that branch of government. The incumbent, Tod R. Caldwell, was their candidate, and without a large black vote he managed to win by a mere 1,899 votes out of 195,361. The Democrats gained control of the General Assembly and could elect the United States senator. Merrimon had been promised that office if he failed in the gubernatorial race, but most Conservatives preferred Zebulon Vance. Republicans, aware that they could not elect one of their own, threw their support to Merrimon as a means of defeating Vance, whom they disliked because he had been the wartime governor. Merrimon then became one of the state's United States senators.

The year 1872 marked the end of the lengthy period of confrontation between Northern politicians and implacable North Carolinians. In their effort to "reconstruct" North Carolina, and with the assistance of a considerable number of native-born whites who were new to the political scene, these newcomers brought experience and ideas of potential value to the state, but they were generally rejected. Attempts to reestablish a system of public schools withered, and plans to prepare freedmen for full citzenship were finally abandoned in the face of native white opposition. The newly created Republican party, even though it counted among its leadership many prewar Whigs and Democrats, was no longer in control.

Local matters began to attract the attention of newly empowered whites. Many of the carpetbaggers who had not already returned to their Northern homes were now getting old. A few, however, had become acclimated and were acceptable to the natives; some, indeed, were even appreciated and either gave up their crusading efforts or, it turned out, had really never been the evil characters they were depicted as being. Many chastened prewar leaders in North Carolina stood ready to play a role in public affairs again.

21

A FRESH START

A S POLITICAL conditions stabilized so did many other aspects of life in the state. The Conservatives—or Democrats, as they came to be called in the mid-1870s—remained concerned about retaining control of both state and local government. There was a lingering uneasiness that small farmers, both white and black, who had many problems in common, might unite and pose a threat to the "elite," as the older native political leaders later were known. In 1870, after the Conservative party took control of the General Assembly, a proposal to call a convention to revise the state constitution was submitted to the people. It was rejected in a referendum the next year by a vote of 95,252 to 86,007.

The Conservatives seized their next opportunity to revise the constitution, this time by the legislative method which required that any proposed amendment be passed at two successive sessions and then approved by the people. During the legislative session of 1870-72 nearly three dozen amendments were considered; eight of them were submitted to a referendum of the people who approved them by a wide margin. Henceforth the legislature would meet every two years instead of annually, and it again had control of the University of North Carolina. Several new offices created in 1868 were also abolished.

The Constitution Amended

In 1875 the General Assembly called a constitutional convention, as it had the authority to do under the 1868 document. In the balloting for delegates 95,191 Republicans voted, followed closely by 95,037 Conservatives—a difference of a mere 154. The delegates elected included 58 Conservatives, 58 Republicans, and 3 Independents. One of the Independents, Dr. Edward Ransom of Tyrrell County, was nominated for president of the convention by the Conservatives; after thirteen tie votes, Ransom voted for himself and was elected. Republicans wanted to adjourn the convention to prevent their party's loss of power in the state, but Ransom's vote foiled their efforts.

This convention, in session for five weeks in the fall, adopted thirty amendments which were approved by a vote of 120,159 to 106,554 on 7 November 1876, to become effective on 1 January 1877. Among other provisions, they called for the creation of a Department of Agriculture; abandoned the simple and uniform court system created in 1868, and gave the legislature authority to determine the jurisdiction of courts inferior to the North Carolina Supreme Court; denied the vote to those guilty of certain crimes; implemented a one-year residency requirement for voting; required "non-discriminatory" racial segregation in public schools; authorized the legislature to revise or abolish the form and power of county and township government; and simplified the method of amending the constitution. Marriages between whites and blacks were prohibited, and secret political organizations were forbidden.

Some of these amendments clearly increased the power of the legislative branch of government, giving it considerable authority over local affairs and enabling the Democratic party to regain virtual control of the state. The party considered local control to be essential—especially in some of the eastern counties with large black populations and in western counties heavily populated by Republicans. The amendments also gave the legislature extensive authority in those counties with a relatively low number of blacks. In either case, insofar as local control of municipal and county government was concerned, this was a backward step.

Conservatives Return to Power as Democrats

To regain complete control of the government, however, the Conservatives hoped to elect the governor in 1876. National victories in 1874 gave the Democrats control of Congress, and the changes made in North Carolina's constitution in 1875 lent credence to predictions that they would "sweep the state." Politicians hit upon three themes to emphasize: Radical Reconstruction, alleged domination by blacks, and the necessity for white supremacy. Each issue appealed to many voters and forced the Republican party into a defensive position. To succeed, the Conservatives needed the support of the national Democratic party, so they gave up the name "Conservative" under which they had operated since the middle years of the war. The designation, after all, was merely cosmetic, one that had been comfortable for cooperating Whigs, who would have been less likely to support "Democrats."

The campaign of 1876 was one of the most dramatic ever witnessed in North Carolina. It pitted the popular Zebulon B. Vance against Thomas Settle of Rockingham County, a highly qualified and experienced political leader and judge, prewar Democrat, Confederate veteran, and one of the founders of the Republican party. Settle's defeat was narrow, yet it signified the end of effective Republican influence in the state for many years. Using a religious and financial term,

Democrats proclaimed Vance's election as evidence that the state had been "redeemed" from the evils of Reconstruction. During the same year Rutherford B. Hayes was elected president, and, although he was a Republican, one of the first acts of his administration in 1877 was to withdraw Federal troops from the South.

"Home rule" was restored, Democrats said. Nevertheless, under acts of the 1877 General Assembly, elected county government was abolished and local power was concentrated in appointed officials. "White supremacy" once again was established as blacks, now without the support of carpetbaggers and Federal troops, ceased to participate in elections or otherwise risk offending dominant whites. Most of the blacks who served in Congress and in the General Assembly during this period did their jobs well; others accomplished little but certainly did no harm. This was generally true of blacks who held local offices in the state. Some, however, were illiterate and totally ineffective in their elected or appointed positions. Racism grew to be a fact of life in North Carolina, as it did in the other Southern states as well as in parts of the North. Reconstruction was over.

Although the Democrats were entrenched, their hold was not so strong as to permit them to relax. In the gubernatorial elections of 1876, 1880, 1884, and 1888, for example, out of an average of 254,801 ballots cast, the Democratic majority was only 13,576. In 1880 Thomas J. Jarvis defeated Ralph P. Buxton by a mere 6,278 votes. The elite continually found it necessary to persuade poorer people to support their bid for leadership and office. Without the Democratic party to manage things in the best interest of the whole state, party leaders maintained, those eastern counties with a majority—or just a large number—of blacks would revert to black control. By this means, and often without showing any deep concern for the well-being of most of their supporters, Democratic leaders kept as firm a grip on the state as their fathers and grandfathers had done "before the late war." Industrialization became their watchword, and they did little more than pay lip service to the small farmers who provided the bulk of their support.

Industrialization

In the depressing days of Reconstruction it seemed that only a dismal future awaited the South, a region perhaps destined to be held captive by the North indefinitely. Many North Carolinians thought that only Northern men and capital could change things. Nevertheless, through the foresight and guidance of some remarkable native businessmen the state and, indeed, the whole region was stirred to action. In textiles, tobacco, and furniture, which in time became the state's most important industries, as well as in the related fields of banking, finance, trade, and transportation, it was largely native North Carolinians who provided the leadership. Sensing the advantages of North Carolina, a few entrepreneurs came from adjoining states or elsewhere in the South.

Only a small number of people from the Northeast played a decisive role in building the state's industry in the period from 1865 to the end of the century. Most of the leaders came from families that had had identical or related interests before 1860, sometimes having produced raw materials and sometimes even manufactured goods. Members of the Duke, Carr, and Hanes families had been associated with tobacco; the Battle, Cannon, Fries, Holt, and Morehead families had had experience in textiles; the Whites, Lambeths, and Wrenns had been involved in furniture; and A. B. Andrews, William J. Hawkins, Robert R. Bridgers, and some of the Pages had been connected with railroads or perhaps just plank roads, but transportation nevertheless.

In some cases prewar factories survived, and on that base enterprise was renewed. Cloth made in the 1850s by the Holt mills in Alamance County was so popular in the North that the fighting had hardly stopped before merchants there were again placing orders. Sometimes it was necessary to start fresh with resources preserved from before the war. Funds invested abroad or in Baltimore, Philadelphia, New York, or Boston, or hard cash held back at the beginning of the war, were quickly employed to build factories. Some enterprises were the result of community efforts. In any case, it did not take a great deal of money to start up a small manufacturing business.

It has been said that many of the fortunes made in industry after the Civil War were instances of the "rags-to-riches" story. A few were, of course, but most of the development in North Carolina was undertaken by sons of the upper or middle class. The upper class alone furnished 49.2 percent of the postwar business leadership, most of which came from the planter stratum. Fathers of 40 percent of these men were themselves businessmen of one sort or another. Textile and tobacco factories had been well established before 1860, although most were not very large. Of the state's forty-nine textile mills in 1880, at least twenty were old ones that had operated more or less continuously since before the war, fifteen were built by men who had been connected with earlier mills, and several others were constructed by those who had married into families with prior industrial connections.

To illustrate, Michael Schenck built the state's first cotton mill in Lincoln County in 1813. He was followed in the business by a grandson, Henry, who opened a mill in Cleveland County in 1873. Henry's daughter married Thomas J. Ramseur, and he became associated with mills in Lincoln County. Henry's son joined Ramseur in operating a mill, and three of Ramseur's grandsons became cotton manufacturers. Five generations of the family were involved from the earliest days into the late twentieth century. The Battle family in Rocky Mount, the Fries family in and around Winston-Salem, the Moreheads of Rockingham

The Duke tobacco factory in Durham in 1895, thirty years after the Dukes, father and sons, began to produce smoking tobacco at their farm outside of town. The family mansion stood beside the factory. (North Carolina Collection, University of North Carolina at Chapel Hill)

and Guilford counties, and the Holts of Alamance are further examples of the same continued participation. Mills in Randolph and adjoining counties are still operated by descendants of those who established them in the 1830s.

A rags-to-riches case, not unlike others in the state, was that of George Alexander Gray, born in Gaston County in 1851, who began to work in a mill at age ten. With limited education but with native ability and hard work, he became an assistant superintendent nine years later. Steadily progressing, he was by the time of his death in 1912 president of sixteen cotton mills.

Virtually the same pattern was repeated in tobacco manufacturing. The Duke, Hanes, Reynolds, and other families continued their association with tobacco after the Civil War, but not always in the same way. The family of Washington Duke in eastern Orange (now Durham) County, which had grown tobacco before hostilities began, processed a little smoking tobacco during the war which was discovered by Federal troops in 1865; soon sons Benjamin and Buchanan (Buck) began manufacturing it in large quantities. The Dukes gradually acquired many other smaller companies, and began using modern machinery to roll cigarettes instead of producing them by hand. In 1890 the

Richard Joshua Reynolds (1850–1918) worked for his father's Virginia tobacco factory until 1874, when he moved to Winston to establish his own firm among the growing industrialists in North Carolina. An astute manager, he developed a flourishing business and soon enlarged its capacity. His Prince Albert smoking tobacco and Camel cigarettes made the R. J. Reynolds Tobacco Company one of the nation's leading producers of tobacco products. (North Carolina Division of Archives and History, Raleigh)

Dukes created the American Tobacco Company; thereafter they developed slogans, trademarks, and worldwide advertising to sell their products. By the early twentieth century their business amounted to more than $200 million a year, and they controlled around 75 percent of the nation's tobacco industry.

R. J. Reynolds's father manufactured tobacco in the 1850s in Patrick County, Virginia; so when young Reynolds moved a few miles across the line into North Carolina in 1874, he was no stranger to the business he would establish in the youthful town of Winston. He was able to prevent the Dukes from taking it over when they began to expand, and the R. J. Reynolds Tobacco Company became another of the state's leading industries. Durham, Reidsville, and Winston-Salem became centers of tobacco manufacturing, but small factories continued to exist across most of North Carolina.

The production of furniture after the war was virtually a new industry. Previously high-quality pieces had been produced in limited quantities for the local market by such men as John Swisegood of Davidson County and Thomas Day, a free black of Caswell County. For many years the commercial production of furniture in America had been centered in the northeastern states and in Michigan.

In the 1880s Ernest Ansel Snow, a lumber salesman from High Point, sold some wood from North Carolina to a furniture factory in Baltimore. Snow was the son of a Union veteran who had passed through North Carolina on his way home after the war and decided that he liked the place. Arriving at his residence in Vermont, the veteran found that his wife was ill and soon in need of a different climate. In 1871 he moved his family to High Point where they became great civic boosters.

After making his sale in Baltimore, young Snow began to think about the difference between the value of wood fresh from the sawmill and the kiln and wood made into furniture. He wondered why there should not be a furniture factory close to the lumber supply. In 1889 he and two local merchants, John H. Tate and Thomas F. Wrenn, pooled their life savings of about $3,000 each to create the High Point Furniture Manufacturing Company. One of the first employees was the very knowledgeable O. C. Wysong, Southern representative of a Cincinnati firm that produced woodworking machinery. Their small factory was described as little more than a shed two stories high, but it was an immediate success. They made so much furniture the first year, Wrenn said, "I thought surely the whole world would soon be supplied . . . and from the amount of lumber we used I was positive that the forests of North Carolina were completely destroyed." When people saw wagons hauling great piles of furniture, "towering in the air like a load of hay," they were convinced that the partners were doing a big business.

As Wrenn observed, "North Carolina factories in those days were accused of selling lumber and not furniture." Most of the workmen had just moved to town from the farm; inexperienced, they knew little or nothing about different kinds of wood and had no knowledge of style. Workers, managers, and owners together learned on the job whatever they needed to know. High Point was in an excellent location. It had good rail transportation, was in the middle of the state's hardwood forests from which raw materials were available, and was surrounded by poor but adaptable rural citizens who were anxious to work for steady wages. In addition, large numbers of people needed new furniture. Not only were

A natural resource ripe for exploitation was found in the vast woodlands of North Carolina. Soon after the war sawmills appeared across the state to provide lumber for new homes, factories, railroad ties, and, above all, the furniture factories that began to spring up along the route of the old North Carolina Railroad. (North Carolina Collection, University of North Carolina at Chapel Hill)

young couples getting married and setting up housekeeping, but also older families had had no opportunity or money to buy furniture since before the war.

At the High Point Furniture Manufacturing Company, total sales for the first year were $75,000 and double that for the second year. The whole town was excited, and furniture and forestry journals around the nation took notice of what was happening in the middle of North Carolina. Furniture factories were being organized by groups of people who could scrape together a few thousand dollars each. As a business flourished, partners branched out and joined others in new companies. Factories began to spring up all along the North Carolina Railroad or its feeder lines in that part of the state—Thomasville, Lexington, Statesville, Morganton, Hickory, Lenoir, and elsewhere from Durham on the east to Asheville in the mountains.

In order to tap the national market, manufacturers had to pay more attention to quality—to use better woods and to apply finer finishes. They began to exhibit their pieces in national furniture markets and to compete with the older firms. Trains made up of long strings of boxcars filled with North Carolina furniture began moving across the continent all the way to California. Sears, Roebuck, and Company signed a contract with one manufacturer to buy everything he produced. Another retailer persuaded a factory to produce parts for furniture to be sold unassembled at a low price and put together by the buyer. In the early years of the new century North Carolina was well on the way to becoming the nation's leading producer of fine furniture, advertised and appreciated around the world. At the Jamestown Exposition in 1907, marking the three hundredth anniversary of England's first permanent American settlement at Jamestown, Virginia, five carloads were tastefully displayed. Such well-known brand names as Drexel, Tomlinson, White, and many others came to be recognized as synonymous with quality. The White Furniture Company of Mebane, established in 1881, is now the oldest furniture manufacturer in the state.

As furniture manufacturing grew in importance, a number of allied industries appeared in the state. Among the new firms were producers of veneers, plywood, varnishes, stains, glue, dowel pins, casters, hinges, drawer pulls, mirrors, lamps, framed pictures, ceramics, and other accessories. Growth also prompted the creation in 1921 of a permanent exhibition and, finally, the construction of the Southern Furniture Exposition Building in High Point which has been enlarged several times. Hickory also has a furniture exposition building, and shows are held several times a year at each.

The state's business leaders, in addition to being largely native, were overwhelmingly Protestant; almost one-third were college graduates, and about one-fifth had at least some college training. Only about 1.5 percent of those for whom information is available had relatively little or no education. Nearly all were members of the Democratic party and most supported educational, religious, and philanthropic causes, donating to churches, schools, orphanages, and hospitals. Some of them in time created research endowments, contributed to the preservation of historic sites, and helped to establish and support art museums. Nevertheless, their own interests as industrialists were paramount. Their concerns were those of capitalism, and many of them, though not all by any means, came to be regarded as self-serving, demanding, and even heartless.

Thomasville came to be known as "the chair town of the South"; in 1907, one of its factories produced 1,500 chairs a day. A giant chair was erected on the town's main street as a monument to its leading industry. This full-page advertisement appeared in the October 1909 issue of *Southern Furniture Journal*. (North Carolina Collection, University of North Carolina at Chapel Hill)

This Charlotte textile mill was typical of countless others, almost identical to it, that opened in the Piedmont section of North Carolina in the late nineteenth and early twentieth centuries. (North Carolina Collection, University of North Carolina at Chapel Hill)

Urbanization

From the end of the Civil War until the opening of the new century the face of North Carolina changed dramatically. The building of mills and factories brought large numbers of rural people to the towns, where many men—although generally dejected at having to change their accustomed life-style—were obliged to seek employment; women and children also began to work for wages, low though they were. It was not unusual for people to work ten to twelve hours a day. Farms were abandoned by tenants but sometimes owners of small farms, if not too far from town, attempted to grow a little cotton in whatever time they could spare from long hours in the mill. Families lived in clusters of mill-owned houses adjacent to the mill and bought on credit from the "company store" whatever food, clothing, and supplies were necessary. Seldom was there anything to spend "foolishly" or for pleasure.

Throughout the state there were large numbers of maimed veterans who had lost an arm or a leg in battle. Women whose husbands had been killed in the war usually lived with their children or other relatives, and there were hundreds of unmarried women whose sweethearts had lost their lives. Children usually grew up in a family that contained several aging female relatives, and talk of "the war" was common. Two or more generations in North Carolina, as in the other Southern states, were thoroughly indoctrinated in family relationships and dislike of Yankees. This contributed not only to clannishness but also to prejudices.

Table 21-1. Growth of Rural versus Urban Population

Year	Rural	Urban
1880	1,345,000	55,000
1890	1,502,000	116,000
1900	1,707,000	187,000

For several decades before 1900 the urban population increased. The 1870 census, inaccurate though it was for the South, recorded only one town in North Carolina with more than 10,000 people. That was Wilmington, which had enjoyed the distinction of being the largest town in the state since the 1830s when it surpassed New Bern. It was destined to hold that rank until 1910 when Charlotte became the largest. In 1900 it was revealed that five more towns had a population of over 10,000—Charlotte, Asheville, Winston, Raleigh, and Greensboro. The number of towns with between 5,000 and 10,000 residents increased from two to six between 1870 and 1900, while those growing from 1,000 to 5,000 rose from fourteen to fifty-two. This change was most noticeable in the Piedmont and mountain sections, and suggested to many that the time was drawing to a close when the old aristocratic, plantation-centered east would be able to dictate policy to the rest of the state. The statistics for rural and urban residents, however, revealed that North Carolina remained overwhelmingly rural at the end of the century.

Limited though it was, the growth of municipalities together with the increasing number of industrial plants called for improvements in rail transportation. Diligent work made it possible to extend the Western North Carolina Railroad from Morganton to Old Fort in 1869 and within two years to complete much of the surveying and grading to extend it to Asheville. Difficulty in financing obliged the private firm responsible for these improvements to sell the railroad in 1875, and the state, in order to rescue its own investment, bought it. Between that time and 1880 the state owned, operated, and extended the line. Elsewhere a line was completed between Charlotte and Shelby and from Raleigh to Hamlet.

At least some of the state's railroads were not profitable, and the treasury could not make up the losses. Beginning in 1871 North Carolina leased some of its railroad property to out-of-state capitalists, and in 1895 it leased more, including a portion of the prewar North Carolina Railroad, to the newly formed Southern Railway Company for ninety-nine years. The state's railroad interests in the far western section of North Carolina were sold to a New York syndicate on condition that it complete the road to Murphy and to the Tennessee line. This was accomplished, and in 1894 it, too, became a part of the Southern Railway system. The state's final railroad property, the Atlantic and North Carolina Railroad from Goldsboro to Beaufort, was leased for ninety-one years in 1910.

By 1900 North Carolina was well served by 3,800 miles of railroad. The legislature, long in the hands of friendly Democrats, had generously exempted railroads from both taxation and regulation as it chartered a number of new lines. Consolidation resulted in the creation of three major companies generally running north and south through the state: the Seaboard Airline Railway, the Southern Railway, and the Atlantic Coast Line Railroad. The early nineteenth-century dream of a railroad from the coast to the mountains through the middle of the state, with lines feeding into it between the Virginia and South Carolina railroads, was dead.

Little attention was paid to roads around the state. The same scheme of planning, construction, and upkeep that had prevailed in the eighteenth century and earlier was still followed throughout most of the nineteenth century. Able-bodied men turned out about six days a year to maintain the roads. A law passed in 1878 levying a tax to provide all-weather roads in three counties was repealed the following year. The legislator who introduced this bill finally got a law enacted affecting just his home county, Mecklenburg, in 1882. In widely scattered sections of the state a few roads were improved, and sometimes convict labor, under contract to the county, was used for specific projects authorized by the General Assembly.

Agriculture Languishes

The final quarter of the century was a period of distress for most farmers. The shift from slave to free labor affected the large farms of the east and those in parts of the Piedmont. It was responsible to a considerable degree for the rise of tenant farming and sharecropping. So long as Federal troops occupied the state, they or members of the Freedmen's Bureau usually supervised the preparation of agreements involving black workers. Before long the prewar assertions of many people were justified—it had long been said that the South would benefit from a system of free labor. With the use of free labor, as revealed in the census returns after the war, agriculture quickly reached and sometimes surpassed old records (see Table 21-2). The production of cotton and oats had recovered by 1870, as did corn, hogs, milk cows, and beef cattle during the next decade. Before 1880 tobacco had resumed its former productivity, and the 1890 census revealed that potatoes had been added to the list. Wheat was the one crop that did not recover.

Table 21-2. Amount of Cotton and Tobacco Produced

Year	Bales of Cotton	Pounds of Tobacco
1860	145,000	33,000,000
1870	145,000	11,000,000
1880	390,000	27,000,000
1890	336,000	36,000,000
1900	460,000	128,000,000

As plantations and larger farms were divided (land was often sold out of the family that had long owned it), the number of farms in the state increased and the average number of acres per farm correspondingly declined (see Table 21-3). With longtime owners retaining at least a portion of their land at the same time that new owners acquired acreage, the number of farms worked by their owners increased from 104,877 in 1880, to 117,000 in 1890, and to 132,000 in 1900. Nevertheless, in 1880 more than a third of the farms in the state were operated by tenants. Although white tenants outnumbered blacks, this unfortunate system of farm operation attracted little public concern until the early twentieth century. It resulted in soil depletion, reduced per-acre production, reliance on a one- or two-crop system, and a lower standard of living. Just as the small farmer had characterized North Carolina in the colonial period, now the tenant farmer seemed to outside observers to represent the typical North Carolinian. At the end of the harvest season or soon after the first of each new year, wagons loaded with the meager possessions of many families could be seen as they moved from one farm to another in hopes of bettering their condition.

Table 21-3. Number and Size of Farms

Year	Number	Average Size
1860	72,203	316 acres
1870	93,565	212
1880	157,609	142
1890	178,359	127
1900	225,000	101

Although industry began once again to show some of its prewar promise in the state, agriculture was by no means abandoned. This scene of North Carolina cotton being taken to market on a two-wheeled cart, along a rutted road, pulled by a mixed team of mules, horse, and ox, with an old cotton press in the background, suggests the poverty of many farmers after the war. (*Harper's Weekly*, 12 May 1866)

Overproduction, low prices for products together with the high cost of farm supplies and exorbitant interest rates, and the difficulty and expense of getting goods to market all resulted in an agricultural depression during the final years of the nineteenth century. Generally obliged to buy on credit from a local merchant, farmers pledged their crop as security. The merchant demanded cotton or some other crop that could be readily sold, so farmers were not free to diversify. These conditions were not limited to North Carolina, for they were common throughout the nation. Agriculture was described as "languishing" while business and industry flourished. For much of this period intellectual and political progress seemed beyond the reach of the rural population.

Education

The outstanding system of public schools that the state had in place by the beginning of the Civil War declined and finally ceased to exist soon after the war ended. The forced repudiation of the Confederate debt resulted in the loss of that portion of the Literary Fund that had been invested in state and Confederate securities, and its bank and railroad stock was virtually worthless. Conservatives, while in control of the government from 1865 until 1868, abolished the office of superintendent of common schools and refused to make state funds available for schools. Although local governments were authorized to levy taxes for this purpose, few of them did so. Widespread poverty, an aversion to taxes, and the old lack of interest on the part of so many people delayed the development of another public school system.

Among the contributions made in the state by carpetbaggers, however, were a number of effective schools. In some cases they were for whites, in others for blacks, and in a few both races attended. The Freedmen's Bureau was especially diligent in breaking the bond of illiteracy that had held back so many black children. Many churches in the North, notably Presbyterians and Quakers, sent women to teach in these schools; they also provided books and supplies. Some 20,000 boys and girls were enrolled in four hundred schools.

The state constitution of 1868 required that a system of free public schools be established and provided a means of support. The next legislature passed a law—similar to the one that existed before the war—requiring that township school boards composed of three members be responsible for the care and management of the schools in their township. The constitution called for a minimum four-month term, established separate schools for the races, and appropriated $100,-000 for support. As superintendent of public instruction the legislature named the Reverend S. S. Ashley, a carpetbagger from Massachusetts and as his assistant, J. W. Hood, a black. Although the tax revenue for schools was $136,000, the General Assembly in 1870 allocated only $38,000. In that year between one-fifth and one-seventh of the school-age children in North Carolina attended school in seventy-four of the state's ninety counties; the remaining counties had no schools. Almost 50,000 boys and girls were enrolled and nearly half of them were black.

When the Conservatives (Democrats) returned to power in 1871, there was virtually no change in the funds allocated for education. Superintendent Ashley's salary was reduced, and he resigned. A special tax was levied for schools to be used in the county in which it was collected. If the amount was not sufficient to operate a four-month term, the county commissioners were not permitted to impose additional taxes. In 1873, however, the tax rate was increased, and, if the voters approved, further county taxes might be levied to maintain a four-month term.

A few schools took advantage of a $3 million fund established in 1867 by George Peabody of Boston and administered by the Peabody Education Board. It offered up to $1,000 a year to free schools for whites or blacks if two to three times that amount were raised locally. Although North Carolina received $87,000, it went to only a few diligent towns where schools were already well maintained.

As political conditions stabilized, the state administration became more concerned about public education. Governor Vance took the lead in looking to the future, and in 1877 the General Assembly created the Fayetteville Colored Normal School (now Fayetteville State University) as a teacher-training institution for blacks. This was the first school of its kind in the South. To help equip more white teachers for the anticipated increase in school enrollment, another pioneer step was taken. The first summer school ever held at a college or university in the United States opened at the University of North Carolina in 1877 in order to train teachers.

Popular indifference to education remained a serious drawback to the success of the program. Of the governors, only Vance and Thomas Jarvis urged the General Assembly to improve educational opportunities. Legislators received little or no encouragement from their constituents and the old goal of keeping taxes low prevailed. None of the superintendents even approached the enthusiasm Calvin H. Wiley had demonstrated many years before.

In 1880 only about one-third of the state's school-age children attended school for the nine weeks of instruction offered by the average institution. By 1900 around 58 percent of the children at least enrolled, yet only about 37 percent of them attended regularly even though the school term was just sixty days. Illiteracy was more prevalent in 1880 than it had been in 1860. North Carolina probably had the highest rate in the United States. Among blacks, of course, it was much improved since few could read and write in the earlier year. Out of an 1880 population of 1,399,750, there were 463,975 illiterates over age ten. Three-fifths of all illiterates were black, and blacks composed one-third of the total population. North Carolina ranked seventh among the states in illiteracy.

In 1881 United States Senator Henry W. Blair of New Hampshire proposed that Congress appropriate a very large sum of money to be distributed to the states based on their illiteracy rate. Over a period of several years different versions of this bill were considered, and North Carolina's senators favored it. At home people were uncertain of its effect. They feared Federal intervention in the operation of schools. Although the bill did not pass, it served a useful purpose—it made people in the state think about education and drove home the fact that there were so many illiterates in North Carolina. In so doing, it laid the groundwork for state legislation in the twentieth century.

Higher education in the state also underwent significant changes in the immediate postwar period. While the University of North Carolina had managed to remain open throughout the war, its student body dwindled to little more than a dozen, and it closed in 1870. Political manipulation and the loss of its endowment through repudiation of the Confederate debt severely lowered public confidence. The changed political scene and a new Conservative board of trustees enabled the university to reopen in 1875 under a new president and faculty. Wake Forest College had closed in 1862 but was able to reopen in 1866. Davidson and Trinity, which both closed in 1865, resumed classes in 1866. Many of the academies remained open during the war, but closed soon afterward.

The decade of the 1880s was one of disappointment for most North Carolinians. Recovery from the losses of war and Reconstruction was not as quick or as complete as they had anticipated. Political leadership was not as vigorous or as forward-looking as it should have been. Clearly, significant change was needed to set the state back on the progressive course that it had enjoyed in the 1850s. In the 1890s people began to look forward to the new century with great anticipation as new plans and new leaders materialized.

22

A TIME OF
READJUSTMENT

THE CREATION OF numerous small farms was one of the most obvious
legacies of the Civil War. As a primarily rural state, North Carolina continued for many decades to be concerned with the resultant problems.
Farmers themselves, of course, felt that the buyers of their cotton, tobacco, corn,
and other crops took advantage of them, because at harvest time they had to
accept whatever the buyer offered. The opening of new land in the West as well as
increased production in Canada, Australia, South America, and elsewhere contributed to lower agricultural prices worldwide. Financial depression in the 1870s
and 1890s only added further distress to an already burdened segment of the
population.

As previously noted, when farmers had to purchase anything—seed, fertilizer, or tools—they either paid whatever the merchant demanded or put up their
unharvested crop as security. They also realized that legislators, congressmen,
and other elected officials did little or nothing to improve their lot. While they
valued their freedom from bosses in "public work," as they called employment
for wages, their independence had disadvantages. During most of the year farmers worked longer hours than cotton mill employees did. Money was scarce, the
country was on the gold standard, and the amount of money in circulation was
closely tied to the national debt. When it was necessary to borrow money, interest was high. A farmer unable to meet his mortgage or to pay his taxes was liable
to lose his land, tools, livestock, and any crops he might have on hand or growing in the field.

The Democratic party, in control of the state's political affairs, was dominated by men of a conservative bent; they were called "Bourbons" because it was
believed that they, like the former ruling French monarchs, were tied to the past
and were not progressive. Many of them, nevertheless, were closely allied to the
railroad and manufacturing interests. These businessmen were powerful in the
realms of both finance and politics, and they supported legislators who favored
them. The General Assembly declined to alter tax laws which pleased business.
And they ignored the pleas of farmers who wanted freight and interest rates regu-

Leonidas L. Polk (1837–92), a native of Anson County, was a leader of the agrarian movement both in North Carolina and nationwide. At the time of his death, the Populist party was seriously considering him as a candidate for president of the United States. (North Carolina Division of Archives and History, Raleigh)

lated, and who sought support for a program that would put more money into circulation.

Farmers' Organizations

In a desperate, but fruitless, effort to unite in order to gain some relief, many farmers joined the Patrons of Husbandry, or the Grange, as it was widely called after its incorporation in North Carolina in 1875. This national organization was begun in 1869 with social as well as economic aims. More than five hundred local "lodges" were formed in the state, but as a whole the Grange was not successful. The members were unable to provide the financial support necessary to carry out an effective program, and after ten years it declined rapidly, although it still exists in North Carolina.

Leonidas L. Polk, a native of Anson County, was a practical farmer who in 1877 became the state's first commissioner of agriculture. He was concerned enough about the plight of farmers that he began publishing a weekly newspaper, the *Progressive Farmer*, in Winston in 1886. After about a year it changed to a magazine format. It soon was widely read and became an influential means of expressing the needs of rural North Carolinians. Among other things, the magazine introduced farmers to new crops and stressed better methods of tilling the soil. Features for women and children increased its popularity.

In 1887 Polk organized the North Carolina Farmers' Association, which flourished for about a year before the National Farmers' Alliance began a membership drive in the state. Members of Polk's group soon transferred to the Alliance, and very quickly nearly 100,000 North Carolinians were enrolled. In 1887 two conventions of the Farmers' Association, attended by an enormous number of delegates, were held in Raleigh. At the first convention, in January, farmers acted on one of Polk's suggestions made earlier in the *Progressive Farmer*— that the funds granted to the University of North Carolina under the Federal Morrill Land Grant Act be transferred to a new institution to teach "practical" subjects. In response to their proposal for the establishment of a new college, the General Assembly later in the year chartered the North Carolina College of Agriculture and Mechanic Arts in Raleigh (now North Carolina State University). The college opened for classes in October 1889.

With such a large membership, the Farmers' Alliance was seen as a useful political organization. Farmers had long commented that neither Raleigh nor Washington paid any attention to their needs; this was the time, they said, to make their strength felt. It had always been the policy of assorted farmers' groups not to discuss religious or political questions because they might divert the members from their main objectives. Now, however, a member wrote: "We don't advise bringing politics into the farmers' organizations, but we do advise taking . . . agricultural questions into politics." "Take these questions into your nominating conventions," members were told, "have them put into your political platforms and see to it that your candidates shall stand strictly and squarely upon them."

Previously the rural element had not succeeded in gaining a voice in the legislature. With new inspiration a great many farmers were elected in 1888 and an Alliance leader became speaker of the house. The next year eight of the state's nine congressmen held Alliance views. In 1889 the North Carolina House of Representatives passed a law to create a railroad commission, but it was defeated in the senate by what the *Progressive Farmer* called the "maneuverings of the wiley old political leaders." At the next election some new senators, with more sympathy for farmers, were elected, and in 1891 a three-member railroad commission was created with authority to determine rates and to eliminate rebates and unjust discrimination of all kinds. Rates were promptly reduced as much as 40 percent, and it was not long before the commission was given authority over passenger, express, and telegraph rates—railroads then operated the telegraph system. This

THANKSGIVING NUMBER.

THE PROGRESSIVE FARMER.

A Farm and Home Weekly for the Carolinas, Virginia, Tennessee and Georgia.

PROGRESSIVE FARMER—VOL. XXI. NO. 42.
THE COTTON PLANT—VOL. XXIII. NO. 41.   RALEIGH, N. C., NOVEMBER 29, 1906.   Weekly: $1 a Year.

[Copyright 1904, by James Arthur and Rural Magazine. Reprinted in Progressive Farmer by special permission.]

Thanksgiving in the Nursery.

Oh, for an hour in that dear place!
Oh, for the peace of that dear time!
Oh, for that childish trust sublime!
Oh, for a glimpse of mother's face!
—*Eugene Field.*

A Song of Thanksgiving.

Have you cut the wheat in the blowing fields,
The barley, the oats and the rye,
The golden corn and the pearly rice?
For the winter days are nigh."
  "We have reaped them all from shore to shore,
  And the grain is safe on the threshing floor."

"Have you gathered the berries from the vine,
And the fruit from the orchard trees?
The dew and the scent from the roses and thyme,
In the hive of the honey bees?"
  "The peach and the plum and the apple are ours,
  And the honey comb from the scented flowers."

"The wealth of the snowy cotton field,
And the gift of the sugar cane,
The savory herb and the nourishing root—
There has nothing been given in vain."
  "We have gathered the harvest from shore to shore,
  And the measure is full and brimming o'er."

Then lift up the head with a song!
  And lift up the hand with a gift!
To the ancient Giver of all
  The spirit in gratitude lift!
For the joy and promise of spring,
  For the hay and the clover sweet,
The barley, the rye, and the oats,
  The rice and the corn and the wheat
The cotton and sugar and fruit,
  The flowers and the fine honeycomb,
The country, so fair and so free,
  The blessings and the glory of home.
—Amelia E. Barr,

And so let us give thanks to God on Thanksgiving Day. Nature is beautiful and fellow-men are dear, and duty is close beside us, and He is over us and in us. What more do we want, except to be more thankful and more faithful, less complaining of our trials and our times, and more worthy of the tasks and privileges He has given us?—PHILLIPS BROOKS.

The *Progressive Farmer* began publication on 10 February 1886, under the editorship of Leonidas L. Polk, to support farmers in their struggle for a better life. It also helped to diversify agriculture by introducing new crops adaptable to the South. After more than a century the paper continues to serve these and other worthwhile causes. (North Carolina Collection, University of North Carolina at Chapel Hill) action resulted in a saving of some half a million dollars to the public. The commission also was authorized to appraise railroad property, and soon the value of such property was raised from $12 to $20 million, thereby producing new tax revenue for the state.

The farmers wanted other programs that the General Assembly was unable to provide. The financial plight of agriculture needed attention from the highest level of government. A Greenville attorney, Harry Skinner, promoted a scheme that came to be known as the "subtreasury plan." It called for the federal government to develop a great system of warehouses throughout the country where farmers, instead of selling their products when prices were low, could store such nonperishable things as tobacco, cotton, and grain under seal. The government would then lend them 80 percent of their crops' market value; when prices rose they could sell their produce, repay the loan, and pocket the difference. Senator Zebulon B. Vance was asked to introduce this plan in Congress, but he agreed to do so only by request. In part because he did not approve of it, the measure was defeated.

Skinner also proposed limiting the production of farm crops as a means of raising prices. Neither of his ideas was acceptable, but strategies very much like both of them became national policy under President Franklin D. Roosevelt half a century later.

From around 1890 the Democratic party came under pressure from two sources. First, agrarian reformers grew more and more insistent that they be heard. And second, North Carolina Republicans—never far from victory, sometimes winning as much as 46 percent of the gubernatorial vote—began to anticipate the possibility of new support both at home and abroad.

The 1884 election of President Grover Cleveland, a Democrat, had demonstrated the importance of strong, united Democratic support from both the North and the South. Party allegiance in such a populous northern state as New York, combined with that of the solid South, assured victory. In 1888, however, the Republicans returned to power. In an effort to retain their lead, two Massachusetts congressmen, Henry Cabot Lodge and George F. Hoar, introduced bills to place congressional elections in the South once more under the supervision of federal officials. Their objective was to regain for their party the votes of southern blacks. Black voting in the South had been restricted by various means such as laying out districts so that they contained a majority of whites, disfranchisement for minor infractions of the law, verbal threats, and a bit of "judicious" cheating in applying election laws and in counting ballots. Known as the "Force bill," the legislation proposed by Lodge and Hoar was passed by the House, but in the Senate a combination of southerners and westerners defeated it. There was no guarantee that such a bill would not be resurrected and passed in the future, and this possibility once more brought the issue of "white supremacy" to the fore. William W. Kitchin of Scotland Neck, a leader of the Democratic party for many years, said in 1888: "You may talk tariff, revenue, corruption, fraud, pensions and every other evil . . . till doomsday and not one man in ten will remember what you said three minutes after you stop. . . . But when you talk negro equality, negro supremacy, negro domination to our people, every man's blood rises to boiling heat at once."

Nevertheless, among North Carolina Democrats two strains of loyalty evolved. Memories of Reconstruction were growing dim for many while some had never been bothered by it, and the alleged threat of "black supremacy" seemed meaningless. People were beginning to demand more of the party in power than protection against alleged "black rule," which, after all, had never been a serious threat. There were more important matters to consider. On the other hand, those accustomed to being in control were certain that the security of the South, at least as they saw it, depended on the strength, unity, and maintenance of the Democratic party; anything that might disrupt party harmony was to be avoided. These new attitudes were apparent in the Farmers' Alliance, and contributed to its dissolution. Even Leonidas L. Polk, although he was a Democrat and had been a Confederate soldier, asserted that the economic reforms so badly needed by farmers were more important than just keeping Democrats in office. Given the difficulty of reforming or reshaping the old parties, leaders of the Alliance concluded that only the creation of a third political party would produce adequate results.

Political Party Fusion

In the late 1880s large numbers of Alliancemen withdrew from the Democratic party, thus suggesting to the Republicans that they had a chance to win the next election. This quickly wrecked the Farmers' Alliance. Polk, however, set about to deliver the Alliance membership to the new People's or Populist party. That party's national platform called for a graduated income tax, an increase in the amount of money in circulation, and government ownership of railroads and telegraph lines among other things.

The lack of opposition had made the Democratic leaders self-satisfied, conservative, and even reactionary. This had not been true before the Civil War when North Carolina had two viable parties with leadership changing from time to time, resulting in new periods of progress for the state. Such postwar leaders as Zebulon B. Vance and Matt W. Ransom, while undoubtedly sincere and patriotic, later seemed to be looking more to the past than to the present or the future.

Leonidas L. Polk, who had served three terms (1889–91) as national president

Marion Butler (1863–1938), a native of Sampson County and a graduate of the University of North Carolina, was forced to give up his ambition to study law in order to operate the family farm after his father's death. As an articulate farmer he rose to positions of leadership in farm organizations, joined the Populist party, and participated in its "fusion" with the Republican party. He was elected to the United States Senate, but thereafter his association with Governor Daniel L. Russell left him without a political future in the state. (North Carolina Division of Archives and History, Raleigh)

of the Farmers' Alliance and was mentioned as the party's candidate for president, died in June 1892. In North Carolina Marion Butler, of Sampson County, as spokesman for the Populists, rejected overtures of the Democrats to obtain his support perhaps because the national program of that party paid little attention to the needs of farmers and appealed more to the industrial and labor interests of its northern supporters. In August 1892 at a Populist meeting in Raleigh it was decided to field a full slate of candidates.

The Farmers' Alliance undertook a number of cooperative ventures such as manufacturing shoes, ordering the ingredients for fertilizer in large quantities, and producing smoking tobacco. Few of them were successful. (North Carolina Division of Archives and History, Raleigh)

To lure their lost members back into the fold, the Democrats nominated a "dirt farmer," Elias Carr, as their candidate for governor. The Populists, most of whom had been Democrats, accepted many Republicans as candidates on their ticket, and this "fusion" of the two parties resulted in the election of sixteen Republicans and eleven Populists to the lower house of the General Assembly. Carr, however, was elected governor and served from 1893 to 1897. The Democrats polled 7,101 *fewer* votes than the combined votes cast for Republicans and Populists. In addition, almost 2,500 votes were cast for a Prohibitionist party candidate. To political leaders of the state these tallies foretold events to come.

Populists and Republicans for the campaign of 1894 joined forces to present a unified, Fusion ticket in which men from each party were candidates for different offices. As a result the Democrats lost control of both houses of the General Assembly, although the vote of blacks had little to do with the Fusionists' victory. One of the first steps taken by the new legislature looked toward the restoration of local self-government, an act favored by Republicans and likely to increase the influence of the black vote. Populists as a whole, however, had no interest in seeing this segment of the population advance politically. Election laws were therefore amended to extend the suffrage. A law passed under Democratic sponsorship many years earlier had required that all ballots be printed on white paper and contain no symbol or illustration indicating political party. This law was repealed so that henceforth ballots could be printed on colored paper and contain a party "device" or picture. Such a change may have been for the simple purpose of making it easier for illiterate persons to vote. But, since this occurred before the adoption of the Australian or secret ballot, there may have been another reason. Illiterate persons now could easily be instructed to "cast the blue ballot" or "the ballot with a picture of a cotton bale on it," and an observer could determine whether instructions were followed. The law also stipulated that election officials from each party be present when ballots were cast and counted; and that, if members of either party felt their party or their race was not fairly represented on election boards, they could petition the local court to make additional appointments. A further change in the election laws provided a longer period for challenging registrations before election day to give officials time to resolve any differences well in advance. This was clearly a more democratic and honest arrangement than that devised by the Democrats.

Since election statistics were not kept by race, it is impossible to determine the effect of these changes on black voting patterns. Nevertheless, in the gubernatorial election of 1892, when Democrats were in control, the total vote was 280,203; in 1896, under Fusion auspices, 330,254 votes were cast. Not all of the additional 50,051 ballots were cast by blacks, of course, but many conservative whites suspected that a large portion of them were.

During this period officeholding by blacks became quite common. The General Assembly of 1895 named some three hundred black magistrates. There were forty in New Hanover County, thirty-one in Edgecombe, twenty-nine in Halifax, twenty-seven in Craven, seventeen in Granville, and sixteen in Bertie. In Craven and Warren counties, black registers of deeds were elected. There also were some black deputy sheriffs, a number of county commissioners, and at least one coroner.

Table 22-1. Number of Black Legislators, 1868–1899

County	Number	County	Number
Bertie	3	Hertford	1
Bladen	1	New Hanover	15
Caswell	5	Northampton	5
Chowan	3	Pasquotank	3
Craven	14	Richmond	1
Cumberland	2	Vance	4
Edgecombe	11	Wake	4
Franklin	1	Warren	9
Granville	9	Washington	1
Halifax	9		

Officeholding by blacks further strained relations between the races as many whites resented having to deal with blacks in the courthouse or town hall on official business. When whites accused blacks of insolence, blacks replied that whites were intolerant. In counties with large numbers of blacks, the breaking point was quickly approached. Even so, the political lineup for the 1896 election was little changed. Despite Democratic appeals, the Populists maintained their alliance with Republicans. All three parties offered candidates for governor, but the Populists and Republicans again shared a ticket for other offices.

Black Officeholders

In 1897 Daniel L. Russell, the Republican candidate, became governor and the Fusion majority continued its hold of the legislature. Some 1,000 blacks were either elected or appointed to office throughout the state. They had filled many public offices in North Carolina since the beginning of congressional Reconstruction, but never in such large numbers; nor had they been concentrated in local offices in so many counties. Between 1868 and the end of the century, 127 blacks served in the General Assembly, usually representing counties with a 50 percent or greater black population; 26 were elected to the senate and 101 to the house of representatives.

Many black legislators were well qualified and rendered effective service in other ways as well. Halifax County was represented in the General Assembly for ten years by Henry Eppes, a popular Methodist minister; Raleigh alderman

James H. Harris, who served as secretary pro tem of the Constitutional Convention of 1868, was also a director of the State School for the Deaf, Dumb, and Blind; William P. Mabson of Edgecombe County, a schoolteacher, served in the Constitutional Convention of 1875; after eight years as a Raleigh city alderman, Stewart Ellison was director of the state penitentiary for four years; and George H. White, besides representing Bladen County for two terms in the General Assembly, was elected to two terms in Congress, serving from 1897 to 1901. His election to a second congressional term came during a particularly bitter "white supremacy" campaign. Three other black congressmen were John Adams Hyman (1875–77), James E. O'Hara (1883–87), and Henry P. Cheatham (1889–93). All were natives of the state except O'Hara, a lawyer and the only carpetbagger among them; he also served in the Constitutional Convention of 1875. Among these men were four college graduates, two with some college training who had also taught school, and a newspaper business manager.

Following the inauguration of Governor Russell in 1897, Fusionists were secure only until the next general election as a Democratic majority in the legislature was elected in 1898. Superintendent of Public Instruction Charles H. Mebane, elected in 1896 as a Populist but not active in politics, was instrumental in removing the public schools from partisan politics, obtaining a law authorizing a special school tax election in each school district every two years until a special tax was approved, and in getting an appropriation of $50,000 for a central school fund. Fusionists also increased appropriations for the state's colleges and normal schools. Their plans and support for education were well received, and once Democrats returned to power this was one part of the Fusionists' program that could not be rejected.

As the restoration of local self-government continued, county government was placed in the hands of a three-man board of commissioners elected by the people who replaced the justices named by the legislature. Fusionists also tried but failed to break the ninety-nine-year lease of the North Carolina Railroad made by the previous Democratic administration. This reinforced the Populists' belief that Democrats favored business over agriculture and small farmers.

Partisan differences and questions of patronage began to split the uneasy political union of people who held many differing views. Republicans, in the minds of many white North Carolinians, were still associated with the terms "Reconstruction," "carpetbaggers," and "scalawags," whereas the farmers who made up the mass of Populists were accustomed to following the lead of their Democratic neighbors whom they often but perhaps silently recognized as their "betters." The growing number of blacks in public office also had its effect.

DANIEL L. RUSSELL,

A caricature of Daniel L. Russell (1845–1908), a native of Brunswick County, who was elected governor as a Republican in 1896. Charges of scandal wrecked his administration, as did his party's election or appointment of a number of blacks to office. (North Carolina Division of Archives and History, Raleigh)

Democratic Campaign Plans

In beginning to plan their return to power, Democrats engaged the services of a young but skillful political genius, Furnifold M. Simmons. A native of Jones County, educated at Wake Forest and Trinity colleges, and a lawyer, Simmons was elected to Congress in 1886 but in 1890 was defeated by a black Republican. In 1898 he was named chairman of the Democratic party in North Carolina, a position he had also held from 1892 to 1894. On assuming that post he promptly planned, launched, and conducted a vicious racist campaign the likes of which the state had never seen. One aspect of it sent persuasive speakers into virtually every community in North Carolina to report on the "evils of

Furnifold M. Simmons (1854–1940) was the consummate political organizer of the Democratic party from 1898, when he led that party into power following the "fusion" of Republicans, Populists, and others; Democratic governors succeeded to the office regularly for many years. He also received credit for prohibition legislation in North Carolina and was himself elected to the United States Senate. (North Carolina Division of Archives and History, Raleigh)

Negro domination." Businessmen and religious leaders were promised legislative favors, pamphlets and broadsides were distributed across the state, cartoonists attacked Republicans and blacks with abandon, and newspaper editors, in the days before libel laws, enlarged upon unsubstantiated reports of wrongdoing by incumbent officeholders and blacks. Appeals were directed to "men of Anglo-Saxon blood" to take action to halt what Democrats considered to be the growing influence of the black race in the state. What followed, of course, was a white supremacy campaign of enormous proportions.

In May 1898 both the Democrats and the Populists held their conventions in

Raleigh. Populist delegates were divided as to whether to continue their coalition with Republicans or to support the Democrats. The Democratic executive committee the previous November had said that "no Southern State can be governed with honor and decency by the Republican party," pointed out that many Republicans were susceptible to bribery, and, on behalf of the Democratic party, promised on its return to power to correct abuses that had arisen in North Carolina government. Aware of these comments, a segment of the Populist delegation under Marion Butler made overtures to the Democrats.

Some Democrats, including Raleigh newspaper editor Josephus Daniels, favored negotiating with the Populists. The majority, however, rejected Butler's feelers, and Simmons continued on his course. In investigating the records of the Fusion administration, he began to uncover some interesting evidence. Under John R. Smith, of Wayne County, the Republican superintendent of the state penitentiary, considerable "squandering and stealing" had occurred. It was further revealed that although he knew of Smith's misconduct, Governor Russell, instead of prosecuting him, remained silent and merely had Smith exchange offices with J. M. Mewborne, of Lenoir County, commissioner of agriculture. Simmons also discovered that neither Smith nor Mewborne made regular reports which were required by law. On writing Mewborne for an explanation, Simmons received a "vicious" letter that he suspected was actually drafted by Russell.

In response, Simmons wrote a letter on 27 July 1898 exposing the "corruption and arrogance of the Republican-Negro rule" and calling upon whites to stand together in support of "White Supremacy." This quickly became the theme of the Democrats' campaign. Over 100,000 copies of Simmons's letter were printed and distributed around the state, and newspapers gave extensive publicity to the contents. Democrats announced that their party had been "washed, purged, and made white as snow," and they began to welcome the return of the recent Populists. This was made easier for them because many of the old, conservative leaders of the party were dead, and the new leadership—which included Charles B. Aycock, Henry Groves Connor, Robert B. Glenn, Claude and William W. Kitchin, Locke Craige, and Cameron Morrison—was younger and more progressive.

As election day, 8 November 1898, drew near, further steps were taken to assure a Democratic victory. One tactic was the introduction of Red Shirts, bands of men wearing bright red shirts, to intimidate black voters. Red Shirts had flourished in South Carolina from 1870 until federal troops were withdrawn in 1877, but they did not appear in North Carolina until October 1898. Armed with rifles, they rode on horseback through communities or neighborhoods where blacks lived; they also showed up at political rallies. However, unlike their earlier counterpart, the Ku Klux Klan, they apparently did not use physical violence nor did they conceal their faces. The Red Shirts were most active in southeastern North Carolina, and undoubtedly their presence contributed to the low turnout of black voters there and elsewhere in the state.

Bankers, millowners, and other businessmen supported particular candidates because they would benefit business, especially by keeping taxes down. Millowner H. F. Schenck, for example, held large fish fries to aid the cause—that "the white property owners of North Carolina" should not "be ruled by a parcel of ignorant negroes." Not surprisingly, the Democrats won a solid victory, electing 134 members to the General Assembly and 5 representatives to Congress. Thirty Republican legislators and 3 congressmen were also elected, while the Populists claimed 6 legislators and 1 congressman. The *Charlotte Observer* was convinced that these results were not entirely due to the race issue but that for the first time business interests made themselves felt in the state.

The Wilmington Race Riot

Nevertheless, strong racial antipathy was demonstrated. In Wilmington Alexander Manly, the mulatto editor of a black paper, the *Daily Record*, replied to a charge by Democrats that Fusion rule had been responsible for certain liberties reported to have been taken by black men with white women. In an editorial of 18 August, Manly observed that some white women were as attentive to black men as white men were to black women. This led to visits by Red Shirts and strong expressions of the determination to end "black rule" in Wilmington. On the day after the election, some local white businessmen, led by Colonel Alfred M. Waddell, met and began to plan to take charge of city government. A letter was sent to a group of black leaders ordering Manly to leave Wilmington within twenty-four hours and to take his printing press with him. Waddell was to be notified by 7:30 the following morning, 10 November, that this had been done.

Since Manly had already left the city, some of his friends arranged to ship his press as quickly as possible and drafted a message informing Waddell of what had happened. Unfortunately, the note was mailed instead of being delivered by hand. Whites waited impatiently as the deadline passed; still no response was received. At nine o'clock a mob of about four hundred men went to Manly's newspaper office, knocked in the door, and broke the presses. Somehow the building "accidentally" caught fire. Witnesses disagreed as to the number of fatalities, but according to the *Wilmington Morning Star* of 12 November a young black fired the first shot into the mob and whites returned the fire, killing four or five blacks. The local militia was called in to stop the riot. State newspapers reported that three white men were wounded; eleven blacks were killed

The press in Alexander Manly's black newspaper after it was burned during the Wilmington Race Riot of 10 November 1898. (North Carolina Collection, University of North Carolina at Chapel Hill)

and twenty-five wounded. Soon afterward large numbers of blacks left Wilmington, including Silas Wright, the duly elected mayor. The few other blacks who held local office were replaced by whites in what was perhaps the bloodiest white supremacist coup d'état in North Carolina history. Blacks, of course, had never constituted a majority of officeholders.

In contrast to the events in Wilmington, and coincidentally in the same year, two black men, John Merrick, a former slave, and Dr. Aaron M. Moore organized the North Carolina Mutual Insurance Company in Durham. Their firm was successful and later established other black-operated businesses, including a bank and a cotton mill. In time the insurance company became the largest black-owned business in America.

Governor Russell's term still had two years to run, and the state's two senators, one a Republican and the other a Populist, continued in office. Federal patronage, for a time, would remain at their disposal. With these exceptions state and local government again fell into the hands of Democrats, who began to accomplish their immediate goal—the removal of blacks from further consideration in the governing of North Carolina. In fact, they had never been given much consideration, and as officeholders at the state level they were relatively rare since, as noted earlier, only 101 had served in the state house and 26 in the senate. Counties with a large black population had elected blacks to local office, but many counties in the state never had even one black official.

Once again the law was changed so that most county officials were appointed, further eliminating the possibility that blacks might be elected in certain counties. A department of insurance was created, and the office of commissioner of agriculture was made elective instead of appointive. The railroad commission, which had served so effectively, was converted into the first corporation commission created in the United States. For the present it supervised railroads, banks, telegraph and telephone companies, street railways, and express companies, but in time its duties were further expanded. The school law of 1869 was repealed, yet an appropriation of $100,000 was made for public schools.

Blacks Disfranchised

Steps to dilute the possible effect of the black vote included new election laws. Under them there was a fresh registration of voters, and the General Assembly named members to a new state board of elections. The law now provided that the state board choose county boards, and that the county boards name local election officials. Legislators had to be careful not to violate the Fifteenth Amendment to the United States Constitution, yet they also wanted to avoid denying the vote to illiterate whites. Taking their cue from schemes developed in Louisiana, Mississippi, and South Carolina, legislators proposed that only those who had paid a poll tax and could read and write any section of the Constitution be permitted to register to vote. So as not to disfranchise whites, the amendment had a grandfather clause stipulating that no one who could vote on or before 1 January 1867, or his lineal descendant, should be denied the right to vote, whether he could read or not, provided that he registered before 1 December 1908. An amendment to this effect was ratified on 2 August 1900 by a vote of 182,217 to 128,285. Thirty-one central and western counties, where there were relatively few blacks, voted against the amendment.

In the minds of Democratic party leaders in North Carolina, the state now was "safe for white rule." A new century was about to begin, and many new Democratic leaders began to talk at length about two things—the "Dawn of a New Day" and "White Supremacy." The latter would be the key to defeating the Republican gubernatorial candidate. The "New Day" that they envisioned promised universal education and that became an important part of their gubernatorial campaign. Improved schools, they stressed, would enable both white and black youths to read and write, and thus ensure their eligibility to vote.

Other progressive programs were developed in due course. Nevertheless, the powerful single party was strongly in control and provided little opportunity for debate, opposition, or the presentation of alternate plans. Even so, the Democratic primary on many occasions came close to becoming more receptive to new ideas at both the local and the state levels. Victory in the spring primary nearly always was tantamount to election in November.[1] Issues might be debated and programs presented before the primary, but once the primary was over the party unified to defeat the weak Republican opposition.

Signs of Progress

The Democratic party's noisy exploitation of racial fears and antipathies tended to draw attention away from other aspects of the state in the years between the end of Reconstruction and the beginning of the twentieth century. In spite of the obstinacy displayed by the Bourbons, or old leaders of the state, a number of programs and institutions of lasting benefit had their origins during that period. Hints, at least, of social and economic reform were heard before they became a reality in the new century.

In 1862, during the Civil War, the federal government adopted a pension plan which was expanded a number of times and extended to dependents in 1887. Southerners, after the war, expressed some bitterness over the use of federal funds for this purpose when Confederate veterans, quite naturally, were excluded. The state of North Carolina, however, began to pay pensions to "disabled and destitute soldiers" in 1885. Soon afterward about 1,000 ex-soldiers and 2,600 widows were receiving modest monthly checks from the state.

The Grand Lodge of Masons established an orphans' home at Oxford in 1872, and in the early 1880s it began to receive support from the state. In 1883 a state-supported orphanage for black children was also established near Oxford. As previously mentioned, an insane asylum was begun in Raleigh in 1853; in 1875 the Western North Carolina Insane Asylum began operations in Morganton, and in 1877 the North Carolina Asylum for the Colored Insane opened in Goldsboro.

The mid-1880s found North Carolina facing an exodus of young people not unlike that of the 1820s and 1830s. A large number of ambitious young men went to Baltimore, Philadelphia, and elsewhere to attend business and professional schools; while some returned to the state, many found interesting and profitable employment in the North. The West beckoned others. North Carolina, like

1. Until the Seventeenth Amendment provided for the popular election of United States senators, they were named by the General Assembly. Beginning in 1900 the North Carolina Democratic primary selected nominees of that party and the winners were then "elected" by the legislature. The first popular election under the new amendment was held in 1914.

the other southern states, was flooded with handbills and attractive brochures, issued for the most part by railroad companies and land colonization projects, describing the benefits to be gained in other parts of the nation by poor but resourceful southern youth. Governor Alfred M. Scales was distressed that some of the best and the brightest young people were leaving; he also saw the roots of growing tenant farming in the movement of others from farm to town. "I have observed with much regret since the war," he once said, "a disposition on the part of educated young men . . . to surrender the farm of their fathers to the hands of tenants and repair to the cities, already overcrowded, to lead a faster, but a less useful and it may be a less manly life."

A related concern was voiced by Walter Hines Page, a native of Cary and a graduate of Trinity College who did further work at Johns Hopkins. After obtaining newspaper experience in New York and elsewhere, he started his own weekly, *The State Chronicle*, in Raleigh in 1883. Through its columns Page attempted to wipe out sectional prejudice and the tendency of many to glorify the past. Too many of the state's leaders, such as the Bourbons whom he also called "Mummies," yearned for "the good old days," he observed, "instead of looking to the promise of the future." An advocate of educational improvement and industrial growth, Page's newspaper proved to be interesting, but at the same time it was irritating and provocative to many. Failing in his primary objective and not making a financial success of his newspaper, Page sold out to Josephus Daniels who in time became one of the state's best known newspaper editors. Page then went to New York and Boston where he enjoyed an outstanding career in publishing and writing; before and during World War I he was the United States ambassador in London. From his base outside the South, he continued his efforts to eliminate sectionalism and to bring the South into the mainstream of American life. He wrote and published a great deal about his native region, particularly in a new magazine that he established, *World's Work*, which was a pioneer in photographic journalism.

The Electric Age also arrived in the decade of the 1880s when electricity began to be used for both lighting and power. Thomas Edison invented the incandescent electric light in 1879. In Philadelphia in 1876 at the exhibition marking the centennial of the Declaration of Independence, a demonstration was presented of an electric current carrying impulses over a wire for the reproduction of the human voice. The telephone thus was born at almost the same time as the electric light. Two crude telephones were installed in Raleigh in 1879, and the first telephone exchange opened in the spring of 1882 with twenty-nine subscribers. Later in the year telephones were installed in Wilmington; they appeared in Asheville in 1886, and in the towns of Winston and Salem in 1890. Salem was the first town in the state, and perhaps in the South, to have electric lights in a manufacturing plant when the Salem Woolen Mills and the new plant of the Arista Cotton Mills owned by F. H. Fries acquired them. Raleigh received electric lights late in 1885 and Wilmington got them in 1886. Winston in 1887 opened a generating plant to provide street lights as well as home lighting.

Public transportation arrived in both Wilmington and Raleigh in 1887, when a system of horse-drawn streetcars began operation. The Wilmington line converted to electric-powered cars in 1892, two years after a similar system was established in Winston and Salem.

Other public utilities began to appear in more towns as the decade advanced. Salem had had a public water system before the close of the colonial period, and one was reportedly being installed in Fayetteville in 1823. In the 1880s waterworks began to replace wells and public pumps in Charlotte, Raleigh, Wilmington, and Winston. By 1894 five cities—Asheville, Charlotte, New Bern, Raleigh, and Winston—had sewerage systems, but half a century or more passed before outdoor privies ceased to be seen behind almost every house, city or country.

Roads and turnpikes at the end of the nineteenth century differed very little from those of a century before. Although Wilmington, Raleigh, Charlotte, and perhaps a few other towns had stone or brick pavement, rural roads were built and maintained through local efforts. A Mecklenburg County legislator, Captain Sydenham B. Alexander in the late 1870s sponsored a good roads law in the house of representatives, but when finally passed it applied to only three counties including his own. His constituents did not like the idea of being taxed for this purpose and defeated Alexander at the next election. In his bid for the senate, perhaps having discussed roads with his neighbors, he was elected and successfully sponsored a bill to construct and improve some rural roads in Mecklenburg County. At the time this was a rare victory, but it perhaps served to make people start thinking about the advantages of better rural roads.

In some places people living in the country began to become aware of the many benefits that people in town enjoyed. Easier access to postal service was one of them, and some of the farmers' organizations included this in their objectives. In 1892, a North Carolina congressman, John S. Henderson of Salisbury, was chairman of the committee on post office and post roads. A bill introduced by a Georgia congressman to appropriate money for the delivery of mail in rural areas of America was defeated, but the next year a bill for a lesser amount to experiment with rural free delivery was passed. The unsympathetic postmaster general said he did not think that was enough, and not until 1896 was he satisfied. In that year, in two places—Charleston, West Virginia, and China Grove, North Carolina—mail began to be carried from the post office to rural residents. Although some people living in China Grove did not like the idea because they thought their neighbors would be able to snoop into their mailboxes and learn more about them than they ought to know, after about a month—and some persuasion from the local postmaster—the idea was accepted. By 1898 rural free delivery of mail was a permanent feature of the postal service.

Another occurrence of the busy year 1898 was the brief Spanish-American

War. United States interests in Cuba had long been dissatisfied with Spanish misrule there, and the sinking of an American battleship in Havana harbor on 15 February offered an excuse to bring about some changes. In North Carolina, for a short time, other concerns were laid aside. To raise an army, President William McKinley called on the states for troops; North Carolina's quota was two regiments of infantry and a battery of artillery. Two regiments of white troops were easily raised, and, instead of the artillery battery, the state furnished three companies of black infantrymen. Only one of the three regiments actually left the state, but some did serve in both Cuba and the Philippines. Two North Carolinians in regular service lost their lives. The death of Ensign Worth Bagley of Raleigh on 11 May was recorded as the first loss of an American naval officer in the war. Army Lieutenant William E. Shipp was killed at the Battle of San Juan on 1 July. The war in Cuba was over in six months, but, although Spain in the treaty of peace ceded the Philippines to the United States, local insurrection there lasted until 1902.

Although often labeled the "Gay Nineties," the decade of the 1890s was far from light-hearted and happy for a majority of North Carolinians. As discussed earlier, the state was confronted with many unpleasant and unfortunate events as it attempted to adjust to changed conditions. Perhaps the adoption of a state motto in 1893, *Esse Quam Videri* (To Be Rather Than To Seem), was a hint that at least some of the state's leaders wanted to be more honest in their actions. Perhaps this changed attitude was reflected as early as February and March 1891 when the General Assembly chartered the State Normal and Industrial School, the first state-supported institution for the higher education of women (now the University of North Carolina at Greensboro) and the State Normal and Training School for blacks (now Elizabeth City State University). Higher education for women and blacks was not offered in every state. The North Carolina School for the Deaf and Dumb at Morganton was also created at the same session of the General Assembly. And one wonders whether the arrival in 1893 of fifty families of French-speaking Waldensians from the Alps of northern Italy in Burke County did not suggest that they regarded North Carolina as an unusually promising place to enjoy a new life. The distressing internal conflicts of the final decade of the century were, perhaps, the birth pangs of the better times that lay ahead.

23

GREAT ANTICIPATIONS
FOR THE
TWENTIETH CENTURY

L OOKING FORWARD to the twentieth century, many of the state's political leaders began to speak of the "Dawn of a New Day." As the nineteenth century drew to a close, changes in the law concerning voting eligibility, including, of course, the grandfather clause effective only until 1 December 1908, ensured the election of a majority of Democrats, thereby setting a pattern in the General Assembly that would remain unbroken for more than a century. For almost seventy-five years, although only Democratic governors were elected, it became customary that they alternate geographically with one coming from the western part of the state one time and from the east the next.[1] Since a governor could not succeed himself, this practice continued until 1977 when the state constitution was amended to permit a governor to serve two successive terms.

In the 1900 campaign Democratic gubernatorial candidate Charles B. Aycock of Wayne County stressed his concern for "universal education" (sometimes also adding "of the white children"), pointing out that all young men would soon be able to meet the literacy test for voting. Although benefiting from the grandfather clause, he himself played down the race issue, but his supporters were not reluctant to mention the subject. A physically grueling campaign brought Aycock the support of seventy-four of the state's ninety-seven counties and gave him a majority of 60,354 votes.

The inauguration of Governor Charles Brantley Aycock on 15 January 1901 did, indeed, mark the beginning of a long period of one-party rule, but a period of change, nevertheless. Aycock's biographer, Oliver H. Orr, Jr., credits the new governor with having "inspired the people with visions of the good government which educated voters might create, the economic prosperity which educated

---

1. Until the election of Robert Morgan from Harnett County in 1974 when Jesse Helms from adjoining Wake County was the other United States senator, it was also a long-standing custom to have one North Carolina senator from the west and the other from the east.

workers might produce, and the cultural heights which an educated people might reach."

The South Dakota Bond Case

In February 1901 Aycock, as had post-Civil War governors before him, received demands from the North for payment of certain bonds issued during Reconstruction. The state earlier had classified these bonds, recognizing some as valid and in 1879 offering to pay them off at 25 percent of par. Most, however, were repudiated as fraudulent and corruptly issued. Ten of the bonds issued in support of the Western North Carolina Railroad came into the possession of Schafer Brothers, a New York brokerage firm, through Governor Daniel L. Russell and Senator Marion Butler, whose Republican-Fusion party had recently been defeated by the Democrats. The brokerage firm tried to have the bonds redeemed but failed even though the state in 1879 had recognized them as valid.

In October 1901 the state of South Dakota (which Schafer Brothers clearly had drawn into its scheme as the firm was named as a party to the suit) applied to the United States Supreme Court for permission to sue North Carolina. Since the Eleventh Amendment (for which James Iredell deserves credit) prohibited a *citizen* of one state from suing another state, the brokers found South Dakota willing to participate in their plan. North Carolina officials became concerned as the value of Reconstruction bonds then was around $80 million, roughly the total value of all personal property in North Carolina.

Governor Aycock, the attorney general, and a staff of legal counsel responded to South Dakota's complaint. Depositions were taken, the General Assembly was informed, and state leaders were confident that North Carolina would emerge victorious. The case was heard in April 1903 and the Supreme Court, by a vote of five to four, ordered North Carolina to pay South Dakota the par value of the bonds plus interest—a total of $27,400. If the state refused, the United States marshal would seize North Carolina Railroad stock and sell it. Aycock felt that the Court could not enforce its judgment; stockholders other than the state might sue. Aycock delayed. The attorney general sought a rehearing but was turned down. Then in 1905 the governor laid the matter before the legislature, suggesting that full payment be made to South Dakota and that Schafer Brothers receive payment on the same basis as had been offered in 1879. However, it fell to Aycock's successor, Governor Robert B. Glenn, to conclude the matter, and the state paid the $27,400 required by the Supreme Court.

Butler, Russell, and their associates formed a syndicate and tried to persuade other states to cooperate with them by bringing suit for the payment of additional bonds. No other state, not even South Dakota which by now recognized that it had been used, would collaborate. North Carolina was saved from a very costly experience.

Impeachment of Two Justices

At the same time the Republican-Populist-Fusion faction was thus attempting to gain revenge, the Democrats were also engaged in partisan activities. The 1899 legislature, dominated by Democrats, reassigned the responsibilities of a minor office—until now independent and filled by a Populist—to an agency under Democratic control. The incumbent involved took his case in turn to both the state's superior and supreme courts and was upheld. Three Republican supreme court justices (one of whom, Chief Justice William T. Faircloth, died on 29 December 1900) ordered the state auditor and the state treasurer to pay the person who had been dismissed as a result of legislative action. This prompted the house of representatives to bring impeachment charges for a technical violation of the constitution against the new chief justice, David M. Furches, and Associate Justice Robert M. Douglas. The charges, introduced by Representative Locke Craig, may have reflected the fear that a Republican-dominated court would order the repayment of Reconstruction bonds. Another reason imputed to the Democrats was simply that they saw this as an opportunity to remove two Republican justices. After a trial that lasted two weeks, the senate failed to obtain the necessary two-thirds majority for conviction.

The Educational Governor

Aycock had been a candidate for office on a platform that emphasized the importance of public school education. A graduate of the University of North Carolina and a practicing attorney, he had served as a school board chairman as well as a county school superintendent. Universal education would lead to universal suffrage, he explained, and with an educated citizenry the race problem in politics might be expected to disappear.

Little progress had been made in the state's school system since the 1870s. Of the 660,000 children of school age in 1900, only about two-thirds were even enrolled and less than half of them attended on a regular basis. Twenty-three counties had cotton mills where many children under age fourteen worked long hours without ever going to school. These facts appalled the new governor and, in public appearances across the state, he set about popularizing his ideas that elementary schools should be supported by local taxes, should be open for four months each year, and should be located within walking distance of children's homes. In favor of schools for all segments of society, he faced a challenge from

Charles Brantley Aycock (1859–1912) was a newspaper editor, a lawyer, and a school administrator before he became governor in 1901. As chief executive he supported extensive improvements in the state's public schools. (North Carolina Collection, University of North Carolina at Chapel Hill)

the legislature soon after his inauguration in 1901. That year bills were introduced to permit whites to tax themselves to improve white schools without doing anything for blacks. Not having the veto power, Aycock announced that he would resign if the bills passed, so they were defeated.

A belief had prevailed in North Carolina since colonial days that the best government was the one that governed the least. It followed, then, that people were most prosperous when taxes were lowest. Aycock attacked this old saying by maintaining that taxes for education represented a wise investment. Educated people meant better industry. Educated workers were more productive, and their prosperity would spread to all levels. The Democratic legislature of 1899 had appropriated $100,000 for education; now in 1901, when that amount was doubled, there was loud cheering on the floor of the legislature.

This session of the General Assembly also began a new program of "equalization" through which money was distributed in inverse proportion to the value of a county's taxable property. This enabled the poor counties to take steps to raise (or equalize) the quality of their schools to at least approach that of the wealthier counties. Wealthy counties, of course, resented having to help carry the burden of "pauper" counties, and for a number of years this was the cause of considerable dispute in the state. Its ultimate resolution, however, produced an excellent solution—maintenance of the school system by the state rather than by the counties.

High school education had been available in North Carolina through a limited number of church-supported schools, private schools, and academies. A few towns had special charters permitting them to establish high schools, but, until a rural high school law was adopted in 1907, children living in the country seldom had the advantage of such education. And although a few towns accepted them as tuition-paying pupils, this arrangement was not widely accepted since most rural boys and girls were poorly prepared. Rural schools were operated only about four months a year, while a school year in town was sometimes as long as ten months.

Within a year after the passage of the rural high school act, nearly 160 high schools were opened in eighty-one of the state's ninety-eight counties, and around four thousand boys and girls took advantage of this new opportunity. About the same time, it was proposed that the school term be extended to six months. A constitutional amendment to that end was submitted to the people in November 1918 and passed by a vote of more than six to one.

Another drive mounted simultaneously anticipated the consolidation of rural school districts of the state into larger units and the transportation of school children to them at public expense. The growing use of automobiles during World War I enabled people to travel farther from home and to do so more frequently. It led many rural residents to observe the differences between city life and their own. While appreciating many of the advantages of living in the country, they envied the educational and cultural opportunities enjoyed by city children. This led to the very significant move to combine many small schools into larger ones that could afford to have chemistry laboratories and better libraries, and to offer instruction in business, home economics, art, drama, foreign languages, and a wider range of courses in the sciences and humanities. With consolidation, of course, came school buses; soon North Carolina had more children riding to and from school each day than did any other state. These changes were being implemented by the mid-1920s at a time when the state assumed responsibility for certifying teachers and approving salary scales. Teachers were thereby freed from local political control and were less likely to be obliged to belong to a particular religious denomination or to conform to some unique local custom.

By the late 1920s many North Carolinians could take pride in the progress of their schools. Not everyone, however, had cause to do so. Although Aycock's original goal had stressed equal educational opportunities for all boys and girls, especially so that young men at age twenty-one could qualify to vote, this often enunciated objective gradually fell by the wayside.

It was the practice in the South, upheld by state laws, to separate the races in all forms of public accommodation, including schools. The North generally followed the same pattern, although more by preference of the majority race than by law. In theory and by verbal assertion, minorities were entitled to and promised equal treatment in all respects, even if physically separate. The decision of a federal court in the case of *Plessy v. Ferguson* (1896) upheld the validity of a state law requiring "equal but separate accommodations for the white and colored races." But just as nothing was done after Reconstruction to see that freedmen were justly treated, so now nothing was done to see that treatment was, in fact, *equal.* Public schools were made available for blacks, but when funds were apportioned those schools received far less than their fair share. Seldom in a position to question their treatment, blacks on the whole submitted, and it was not until the 1950s that their appeals for consideration began to be heard.

The Crime of Lynching

An unfortunate blot on the record of North Carolina, yet much less widespread than elsewhere in the South, was not eradicated during Aycock's administration although it showed signs of disappearing. This was the crime of lynching. While black men were most often the victim, occasionally white men were hanged or shot under similar circumstances. The state bar defined this act as the "killing or aggravated injury of a human being by act or procurement of a mob." It nearly always took place in an isolated, rural spot. The typical county in which lynching occurred was described as one having fewer than 10,000 residents with a lower-than-average education. Most lynch mobs were composed of illiterate youths under twenty-five with a sprinkling of "older but even more barbarous leaders." Between 1889 and 1936 there were 68 lynchings in North Carolina; during the same period there were 4,643 throughout the nation. The peak year in the state was 1892, when 5 were committed. By the mid-1930s this offense had almost ceased; there was only 1 lynching in the state in 1930 and 2 in 1935. Elsewhere in the nation, however, there were 28 in 1933 and 15 in 1934.

State Literary and Historical Association

To get the new century off to a good start intellectually, a group of concerned citizens met in Raleigh on 18 September 1900 to talk about forming an organization "to stimulate literary and historical activity in North Carolina." At a public meeting called a few weeks later the State Literary and Historical Association was founded. Its constitution set forth a most ambitious goal: to collect, preserve, produce, and disseminate the literature and history of the state. The association intended to do this by encouraging the creation of public and school libraries, establishing a historical museum, fostering a literary spirit among the people, correcting printed errors about North Carolina, and "engendering . . . an intelligent, healthy State pride in the rising generation."

Membership was open to all who wanted to support this program, and at their annual meetings members heard addresses by distinguished leaders, national and international, in many related fields, as well as by North Carolinians. Officers and members spoke and wrote on literary and historical subjects pertaining to the state and encouraged others to do likewise. In 1901 the association was responsible for a law establishing "North Carolina Day" in the public schools when a special topic concerning the state would be featured. A booklet on each year's topic was prepared, published, and widely distributed; this custom continued for more than twenty-five years. Rather than spread itself too thin, the association encouraged the formation of related groups of which it became a kind of sponsor. In response to an association resolution of 3 January 1903, the General Assembly on 9 March authorized the creation of the North Carolina Historical Commission; this agency evolved into the North Carolina Division of Archives and History, a model state archival agency whose first director, R. D. W. Connor, became the first archivist of the United States. The association's policy further resulted in the organization of societies devoted to folklore, poetry, art, historic preservation, music, and county and local history. The Hall of History (now the North Carolina Museum of History) was one of the first visible results.

Another outgrowth of the work of this young organization was an awareness of the need for libraries; these were established in many places—often by local women's clubs. The State Art Society and the ultimate product of its efforts, the present North Carolina Museum of Art, are also offspring of the association, as are the North Carolina Symphony and the Historic Preservation Foundation of North Carolina.

Mount Mitchell State Park

The initial step toward a program that in time would benefit thousands of people was taken on 28 January 1915 when Representative Gaston P. Deyton of Yancey County (in his only term in the General Assembly) introduced a bill authorizing the appointment of a commission to acquire a portion of Mount Mitchell and the creation of "a public park for the use of the people of the State of North Carolina." On 19 February Senator Zebulon Weaver of Buncombe County introduced an identical bill in the upper house. Before adjournment on 9 March, this bill became law and Governor Locke Craig was authorized to spend $20,000 for that purpose.

In May surveyors rode a logging train to a camp within a mile of the peak, spent the night, and the following day hiked to the top. The logging company that had been clearing much of the area had already stopped cutting in anticipation of this step. It took sixteen "long days" to survey a tract three miles long and a quarter of a mile wide including the peak; a few years later the state's holdings were increased. Mount Mitchell State Park in 1915 became the first of more than thirty state parks and recreation areas.

Wireless Experiments

Two entirely unrelated events, little noticed at first in North Carolina or elsewhere yet destined to affect the whole world, took place on the Outer Banks during the first three years of the twentieth century. The first of these originated from a base on the northern end of Roanoke Island only a short distance from the site of the settlement of Sir Walter Raleigh's colonists. Experimenting between December 1900 and August 1902, Reginald A. Fessenden, a Canadian who had once worked briefly with Thomas A. Edison, succeeded in sending wireless (pioneer radio) messages by code from a tower on Roanoke Island to Cape Hatteras on the Outer Banks and to Cape Henry, Virginia. He also received musical notes transmitted from Cape Hatteras. From refinements of Fessenden's system came the radio.

First Airplane Flight

The second epoch-marking event occurred on 17 December 1903. This was the first manned flight of an airplane. Orville and Wilbur Wright, who owned a bicycle shop in Dayton, Ohio, had been interested in the possibility of manned flight for several years. Building kites and gliders, watching the flight of birds, compiling records of air pressure, and studying ship propellers prepared them for several visits to Kitty Hawk, North Carolina. There they found the terrain, the wind, the air pressure, and the absence of curious onlookers to be especially suitable for conducting experimental flights.

On their first visit in September 1900 the Wright brothers tested a glider with a man on board, and in July 1901 they made several hundred long glider flights. In August 1902 they assembled and tested a new glider developed from their own air pressure tables and wind tunnel experiments, afterward patenting the vehicle. Back in Dayton they began constructing an even larger machine to be powered by a twelve-horsepower engine that they designed to drive two propellers. Returning to Kitty Hawk in September 1903 they encountered bad storms and had to postpone the testing. By December, conditions had improved and the first flight lasting twelve seconds took the plane under its own power a distance of 100 feet. Three more flights followed, with the last covering 852 feet in fifty-nine seconds. In Dayton heavier and stronger airplanes were built and tested, and in 1905 a round-trip flight of twenty-four miles was made. Transportation by air thus became a reality as a result of the successful flight at Kitty Hawk.

Alcoholic Beverage Control

Of long-standing concern to many North Carolinians was the availability, manufacture, and consumption of alcoholic beverages. Legislative involvement with this issue dated back to 1715, when attempts were made to eliminate the "odious and loathsome Sin of Drunkeness." Apprehensions had grown after the Tuscarora War of 1711–12, when Indians could get rum or some other alcoholic drink. Neither efforts to punish drunks nor schemes to make alcoholic beverages difficult to obtain by raising prices had much effect. Costly licenses for the sale of liquor were also ineffective, since all sorts of drinks were readily available from many sources. Before the Civil War, when a temperance movement flourished, people joined organizations committed to sobriety. Called Sons of Temperance, Daughters of Temperance, and, for children, Cadets of Temperance, some of these groups attracted a large membership, but whatever effect they had was lost with the coming of war.

In the late nineteenth and early twentieth centuries those who opposed the consumption of alcoholic beverages pinned their hopes on Prohibition. The idea had been proposed in North Carolina as early as 1852, when a petition seeking statewide Prohibition was presented to the General Assembly. Supporters pointed out that intemperance led to murder, fights, and domestic violence; personal income spent on liquor deprived children of adequate support; and the practice of offering whiskey as a bribe at political meetings contributed to inefficient government. Since few of the petition's 20,000 signers were prominent in ruling circles, the legislature paid little attention to their request.

Subsequent appeals were no more successful, although local elections were authorized in the late 1850s to determine whether to license saloons. A few were established. During the Civil War, however, the use of grain to distill liquor was prohibited on the grounds that grain was needed for food and liquor was an unnecessary luxury. After the war, the legislature outlawed the manufacture and sale of liquor near churches and schools. If a town approved, liquor could be sold at a "dispensary" under the strict supervision of town-appointed commissioners. Laws of 1903 and 1905 finally extended Prohibition to all of rural North

Carolina. Municipalities were exempt, and saloons and dispensaries continued to operate in those cities and towns that did not prohibit them through a local referendum.[2]

The Prohibition issue grew in significance both in the state and across the nation. In 1881 an Anti-Prohibition-Liberal party flourished, partly under the sponsorship of the Republican party. A few years later the National Prohibition party appeared and even offered a candidate for governor. Early in the twentieth century an Anti-Saloon League became active in North Carolina, making Democratic party leaders uncomfortable. The possibility existed that a new Fusion movement might occur—to the detriment of the Democrats if they did not support Prohibition. But by 1906, men with temperance leanings had assumed control of the Democratic party and supported a move toward total Prohibition in the state. At a special session of the General Assembly in 1908, legislators yielded to popular demand and called for a referendum on the question. Leading Democrats jumped on the bandwagon where they were joined by nearly all of the state's most prominent businessmen and educators. Members of the clergy were already aboard and might even be said to have been driving. At the polls the drys won by a margin of nearly five to three, carrying more than three-fourths of the counties. North Carolina was proclaimed to be "the first state in the Union to banish the liquor traffic by popular vote." As Prohibition swept the state, it was believed that a two-hundred-year-old problem had been solved.

In this instance North Carolina was in the vanguard. Prohibition became national policy in January 1919 with the ratification of the Eighteenth Amendment to the United States Constitution. It prohibited the use or sale of intoxicating beverages except under very limited circumstances—liquor prescribed by physicians could be sold in drugstores or used in hospitals in treating alcoholics, and wine could be obtained for sacramental use. Certainly for the time being the opponents of liquor were placated.

Farmers' Organizations

The beginning of a new century did not erase the financial hardships about which farmers had complained with so little effect in the final years of the old. The role of farmers among the Democrats who joined in the "fusion" with the Republican party cost them the wholehearted confidence of the chastened

2. To evade Prohibition some rural distillers incorporated their farms as if they were municipalities. The owner might be named mayor, a son chief of police, another son the treasurer, and so on. Some of these "paper towns" survived, at least in the records, until the General Assembly enacted the state's first "Sunset Law" in 1977 and subsequently deleted these and other obsolete provisions from the General Statutes.

Democratic party. In an effort to solve their own problems, some 155,000 North Carolina farmers joined the Farmers' Educational and Cooperative Union beginning in 1905. This new organization continually admonished its members to "keep out of politics." The discussion of any matter of "a sectarian or partisan nature" was grounds for dismissal.

Some of the programs of the Farmers' Union, as the group was generally called, were effective. Through one program, the union purchased nitrogen, potash, and the other ingredients for fertilizer, minus the "filler" necessary to spread it, and sold them to farmers at cost. Without the filler, often ground-up brick and sand which they could add themselves, the cost of freight was greatly reduced. The union's interest in the improvement of public education was strong enough to gain legislative support. On the other hand, it was unable to reduce the cost of jute bagging (necessary for baling cotton) because its sale was controlled by one of the "trusts"—a giant combination of businesses able to regulate both production and sale. Several of the union's cooperative business ventures also failed. These, combined with rising farm prices and the market changes wrought by World War I, resulted in a slow decline in union membership. No lasting improvement was apparent to alleviate the farmers' longstanding complaint that they had no control over what they received for their crops or what they paid for whatever was needed to produce them.

Organized Labor

Laborers in textile mills had equal cause for complaint. Low wages, long hours, night work, and unhealthy conditions were all valid reasons for grumbling and discontent, yet most were glad to be gainfully employed at all and many remembered even longer hours and harder work on the farm. Gratitude to the millowner for a job and such small favors as being able to live in a mill village and run a charge account at the company store kept grievances at a minimum.

In 1884 in Raleigh the Knights of Labor organized the first "assembly" in the state and three years later claimed that many more had been formed. Among its members were bricklayers, masons, plasterers, locomotive engineers and railway conductors, typesetters, and bookbinders; however, no employees of textile, tobacco, or furniture factories were represented. The assembly in Raleigh included such diverse occupations as teacher, preacher, retail clerk, printer, butcher, and even the owner of a large publishing house. Minutes of the meeting indicate a strong concern for ill members, those who had suffered some personal loss, widows and orphans, and entertainment for the membership. In brief, the purposes seem to have been largely humanitarian and social. Harmonious conditions apparently prevailed between labor and management in the occupations represented.

By the early twentieth century, as industrialization flourished, differences between management and labor arose. Occasionally disputes were resolved through collective bargaining, but most employers were opposed to this action, maintaining that the working conditions they provided and the wages they paid were as high as they could afford in the face of competition from northern manufacturers.

The widely scattered location of mills and the abundant supply of unskilled but willing workers, together with public opposition to labor unions and the general indifference or outright hostility of the state government, weakened the movement to organize labor in North Carolina. Strikes in Durham, Fayetteville, Gibsonville, and Raleigh all failed, and the North Carolina State Federation of Labor, organized in 1905, was virtually ineffective because of widespread anti-union sentiment. While the United Textile Workers engaged in a vigorous campaign to organize the South between 1913 and 1918, they made no effort to enter North Carolina until about 1919. Soon around 30,000 workers formed forty-three unions in the state. A few strikes occurred in the early 1920s, at least one of which lasted for three months, but nearly all of them were unproductive. One in Charlotte was resolved by joint committees of union workers and manufacturers. On that occasion, the workweek was reduced from sixty to fifty-five hours with no change in pay but with the loss of a bonus. The latter was partly compensated for by free rent in company houses during a lockout when management had closed the plant because of the strike.

From the mid-1920s wages declined and workers became more dissatisfied with their conditions of employment. Aware of these conditions, the Communist-run National Textile Workers Union sent thirty-three-year-old Fred E. Beal, a native of Massachusetts and a skilled union organizer, to Charlotte. By playing down his Communist beliefs and overcoming the workers' distrust of himself as a northerner, Beal was able to organize a small, secret union in the Loray textile mill in Gastonia. The mill management had recently brought in an "efficiency expert" who was responsible for reducing the number of workers, cutting pay scales, and increasing the daily output, thus expecting fewer workers to oversee more looms. (This practice came to be called the "stretch-out.") On 30 March, after five mill employees were discharged for being members of the Communist party, two hundred workers walked off the job in protest. Soon employees at five other mills became involved in the dispute, and about a thousand workers were on strike. Five companies of the North Carolina National Guard were sent to Gastonia to control the resulting disorder.

Shooting broke out between the strikers and the city police, and the chief of police was killed. Anti-Communist sentiment was rampant. In a trial before a packed courtroom, Beal and six others were found guilty of conspiracy to murder. Sentenced to up to twenty years, Beal was free on bail pending an appeal when he left to visit Russia; disappointed in what he saw, he returned home but skipped bail again to go back to Russia. This time he missed the freedom that he had enjoyed at home and abandoned his Communist ideals, so he returned to North Carolina to begin serving his sentence. After four years he was paroled for good behavior and on the grounds that he had not received a fair trial.

Another casualty of these troubled times was Ella May Wiggins, a mountain-born textile worker in Bessemer City, a few miles from Gastonia. Obliged to work the night shift in order to care for her five children during the day after her husband abandoned her, she was a victim of the stretch-out. A naturally friendly person, she began appealing to her friends and neighbors, black as well as white, to unite and oppose the exhausting work schedule. She composed songs expressing the deepest feelings of the workers, spoke and sang at union rallies, and in other ways participated in the strike. On the way to a meeting of strikers, she was riding with others in the back of a truck that was stopped by a carload of unidentified men when she was fatally shot.

The National Textile Workers Union proclaimed Ella May Wiggins a martyr for their cause, and strikers brought further pressure to bear on management. Subsequently, the workweek was reduced to fifty-five hours, conditions in the mills were improved, and welfare work in the mill villages was expanded. Five Loray mill employees were indicted for her murder, but in a trial in Charlotte the following March they were acquitted.

Child Labor

Closely related to the struggle to improve working conditions in general was the especially sad plight of children who were employed for long hours in textile mills at very low wages. In previous centuries, when farms were family-operated, it was customary for children to join in almost every task; but then they worked alongside parents and siblings. This changed with industrialization, which adopted the same practices of child labor that had prevailed earlier in England and in the mills of Massachusetts. When the much acclaimed New Day dawned over North Carolina, 24 percent of the state's textile workers were children. Young girls, both black and white, were employed in cigarette manufacturing.

The evils of child labor were publicized late in the nineteenth century, and in 1903 the state adopted its first child labor law, weak though it was. No longer could children under age twelve be employed in factories nor could those under eighteen work more than sixty-six hours a week. Compliance with this law was at the employer's discretion, however, since no machinery was provided for its enforcement. The next year, when the Reverend Alexander J. McKelway, a Presbyterian minister from Charlotte, became southern secretary of the National

The employment of children in mills was widespread around the turn of the century. The unhealthy conditions are suggested by the lint on this girl's hair and clothes. Much of the complicated machinery was dangerous and the hours were long. In 1903, North Carolina passed its first child labor law prohibiting the employment of children under twelve and restricting those under eighteen to a maximum sixty-six-hour week. (Courtesy of Edward L. Bafford Photography Collection, University of Maryland Baltimore County Library)

Child Labor Committee, a new campaign for a better law got under way. Josephus Daniels, editor of the Raleigh *News and Observer*, played an active role in the campaign, as did Governor Charles B. Aycock. Their goal was a statute prohibiting the employment of girls under fourteen, and requiring (1) that the ages of working children be certified by their teachers and (2) that working boys under fourteen be able to read and write. The latter, Aycock believed, would tend to reduce illiteracy, and he referred to it as a form of "compulsory education."

The bill introduced in 1905 contained the fourteen-year age limit for girls as well as a sixteen-year limit on night work for both boys and girls; it also reduced the workweek for children under sixteen to sixty hours, required age certification from school officials, and stipulated that the state commissioner of labor or his deputy be named the factory inspector. But the combined opposition of the

Many workers in the textile mills of North Carolina, as elsewhere in the South, had formerly lived on farms. Wages were low and it often was necessary for whole families to work. In this photograph of workers at the West Monbo Manufacturing Co. on the Catawba River in Catawba County, nearly all of the men are wearing suspenders and the boys are barefooted. The owner of the mill named the site "Mont Beau" but local people soon called it "Monbo." (North Carolina Collection, University of North Carolina at Chapel Hill, from original owned by Una Mae Brown, Catawba, N.C.)

North Carolina Cotton Growers' Association, a number of individual industrialists, and those who criticized the National Child Labor Committee for its "Northern connections" could not be overcome. A few days before the bill was sent to committee, some mill operators went to Raleigh to lobby against it, and it was defeated. To dismiss at least the accusation of northern influence, a North Carolina Child Labor Committee was formed in 1906 with Episcopal bishop Joseph Blount Cheshire as chairman and popular educator Charles L. Coon as secretary. It was a committee of Tar Heels born and bred.

Perhaps to frighten adult workers, manufacturers began to complain of a labor shortage and to talk of the need for immigrant labor. Realizing, however, that some form of restrictive legislation would be presented to the 1907 session of the General Assembly, they drew up a bill minimally acceptable to themselves. It provided that no children under thirteen would be employed except as an apprentice, although twelve- to thirteen-year-olds might work for four months if they had attended school for six months; from fourteen to fifteen they might work seven months and go to school for three, and from fifteen to sixteen they might work ten months and attend school for two. No child under sixteen would work more than sixty-six hours a week, and none under fourteen would work between 8:00 P.M. and 5:00 A.M. The manufacturers' bill passed, although the state Child Labor Committee considered its provisions to be inadequate. Features designed to strengthen it were considered in 1909 but rejected because some manufacturers who originally agreed to support the bill later withdrew.

Not until 1913 did the General Assembly enlarge the law to provide that no person under sixteen could work in a factory or manufacturing establishment between 9:00 P.M. and 6:00 A.M., that the age of children should be certified by school officials, and that county school superintendents would be responsible for inspecting mills to ensure that the law was obeyed. In 1917 the threat of a federal inspection law resulted in the creation two years later of a state Child Labor Commission to inspect mills for compliance. This law also required children between the ages of eight and fourteen to attend school for a full term, and it prohibited the employment of children under fourteen. Efforts made in 1927 to further regulate child labor failed, in part because Governor Angus W. McLean did not support them. Finally, however, a federal law in 1933 abolished child labor altogether.

Academic Freedom

An instance of support for "free speech" as well as academic freedom at Trinity College drew national attention to North Carolina in 1903. Professor John Spencer Bassett, a native of Tarboro and a graduate of both Trinity and the Johns Hopkins University, founded and was editor of the *South Atlantic Quarterly*, a journal inviting serious contributions concerning the literary, historical, and social development of the South. Intending to inspire objective discussion of the problem of race, Bassett published an article reviewing the history of relations between whites and blacks; in it he described Booker T. Washington, a black, as "the greatest man, save General Lee, born in the South in a hundred years." Copies of the *Quarterly* had hardly been delivered when a storm of protest erupted. Newspaper editors, including Josephus Daniels of the Raleigh *News and Observer* who printed his name as "bASSett," joined in the demand for his dismissal. Parents were called upon to withdraw their children from Trinity College if he remained. The students, however, threatened to leave of their own accord if Professor Bassett were fired.

Bassett offered to resign, but the president and the faculty stood firmly behind him. They indicated, in fact, that they would also leave if Bassett were discharged. In what must have been a very difficult meeting, the trustees voted 18 to 7 to reject Bassett's letter of resignation. This action was termed "one of the greatest victories for academic freedom ever won in the United States."

World War I

These and other compelling concerns at home were laid aside for a few years when world events demanded the attention of all Americans. The changes precipitated by these events were so pervasive that North Carolina would never again be the same. In June 1914 in the small mountain town of Sarajevo (now in Yugoslavia), a place not even the schoolteachers had ever heard of or could pronounce, the heir to the Austro-Hungarian throne was assassinated. A relatively unimportant crime in itself except for those immediately involved, it became an excuse for one European nation to attack another, and for others to come to the defense of a neighbor. In rapid succession Germany, France, Russia, Italy, Great Britain, Turkey, Bulgaria, and other countries entered a general European war.

Far removed from the scene, the United States attempted to remain neutral and show favoritism to no nation but above all to keep out of the war. Individuals, nevertheless, went abroad to assist in many ways; some drove ambulances while others joined the French air force. Financial loans and the sale of supplies to the Allies—England, France, Russia, and Italy—as well as effective propaganda reflected American sympathy to the Allied cause. Germany's unprovoked action in permitting its submarines to sink passenger liners and attack neutral shipping, however, led the United States after three years to declare war on 6 April 1917. This was called "the war to end all wars" or "the war to make the world safe for democracy."

Walter Hines Page was ambassador to England, and many other North Carolinians were poised in the national administration to play significant roles in the war. Josephus Daniels was secretary of the navy and thus head of the department responsible for transporting more than 2 million American troops overseas. President Woodrow Wilson's secretary of agriculture, David Houston, was a native of North Carolina though a resident of Missouri when he was appointed to the cabinet. In Congress the Democratic leader of the House of Representatives was Claude Kitchin, and Furnifold Simmons was chairman of the Senate Finance Committee. In combat the state provided one major general, three brigadier generals, and three rear admirals. To the armed forces North Carolina sent 86,457 men, of whom 20,350 were black. Also serving were 195 nurses from the state. Losses included 629 killed in action, 204 deaths from wounds, and 1,542 deaths from disease.

Three training camps were established in the state: Camp Greene in Charlotte, Camp Polk in Raleigh, and Camp Bragg near Fayetteville. After the war the first two were closed, but the third was retained and as Fort Bragg it became the largest artillery base in the world. In recent years it has served other units, particularly airborne forces.

People at home also did their share to support the war effort. Shipyards at Wilmington and at Norfolk, Virginia, and factories making ammunition in Petersburg, Virginia, in Raleigh, and elsewhere drew workers from across the state. Men and women served with the Red Cross, the YMCA, and similar agencies. Women took over jobs formerly held by men in offices, factories, and shops, demonstrating their ability to perform well in unexpected places. Farmers and city dwellers alike joined in planting Victory gardens and in drying, canning, or otherwise preserving food. They did without certain things or found substitutes to permit scarce and essential supplies and food to be sent overseas.

Many North Carolinians served on battleships and troop transports, while both men and women worked in medical units. Several units were composed almost totally of North Carolinians—notably the Thirtieth Division and assorted groups of field artillery, engineers, and machine gun battalions. The men were involved in the exhausting trench warfare in France as the Germans attempted to take Paris. Rain, snow, wind, and smoke from exploding shells, or in season the dirt and dust, and at times poison gas, contributed to the misery of the men at the front. In the spring of 1918, when the Germans began a major offensive, the losses were heavy on both sides. Extended coils of barbed wire tore clothes and skin, and delayed movement as soldiers became targets for the enemy. More than 100,000 American troops helped to halt the Germans, however, and from late September until early November the Allies took the offensive. Germany was defeated, and an armistice was signed on 11 November.

From time to time since the colonial period there had been epidemics of influenza, sometimes affecting large parts of the world. But between September and November 1918, an especially virulent strain killed an estimated 15 million people worldwide of whom about 450,000 were Americans. Occurring largely among young adults between the ages of twenty and forty, the disease took a toll of 13,644 in North Carolina. The new president of the University of North Carolina, Edward Kidder Graham, was a victim just a few days past his forty-second birthday. Sometimes whole families were struck down. Public meetings, often including church services, were canceled and schools were closed. Private funerals became the rule as attempts were made to halt the spread of the disease.

The young men and women who had served in the armed forces began to return home with accounts of faraway places. Some had been in other states for training and many had served in England and on the Continent. A lot of them had even been to Paris. They had made friends in those places, and some of the men found wives while they were overseas. For many foreign travel was quite revealing, and they became critical and dissatisfied with conditions at home. Some now had a more progressive outlook and supported drives for improvements in the state. Others became more tolerant of those whose ideas differed from theirs. All in all, many aspects of life in North Carolina changed significantly after World War I.

Woman Suffrage

Despite the fact that the war had altered the perspectives of many North Carolinians, the General Assembly reacted with little interest to a proposal that had been introduced many years before—that it grant the vote to women. Very much as their predecessors had done in the 1850s when considering free manhood suffrage, North Carolina legislators of the early twentieth century hesitated to extend the suffrage to women. In the colonial period and even for a time afterward, women had been permitted to vote in New York, New Jersey, and a few other places. While a new constitution was being prepared in North Carolina in 1868, someone asked why women should not be granted the right to vote, especially if black men were to be enfranchised, but no one paid any attention. Yet the following year, women were permitted to vote in Wyoming when it was organized as a territory. The question, then, was by no means new.

In 1884, Margaret Richardson attended a National Suffrage Association convention in Washington, D.C. She was probably the first North Carolinian to demonstrate a personal concern in the matter. Thereafter suffrage associations were formed in some of the states, but not until the winter of 1894 was North Carolina among them. At the call of Helen Morris Lewis, a local music teacher, forty-five men and women met in the Buncombe County courthouse and, under the guidance of Mayor Thomas W. Patton, organized the North Carolina Equal Suffrage Association. Its newly elected president, Helen Lewis, then began a speaking tour of some of the western counties to make known the wishes of at least some women to have the vote. In the General Assembly early in 1897 Senator J. L. Hyatt, a Yancey County Republican, introduced a woman suffrage bill. Many of the all-male legislators probably were surprised at such a proposal, and perhaps applauded the decision to send it to the committee on insane asylums where it died.

The whole idea of votes for women ceased to be a viable option for fifteen years. In the summer of 1913 a local suffrage league was formed in Morganton, and again some men thought that was an appropriate site since Morganton was also the home of an insane asylum. But the revived proposal began to take root—another chapter was formed in Greenville—and the state suffrage league went to work. In November a convention was held and a president elected; soon women from South Carolina and Virginia arrived to assist in recruiting new members. Charlotte followed Greenville with a large local league, and by the end of 1914 the list included sixteen towns. In Reidsville T. Wingate Andrews, superintendent of schools, was president, and in Chapel Hill fourteen of the twenty-nine members were men. Newspaper publicity was generous but not always complimentary. The morning dailies in Charlotte and Raleigh, however, were very supportive. Chief Justice Walter Clark spoke often and forcefully in favor of woman suffrage, stressing that the most aggressive opponents were the liquor interests and the political machines who might well expect to be put out of business by the votes of women.

When they failed to achieve their goal, women in the state suffrage movement lowered their sights and sought the right to vote just in presidential and municipal elections. To equip themselves for the campaign, many of them attended courses in public speaking, parliamentary law, publicity organization, and fund-raising. Nevertheless, the General Assembly of 1917 rejected both a bill to grant municipal suffrage and another one to grant suffrage in presidential elections, the latter by a closer vote than the former.

After the United States declared war on Germany in the spring of 1917, women demonstrated their patriotism by taking jobs vacated by men who had gone to fight. Their contributions and effective leadership earned the gratitude of many who had for so long referred to women as "the weaker sex." Having thus been accepted in business and industry where many remained, women renewed their campaign for women's rights in the political arena. Membership in the Equal Suffrage League increased dramatically.

When Congress began to consider an amendment to the United States Constitution in 1918 to grant the vote to women, many women in North Carolina wrote to their state's representatives urging them to support it. However, only one congressman from North Carolina endorsed the proposed amendment. At home, those who supported universal suffrage tried to have both political parties include a plank to that effect in their platforms. The Republicans complied without opposition, but the Democrats declined to do so, maintaining that the issue was too divisive for the party to take a stand. Not surprisingly, in view of the Democrats' attitude, an attempt to obtain municipal suffrage for women failed in 1919. Three months after the General Assembly adjourned, however, the Congress submitted the text of a proposed amendment providing for woman suffrage.

The Nineteenth Amendment was approved by one state after another, and in the summer of 1920 the General Assembly of North Carolina was called into special session to consider this and other important matters. Hope was high that the state would support the amendment, as by that time only one more acceptance was needed for it to take effect. The legislature of Tennessee was also in

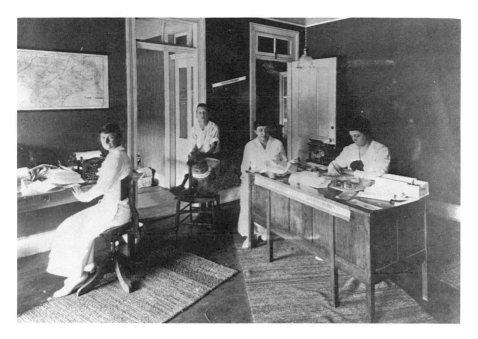

Workers in the woman suffrage campaign of 1920 had hopes that the special session of the General Assembly would join other states in ratifying the Nineteenth Amendment. The approval of just one more state was needed, but the legislators of North Carolina disappointed them. On 26 August 1920, with Tennessee's ratification, the amendment became a part of the United States Constitution anyway. (North Carolina Division of Archives and History, Raleigh)

session for the same purpose, and many North Carolinians wanted their state to have the distinction of taking the decisive step. Legislators, however, were not stirred by the urgent appeals from both men and women. Instead of accepting the inevitable, they sent a "round robin petition"—with names signed in a circle so no one could tell who signed it first—asking their counterparts across the mountains to reject the amendment. This cowardly device was ineffective, and Tennessee ratified anyway. The woman suffrage amendment became a part of the United States Constitution on 26 August 1920. Women acquired the right to vote with no thanks to the North Carolina General Assembly. The legislature, in a meaningless action, finally ratified the amendment in 1971.

The Roaring Twenties

In numerous ways the decade of the 1920s created such profound changes in the attitudes and the habits of many North Carolinians that some spoke of it as "a bloodless revolution." Others felt the events of those years represented "a new phase" or "a new day," and they were not pleased with the changes. The period that became known as the Roaring Twenties was a time of carefree living and disregard for the present laws and the moral standards of the recent past. Even though Prohibition was the law of the land, illicit distilleries flourished and many people gathered at speakeasies to drink, much as they had done before in the saloons. Women shed their "crowning glory," long hair worn in a bun on the nape of the neck, and appeared in newly established "beauty parlors" or even in men's barbershops to have their hair "bobbed." They also painted their cheeks and fingernails, wore lipstick, and bought dresses with hems above the knees. Worse yet, young women—as well as young men—began to smoke cigarettes.

Automobiles, which first appeared near the end of the nineteenth century, could now be seen and heard all around the state; the younger generation took off for distant places and came home late at night. Even women began to drive. Where they went and exactly what they did, no one was quite prepared to say, but many were aware that they were not at church on Sunday morning or at prayer meeting on Wednesday night.

The Evolution Controversy

The vast majority of North Carolinians still believed in an old-fashioned orthodoxy. The population was predominantly rural. People went to church on Sunday, and most of them accepted the Bible as the literal word of God. North Carolina, they were convinced, was a "Christian Commonwealth." It disturbed them, therefore, when evangelists began to use the word *evolution* and to condemn the theory that it represented. Charles Darwin's theory was not explained to them nor did they understand it, yet they got the idea that it said that human beings were descended from monkeys. "God-or-gorilla" seemed to be the choice.

Talk of evolution was heard everywhere; newspaper editorials discussed it, and popular magazines carried long articles on the subject. Bible conferences, denominational disputes, and debates by professors, preachers, and politicians spread the word. But, above all, it was the evangelists—while traveling around the South, preaching under large tents or in the courthouse or a tobacco warehouse—who publicized Darwin's theory. It was they, in large measure, who created the fury that aroused virtually the whole state in the mid-1920s.

In 1924 Governor Cameron Morrison, as ex officio chairman of the State Board of Education, banned a biology textbook from the public high schools because it discussed the theory of evolution. Soon afterward religious fundamentalists launched a campaign to eliminate from the faculty of church-related colleges all "evolutionists" and to introduce Bible courses in the public school curriculum. This, they maintained, would help defeat "the forces of the devil."

At the notorious "Monkey Trial" held in Tennessee in June 1925, a high school teacher, John Thomas Scopes, was tried for teaching the theory of evolution in violation of a state law. The trial, held out-of-doors because it was feared the large crowd would cause the floor of the courtroom to collapse, made Tennessee the laughing stock of the nation. Yet Scopes was found guilty and fined. On appeal to the state supreme court the verdict was set aside.

In the 1925 session of the North Carolina General Assembly, Hoke County representative D. Scott Poole, a newspaper editor and noted Presbyterian layman, introduced a bill to prohibit public schools from teaching "as a fact either Darwinism or any other evolutionary hypothesis that links man in blood relationship with any lower form of life." Also in the legislature the University of North Carolina was loudly condemned for its classroom discussion of the "infidel" theory.

Advocates pointed out that the Poole bill was not an attack on the freedom of speech nor an attempt to regulate religious beliefs; rather, it was an admonition that a theory not be taught as the truth. Representative Samuel J. Ervin, Jr., of Burke County, maintained that all it did was "absolve monkeys from all responsibility for the human race," but it did, nevertheless, curb free speech. R. O. Everett of Durham objected to such an attempt by the legislature to regulate religious views, and he moved to have the bill tabled. Although his motion was rejected, the measure itself was defeated by a vote of 67 to 46.

National antievolution forces, after their recent victories in Tennessee, Mississippi, and Arkansas, were anxious to prevail in the Tar Heel state. In time, they anticipated, they would secure national legislation to prohibit the teaching of evolution throughout the country. To that end, speakers from Tennessee, Texas, Mississippi, and elsewhere joined local supporters in a North Carolina crusade; leaders of the Anti-Evolution League of America also appeared in the state. At a meeting in Charlotte in May 1926, a Committee of One Hundred made up of native fundamentalists was formed to conduct a statewide campaign. Newspaper reporters described the gathering as intemperate and disorderly, and adverse publicity limited the committee's effectiveness. Both Harry Woodburn Chase, president of the University of North Carolina, and William Louis Poteat, president of Wake Forest College, were supported by their respective alumni after being harshly criticized for permitting Darwin's theory to be discussed in classes.

As part of the fundamentalist campaign, local antievolution societies were formed and a number of city and county school boards directed teachers not to discuss Darwin's theory in their classes. Public meetings were also held. These were often poorly attended, and it was not unusual for members of an audience to leave before a speaker had finished. One meeting that drew attention, however, was a debate planned for Charlotte between a prominent Mississippi evangelist and an atheist from Detroit. When Charlotte officials refused to permit an atheist to speak in the city, the confrontation had to be moved to a rural site. The atheist used a monkey named "Genesis" to illustrate his remarks, and it was reported that the presentation in some respects resembled a vaudeville performance. The *Charlotte Observer*, usually supportive of fundamentalism, noted that the antievolution crusade had turned "into a cheap show of the common order."

The evolution debate became an issue in the political campaign of 1926 when the antievolutionists declared that they were going to elect legislators sympathetic to their views. The Democratic party declined to include any mention of the subject in their platform, but the Committee of One Hundred demanded that every candidate take a public stand on the question. Unopposed in Hoke County, D. Scott Poole took the lead in advocating antievolution legislation, and the vote in Mecklenburg County, considered "the mecca of fundamentalism," attracted considerable attention. In a runoff primary, Julia Alexander, a Presbyterian who was closely identified with the Committee of One Hundred, was defeated by Carrie MacLean, an attorney and a Baptist who opposed attempts to restrict freedom of speech.

Once again Representative Poole introduced a bill to prohibit the teaching of the evolution theory. It was referred to the committee on education where it was soundly rejected. Antievolutionists got the message and they made no attempt to get the measure to the floor of the house on a minority report. It was clear, nevertheless, that a majority of North Carolinians were fundamentalists and that they would have been pleased never again to hear of Charles Darwin or his strange theory. But a law to prohibit the discussion of any subject, even evolution, was another matter. To appear to offer legislative support to a particular religious belief, as Poole's bill certainly did, was also unacceptable. Even more dreaded was the possibility that North Carolina might become the target of derisive remarks from other states if it passed such a measure.

Higher Education

At the end of the nineteenth century there were nearly sixty colleges of varying quality in North Carolina including one for Indians established in Robeson County in 1887, a dozen for blacks, and nearly fifteen for women. Most, even those created by the state, operated on very limited budgets and depended largely on tuition for support. A majority of them were church-related and provided free or inexpensive tuition for young men preparing for the ministry. Several were teacher training institutions and a few also offered instruction at the high school level. Libraries and laboratories, judged by later standards, were inadequate, but many were motivated to improve themselves when the Carnegie Foundation for the Advancement of Teaching drew up a set of standards for college admission, and the General Education Board, a Rockefeller benefaction, offered matching grants to those who met the challenge.

By 1914 Trinity, Davidson, Salem, Wake Forest, and Meredith—all denominational colleges—had raised significant sums for their improvement. The General Assembly between 1901 and the 1920s increased appropriations to the University of North Carolina from $155,000 to more than $2 million; it also provided about $2 million more for permanent improvements. With additional support, the university upgraded and expanded its graduate and professional training. More than a dozen new buildings were erected on the Chapel Hill campus by the end of the 1920s with funds for three of them coming from private sources. The North Carolina College of Agriculture and Mechanic Arts had added four new buildings by 1912, and both state institutions began to serve North Carolina in new ways. Extension departments took members of the faculty across the state to teach and consult, and publications and public programs made the results of practical and scholarly research available to a wide range of citizens. State appropriations for the teachers' colleges also grew, resulting in enlarged campuses and improved programs.

One of the outstanding improvements in higher education occurred in Durham. Trinity College, supported by the Methodist denomination, had moved there in 1892 from a rural setting in Randolph County where it had been organized as an academy in 1838 and a dozen years later elevated to college status. Durham businessmen Julian S. Carr and Washington, Benjamin, and James Buchanan (Buck) Duke contributed generously to the support of Trinity. In 1924 James B. Duke endowed the college, and its name was changed to Duke University. A new campus was laid out and many handsome Gothic-style stone buildings, including a very large chapel, were constructed.

Books and Writers

The first three decades of the twentieth century, in addition to producing extensive economic growth, also saw the development of equally significant cultural changes. While a number of small, local newspapers ceased publication, many of the larger dailies such as those in Charlotte, Greensboro, and Raleigh increased their circulation, served a regional rather than a strictly local area, and helped create a statewide outlook among the people. Professional journalists rather than mere printers became involved, and men like Joseph P. Caldwell, Josephus Daniels, Gerald W. Johnson, and Walter Hines Page—some of them more liberal than most of their readers—influenced the attitudes on public questions of a large segment of the population as well as the decisions of many state and local officials. Disregarding their dependence on revenue from advertising, editors often spoke out against such things as child labor, business trusts that worked to the detriment of farmers, and the liquor question. They also played a role in the campaign against lynching, usually of blacks, by unruly and frequently unprosecuted mobs, and against the leasing of convict labor to individuals or businesses. Newspapers began to review books and to publish essays, poems, and short stories by local writers. From October 1909 to April 1913 the Raleigh *News and Observer* published a weekly supplement, the *North Carolina Review*, to which many prominent state and regional writers contributed historical, biographical, and literary pieces; it also contained information of current reference value.

Early in the century civic-minded individuals or groups undertook to establish libraries in the towns for the benefit of local residents. Women's clubs were especially active in this work. Durham in 1897 actually had the first tax-supported public library in the state, but close behind were Greensboro (1902), Charlotte (1903), and Winston (1906). Durham also was a pioneer in delivering books to patrons through its "book auto"—an early version of the bookmobile—which was in service by 1923. Although the legislature made an annual appropriation for books for a state library as early as 1819, the miscellaneous collection of books, documents, and other materials kept in the office of the secretary of state was not organized until after 1902, when Carrie L. Broughton became assistant state librarian; in 1918 she became state librarian, the first woman to be named head of a state department. In 1909 the General Assembly created the Library Commission to give assistance, advice, and counsel to all libraries in the state. Under the chairmanship of Louis R. Wilson, librarian at the University of North Carolina, the commission reorganized many old libraries as public libraries and established new ones. State aid, limited at first but soon increased, made possible the opening of free public libraries in thirty-five of the state's largest towns by 1922.

With better public schools, more opportunities for higher education, and the encouragement of intellectual pursuits by the Literary and Historical Association and the organizations it sponsored, North Carolinians began to "dip pen into ink," as one critic commented. The state's tradition of writing and publishing rarely gained fame beyond its borders. John Lawson's *A New Voyage to Carolina* (1709), John Hill Wheeler's *Historical Sketches of North Carolina* (1851), and Frances Fisher Tiernan's *Land of the Sky* (1876) may suggest the limited contributions ranging from contemporary accounts, through researched history, to fiction, respectively. The twentieth century, however, saw an abundance of pamphlets and books by North Carolina writers in such widely divergent classifications as politics and religion, sociology and science, history and fiction, and biography and creative literature. The latter continued the poetic tradition that had existed more or less anonymously since 1698, when a Perquimans County Quaker, Henry White, composed a long but untitled poem on the fall and redemption of man. In fact, during the 1900s some of the nation's most talented writers were North Carolinians.

Historians benefited greatly from the publication of ten volumes of the *Colonial Records of North Carolina* between 1886 and 1890 under the editorship of William L. Saunders and sixteen volumes of *State Records of North Carolina*, edited by Walter Clark, which appeared between 1896 and 1906. In addition, Stephen B. Weeks prepared a four-volume index, published between 1909 and 1914. These newly available documentary sources led Samuel A. Ashe to publish a two-volume *History of North Carolina*, the first comprehensive history of the state; the first volume appeared in 1908 and the second in 1925. Ashe also was editor of the eight-volume *Biographical History of North Carolina* (1905–17). In 1903 Marshall De Lancey Haywood published *Governor William Tryon*, a new biographical appraisal of the royal governor based on contemporary sources; it revealed that Tryon was not the tyrant he had so long been pictured.

Walter Hines Page's novel, *The Southerner* (1909), was intended to persuade people that many of the old prejudices of the past should now be laid aside. John Henry Bonner, John Charles McNeill, and Henry Jerome Stockard were popular Tar Heel poets of the early 1900s whose contributions to the newspapers were widely appreciated. Their collected poems also appeared in book form. Novelist Thomas Dixon, born in Cleveland County, wrote a great many books including *The Leopard's Spots* (1902) and *The Clansman* (1905); the latter was the basis of the country's first important full-length epic film, *The Birth of a Nation*. Guilford County native William Sydney Porter, better known by his pseudonym, O. Henry, was the author of numerous popular short stories published in national magazines of the early 1900s. Afterward collected in many editions, they remained popular for a very long time and were frequently reprinted after the copyright on them expired. Some of them also were the basis for motion pictures. A black author, Charles Waddell Chesnutt, whose family had come from Fayetteville where he spent his youth, wrote five widely read books between 1899 and 1905, including a collection of folk tales, a group of short stories, and three racial novels. Chesnutt is considered to be the first black American writer to merit serious attention for the literary quality of his work.

Politics

While events on the literary plane were attracting attention, in other spheres activity continued apace. Politicians never ceased forming strategies to interest the electorate nor overlooked a subject with popular appeal. Since ballot boxes were brought out every two years, there was never time to rest on one's laurels. Women were now making their presence known in the public service arena, and by 1921 one of them, Harriet Morehead Berry of Hillsborough, was regarded as "the best woman politician in the state." An 1897 graduate of the State Normal and Industrial School (now the University of North Carolina at Greensboro), she became secretary of the North Carolina Geological and Economic Survey, headed by Joseph Hyde Pratt with offices in Chapel Hill. This agency, which was concerned with the conservation of natural resources and the construction of better roads, provided valuable assistance to the North Carolina Good Roads Association. When Pratt left for military service in 1917, Harriet Berry became acting head of the survey. In this capacity she played an effective role in planning and securing legislation for a road-building program. News releases, letters, petitions, circulars, and a great variety of publications blanketed the state, publicizing the plan and laying the groundwork for legislative support. The idea was to have an extensive network of all-weather roads connecting every county seat town with its neighboring county seats; all state institutions not in a county seat would also be included in this great spiderweblike design.

A "mere woman" alone, of course, could not attain such an ambitious goal without the assistance of professional politicians who were anxious to attract personal attention and to make a name for themselves. As had happened so many times in the past and as would often be the case again, North Carolina was fortunate to have the right people in positions of authority at the critical time. One such person was Cameron Morrison, a native of Richmond County and governor from 1921 to 1925. As a very young man he had followed his father's lead into the Republican party, but soon changed his registration to Democrat and a few years later participated in the Red Shirt movement. He became mayor of Rockingham and at the turn of the century was a member of the state senate. Remaining active in state politics, in 1920 he became his party's candidate for governor, having defeated the incumbent lieutenant governor, O. Max Gardner, for that honor. Although Morrison was a colorful public figure, described as "bluff and hearty in his bearing and manner," no one expected more than "unimaginative, routine leadership from him." Much to the surprise of his friends, his administration was one of the most progressive the state had known.

Morrison took his first forward step a few months after he was inaugurated. Between the election and that date he had been busy lining up support for the program of good roads that would make him long remembered. He became the first of several to claim to be the "Good Roads Governor." With the help of his longtime friends in the General Assembly, committee chairmen were carefully selected. Those who might have opposed his program were placated and their vanity carefully stroked. Men of influence and ability were placed in positions

Heriot Clarkson, chairman of the legislative committee of several organizations supporting a system of good roads, and Hattie Morehead Berry, a vital leader in the North Carolina Good Roads Association. It was largely through her efforts that a State Highway
Commission was created in 1921 and the state was committed to the construction of a
system of modern highways. (North Carolina Division of Archives and History, Raleigh)

where these qualities would be useful. As a result the legislature in 1921 created a
powerful state highway commission and committed North Carolina to the construction of a thoroughly modern system of highways 5,500 miles in extent. To
accomplish this a $50 million bond issue was authorized and two years later an
additional $15 million was approved.

Harriet Berry was not forgotten in the political maneuvering that made this possible. She came to be recognized as the "Mother of Good Roads in North Carolina," and was often commended for her foresight and ability. Having achieved this victory, she joined the staff of the *Greensboro Daily News* as editor of the Department of Industries and Resources to campaign for better schools and to publicize North Carolina's attractions for industry, tourists, and new residents, all of which would contribute to the orderly development of the state's resources.

Governor Morrison enjoyed equal success with other programs. Under his leadership the legislature funded a six-year, $20 million program to expand the overcrowded state institutions of higher education and to improve the state insane asylums, reformatories, sanatoriums, and schools for the deaf, dumb, and blind.

Routine operating funds for the State Board of Health were also increased, and greater appropriations were made for the public schools. A loan fund for the construction of new school buildings was increased from $1 million to $10 million, and the laws regulating county support for schools were altered to compel more generous appropriations.

In general Morrison's views of relations between the races were no different than those of the vast majority of his constituents. Nevertheless, in 1921 he called a meeting of prominent black and white citizens to discuss ways to improve race relations. Out of this came the North Carolina Commission on Interracial Co-operation. He also was an ardent opponent of lynching, and, because of his policy of calling out state troops at the slightest hint of impending violence, there were no lynchings in the state during the last three and a half years of his administration.

Morrison's successes far outranked his failures; even his programs that were rejected suggest that he was a man of vision. In 1923, for example, he proposed that a State Department of Commerce and Industry be created and that a bond issue of $8.5 million be approved for the construction of state-owned port terminal facilities. Both plans were turned down.

The policies inaugurated up to 1925 were continued until the end of the decade. In the public school system many new buildings were erected; libraries, laboratories, and cafeterias were added; and the term of instruction was extended to at least six months but even longer in most city systems. A particularly significant accomplishment in 1925, early in the administration of Governor Angus W. McLean, Morrison's successor, was the creation of the State Budget Bureau with the governor as ex officio head. It then became the duty of the governor to prepare a balanced budget for submission to the General Assembly. At the same time an Advisory Budget Commission was established to consist of the chairmen of the appropriations and finance committees of the house and the senate as well as two other persons to be named by the governor. Almost as if in anticipation of the hard times that lay ahead, some state government agencies were consolidated. The number of state employees was reduced and a commission created to establish salaries and wages. As Governor Morrison had proposed, a Department of Conservation and Development was created. Two years later the General Assembly made provisions for the establishment of a tax commission to gather and classify data on taxation; an advisory commission to improve and simplify many operations of county government; and a State Board of Equalization in connection with the taxation of property to support county schools.

A little more than a quarter of a century after the "Dawn of a New Day" the state showed many signs of progress. Except in the area of race relations, North Carolina and most of the other southern states were not very different from most states in other parts of the country. The losses suffered by many families during the Civil War and the heavy hand of Reconstruction were seldom mentioned. Few had any recollection of those years, and most people looked optimistically to the future.

24

DOWN BUT NOT OUT: THE STATE SURVIVES THE GREAT DEPRESSION

WHEN Angus W. McLean succeeded Cameron Morrison as governor in 1925, many North Carolinians, except farmers, were enjoying a period of rising prosperity. The state was laying the foundation for what would soon become one of the best highway systems in the nation. The University of North Carolina and the state-maintained colleges were receiving more generous support than ever, and the private and church-related colleges were also flourishing. The munificent Duke Endowment was providing support not only for the newly created Duke University, but also for Davidson College and Johnson C. Smith University, many hospitals and orphanages, and to aid retired Methodist ministers. Under Governor Morrison's leadership public schools had been improved and the length of the term extended. The electorate was given an opportunity to vote on a plan to improve the state's ports but rejected it. Business was healthy and for most workers income was reliable and steady. Farm prices, however, had recently declined; and while the number of farms increased, the average size decreased.

In North Carolina it had long been the practice of the people to manage their own affairs as they pleased, and to keep both state and local taxes low and all levels of government as nearly invisible as possible. As the first quarter of the twentieth century passed, however, this attitude toward government began to change. It was not only individuals who came to expect the government to take the lead in charting the state's future, but business, professional, and social groups as well. People began to approve the creation of new state agencies with programs unimagined a few years before.

Governor McLean, born on a farm in Robeson County, was a lawyer who had represented the Atlantic Coast Line Railroad for many years and had played a key role in building a rail connection between that line and his hometown, Lumberton. He served two terms on the town board of commissioners, was a member of the state executive committee of the Democratic party, and, because of his role in raising funds for Woodrow Wilson's presidential campaign in North Carolina, he was named assistant secretary of the treasury in 1920. A Scotsman by heritage, he was a founder of three textile mills and a profitable bank, and his reputation for thrift and his commercial acumen made him attractive to voters when he ran for governor in 1924.

The "Businessman's Governor"

When the General Assembly met in January 1925, McLean proposed the creation of an executive budget system, much as his predecessor had advocated. This time it was approved, and the governor henceforth became ex officio director of the budget. Through the Advisory Budget Commission, he would be responsible for preparing a state budget to be approved by the General Assembly. Beginning with that act, legislative appropriations were budgeted to the various state agencies, and since then North Carolina has enjoyed the security of a balanced budget. All revenue collecting activities were consolidated in the State Department of Revenue, and deposits were made daily in an officially designated bank. Interest earned became a part of the state's revenue, and, due to this new financial arrangement, when McLean's term ended in 1928 there was a surplus of $2.5 million in the treasury. According to his successor, this saved the state from bankruptcy during the financial crisis that began the next year.

McLean was called the "businessman's governor," and his sound policies were appreciated by people across the state. Through his guidance the General Assembly drew up a new state personnel policy under which a uniform salary and wage schedule was adopted and state employees were classified. The responsibilities of the Corporation Commission were defined to include the supervision and regulation of business, financial, and industrial organizations. Previously lawyers had been retained by various state agencies as needed, but as an economy measure new provisions centralized all legal activities under the attorney general. The old Geological and Economic Survey, whose origin could be traced back through several changes of name to 1823, was succeeded by the Department of Conservation and Development, an agency that Governor Morrison had also envisioned but failed to have approved.

Under his predecessor, McLean had served on a commission charged with recommending changes in the laws pertaining to county government. Now that he was governor, McLean set about implementing the commission's recommendations. As a result, the 1927 General Assembly provided a new, clear definition of the responsibilities of county commissioners; placed counties on a budget system and provided machinery for annual tax levies and appropriations; regulated the borrowing and repayment of money; required that local taxes be collected and settlement completed in the same fiscal year in which the levy was passed; and amended the laws covering tax deeds and foreclosures.

While efficiency in government was McLean's primary goal, he was also concerned that the youth of the state be well educated. He wanted to see a new generation of leaders who would ensure North Carolina's predominance among southern states in terms of industrial growth. At the same time he believed that rural schools should play a leading role in improving agriculture. Responding to the governor's wishes, the General Assembly increased the Equalization Fund to $3.25 million, the largest appropriation made for education up to that time. During his term North Carolina completed a six-year, $20 million program of expansion for its institutions of higher learning. In 1927 funds were also made available to enlarge the teacher training programs at state-supported colleges. By the end of this administration more than 52 percent of the state's tax revenues was being applied to education, a percentage exceeded by only four other states in the country.

As a businessman, Governor McLean naturally took an interest in programs that would enhance the commercial advantages of the state. Surveys begun following the creation of the Department of Conservation and Development led to the quarrying of building stone and the establishment of clay products industries. McLean promoted improved methods of marketing and diversification in agriculture and industry which laid the foundation for more prosperous years ahead. After the price of cotton dropped, farmers supported his campaign to reduce its production and to expand other crops for which there was a market. The state also launched a significant publicity campaign to attract new capital and new industries.

Roads and Transportation

Again following the lead of Cameron Morrison, Governor McLean lent his support to the Good Roads Campaign. From his first legislature he requested $20 million in bonds for highways, and in 1927 he supported a bond issue of $30 million to complete the system as well as to take over at least 10 percent of the 6,000 miles of county roads for maintenance and improvement. This program of road building in the 1920s, however, supported by an unprecedented bond issue of considerably more than $178 million, proved to be a considerable burden for the state during the depression. Fortunately it was never obliged to default on the bond payments, but it did have to reduce expenses in every way possible.

Automobiles, trucks, buses, and motorcycles came into common use during the twenties. In 1909 automobiles (at that time often referred to as "machines" but soon afterward as cars from the words *carriage* or *cart*) were first registered;

by 1929, 422,612 cars and 52,633 trucks, buses, and motorcycles were registered by North Carolinians. The number of new cars being purchased declined in the 1930s as the economic depression continued. Many people could no longer afford to operate their car and it was put up on blocks to await better times. It was not uncommon to see a car being pulled by horses or mules when money was not available for gasoline, and sometimes the axle and wheels were used to make a cart—called a "Hoover cart," since President Herbert Hoover was blamed for the depression.

During this period a statewide bus system was developed, and street railways (trolley cars or streetcars, as they were also called), which had long operated in the towns, were soon supplanted by motor buses. Many municipal governments operated trolley lines, and this contributed to the growth of cities and the development of suburbs. In April 1903 the Southern Car Company was established in High Point to build trolley cars; the first ones ran in that city in 1911. Although this company closed in 1914, production was continued by the Thomas Car Works established by Perley A. Thomas, and in time it became the nation's largest manufacturer of school bus bodies and other specialized vehicles. The convenience of bus transportation contributed to a reduction in railway passenger service after World War II. Trucks began to haul more freight and the use of railroads further declined.

Aviation also came into its own as the twenties drew to a close. The state's first airmail service was established at Lindley Field, Greensboro, on 1 May 1928. In September 1929 Raleigh began to be served by commercial airplanes. One line flew passengers to New York and another offered service to Atlanta and Charlotte. Soon a Richmond-Atlanta flight stopped in Greensboro and Charlotte; and a Richmond-Jacksonville, Florida, flight, in Raleigh. By October 1931 North Carolina was served by a line that flew from New York to Miami one day and the reverse route the next.

Although his fiscal and administrative reforms entitled him to rank among the most progressive governors of the nation, McLean was a conservative when it came to social and political reform. He declined to support bills offered in 1925 and 1927 to provide workmen's compensation and neither was passed. The same was true of attempts to improve the state's child labor laws and to introduce the secret ballot.

A Rise in Republican Strength

In 1924, there were 480,068 ballots cast in the gubernatorial election when McLean defeated his Republican opponent by 108,814 votes. Four years later 651,424 people voted, and O. Max Gardner, a lawyer and millowner from

Cleveland County, won by 72,594 votes against the Republican candidate. Gardner, it has been said, was "the first governor elected in North Carolina on a platform which did not look back in some particular to Reconstruction."

The 1928 election was influenced by the national presidential race, which pitted Democratic candidate Alfred E. Smith against Republican Herbert C. Hoover. Smith, former governor of New York, was a Roman Catholic who believed that Prohibition had failed and should be abandoned; Hoover, the current secretary of commerce, was a Quaker, an advocate of Prohibition, and noted for his role in relief work in Europe after World War I. North Carolinians voted overwhelmingly for Hoover (348,923 [R] to 286,227 [D]) and also elected two Republicans to Congress and forty-seven to the General Assembly, a greater number than had served there in many years. Since 16,274 more people voted in the gubernatorial election than in the presidential election, it appears that many Democrats chose not to vote at all rather than to cast their ballot for a Republican presidential candidate.

Governor Gardner's Program

Gardner's administration was largely influenced by economic conditions that had their origin outside the state. Although when he assumed office on 11 January 1929 North Carolina was still prosperous, there were hints of changes on the horizon. Farm prices recently had been declining and there were signs of industrial distress. His term would also encounter labor unrest in Gastonia and Marion.

In his inaugural address the new governor recommended that land taxes be reduced, and that the Equalization Fund for schools be increased. He also endorsed the secret ballot and workmen's compensation. All of these proposals were loudly applauded. The Australian, or secret, ballot was supported in the General Assembly by Senator J. Melville Broughton of Wake County, and in the press by Josephus Daniels, influential editor of the Raleigh *News and Observer*. Adopted in 1929, it was intended to reduce vote-buying since the buyer would no longer be able to see that he got what he had bought.

Workmen's compensation had been proposed in the Democratic party's platform since 1913. It became law as a result of consultation with spokesmen for both labor and industry, and with the support of the North Carolina Conference for Social Service headed by Professor Frank P. Graham of the University of North Carolina. Gardner named the president of the North Carolina State Federation of Labor to direct the Industrial Commission, created to administer the new law. Although the state invested generously in schools and roads, it did not consider regulating business or meddling in social welfare beyond the program of workmen's compensation.

Table 24-1. Party Representation in the General Assembly

| | Senate | | House | | |
	Republican	Democrat	Republican	Democrat	Independent
1917	9	41	21	98	1
1919	10	40	27	93	
1921	11	39	27	93	
1923	3	47	9	111	
1925	3	47	20	100	
1927	3	47	16	104	
1929	12	38	35	84	1
1931	2	48	5	115	

Half of the increased Equalization Fund for schools provided by the General Assembly came from land taxes, and a new source of revenue—a tax on soft drinks, movie admissions, and electric light bills—provided the remainder. Teachers were forced to take a salary cut, but with the addition of two months to the school year they actually received a larger income.

In all of these matters, as in others, Gardner was an astute politician. He often filled vacancies with former opponents, naming one of them state treasurer, another revenue commissioner, and still another superintendent of the state prison. One incumbent opponent, however, who wrote the governor that he intended to retain his office, was obliged to step down; he was replaced by a person of considerable political influence who had previously opposed Gardner. The governor went so far as to name a woman, Annie Kizer Bost, to head the Welfare Department. She happened to be the wife of a popular newspaper reporter who covered state government. At the governor's recommendation, the agriculture and highway departments were placed under the State Budget Bureau, which, of course, the governor controlled.

One legislative proposal that the governor opposed never got very far. To cut expenses, it was suggested that the North Carolina College for Negroes in Durham and the Agricultural and Technical College in Greensboro be combined. Working behind the scenes, Gardner was able not only to stop further discussion of this idea but also to secure a substantial appropriation for the Durham school (now North Carolina Central University). Like Governor Charles B. Aycock many years earlier, Gardner also refused to support a proposal that revenue for public schools be apportioned according to the race from which it came. In the summer of 1929 he was photographed with two high

O. Max Gardner (1882–1947) of Shelby was governor from 1929 until 1933. His term was marked by serious labor unrest as well as problems growing out of the depression. (North Carolina Division of Archives and History, Raleigh)

school students, a white boy and a black girl, each a winner in a "Live at Home" essay contest, part of a campaign to encourage people to become self-sufficient by growing their own food. When criticized for posing with a black, he commented that in any future political campaign he would make use of the picture himself.

Gardner, having demonstrated his political skills in the General Assembly, set about gaining the confidence of the people. Resorting to a rather new device, he made radio addresses explaining his program, praising the legislature, and pointing out conditions that likely would concern citizens in the next few years. Gardner was such an astute politician that he came to be regarded as the founder of the "Shelby Dynasty," named for his hometown in Cleveland County. He and a significant number of other men from there, and some women as well, made their influence felt in the state for several decades—particularly through the use of political patronage. Gardner's brother-in-law, Clyde R. Hoey, became governor and a United States senator, while R. Gregg Cherry from adjoining Gaston County became governor. Gardner practiced law in Washington, D.C., where he became undersecretary of the Treasury. He later was named United States ambassador to the Court of St. James but died on the eve of sailing.

Economic Hardships

The panic of 1929, or the Great Depression, followed a period of large export trade in manufactured goods through foreign lending. A reduced domestic demand for goods kept private and corporate savings from being invested in further production which would have created new jobs. Growing mortgage debts, particularly on speculative property, and new local government indebtedness, especially for roads and streets in new developments, and, of course, the continuing decline in farm income combined to bring an end to the especially prosperous years between 1924 and 1926. A decline in the sale of automobiles began in 1927, yet a speculative construction boom—in the mountains of North Carolina, among other places—gave no hint of the disaster to follow.

"Easy money" led to speculation in stocks and bonds and in the mortgage market. Banks made large loans on inadequate security. In June 1929 some bankers became concerned about the steadily rising stock market, and the Federal Reserve Board raised the discount rate to tighten credit. Lenders began to call in loans that had been made for the purchase of stock. A slight decline in the stock market came late in September, followed by further declines in early and mid-October. The "crash" came on 29 October when banks that had made loans were called on to cover the difference between the loans and the actual value of stock put up as collateral. The financial system of the nation virtually collapsed. Hardly a bank anywhere escaped, and businesses of all kinds suffered—many being forced to shut down.

Whereas 98 banks closed in North Carolina in the 1920s, 194 shut down between 1930 and 1933. In 1930 alone, 88 banks failed. In the latter year, 233 building and loan associations also folded; 209 did so in 1933. As a result of these closures, many people lost their homes as well as their businesses. Many communities, particularly some depending on a rural trade, had no banking facilities.

One of the most serious causes of bank failures was "runs" on the bank when people became concerned about their money on deposit and began to withdraw it. With funds out on loan or invested, banks could seldom meet this sudden demand and they had no choice but to close. Also contributing to the crisis were the acceptance of inadequate collateral for loans, embezzlement by bank officials, and poor management. More careful supervision of banking practices by the state might have prevented some of the closings, but the Corporation Commission was not always diligent in performing its duties. On the other hand, sometimes when the bank inspector reported signs of weakness, no action was taken. Some bank officials, either because they were actually guilty of improper practices or because they felt burdened by the suffering in the community, committed suicide.

Not all of the banks that closed were in serious trouble. Some discontinued operations temporarily to protect their depositors. Once closed, however, a bank could not reopen until the state commissioner of banks examined its records and certified it to be sound. Many weathered this process and then carried on with the full confidence of their clientele. Others were reorganized and in time met their obligations, although not always totally. While some depositors received all of their deposits, some received nothing. The amount recovered from many banks ranged from 10 to 75 percent, sometimes paid over a period of several years.

Among the earliest agencies of government to feel the effects of the depression were the counties. Public revenue, deposited in many local banks, was sometimes lost as a result of the crash. In certain counties where incumbent officials might have held office for years, government had become inefficient and petty corruption was ignored. Under the direction of the governor, the General Assembly of 1931 created the Local Government Commission as a refinement of the 1927 County Government Advisory Commission. The older body had provided only limited assistance, such as information on budget classifications and audits. In contrast, the new commission was not only advisory in nature but it also was charged with approving or rejecting the issuance of bonds or notes by local governments and with auditing their accounts. The commission had the power to enforce its decisions by suits in the superior court; in addition, it was the agency through which earlier laws pertaining to local government were enforced.

With the depression exerting its full force on the people of his state, Governor Gardner in the early summer of 1930 turned to the Brookings Institution in Washington, D.C., for advice on how "more effectively to promote increased efficiency and economy in the conduct of the governmental affairs of the State." In response to his request this independent organization, privately funded to study problems of government and to make recommendations, investigated and analyzed conditions in North Carolina. It then presented a carefully prepared study of the structure and administration of state government together with reasonable suggestions for improvement. Copies of the Brookings Institution report were received in December and distributed to members of the legislature as well as to state officers, the press, and other interested individuals. In his address to the General Assembly on 9 January 1931, the governor recommended favorable action on a number of the institution's proposals. Surprisingly, nearly all of them were enacted into law. As a rule North Carolina governors had difficulty in obtaining approval of recommendations made to the second legislative session of their administration, but in these troubled times quibbling was laid aside.

University Consolidation

Leading the list of changes recommended by Brookings and approved by the legislature was the consolidation of the University of North Carolina (Chapel Hill), North Carolina State College (Raleigh), and the North Carolina College for Women (Greensboro) into a greater University of North Carolina. After 1 July 1932, a single board of trustees of one hundred members had the authority to control and manage all three branches as one university. It was anticipated that, by ending the duplication of programs and educational rivalry, these institutions could provide more effective service at a substantially reduced cost. A Commission on Consolidation was designated to plan the transition, and on 14 November 1932 Frank P. Graham became president of the Consolidated University of North Carolina. He had been president of the University at Chapel Hill since 1930. In 1938 the School of Engineering was moved from Chapel Hill to North Carolina State College in Raleigh, creating resentment among some Chapel Hill alumni.

New State Government Agencies

The General Assembly also created a Division of Purchase and Contract within the governor's office and gave it broad power over state purchases. Considerable economy resulted from the division's work in identifying sources of supplies, materials, and equipment and its adoption of a system of competitive bidding. Additional tasks included maintaining an inventory and overseeing the profitable disposal of obsolete or unused state property. This agency very quickly proved its effectiveness by saving the state more than $400,000 in the first year.

Another new agency, a Department of Personnel, was directed to survey the personnel needs of all state departments and bureaus, and to determine the cost and value of each organization. Salaries and wages were to be set and the qualifications of applicants certified. The personnel director would now examine budgets to ensure that expenditures were properly allotted. The bill also covered the personnel needs of cities, towns, and counties for all positions except teachers.

The recent failure of so many banks contributed to a general distrust of the Corporation Commission. This led to the creation of a Department of Banking to take over the banking supervision function previously assigned to the commission and the chief state bank examiner. In addition to banks, the new agency would supervise the state's insurance industry. The state treasurer and the attorney general were made members of a five-member body to advise the commissioner of banking.

The old Department of Labor and Printing became the new Department of Labor with provisions for a Division of Statistics, a Division of Standards and Inspections (to supersede the Child Welfare Commission), and a Division of Workmen's Compensation.

The State Board of Health, first created by the General Assembly in 1877, was in effect dismissed because of friction that developed among its members in 1930, and a totally new board was named. The secretary-treasurer, formerly the head administrative officer, would henceforth be named by the board with the approval of the governor; such approval had not been required under the old law. One of the largest and most important state departments, the board was charged with making and enforcing the state's public health policy including guidelines for quarantine and immunization.

The most sweeping Brookings recommendation called for the "short ballot." Under this system only a few state officials would be elected, leaving the governor to make a great many appointments. If he were to be responsible for a broad program, it was stressed, he should have authority to appoint the officials who would carry it out. Because this represented such a major shift in policy and would have required a constitutional convention, it received little consideration from the 1931 General Assembly.

The Brookings Institution report proposed a great many other changes as well, and some of them were implemented over a long period of time. For the present, however, it seemed that the secret ballot, workmen's compensation, consolidation of the three institutions of higher education, state maintenance of roads, increased support of education, and other changes made by Gardner's first legislative session, together with the creation of the local government commission in 1931, were enough.

Virginia's government had recently been reorganized in line with recommendations of the Brookings Institution, and Governor Gardner invited Virginia Governor Harry F. Byrd to address a joint session of the legislature on his state's experience. Illinois and Tennessee adopted similar administrative reorganization codes. In North Carolina a joint resolution of both houses of the General Assembly established a nine-member commission to study the state constitution and to report to the 1933 session. At the appointed time, the commission delivered its draft of a revised constitution, which was approved by the legislature for submission to a referendum of the electorate. However, because of an advisory opinion of the North Carolina Supreme Court it was never put to the people.[1] The draft proposed a number of significant changes including the granting of the veto to the governor. Among other provisions, one would have removed most of the limitations on the power of the General Assembly to tax. Another created an appointed State Board of Education with broader jurisdiction over the public schools, while still another granted authority to the Judicial Council, composed of all the judges of the supreme and the superior courts, to make rules of practice and procedure in the courts inferior to the supreme court.

Governor Gardner accomplished a great deal to help North Carolina survive the depression. Four achievements attracted national attention: assuming responsibility for the maintenance of county roads, thereby relieving local government of that expense; stabilizing the credit of counties and towns through the Local Government Act and keeping their credit good; uniting the three state-supported institutions of higher education as the Consolidated University of North Carolina; and taking responsibility for operating the public schools for the required six-month term, further easing the burden on local government. Continuation of the latter was possible largely through the adoption very early in the next administration of a 3 percent sales tax on virtually everything people bought except bread, flour, and meat. Nevertheless, necessary economies affected many school systems. There was talk of closing all public schools for a year or two while money was saved to maintain the same standard as before; instead of closing completely, however, some schools shut down their cafeterias, ceased to have chemistry laboratories and instead had teachers conduct experiments before the class, and discontinued the teaching of Latin and other foreign languages, music, art, typing, home economics, and other subjects not regarded as strictly essential.

The depression imposed numerous other hardships as well. The state budget was reduced by one-third, and the salaries of state employees were reduced

---

1. Governor J. C. B. Ehringhaus, Gardner's successor, asked the state supreme court whether the "election" (referendum) to decide the fate of the new constitution would meet the requirement that it be submitted to the next "general election" after its approval by the General Assembly. Since the end of the last session a referendum had already been held on the question of repealing the Eighteenth Amendment to the United States Constitution. The court advised the governor that another election would not meet that constitutional requirement.

by 20 percent under Gardner and by an additional 25 percent under J. C. B. Ehringhaus, governor from 1933 to 1937. However, agriculture—the mainstay of so many North Carolinians—was most drastically affected. During the good times from 1919 to 1923 cotton sold for more than 30 cents a pound, but by 1932 it had dropped to a mere 6½ cents. And whereas the state produced $62.4 million worth of cotton in 1929, it received only $19.5 million in 1932. Tobacco farmers also suffered as the price they received declined from a high of 26 cents a pound in 1926 to just 9 cents in 1932. A crop worth $88.6 million in 1929 dropped to $34.8 million in 1932. Most farmers received less for their crops than it cost to produce them, and as a result they could pay neither their fertilizer bill nor their taxes. Mortgages were foreclosed, property was sold for nonpayment of taxes, and sometimes land was simply abandoned because farming was so unproductive.

Widespread Suffering

Large numbers of rural people moved into the towns hoping to find employment. Relatives often did their best to take in desperate members of their family, and those with anything to share usually were generous in providing what relief they could. Hunger was rampant not only in the country but also in the towns; often families were obliged to survive on two or perhaps even one inadequate meal a day. Sometimes the only food available for days at a time might be cornmeal mush and fatback, collards only, or some other monotonous and unbalanced fare, and naturally the health of many, particularly children, deteriorated. In 1929 and 1930 public health doctors found that out of the 140,000 school children they examined in forty-one counties, 23,000 were suffering from malnutrition.

Driven to desperation, once scrupulously honest men stole to feed and clothe their families. Smokehouses in the country were broken into, orchards were raided, and in town milk delivered before daybreak often disappeared from front porches. A woodpile or clothes left to dry on a line after dark were too tempting to be resisted by someone whose children were cold. In the spring the tender leaves of dandelions and pokeweed furnished greens, and a little later in the season patches of wild blackberries and huckleberries were picked clean. The conditions of the early 1930s had not been known since the shortages experienced during the Civil War, and people became frantic in the face of what seemed to be a bleak future indeed. Even so, North Carolina fared much better than some of the other states. There were no dust storms like those that ravaged the midwestern states, where fertile topsoil blew away and barns, houses, and farm equipment were all but covered by dry soil blown by the wind. Although some North Carolina farmland had already been spoiled by constant use and soil erosion produced deep gullies, the problem was less serious than it was in Georgia, Alabama, and other southern states.

As farmers quickly felt the effects of hard times and as banks closed, industry also declined. The tobacco industry was slower to show signs of depression than were textiles and furniture. There was little competition in the tobacco industry, prices were reduced, and demand increased—a bag of Bull Durham tobacco, with which smokers rolled their own cigarettes, dropped to five cents. Utilities also escaped to a certain extent. By reducing rates and improving service, some of the telephone companies remained secure. Electric companies were able to offer service in new regions, and they also began to sell electrical appliances.

Unemployment and Labor Problems

Furniture manufacturing—the fourth most important industry in the state—was extremely hard hit by the recession of the 1930s. Production fell from some $53.6 million in 1929 to $26.6 million in 1933. Some plants had to close for as long as six months when the demand for furniture declined, and in other cases firms merged in an effort to survive.

The textile industry experienced the most serious loss in the number of workers. Profits had declined for several years, partly because of the change in women's styles; in 1910 and earlier a woman's dress required ten yards or more of cloth, but in the 1920s around two yards would suffice. Rapid changes in styles, particularly as they concerned prints and colors of cloth, often made material obsolete and required a quick change in production. Few American mills continued to produce for the foreign market, as they were supplanted by mills in Japan, India, and Great Britain. Efforts by management to reduce expenses and increase production were responsible for some of the complaints that led to labor unrest. Low wages and the stretch-out, the threat of millowners to bring in foreign workers when it seemed that child labor might be prohibited, and the appearance of labor organizers all contributed to the problems of the 1920s.

There were some 209,000 industrial workers in North Carolina about the time of the stock market crash. The rapid decline in the wage rate—to twelve cents an hour in one mill—and the total loss of employment by many people resulted in considerable labor unrest. The American Federation of Labor and the Textile Workers' Union of America sent organizers into the state to aid local workers in their efforts to obtain more reasonable wages and hours of work. Some of these organizers were, or were suspected of being, Communists; and soon after their arrival in North Carolina, it became apparent that they were not welcome by local labor, management, or government. Although intending to establish their headquarters in Charlotte as a base from which to organize the

South, they departed early in 1931 for Birmingham, Alabama, which proved to be more hospitable. North Carolina workers were left to fend for themselves.

In addition to the earlier strikes at Gastonia and Marion (where some lost their lives), there was unrest throughout the state. At mills in Greensboro 4,000 workers called for help. When union organizers appeared at the various mills, owners often fired workers who offered their support. Violence occurred in Wilmington, Raleigh, Leaksville, Draper, Spray, Winston-Salem, Bessemer City, and many other places. On a hot summer day in 1932, mobs of unemployed men drove from mill to mill in High Point, Jamestown, Kernersville, Lexington, and Thomasville cutting off electricity and trying to get workers to strike; occasionally they picked up reluctant employees and carried them outside. So successful were these mobs that 150 factories were closed and 15,000 workers walked out, although they nearly all returned the next day.

During these troubled times the governor sometimes was asked to call up the state guard, but he refused. Now and then, however, highway patrolmen were dispatched to keep order; once when this happened the unsympathetic Raleigh *News and Observer* referred to them as "North Carolina's Mounted Industrial Police." In some cases Gardner sent in a negotiator to arbitrate between management and labor. In at least one instance he assisted in making free flour available to strikers. Some strikes were ended through arbitration and others averted. Management sometimes gave in to the laborers' demands; it was also known to withdraw threats of dismissal or to rescind directives that had contributed to the unrest.

Relief

Under the leadership of Governor Gardner, the state initially believed that private agencies and local government would know best how to provide relief from the economic hardships of the depression. Those in need ought to have an opportunity to work rather than receive a handout, and people should be encouraged to help themselves. To that end, the governor introduced his "Live at Home" program soon after taking office. For a long time farmers had grown crops to be sold for cash; now it was recommended that they produce hay, corn, and other grains for their livestock and food for their families. By drying and preserving what was not needed immediately, it would be possible to provide subsistence over the winter. Home demonstration agents under the direction of North Carolina State College offered advice and encouraged the planting of gardens. (In 1929 schoolchildren across the state had already participated in an essay contest on the means and the benefits of living at home.) As a result of this program, in two years the land devoted to cotton declined by 536,000 acres and

Durham County women, under the direction of a Home Demonstration Agent, prepare corn for canning in the summer of 1933 during the depths of the depression. (North Division of Archives and History, Raleigh)

the production of corn increased by 10 million bushels. Women canned more fruits and vegetables than ever before, and the production of molasses increased by more than a million gallons.

In December 1930 the governor appointed a Council on Unemployment and Relief, which organized relief committees in eighty-two counties. Needs were identified and local governments were encouraged to create work-relief jobs. Funds were raised and distributed, generally through the Red Cross, the Community Chest, the Salvation Army, and similar organizations. A small amount of money from the State Emergency Fund was made available for the council's expenses but no salaries were paid. Free school lunches were provided and, in exchange for modest work, the itinerant poor were given hot meals and a temporary place to sleep. In some areas milk was made available for babies, local civic groups gave clothes to schoolchildren, and college students donated their Sunday evening meals to the needy. Several hospitals, notably the Baptist Hospital in Winston-Salem and Duke Hospital in Durham, reserved beds for the indigent, and the Duke Endowment helped to support charity cases in other hospitals. Many physicians gave free medical care to those unable to pay.

The roots of the depression, of course, lay outside of North Carolina, and local attempts to meet the needs of so many could not provide permanent solutions. Recognizing this problem, Congress established the Reconstruction Finance Corporation (RFC) to make funds available to the states. On 1 July 1932 the governor's Council on Unemployment and Relief was discontinued, and a new agency, the Governor's Office of Relief, headed by Fred W. Morrison, was created in September to direct relief activities in the state with these new federal funds. Between October and the end of the year, North Carolina received and allocated to the counties over $1.3 million in RFC grants for public works of permanent value. All money was used for wages, while necessary materials were purchased from local public and private funds. Among the projects undertaken were highway and road maintenance, construction and repair of public buildings, drainage, water and sewer extension, and farm and garden work to benefit communities at large.

In the summer of 1932, Franklin D. Roosevelt, an advocate of economy in government, was named his party's candidate for president. Speaking to the Democratic National Convention in Chicago on 2 July, he used the term "New Deal" to describe his projected program of relief, recovery, and reform for the nation. Immediate relief from the hardships that had grown steadily more severe since the fall of 1929 was essential; and then the nation should take action, he said, to recover from the hard times. Finally, if elected, he and his advisers would implement a program to make the national government better serve the "common good" of the people. In November, Roosevelt was the overwhelming choice of the nation. His victory in North Carolina was of the same magnitude—he received 497,566 votes to 208,344 for Herbert Hoover, the Republican candidate. Hoover carried only Avery and Yadkin counties although the vote was fairly close in a number of other Mountain and a few Sandhill counties.

Inaugurated in March 1933, the new president acted decisively and effectively. Just a few days after his swearing-in, Roosevelt ordered that certain categories of banks be closed. Then he called a special session of Congress where an Emergency Banking Act was passed giving him the authority to reorganize insolvent banks. This and related acts restored a degree of confidence in business nationwide.

Congress granted Roosevelt unprecedented powers, and he began a series of costly programs, some of which overlapped. Their objectives were not always clear, but most of them were intended to get money into the hands of desperate Americans as quickly as possible. The first New Deal agency was the Civilian Conservation Corps (CCC), established in March 1933 to provide jobs for single young men between the ages of seventeen and twenty-five, mostly from families on relief. They lived in temporary camps, wore drab uniforms, were organized (usually with the assistance of the army) into companies of around two hundred men each, and received $30 a month, of which $25 was sent to their families. There were sixty-one CCC camps in North Carolina from which young men went out daily to perform a variety of tasks such as planting trees, controlling erosion, constructing field terraces, reclaiming eroded land, eradicating pests,

A federal program with considerable influence in North Carolina was the Civilian Conservation Corps, which enabled young men to undertake a period of public service to acquire training and to help provide an income for their families. This CCC camp was at Globe in Caldwell County. (North Division of Archives and History, Raleigh)

laying out trails in public forests, and engaging in fire prevention activities. This proved to be very popular program and one that accomplished a great deal that was of lasting value; it was discontinued in 1942 when the employment picture had improved dramatically and the nation's involvement in World War II made it unnecessary.

For young people still in school, both high school and college, the National Youth Administration (NYA) was formed to provide funds to pay them for part-time work. The jobs were usually of a clerical nature and at school—such as in libraries and school offices. This enabled many of them to continue their education when their parents could not afford for them to do so.

Another early federal agency was the Federal Emergency Relief Administration (FERA), which operated for four and one-half years. Through this program, money appropriated by Congress was channeled to the states so they could provide work for the unemployed in worthwhile public projects. It was national policy to require those states that could do so to match the federal funds. North Carolina was already using funds raised locally, both public and private, under the Governor's Office of Relief; in addition, it was engaged in a highway construction program using a large number of otherwise unemployed laborers.

When federal officials insisted that North Carolina match the funds they provided, Governor J. C. B. Ehringhaus protested. The state, he maintained, was already doing all it could. The director of the FERA threatened to cut off funds to North Carolina but his warning had no effect. Realizing that termination of the program would only hurt the unemployed, he relented and the state continued to receive a portion of the federal funds, although never as much as most other southern states. The federal projects funded by the FERA were, therefore, not as numerous in North Carolina. Although administered by the state, the expenditure of these funds was supervised by federal officials. Under the program work projects were included, but some of the resources were used for cash grants as well as food and shelter.

Other federal agencies created to combat the effects of the depression included the Civil Works Administration (CWA), the Public Works Administration (PWA), and the Works Progress Administration (WPA). The latter was perhaps the most effective; in North Carolina it was funded at $175 million and employed thousands of men and women between July 1935 and December 1938. WPA projects included the construction of schools, armories, and post offices; the development of municipal and state parks, trails, and recreation areas; and the building of sidewalks and streets. One project that attracted a great deal of attention was the construction of 63,311 outdoor privies as well as the laying of sewerage lines in a number of municipalities. Artists were hired to paint murals for public buildings and to record the contemporary scene; musicians both composed and performed music (the North Carolina Symphony was a benefactor of this program); actors presented dramatic performances; writers recorded folklore and recollections of old-timers (an especially valuable undertaking was a series of interviews with former slaves to document their recollections); historians prepared local histories as well as a detailed guidebook for the state and a few cities; clerical workers contributed countless hours of special work in libraries, schools, and colleges, and in compiling statistics; and educators conducted classes in many useful subjects, often teaching the illiterate to read and write.

The Civil Works Administration provided 90 percent of the cost when localities furnished the remainder to build airfields, bridges, sidewalks, walls around public cemeteries, and schools; to lay sewer lines; and to undertake similar construction projects. Workers were engaged by the day for a thirty-hour week rather than under contract, and whenever practicable human labor rather than machinery was used. The CWA largely benefited people who lived in towns.

Rural areas were greatly aided by another agency, the Rural Electrification Administration (REA). Established in May 1935, the REA provided low-interest loans to farmers' cooperatives for building power (and later telephone) lines with

WPA labor in places where private power companies felt unjustified in offering service. This brought electricity to a large part of rural North Carolina, enabling farmers to have electric lights and numerous electric household appliances. It also permitted them to use many laborsaving devices, particularly milking machines and water pumps.

Agriculture was also of serious concern in Washington, D.C., and the Agricultural Adjustment Administration (AAA) was created to deal with that aspect of the nation's economy. This was one of the first programs aimed at recovery rather than relief and was controversial almost from the day of its adoption in May 1933. At first subsidies were offered to those who reduced the production of livestock and certain crops, but in response to objections it was changed to make payments to those who complied with the AAA programs and also carried out soil conservation measures. Allotments were provided for the production of wheat, cotton, tobacco, and other crops, and credit was granted for a variety of constructive programs such as terracing hillside land, planting soil-enriching crops, and converting exhausted fields to pastureland. Quotas were established for marketing as a means of controlling production and raising prices. Some of these features were reminiscent of proposals made by farm leaders many years before.

The National Recovery Administration (NRA) was established in June 1933 to bring government into business planning. It set minimum wages and hours of work, guaranteed the right of collective bargaining, provided codes to end wasteful competition, and provided for the licensing of business by government. The NRA was unpopular with many businessmen, and in May 1935 the Supreme Court ruled unanimously that "Congress cannot delegate legislative power to the President to exercise an unfettered discretion to make whatever laws he thinks may be needed or advisable for the rehabilitation and expansion of trade or industry." Shortly afterward Congress passed an act with virtually the same objectives as the NRA. Its primary goal was to reduce unemployment by spreading work among more people through shorter working hours. Although this program was promulgated by Congress, it was largely enforced by the states, and toward that end North Carolina created an Unemployment Compensation Commission in 1936. Congress in 1938 passed a Wages and Hours Act providing a minimum wage and a maximum workweek of forty-four hours for industries that manufactured goods that moved in interstate commerce. This new federal authority henceforth would make itself felt in the nation's business.

One more program of the Roosevelt administration to leave a lasting impression on the country was the Social Security system. Implemented in August 1935, it was intended to provide relief on a more permanent basis against the loss of income from death, old age, retirement, unemployment, or sickness and to aid dependent children. Basically, however, it was a program of old-age assistance

A tenant farmer in Chatham County in July 1939. Agricultural programs implemented during the depression not only helped a great many farmers to overcome personal hardships but also taught them new skills and introduced them to new crops. (North Carolina Division of Archives and History, Raleigh)

and initially applied to a limited number of situations. A survey in 1935 revealed that only 65,206 people were eligible to participate in the program. Over the years its coverage was extended until by 1972 nearly all gainfully employed workers except federal employees fell under its provisions. "Contributions" to the Social Security system were collected from the wages of workers, and on retirement or disability, under the regulations of the system, those eligible began to receive monthly payments.

The New Deal programs in North Carolina, as well as in most of the nation, accomplished their purpose. Some, such as the CCC, the WPA, the NYA, and the CWA, were discontinued between 1938 and the early 1940s. Others, however, such as the REA, wage and hour legislation, farm production and marketing restrictions, and, of course, Social Security became firmly entrenched. Most of them served the state well, contributing in an important way to rescuing the people from the degradation of the depression. Government loans enabled large numbers of farmers either to save their farms or, in the case of tenant farmers, to acquire land of their own. Young people through the CCC and the NYA could continue their education. Jobs became available, and people were able to resume a normal, respectable life. Because the Roosevelt administration had had to rely heavily on the states for program implementation and enforcement and because conditions returned to normal after a relatively short time, some aspects of the social reform did not become permanent. Millowners and farmers returned to many of their former practices—labor unions did not flourish, and farmers resumed the planting of their customary "money crops."

During these years several North Carolinians rendered useful service in the national government. Congressman Robert L. Doughton was chairman of the House Ways and Means Committee; Lindsay C. Warren was comptroller general of the United States; Josephus Daniels, who had been secretary of the navy in World War I when Roosevelt was assistant secretary, served as ambassador to Mexico; and R. D. W. Connor, first head of the North Carolina Historical Commission and more recently a professor of history at the University of North Carolina, was named first archivist of the United States in 1934 and organized that new agency of the federal government.

25

NEW POINTS TO PONDER
IN A RESTLESS WORLD

NORTH CAROLINA was one of the last states to feel the full effects of the depression, and it was one of the first to enjoy a return to normalcy. Tobacco prices were good in 1937 and brought farmers $154 million. Textile plants had begun to receive orders by the summer of 1938 and many were operating full-time. Although cotton prices were low, food crops were beginning to contribute significantly to farm income as a result of diversification. In cash received from all crops, North Carolina stood third in the nation. Poultry raising, cattle, and dairying were becoming increasingly important. During the first ten months of the year, 120 new industries were established in the state and 68 existing plants were enlarged. The Ecusta Paper Corporation, with threats of war in Europe, moved from France and established a $2 million plant at Brevard primarily to produce cigarette paper but writing paper and other products as well. Altogether these new industries added $10 million annually to the payrolls of the state.

Signs of Progress

North Carolina could take pride in many other recent accomplishments. No longer did counties maintain chain gangs using prisoners to work on roads or under contract to private employers. Now the state operated the prison system. It also maintained a 58,000-mile network of highways, transported more students to school than any other state in the nation, provided free schoolbooks for the elementary grades, and supported an eight-month school term. Each month 32,000 checks were sent to persons entitled to old-age assistance and over 20,000 went to aid dependent children. Provision was also made to assist the blind, and Confederate veterans and widows were more generously supported "by a grateful state" than previously, the governor reported.

Twenty years after gaining the suffrage, women were taking considerable interest in government. They cast a significant percentage of the total vote in the state and served in various capacities with such agencies as the Board of Charities and Public Welfare, the Board of Agriculture, the State Planning Board, the Industrial Commission, the Rural Electrification Authority, the Committee on Roadside Control and Improvement, the State Board for Vocational Education, the Textbook Commission, and the State Council for National Defense. Women were also represented on the board of directors of the North Carolina Railroad; on the boards of trustees of nearly all of the state institutions of higher education, asylums, hospitals, and correctional institutions; and on assorted study commissions.

The state was in the midst of an extensive building program. In some cases it provided 55 percent of the cost, the remainder being covered by a federal grant, frequently under the Works Progress Administration. In other cases the cost was covered by a bond issue. Among the buildings completed in Raleigh were the Education Building, the State Highway Building, the Supreme Court Building, and the Revenue Building. State hospitals, schools and colleges, and various custodial institutions around the state also were included in this program. On the three campuses of the University of North Carolina some thirty new buildings were constructed. No additional taxes were levied, and the sales tax on food was eliminated. At the same time the state was able to reduce its bond indebtedness by the payment of over $30 million in 1938.

Among the new topics of concern or emphasis were adult education, public welfare, general health measures including a campaign to eradicate venereal diseases and to encourage birth control, juvenile delinquency, highway safety, and protection against crime. In connection with the latter, the State Bureau of Investigation was organized "for the investigation of crime and apprehension of criminals . . . [and] to assist local officials in counties and municipalities." An officers' fund was established for those killed or injured in service.

On 2 September 1939 the Great Smoky Mountains National Park was dedicated by President Roosevelt. This was the culmination of activity that had begun forty years earlier when the Asheville Board of Trade organized the Appalachian National Park Association. North Carolina and Tennessee, through legislative generosity and gifts from numerous individuals, notably John D. Rockefeller, acquired and turned over to the United States secretary of the interior 463,000 acres of land at a cost of $12 million. Some federal relief agencies, especially the Civilian Conservation Corps, were involved in laying out roads, camp sites, and picnic areas, and in protecting the land from poachers. This reserve was destined to become the most popular national park in America.

Before leaving office in 1940, Governor Clyde R. Hoey reflected on the recent achievements of North Carolina. As a result of the state's new advertising program, he observed, tourism during the past four years had grown from a $36 million to a $102 million industry. Another recent program was the renting of textbooks for high school use. The General Assembly had also provided funds for a forestry service and a mineral assay office in the Department of Conservation and Development. Hoey was especially pleased with the modern probation system, which enabled more than 32,000 offenders to be gainfully employed instead of going to prison. Commending the religious and educational work among prisoners and particularly the reclamation program, he reported that North Carolina's parole system was considered to be among the ten best in the nation. Through local religious, business, and civic groups, efforts were made to obtain jobs for prisoners when they were discharged. The highway patrol had been increased from 121 to 188 officers and improved by equipment and training. Graduate courses were offered at the colleges for blacks, and a program was instituted to erase the salary gap between white and black teachers.

Although the Prohibition Amendment to the United States Constitution had been repealed in 1933, soon after which "light" wine and some beer became available, North Carolina generally remained "dry" until 1935. In 1937 a statewide county option liquor bill was enacted, and the first State Board of Alcoholic Control was named. Many North Carolinians, however, regarded "liquor as Public Enemy Number 1."

Military Maneuvers in the State

Many residents had an opportunity, whether they realized it or not, to glimpse the future during the period 3–17 October 1938 when a joint Antiaircraft-Air Corps exercise, involving both army and navy personnel and planes, was held in the region of the state lying between Fort Bragg, where headquarters were established, and the coast. With some three hundred "stations" participating, this was the most extensive military training exercise ever held in the United States. While the announced goal of this undertaking might have concerned some people, there was as yet no cause for alarm. "Its purpose," newspapers reported in August, "will be to observe the approach of enemy airplanes and to report promptly to the Defense Commander at Fort Bragg the strength, types of planes, altitude, speed, and direction of movement of the attacking air force, in order that the defending pursuit aviation may be able to intercept this force and in order that the defending antiaircraft artillery may be warned in advance of its approach." Civilian volunteers, in much the same capacity as later air raid wardens, were also involved.

While occupied with affairs at home, neither individual North Carolinians nor their government was oblivious to events abroad. By 1939 the national policy of isolationism was obsolete. Japan for a number of years had been busily purchasing scrap iron, brass, copper, and other metals from the United States, and it was clear from newspaper accounts that militarists controlled that country. In addition to secretly fortifying isolated Pacific islands in violation of treaties made in 1921, Japan in the early 1930s invaded Manchuria, Tientsin, and finally Shanghai.

In postwar Europe, Germany gradually was taken over by some extreme nationalists. Under the National Socialists, or Nazis, the nation rearmed and began a series of attacks on its neighbors, entering the Rhineland in March 1936. After forcing a reluctant Austria into collaboration and grabbing Czechoslovakia, Germany overran Poland in the fall of 1939. France and Great Britain, having previously pledged to protect Poland's independence, were drawn into the conflict.

In mid-September 1939, on the eve of a session of Congress called to review the nation's commitment to neutrality, Governor Hoey endorsed a proposal that the United States make available to Great Britain and France the military supplies to defeat Germany and Russia, the latter two having formed a nonaggression pact to protect Germany's eastern frontier. Such a plan, Hoey maintained, would not involve America in the war. "Our example and our action would have a wholesome effect upon the other neutrals and a sobering influence upon Germany," he anticipated. "It is safer to sell supplies than to send men and if England and France can win this war that is our best security for peace." A few days later he again spoke in favor of altering the neutrality policy. "I am thoroughly devoted to the ideals of peace and I do not subscribe to the view that this country will inevitably be drawn into this war," he said. "I am not ready for Hitler to dictate the policy of America. I believe in building our defenses at home so strong that we can take care of ourselves in any war that might be forced upon us. We shall not go to foreign shores, but we shall maintain and defend our rights at home."

Events moved inexorably toward war. Regular army recruiting stations opened across the state, and some towns even had quotas that they were asked to fill. In July and August 1940 the National Guard held a twenty-one-day camp of field instruction. On 16 September Congress passed the Selective Service Act, and on 16 October, when all men between the ages of twenty-one and thirty-six were required to register, more than 450,000 in North Carolina did so; election officials, assisted by countless volunteers, conducted the registration in a single day. Speaking to the Southern Society of New York on 6 December 1940, Hoey observed that "America is now thoroughly aroused and patriotically united." Under a lend-lease arrangement the United States made military supplies available to Great Britain (France had surrendered to Germany in June 1940), and, before the draft ended, millions of young Americans had entered the various branches of the military service. It appeared that while the United States vigorously prepared for war and assisted Great Britain to the fullest extent short of combat, most Americans idealistically expected to remain merely a witness to battle.

In Washington, D.C., however, there was quiet talk—as early as 1938—of the possibility of becoming involved in a two-ocean war. Having agreed not to fortify the Pacific islands, the United States realized that it could not hold the Philippines or Guam. But Alaska, Hawaii, and Panama must be secure. By invading Russia in June 1941, Germany violated its own recent treaty. In the fall of 1941 extensive military exercises on an unprecedented scale were conducted across much of the middle section of the two Carolinas; more than 400,000 men participated. A force of 196,000 "Blue" troops from North Carolina attacked a "Red" force not quite as large that was defending Camden, South Carolina. This exercise, which employed tanks and infantry, foretold action soon to occur in Europe, but especially in North Africa.

World War II

On 7 December 1941 Japanese planes from a fleet of carriers, which had crossed the Pacific Ocean undetected, bombed and strafed the United States fleet at Pearl Harbor, Hawaii, virtually sealing the fate of American forces in the Philippines and elsewhere in the Pacific. Congress declared war on Japan the following day and on the eleventh Germany and its ally, Italy, declared war on the United States. World War II, in which most of Europe had been embroiled since 1939, now engaged the United States as well. After recently preparing itself for this eventuality, the United States began frantically to adjust to the new conditions.

Coastal North Carolina became involved in the conflict almost immediately. The Atlantic Ocean off Cape Hatteras soon came to be called "Torpedo Junction" because of the activity of German submarines there. Tankers transporting oil from the Gulf Coast were particularly vulnerable between January and May 1942, when some 4,000 seamen lost their lives. Burning oil slicks were common sights, and it was not unusual for a German submarine to surface and fire on men struggling in the water. Regional hospitals treated large numbers of badly injured and burned sailors. Many bodies were washed ashore; those of some English sailors were buried in a small cemetery established at Ocracoke. Rumors circulated of German sailors landing under cover of darkness, and of German newspapers being left on seats in movie theaters in coastal towns, but none of these could be verified.

Construction had been under way for some time before the Japanese attack to accommodate more troops at Fort Bragg, a regular army post since World War I, and at Cherry Point Marine Air Station, begun in July 1941 and opened in March 1942. Camp Davis, an antiaircraft and artillery training base, opened in April 1941 and attained a maximum capacity of 60,000. For a time it attracted

For many years before the Japanese attack on Pearl Harbor on 7 December 1941, Japan had purchased large quantities of scrap metal from sources in the United States. These were used largely to manufacture and stockpile munitions of war. Once the United States entered World War II, however, the collection of scrap metal was renewed with vigor, this time to supplement the resources of the Allies. This large quantity of assorted metal was photographed in Raleigh in 1942. (North Carolina Division of Archives and History, Raleigh)

considerable local attention as giant balloons, a part of antiaircraft defense, could be seen tethered above the base. Seymour Johnson Air Base at Goldsboro was also established in 1941 as an Army Air Force Technical Training School. The following year construction began on the 173-square-mile site that became Camp Lejeune, a marine base. Soon more than a dozen other bases around the state, such as Camp Butner north of Durham and the Overseas Replacement Depot in Greensboro, were ready to receive, process, and train men and women. Before the war ended in 1945, more fighting men had been trained in North Carolina than in any other state. Sometimes Allied soldiers also received special training at North Carolina bases.

A double row of army barracks at Fort Bragg during World War II. (North Carolina Division of Travel and Tourism, Raleigh)

A "defense boom" dealt the final blow to the depression throughout most of the nation. Federal contracts for $10 billion went largely to shipyards and aircraft plants, but to lesser suppliers as well. Around $2 billion of this came to North Carolina for goods made by nearly a million men and women engaged in defense work. As during World War I, women worked alongside men in manufacturing, construction, and other types of work that formerly had been regarded as unsuitable for them.[1] Shipyards at Elizabeth City, New Bern, and Wilmington built submarine chasers, minesweepers, and merchant ships. Textiles that had long been produced in the state for world trade were now provided for the government—including sheets, towels, canvas, socks, parachutes, blankets, underwear, material for outer clothing, and even shoelaces. A federal official, commenting on the state's war efforts, said "so wide is the variety of production . . . that every soldier and sailor in the service of the Nation either wears or carries some article manufactured in North Carolina."

Some manufacturers converted from peacetime goods to such things as

---

1. Safety regulations for hazardous positions sometimes required that female workers wear slacks. This marked the beginning of a new fashion in women's apparel.

During World War II several camps were established in North Carolina for prisoners of war, who occasionally were permitted to work for modest wages on adjoining farms. Some of them returned to the state many years later as tourists. These German prisoners of war were photographed at Fort Bragg in May 1942. (North Carolina Division of Archives and History, Raleigh)

ammunition, rockets, bomb clusters, and radar components. Lumber for barracks, bunks, and boxes also came from North Carolina as did crushed stone for roads and mica for insulation. In Vance County a newly discovered source of tungsten, used in hardening steel, replaced European sources when they were cut off. The state's commissioner of agriculture, W. Kerr Scott, commended farmers for their diligence in providing "food, feed, and fibre" for the war effort. Wheat production doubled, even in the face of a labor shortage, and the quantity of peanuts, hay, and both Irish and sweet potatoes increased dramatically. North Carolina ranked either third or fourth in the nation in the volume and value of its agricultural crops.

The scarcity of farm labor was a serious handicap for farmers, but an unusual solution to the problem was found. There were a number of unpublicized prisoner of war camps in the state, and from several of them prisoners were recruited to pick cotton and harvest peanuts for very modest pay. In the fall of 1943 the commanding officer of a field artillery battalion at Fort Bragg was thanked for providing troops to guard Italian prisoners who worked for thirty days in eastern North Carolina. Many years later some of these former prisoners of war returned to renew their acquaintance with the families they had worked for during the war.

In the spring of 1944 the North Carolina Pharmaceutical Association conducted a special sale of war bonds in order to buy five ambulance planes for the war effort. The drive was unusually successful: more than $2.3 million was raised—almost $1 million more than in any other state—and fourteen planes were purchased. The next greatest number purchased by another state was nine.

Among the numerous changes that occurred in daily life during the war was the rationing of food and other scarce commodities. A federal agency, the Office of Price Administration (OPA), with the cooperation of state agencies, directed the activities of rationing boards. Footwear, gasoline, coffee, sugar, meat, and rubber goods were among the scarcest consumer goods. Prices were controlled through the OPA. The planting of Victory gardens and the canning of food were encouraged; and collecting points were established for the recycling of scrap rubber, tin, paper, and other scarce material. Substitutes were developed for some things; "leisure" shoes requiring little or no leather, for example, resulted in the later popularity of footwear made of plastic, canvas, and other material. The scarcity of lead for such containers as tubes for toothpaste, salves, and lotions led to the development of soft plastic containers.

The civilian population was also required to observe a blackout in some parts of the state, particularly those within twenty miles of the coast. People everywhere were encouraged to conserve electricity. Air raid drills were held, and home guard units were organized in the coastal region and at the sites of potential sabotage elsewhere.

In previous wars—from the colonial period through World War I—military organizations had often been formed in a community under local officers, and the men remained together as a unit throughout the conflict. Thus, when a unit suffered heavy losses in battle, the "manhood" of a whole community might be virtually eliminated, and for a generation it would be marked by large numbers of widows and unmarried women. In World War II, however, except for a few National Guard units called into service at the beginning, this practice was abandoned. Men from a particular community or even from a single state—especially those who were drafted as well as many volunteers—would be scattered throughout many military units intended for different zones of action. Because of this policy few men from North Carolina served together; as a result, they made friends from widely different places and many displayed a more cosmopolitan attitude after they returned home.

Women were not drafted, but auxiliary services were created through which they assisted the army, navy, or marines. They often relieved men for combat.

Wartime shortages necessitated the rationing of many items, and books of coupons were issued to ensure equitable distribution. Foods such as coffee, sugar, butter, and most meats were rationed, as well as gasoline, shoes, and other clothing. There were quotas or restrictions on certain products, and in some cases it was necessary to turn in the used item to get a replacement—for example, the soft metal toothpaste tubes then in common use. (North Carolina Division of Archives and History, Raleigh)

Among the positions they filled were those of driver, teletypist, telephone operator, weather observer, aircraft mechanic, control tower assistant, parachute rigger, aerial gunnery instructor, hospital technician, personnel and payroll clerk, musician, chaplain's assistant, and cook. And, of course, nurses were much in demand in all theaters of action. There were also female physicians. Dr. Margaret O. Craighill, of Southport, was the first woman to attain that distinction when she was commissioned a major in the Army Medical Corps.

It was usually as individuals rather than in large groups that North Carolinians were sent to different camps for basic training. Afterward they might be dispersed around the world. Since it was national policy to try to end the war in Europe first, many men were sent to England for a bit of "polishing" before serving in the European theater. There they witnessed the extensive damage suffered in English cities from German bombs and rockets. After the Allied landing in Europe in June 1944, American troops joined the Allies in France, Italy, Germany, and elsewhere in Europe, or in North Africa. Others wound up in the Pacific having first spent some time in Hawaii or Australia, but many went directly to New Guinea or one of the other islands in a campaign of "island hopping" that finally led by way of the Philippines to Japan. India, Burma, and even China claimed others, often requiring their services for two or three years at a stretch without a furlough.

Those in the navy also saw service around the world, sometimes aboard troopships ferrying soldiers and marines, sometimes on submarine duty, or aboard a battleship or aircraft carrier. Still others were pilots, navigators, bombardiers, or mechanics, or held other assignments with the army or navy air corps.

After a period of hard fighting and rapid movement across Germany in the early spring of 1945, the Allies forced the Nazis to surrender on 7 May 1945. In the Pacific successes at sea, from the air, and finally by invasion of Japanese-held territory, costly though they were in life and matériel, took the Allies closer to Japan. A lone bombing raid on Tokyo in March 1945 leveled sixteen square miles, killed 80,000 people, and left another 1.5 million homeless, yet the Japanese were determined to continue the fight. In late July, Japan was called upon to surrender and warned of the impending destruction of eleven more cities. When Tokyo ignored this warning, American troops in the Philippines were issued equipment for a fall or early winter invasion of Japan.

With President Franklin D. Roosevelt's approval, scientists had been developing a bomb that used atomic fission. Following the death of Roosevelt in April, President Harry S Truman made the decision to drop the first atomic bomb on Japan. On 6 August 1945 Hiroshima was the target, and 75,000 people died. After further warnings which the Japanese again ignored, a second atomic bomb was dropped on the ninth; this time Nagasaki was hit and 39,000 people lost their lives. In both instances, of course, large numbers were also badly hurt. On 14 August Japan at last capitulated, and aboard an American battleship anchored in Tokyo Bay a formal instrument of surrender was signed on 2 September.

Around 258,000 men and women from North Carolina served in the army, 90,000 in the navy, and 13,000 in the marines.[2] Of these 4,088 were killed in action. North Carolinians won the Congressional Medal of Honor, the Navy

---

2. The air force did not become an independent branch of the United States military establishment until 1947, when the National Security Act created the Department of Defense to consist of the army, the navy, and the air force. The navy, however, retained control of naval and marine aviation.

Cross, the Distinguished Flying Cross, the Air Medal, and countless other medals and decorations.

Wartime Accomplishments and Postwar Planning

The state's primary wartime chief executive was J. Melville Broughton. Elected governor in November 1940, he was the only native of Raleigh ever to hold that post. In his inaugural address on 9 January 1941 Broughton laid out a progressive program, which, above all else, stressed the importance of a balanced budget, a tradition he insisted be continued. Most of his proposals were implemented during the next four years.

Near the end of his term Broughton delivered a radio message reviewing some of the accomplishments of the state since he had taken office. The people had been unusually generous in their support of the nation's war effort, particularly in purchasing war bonds. Nearly 350,000 North Carolinians, he noted, were then in the armed services while uncounted numbers of men and women from elsewhere had been trained at camps and bases in the state.

Farmers had met all of the demands made on them by the federal government in spite of labor shortages, restrictive regulations, and the unavailability of adequate farm machinery. Singling out the dairy industry, the governor reported that in 1944, for the first time in the state's history, North Carolina produced enough milk for both home consumption and export to other states. The future of dairying was assured by a Council of State allocation of $115,000 for the improvement of dairy equipment and laboratory facilities at North Carolina State College. Progress was anticipated in another area as well since the newly organized North Carolina Engineering Foundation, Inc., had as its goal the improvement of the Engineering Department at the college.

In public education the year 1944 saw the inauguration of the first full nine-month school year. Equal salaries were now provided for both black and white teachers with the appropriation of over a million dollars annually to supplement the salaries of blacks. A twelfth year had been added to the curriculum, and public school activities had been consolidated under the direction of a new State Board of Education. Also during the Broughton administration, the General Assembly devised a retirement system for teachers and state employees, and the North Carolina Textile Vocational School was established in Belmont.

The operations of training and correctional institutions had been consolidated under a newly created State Board of Correction and Training. This had resulted in some economies, but more importantly in better care for the inmates of various institutions. Broughton anticipated that, with the recent opening of a new facility for black girls, it would be possible to provide a more effective program of rehabilitation.

A particularly significant achievement was a comprehensive survey of the state's mineral resources. Long known as "Nature's Sample Case" because of its great variety of minerals, North Carolina proved to be a valuable source for scarce and important natural resources during the war. With the assistance of the United States Bureau of Mines and an allocation of $300,000, both tungsten, already mentioned, and manganese were discovered, and more than four hundred mines of various kinds were opened and operated. A research laboratory was also established at North Carolina State College in Raleigh.

The state's various institutions of higher education made substantial contributions in spite of wartime limitations. The Naval Pre-flight School at Chapel Hill was nationally recognized; State College trained army air cadets, and offered naval engineering training and specialized training for other military units; and the Agricultural and Technical College for Negroes in Greensboro became a training station for black soldiers in different branches of the armed forces.

During the war years the state's leadership continued to look to the future and to make plans for peacetime. On one occasion Governor Broughton pointed out that, when the war was over and many of the military installations were closed, surplus equipment and buildings undoubtedly would become available to counties and municipalities. Schools, libraries, and hospitals, he mentioned particularly, might better serve the public if early plans were made to acquire this property. During this period some of the state's cultural leaders were assembled to plan for the postwar development of the North Carolina Symphony and a state art museum. Planning committees were named, and in due time this foresight bore fruit.

Since North Carolina governors could not succeed themselves, each served only for a four-year term. They also lacked the veto power, which further limited their effectiveness. Their accomplishments and the success of the program they presented to the General Assembly depended on their influence or support in the legislature. If a majority of the legislators belonged to the same party as the governor and if they were of the same political philosophy, he was likely to prevail. Since the late 1930s all but four of the dozen governors who served through 1978 had also been legislators; of the four who had not, two had presided over the senate as lieutenant governor. This meant that they could count on considerable support from their recent colleagues in the General Assembly. During the same period some Democratic legislators had served as many as thirteen terms; none had served less than four. Party loyalty and a willingness to exchange favors or to "make a bargain" in the hope of future support often determined the course of events in North Carolina government. Because of the strength of the Democratic party, it was unlikely that a Republican administration would have the wholehearted backing of the General Assembly.

In the 1944 general election Democrat R. Gregg Cherry of Gastonia was elected by the customarily large margin over his Republican opponent. Cherry had served seven terms in the legislature. Inaugurated on 4 January 1945, the new governor proposed that the General Assembly enact a sound policy for the state. The general fund surplus, accumulated since the war began, should, he suggested, be held in part to pay the state's bond indebtedness when it matured and the remainder held as a postwar reserve fund for use as a cushion against a sudden decline in revenue or for whatever purpose the legislature might decide in the future. Schools were a major concern, and Cherry advocated higher salaries for teachers with A-grade certificates and for superior teachers, free eighth-grade textbooks and minimum rent for those used in the ninth grade and above, and enforcement of compulsory attendance. Matters of statewide interest that had been laid aside during the war, such as the needs of higher education, highways, agriculture, and rural electrification and telephone extension, should be considered as well. Anticipating the end of the war, the new governor discussed the role of the state in the readjustment of returning service people. He suggested that action should be taken to prepare for the thousands of men and women who would be attending school under what he called the "G.I. Plan"—federal provisions to pay tuition and living expenses for honorably discharged veterans who wanted to continue their education. Care for the physically and mentally ill, economic development, public welfare, the preservation of historical records, fair treatment for labor, and the problems of public safety were also among the topics that Cherry suggested be addressed.

Public health, long a matter of concern to the state, was assigned a higher priority as the State Board of Health initiated programs to alleviate or eradicate diphtheria, hookworm, malaria, rabies, smallpox, syphilis, tuberculosis, and typhoid fever. In time the state also sought to eliminate such health hazards as dust, industrial waste, and water pollutants.

Experimental Rockets Tested

Although Camp Davis in North Carolina closed near the end of the war, the navy retained its lease on the coastal portion of the base that included Topsail Island. Lying between the Intracoastal Waterway and the Atlantic Ocean, the narrow island is about twenty-five miles long between New River Inlet on the north and New Topsail Inlet on the south. In 1947 at this isolated spot, off limits to prying eyes, the Naval Ordnance Testing Station—with the cooperation of the

Kellet Corporation and the staff of the applied physics laboratory of the Johns Hopkins University—began work on a secret project. A launching pad was built near the northern end of the island, and at regular intervals along the edge of the ocean seven tall, thick concrete towers were erected with apertures in which cameras were placed to record the passage of experimental rockets. When a rocket was fired, the cameras were activated by wires from the firing pad. A second-stage firing while it was in flight accelerated the rocket's speed, and the cameras were set to record it. After studying the film, scientists could make adjustments. Soon rockets overshot the length of Topsail Island, and the project was transferred to White Sands, New Mexico. Eventually, this early experimentation in rocketry led to manned space flights and a moon landing. To many North Carolinians, the pioneering work at Topsail Island was a suitable follow-up to the Wright brothers' success at Kitty Hawk earlier in the century.

Polio Epidemic

Poliomyelitis posed a particularly difficult problem when it struck 2,498 North Carolinians in 1948. Little was known about the disease, and when it raged through the state public meetings were frequently canceled, theaters and swimming pools were closed, people avoided crowds, and those who could manage to do so lived in isolation in sometimes vain attempts to avoid it. A serious, crippling, and even fatal illness, polio had appeared in North Carolina since at least 1918 when 23 cases were reported. For the next half century seldom were fewer than 20 cases reported annually, and in some years the incidence was very high: 675 cases in 1935, 861 in 1944, 756 in 1950, and 313 in 1959. Many victims of infantile paralysis, as the disease was generally known, were treated at the State Orthopedic Hospital in Gastonia. In 1959 North Carolina became the first state in the nation to require the inoculation of all children, and it played a significant role in the distribution of the newly developed Salk poliomyelitis vaccine. No cases were reported in 1965 and rarely since has even a single case been diagnosed. Yet for many years thousands of people who had been maimed by the disease continued to serve as vivid reminders of its often devastating effects.

Expanded Role of the Federal Government

In the light of subsequent developments, it is interesting to recognize the foresight of three of the governors of North Carolina who were closely associated with the Great Depression and World War II. As time passed the federal government assumed an ever-expanding role in areas that were either previously untouched by that level of government or considered to be the province of the state. This included trade, labor, production, education, housing, social relations, and other aspects of daily life. Some actions taken by the national government, to be sure, were essential to safeguard against the total breakdown of law and order and to facilitate the return of full employment and prosperity, but most North Carolinians expected that the policies adopted to accomplish these desirable ends were temporary.

In a speech presented at a national governors' conference in 1937, Governor Clyde R. Hoey cited the new and growing use of federal funds for schools, highway construction, relief of the poor, the regulation of labor and agriculture, crime control, and other activities formerly managed by the states. In the continued use of federal funds, Hoey anticipated the demand for federal control, and he warned his fellow governors that if they did not regain control of the proper functions of the states they must expect "assumption of authority by the Federal Government."

Subsequently Governor J. Melville Broughton, in a January 1943 address before the Council of State Governments, echoed his predecessor's remarks. "If Thomas Jefferson were alive today . . . he would doubtless be greatly disturbed by the vast powers which the Federal government has appropriated from the states," Broughton stated. "He would probably invoke the Tenth Amendment which he hoped would be the shield and the buckler of the rights of the states. The Tenth Amendment is, of course, the most meaningless section of our Constitution." In April, speaking at the Southern Regional Council, the governor further observed that "there has been a vast expansion of Federal power" which he characterized as "alarming." In his opinion, just as it may have been in Hoey's, the depression and the war were responsible for much of this, yet "unsound thinkers in government have undoubtedly sought to use the emergency to exploit schemes that are abhorrent to our form of government—schemes that would wither in the normal light of true American principles." Although Hoey lacked the benefit of foresight, he did recognize that his state was being pulled most reluctantly into twentieth-century political reality. Governor Broughton also understood what was happening. He urged that for the time being the states put forth their best efforts to win the war but afterward to be ready "to take over every responsibility which they can handle better than the National government."

Finally, Governor R. Gregg Cherry in his inaugural address touched on the same subject. "The Tenth Amendment of the Federal Constitution," he reminded the legislators and his other listeners, "was intended to define and to maintain the line of demarcation between the powers expressly granted to the Federal union and those reserved to the states or to the people." Although he urged cooperation with the federal government in its "true functions," he noted that "the Federal republic owes us the duty of recognizing the functions and the duties not expressly assigned to the republic." He hoped that North Carolina would not "acquiesce in a policy, the consequence of which is to impair the revenue of the state or to determine the character of its social institutions." The warnings of all three governors were prophetic, of course, but to no avail. Power, once yielded, can be regained only through great effort, and the states lacked the unity necessary to recover what they had lost.

Health Concerns

Governor Cherry often spoke of "human values," and his concern for the welfare of people marked many of his public addresses. He was particularly effective in promoting his Good Health Program. Under his leadership the state acquired hospital facilities at the site of Camp Butner north of Durham, a training school to accommodate two hundred mentally deficient children was opened, and a hospital to treat more than a thousand mentally ill was established. The number of health care personnel in North Carolina increased significantly, new hospitals and medical clinics opened, and the General Assembly provided more than $9 million for permanent improvements in existing facilities. Funds were appropriated in 1947 to create the Division of Health Affairs at the University of North Carolina, and two years later schools of dentistry and nursing were added. In 1952 North Carolina Memorial Hospital also opened in Chapel Hill.

Labor, Unions, and Strikes

A Department of Labor and Printing, created by the General Assembly in 1887, had done little more than compile statistics, issue reports, and make recommendations. In 1931 its printing function was transferred to another department, and in 1943 by constitutional amendment the commissioner of labor (together with the commissioner of agriculture) was made a member of the Council of State, thereby increasing the department's significance. As industrial development flourished after the war, various questions relating to labor became more urgent—among them health and safety, accident prevention and compensation, wages and hours, employment, labor-management relations, and standards for women and children.

In view of these concerns, the Department of Labor began to issue more binding guidelines and to conduct more inspections. Although during the postwar period no labor disputes reached the breaking point, such as those earlier in Gastonia and Marion, there were prolonged strikes and less serious confrontations at the Erwin Mills in Durham, the Harriet-Henderson mill at Henderson, and elsewhere. Local police, the state highway patrol, and even the National Guard on occasion were required to preserve the peace before satisfactory adjustments could be made between labor and management. Union membership grew slightly for a time but soon declined. Under federal supervision workers voted on whether to have union representation but more times than not they rejected it.

In 1946 a textile strike in Durham lasted for five months when neither state nor federal conciliators could bring the opposing parties to terms. Time and again negotiations broke down over what seemed to observers to be trivial points. Finally, Governor Cherry telephoned the president of the Textile Workers' Union of America in New York and asked him to come to Raleigh; the governor also invited the vice-president of the mill to join them. In a conference room in the Justice Building the three men discussed the impasse while aides, legal advisers, and top officials on both sides waited just outside the door. After a time Cherry left the room, telling its other two occupants that he expected them to remain until they resolved the dispute. Within twenty minutes they reached an agreement.

Communist Hunt

North Carolina did not totally escape the public fear of Communist activities that pervaded the country from the late 1940s into the 1950s. The revelation that a network of Soviet espionage existed in Canada in 1946 led to the arrest and conviction of several spies in the United States. In Congress the House Committee on Un-American Activities conducted investigations and hearings, and in 1952 Wisconsin senator Joseph R. McCarthy, as chairman of the Senate Committee on Government Operations, plunged heedlessly into attacks on officials whom he suspected of being "soft on communism."

North Carolina's reaction to the national hysteria may be seen in the charges leveled against Junius I. Scales, a 1947 graduate of the University of North Carolina. In July of that year newspapers reported that Scales was head of Communist activities at the university, and sometime afterward the Federal Bureau of Investigation (FBI) began an investigation. In 1952 it was reported that Scales had distributed hundreds of Communist pamphlets. Two years later the FBI accused him of directing a Red conspiracy in Tennessee, North Carolina, and South Carolina, and he was arrested and charged with violating the Smith Act (Subversive Activities Control Act). This act prohibited membership in any organization that taught or advocated the overthrow of the United States government. Scales admitted his membership in such an organization at his trial in Greensboro in the spring of 1955 and was convicted. Sentenced to a six-year term, he appealed all the way to the United States Supreme Court where his conviction was set aside on the grounds that in the trial he did not have access to FBI records. At a new trial in 1960, he was again convicted and given an identical sentence from which he fruitlessly appealed. In July 1961 Scales began to serve his term but obtained a pardon in December 1962 from President John F. Kennedy. In time Scales renounced any support for communism.

Progressive Developments

Cherry's successor as governor was the recent commissioner of agriculture, W. Kerr Scott, a dairy farmer from Alamance County who was portrayed as a country boy tackling the Democratic party machine. The election of 1948 proved to be an exciting one, with a runoff required in the gubernatorial race. The candidates of the "machine" lost several contests, suggesting a decline in the allegiance of some of the party faithful. For one thing the old custom of providing governors alternately from the eastern and western parts of the state was ending; the practice of having one United States senator from each of the two sections was also in its last days.

With no political debts to pay, Scott set off on his "Go Forward" program unencumbered. The 1949 General Assembly generously funded appropriations for the operation of state agencies and institutions, school construction, and bonds to improve facilities for oceangoing ships at the state ports of Wilmington and Morehead City. The terminal facilities at the ports were completed in 1952. The people also voted a special tax for road construction—later called a farm-to-market program—to pave a very large proportion of the state's unnumbered, rural roads. In the first year of Scott's administration 4,658 miles were paved toward his goal of 12,000 miles. At the governor's insistence, public utility companies extended their power and telephone lines into the countryside, and after a year more than 88 percent of the farms in the state had electricity and more than 83,000 new telephones had been installed. Also during this administration the $24 million du Pont plant near Kinston opened to manufacture a new "Fibre V." At Pisgah Forest Olin Industries opened a $20 million plant to produce cellophane, and a $3.5 million plant of the Woonsocket Falls Mills began producing upholstering materials near Wilmington.

Scott was progressive in other ways as well. He appointed the first black to serve on the State Board of Education, eliminated salary discrimination between white and black staff members at the state mental hospitals, and named Susie Sharp as the first female superior court judge in the state. He also recommended lowering the voting age to eighteen, a statewide liquor referendum, stream pollution control, minimum wage legislation, and restoring a motor vehicle inspection law that had been recently repealed.

Among the long-range programs to originate with the Scott administration was the "Nickels for Know-How" Program, implemented when farmers voted in favor of an assessment of five cents per ton on feed and fertilizer to support agricultural research at North Carolina State College and at experiment stations throughout the state. This administration also saw the beginning of a continuing program of water conservation and wildlife restoration. Other innovations included folk festivals and Harvest Days. In response to an urgent appeal from Governor Scott, the General Assembly appropriated $1 million in matching funds to obtain a gift of like value from the Samuel H. Kress Foundation to acquire pieces for the North Carolina Museum of Art. The foundation's purpose was to make the art museum in North Carolina one of the best in the country, and the people of the state took up the challenge. In 1956 the museum opened in downtown Raleigh in a building remodeled for that purpose and quickly won national recognition for the quality of its holdings.

The Graham-Smith Campaign

Following the death of United States senator J. Melville Broughton, Scott named as his successor Frank P. Graham, president of the University of North Carolina and perhaps the best known liberal in the South. Graham was a long-time—though not particularly active—advocate of civil rights and a supporter of labor unionization. He served only from 29 March 1949 to 26 November 1950, losing the Democratic nomination for a full term to Willis Smith after a heated campaign.

Smith, a conservative Democrat, was a former president of the American Bar Association. His supporters had made an issue of civil rights as well as the social and economic policies of the national administration. In an editorial of 26 May 1950, the Raleigh *News and Observer* noted that Smith conducted a "high-powered and high-priced campaign of insinuations against Frank Graham's patriotism." For the first time since the white supremacy campaign of 1900, race was a live issue. A young Raleigh radio and television reporter, Jesse Helms, worked on his own time in the Smith campaign, reportedly preparing drafts of news releases.

Korean War

During the last three years of the Scott administration, an unfortunate number of North Carolinians were involved in a new military conflict far from America's shores. In 1943 the Allies, including Russia, had agreed that at some time after World War II Korea—a Japanese colony since 1910—would again become an independent nation. In 1945 it was decided that Russia would temporarily occupy the northern portion to the thirty-eighth parallel and the United States, with limited assistance from fifteen other United Nations countries, the lower portion. Russia immediately stopped movement between the two sections; cut roads, telephone lines, and rail connections; and fortified the frontier. Communists further provoked disorders to the extent that no plans could be made to unify the country. Some United States officials recommended that troops be withdrawn since the area was of no strategic significance, realizing, however, that such an action would enable Russia to occupy the whole country. To withdraw gracefully, the United States prevailed upon the United Nations to supervise an election to establish a unified Korea. Before this could be accomplished, North Korea invaded South Korea, and the United States found it necessary to attempt to halt the invasion in order to demonstrate that it would support its allies in case of future Russian attacks; also if South Korea were abandoned, Russia might strike elsewhere.

The result was a long struggle that neither side seemed likely to win. A presidential election in the United States and the death of Joseph Stalin, the Russian dictator, may have been responsible for the changes that followed. The new president, World War II general Dwight D. Eisenhower, went to Korea and made veiled suggestions that the atomic bomb might be used. With assurance that the United States would continue to provide economic and military aid to South Korea, it was agreed to retain the thirty-eighth parallel as the division between the free and the Communist portions of Korea.

The Korean War was unpopular in the United States. Troops suffered from long and seemingly pointless action, from the lack of enthusiastic support from home, and from a harsh climate and disease. The exact number of North Carolinians who served in Korea is uncertain, but in 1958 it was reported that there were 121,000 veterans of whom 25,000 had also seen service in World War II. Approximately 876 North Carolinians were either killed in action or died in service.

*   *   *

The events that occurred in North Carolina during the quarter century after 1940 probably made a greater impression on the state than any like period in its history. From an isolated, self-satisfied people, North Carolinians had become aware of influences beyond their control; they would never again return to the attitudes of the past.

26

A NEW FACE
FOR THE STATE

FOLLOWING BOTH the Civil War and World War I, which together lasted
less than half a dozen years, great changes took place in North Carolina.
Among them, after 1865, were freedom for over 300,000 people previously
held in slavery, a new system of agricultural labor, and a modified state constitution with sweeping changes in government. After 1918, over the objections of the
General Assembly, women won the right to vote; people started to question the
ideals and beliefs of the older generation; and automobiles in larger numbers
appeared on newly paved highways, while tractors began to replace mules in the
fields. Young people left the farm to work in town or even in some other state,
and interest in "culture"—art, dance, history, literature, and music—began to
take root. Radio and motion pictures were perfected and soon, like other forms
of education and entertainment available nationwide, they exerted a leveling
influence on people throughout the country. North Carolinians began to lose
some of the characteristics that made them unique. They became less provincial,
grew more tolerant of "outsiders," paid more attention to news of national and
world significance, and welcomed industrial growth. With the Great Depression
of the 1930s also came a realization that they shared countless problems in common with the rest of the nation. Racial segregation, for the most part, was the law
in the South; in the North it was in many places merely the custom.

After World War II some of these traits were expanded. Numerous soldiers
and sailors stationed overseas during the conflict brought home "war brides,"
whose presence contributed to a more cosmopolitan attitude in the state. The
"G.I. Bill of Rights" provided educational opportunities to honorably discharged service personnel, and thousands attended colleges or received technical
training for new careers. This contributed to the creation of a better educated
citizenry, and more people than ever before began to take an active interest in
local and state government and to participate as volunteers in the work of public
service agencies. In numerous ways North Carolina began to reflect a more progressive attitude in its programs.

Race Relations

One problem which faced the state in the late 1940s had its roots deep in the past, and a satisfactory solution still lies in the future. Attempts to solve it proved to be costly in terms of dollars, but more significantly in terms of human life and relationships. This was, of course, the all-pervasive issue of race relations among the diverse people of the United States. The magnitude of the problem was proportional to the majority-minority ratio among the population of each state. It was more serious in the states of the Deep South than it was in North Carolina and less serious in some of the northern states.

For a long time people had been aware of the injustices to blacks, native Americans, and other minority groups. Yet because the few who cared were in a minority themselves, they could do little. On occasion, of course, the victims of racial prejudice spoke out or wrote about what they endured or witnessed. But in North Carolina, as elsewhere, the rights of blacks generally, and sometimes of Indians, were either ignored or violated—at the ballot box, on buses and trains, in hotels and restaurants, in schools, at theaters and stores, on the sidewalk in some towns, and even at the State Fair in Raleigh.

During the depression and in World II some white North Carolinians had an opportunity to associate with blacks under new conditions. They worked together on federally sponsored projects, and as young people in uniform they occasionally served in the same military unit. (Yet not until President Harry S Truman's executive order of 1948 were the armed forces desegregated.) In many cases each came to accept the other as a person and not necessarily as a member of a particular race. Instances of genuine friendship were not unique. In the early 1950s, the integration of schools, public transportation, recreation facilities, restaurants, housing, and other areas where segregation of the races was the custom throughout much of the country became a live issue. Indeed, one of the nation's most pressing problems was the involved question of civil rights.

Segregation had been practiced for a long time in America, but since 1896 it had been sanctioned by a decision of the United States Supreme Court. The case of *Plessy v. Ferguson* in that year was the basis of the principle that separate accommodations were permitted so long as they were equal. The separate-but-equal doctrine then came to be cited to support all forms of racial segregation with little or no regard for the *equal* portion of the equation. By various devious means blacks had also been denied the vote in many places, so minorities included suffrage in their appeal for civil rights.

As blacks were denied the full privileges of citizenship in the South to a greater degree than in the North, there was a great exodus to northern cities. Large numbers moved to Baltimore, Philadelphia, New York, Chicago, Detroit, and elsewhere much as blacks had done in the 1870s when they were referred to as "exodusters." While conditions there were usually more to their liking than they had been in the South, they were still far from ideal. An organization formed in New York City in 1910, the National Association for the Advancement of Colored People (NAACP), sought through legal means to secure the constitutional rights of all people. The National Urban League was established the following year for the same purpose. Both also helped newly arrived migrants adapt to city life.

In 1942 the Congress of Racial Equality (CORE) was formed in Chicago. Like the two earlier organizations, it advocated peaceful action through interracial cooperation, but it intended to go directly to the root of the problem. Within a year CORE sponsored sit-ins and stand-ins in Chicago, and in 1947, in a "Freedom Ride" across the South, it tested segregation in interstate bus terminals which the Supreme Court had declared unconstitutional. Financial support for these civil rights organizations came largely from a small, elite group of northerners.

The Democratic party's national platform in 1948 contained a strong civil rights plank, and in the same year President Truman took formal steps to desegregate personnel in both the civil and military services. By 1950, partly as a result of a threatened march on Washington, D.C., blacks had won a number of concessions. Some state laws were being changed on their behalf, and more blacks were participating in the political primaries. Among other rights, they also gained admission to graduate and professional schools formerly closed to them. In 1957 Congress established a Commission on Civil Rights to investigate charges regarding infringement of the right to vote, and to study and report on equal protection of the law under the Constitution.

It is not surprising that the first significant action leading to such sweeping changes concerned education. Few blacks before 1865 ever had an opportunity to learn to read and write, especially in the South, and fewer still obtained further education. Their eagerness to learn was demonstrated in North Carolina at the end of the Civil War when, for a few years, they attended schools maintained by northern churches, philanthropic organizations, and the Freedmen's Bureau. The literacy rate of the state rose dramatically. In 1877, during the administration of Governor Zebulon B. Vance, the General Assembly began to support the Howard School established ten years earlier in Fayetteville to train black teachers (it is now Fayetteville State University). Nevertheless, schools for blacks were poorly supported and open for only two or three months a year. In 1890 the black school-age population was 235,911, yet only 117,017 were enrolled in the public schools. After 1900, however, Governor Charles B. Aycock's educational program enabled more black children to receive at least some education.

In North Carolina and elsewhere in the South, the dual systems of public schools—one for whites and another for blacks—were maintained under the illusion that the Supreme Court decision in *Plessy v. Ferguson* prevailed—that separate schools, if they were equal, might exist. During the presidential administration of Franklin D. Roosevelt, however, particularly in the late 1930s, the Supreme Court recognized—in various decisions—that opportunities for higher education and professional study were not the same for all races. One effect of these decisions was the creation of a graduate school at the North Carolina College for Negroes in Durham in 1939 to offer programs in the liberal arts and the professions. A law school was opened in 1940 and a school of library science the following year. Professors from Chapel Hill went to the Durham school on a regular schedule to teach many of these classes. These and other modest gains by blacks were the result of their own initiatives. Legal action or the threat of it became their most effective tool. In March 1951, for example, the United States Circuit Court of Appeals reversed a decision by the Middle District Court of the previous October, and in the summer and fall sessions of the University of North Carolina blacks were admitted to the law, medical, and graduate schools in Chapel Hill.

Even though a large share of the financial support came from state revenue, the North Carolina public school system was largely controlled by county and city school boards. The State Department of Public Instruction set certain standards for all of the public schools, participated in the selection of textbooks, and provided a broad range of assistance to the local systems. Because of the state's role in education it was not necessary for it to defend the policy of segregation nor, in time, to adopt a statewide policy of integration. Each county and city school system made its own plans.

In the case of *Brown v. Board of Education* arising in Topeka, Kansas, the United States Supreme Court on 17 May 1954 rejected the "separate but equal" ruling that had stood for nearly sixty years. It now determined that "separate education facilities are inherently unequal." Based on data presented by an educator and a psychologist, the Court concluded that segregated schools were harmful to black students, giving them a sense of inferiority. Henceforth, it directed, suits against tax-supported school systems were to be decided by district courts and blacks were to be admitted to public schools "on a racially nondiscriminatory basis with all deliberate speed."

In parts of the nation whites reacted to the Supreme Court's ruling in shocked disbelief. There was violent resistance in some states, particularly Arkansas, Mississippi, and South Carolina as well as in a few northern cities, notably Boston and Detroit, when they eventually were forced to comply with the order.

In North Carolina, some political leaders attempted to delay implementation of the new federal directive until the mood of the people could be determined and, if necessary, altered. They debated the meaning of the Court's words—"with all deliberate speed." Governor William B. Umstead was ill in the spring of 1954, and following his death on 7 November it fell to his successor, Luther H. Hodges, to deal with the problem. His challenge was twofold: to develop a workable program for the people of North Carolina yet ensure its acceptability to the United States Supreme Court. With two masters, for the most part holding opposing views, the crisis faced by the white leadership of the state was very grave indeed. Hodges, a distinguished businessman but with only limited political experience, was determined above all else to see that the public schools of the state remained open. In a television broadcast, he announced that North Carolina would not violate the Constitution. His position, as a moderate conservative, was in sharp contrast to the views of Orval Faubus in Arkansas and public spokesmen elsewhere from Virginia to Mississippi. North Carolinians, characteristically, took a more reasoned approach than many people elsewhere.

On 30 December 1954 the Special Advisory Committee on Education, which had been named by Governor Umstead, recommended "that North Carolina try to find means of meeting the requirements of the Supreme Court's decision within our present school system before consideration is given to abandoning or materially altering it." In response, the General Assembly in March 1955 adopted a pupil assignment plan affirming that local school boards had power over the enrollment and assignment of children in the public schools and on school buses throughout the state. By September, it appeared to some members of the governor's staff that "the people of this state are still, in the main, apathetic in regard to this problem. . . . There is also a feeling among many that there is no way to head off integration in schools and that we should attempt to work out plans for gradual integration."

The Pearsall Plan

At a special session in July 1956, the General Assembly adopted the "Pearsall Plan," named for Thomas J. Pearsall, of Rocky Mount, chairman of the Special Advisory Committee. Embodied in a constitutional amendment, it provided for the payment of education expense grants from state or local public funds for the private schooling of any child assigned against the wishes of his or her parent or guardian to an integrated school. In addition, local communities would be permitted—by majority vote—to suspend the operation of public schools if conditions became intolerable because of forced integration. Early in September the people ratified this proposal by a vote of 471,657 to 101,767.

Needless to say, the Pearsall scheme stirred up strong reactions. To supporters, it presented a middle ground, a "safety valve" against integration and a way to avoid the kind of violence that had flared in the Deep South. State senator Terry Sanford believed the plan to be a step toward "moderation, unity, understanding and goodwill." Others considered it a form of nullification, a means of evading the law, and, in the words of philosopher-playwright Paul Green, "the old familiar message of an ancient and reactionary South."

Around the state editorial reaction was also mixed, but generally favorable to the plan. Most papers recognized it for what Hodges and Pearsall probably intended it to be—a way to give potential (but never identified) troublemakers time to cool off. Even the plan's drafters realized that integration could not be prevented. The *Fayetteville Observer* called it "a fire extinguisher." The *Greensboro Daily News*, writing of the "tortuous and narrow" path ahead, suggested that the Pearsall Plan would enable North Carolina to "tread it safely." On the other hand, Reed Sarrat of the Winston-Salem *Journal-Sentinel* had found a great many North Carolinians who favored full compliance with the demands of the Supreme Court. There were reports that local school boards in at least seven cities were prepared to integrate their schools. A Duke University historian, reflecting on the events of 1955–56, suggested in 1980 that the actions of Hodges and Pearsall were politically motivated. He pointed out that the Federal Bureau of Investigation had infiltrated the Ku Klux Klan and that neither the Klan nor any other "redneck" organization posed a serious threat to integration.

Token School Integration

When schools opened in the late summer of 1957 in Charlotte, Greensboro, and Winston-Salem, a dozen black students were enrolled in previously all-white schools. All three systems announced their action at the same time to limit to a single occasion the response of those who might object rather than give them three opportunities to protest. There were demonstrations by recalcitrant whites, of course, including members of the Ku Klux Klan and the White Patriots, yet all three cities were criticized by others for not enrolling a greater number of blacks. Nevertheless, the northern press observed that this small step was significant and indicative of future action.

In a very modest way integration continued, with a few blacks entering the schools of Havelock–Craven County, Wayne County, Durham, and High Point in the fall of 1959 and of Chapel Hill, Raleigh, and Yancey County the next year. In 1961, when Terry Sanford became governor, over two hundred blacks were enrolled in eleven districts—not a great number, to be sure, but the pattern was set and the change was being made peacefully. Time began to heal the wounds that many people nursed privately and a few publicly. To speed the integration of public schools, Congress in 1964 passed a Civil Rights Act with provisions to withhold federal funds for education in school districts where racial discrimination continued to be practiced.

The Charlotte-Mecklenburg School Case

To combat discrimination in the schools, the Legal Defense Fund of the NAACP filed a number of lawsuits across the state. When one suit came before the federal court in Mecklenburg County in 1969, the district judge, James B. McMillan, after examining the records of the school concerned, ordered the local school system to employ "any and all known ways of desegregation, including busing." McMillan was a graduate of the University of North Carolina (1937) and the Harvard Law School; he had served in the navy during World War II. Described as a southern liberal and an idealist, he was a member of the United World Federalists, advocates of world government, and somewhat outside the mainstream of North Carolina political philosophy. As a result of his ruling in 1969, McMillan's life was threatened and he was placed under police protection. Threats were also made against attorney Julius Chambers, a black graduate of the University of North Carolina, who had also participated in the case. His law office was burned.

The Charlotte-Mecklenburg Board of Education had already fought busing through the lower courts and had reluctantly transported pupils in accordance with their directives. Even before the federal court order, schools in the system were busing 23,600 children on trips that averaged one hour and fourteen minutes each way. In 1963, under the skillful leadership of Mayor Stan R. Brookshire, Charlotte had desegregated its auditorium and coliseum, schools, library, buses and bus drivers, police department, parks and swimming pools, community services, and medical association; later in the year hotels, motels, and most of the restaurants and theaters were opened to blacks. School integration, nevertheless, was not at the same ratio as the white-to-black population, and supporters of a more equitable ratio persisted. Approximately 71 percent of the school-age children were white and 29 percent were black; Judge McMillan ruled that each school in the district should have that proportion.

The Charlotte school desegregation order was appealed to the United States Supreme Court in 1970, thereby attracting national attention. Even President Richard M. Nixon and Secretary of Health, Education, and Welfare Robert Finch denounced McMillan's decision. At the time, the *Washington Post* called school busing "the country's most volatile domestic political issue."

The justices of the Supreme Court were deeply concerned about the decision they must make. They recognized that a difference existed between *desegregation* (as *Brown v. Board of Education* mandated) under which minorities would be admitted where they formerly had been excluded, and *integration* under which a precise ratio of minority to majority must be maintained. Judge McMillan had drastically altered school attendance zones in requiring the busing of 13,000 more pupils to reach a "racial balance" in each school. This was a new concept, and support for it came only after the summer session of the Court was canceled to give the justices an opportunity to consider several busing cases. Chief Justice Warren E. Burger announced, however, that *Swann v. Charlotte-Mecklenburg Board of Education* would be argued first in the new term.

Consideration ranged all the way from advocating only attendance at the nearest school to supporting McMillan's decision. Justice Potter Stewart regretted McMillan's ruling and the position in which he had placed the nation's highest court. Until this time all Supreme Court decisions pertaining to segregation had been unanimous. To maintain that tradition much soul-searching and considerable persuasion were required.[1] Several possible versions of a decision were prepared and circulated, ranging from reversing McMillan's decision to affirming it. Finally the United States Supreme Court in 1971 upheld the ruling, and busing came to be a tool not only to desegregate schools but also to integrate them—throughout the nation as well as in North Carolina.

Busing was resisted in many parts of the country. Boston and Detroit, among other cities, were the scene of considerable opposition. Strong resistance to integration was reflected in the thousands of white students whose parents took them out of public schools and sent them to hastily established private institutions.

Already the University of North Carolina at Chapel Hill, under court order, had admitted black undergraduates in 1955; Davidson and Mars Hill colleges and Duke University admitted their first black students in 1961. Thereafter the state's colleges and universities seldom declined to admit minorities if they were otherwise fully qualified. In some cases, remedial courses were offered to assist those who did not meet admission standards.

Despite desegregation the racial identity of institutions of higher education in North Carolina continued. Under pressure to meet deadlines promulgated by federal officials, quotas were established and special recruiting programs implemented. Tuition grants and scholarships were offered to induce young people to attend a college traditionally attended by those of a different race.

In 1966 the Pearsall Plan was declared to be unconstitutional, although it had not been used in a single school system. Whether the plan was necessary is, of course, debatable, but it seem to have been the "safety valve" its creators intended rather than an instrument to "forestall integration." Fortunately it had not been needed as a "fire extinguisher" either, so perhaps it might be compared to the umbrella carried on a clear day to keep the rain away.

Greensboro Lunch Counter Sit-Ins

The landmark decision in *Brown v. Board of Education* was promptly interpreted by many people as applying to accommodations in all public facilities, not

1. For the details see Bob Woodward and Scott Armstrong, *The Brethren Inside the Supreme Court* (1979), pp. 95–112 and passim.

just public schools. The Supreme Court upheld this view in later cases. In Montgomery, Alabama, in 1957, a successful boycott of city buses led to the creation of the Southern Christian Leadership Conference (SCLC) under the aegis of the Reverend Martin Luther King, Jr. It was his plan, in a nonviolent manner following the pattern set by CORE, to "create such a crisis and foster such a tension" in communities that refused to negotiate over the question of segregation as to force them to "confront the issue."

This policy was first applied on a Monday, the first day in February 1960, in Greensboro when four black students from the North Carolina Agricultural and Technical College went downtown to the lunch counter at Woolworth's. Having sat down and asked for a cup of coffee, they were told that only whites were served there. But the students sat at the counter until the store closed at the end of the day and returned the next day to resume their wait. Soon they were joined by other blacks, who eventually occupied sixty-three of the sixty-five seats at the counter. Large crowds gathered, some to support the sit-in and others to jeer and threaten. Among them were many students, white hecklers, and newspaper, radio, and television reporters including some from the national networks and newsmagazines. After four days the sit-in spread to another store, and by the end of the week more than three hundred students were involved as were additional stores that served food.

The following week there were sit-ins in Winston-Salem and Durham and, a few days later, in Chapel Hill, Charlotte, and Raleigh. In the latter city students from Shaw University formed the Student Non-Violent Coordinating Committee (SNCC) to plan and execute their activities, and the idea as well as the name spread to other institutions. Soon black students, sometimes joined by white students, were involved in similar demonstrations across the state. Although the sit-ins were condemned by the state attorney general, they found support in a number of quarters. The North Carolina AFL-CIO commended the students' efforts to desegregate lunch counters, as did the presidents of the Baptist State Convention and the North Carolina Council of Churches. Local white business and civic leaders began to negotiate with the students, college officials, and managers of various downtown businesses. After several breakdowns in these talks, all the stores agreed to open their food service to the public without regard to race. On 25 July 1960, the first black was accommodated at the lunch counter where the sit-ins had begun in February. The ultimate results of the "coffee party" in Greensboro have sometimes been compared to the results of the tea parties in Boston, Edenton, Rhode Island, and elsewhere on the eve of the American Revolution.

For what seemed to many to be interminable years after the Supreme Court decision in 1954, there was extensive unrest in North Carolina as well as throughout the nation. Much of it had its roots in racial concerns, but some was also political, particularly with respect to the real or imagined threat of communism.

Four members of the original sit-in group leaving Woolworth's on 1 February 1960 (*left to right*): David Richmond, Franklin McCain, Ezell Blair, Jr., and Joseph McNeil. (Photograph by Jack Moebes, *Greensboro News & Record*)

The national press focused a great deal of attention on this unrest, particularly in the South, and events in North Carolina were the subject of considerable comment—some from as far away as Moscow. Both school integration and the sit-ins inspired much marching, singing, shouting, and jeering. Nevertheless, the non-violent sit-in proved to be an effective tool in integrating public facilities.

Similar activities by young blacks and others opened the state's theaters, hotels, motels, and restaurants to both races in 1963. The General Assembly in the same year voted to desegregate the National Guard. Protests such as the sit-ins, generally peaceful, succeeded not only in North Carolina where they began but across the country as well. The Civil Rights Act of 1964, which contained a provision relating to education, also prohibited discrimination in most public facilities. Soon municipal cemeteries were integrated as well.

The "tortuous and narrow" path of desegregation described by the *Greens-*

boro Daily News was finally open, but it also proved to be a long and uneven path, sometimes blocked by briars. After many years, still winding its way through the thickets of tradition and protest but crossing the bridges of justice and equality, we may hope that it leads to fertile fields for all of the laborers who follow it.

Violence in Wilmington

A widely publicized incident in Wilmington on 6 February 1971 was precipitated by the firebombing of a white-owned grocery story in a black neighborhood. It followed a period of unrest resulting from claims by black students that racism flourished both in classes and on the sports fields in local high schools. Charges and countercharges were hurled, and black youths began a school boycott. When local officials lost control of the situation, outsiders moved into the fray—among them Ben Chavis, a black man working with the Commission for Racial Justice, and members of the Ku Klux Klan. Elements of each side coalesced, and word spread that many of the blacks and some of their white supporters were armed and barricaded in a church. It was also reported that they were responsible for bombing the nearby grocery store. When firemen and police arrived at the scene, they were fired upon from the church.

Confusion reigned and a year passed before nine black men and a white woman were arrested, tried, and convicted of burning the grocery store. The "Wilmington Ten," as they were called in the press, were sentenced to long prison terms. Loud protests were heard from around the country, but the state court of appeals found no error in the trial. Governor James B. Hunt refused to pardon them, but he did reduce their sentences. Finally in 1980 the federal court of appeals overturned their conviction on technical grounds. *Izvestia* carried the story in the Soviet Union, and, for a time afterward, Russian nationals told American officials that this was an instance of political prisoners being held by the United States government.

"Death to the Klan" Rally

Another incident attracting world attention occurred in Greensboro on 3 November 1979, when members of the Communist Workers party, some of whom were black, scheduled an anti-Klan meeting at a public housing project in Greensboro. Hailed as a "Death to the Klan" rally and widely publicized in advance, it attracted people of vastly different viewpoints. Klan members, joined by a group of neo-Nazis, rushed into the rally, killing five members of the Communist Workers party; among the dead were two physicians and an honors graduate of Duke University. Six Klansmen were cleared of murder charges in a trial the following year, although it was rumored that some public officials had conspired with the Klan against the Communists. A private investigation ten years later revealed no evidence of a conspiracy.

Black Candidates for Office

In the 1960s blacks began to consider running for public office, and in 1968 a Charlotte dentist, Reginald A. Hawkins, became the first of his race in the twentieth century to run for a statewide office. As a candidate for governor in the Democratic primary, he received 129,808 votes while two white candidates, both of whom were sons of former governors, together received 571,292 votes. In the fall elections that year Henry E. Frye of Guilford County was the first black to be elected to the General Assembly in the twentieth century. (In 1983 Frye became the first black to sit on the North Carolina Supreme Court.) Chapel Hill was the first predominantly white southern town to elect a black mayor when it chose Howard N. Lee in 1969. (Lee also became the first of his race to hold a cabinet position in North Carolina when Governor James B. Hunt in 1977 named him secretary of the Department of Natural Resources and Community Development.) In 1973 the voters of Raleigh also selected a black mayor. In 1985 a black was named head of the state prison system. As historian H. G. Jones has pointed out, "These victories reflected more than a growing black vote; they also reflected the willingness of many whites to vote for minority candidates." Nevertheless, Jones noted that in 1981 blacks constituted 22 percent of the population of the state, yet they filled only 255 or 5 percent of its 5,037 elective offices.

As the 1980s progressed, blacks still had not attained full acceptance in all parts of the state. Even so, in 1983 a black woman, Deneen Graham of North Wilkesboro who was a junior at the North Carolina School of the Arts, was chosen Miss North Carolina. By then people of all races were serving on various boards, commissions, and committees and dealing objectively with matters of statewide concern. Signs of acceptance of integration were frequently observed across the state in such simple incidents as a crew of telephone linesmen, black and white, sitting down to eat their midday "dinner" together at the only restaurant in a small county seat town, laughing and joking with each other; or a group of young people, players and cheerleaders, urging their friends to victory regardless of race. Black football, baseball, and basketball players, both in collegiate and professional sports, undoubtedly influenced public attitudes.

Because of the changed racial climate in North Carolina, numerous blacks returned "home" to the state after having lived in the North for many years. Between 1970 and 1980, 107,952 of them followed the reversed trail of the old "exodusters." Many said that they considered North Carolina a better place to

When Henry E. Frye (b. 1932), a native of Ellerbe, was elected to the North Carolina House of Representatives in 1968, he became the first black to sit in that body in the twentieth century. After six terms in the house he was elected to the state senate, and in 1983 he became an associate justice of the North Carolina Supreme Court. (Courtesy of Justice Frye)

raise their children. Although it took thirty years to bring about the changes making this possible, and it may require that many or more to wipe out the last vestige of more than three centuries of discrimination, those who predicted in 1954 that white North Carolinians would never consent to integration clearly were wrong.

The Research Triangle Park

The successful creation of one of the most unusual and valuable features of late twentieth-century North Carolina—and, indeed, of the nation—was initially closely tied in with integration. This was the Research Triangle Park. When it was first being discussed, some its planners were faced with the necessity of interesting outsiders in the concept. Some potential backers also considered Virginia and Georgia as likely sites but concluded that the "massive resistance" to school integration in Virginia and the indecisiveness of Georgia would be hindrances. North Carolina was a more tolerant state, they reasoned, and the unequivocal declaration by Governor Hodges that its schools would remain open proved to be decisive.

Even as lieutenant governor under William B. Umstead, Luther H. Hodges, formerly a businessman, had considered what steps might be taken to expand North Carolina's industry in more profitable ways. And as early as 1952, during the administration of Governor W. Kerr Scott, there had been talk of bringing together research and industry in a research institute that would benefit the entire state. When Hodges became governor in 1954 after Umstead's death, he was able to pursue this idea more forcefully. With the assistance of Romeo H. Guest, planner and builder of Greensboro, Robert M. Hanes, president of Wachovia Bank in Winston-Salem, and Howard W. Odum and George L. Simpson, Jr., sociologists of Chapel Hill, firm plans began to appear. Administrators and faculty members from Duke University in Durham, North Carolina State College in Raleigh, and the University of North Carolina were drawn into the project. They not only helped develop the idea but also offered to participate in future programs.

To acquire a suitable tract of land roughly equidistant from the three campuses, a nonprofit group, the Research Triangle Committee, was formed in 1956. When a $1.5 million contribution was made to the committee, it changed its name to the Research Triangle Foundation. The foundation had no connection with either state or local government, although it has always provided invaluable service to the state. Incorporated in December 1958, it began acquiring land on which an option had been taken in 1957 by some of the officers. Karl Robbins, a retired manufacturer from New York, quietly assisted with land purchases as well as options to buy land, and in time he also contributed to the installation of utilities. Soon the foundation possessed 5,600 acres of eroded, rolling land covered with a few hardwood trees and some tall pines but largely by scrub pines, broomsedge, and briars. It lay largely in Durham County with a small portion in Wake County. Gently curving roads were designed and sizable parcels of land marked off to await the arrival of tenants. Ample space was reserved between potential building sites to retain a parklike atmosphere, trees and vegetation would serve as shields between them, and there would be adequate space for research and work of a scientific nature. Rules for occupancy were established. Among other things heavy manufacturing would be excluded from the park, nor would fumes, noise, radiation, dust, smoke, or odors be allowed if they spread beyond the boundaries of the land held by the company responsible for creating them. This set a pattern for future development throughout the state when "high tech" industry would be lured to supplement and eventually to supersede older industries.

Archie K. Davis, a Winston-Salem banker, was instrumental in raising funds to enable the Research Triangle Foundation to begin its work. With George Simpson as director and Elizabeth Johnson Aycock as secretary, the foundation set out to convince suitable businesses either to move to the park from elsewhere or to establish new facilities there. The first tenant was the Research Triangle Institute, a nonprofit corporation that engages in contract research conducted by specialists from the three nearby universities. At the time there were nine other such research institutes in the United States, but this one was better equipped and offered a wider variety of services. Thanks to a generous gift from George Watts Hill of Durham, Professor Gertrude Cox of the University of North Carolina established a statistical laboratory at the institute in 1958. The institute operated out of rented quarters in Durham until its building at the park was completed in 1961.

Late in 1958 it was announced that a second facility—the research laboratory of the United States Forestry Service—would be constructed in the Research Triangle Park. Foundations and individuals soon donated funds to assist in the park's further development, and the General Assembly contributed a grant-in-aid on two occasions totaling $500,000. The first large tenant was secured in 1959 when Chemstrand Corporation, a subsidiary of Monsanto Chemicals, decided to establish facilities for the development of artificial fibers. Other organizations followed—among them the American Association of Textile Chemists and Colorists.

North Carolinians, never hesitant to take advantage of political associates or to extract payment for past favors, were in a particularly fortuitous position at this time. When Governor Hodges' term ended in 1961, he became secretary of commerce in the cabinet of President John F. Kennedy. This provided an ideal base from which to promote the Research Triangle Park nationwide. The fact that the incumbent governor, Terry Sanford, had endorsed Kennedy's candidacy at the Democratic National Convention in 1960 also helped. It has been suggested that Sanford "cashed in his chips" to gain support for locating some federal research agencies at the park. In 1965 it was announced that the National Institute of Environmental Health Sciences would be established there on five hundred acres of land; it would employ 2,000 people in buildings costing around $25 million.

The publicity resulting from this announcement as well as the recognized advantages of the park soon attracted a long list of tenants. A firm making units for computers rented space for a time and then bought land for its own building. International Business Machines was also an early arrival to develop and build its Data Communication System in a $15 million plant employing 2,500 people. A British pharmaceutical company, Burroughs Wellcome, one of the world's foremost research and manufacturing firms in this field, moved its New York facility to the Research Triangle Park in 1970. Its handsome contemporary building has attracted much favorable comment and has been the setting for at least one futuristic motion picture. It is said that the architect was concerned about how staid North Carolinians might react to the building, so with the earliest drawings of his design he announced that it would look like "a stack of front porches!"

Also located at the park are the National Center for Health Statistics Laboratory, Northern Telecom, Inc., Ciba-Geigy Biotechnology Research, the Environmental Research Center of the United States Environmental Protection Agency, the Chemical Industry Institute of Toxicology, Family Health International, General Electric Company's Semiconductor Division, Glaxo, Inc., Union Carbide's Agricultural Products Technical Center, Underwriters Laboratories, Inc., the international headquarters of the Instrument Society of America, Microelectronics Center of North Carolina, Airco Industrial Gases' Special Products department, the Triangle Universities Computation Center, DuPont's Electronics Development Center, and many others.

Perhaps most significantly, the park is the home of the National Humanities Center, created by a special committee of the American Academy of Arts and Sciences and the Triangle Universities Center for Advanced Studies. Here, scholars from all over the world come for study and research, but especially to write in the field of the humanities as well as in law, medicine, business, and other areas. Seminars and lectures provide opportunities for the exchange of ideas in a variety of disciplines and on countless topics and issues.

The National Humanities Center in the Research Triangle Park has attracted scholars from across the nation as well as from abroad. Here they engage in the exchange of ideas, research, and writing in the fields of history, biography, literature, sociology, politics, and related areas. They also participate in public seminars and frequently are guest speakers in the region. (Courtesy of JoAnn Sieburg-Baker, Photographer, Charlotte)

The Vietnam War

While North Carolinians at home were concerned with the intricacies of integration, with plans to bring new sources of income to the state, and with a host of other matters, halfway around the world others faced threats to life and limb in rice paddies, swamps, and jungles. Between 1957 and 1975 the United States was involved in still another undeclared war in Asia. The Geneva Accords of 1954, drawn in haste and not clearly expressed, were intended to end the fighting in Vietnam and unify that war-torn country. The United States had assisted France in establishing a stable government in former French colonial territory in the hope of preventing the spread of communism in Southeast Asia. In that area Vietnam was divided by a demilitarized zone intended to separate opposing military forces—Communists in the north and non-Communists in the south.

American military advisers were sent to South Vietnam in 1955, and the French withdrew in 1957. The government, however, became autocratic, opposition arose, and a succession of insecure governments followed.

Communists began to infiltrate South Vietnam where they found considerable local support, and war broke out between the two divisions. United States involvement grew from merely advising the South Vietnamese government to sending increasingly large numbers of American troops into what proved to be a hopeless, undeclared, and unwinnable war. (In the summer of 1988 a bill was introduced in the United States Senate declaring that the war officially began on 28 February 1961.) As ununiformed Communist soldiers moved among the civilian population, it became virtually impossible to determine enemy from friend. Thick tropical foliage provided cover for the Communists' hit-and-run raids, land mines, and booby traps that inflicted cruel wounds; it also made movement across the land difficult. Climate and disease added to the misery of the fighting men. Eventually the United States forces used chemicals to defoliate trees and strip the land of cover for the enemy. These chemicals caused illness in humans who came in contact with them; some had long-lasting effects.

The mass of American people showed little interest in the struggle, yet in 1972 the nation's highest percentage of volunteers for service came from eastern North Carolina. While many North Carolinians gave the war little or no support, large numbers actually opposed it in vocal and graphic ways. Draft evasion was common. Some young men moved to Canada while others openly defied the law and participated in public demonstrations against both the draft and the war itself. The nation was seriously divided, and this, too, affected the morale of the troops. American policy prohibited the pursuit of the enemy when it fled into neighboring Cambodia, and this frustrated the fighting men. With Russian tanks and other equipment, the North Vietnamese launched unusually heavy attacks on several occasions which proved costly to both sides in dead, wounded, and captured. Finally, secret discussions by a special adviser to President Richard M. Nixon led to a cease-fire agreement effective in January 1973, and soon afterward American troops began to be withdrawn.

North Vietnam retained control of the northern part of the country, leaving many troops in the south as well. In violation of their agreement, the northern government conducted a series of offensives in the south and by the end of April 1975 had taken the whole of Vietnam. Remaining American troops, diplomatic personnel, and others escaped from the capital of South Vietnam just minutes before the city was occupied. Accompanying them were large numbers of prominent South Vietnamese who probably would have been executed by the occupying forces. Estimates suggest that around 4,500 Vietnamese and Laotian refugees settled in North Carolina after they reached the United States.

Most of the North Carolinians engaged in this war were nineteen- and twenty-year-olds who had been drafted. The first known casualty was Floyd Milton Frazier, an air force technical sergeant from Waynesville, who was killed in February 1962. Of the 543,000 Americans who served in Vietnam, 46,397 were lost in combat. Among the casualties, 1,282 North Carolinians were killed in battle and 290 died of other causes. In addition, when the war was over 1,333 Americans were missing.

Student Unrest

In large measure as a result of the Vietnam War, there was extensive student unrest across the United States. In North Carolina, however, it was largely confined to those colleges and universities with a large and diverse student body, attended by at least some out-of-state students, and where the educational goals and concerns of the institution were directed to society at large more than to the individual. The presence of graduate students on campus also was influential. Demonstrations occurred most frequently and violently at the University of North Carolina at Chapel Hill, Duke University, and North Carolina State University, although they also flared on other college campuses and at a few high schools.

The war in Vietnam was the primary focus. At many colleges students objected to the military draft and to the presence on campus of recruiters from business firms holding government contracts for war materials. "Flower children" thrived here and in many other parts of the world with the aim of correcting all of the world's "evils" overnight. The counterculture of the late 1960s and early 1970s grew out of the recent "beat" or hippie movement representing a basic lack of respect for and disregard of traditional values and behavior. Long hair on males, unconventional dress, and communal living were much in evidence, as was the use of marijuana and psychedelic drugs.

In some instances local causes were also adopted. Student activists, for example, opposed the low wages paid to food service workers and other unskilled employees. Their agitation at the University of North Carolina in Chapel Hill was typical of protests around the state and nation. Police protection became necessary to keep the student cafeteria open; it finally closed after a strike in February 1969 and its operation was later contracted to a private firm.

Student government came under attack for representing the "Establishment." At the Chapel Hill campus black students in 1968 demanded a black student court, and they became increasingly alienated from the student body as a whole; yet four years later, in the spring of 1972, Richard Epps of Wilmington—a black—was elected president of the student body. In a confrontation between white and black students on 16 January 1975, more than two hundred black students marched down the aisles, shouted, and clapped, preventing Ernest David

Duke, national information officer of the Knights of the Ku Klux Klan, from speaking at a meeting sponsored by the Carolina Forum in Memorial Hall. In the spring of 1977 Darrell Hancock, a black law student from Salisbury, as attorney general in the student government, swore in Jimmie Phillips, a white from Lexington, as president of the student body.

The trustees of the University of North Carolina at Chapel Hill in the spring of 1969 adopted regulations to suspend or expel any student or to discharge any faculty member for participating in activities impairing, impeding, or disrupting the educational processes of the university. Early in May 1970 at Kent State University in Ohio, following a series of outbursts and demonstrations over a period of several days, National Guardsmen fired into a mob of approaching students. Four students were killed and thirteen wounded. The repercussions on campuses nationwide were severe, and around seven hundred colleges and universities closed, some for the remainder of the semester. At almost exactly the same time, the Vietnam War escalated with the U.S. invasion of Cambodia. The reaction on North Carolina campuses was swift. Class attendance fell off dramatically (some said due to spring fever, however), and in Chapel Hill on one occasion thousands of students marched around campus and through classroom buildings, yelling and banging on pans or anything else that would make a disruptive noise. The participants shouted: "On strike! Shut it down!" A few students fled classrooms for safety's sake but others joined the mob. Some classroom doors were locked to keep the strikers out.

Greatly outnumbered, of course, faculty members hastily assembled to discuss the situation. As a result of their deliberations, they adopted a resolution offering students three alternatives for completing the term, which was almost over: (1) take a grade for their courses on the basis of work to date; (2) complete the requirements for their courses, but do so beyond the current semester; or (3) complete their courses in the normal manner. Many classes continued as scheduled and the term ended peacefully. Soon afterward, the war in Vietnam wound down and orders from draft boards ceased. The Twenty-sixth Amendment to the United States Constitution, extending the right to vote to eighteen-year-olds, was proposed in Congress on 12 March 1971 and ratified in record time—on 30 June of the same year. The recent protesters promptly calmed down and began to work within "the system," participating in voter registration programs and political campaigns.

Communism and the Speaker Ban

The role of Russia in both the Korean and Vietnam wars understandably concerned Americans. Communism was a term that aroused considerable fear and mistrust in North Carolina. The reluctance of numerous young men—

Following the enactment of the "Speaker Ban Law" by the legislature in 1963, persons prohibited from speaking on campus appeared on Franklin Street, in Chapel Hill, just across the wall along the northern edge of the University of North Carolina campus. (North Carolina Collection, University of North Carolina at Chapel Hill)

throughout the country and in some parts of North Carolina, of course—to serve in these wars, unlike their predecessors during World War II when the defense of democracy was clearer, troubled many of the state's political leaders. In an apparent move to secure the future of the state, the General Assembly rushed through a law on 26 June 1963, the next to the last day of the legislative session, which to many people became a "symbol of resistance to Communism." Known as the "Speaker Ban Law," it required boards of trustees of all state-supported colleges and universities to prohibit any known Communist from speaking on campus. Also covered was anyone who advocated the overthrow of the United States or of North Carolina, or who had pled the Fifth Amendment of the United States Constitution in refusing to answer questions about his or her possible Communist or subversive past. Visiting speakers of questionable eligibility were now obliged to speak from the sidewalk bordering the campus or somewhere else off university property.

Before long an agency of the Southern Association of Colleges and Schools indicated that this bill jeopardized the academic accreditation of the University of North Carolina and other state-supported institutions of higher learning in North Carolina. According to the agency, it threatened academic freedom as well as the independence of the institutions. At the recommendation of Governor Dan K. Moore, the General Assembly in June 1965 created a commission to study "the Statutes Relating to Visiting Speakers at State Supported Educational Institutions." The commission reported to the governor on 5 November, and he promptly called a special session of the General Assembly for 15 November. Between 6 and 12 November the trustees of the state-supported colleges and universities approved the policy statement of the commission. When the legislators met some demanded that the ban be strengthened, whereas others maintained that it should be totally rescinded. Based on the commission's recommendation, however, the law was amended on 17 November to provide that the governing body of each affected institution draw up its own regulations concerning the use of campus facilities by communistic or subversive speakers, thus eliminating the threatened loss of accreditation.

In an attempt to meet the intent of the General Assembly, trustees of the University of North Carolina formulated regulations applicable to all campuses of the system. Their action did not please certain students and some from Chapel Hill appealed to the court. In February 1968 the law was declared unconstitutional. This decision, however, did not affect a much earlier statute prohibiting the use of state facilities to advocate the overthrow of the government by force or violence. At their next session the trustees decided not to appeal the court's ruling or to try to ban any speaker in the future. But they did insist that all forums be open to the public, that all sides of controversial issues be presented, and that there be an opportunity to question or differ with speakers.

Governor Sanford's Progressive Program

While college and university students vigorously protested the Vietnam War and the ills that they saw around them, and while learned faculties debated the impact of the speaker ban on their campuses, Governor Terry Sanford was laying the foundations for a program to break the cycle of poverty that for so long had held large numbers of North Carolinians in its grip. His plans began to bear fruit in July 1963, when he announced the creation of the North Carolina Fund "to seek out the poor and help them become self-respecting and self-supporting." At his invitation, members of the Ford Foundation came to the state to study his proposal and advise him. Impressed by what its representatives had seen, the

Ford Foundation announced that it would contribute $7 million to the fund. Other gifts included $1,625,000 from the Z. Smith Reynolds Foundation and $875,000 from the Mary Reynolds Babcock Foundation.

Organized as a nongovernmental corporation, the directors of the North Carolina Fund sought to create a spirit of community effort and voluntary involvement of state and local officials as well as of religious, business, educational, and other community action leaders. In the summer college students, under the designation "North Carolina Volunteers," worked on projects that the fund supported. The goal was to identify regions of greatest poverty and need, and to implement programs to overcome the factors that created them. Each of North Carolina's one hundred counties was asked to identify specific problems and to submit suggestions or plans to resolve them. Fifty-one responded, and the fund chose eleven different kinds of projects in different sections of the state for assistance.

Local leadership was developed, and projects were planned and executed to serve as models for programs that could be organized by volunteers elsewhere or continued after the fund ceased to exist. Among them was a farmers' cooperative established in an abandoned county prison. With the help of the State Board of Education a School Improvement Program was developed to bring new hope to culturally disadvantaged children. Adults were taught to read and write, and children were introduced to art and literature. In a depressed mountain area artisans were encouraged to pursue their traditional handicrafts; a cooperative marketing system was created; and soon the demand for many of their products was greater than the supply. Architects also designed low-cost housing for low-income families. Other projects included studies and programs relating to voter education, health, hunger, and labor mobility.

Reports and booklets were issued to extend the influence of the fund's staff. Having served its purpose, the North Carolina Fund concluded operations in November 1968. During its existence the corporation accomplished its objectives by demonstrating how serious local areas of poverty could be eliminated. It also served as a model for the national War on Poverty program, and, through the North Carolina Volunteers, it was a prototype of the Peace Corps.

Environmental Concerns

In 1962, the publication of *Silent Spring* by Rachel Carson brought to the fore a subject of both national and local concern which previously had received little attention. Among other facts the author pointed out that bluebirds had become a rare species, that the call of birds heralding the arrival of spring had all but ceased in many parts of the country. The extensive use of sprays, dusts, and aerosols, she noted, had poisoned much of the nation's wildlife. If wildlife could be harmed, so could humans, and her book provoked a wide-ranging demand for environmental control.

In North Carolina the seeds for a response had been planted many years earlier. In 1911 the state began to purchase land containing the headwaters of certain rivers in order to protect water supplies, and in the 1920s zoning laws expanded public control over private property to assure compatible uses of land. Many municipalities had long before declared themselves to be bird sanctuaries and passed ordinances to protect birds, particularly from boys with BB guns. Audubon societies and bird clubs flourished, bird watching became a favored pastime, birdhouses were placed on trees and posts around the state, and bird feeders appeared outside countless windows.

The people of North Carolina became aware that something was awry in the environment when the ancient chestnut trees in the mountains began to die around 1922. A blight quickly wiped them all out. A fungus first attacked mimosa trees at Tryon in 1930, and within a few years only a few survived. Dutch elm disease pushed south from New England by the late 1930s and did its deadly work until only a rare elm tree survived. When spruce, balsam, and fir trees in the mountains began to lose their bright green sheen and finally to shed their needles in the late 1970s and the 1980s, scientists were called in to determine the cause. Blame was placed on acid rain. Harmful chemicals in the air from industrial waste had drifted into the mountains and rain washed them out onto the trees, killing them. The elimination of air pollution became an international concern, addressed by many leaders. Still another enemy of trees, attacking individual specimens as well as large tracts, has been the southern pine beetle. It can kill a tree in just a few days as it bores beneath the bark to "starve" the tree.

Soil conservation, a popular program of the Agricultural Adjustment Administration in the 1930s, was naturally a part of the new interest in the environment. Terraces in fields channeled run-off rainwater and held back topsoil. In 1971 statewide land use planning was implemented in compliance with the Environmental Policy Act of that year. Its stated purpose was "to seek, for all [North Carolina] citizens, safe, healthful, productive and aesthetically pleasing surroundings; to attain the widest range of beneficial uses of the environment without degradation, risk to health or safety; and to preserve the important historic and cultural elements of our common inheritance." The State Planning Commission's report in 1972 pointed out that "property rights are not static; they are fluid. They include both the rights of private individuals and the rights of the larger society. As society changes, so too do the rights in land." The General Assembly in 1973 created the Environmental Management Commission as a part of the Department of Natural and Economic Resources. The Coastal Management Act of 1974 required the twenty coastal counties to prepare land use plans, and four years later North Carolina became the first southern state to be recognized by the national Office of Coastal Zone Management through the granting of funds to carry out its work.

Laws were passed late in the century requiring contractors and builders to enclose excavated sites to prevent loose soil from being washed into streams. This not only prevented soil erosion, but it also helped to keep creeks and rivers clean. Until the 1950s most of the rivers in the western two-thirds of the state were red from the clay soil washed into them. During the last quarter of the century most of them were so clear that the sand and rocks at the bottom were clearly visible.

Further evidence of concern for the state's environment is provided by the successful effort to prevent a power company from constructing a dam in Virginia that would have flooded the New River in northwestern North Carolina.[2] Many herbicides, pesticides, and other chemicals have been banned by state law while others are prohibited by federal law. North Carolina chapters of the Nature Conservancy, the Sierra Club, and other organizations warn citizens of potential harm to the environment as well as take title to land, swamps, lakes, or other property to ensure their protection. State and local organizations also exist to protect and manage particular sites such as the Eno River in Durham and Orange counties and Weymouth Woods in Moore County. Plants and wildlife likely to disappear are safeguarded by private groups as well as by the state. The North Carolina Botanical Garden at Chapel Hill and the State Zoological Park near Asheboro play similar roles. State agencies are charged with testing and protecting land, air, and water resources, and safeguards have been implemented to control the disposition of harmful chemicals and radioactive waste.

Crime

For several centuries most North Carolinians felt secure in their homes and in the possession of their property. Doors were seldom locked. The final quarter of the twentieth century, however, saw this confidence evaporate even though the crime rate in North Carolina was considerably below the national average. In 1971 the state had approximately 1,900 crimes per 100,000 persons as opposed to 2,800 for the same group nationwide.

Many people believed that the misuse of drugs, as well as alcohol, accounted for much of the crime in the state. Drug addiction was expensive, and users might steal to support their habit. Sometimes robbery or attempted robbery

---

2. The river received its name in 1749 when it was discovered in a region so rough and inaccessible that it had never before been explored. Geologists consider the New River to be one of the oldest on the continent.

Table 26-1. Incidence of Crime in North Carolina.

	1975	1980	1985
Murder	668	608	504
Rape	852	1,306	1,450
Robbery	4,413	4,754	4,783
Motor vehicle theft	9,519	12,474	11,635
Aggravated assault	17,214	19,477	18,773
Burglary	65,964	82,011	69,872
Larceny	99,830	146,738	142,948

ended in homicide. Drug addicts, just as drunken drivers, might be responsible for automobile accidents.

Economic conditions, of course, contributed to the problem—the loss of a job, for instance, could drive a person to crime. So-called white-collar crimes such as embezzlement resulted from assorted causes including greed, living beyond one's means, or simply yielding to temptation, while the willful burning of property might be prompted by a desire for revenge, envy, or other causes. Crime statistics compiled by the state between 1975 and 1985 reveal that, whereas cases of rape and larceny increased significantly, the number of murders declined.

In 1977, at the request of Governor James B. Hunt, Jr., the General Assembly created the Department of Crime Control and Public Safety. Its purpose, together with the Governor's Crime Commission, Hunt said, was to provide "a focus for comprehensive planning and coordination of our criminal justice system." Juvenile offenses were identified as the fastest growing area of crime and steps were taken to revise the juvenile code. Community Watch programs were implemented in neighborhoods across the state. Local government officials were invited to cooperate with the state agencies, and brochures, television and radio advertisements, and films were made available.

Renewed efforts at federal, state, and local cooperation in law enforcement, investigation of the sources of crime, and prosecution of those convicted were effective. New municipal and county jails as well as new buildings at the state penitentiary were constructed. In 1987, the state budgeted $262 million to maintain its eighty-five prisons and $30 million for prison construction. To reduce the number of prisoners who did not commit violent crimes—about half of those being held—a new program was implemented. Referred to as the "Community Penalties Program," it required offenders to repay the victim by performing community service assignments as well as to obtain counseling for mental health and educational problems. In these cases the offender remained in the community and continued to work and pay taxes.

Historical Observances

While the state was preoccupied with foreign wars, the speaker ban, the North Carolina Fund, integration, and a host of other concerns, three significant historical events were commemorated. Each required considerable planning for several years before the actual celebration. The first of these was the centennial of the Civil War, observed between 1961 and 1965 under the direction of the North Carolina Confederate Centennial Commission. During this period educational programs presented historical facts through drama, music, film, and print; in many communities anniversaries were marked with programs developed by local citizens. Some of the commission's work made lasting contributions to the state. A survey of contemporary sources pertaining to the Civil War was completed, several historical works of merit were published, and the compilation of a new roster of Confederate soldiers from North Carolina was begun; volumes of the roster continued to appear in succeeding years through a project that was still under way in 1988. An archaeological team recovered the Confederate gunboat *Neuse* from the Neuse River near Kinston; it has been stabilized and is on display in a museum nearby. The Centennial Commission also designed and erected a number of large explanatory markers at sites around the state where significant events occurred during the war.

In 1963, the state commemorated the tercentenary of the Carolina charter under which eight Lords Proprietors were granted the territory of Carolina. A mobile museum—with exhibitions pertaining to the colonial period—visited many schools in the state, and a special exhibition at the Museum of History illustrated the seventeenth-century history of North Carolina. Musical compositions, dances, and dramas were also created for the observance. The commission that planned and executed the celebration made a number of lasting contributions as well. It formed a private corporation—still active in 1988—to help finance a project to locate and copy historical documents, particularly those in Great Britain, relating to colonial North Carolina. As a result of this work, xerographic and microfilm copies of thousands of pages of documents have been added to the holdings of the State Archives. In addition to publishing seven pamphlets on various aspects of early North Carolina history, the Carolina Charter Tercentenary Commission began a new series of *Colonial Records* which was continued by the State Department of Archives and History (now the Division of Archives and History).

Finally, between 1984 and 1987 the state observed America's Four Hundredth Anniversary commemorating the quadricentennial of the attempts by Sir Walter Raleigh to discover and settle the area that became North Carolina and the United States. A splendid exhibition at the British Museum in London, later moved to the Museum of History in Raleigh and to the New York Public Library, brought to America many artifacts of the sixteenth century. A publications program produced a series of pamphlets on aspects of the region's history, several volumes of history including one reproducing the watercolors of John White, and a bibliography of works by and about Sir Walter Raleigh. Scholars from both sides of the Atlantic attended a symposium on Raleigh in Chapel Hill, and the papers presented on that occasion were published in a single volume. A full-size representation of a ship of the period, *Elizabeth II*, was constructed and docked at a new State Historic Site on an island opposite the town of Manteo on Roanoke Island. A number of permanent historical markers were erected on Roanoke Island as well as in England, and the Four Hundredth Anniversary Committee lent support to a folk festival and to an educational television production, *Roanoak*, which was telecast nationwide. An archaeological program resulted in a new search for the sites of English habitation on Roanoke Island as well as for Indian villages known to the Roanoke colonists of the sixteenth century.

Reorganization of State Government

During the last half of the twentieth century North Carolinians witnessed a variety of progressive changes in their state involving larger numbers of its citizens in activities of many kinds. As we have seen, these served the general population in special educational programs, cultural opportunities, environmental concerns, and crime protection. Ranging from such serious matters as adjusting state government to altered conditions to establishing one of the nation's most promising zoos, North Carolina might be said to have changed from A to Z.

The necessity for revising the machinery of state government was acknowledged in 1953, when the General Assembly passed the first of a series of almost biennial resolutions creating and continuing a Commission on the Reorganization of State Government. This commission thereafter issued biennial reports on a wide range of topics as they were studied. Among them, but by no means all, were such subjects as state printing, the Museum of Art, the General Assembly, commercial fisheries, the State Ports Authority, agricultural marketing, mental health clinics, gubernatorial succession, correctional agencies, historic sites, education, control of alcoholic beverages, interstate cooperation, planning

The North Carolina House of Representatives meeting in the State Legislative Building, the first building in the United States devoted exclusively to the legislative branch of state government. Funds were appropriated in 1959, construction began in 1961, and the building was occupied in 1963. (North Carolina Division of Travel and Tourism, Raleigh)

agencies, public records management, state land management, water resources management, licensing boards, building regulations, and personnel management. Having investigated and reported to the General Assembly on virtually every aspect of state government over a sixteen-year period, the commission's work came to fruition. In 1969 the General Assembly drew up an act to amend the constitution so as to reduce the number of state administrative departments to no more than twenty-five and to authorize the governor to reorganize them subject to legislative approval. This amendment was ratified by the people on 3 November 1970, and between 1971 and 1973 the General Assembly enacted laws to streamline state government.

One of the first recommendations made by the Commission on the Reorganization of State Government was to build new quarters for the General Assembly. In the 1950s the legislature still occupied the same chambers that had been used in 1840. Space for committee meetings as well as for regular sessions was inadequate, the presiding officers had no offices, and there was little room for visitors. On the commission's advice, the 1959 General Assembly made an appropriation to construct a legislative building. Several blocks of Halifax Street running north from the capitol were closed, and the nation's first structure to be erected solely for a state legislature was built on Jones Street facing the capitol astride the former Halifax Street. It was first used in 1963. Soon additional buildings to house state agencies and to provide office space for legislators were constructed on a landscaped plaza between Jones and Peace streets.

Constitutional Reform

Governor Dan K. Moore in 1967 suggested that the North Carolina State Bar undertake a study to determine how the state constitution might be revised in order to conform with changed conditions. Since 1869 there had been ninety-seven proposals for amending the constitution, of which sixty-nine had been ratified by the voters. Certain provisions were outdated because of federal action, and some of the language was either out of date or vague. In response to Moore's recommendation, the State Bar and the Bar Association established the North Carolina State Constitution Study Commission of twenty-five members under the chairmanship of former state chief justice Emery B. Denny.

The commission produced a revised text of the constitution incorporating both editorial and substantive changes, none of which were likely to be controversial when submitted to a vote of the people. This document, approved in 1970, took effect the next year and became known as the Constitution of 1971. In addition to this document, the study commission drew up ten separate proposals that either were potentially controversial or represented fundamental changes; these were submitted to a referendum of the people as separate items. The latter included extensive revision of the finance article of the constitution. The basic organization of the constitution was retained, as was the declaration of rights dating largely from 1776. Obsolete references to race were eliminated, scattered statements concerning the duties of the governor were combined, and the Council of State was enlarged to include the governor, the lieutenant governor, and the attorney general as ex officio members. The poll tax was eliminated and references to education were consolidated. Other revisions further modernized the document, and the General Assembly was authorized to implement some organizational changes.

In carrying out the mandate of the people, the General Assembly passed the Executive Organization Act of 1971 whereby more than 350 separate agencies, boards, and commissions were combined into fewer than 20 executive departments, many with new names, each to be headed by a Secretary appointed by the governor. The objectives of the act—to streamline the operations of administrative departments, reduce the number of employees, and bring more professionalism into the operation of state government—did not materialize in every case, however. Many of the departments soon began to increase the top level of management as political appointees required professional assistance in managing their responsibilities. In more and more instances politics came to play a role in the selection of even lower-echelon state employees. Changes in administration, whether of the same party or of the other, frequently brought not just a change of incumbent but often a change of policy as well, even in the case of work generally considered professional.

Higher Education

The face of North Carolina was further modified in the field of higher education. In 1963 the General Assembly changed the names of two branches of the University of North Carolina to the University of North Carolina at Chapel Hill and the University of North Carolina at Greensboro, and in 1965 the Raleigh campus was named North Carolina State University at Raleigh. Charlotte College became the University of North Carolina at Charlotte in 1965, while in 1969 Asheville-Biltmore College and Wilmington College became the University of North Carolina at Asheville and the University of North Carolina at Wilmington, respectively. In 1971 the remaining ten state-supported institutions of higher education were brought into the university system as was the North Carolina School of the Arts in Winston-Salem. All came under the supervision of a thirty-two-member board of governors.

Educational television began in North Carolina on 8 January 1955 when the University of North Carolina opened studios on the campuses at Chapel Hill, Greensboro, and Raleigh. In time other transmitters were installed across the state from Wilmington and Columbia in the east to Linville and Asheville in the west. Educational programs for all ages were regularly scheduled as were programs of general interest, drama, music, dance, and public service.

With fifty-eight institutions, the North Carolina system of community colleges was the third largest in the nation. In 1985 it enrolled more than half a million students on campuses that were within thirty miles of 99.2 percent of the state's population. The system began in 1957 when the General Assembly passed the Community College Act. By 1963 six junior colleges had been established, soon to be joined by industrial educational centers; the latter were given the option of calling themselves technical colleges or technical institutes. Some community colleges offered transfer programs for students who intended to con-

Students in the dance studio of the North Carolina School of the Arts. Authorized by the General Assembly in 1963, the first state-supported residential school for the performing arts opened in 1965. (North Carolina School of the Arts, Winston-Salem)

tinue their education at a four-year institution, whereas others provided technical and vocational training, continuing education programs, and basic adult and general education programs. Industry service programs provided specialized training for potential employees of new businesses that moved into a community.

Great and Unexpected Changes

North Carolina kept pace with the changing scene by creating means of dealing with assorted new questions. For example, a highway safety program was established to study the serious problem suggested by its name. It issued publications, compiled statistics, and made recommendations to the General Assembly. With a grant from the Richardson Foundation in 1963 the North Carolina Film Board was created both to produce films about North Carolina and to encourage the production of commercial films in the state. In time, a number of movies were made in North Carolina by national producers. Asheville, Chapel Hill,

Durham, Raleigh, Shelby, Statesville, and Anson County were discovered to be excellent settings, and companies intending to produce films on a long-term basis established offices in Wilmington and Shelby. Later, when it became part of the Department of Commerce, the Film Board was renamed the North Carolina Film Office. A Commission of Indian Affairs was established to provide aid and protection for the state's native Americans, to assist their communities in social and economic development, to help them preserve cultural and religious traditions, and to bring into focus local, state, and federal resources that could be used to their advantage.[3]

Many North Carolinians participated in the formation of the North Carolina Zoological Society, a nonprofit organization that bought 1,371 acres in Randolph County—including 947-foot Purgatory Mountain—on which to establish a state zoo. In 1969 the General Assembly appropriated $250,000 for the project; construction began soon after it approved the site in 1971. An interim zoo was completed in September 1974, and in the following decade new segments were opened as they were ready. Plans for expansion will carry construction into the next century. Outdoors there are herd areas as well as sections designed as special habitats. Others provide a controlled environment indoors, a forest aviary, and an African pavilion. Supported in part by private funds, this facility is anticipated to be one of the nation's most outstanding zoos.

The North Carolina Museum of Art rapidly came to be known for possessing one of the country's top-ranked collections, particularly in the Renaissance and baroque periods. In April 1983 it opened in a new building situated in a parklike setting in west Raleigh.

In the mid-1970s religious fundamentalists organized a movement to challenge the perceived attitude of many governmental leaders and a large portion of the American public regarding moral and religious issues. This segment of the population, commonly referred to as the "New Christian Right" or the "Moral Majority," was also allied to the ultra-conservative wing of the Republican party in North Carolina led by Senator Jesse Helms. Adherents of the movement opposed abortion, pornography, sex education, the gay rights movement, homosexual teachers in public schools, the Equal Rights Amendment, drug abuse, drinking, X-rated films and bookstores, topless dancers in lounges, and gambling. They advocated prayer in public schools and the teaching of creationism, as well as policies of free enterprise at home and unyielding opposition to communism abroad. The survival of the American family, they maintained, depended on the elimination of the evils that they identified.

Members of the New Christian Right pursued their goals through radio and

---

3. For further examples of state boards, commissions, and other agencies, see the current issue of the *North Carolina Manual* published by the Office of the Secretary of State.

television evangelism and by persuading local civic and business leaders in many communities to do their bidding. They succeeded in eliminating certain "objectionable" books from schools and libraries and in closing some motion picture theaters, lounges, and massage parlors. They conducted registration drives and managed to elect like-minded candidates to office. Supporters claimed that they were instrumental in the election of Ronald Reagan as president in 1980. Their support of the National Congressional Club and Political Action Committees provided resources for candidates who reflected their views.[4]

Governor James B. Hunt, Jr., in the late 1970s strongly supported the Equal Rights Amendment to the United States Constitution which was presented to the states in 1972. Its avowed purpose was to prevent discrimination against women in the workplace, and by 1975 it had been ratified by thirty-four states. After wide discussion around the state and many public demonstrations both for and against the amendment, the North Carolina General Assembly in 1979 referred the matter to two different committees; it died in one and was given an unfavorable report in the other. Two bills introduced to authorize a statewide referendum on the question met similar opposition in the committees. The amendment was never ratified even though the time limit for ratification was extended.

Near the end of the American Revolution there was a popular song about "the world turned upside down." North Carolina's political leaders might well have quietly hummed the tune on many occasions two hundred years later. Those who said that the public schools would never be integrated or that busing would be resisted to the bitter end had to eat their words. Those who refused to ratify the Nineteenth Amendment, and their counterparts who rejected the Equal Rights Amendment, lived to see women prove that they were equal to men in countless ways. They saw Judge Susie Sharp sitting on the North Carolina Supreme Court and Grace J. Rohrer as Secretary of the Department of Art, Culture, and History, the first woman to hold a cabinet-level post, to say nothing of numerous other women in policy-making positions at every level of government. The sight of eighteen-year-olds casting their ballots at the polls would never have been dreamed of earlier in the century.

In 1973, for the first time in the century, a Republican, James E. Holshouser, Jr., became governor, thereby inaugurating a new day for two-party politics in the state. His Democratic successor, James B. Hunt, Jr., in 1977 obtained an

4. I am indebted to Professor Anthony Oberschall of the Department of Sociology, University of North Carolina at Chapel Hill, for permitting me to read his unpublished paper, "The Old and the New Right in North Carolina," delivered at the annual meeting of the Society for the Scientific Study of Religion, held in Providence, Rhode Island, on 22 October 1982. He was assisted in this study by Steve Howell, a graduate student.

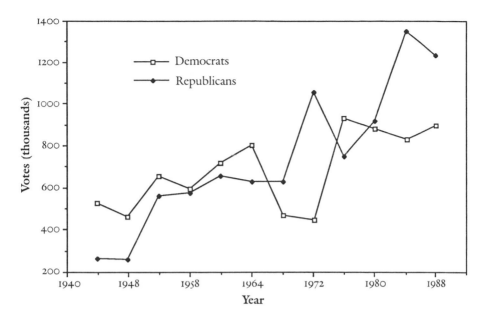

Presidential Election Statistics: 1944–1988

amendment to the state constitution permitting the governor to serve two consecutive terms, and then was elected to succeed himself. But at the end of his eight years in office he was followed by another Republican, James G. Martin, further strengthening the two-party concept. Hunt was defeated in his bid for a seat in the United States Senate by the Republican incumbent, Jesse Helms, in the most expensive senatorial campaign ever waged in the United States. It was reported that the victor spent $14 million. Helms, who was first elected to the Senate in 1972, became known for his conservative stance. Although some of his stands were rejected nationally as well as at home, he remained popular with a majority of the voters. He favored such issues as prayer in public schools, the tobacco support program, and a balanced national budget. He opposed the Equal Rights Amendment, cross-busing to achieve racial balance in schools, abortion for any reason, and the Voting Rights Act.

Finally, old-time politicians would have been amazed at the number of blacks elected to public office in North Carolina from the supreme court, through the General Assembly, down to the local level—mayors and aldermen, members of school boards, and even sheriffs.

The face of North Carolina was also changed by the appearance of new industry scattered across the countryside, as well as in cities and towns. In well-landscaped settings and in attractive buildings, clean industry appeared thanks in large measure to forward-looking regulations drafted by concerned legislators. Industry hunters from the governor to chambers of commerce traveled not only from coast to coast but also to Europe and Asia to lure desirable firms to the state.

The arrival of new industry was partly responsible for an increase in population. Charlotte, Greensboro, and Raleigh continued to grow as they had in recent decades, but so did Fayetteville, Rocky Mount, Greenville, Wilson, Chapel Hill, Goldsboro, Cary, and Havelock. A few cities, however, lost population—Asheville, Wilmington, Statesville, and Concord among them.

Economic growth, combined with the increase in population and the improved opportunities for higher education, also altered the cultural climate of the state. Programs of music, drama, and dance increased as state sponsorship grew and local productions were organized. Museums displaying art, historical artifacts or documents, and local or regional crafts were established. Young architects began to experiment with new materials and design to change the scene in town and country. Business and residential structures added to the attractions of the state.

A further surprise was the availability of new sources of power. Solar panels atop houses and commercial buildings would have suggested a science fiction story with a twenty-first-century setting just thirty years before they actually appeared. Nuclear power plants such as those constructed by the Carolina Power and Light Company in Brunswick and Wake counties and by Duke Power Company on Lake Norman would have seemed equally as futuristic. The latter were widely protested by those concerned about the environment.

Through surveys, sociologists found that the vast majority of native North Carolinians were highly satisfied with their state. A large percentage of newcomers were also at least content to live in North Carolina. A number of national polls reported it to be one of the states most favored by retirees. Yet it was not unusual for a native, nor rare for a newcomer, to suggest that "enough is enough, let's halt the movement of any more 'outsiders' to the state!"

27

THE STATE LOOKS
TO THE FUTURE

ORTH CAROLINIANS on a number of occasions, especially when the
present was not particularly promising, have looked to the future. The
Roanoke colonists of the 1580s took a great risk in leaving England for a
different kind of life in the New World wilderness, and as it turned out most of
them paid with their lives. In the 1670s those who took matters into their own
hands at the time of Culpeper's Rebellion obtained the reforms they sought and
so did those who drew up the Halifax Resolves and who cast their lot with John
Harvey, Cornelius Harnett, and other revolutionists near the beginning of the
last quarter of the eighteenth century. Archibald DeBow Murphey in the second
decade of the nineteenth century, recognizing that North Carolina suffered
from a backward, parochial view toward public affairs, drew up a progressive
program; his strategy did, indeed, change conditions in the state even though it
was not adopted promptly or in its entirety. Nearly half a century later Southerners lost their struggle to secure the freedom they believed was guaranteed to
them in the Tenth Amendment to the United States Constitution in the original
Bill of Rights. As the nineteenth century drew to a close Charles B. Aycock
predicted the "Dawn of a New Day" with his program for progress based on
universal education. In theory Aycock's proposal was sound, and insofar as it was
implemented it did make a difference. The creation of the Research Triangle Park
beginning in the mid-1950s was a step into the future based on faith.

The state's experience in gazing into the future, however, has had mixed
results. If converted into a graph it would display peaks and valleys; it would also
demonstrate that projected goals are seldom realized, yet in the attempt to reach
them some progress is achieved.

With the twentieth century nearing an end, Governor James B. Hunt, Jr.,
on 1 June 1981 by executive order, created the Commission on the Future of North
Carolina to implement a project known as "NC 2000." About six months earlier
he had asked the State Goals and Policy Board to begin planning for long-term
problems and opportunities in the state; subsequently, it was determined that
such a program could best be accomplished by a special commission established

for that purpose. In announcing his plans, the governor said: "Our task today is to anticipate and prepare for the North Carolina our children will encounter tomorrow. . . . We must take responsibility for making the world what we want it to be, for ourselves and for our children. And that requires looking into the future *now*. Looking at the future can help us anticipate changes and make decisions. It can prepare us for what lies ahead and put *us* in the driver's seat, to chart the course for North Carolina."

William C. Friday, president of the Consolidated University of North Carolina, was named chairman of the 69-member commission. Also appointed to work with this group was at least one representative from each of the state's one hundred counties. For local perspectives, 114 county chairs and co-chairs were authorized to seek the assistance and advice of leaders in their counties. Sixty-eight counties actually participated in the preparation of the commission's report, which also drew on the responses of 113,000 North Carolinians to a lengthy questionnaire. Public meetings were held in many parts of the state, at which knowledgeable individuals were consulted from time to time.

The concerns and the desires of North Carolinians, as determined by the commission members, revealed a great deal about the North Carolina of 1982. People hoped that by the year 2000 the weaknesses or needs apparent in their own lifetime would be redressed. Several interim reports were issued and a final report was published in 1983.

Press reaction to both the creation of the commission and its final report was mixed. One highly critical newspaper considered NC 2000 to be a political ploy of the governor so that he could "boast about the commission he appointed to study the future of North Carolina." Although the commission's report "is supposed to pave the way to the future," the writer continued, it "is actually a stunning indictment of the past failures of state government—both before and during the nearly 12-year reign of Hunt as majority party leader." Another newspaper, however, was more optimistic, citing the governor's predictions that if the commission's recommendations were followed North Carolina would be well served in the next century. It emphasized a number of positive proposals concerning education, business, land use, and the preservation of natural resources. A Raleigh columnist, often critical of state government, commented that "the next governor, Council of State and Legislature will . . . have slipped up if they don't take seriously the economic, social and environmental challenges identified" by the commission.

The first broad category of needs addressed by the commission related to *people*—specifically their health, housing, education, economic opportunity, justice, and self-fulfillment. Education was determined to be a high priority, and four aspects were emphasized: (1) the accessibility of a basic education to all citizens; (2) the availability of specialized services and quality day-care to meet the developmental needs of preschool children; (3) the quality of postsecondary education; and (4) training for new workers and for those required to learn new skills. Anticipated problems with the financing of an educational system to meet these goals were discussed, as was the question of teacher quality. Curriculum relevance at various levels, the educational needs of adults, and the role of business and industry in planning to provide people with job skills were all considered in great depth before recommendations were drawn up.

As a part of its concern with the health of North Carolinians, the commission observed that the increasing number of older people in the state would create a need for special services. By 2000, it predicted, one out of every eight residents of the state would be over sixty-five. This suggested the necessity of planning for an effective program to meet their needs for proper food, medical attention, and special equipment such as wheelchairs and beds. At the same time improved nutrition, sanitary conditions, and immunization had increased the number of infants and young people who survived, and the benefits of these should be available to all. Lifestyle-created diseases—from smoking, drinking, substance or drug abuse, hazards of the workplace, and other sources—required special attention, however, particularly by educating those who were susceptible. The control of hazardous substances was predicted to be an especially critical problem in the twenty-first century. In 1982 it was estimated that companies in the state generated some 1.8 billion pounds of hazardous waste and more than 200,000 cubic feet of low-level radioactive waste annually. Chemicals, dust, minerals, and other materials producing acute or chronic illness would have to be managed. This point was emphasized by the critical press, which pointed out that some recently recruited industries were contributing to this problem and that hazardous waste had been dumped in city and county landfills and on military bases. Health care, it was concluded, must be affordable and available to all North Carolinians.

The commissioners agreed that safe, sanitary, and decent housing must be available to families of low and moderate income through "innovative financing and construction techniques." Changes in restrictive zoning ordinances and in building codes (to permit the use of new materials) were recommended as possible aids.

In its report, the commission noted that the incidence of poverty, after a low point in 1973, appeared to be rising by 1982, but it offered no specific recommendations other than suggesting that "a closer look at . . . age, race, gender, and household type . . . may identify possible approaches for helping the poor." It was also found that the poverty rate for those sixty-five and older was higher in North Carolina than elsewhere in the nation—24 percent in the state as opposed to 15 percent nationwide. For those under eighteen, the state's poverty rate was two points higher—18 percent versus 16 percent.

The second topic of general concern was the *economy*. In broad terms the commission recommended a number of steps to maintain a favorable economic climate and to make capital available to small businesses, industry, agriculture, and fisheries. In line with some of the points mentioned in connection with education, it was hoped that by 2000 improved training institutions would help workers prepare for employment in new technical industries and that increased opportunities for women would enable them to remain in the labor force. Also related to education was the proposal that public schools offer "job-readiness training" to acquaint young people with the realities of daily employment. Without defining their precise goals, the commission suggested that young men and women be encouraged to enter nontraditional occupations and that guidance counselors be made aware of this possibility. To support a growing economy it was anticipated that improved public transportation, sources of energy, clean water, facilities for treating wastewater, and a network of information, communication, and technical advice would be required.

The recent growth in service industries prompted the commission to recommend this type of employment for future study. Included were recreational services, professional and technical services, personal services, wholesale and retail trade, and services to the growing retired population. Also mentioned for special consideration were tourism and agriculture. The tremendous recent decline in textiles and lesser drops in tobacco, food, wood, and apparel were represented in a graph which further indicated that relatively new fields of manufacturing in North Carolina—such as machinery, electrical components, chemicals, fabricated metals, instruments, rubber, and printing—might offer good job opportunities as the new century approached.

Third among the topics considered was *natural resources*. Article Fourteen of the state constitution directs the state to "conserve and protect all lands and waters for the benefit of all its citizenry and . . . to control and limit the pollution of our air and water, to control excessive noise, and in every other appropriate way to preserve as a part of the common heritage of this state its forests, wetlands, estuaries, beaches, historical sites, open lands, and places of beauty." The commission reaffirmed this constitutional mandate and its further elaboration by the state's Environmental Policy Act. More than eight hundred people from all parts of the state attended a meeting in December 1982 to discuss the environment. Their input was essential in the preparation of the commission's recommendations. It is noteworthy that participants suggested that the program proposed be implemented immediately rather than by the year 2000.

A number of precise goals were set: (1) clean up air and water pollution hazards, and prevent new ones from occurring; (2) ensure an adequate supply and equitable allocation of water resources; (3) stop erosion and the loss of fertile soil, and reduce water pollution from sedimentation; (4) increase the productivity of economically valuable resources up to their sustainable potential; (5) foster energy conservation and encourage the transition to renewable sources of energy; (6) preserve the special qualities of the natural landscape; (7) increase public access to outdoor recreational opportunities; (8) improve understanding of natural resources; (9) protect legitimate public interests in land-use decisions; and (10) simplify, improve, and adequately fund the management of natural resources.

The treatment of wastewater was determined to be a serious problem. It was discovered that in 1982 only half of the municipal waste treatment plants complied with water quality standards, and funds for improvements were decreasing. Some pollutants, such as sediment, were not treated by these plants. State tests of water resources were also found to be inadequate; rivers were tested for only 10 out of an estimated 55,000 chemicals used in the state. Both streams and groundwater were contaminated by surface mining, highway and other construction, sanitary landfills, livestock, and other sources such as runoff from fields where fertilizers or pesticides had been applied. These, of course, required attention.

The commission noted that large quantities of hazardous wastes were treated, stored, or disposed of in the state. At the end of 1981, for example, more than 79 million pounds were in storage. It also referred to "small" producers of similar, and equally dangerous, materials on which no information was regularly available. All of this material, the commission agreed, should be safely recycled, neutralized, or destroyed—at the site where it was created, if possible.

Interstate aspects of the pollution issue were considered. Acid rain damaging lakes, trees, rivers, and crops in North Carolina originated from industrial air pollution in New Jersey, Ohio, Alabama, and elsewhere. Rivers were polluted by material discharged into them in adjacent states. Beach pollution might come from adjoining states or from ships. The commission urged that negotiations be opened among governors to find solutions to these problems.

Among the state's important natural resources were its woodlands and streams for fishing, both sport and commercial. Long ago cited as "Nature's Sample Case," the mineral resources of North Carolina were a precious heritage. Scenic beauty, to be observed at many points along the more than five hundred miles between the ocean and the mountains, was also considered by the commission and listed as one of the state's natural resources to be protected for the future. The introduction of special incentives to private owners was especially commended as a possible way to protect natural areas.

Finally, the commission considered the subject of *community*, defined as "a group of people living in a given locale who share some common activities, attitudes, and interests." In an address to commission members, journalist Edwin Yoder said: "Amid the turbulence and impersonality of late twentieth-century life, this state clings doggedly to the idea of community, an asset to be prized." This definition may be applied to a neighborhood, a town or city, a county, or the whole state. Outsiders who moved to North Carolina frequently observed a feeling of closeness among the people, and this proved to be one of the attributes of the state that appealed to them.

To maintain this sense of "community" in the twenty-first century, the commission drew up ten goals and recommendations: (1) improve existing community physical environments; (2) ensure that new development enhances communities, while accommodating the expanding populations; (3) increase opportunities for recreational activities; (4) ensure access to adequate library facilities and services as well as their effective use in enriching the lives of citizens; (5) preserve and enhance the availability, accessibility, and diversity of community cultural opportunities; (6) reduce the incidence of crime and its effects on individuals by improved prevention and law enforcement efforts; (7) establish a more effective and equitable system of dealing with criminal offenders; (8) ensure a public policy formulation and decision-making process that is responsive to citizen concerns and equitable in the allocation of public resources; (9) organize and administer public services in an efficient and productive manner, and pursue, where feasible, fundamental program changes that achieve major and continuing cost reductions; and (10) establish and maintain adequate and equitable means for supporting necessary public functions.

These issues boiled down to four main aspects of community life. People wanted to retain the character of the place where they lived, but at the same time ensure that the changing physical needs were met. In this category they wished to support all worthwhile functions of the community from social participation to resource conservation. They desired the resources to support their intellectual and physical well-being while enjoying the satisfaction and the diversity of community life. They wanted to be secure and enjoy the feeling of protection for all those who lived there; at the same time they hoped to see law-breakers rehabilitated and socially acceptable behavior restored. Finally, to contribute to the sense of community, the commission sought to establish a stable community government to carry out the goals of those whom it governed.

Specific recommendations related to the rehabilitation or replacement of public works such as roads, bridges, water systems, police and fire stations, schools, and hospitals. The renewal and stabilization of downtown business areas and neighborhoods were mentioned along with new schools, libraries, and parks. Recreational facilities, the preservation of historic, cultural, and ethnic heritage, accessibility of the arts, crime prevention, and greater citizen participation in government all found a place in the report of the NC 2000 Project.

This comprehensive look at the North Carolina of the 1980s and carefully drawn image of the next century was presented to Governor Hunt in 1983 while the General Assembly was in session. The only legislative response, one newspaper reported, was "a bland joint resolution encouraging the continuation of the N.C. 2000 process." The legislators "produced nothing to deal with the most critical aspects of this report." Subsequently, the governor directed the state agencies to consider what they might include in their next budget request to accomplish some of the most crucial recommendations.

Chairman William C. Friday noted that the report of the commission could never be regarded as complete and that areas of concern to North Carolina in the 1980s had not been addressed. He believed, nevertheless, that the report did "capture the spirit of the citizens of the state in their aspirations for the future, and the commissioners share . . . their convictions about a future for North Carolina that they wish to enjoy and a quality of life they fervently hope that their children and grandchildren will experience."

At about the midpoint of his second term, Governor Hunt met with department heads of his administration and later with members of the State Goals and Policy Board to plan a transition to his successor. Specific recommendations were made for certain goals that might represent the state's action agenda for the balance of the century. These received attention for the final two years of Hunt's incumbency.

A staff member who had been closely involved with NC 2000 was retained in the administration of Governor James G. Martin, and a thread of continuity was maintained. The concerns and recommendations of the Commission on the Future of North Carolina continued to receive attention, and a number of them were soon acted upon. Educational needs appeared at the head of the list, as they had so often in the past. Support for the community college system, faculty salaries generally, the problems of poverty, the decline in the textile industry, the environment, the disposal of hazardous wastes, the quality of water, health care, and energy also held high priority for action as the state rounded out four hundred years.

APPENDIXES

APPENDIX A

British Monarchs during Exploration, Settlement, and the Colonial Period

Elizabeth I   1558–1603
James I   1603–25
Charles I   1625–49
     [Commonwealth 1649–60]
Charles II   1660–85
James II   1685–88
William III   1689–1702   and Mary   1689–94
Anne   1702–14
George I   1714–27
George II   1727–60
George III   1760–76

APPENDIX B

Chief Executives of North Carolina

Governors of "Ould Virginia"

1585–86	Ralph Lane	Appointed by Sir Walter Raleigh
1587–90	John White	Appointed by Sir Walter Raleigh

Commander of the Southern Plantation

1662–64	Samuel Stephens	Appointed by the Council in Virginia

Governors of Albemarle County under the Lords Proprietors

1664–67	William Drummond	
1667–70	Samuel Stephens	
1670–72	Peter Carteret	
1672–75	John Jenkins	Appointed deputy by Peter Carteret
1675–76	Thomas Eastchurch	Speaker of the Assembly
1676–77	John Jenkins	Deputy for Eastchurch who was appointed by the Lords Proprietors but did not serve
1677	Thomas Miller	Deputy
1678	Seth Sothel	Commissioned by the Lords Proprietors but did not serve
1678	John Jenkins	President of the "rebel" council
1679	John Harvey	President of the Council
1680–81	Henry Wilkinson	Commissioned by the Lords Proprietors but did not serve
1680–81	John Jenkins	President of the Council
1682–89	Seth Sothel	
1683–86	John Archdale	Acting governor
1689	John Gibbs	Governor by virtue of his rank as a cacique

Appendixes

Governor under the Lords Proprietors of "That Part of the Province of Carolina That Lies North and East of Cape Fear"

1689–91   Philip Ludwell

Deputy Governors of the Northern Part of Carolina for the Governor of Carolina Resident in Charles Town

1691–94	Thomas Jarvis	
[1694–96	John Archdale	Governor of both parts of Carolina]
1696–99	Thomas Harvey	
1699–1704	Henderson Walker	President of the Council
1704–5	Robert Daniel	
1705–6	Thomas Cary	
1706–8	William Glover	President of the Council
1708	Edward Tynte	Commissioned by the Lords Proprietors but died in Charles Town before taking office
1708–11	Thomas Cary	President of the Council
1711–12	Edward Hyde	President of the Council

Governors of North Carolina under the Lords Proprietors

1712	Edward Hyde	
1712–14	Thomas Pollock	President of the Council
1714–22	Charles Eden	
1722	Thomas Pollock	President of the Council
1722–24	William Reed	President of the Council
1724–25	George Burrington	
1725–29	Sir Richard Everard	

Royal Governors of North Carolina

1729–31	Sir Richard Everard	Remained in office until the first royal governor arrived from England
1731–34	George Burrington	

1734–52	Gabriel Johnston	
1752–53	Nathaniel Rice	President of the Council
1753–54	Matthew Rowan	President of the Council
1754–65	Arthur Dobbs	
1765–71	William Tryon	
1771	James Hasell	President of the Council
1771–75	Josiah Martin	

Presidents of the Council under the Revolutionary Government

1775–76	Cornelius Harnett
1776	Samuel Ashe
1776	Willie Jones

Governors of the State of North Carolina[1]

		Home County
1776–80	Richard Caswell	Dobbs (now Lenoir)
1780–81	Abner Nash	Craven
1781–82	Thomas Burke	Orange
1782–84	Alexander Martin	Guilford
1784–87	Richard Caswell	Dobbs (now Lenoir)
1787–89	Samuel Johnston	Chowan
1789–92	Alexander Martin	Guilford
1792–95	Richard Dobbs Spaight	Craven
1795–98	Samuel Ashe	New Hanover
1798–99	William R. Davie	Halifax
1799–1802	Benjamin Williams	Moore
1802–5	James Turner	Warren
1805–7	Nathaniel Alexander	Mecklenburg
1807–8	Benjamin Williams	Moore
1808–10	David Stone	Bertie
1810–11	Benjamin Smith	Brunswick
1811–14	William Hawkins	Warren
1814–17	William Miller	Warren
1817–20	John Branch	Halifax

1. Elected by joint ballot of both houses of the legislature for one-year terms during the period 1776–1835; elected by the qualified voters for two-year terms, 1836–68; and elected by the voters for four-year terms since 1868.

Appendixes

1820–21	Jesse Franklin	Surry
1821–24	Gabriel Holmes	Sampson
1824–27	Hutchins G. Burton	Halifax
1827–28	James Iredell	Chowan
1828–30	John Owen	Bladen
1830–32	Montfort Stokes	Wilkes
1832–35	David L. Swain	Buncombe
1835–36	Richard Dobbs Spaight, Jr.	Craven
1836–41	Edward B. Dudley	New Hanover
1841–45	John M. Morehead	Guilford
1845–49	William A. Graham	Orange
1849–51	Charles Manly	Wake
1851–54	David S. Reid	Rockingham
1854–55	Warren Winslow	Cumberland
1855–59	Thomas Bragg	Northampton
1859–61	John W. Ellis	Rowan
1861–62	Henry T. Clark	Edgecombe
1862–65	Zebulon B. Vance	Buncombe
1865	William W. Holden[2]	Wake
1865–68	Jonathan Worth	Randolph
1868–71	William W. Holden[3]	Wake
1871–74	Tod R. Caldwell	Burke
1874–77	Curtis H. Brogden	Wayne
1877–79	Zebulon B. Vance	Mecklenburg
1879–85	Thomas J. Jarvis	Pitt
1885–89	Alfred M. Scales	Rockingham
1889–91	Daniel G. Fowle	Wake
1891–93	Thomas M. Holt	Alamance
1893–97	Elias Carr	Edgecombe
1897–1901	Daniel L. Russell	Brunswick
1901–5	Charles B. Aycock	Wayne
1905–9	Robert B. Glenn	Forsyth
1909–13	William W. Kitchin	Person
1913–17	Locke Craig	Buncombe
1917–21	Thomas W. Bickett	Franklin
1921–25	Cameron Morrison	Mecklenburg
1925–29	Angus W. McLean	Robeson
1929–33	O. Max Gardner	Cleveland
1933–37	J. C. B. Ehringhaus	Pasquotank
1937–41	Clyde R. Hoey	Cleveland

2. Appointed by President Andrew Johnson under his plan of Reconstruction.

3. Impeached and removed from office in 1871; he was succeeded by the lieutenant governor, Tod R. Caldwell.

1941–45	J. Melville Broughton	Wake
1945–49	R. Gregg Cherry	Gaston
1949–53	W. Kerr Scott	Alamance
1953–54	William B. Umstead	Durham
1954–61	Luther H. Hodges	Rockingham
1961–65	Terry Sanford	Cumberland
1965–69	Dan K. Moore	Jackson
1969–73	Robert W. Scott	Alamance
1973–77	James E. Holshouser, Jr.	Watauga
1977–85	James B. Hunt, Jr.+	Wilson
1985–	James G. Martin	Iredell

4. An amendment to the state constitution during Hunt's administration permitting a governor to succeed himself for a second four-year term made it possible for him to serve two terms.

APPENDIX C

North Carolina Counties

Name	Date of Formation	Named For	County Seat	Land Area in Sq. Miles	1980 Population
Alamance	1849	Probably of Indian origin	Graham	433	99,319
Alexander	1847	William J. Alexander	Taylorsville	259	24,999
Alleghany	1859	Indian origin	Sparta	234	9,587
Anson	1750	Admiral George Anson, Baronet	Wadesboro	533	25,649
Ashe	1799	Samuel Ashe	Jefferson	426	22,325
Avery	1911	Waightstill Avery	Newland	247	14,409
Beaufort	1712	Duke of Beaufort	Washington	826	40,355
Bertie	1722	James and Henry Bertie	Windsor	701	21,024
Bladen	1734	Martin Bladen	Elizabethtown	879	30,491
Brunswick	1764	Town of Brunswick	Bolivia	861	35,777
Buncombe	1791	Edward Buncombe	Asheville	659	160,934
Burke	1777	Thomas Burke	Morganton	505	72,504
Cabarrus	1792	Stephen Cabarrus	Concord	364	85,895
Caldwell	1841	Joseph Caldwell	Lenoir	471	67,746
Camden	1777	Earl Camden	Camden Courthouse	241	5,829
Carteret	1722	Sir John Carteret	Beaufort	525	41,092
Caswell	1777	Richard Caswell	Yanceyville	427	20,705
Catawba	1842	Catawba Indians	Newton	396	105,208
Chatham	1771	William Pitt, Earl of Chatham	Pittsboro	708	33,415
Cherokee	1839	Cherokee Indians	Murphy	452	18,933
Chowan	1668	Chowan Indians	Edenton	181	12,558
Clay	1861	Henry Clay	Hayesville	214	6,619
Cleveland	1841	Benjamin Cleaveland	Shelby	468	83,435
Columbus	1808	Christopher Columbus	Whiteville	939	51,037
Craven	1705	William, Earl of Craven	New Bern	702	71,043
Cumberland	1754	William, Duke of Cumberland	Fayetteville	657	247,160
Currituck	1668	Indian word	Currituck	256	11,089

Name	Date of Formation	Named For	County Seat	Land Area in Sq. Miles	1980 Population
Dare	1870	Virginia Dare	Manteo	391	13,377
Davidson	1822	William Lee Davidson	Lexington	548	113,162
Davie	1836	William R. Davie	Mocksville	267	24,599
Duplin	1750	Thomas Hay, Viscount Dupplin	Kenansville	819	40,952
Durham	1881	Town of Durham	Durham	298	152,785
Edgecombe	1741	Richard Edgecumbe	Tarboro	506	55,988
Forsyth	1849	Benjamin Forsythe	Winston-Salem	412	243,683
Franklin	1779	Benjamin Franklin	Louisburg	494	30,055
Gaston	1846	William Gaston	Gastonia	357	162,568
Gates	1779	Horatio Gates	Gatesville	338	8,875
Graham	1872	William A. Graham	Robbinsville	289	7,217
Granville	1746	John Carteret, Earl Granville	Oxford	534	34,043
Greene	1799	Nathanael Greene	Snow Hill	266	16,117
Guilford	1771	Francis North, Earl of Guilford	Greensboro	651	317,154
Halifax	1759	Earl of Halifax	Halifax	724	55,286
Harnett	1855	Cornelius Harnett	Lillington	601	59,570
Haywood	1808	John Haywood	Waynesville	555	46,495
Henderson	1838	Leonard Henderson	Hendersonville	375	58,580
Hertford	1760	Earl of Hertford	Winton	356	23,368
Hoke	1911	Robert F. Hoke	Raeford	391	20,383
Hyde	1705	Governor Edward Hyde	Swanquarter	624	5,873
Iredell	1788	James Iredell	Statesville	574	82,538
Jackson	1851	Andrew Jackson	Sylva	490	25,811
Johnston	1746	Gabriel Johnston	Smithfield	795	70,599
Jones	1779	Willie Jones	Trenton	470	9,705
Lee	1907	Robert E. Lee	Sanford	259	36,718
Lenoir	1791	William Lenoir	Kinston	402	59,819
Lincoln	1779	General Benjamin Lincoln	Lincolnton	298	42,372
McDowell	1842	Joseph McDowell	Marion	437	35,135
Macon	1828	Nathaniel Macon	Franklin	517	20,178
Madison	1851	James Madison	Marshall	451	16,827
Martin	1774	Josiah Martin	Williamston	461	25,948
Mecklenburg	1763	Princess Charlotte of Mecklenburg	Charlotte	528	404,270
Mitchell	1861	Elisha Mitchell	Bakersville	222	14,428
Montgomery	1779	Richard Montgomery	Troy	490	22,469
Moore	1784	Alfred Moore	Carthage	701	50,505
Nash	1777	Francis Nash	Nashville	540	67,153

Name	Date of Formation	Named For	County Seat	Land Area in Sq. Miles	1980 Population
New Hanover	1729	House of Hanover	Wilmington	185	103,471
Northampton	1741	Earl of Northampton	Jackson	538	22,584
Onslow	1734	Arthur Onslow	Jacksonville	763	112,784
Orange	1752	William V of Orange	Hillsborough	400	77,055
Pamlico	1872	Pamlico Sound	Bayboro	341	10,398
Pasquotank	1668	Indian tribe	Elizabeth City	228	28,462
Pender	1875	William D. Pender	Burgaw	875	22,215
Perquimans	1668	Indian tribe	Hertford	246	9,486
Person	1792	Thomas Person	Roxboro	398	29,164
Pitt	1761	William Pitt, Earl of Chatham	Greenville	656	90,146
Polk	1855	William Polk	Columbus	238	12,984
Randolph	1779	Peyton Randolph	Asheboro	789	91,728
Richmond	1779	Duke of Richmond	Rockingham	477	45,481
Robeson	1786	Thomas Robeson	Lumberton	949	101,610
Rockingham	1785	Marquis of Rockingham	Wentworth	569	83,426
Rowan	1753	Matthew Rowan	Salisbury	519	99,186
Rutherford	1779	Griffith Rutherford	Rutherfordton	568	53,787
Sampson	1784	John Sampson	Clinton	947	49,687
Scotland	1899	Scotland	Laurinburg	319	32,273
Stanly	1841	John Stanly	Albemarle	396	48,517
Stokes	1789	John Stokes	Danbury	452	33,086
Surry	1771	County of Surrey, England	Dobson	539	59,449
Swain	1871	David L. Swain	Bryson City	526	10,283
Transylvania	1861	Latin words	Brevard	378	23,417
Tyrrell	1729	Sir John Tyrrell	Columbia	407	3,975
Union	1842	County made from parts of two others	Monroe	639	70,380
Vance	1881	Zebulon B. Vance	Henderson	249	36,748
Wake	1771	Margaret Wake Tryon	Raleigh	854	301,327
Warren	1779	Joseph Warren	Warrenton	427	16,232
Washington	1799	George Washington	Plymouth	332	14,801
Watauga	1849	Watauga River	Boone	314	31,666
Wayne	1779	Anthony Wayne	Goldsboro	554	97,054
Wilkes	1778	John Wilkes	Wilkesboro	752	58,657
Wilson	1855	Louis D. Wilson	Wilson	374	63,132
Yadkin	1850	Yadkin River	Yadkinville	336	28,439
Yancey	1833	Bartlett Yancey	Burnsville	314	14,934

Total Land Area in Sq. Miles 48,843

Total 1980 Population 5,881,766

Population of North Carolina

Year	Total Population[1]	Urban	Rural	Percent Urban	Blacks Free	Slave
1675	4,000					
1700	10,720					
1710	15,120					
1729	35,000					
1752	100,000					
1765	200,000					
1786	350,000					
1790	393,751				4,975	100,572
1800	478,103				7,043	133,296
1810	555,500				10,266	168,824
1820	638,829	12,502	626,327	2.0	14,612	205,017
1830	737,987	10,455	727,532	1.4	19,543	246,462
1840	753,409	13,310	740,109	1.8	22,732	245,817
1850	869,039	21,109	847,930	2.4	27,463	288,548
1860	992,622	24,554	968,068	2.5	30,463	331,059
1870	1,071,361	36,218	1,035,143	3.4	391,650	
1880	1,399,750	55,116	1,344,634	3.9	531,277	
1890	1,617,947	115,759	1,502,190	7.2	561,018	
1900	1,893,810	186,790	1,707,020	9.9	624,469	
1910	2,206,287	318,474	1,887,813	14.4	697,843	
1920	2,559,123	490,370	2,068,753	19.2	763,407	
1930	3,170,276	809,847	2,360,429	25.5	918,647	
1940	3,571,623	974,175	2,597,448	27.3	981,298	
1950	4,061,929	1,238,193	2,823,736	30.5	1,047,353	
1960	4,556,155	1,801,921	2,754,234	39.5	1,116,021	
1970	5,082,059	2,285,168	2,796,891	45.0	1,126,478	
1980	5,881,766	2,823,180	3,058,586	48.0	1,318,857	

1. Only estimates are available for the period before 1790; thereafter, official United States census returns are cited.

Appendixes

North Carolina's Twenty-five Largest Cities

	Population	
	1980	1970
Charlotte	314,447	241,420
Greensboro	155,642	144,076
Raleigh	150,255	122,830
Winston-Salem	131,885	133,683
Durham	100,831	95,438
High Point	63,380	63,229
Fayetteville	59,507	53,510
Asheville	53,583	57,820
Gastonia	47,333	47,322
Wilmington	44,000	46,169
Rocky Mount	41,283	34,284
Burlington	37,266	35,930
Greenville	35,740	29,063
Wilson	34,424	29,347
Chapel Hill	32,421	26,199
Goldsboro	31,871	26,960
Kinston	25,234	23,020
Salisbury	22,677	22,515
Cary	21,763	7,640
Hickory	20,757	20,569
Statesville	18,622	20,007
Lumberton	18,241	16,961
Havelock	17,718	3,012
Jacksonville	17,056	16,289
Concord	16,942	18,464

APPENDIX E

Sites of Meetings of the Legislature

1707	Little River [Perquimans County]
1708	Perquimans Precinct
1709	Little River
1715–16	Little River
1722–37	Edenton
1739–40	New Bern
1740–41	Edenton
1741	Wilmington
1743	Edenton
1744	Bath
1744–46	New Bern
1746	Wilmington
1747–52	New Bern
1752	Bath
1753	New Bern
1754	Wilmington
1754–60	New Bern
1760–64	Wilmington
1761	Brunswick
1765–78	New Bern
1778	Hillsborough
1779	Halifax
1779	Smithfield
1779	Halifax
1780	New Bern
1780	Hillsborough
1781	Halifax
1781	New Bern
1781	Wake Court House
1781–84	Hillsborough
1784–85	New Bern
1786–87	Fayetteville
1787	Tarboro
1788–90	Fayetteville
1791–93	New Bern
1793–94	Fayetteville
1794	New Bern
1794–	Raleigh

APPENDIX F

Chronology

1492	Columbus discovers the New World.
1497–98	Cabot discovers North America.
1497–1503	Voyages by Amerigo Vespucci.
1524	Verrazano explores North Carolina coast.
1526	D'Ayllón attempts settlement on Carolina coast.
1540	De Soto explores mountains of southwestern North Carolina.
1561	De Villafañe visits Cape Hatteras.
1566	De Coronas lands at Currituck.
1566–67	Pardo and Boyano in the mountains of North Carolina.
1578	Sir Humphrey Gilbert goes to Newfoundland with a colony; returns to England.
1584	25 March. Walter Raleigh obtains a patent for New World settlement.
	27 April. Amadas and Barlowe sail from England.
	13 July. They take formal possession of some 1,200 miles of North American coast and begin exploration.
	September. They return to England, and the new land is named "Virginia."
1585	6 January. Raleigh is knighted.
	19 April. Seven ships under Sir Richard Grenville take colonists and Governor Ralph Lane to Roanoke Island.
	26 June. Lane colony reaches Outer Banks.
	17 August. Fort is completed and Lane takes command over 107 men who compose England's first New World colony.
	25 August. Grenville returns to England.
	October (?). Detachment goes to Chesapeake Bay to spend the winter.
1586	March–April. Exploration of Albemarle Sound, Chowan and Roanoke rivers.
	Late April or early May. Grenville leaves England with supplies for the Lane colony.
	8 June. Sir Francis Drake's fleet is sighted off Outer Banks.
	10 June. Lane attacks mainland Indian village and kills Wingina. Drake arrives and offers Lane reinforcements and a ship.
	13 June. Hurricane strikes.
	16 June. Lane decides to take colony home to England.
	18 or 19 June. Colony sails with Drake, abandoning three men who were away on reconnaissance.

Late June. An unidentified ship arrives at Roanoke Island with supplies and finds colony gone.

Late July or early August. Grenville reaches Roanoke Island, explores region, leaves 15 or 18 men, and sails for home.

September or later. Garrison is attacked by Indians; 2 men are killed, 13 escape and disappear.

1587   7 January. "Cittie of Ralegh" in Virginia is incorporated under license from Raleigh.

8 May. Three ships sail with a colony of 91 men, 17 women, and 9 boys (at least one of whom was a baby). John White is governor.

22 July. Colony arrives off North Carolina coast; men begin repairs on houses left by Lane.

13 August. Manteo is baptized and given title of "Lord of Roanoke."

18 August. Virginia Dare is born, the first English child born in America. Harvey child is born a few days later.

22 August. Colonists insist that White return to England with fleet to rush supplies.

27 August. White sails for England.

1588   February. Thomas Harriot's *A briefe and true report* is published.

31 March. New colonizing expedition is nearly ready to sail.

April. No ships are allowed to sail from England due to Spanish threat.

27 April. White is permitted to sail, taking 7 men and 4 women to join colony, but after attack by pirates he is forced to return to England.

June. Spanish Armada is defeated.

1590   20 March. White sails with a privateering fleet that will stop by Roanoke Island when it is ready to return home.

18 August. White reaches Roanoke Island and finds the settlement abandoned.

20 August. Bad weather, perhaps a hurricane, forces ships to sail without further searching.

24 October. White arrives at Plymouth.

1602   Spring. Samuel Mace sails in March to search for the 1587 colonists, but visits only the Cape Fear when a storm drives him away.

1606   Charter from King James I to the Virginia Company of London includes region that became North Carolina.

1607   Jamestown on the Chesapeake Bay (where the 1587 colony was directed to settle) is established as the first permanent English colony in America.

1608   John Smith attempts to send two men to the Chowan region in search of the 1587 colonists.

1618   29 October. Raleigh is beheaded in London by order of James I.

1619   30 July–4 August. First representative legislature in America meets in Jamestown.

Late August. A Dutch ship brings the first blacks in North America to Jamestown.

1620	26 December. Pilgrims land at Plymouth, Massachusetts.
1622	February. John Pory from Virginia explores the region around Chowan River and praises it highly.
	First newspaper printed in England.
1624	Virginia Company's charter is withdrawn and its territory becomes subject to the Crown's disposal.
1625	James I dies and is succeeded by Charles I.
1629	30 October. Charles I grants Carolana to Sir Robert Heath.
1638	County of Norfolk is formed by Virginia to include territory as far south as 35°N latitude.
1639	First printing press in North America, at Cambridge, Massachusetts.
1642–49	Civil war in England.
1646	Expedition from Virginia against Indians along Chowan River.
1648 (?)	Several Virginians buy land from Indians along Roanoke River.
1649	30 January. Charles I is executed.
1649–60	Commonwealth in England.
1650	Approximate year first settlers from Virginia arrived in northeastern North Carolina.
1653	Virginia Assembly grants land along Roanoke and Chowan rivers to Roger Green.
1654	Francis Yeardley's company of six men visit Currituck Sound–Roanoke Island area.
1656	Captain Thomas Francis and Colonel Thomas Dew are commissioned by Virginia Assembly to explore between Cape Hatteras and Cape Fear.
1657	By this time Nathaniel Batts, the first known permanent white settler in North Carolina, has a house at the western end of Albemarle Sound.
	Nicholas Comberford, London mapmaker, prepares a map of the "south part of Virginia."
1660	Charles II becomes king of England with the restoration of the monarchy.
	24 September. Oldest recorded North Carolina deed—from Indians to Nathaniel Batts.
1661	4 August. Grant of land from King Kilcocanan to George Durant is recorded.
1662	9 October. Samuel Stephens is appointed "commander of the southern plantation" by the Virginia Council.
1663	24 March. Carolina (first official use of the name) is granted by Charles II to eight Lords Proprietors.
	William Hilton and others explore Cape Fear region.
	A small party of New Englanders settle along Cape Fear River but remain only a short time.
1664	Proprietors plan three counties in Carolina: Albemarle, Clarendon, and Craven.
1664–67	William Drummond is appointed the first governor of Albemarle County, Carolina.

1665	30 June. Proprietors receive a new charter extending their territory north and south.
	Colony from Barbados settles along lower Cape Fear River, establishes Charles Town (site now in Brunswick County, N.C.) in Clarendon County. Sir John Yeamans is named governor.
	First Albemarle legislature meets.
	15 November. Oldest recorded will in North Carolina—that of Mrs. Mary Fortsen, dated and signed by her on January 1664—is proved.
1666	Carolina is represented at a council held at St. Mary's, Maryland, concerning the quality of tobacco in Maryland, Virginia, and Carolina.
1667	Clarendon County is abandoned after attaining a population of around 800.
1667–70	Samuel Stephens is governor of Albemarle County.
1668	About this time Chowan, Currituck, Pasquotank, and Perquimans precincts, Albemarle County, are formed.
1669	21 July. Fundamental Constitutions are approved by the Proprietors.
1670	Settlement of Craven County on Ashley River as beginning of South Carolina.
1672	Quakers William Edmundson and George Fox preach in the Albemarle area.
1675–77	Chowanoc Indian war.
1677	Culpeper's Rebellion, a revolt against acting governor Thomas Miller.
1689	Albemarle County as a unit of government ceases to exist, and Carolina "North and East of Cape feare" is established.
1690	Gibbs's Rebellion over title to office.
	Colony of French from Virginia settle on Pamlico River.
1691	Proprietors unite all of Carolina under one governor in Charles Town, with a deputy governor in the Albemarle region.
1696	Bath County is formed.
1699	The Reverend Thomas Bray sends three collections of books from England as libraries for the Albemarle area.
1701	Vestry Act is passed to establish Anglican church in the colony.
	15 December. Chowan parish (now St. Paul's, Edenton) is established.
1705–8	Charles Griffin, of Pasquotank Precinct, has first known school in the colony.
1706	Bath is incorporated, the first town in the colony.
1710	New Bern is founded.
1711	Cary's Rebellion.
	22 September. Beginning of Tuscarora Indian war.
1712	Separation of North Carolina and South Carolina with the commissioning of Edward Hyde as the first governor of North Carolina. Christopher Gale is named the first chief justice of the colony.
1713	Beaufort is laid out (incorporated in 1723).
	First paper money is issued by the colony.

1713–15	Continuation of Tuscarora war.
1715	Town on Queen Anne's Creek is established (name changed to Edenton in 1722).
1718	Piracy ends with killing of Blackbeard and capture of Stede Bonnet.
1725	3 June. Patents are first issued for land in the lower Cape Fear.
1726	Town of Brunswick is laid out.
1728	7 March. Surveyors begin marking the North Carolina-Virginia line.
1729	25 July. King George II purchases seven of the eight Proprietors' shares of Carolina.
1733 (?)	Settlement begins that becomes Wilmington.
1734	St. Thomas Church, Bath, the oldest surviving church in North Carolina, is built.
1735	North Carolina-South Carolina boundary survey begins.
1738–39	First post road for regular postal service.
1739–48	England, Spain, and France are at war. Colonies, including North Carolina, furnish some troops.
1739–76	Highland Scots settle in Cape Fear Valley.
1744	Granville District is created but only partially surveyed.
1747–48	Spanish attack Brunswick and Beaufort.
1749	24 June. James Davis begins operation of first printing press in North Carolina.
1751	August. *North Carolina Gazette*, the first newspaper in the colony, comes from Davis's press.
1752	7 September. England and the colonies adopt the Gregorian calendar.
1753	Moravians from Pennsylvania purchase 98,985 acres from Earl Granville and name tract "Wachovia." They soon establish the towns of Bethabara, Bethania, and Salem.
1754–63	French and Indian War.
1755	Sandy Creek Church is founded, the "Mother of Southern Baptist Churches."
	Fort Dobbs is built on the frontier for protection against raiding Indians.
1759	Riots in Granville District against Francis Corbin.
1760	An academy opens in Wilmington.
1763	England adopts "New Colonial Policy" at end of French and Indian War; royal proclamation prohibits settlement beyond crest of mountains.
1764	Parliament passes Sugar Act levying tax.
	10 October. William Tryon arrives as lieutenant governor.
1765	Selwyn land riots—the War on Sugar Creek in Mecklenburg County.
	22 March. Stamp Act is passed, effective 1 November.
	25 March. Quartering Act is passed.
	28 March. Governor Dobbs dies.
	April. Tryon becomes governor.
	6 June. George Sims's address in Granville County.
	7–25 October. Stamp Act Congress is held in New York.

28 November. *Diligence* arrives in Cape Fear with stamped paper.

1765–66 November–February. Stamp Act is resisted in North Carolina.

1766 January. Captain Jacob Lobb of *Viper* seizes two ships.

18 March. Stamp Act is repealed, effective 1 May.

November. Orange County meeting to get accounting of local government.

1767 David Caldwell's school opens.

January. Construction of Tryon Palace begins.

29 June. Townshend Revenue Acts are passed by Parliament.

1768 11 February. Massachusetts Circular Letter.

4 April. Regulators organize in Orange County.

Daniel Boone explores Kentucky.

1769 18 May. Virginia Non-Importation Association.

6 November. "Convention" is called to support Non-Importation Association.

1770 Tryon Palace is completed.

1771 15 January. Queen's College is chartered.

16 May. Battle of Alamance.

1 July. Governor Tryon leaves for New York.

July–August. James Hasell is acting governor.

12 August. Josiah Martin qualifies as governor.

1772 Salem Female Academy is established.

1773 8 December. North Carolina Committee of Correspondence is appointed.

15 December. Boston Tea Party.

1774 31 March–22 June. "Intolerable Acts" are passed by Parliament.

4 August. Rowan County freeholders adopt resolves opposing slave trade.

25–27 August. First Provincial Congress, New Bern.

September–October. First Continental Congress, Philadelphia.

25 October. Edenton Tea Party.

1774–89 Continental Congress.

1775 3–7 April. Second Provincial Congress, New Bern.

8 April. Last royal Assembly is dissolved by Governor Josiah Martin.

19 April. Battles of Lexington and Concord, Massachusetts.

[20 May. "Mecklenburg Declaration of Independence".]

31 May. Mecklenburg Resolves.

31 May. Governor Martin flees the palace in New Bern.

2 June. He arrives at Fort Johnston.

23 June. He calls an Assembly which does not convene.

18 July. He escapes to British warship in Cape Fear River.

18 July. Fort Johnston is burned by Patriots.

20 August–10 September. Third Provincial Congress, Hillsborough.

23 August. Parliament declares the colonies to be in revolt.

1775–76 May 1775–December 1776. Second Continental Congress.

1776 27 February. Battle of Moore's Creek Bridge.

4 April–14 May. Fourth Provincial Congress, Halifax.

12 April. Halifax Resolves authorize North Carolina delegates in Continental Congress to "concur with the delegates of the other Colonies in declaring Independency."

Summer. Expedition against the Cherokees.

1 August. Cornelius Harnett publicly reads the Declaration of Independence at Halifax.

2 August. Declaration of Independence is signed on behalf of North Carolina.

12 November–23 December. Fifth Provincial Congress, Halifax.

17 December. Declaration of Rights are adopted by the Provincial Congress.

18 December. State constitution is adopted by the Provincial Congress.

22 December. Richard Caswell is chosen governor by the Provincial Congress.

1777   6 February. Josiah Martin's property is sold at auction in New Bern.

7 April. First state legislature meets at Tryon Palace, now the state capitol.

18 April. Richard Caswell is elected governor by the General Assembly.

15 November. Continental Congress adopts Articles of Confederation.

1778   6 February. France recognizes independence of the United States.

24 April. North Carolina ratifies Articles of Confederation.

1780   20 June. Battle of Ramsour's Mill.

16 August. Battle of Camden, South Carolina.

9 September. Patriots attack Tories at Wahabs in present Union County.

28 September. Defense of Charlotte against approaching British.

7 October. Battle of King's Mountain, South Carolina.

1781   January. British Major James H. Craig occupies Wilmington.

17 January. Battle of Cowpens, South Carolina.

31 January. Engagement at Cowan's Ford.

23 February. Pyle's Massacre, defeat of Tories near Hillsborough.

1 March. Last state ratifies Articles of Confederation.

6 March. Engagement at Wetzel's Mill.

15 March. Battle of Guilford Court House.

4 August. Engagement at Beatty's Bridge.

5 August. Engagement at the House in the Horseshoe.

29 August. Battle of Elizabethtown.

1 September. Engagement at Raft Swamp.

12 September. Tories under David Fanning capture Governor Thomas Burke at Hillsborough.

13 September. Battle of Lindley's Mill on Cane Creek.

19 October. Cornwallis surrenders at Yorktown, Virginia.

18 November. Major Craig evacuates Wilmington.

1782   May. David Fanning leaves the state.

1783   19 April. Governor Alexander Martin informs the legislature that Britain acknowledges independence.

3 September. Treaty of Paris ends war between Great Britain and the United States.

1784	April. North Carolina cedes its western land to the United States but in October revokes this act.
	8 November. Bill is presented to legislature to establish a state university but is rejected.
1785	State of Franklin is created in North Carolina's western country.
	19 April. Methodist church holds its first annual conference in the United States in Louisburg at the home of Green Hill.
1787	25 May–14 September. United States Constitution is drawn up in Philadelphia.
	November. *Bayard v. Singleton* is the first court decision to declare a law unconstitutional.
	Franklin Academy is chartered; evolves into Louisburg College.
1788	21 July–4 August. Convention in Hillsborough declines to ratify United States Constitution, suggesting many amendments.
	2 August. Convention agrees to locate new capital within ten miles of Isaac Hunter's plantation in Wake County.
1789	16–23 November. Convention in Fayetteville ratifies United States Constitution.
	11 December. General Assembly charters the University of North Carolina.
	State's western land is ceded to the United States.
1790	Dismal Swamp Canal is chartered to join Albemarle Sound and Chesapeake Bay.
	10 February. James Iredell is appointed to United States Supreme Court.
	August. Taking of first United States census begins.
1791	May–June. George Washington visits a number of North Carolina towns during his southern tour.
1792	Site for state capital is located and named "Raleigh."
1793	18 February. Judge Iredell dissents to the decision in *Chisholm v. Georgia* in a pioneer stand for states' rights that results in the Eleventh Amendment.
	12 October. Cornerstone is laid for the first building at the University of North Carolina.
1794	30 December. General Assembly convenes in the newly completed state capitol.
1795	15 January. University of North Carolina officially opens.
	12 February. Hinton James, the first student, arrives to enter the university.
1797	Asheville is incorporated.
1799	Seventeen-pound chunk of gold is found in Cabarrus County by 12-year-old Conrad Reed.
	28 June. North Carolina–Tennessee boundary survey is completed.
	22 October. *Raleigh Register* begins publication.
1804	First locomotive steam engine runs in Wales.
	Bank of Cape Fear and Bank of New Bern are chartered as the first banks in North Carolina.

1804–7	Walton War on North Carolina-Georgia boundary.
1807	Robert Fulton operates the first successful commercial steamboat on Hudson River.
1808	Importation of slaves ceases.
1810	Bank of North Carolina is chartered.
1812	State Library is established.
1812–15	War of 1812.
1813	Michael Schenck cotton mill, the first in the state, is built in Lincoln County. (Three years later Absolam Warlick joined in its operation.)
	12–16 July. British fleet occupies Portsmouth and Ocracoke.
1815	Archibald D. Murphey reports to General Assembly on internal improvements.
	Roanoke Navigation Company is chartered.
1816	Murphey reports to General Assembly on education.
1817	Former Anglicans organize Episcopal church in North Carolina.
	Joel Battle and H. A. Donaldson build a cotton mill at the Falls of Tar River [Rocky Mount].
1818	Neuse River Navigation Company operates a steamboat between New Bern and Elizabeth City.
	Battle family erects a cotton mill at Rocky Mount.
	Prometheus is the first steamboat built in the state (at Beaufort); operates on Cape Fear River.
	State supreme court is reorganized.
1819	Murphey publishes his *Memoir on Internal Improvements*.
	Western boundary with South Carolina and Georgia is determined as 35th parallel.
	Cherokee Indians cede a large amount of land to North Carolina.
	24 December. Canova statue of George Washington is unveiled in the state capitol.
1825	State Literary Fund is created and Literary Board is named to manage it.
	Tiny steam locomotive is operated briefly and privately in New Jersey.
1826	Three-mile railway using horses is built in Quincy, Massachusetts, to haul stone for Bunker Hill monument.
1828	1 August. First meeting in North Carolina to promote railroads is held on the farm of William Albright in Chatham County.
	Experimental railroad is laid in Fayetteville from Cape Fear River up Bridge and Person streets to haul freight to a warehouse by horse power.
1829	8 August. Steam locomotive imported from England proves to be too heavy for tracks in Delaware experiment.
1830	January. In Maryland, the first railroad passengers are carried in cars drawn by horses.
	Baptist State Convention is organized.
	25 December. On a line running six miles out of Charleston, South Carolina, the first steam locomotive in America is operated.

1831	21 June. State capitol burns.
	Christopher Bechtler establishes a private mint in Rutherford County.
1833	4 June. Cornerstone is laid for new capitol.
	Experimental railroad is laid 1¼ miles to haul—by horse power—stone from the quarry to the site of the new capitol.
	John W. Leak mill is built at Great Falls.
	Mount Hecla Mills, opened at Greensboro, is the first steam-powered cotton mill in North Carolina.
1834	Wake Forest Institute (now University) is founded.
	Wilmington and Raleigh Railroad is chartered.
1834–35	Whig party is formed in North Carolina.
1835	4 June–11 July. Constitutional convention revises 1776 state constitution.
	Wilmington and Raleigh Railroad is rechartered as Wilmington and Weldon.
	Raleigh and Gaston Railroad is chartered.
1836	Francis Fries and Dr. F. H. Schumann erect a mill at Salem.
	31 December. Edward B. Dudley qualifies as the first governor elected by popular vote.
1837	Davidson Colleges opens.
	New Garden Boarding School (now Guilford College) is founded.
	United States branch mint opens in Charlotte.
	E. M. Holt mill is built on Alamance Creek and in 1853 produces the first factory-dyed cotton cloth in the South.
1838	Union Institute (which evolved into Trinity College and in 1924 became Duke University) is formed in Randolph County.
	Most of the Cherokee Indians are removed from North Carolina to Indian Territory across the Mississippi River.
	John Motley Morehead erects a mill at Leaksville.
1839	8 January. General Assembly passes the state's first free public school law.
	Stephen Slade, a slave, discovers method of curing bright leaf tobacco.
1840	7 March. Wilmington and Weldon Railroad is completed.
	Raleigh and Gaston Railroad is completed.
	New capitol is completed.
	First public schools open.
1845	School for the deaf is established in Raleigh.
1846	Greensboro Female College opens.
1846–48	War with Mexico.
1849	Construction of State Hospital for the Insane begins in Raleigh.
	North Carolina Railroad is chartered.
	Fayetteville and Western and other plank roads are begun.
1850–51	*Raleigh Register* and *Wilmington Daily Journal* are the state's first daily newspapers.

1851	A department for the blind is opened in Raleigh at the school for the deaf.
1853	Calvin H. Wiley becomes the first superintendent of common schools.
	Holt mill in Alamance County produces the first colored cloth in the South—"Alamance plaid."
	17 April. Fayetteville-to-Salem plank road is completed, the longest in the world.
	18–21 October. The first State Fair is held in Raleigh.
1855–58	Thalian Hall (theater) is built in Wilmington.
1856	North Carolina Railroad is completed from Goldsboro to Charlotte.
	Albemarle and Chesapeake Canal is begun (later a part of Intracoastal Waterway).
	29 April. State Hospital for the Insane opens.
1857	Free suffrage amendment is adopted.
1859	Raleigh Workingmen's Association is formed.
	Cape Lookout Lighthouse is built.
1861	20 May. Secession Convention takes North Carolina out of the Union.
	10 June. Henry Lawson Wyatt, the first Confederate soldier to die in battle, is killed at Big Bethel.
	29 August. Federal forces take forts Hatteras and Clark.
1862	8 February. Roanoke Island falls to Federal forces.
	14 March. New Bern is taken by Federal forces.
	21 March. Washington is taken by Federal forces.
	26 April. Fort Macon falls.
	8 September. Zebulon B. Vance becomes governor.
	11 December. Plymouth is taken by Federal forces.
1863	July. Construction of the Confederate ram *Albemarle* begins.
	1–3 July. Battle of Gettysburg, Pennsylvania.
	4 July. Vicksburg, Mississippi, falls.
1864	17–20 April. Plymouth is retaken by Confederates.
	27 October. *Albemarle* is blown up at Plymouth by Federal forces.
1865	15 January. Fort Fisher falls.
	22 February. Wilmington is taken by Federal forces.
	11–14 March. Federal general William T. Sherman occupies Fayetteville.
	16 March. Battle of Averasboro.
	19–21 March. Battle of Bentonville.
	March–April. "Stoneman's Raid" through western North Carolina destroys much property.
	13 April. Sherman occupies Raleigh.
	26 April. Confederate general Joseph E. Johnston surrenders to Sherman at the Bennett house near Durham.
	6 May. Near Waynesville, General J. G. Martin surrenders the last Confederate forces in North Carolina.
	22 May. President Andrew Johnson appoints W. W. Holden provisional governor of North Carolina.

4 October. Ordinance of secession repealed.

5 October. Ordinance is passed forever prohibiting slavery in the state.

15 December. Jonathan Worth takes office as governor.

18 December. North Carolina ratifies Thirteenth Amendment to the United States Constitution abolishing slavery.

1866   22 December. Jonathan Worth begins second term.

1867   2 March. Congressional Reconstruction Act is passed and North Carolina becomes a part of the Second Military District.

Jewish congregation is established in Wilmington.

1868   14 January–17 March. Constitutional convention meets in Raleigh.

21–23 April. New state constitution is ratified by vote of those eligible under Reconstruction Act.

1 July. W. W. Holden becomes governor.

4 July. North Carolina ratifies Fourteenth Amendment concerning citizenship, representation, and other subjects.

4 July. North Carolina is readmitted to the Union.

1869   5 March. North Carolina ratifies Fifteenth Amendment concerning right to vote.

1869–70   Cape Hatteras Lighthouse is built.

1870   Governor Holden proclaims Alamance and Caswell counties to be in a state of insurrection and calls in troops. Kirk-Holden War results.

9 December. Resolution of impeachment is drawn up against Holden.

1871   1 February. University of North Carolina is closed.

2 February–23 March. Holden is tried, found guilty on six of eight charges, and removed from office.

1872   Standard time zones are established.

1873   7 August. Eight amendments to state constitution are approved.

1874   Tobacco factories are built in Winston and Durham by R. J. Reynolds and Washington Duke.

1875   15 September. University is reopened.

6 September–11 October. Constitutional convention; thirty amendments are added.

State Grange is incorporated.

1875–76   Temple of Israel, Wilmington, is the first house of worship built by Jews in North Carolina.

1876   7 November. Thirty amendments to the state constitution are approved.

1877   1 January. Zebulon B. Vance becomes governor and Democrats regain control of state government.

Federal occupation troops are withdrawn from the South by order of President Rutherford B. Hayes.

General Assembly establishes State Colored Normal School (now Fayetteville State University), the first teacher-training school for blacks in the South.

State Department of Agriculture is organized.

12 February. State Board of Health is authorized by General Assembly.

1879	October. The state's first telephone exchanges are opened in Raleigh and Wilmington.
1881	Statewide prohibition of alcoholic beverages is defeated by a large vote.
1883	18 November. Standard time goes into effect.
1886	31 August. Charleston earthquake, felt in North Carolina.
1887	North Carolina College of Agriculture and Mechanic Arts (now North Carolina State University) is chartered.
	Normal school for Indians (now Pembroke State University) is established in Robeson County.
	Farmers' Alliance begins in North Carolina.
	James W. Cannon builds cotton mill in Concord.
1889	North Carolina College of Agriculture and Mechanic Arts opens in Raleigh.
1890	31 January. American Tobacco Company is formed by James B. Duke.
	2 July. Sherman Anti-Trust Act passed by Congress.
1891	February. General Assembly charters State Normal and Industrial College (now the University of North Carolina at Greensboro), the first state-supported institution for the higher education of white women. (Opened 1892.)
	3 March. State Normal and Training School for blacks (now Elizabeth City State University) is chartered. (Opened January 1892.)
	North Carolina School for the Deaf and Dumb is established at Morganton.
1892	People's (Populist) party is formed.
	Trinity College moves from Randolph County to Durham.
1893	*Esse Quam Videri* is made state motto by General Assembly.
	Fifty families of Waldensians from Alps of northern Italy settle in Burke County and form the town of Valdese.
1894	Populists and Republicans fuse and gain control of state government.
	Southern Railway Company is organized.
	November. North Carolina Equal Suffrage Association is formed.
1896	Daniel L. Russell, a Republican, is elected governor on the Fusion ticket.
	23 October. First rural free delivery of mail in the state out of China Grove.
	Plessy v. Ferguson confirms "separate but equal doctrine."
1898	Red Shirt campaign enables Democrats to regain control of legislature.
	Spanish-American War.
	North Carolina Mutual Insurance Company is organized.
	11 May. Worth Bagley of North Carolina is the first American officer to be killed in Spanish-American War.
	1 September. First forestry school in the United States begins at Biltmore under the direction of Carl A. Schenck.
	10 November. Race riots in Wilmington.
1900	21 February. Constitutional amendment is adopted providing for a literacy test but also containing the grandfather clause.
	White Supremacy campaign is mounted by Democrats.

Atlantic Coast Line Railroad and Seaboard Airline Railway Company are formed.

State Literary and Historical Association is organized.

1900–1902 Reginald A. Fessenden conducts successful experiments to transmit wireless (radio) messages from Roanoke Island to stations at Cape Hatteras and at Cape Henry, Virginia.

1901 Supreme court justices are impeached.

1901–05 South Dakota bond case.

1902 North Carolina Federation of Women's Clubs is organized.

Good Roads Association is organized.

1903 North Carolina Historical Commission (now Division of Archives and History) is created by legislature.

First state child labor law is enacted.

17 December. Wilbur and Orville Wright fly first power-driven airplane at Kill Devil Hills.

1904 Southern Power Company (now Duke Power Company) is organized.

1906 Norfolk and Southern Railway Company is organized.

1908 Statewide prohibition of alcoholic beverages.

1913 Seventeenth Amendment is ratified providing for the popular election of United States senators.

1915 State Highway Commission is created.

Mount Mitchell is made the first state park in North Carolina.

1916 Federal Highway Act inaugurates federal aid for highway construction.

1917 6 April. United States declares war on Germany.

1918 State-supported school term is increased from four to six months.

Fort Bragg is established as a field artillery training center.

Carolina Playmakers is organized.

Carrie L. Broughton is named state librarian, the first woman to head a state department.

September–November. Influenza epidemic.

11 November. Armistice ends World War I.

1920 26 August. Nineteenth Amendment, giving women the vote, goes into effect.

1921 Program of state highway construction begins.

First commercial radio broadcast in the state, by WBT, Charlotte.

1924 Trinity College, Durham, is endowed by James B. Duke and changes name to Duke University.

State Art Society is formed.

1925 Department of Conservation and Development is created.

Parole Commission is created.

1927 "Talking movies" arrive.

1929 30 March. Strike at Loray Mill, Gastonia.

18–29 October. Stock market decline leads to start of Great Depression.

State Highway Patrol is organized.

State Art Gallery is opened.

	Australian, or secret ballot, law is enacted.
1931	State assumes control of entire highway system, relieving counties of some maintenance.
	General Assembly passes Workmen's Compensation Act.
	General Assembly adopts secret ballot.
	Administration of the University of North Carolina, State College at Raleigh, and Woman's College at Greensboro is consolidated.
	1 April. First regularly scheduled airline passenger service from New York to Miami, with stopover in Raleigh.
1932	14 May. North Carolina Symphony is organized.
1933	State program is adopted for financing an eight-month public school term.
	President Franklin D. Roosevelt inaugurates New Deal program.
1935	Statewide prohibition ends; under special legislation, sixteen eastern counties vote to establish liquor stores.
1936	Intracoastal Waterway is completed.
	Honorary post of poet laureate is created.
1937	First general law is adopted to limit hours of labor in industry.
	Local option law permits counties to establish liquor stores.
	Old-age pensions and unemployment insurance are established.
	4 July. First presentation of outdoor drama, *The Lost Colony*, on Roanoke Island.
1939	State provides free textbooks for public school elementary grades and rental plan for high schools.
	World War II begins in Europe.
1940	2 September. Great Smoky Mountains National Park is dedicated.
1941–45	World War II.
1941	Teachers' and state employees' retirement system is established.
	Seymour Johnson Air Base, Goldsboro, is begun.
	Cherry Point Marine Air Station is begun.
	27 July. Daylight saving time goes into effect.
1942	Camp Lejeune, Jacksonville, is begun.
1943	A ninth month is added to school term.
1946	Bequest by Reynolds family to Wake Forest College; plans are begun to transfer the school to Winston-Salem.
1947	State inaugurates Good Health Program.
	Rocket research begins at Topsail Island.
1948	First commercial television broadcast in the state, by WBTV, Charlotte.
	State reports 2,498 cases of polio.
1949	Bond issue votes $200 million for secondary roads and $50 million for public school buildings.
	Susie Sharp becomes first female superior court judge.
1950	Frank P. Graham is defeated in senatorial primary by Willis Smith after race issue raised in campaign.

1950–53	Korean War.
1951	Construction begins on new Wake Forest College campus at Winston-Salem.
	University of North Carolina is ordered by federal courts to admit blacks to law, medical, and graduate schools.
1953	Bond issue votes $50 million for public schools and $22 million for mental institutions.
1954	15 October. Hurricane Hazel strikes, the most destructive storm in the state's history.
	In *Brown v. Board of Education*, United States Supreme Court orders schools to be racially integrated "with all deliberate speed."
	Junius I. Scales is arrested for Communist activities.
1955	Pupil assignment plan is adopted for public schools.
	Governor Luther Hodges takes lead in development of Research Triangle Park.
	Board of Higher Education is established.
1956	Pearsall Plan for school attendance is adopted.
	North Carolina Museum of Art opens in new quarters in downtown Raleigh.
1957–75	Vietnam War.
1959	Voters approve over $34 million bond issue for capital improvements.
	A few blacks are admitted to formerly white public schools.
1960	1 February. The nation's first lunch counter sit-in begins in Greensboro.
	Governor Terry Sanford's "Go Forward" program emphasizes "quality education."
	Student Non-Violent Coordinating Committee is formed in Raleigh.
1961	2 October. Battleship *North Carolina* is berthed at Wilmington as a museum and war memorial.
1962	Judge Susie Sharp becomes first woman to serve on state supreme court.
	Court reform amendment is adopted.
1963	General Assembly convenes in new legislative building, the first ever constructed by a state for exclusive use of legislature.
	"Speaker Ban Law" is enacted to prevent known Communists from speaking at state-supported institutions of higher education.
	North Carolina School of the Arts is created by General Assembly.
	Initial (summer) session of Governor's School for gifted children opens in Winston-Salem.
	18 July. Governor Sanford announces creation of the North Carolina Fund.
1964	2 February. Learning Institute of North Carolina is established.
	8 November. Advancement School for eighth graders opens in Winston-Salem.
1965	Charlotte College becomes University of North Carolina at Charlotte and names of three other campuses of the university system are changed.
	Minimum wage law is enacted.

	Judicial system is reorganized with creation of Court of Appeals; justice of the peace system is abolished and replaced by magistrates.
1966	Special legislative session reapportions seats in General Assembly. Speaker Ban Law is modified.
1967	"Brown bagging" is legalized to permit alcoholic beverages in restaurants. Four new "regional universities" are created.
1968	Reginald A. Hawkins is the first black candidate for Democratic gubernatorial nomination. Federal courts declare Speaker Ban Law unconstitutional.
1969	Cigarettes are taxed for the first time; a tax is also levied on soft drinks. Five additional colleges are named "regional universities."
1970	State population for the first time exceeds 5 million.
1971	In accordance with federal court requirements, the General Assembly reapportions the state's eleven congressional districts to comply with "one man, one vote" directive. Busing in Charlotte becomes a tool in school integration. 6 February. Burning of a grocery store in Wilmington sparks racial violence. February. Site near Asheboro is approved for state zoo.
1972	James E. Holshouser, Jr., is the first Republican elected governor of North Carolina in the twentieth century.
1974	September. State zoo opens. Susie Sharp becomes the first woman to be elected chief justice of state supreme court.
1977	General Assembly declines to ratify Equal Rights Amendment.
1978	Windmill is erected near Boone to produce electric power.
1979	3 November. Communist Workers party and Ku Klux Klan clash in Greensboro.
1981	1 June. Commission on the Future of North Carolina is named.
1982	School of Science and Mathematics graduates its first class. School of Veterinary Medicine at North Carolina State University admits its first class. North Carolina Museum of Art moves to new building in west Raleigh.
1984	Senatorial race between Jesse Helms and James B. Hunt, Jr., costs a record $25 million. Henry E. Frye is the first black elected to state supreme court. *Elizabeth II*, the representation of a sixteenth-century sailing vessel, is christened.
1985	Legal drinking age is raised to nineteen. Seat belt law is enacted.
1987	General Assembly adopts Martin Luther King holiday.
1988	George H. Hutchings and Gertrude Elion of the Research Triangle Park win Nobel Prize in medicine. James G. Martin reelected governor, the first time that a Republican governor was reelected to succeed himself.

FURTHER READING

ANYONE who wants to look further into the history of North Carolina will find a wide range of options. There are books covering certain periods of time, specific events, counties, cities, churches, schools, businesses, or families, as well as civic, professional, and historical organizations. Biographies of individuals and volumes of collected biographies are numerous. Other books contain such printed source materials as charters and constitutions; selected correspondence of individuals and organizations; minutes of legislative bodies, committees, and professional organizations; and military records. Many newspapers and periodicals from the eighteenth century to the present survive in original form and some are available on microfilm as are many manuscript records from county courthouses, a few of which date from as early as the late 1600s.

Selected source materials have been indexed by individuals, libraries, and archival agencies. In a few instances these indexes have been published, but in others they are available only at the creating agency. For example, the North Carolina Collection at the University of North Carolina at Chapel Hill has a card index of biographies found in several hundred obscure volumes, and the public libraries in Charlotte, Durham, and Greensboro have indexes of the morning daily newspaper in their city.

The outstanding repository of printed materials relating to the state is the North Carolina Collection, but there also are fine collections at the University of North Carolina at Charlotte and at East Carolina University. Most of the other universities and colleges in the state have special collections as well. Western Carolina University at Cullowhee and Appalachian State University at Boone have good collections of regional material. In addition, many public libraries have unusually complete collections—notably those in Asheville, Charlotte, Greensboro, Salisbury, Wilmington, and Winston-Salem. The State Library in Raleigh contains much documentation, but it is not designated as a special collection. At the Elizabeth II State Historic Site, the Outer Banks History Center contains an extensive collection developed by David Stick, with emphasis on the state's coastal history.

Manuscript records may be consulted at the State Archives in Raleigh where colonial and state archives as well as many county and local records are located. Numerous photocopies of documents from repositories in Great Britain are available there as well. Some private manuscripts, such as personal and business correspondence, are also in the State Archives, but an even wider range will be found in the Southern Historical Collection at Chapel Hill, in the Manuscripts Department at the Duke University Library in Durham, and in the manuscript collections at East Carolina University at Greenville and Wake Forest University at Winston-Salem, as well as at some other colleges and regional universities. Extensive records of the Presbyterian church are located at Montreat, while Moravian archives dating from 1752 are at Winston-Salem. Smaller Methodist collections are at Lake Junaluska and States-ville, while Episcopal records are in Raleigh, Lutheran and German Reformed records at Salisbury, Quaker records at Guilford College, and others elsewhere but especially in the larger manuscript collections already mentioned in Chapel Hill, Durham, and Raleigh. The state's universities as well as some of the colleges have archivists to maintain the official records of their institution, whereas alumni associa-tions usually keep records of former students.

Books, pamphlets, and periodicals dealing with North Carolina are numerous, and many more are being published each year. An attempt to list all of these would be futile, yet the citation of a few general works may suggest the variety. Long consid-ered the leading book for a survey of North Carolina is *North Carolina: The History of a Southern State* by Hugh Talmage Lefler and Albert Ray Newsome, published by the University of North Carolina Press in 1954 with modest revisions in 1963 and 1973. Lefler also was the editor of *North Carolina History Told by Contemporaries* containing selections from sources and intended for use in North Carolina history classes. Pub-lished in 1934, it was revised four times, the last in 1965, with the addition of docu-ments to bring it up to date. Editors Lindley S. Butler and Alan D. Watson, combin-ing both features of Lefler's two works, prepared *The North Carolina Experience: An Interpretive and Documentary History*, published by the University of North Carolina Press in 1984. Covering the state's history in nineteen chapters, each with a different author, this book contains readable narratives, extracts from contemporary docu-ments, and suggested readings. William S. Powell's *North Carolina: A Bicentennial History* (1977) is a concise narrative history intended for the general reader. Especially appealing to the casual reader is *North Carolina Illustrated, 1524–1984*, by H. G. Jones, which relates the history of the state in word and picture.

Lefler and Powell collaborated to produce *Colonial North Carolina* (1973), a close examination of the colony before the American Revolution. Harry Roy Merrens's *Colonial North Carolina in the Eighteenth Century* (1964) is a study in historical geogra-phy touching on the setting, the economy, and demographic changes of the colony. Two special studies focus on opposite ends of the province: Lawrence Lee's *The Lower Cape Fear in Colonial Days* (1965) and Robert W. Ramsey's *Carolina Cradle: Settlement of the Northwest Carolina Frontier, 1747–1762* (1964). Using local records and based on long personal acquaintance with the region, each author carefully depicts the pioneers and the life they lived. A. Roger Ekirch in *"Poor Carolina": Politics and Soci-ety in Colonial North Carolina, 1729–1776* (1981) undertakes to account for the political unrest that marked North Carolina as a British colony.

Readers and writers of North Carolina history and biography are fortunate in having many printed primary sources readily available. Chief among them are the ten volumes of *Colonial Records* edited by William L. Saunders and the sixteen volumes of *State Records* edited by Walter Clark, together with a four-volume index prepared by Stephen B. Weeks, all published between 1886 and 1914. A new series of colonial records was begun in 1963 by the Carolina Charter Tercentenary Commission and continued by the State Department of Archives and History. That agency and its successor under different names over the years has published a variety of source material including eleven volumes of *Records of the Moravians* and personal and official papers of such significant leaders as John Gray Blount, John W. Ellis, William A. Graham, James Iredell, Archibald D. Murphey, William Tryon, Zebulon B. Vance, and many others. A collection of seventeenth-century documents of the Proprietary period and the Civil War diary of Catherine Anne Devereux Edmondston suggest the range in time of these documentary volumes. Facsimiles of maps and significant historical documents have also been issued. At the end of each governor's term, the state, through the Division of Archives and History, publishes a selection of the chief executive's significant papers; included are speeches, correspondence, lists of appointments to boards, commissions, and other agencies, and other documents considered to be important in understanding the administration.

Anyone undertaking to read and enjoy the history of North Carolina should have at hand a good history of the United States and for easy reference a work such as the *Dictionary of American History*. The *Atlas of North Carolina* (1967) prepared by Richard E. Lonsdale and others, the 1975 *North Carolina Atlas: Portrait of a Changing Southern State*, a recent map of the state, and a dictionary—preferably one on historical principles to explain words found in documents of the time but no longer in use—are also recommended. *The North Carolina Gazetteer* will be helpful in locating and identifying natural features, counties, townships, and municipalities, as well as many obsolete designations such as districts, former counties, parishes, and ports of entry. *North Carolina Government, 1585–1979: A Narrative and Statistical History*, compiled by John L. Cheney, Jr., is an indispensable tool for understanding the government of the colony and state; its lists of officials and its election statistics will clarify many obscure points.

To help identify people and explain many family ties, such works as the *Dictionary of National Biography* for British persons including many colonial Americans, the *Dictionary of American Biography* for prominent people in both the colonial and national periods, and the *Dictionary of North Carolina Biography* will be of use. An older work but still interesting is the *Biographical History of North Carolina*, published in eight volumes between 1905 and 1917.

Those interested in the historiography of North Carolina—the history of historical writing—will find two books to be illuminating. *For History's Sake: The Preservation and Publication of North Carolina History, 1663–1903*, by H. G. Jones, discusses the keeping of records from the colonial period to the twentieth century, relating the fate of lost records as well as of many that have survived. Also covered are the work of pioneer historians, editors of documents and collected works, and the goals of early historical societies and individuals. Jeffrey J. Crow and Larry E. Tise edited *Writing North Carolina History*, a volume containing eight essays by modern historians of the state who discuss historians of the past from 1585 to 1976. Their work is appraised, their successes applauded, and their failures commented on. The methods used by earlier historians and their interpretations are considered, and opportunities are suggested for further investigation of the state's past.

Chapter 1: Natural Features and Native Peoples

Blu, Karen L. *The Lumbee Problem: The Making of an American Indian People* (1980).
Camp, Cordelia. *The Influence of Geography upon Early North Carolina* (1961).
Dean, Jim, and Lawrence S. Earley. *Wildlife in North Carolina* (1987).
Dunbar, Gary S. *Geographical History of the North Carolina Outer Banks* (1955).
Finger, John R. "The Saga of Tsali: Legend versus Reality." *North Carolina Historical Review* 56 (January 1979).
French, Laurence, and Jim Hornbuckle, eds. *The Cherokee Perspective* (1981).
Ganyard, Robert L. "Threat from the West: North Carolina and the Cherokee, 1776–1778." *North Carolina Historical Review* 45 (January 1968).
Johnson, Douglas. *Origin of the Carolina Bays* (1942).
Kirk, Paul W., Jr., ed. *The Great Dismal Swamp* (1979).
Lawson, John. *A New Voyage to Carolina*, edited by Hugh T. Lefler (1967).
Lemert, Ben F. "Geographic Influences in the History of North Carolina." *North Carolina Historical Review* 12 (October 1935).
Mathis, Mark A., and Jeffrey J. Crow, eds. *The Prehistory of North Carolina: An Archaeological Symposium* (1983).
Paschal, Herbert R. "The Tragedy of the North Carolina Indians." In Lindley S. Butler and Alan D. Watson, eds., *The North Carolina Experience* (1984), pp. 3–27.
Perdue, Theda. *Native Carolinians: The Indians of North Carolina* (1985).
Pomeroy, Kenneth B., and James B. Yoho. *North Carolina Lands: Ownership, Use, and Management of Forest and Related Lands* (1964).
Rights, Douglas L. *The American Indian in North Carolina* (1957).
Simpson, Marcus B., Jr., and Sallie W. Simpson. "The Pursuit of Leviathan: A History of Whaling on the North Carolina Coast." *North Carolina Historical Review* 65 (January 1988).
Stick, David. *Graveyard of the Atlantic* (1952).
———. *Outer Banks of North Carolina* (1958).
Stuckey, Jasper L. *North Carolina: Its Geology and Mineral Resources* (1965).
Swanton, John R. *The Indians of the Southeastern United States* (1946).
Wetmore, Ruth Y. *First on the Land: The North Carolina Indians* (1975).

Chapter 2: Exploration and Early Settlement

Briceland, Alan Vance. *Westward from Virginia: The Exploration of the Virginia-Carolina Frontier, 1650–1710* (1987).
Butler, Lindley S. "The Early Settlement of Carolina: Virginia's Southern Frontier." *Virginia Magazine of History and Biography* 79 (January 1971).
Cumming, William P. *Mapping the North Carolina Coast: Sixteenth-Century Cartography and the Roanoke Voyages* (1988).
———. *The Southeast in Early Maps* (1962).
Foss, Michael. *Undreamed Shores: England's Wasted Empire in America* (1974).

Further Reading

Hoffman, Paul E. "New Light on Vicente Gonzalez's 1588 Voyage in Search of Raleigh's English Colonies." *North Carolina Historical Review* 63 (April 1986).

———. *Spain and the Roanoke Voyages* (1987).

Hulton, Paul. *America 1585: The Complete Drawings of John White* (1984).

Humber, John L. *Backgrounds and Preparations for the Roanoke Voyages, 1584–1590* (1986).

Johnson, Gerald W. *Our English Heritage* (1949).

Kopperman, Paul E. "Profile of Failure: The Carolana Project, 1629–1640." *North Carolina Historical Review* 59 (January 1982).

Kupperman, Karen O. *Roanoke: The Abandoned Colony* (1984).

McPherson, Elizabeth G. "Nathaniell Batts: Landholder on Pasquotank River, 1660." *North Carolina Historical Review* 43 (January 1966).

Miller, Helen H. *Passage to America* (1983).

Powell, William S. "Carolana and the Incomparable Roanoke: Explorations and Attempted Settlements, 1620–1663." *North Carolina Historical Review* 51 (January 1974).

———. "An Elizabethan Experiment." In Lindley S. Butler and Alan D. Watson, eds., *The North Carolina Experience* (1984), pp. 29–51.

Quinn, David B. *The Lost Colonists: Their Fortune and Probable Fate* (1984).

———. *Set Fair for Roanoke: Voyages and Colonies, 1584–1606.* (1985).

———, ed. *The Roanoke Voyages, 1584–1590.* 2 vols. (1955).

———, and Alison M. Quinn. *The First Colonists* (1982).

Sally, Alexander S., ed. *Narratives of Early Carolina, 1650–1708* (1911).

Shirley, John W. *Sir Walter Raleigh and the New World* (1985).

Stick, David. *Roanoke Island: The Beginnings of English America* (1983).

Vigneras, L. A. "A Spanish Discovery of North Carolina in 1566." *North Carolina Historical Review* 46 (October 1969).

Chapter 3: A Proprietary Colony, 1663–1729

Butler, Lindley S. "Culpeper's Rebellion: Testing the Proprietors." In Lindley S. Butler and Alan D. Watson, eds., *The North Carolina Experience* (1984), pp. 53–78.

———. "The Governors of Albemarle County." *North Carolina Historical Review* 46 (July 1969).

Byrd, William. *The Prose Works of William Byrd of Westover*, edited by Louis B. Wright (1966).

Crane, Verner W. *The Southern Frontier, 1670–1732* (1929).

Crittenden, Charles C. "The Surrender of the Charter of Carolina." *North Carolina Historical Review* 1 (October 1924).

Graffenried, Christoph von. *Christoph von Graffenried's Account of the Founding of New Bern*, edited by Vincent H. Todd (1920).

Hudson, Arthur P. *Songs of the Carolina Charter Colonists* (1962).

Lee, E. Lawrence. *Indian Wars in North Carolina, 1663–1763* (1963).

Parker, Mattie Erma E. "Legal Aspects of Culpeper's Rebellion." *North Carolina Historical Review* 45 (January 1968).

Parramore, Thomas. "The Tuscarora Ascendancy." *North Carolina Historical Review* 59 (October 1982).

Powell, William S. *The Proprietors of Carolina* (1968).

————, ed. *Yᵉ Countie of Albemarle in Carolina: A Collection of Documents, 1664–1675* (1958).

White, Steven J. "From the Vestry Act to Cary's Rebellion: North Carolina Quakers and Colonial Politics." *Southern Friend: Journal of the North Carolina Friends Historical Society* 8 (Autumn 1986).

Wolf, Jacquelyn H. "Patents and Tithables in Proprietary North Carolina, 1663–1729." *North Carolina Historical Review* 56 (July 1979).

Chapter 4: Royal Government

Bailyn, Bernard. *Voyagers to the West* (1986).

Clarke, Desmond. *Arthur Dobbs, Esquire, 1689–1765* (1957).

Connor, R. D. W. *Race Elements in the White Population of North Carolina* (1920).

Dill, Alonzo T. *Governor Tryon and His Palace* (1955).

Ekirch, A. Roger. *"Poor Carolina": Politics and Society in Colonial North Carolina, 1729–1776* (1981).

Fenn, Elizabeth A., and Peter H. Wood, eds. *Natives and Newcomers: The Way We Lived in North Carolina before 1770* (1983).

Greene, Jack P. *The Quest for Power: The Lower Houses of Assembly in the Southern Colonies, 1689–1776* (1963).

Kay, Marvin L. Michael. "The Payment of Provincial and Local Taxes in North Carolina, 1748–1771." *William and Mary Quarterly* 26 (April 1969).

————. "Provincial Taxes in North Carolina during the Administrations of Dobbs and Tryon." *North Carolina Historical Review* 42 (October 1965).

Lee, E. Lawrence. *The Lower Cape Fear in Colonial Days* (1965).

London, Lawrence F. "The Representation Controversy in Colonial North Carolina." *North Carolina Historical Review* 11 (October 1934).

McCain, Paul M. *The County Court in North Carolina before 1750* (1954).

Price, William S., Jr. "'Men of Good Estates': Wealth among North Carolina's Royal Councillors." *North Carolina Historical Review* 49 (January 1972).

————. "North Carolina in the First British Empire: Economy and Society in the Eighteenth Century." In Lindley S. Butler and Alan D. Watson, eds., *The North Carolina Experience* (1984), pp. 79–99.

————. "A Strange Incident in George Burrington's Royal Governorship." *North Carolina Historical Review* 51 (April 1974).

Ramsey, Robert W. *Carolina Cradle: Settlement of the Northwest Carolina Frontier, 1747–1762* (1964).

Rankin, Hugh F. *The Pirates of Colonial North Carolina* (1960).

Robinson, Blackwell P. *Five Royal Governors of North Carolina, 1729–1775* (1968).
Smith, Mary P. "Borough Representation in North Carolina." *North Carolina Historical Review* 7 (April 1930).
Watson, Alan D. *Money and Monetary Problems in Early North Carolina* (1980).

Chapter 5: Colonial Society and Culture, 1729–1776

Allcott, John V. *Colonial Homes in North Carolina* (1963).
Bivins, John. *The Furniture of Coastal North Carolina, 1700–1820* (1988).
Crittenden, Charles C. *North Carolina Newspapers before 1790.* James Sprunt Studies in History and Political Science, vol. 20 (1928).
Davis, Richard Beale, ed. "Three Poems from Colonial North Carolina." *North Carolina Historical Review* 46 (January 1969).
Fries, Adelaide L. "The Moravian Contribution to Colonial North Carolina." *North Carolina Historical Review* 7 (January 1930).
Gehrke, William H. "The Transition from the German to the English Language in North Carolina." *North Carolina Historical Review* 12 (January 1935).
Hammer, Carl, Jr. *Rhinelanders on the Yadkin* (1965).
Johnston, Frances B., and Thomas T. Waterman. *The Early Architecture of North Carolina* (1941).
London, Lawrence F., and Sarah M. Lemmon, eds. *The Episcopal Church in North Carolina, 1701–1959* (1987).
Meyer, Duane. *The Highland Scots of North Carolina* (1961).
Newsome, Albert R., ed. "Records of Emigrants from England and Scotland to North Carolina, 1774–1775." *North Carolina Historical Review* 11 (January, April 1934).
Nixon, Joseph R. *The German Settlers in Lincoln County and Western North Carolina.* James Sprunt Studies in History and Political Science, vol. 11 (1912).
Rouse, Parke, Jr. *The Great Wagon Road from Philadelphia to the South* (1973).
Schaw, Janet. *Journal of a Lady of Quality*, edited by Evangeline Walker Andrews and Charles M. Andrews (1939).
Smith, Abbot E. *Colonists in Bondage: White Servitude and Convict Labor in America, 1607–1776* (1947).
Spindel, Donna J., and Stuart W. Thomas. "Crime and Society in North Carolina, 1663–1740." *Journal of Southern History* 49 (May 1983).
Spruill, Julia Cherry. *Women's Life and Work in the Southern Colonies* (1938).
Watson, Alan D. *Society in Colonial North Carolina* (1982).
———. "Women in Colonial North Carolina: Overlooked and Underestimated." *North Carolina Historical Review* 58 (January 1981).
Whitener, Daniel J. *Prohibition in North Carolina, 1715–1945.* James Sprunt Studies in History and Political Science, vol. 27 (1945).

Chapter 6: Colonial Economy: Agriculture, Trade, and Communication

Cappon, Lester J. "Iron-Making—a Forgotten Industry of North Carolina." *North Carolina Historical Review* 9 (October 1932).
Cathey, Cornelius O. *Agriculture in North Carolina before the Civil War* (1966).
Crittenden, Charles C. *The Commerce of North Carolina, 1763–1789* (1936).
Merrens, Harry R. *Colonial North Carolina in the Eighteenth Century* (1964).

Chapter 7: Sectional Controversies in the Colony

Adams, George R. "The Carolina Regulators: A Note on Changing Interpretations." *North Carolina Historical Review* 49 (October 1972).
Ekirch, A. Roger. "'A New Government of Liberty': Hermon Husband's Vision of Backcountry North Carolina, 1755." *William and Mary Quarterly* 34 (October 1977).
———. "The North Carolina Regulators on Liberty and Corruption, 1766–1771." *Perspectives in American History* 11 (1977–78).
Fanning, David. *The Narrative of Col. David Fanning*, edited by Lindley S. Butler (1981).
Kay, Marvin L. Michael. "The North Carolina Regulation, 1766–1776: A Class Conflict." In Alfred F. Young, ed., *The American Revolution: Explorations in the History of American Radicalism* (1976).
Watson, Alan D. "The Regulation: Society in Upheaval." In Lindley S. Butler and Alan D. Watson, eds., *The North Carolina Experience* (1984), pp. 101–24.
Whittenburg, James P. "Planters, Merchants, and Lawyers: Social Change and the Origins of the North Carolina Regulators." *William and Mary Quarterly* 34 (April 1977).

Chapter 8: A Decade of Dispute

Butler, Lindley S. *North Carolina and the Coming of the Revolution, 1763–1776* (1976).
Current, Richard N. "That Other Declaration: May 20, 1775–May 20, 1975." *North Carolina Historical Review* 54 (April 1977).
Frech, Laura P. "The Wilmington Committee of Public Safety and the Loyalist Rising of February, 1776." *North Carolina Historical Review* 41 (January 1964).
Ganyard, Robert L. *The Emergence of North Carolina's Revolutionary State Government* (1978).
Lee, E. Lawrence. "Days of Defiance: Resistance to the Stamp Act in the Lower Cape Fear." *North Carolina Historical Review* 43 (April 1966).
Mathews, Alice E. *Society in Revolutionary North Carolina* (1976).
Price, William S., Jr. *Not a Conquered People: Two Carolinians View Parliamentary Taxation* (1975).

Skaggs, Marvin L. *North Carolina Boundary Disputes Involving Her Southern Line*. James Sprunt Studies in History and Political Science, vol. 25 (1941).

Spindel, Donna J. "Law and Disorder: The North Carolina Stamp Act Crisis." *North Carolina Historical Review* 57 (January 1980).

Chapter 9: Attaining Independence

Calhoon, Robert M. *Religion and the American Revolution in North Carolina* (1976).

Crow, Jeffrey J. *The Black Experience in Revolutionary North Carolina* (1983).

———. *A Chronicle of North Carolina during the American Revolution, 1763–1789* (1975).

———. *A Guidebook to Revolutionary Sites in North Carolina* (1975).

———. "Tory Plots and Anglican Loyalty: The Llewelyn Conspiracy of 1777." *North Carolina Historical Review* 55 (1978).

Davie, William R. *The Revolutionary War Sketches of William R. Davie*, edited by Blackwell P. Robinson (1976).

DeMond, Robert O. *The Loyalists in North Carolina during the Revolution* (1940).

Higginbotham, Don. *Daniel Morgan: Revolutionary Rifleman* (1961).

———. "Decision for Revolution." In Lindley S. Butler and Alan D. Watson, eds., *The North Carolina Experience* (1984), pp. 124–46.

Hoyt, William Henry. *The Mecklenburg Declaration of Independence* (1907).

Kay, Marvin L. Michael. "Class, Mobility, and Conflict in North Carolina on the Eve of the Revolution." In Jeffrey J. Crow and Larry E. Tise, eds., *The Southern Experience in the American Revolution* (1978).

Lumpkin, Henry. *From Savannah to Yorktown: The American Revolution in the South* (1981).

Lutz, Paul V. "A State's Concern for the Soldiers' Welfare: How North Carolina Provided for Her Troops during the Revolution." *North Carolina Historical Review* 42 (July 1965).

Morgan, David T. "Cornelius Harnett: Revolutionary Leader and Delegate to the Continental Congress." *North Carolina Historical Review* 49 (July 1972).

Nelson, Paul D. "Horatio Gates in the Southern Department, 1780: Serious Errors and a Costly Defeat." *North Carolina Historical Review* 50 (July 1973).

O'Donnell, James H., III. *The Cherokees of North Carolina in the American Revolution* (1976).

Parramore, Thomas C. "The Great Escape from Forten Gaol: An Incident of the Revolution." *North Carolina Historical Review* 45 (October 1968).

Rankin, Hugh F. *Greene and Cornwallis: The Campaign in the Carolinas* (1976).

———. "The Moore's Creek Bridge Campaign, 1776." *North Carolina Historical Review* 30 (January 1953).

———. *North Carolina in the American Revolution* (1959).

———. *The North Carolina Continental Line in the American Revolution* (1976).

———. *The North Carolina Continentals* (1971).

Robinson, Blackwell P. *William R. Davie* (1957).

Sellers, Charles G., Jr. "Making a Revolution: The North Carolina Whigs, 1765–1775." In J. Carlyle Sitterson, ed., *Studies in Southern History*, pp. 23–46. James Sprunt Studies in History and Political Science, vol. 39 (1957).

Smiley, David L. "Revolutionary Origins of the South's Constitutional Defenses." *North Carolina Historical Review* 44 (July 1967).

Still, William N., Jr. *North Carolina's Revolutionary War Navy* (1976).

Stumpf, Vernon O. "Josiah Martin and His Search for Success: The Road to North Carolina." *North Carolina Historical Review* 53 (January 1976).

————. *Josiah Martin: The Last Royal Governor of North Carolina* (1986).

Thorne, Dorothy Gilbert. "North Carolina Friends and the Revolution." *North Carolina Historical Review* 38 (July 1961).

Treacy, M. F. *Prelude to Yorktown: The Southern Campaign of Nathanael Greene, 1780–1781* (1963).

Troxler, Carole W. *The Loyalist Experience in North Carolina* (1976).

Watson, Alan D., and others, eds. *Harnett, Hooper and Howe: Revolutionary Leaders of the Lower Cape Fear* (1979).

White, Steven J. "Friends and the Coming of the Revolution." *The Southern Friend: Journal of the North Carolina Friends Historical Society* 4 (Spring 1982).

Chapter 10: A Free State

Hecht, Arthur. "Postal History of North Carolina, 1789–1795." *North Carolina Historical Review* 35 (April 1958).

Hendricks, J. Edwin. "Joining the Federal Union." In Lindley S. Butler and Alan D. Watson, eds., *The North Carolina Experience* (1984), pp. 147–70.

Howard, Lucille. *North Carolina: Our State Government* (1983).

Ketcham, Earle H. "The Sources of the North Carolina Constitution of 1776." *North Carolina Historical Review* 6 (July 1929).

Liner, Charles D., ed. *State-Local Relations in North Carolina* (1985).

Morris, Francis G., and Phyllis M. Morris. "Economic Conditions in North Carolina about 1780." *North Carolina Historical Review* 16 (April, July 1939).

Newsome, Albert R. "North Carolina's Ratification of the Federal Constitution." *North Carolina Historical Review* 17 (October 1940).

Trenholme, Louise I. *The Ratification of the Federal Constitution in North Carolina* (1932).

Williams, Samuel C. *History of the Lost State of Franklin* (1924).

Zornow, William F. "North Carolina Tariff Policies, 1775–1789." *North Carolina Historical Review* 31 (April 1955).

Chapter 11: A Jeffersonian Republic

Broussard, James H. "The North Carolina Federalists, 1800–1816." *North Carolina Historical Review* 55 (January 1978).

Davis, Robert Scott, Jr. "The Settlement at the Head of the French Broad River, or the Bizarre Story of the First Walton County, Georgia." *North Carolina Genealogical Society Journal* 7 (May 1981).

Fordham, Jeff B. "Iredell's Dissent in *Chisholm v. Georgia*: Its Political Significance." *North Carolina Historical Review* 8 (April 1931).

Foreman, Grant. *Indian Removal* (1953).

Lemmon, Sarah M. "Dissent in North Carolina during the War of 1812." *North Carolina Historical Review* 49 (April 1972).

———. *Frustrated Patriots: North Carolina and the War of 1812* (1973).

———. *North Carolina and the War of 1812* (1984).

Reidinger, Martin. "The Walton War and the Georgia–North Carolina Dispute." Typescript, North Carolina Collection, University of North Carolina Library, Chapel Hill, 1981.

Watson, Harry L. *An Independent People: The Way We Lived in North Carolina, 1770–1820* (1983).

Chapter 12: A State Asleep

Cathey, Cornelius O. *Agricultural Development in North Carolina, 1783–1860.* James Sprunt Studies in History and Political Science, vol. 38 (1956).

Franklin, John Hope. *The Free Negro in North Carolina, 1790–1860* (1943).

Johnson, Guion G. *Ante-Bellum North Carolina* (1937).

Newsome, Albert R. *The Presidential Election of 1824 in North Carolina.* James Sprunt Studies in History and Political Science, vol. 23 (1939).

Patton, James W. "Glimpses of North Carolina in the Writings of Northern and Foreign Travelers, 1783–1860." *North Carolina Historical Review* 45 (July 1968).

Watson, Harry L. "'Old Rip' and a New Era." In Lindley S. Butler and Alan D. Watson, eds., *The North Carolina Experience* (1984), pp. 217–40.

———. "Squire Oldway and His Friends: Opposition to Internal Improvements in Antebellum North Carolina." *North Carolina Historical Review* 54 (January 1977).

Chapter 13: The Vision of Archibald D. Murphey

Hoffmann, William S. *Andrew Jackson and North Carolina Politics.* James Sprunt Studies in History and Political Science, vol. 40 (1958).

Hoyt, William Henry, ed. *The Papers of Archibald D. Murphey.* 2 vols. (1914).

Noble, Marcus C. S. *A History of Public Schools in North Carolina* (1930).

Turner, Herbert S. *The Dreamer: Archibald DeBow Murphey, 1777–1832* (1971).

Weaver, Charles C. *History of Public Improvements in North Carolina Previous to 1860* (1903).

Chapter 14: *The Constitutional Convention of 1835*

Counihan, Harold J. "The North Carolina Constitutional Convention of 1835: A Study in Jacksonian Democracy." *North Carolina Historical Review* 46 (October 1969).

Green, Fletcher M. *Constitutional Development of the South Atlantic States, 1776–1860* (1930).

Jeffrey, Thomas E. "National Issues, Local Interests, and the Transformation of Antebellum North Carolina Politics." *Journal of Southern History* 50 (February 1984).

Schauinger, Joseph H. "William Gaston: Southern Statesman." *North Carolina Historical Review* 18 (April 1941).

Watson, Harry L. *Jacksonian Politics and Community Conflict* (1981).

Chapter 15: *The Whig Era, 1835–1850*

Brooks, Aubrey L. "David Caldwell and His 'Log College'." *North Carolina Historical Review* 28 (October 1951).

Green, Fletcher M. "Gold Mining: A Forgotten Industry in Ante-Bellum North Carolina." *North Carolina Historical Review* 14 (January, April 1937).

Hamilton, J. G. de Roulhac. *Party Politics in North Carolina, 1835–1860*. James Sprunt Studies in History and Political Science, vol. 15 (1916).

Hoffmann, William S. "The Election of 1836 in North Carolina." *North Carolina Historical Review* 32 (January 1955).

———. "John Branch and the Origins of the Whig Party in North Carolina." *North Carolina Historical Review* 35 (July 1958).

———. *North Carolina in the Mexican War* (1969).

Jeffrey, Thomas E. "Internal Improvements and Political Parties in Antebellum North Carolina, 1836–1860." *North Carolina Historical Review* 55 (April 1978).

Kruman, Marc W. *Parties and Politics in North Carolina, 1836–1865* (1983).

McCulloch, Margaret C. "Founding the North Carolina Asylum for the Insane." *North Carolina Historical Review* 13 (July 1936).

Norton, Clarence C. "Democratic Newspapers and Campaign Literature in North Carolina, 1835–1861." *North Carolina Historical Review* 6 (October 1929).

———. *The Democratic Party in Ante-Bellum North Carolina, 1835–1861*. James Sprunt Studies in History and Political Science, vol. 21 (1930).

Reid, Paul A. *Gubernatorial Campaigns and Administrations of David S. Reid, 1848–1854* (1953).

Wallace, Carolyn A. "David Lowry Swain, the First Whig Governor of North Carolina." In J. Carlyle Sitterson, ed., *Studies in Southern History*, pp. 62–81. James Sprunt Studies in History and Political Science, vol. 39 (1957).

Wallace, Lee A., Jr. "Raising a Volunteer Regiment for Mexico, 1846–1847." *North Carolina Historical Review* 35 (January 1958).

Williams, Max R. "The Foundations of the Whig Party in North Carolina: A Synthesis and a Modest Proposal." *North Carolina Historical Review* 47 (April 1970).

Chapter 16: A Change in Midstream

Braverman, Howard. "Calvin H. Wiley's *North-Carolina Reader.*" *North Carolina Historical Review* 29 (1952).

Jeffrey, Thomas E. "Free Suffrage Revisited: Party Politics and Constitutional Reform in Antebellum North Carolina." *North Carolina Historical Review* 59 (January 1982).

Kruman, Marc W. "Thomas L. Clingman and the Whig Party: A Reconsideration." *North Carolina Historical Review* 64 (January 1987).

Morrill, James R. "The Presidential Election of 1852: Death Knell of the Whig Party in North Carolina." *North Carolina Historical Review* 44 (October 1967).

O'Brien, Gail W. "Power and Influence in Mecklenburg County, 1850–1880." *North Carolina Historical Review* 54 (April 1977).

Williams, Max R. "Reemergence of the Two-Party System." In Lindley S. Butler and Alan D. Watson, eds., *The North Carolina Experience* (1984), pp. 241–64.

Chapter 17: The Economy and Antebellum Society

Allen, Jeffrey B. "The Racial Thought of White North Carolina Opponents of Slavery, 1789–1876." *North Carolina Historical Review* 59 (January 1982).

Brown, Cecil K. *A State Movement in Railroad Development* (1928).

Censer, Jane T. *North Carolina Planters and Their Children, 1800–1860* (1984).

Clark, Ernest J., Jr. "Aspects of the North Carolina Slave Code, 1715–1860." *North Carolina Historical Review* 39 (April 1962).

Elliott, Robert N., Jr. "The Raleigh Register, 1799–1863." James Sprunt Studies in History and Political Science, vol. 36 (1955).

Griffin, Frances. *Less Time for Meddling: A History of Salem Academy and College, 1772–1866* (1979).

Jacobs, Harriet A. *Incidents in the Life of a Slave Girl Written by Herself*, edited by Jean Fagan Yellin (1987).

Johnson, Guion G. *Ante-Bellum North Carolina* (1937).

Konkle, Burton A. *John Motley Morehead and the Development of North Carolina, 1796–1866* (1922).

Lane, Mills. *Architecture of the Old South: North Carolina* (1985).

Noble, Marcus C. S. *A History of the Public Schools of North Carolina* (1930).

Parramore, Thomas C. *Launching the Craft: The First Half-Century of Freemasonry in North Carolina* (1975).

Robert, Joseph C. "The Tobacco Industry in Ante-Bellum North Carolina." *North Carolina Historical Review* 15 (April 1938).

Roberts, Bruce. *The Carolina Gold Rush* (1971).

Scott, Paul D. *Slavery Remembered: A Record of Twentieth-Century Slave Narratives* (1979).

Sowle, Patrick. "The North Carolina Manumission Society, 1816–1834." *North Carolina Historical Review* 42 (January 1965).

Standard, Diffee W., and Richard W. Griffin. "The Cotton Textile Industry in Ante-bellum North Carolina." *North Carolina Historical Review* 34 (January, April 1957).

Starling, Robert B. "The Plank Road Movement in North Carolina." *North Carolina Historical Review* 16 (January, April 1939).

Taylor, Rosser H. "Humanizing the Slave Code of North Carolina." *North Carolina Historical Review* 2 (July 1925).

———. "Slave Conspiracies in North Carolina." *North Carolina Historical Review* 5 (January 1928).

———. *Slaveholding in North Carolina: An Economic View*. James Sprunt Studies in History and Political Science, vol. 18 (1926).

Tise, Larry E. "Confronting the Issue of Slavery." In Lindley S. Butler and Alan D. Watson, eds., *The North Carolina Experience* (1984), pp. 193–216.

———. *Proslavery: A History of the Defense of Slavery in America, 1700–1849* (1987).

Chapter 18: The Coming of the Civil War

Crenshaw, Ollinger. "The Psychological Background of the Election of 1860 in the South." *North Carolina Historical Review* 19 (July 1942).

Gaither, Gerald, and John Muldowny, eds. "Hinton Rowan Helper, Racist and Reformer: A Letter to Senator John Sherman of Ohio." *North Carolina Historical Review* 49 (October 1972).

Johnson, Clifton H. "Abolitionist Missionary Activities in North Carolina." *North Carolina Historical Review* 40 (July 1963).

London, Lawrence F. "George Edmund Badger and the Compromise of 1850." *North Carolina Historical Review* 15 (April 1938).

Sitterson, J. Carlyle. "Economic Sectionalism in Ante-Bellum North Carolina." *North Carolina Historical Review* 16 (April 1939).

Smiley, David L. "Revolutionary Origins of the South's Constitutional Defenses." *North Carolina Historical Review* 44 (July 1967).

Tolbert, Noble J. "Daniel Worth: Tar Heel Abolitionist." *North Carolina Historical Review* 39 (July 1962).

Chapter 19: The Civil War

Auman, William T., and David D. Scarboro. "The Heroes of America in Civil War North Carolina." *North Carolina Historical Review* 58 (October 1981).

Bardolph, Richard. "Inconstant Rebels: Desertion of North Carolina Troops in the Civil War." *North Carolina Historical Review* 41 (April 1964).

Barrett, John G. *The Civil War in North Carolina* (1963).

———. *North Carolina as a Civil War Battleground, 1861–1865* (1960).

———. "Sherman and Total War in the Carolinas." *North Carolina Historical Review* 37 (July 1960).

———. *Sherman's March Through the Carolinas* (1956).

Bradley, Jesse N. "A Rebel Officer's Revenge, in Spades, against the Navy." *Smithsonian* 7 (November 1976).

Brown, Louis A. *The Salisbury Prison: A Case Study of Confederate Military Prisons, 1861–1865* (1980).

Brown, Norman D. "A Union Election in Civil War North Carolina." *North Carolina Historical Review* 43 (October 1966).

Davis, Archie K. *Boy Colonel of the Confederacy: The Life and Times of Henry King Burgwyn* (1985).

Davis, Burke. *Sherman's March* (1980).

Delaney, Norman C. "Charles Henry Foster and the Unionists of Eastern North Carolina." *North Carolina Historical Review* 37 (July 1960).

Escott, Paul D. "Poverty and Governmental Aid for the Poor in Confederate North Carolina." *North Carolina Historical Review* 61 (October 1984).

———. "Unwilling Hercules: North Carolina in the Confederacy." In Lindley S. Butler and Alan D. Watson, eds., *The North Carolina Experience* (1984), pp. 265–83.

Gallagher, Gary W. *Stephen Dodson Ramseur* (1985).

Luvaas, Jay. "Johnson's Last Stand—Bentonville." *North Carolina Historical Review* 33 (July 1956).

Mitchell, Memory. *Legal Aspects of Conscription and Exemption in North Carolina, 1861–1865.* James Sprunt Studies in History and Political Science, vol. 47 (1965).

Moser, Harold D. "Reaction in North Carolina to the Emancipation Proclamation." *North Carolina Historical Review* 44 (January 1967).

Nichols, Roy F. "Fighting in North Carolina Waters." *North Carolina Historical Review* 40 (January 1963).

Price, Charles, and Claude C. Sturgill. "Shock and Assault in the First Battle of Fort Fisher." *North Carolina Historical Review* 47 (January 1970).

Scarboro, David D. "North Carolina and the Confederacy: The Weakness of States' Rights during the Civil War." *North Carolina Historical Review* 56 (April 1979).

Van Noppen, Ina W. "The Significance of Stoneman's Last Raid." *North Carolina Historical Review* 38 (January, April, July 1961).

Yearns, W. Buck, and John G. Barrett, eds. *North Carolina Civil War Documentary* (1980).

Further Reading

Chapter 20: A State Made New

Alexander, Roberta S. "Hostility and Hope: Black Education in North Carolina during Presidential Reconstruction, 1865–1867." *North Carolina Historical Review* 53 (April 1976).

———. *North Carolina Faces the Freedman* (1985).

———. *Race and Politics in North Carolina, 1872–1901* (1981).

Atchison, Ray M. "*The Land We Love*: A Southern Post-Bellum Magazine of Agriculture, Literature, and Military History." *North Carolina Historical Review* 37 (October 1960).

———. "*Our Living and Our Dead*: A Post-Bellum North Carolina Magazine of Literature and History." *North Carolina Historical Review* 40 (October 1963).

Balanoff, Elizabeth. "Negro Legislators in the North Carolina General Assembly, July 1868–February 1872." *North Carolina Historical Review* 49 (January 1972).

Clayton, Thomas H. *Close to the Land: The Way We Lived in North Carolina* (1983).

Daniels, Jonathan. *Prince of Carpetbaggers* (1958).

Evans, William M. *To Die Game: The Story of the Lowry Band, Indian Guerrillas of Reconstruction* (1971).

Haley, John. *Charles N. Hunter and Race Relations in North Carolina*. James Sprunt Studies in History and Political Science, vol. 60 (1987).

Hamilton, J. G. de Roulhac. *Reconstruction in North Carolina* (1914).

Harris, William C. *William Woods Holden: Firebrand of North Carolina Politics* (1987).

———. "William Woods Holden: In Search of Vindication." *North Carolina Historical Review* 59 (October 1982).

Heyman, Max L., Jr. " 'The Great Reconstruction': General E. R. S. Canby and the Second Military District." *North Carolina Historical Review* 32 (January 1955).

Mabry, William A. " 'White Supremacy' and the North Carolina Suffrage Amendment." *North Carolina Historical Review* 13 (January 1936).

McKinney, Gordon B. *Southern Mountain Republicans, 1865–1900: Politics and the Appalachian Community* (1978).

Mobley, Joe A. *James City: A Black Community in North Carolina, 1863–1900* (1981).

Morrill, James R. "North Carolina and the Administration of Brevet Major General Sickles." *North Carolina Historical Review* 42 (July 1965).

Olsen, Otto H. "Albion W. Tourgée: Carpetbagger." *North Carolina Historical Review* 40 (October 1963).

———. *Carpetbagger's Crusade: The Life of Albion W. Tourgée* (1965).

———. "The Ku Klux Klan: A Study in Reconstruction Politics and Propaganda." *North Carolina Historical Review* 39 (July 1962).

Paludan, Phillip S. *Victims: A True Story of the Civil War* (1981).

Raper, Horace W. *William W. Holden: North Carolina's Political Enigma*. James Sprunt Studies in History and Political Science, vol. 59 (1985).

Trelease, Allen W. "Reconstruction: The Halfway Revolution." In Lindley S. Butler and Alan D. Watson, eds., *The North Carolina Experience* (1984), pp. 285–307.

————. "Republican Reconstruction in North Carolina: A Roll-Call Analysis of the State House of Representatives." *Journal of Southern History* 42 (August 1976).

————. *White Terror: The Ku Klux Klan Conspiracy and Southern Reconstruction* (1971).

Tucker, Glenn. *Zeb Vance: Champion of Personal Freedom* (1965).

Whitener, Daniel J. "Public Education in North Carolina during Reconstruction, 1865–1876." In Fletcher M. Green, ed., *Essays in Southern History*, pp. 67–90. James Sprunt Series in History and Political Science, vol. 31 (1949).

Zuber, Richard L. *North Carolina during Reconstruction* (1969).

Chapter 21: A Fresh Start

Billings, Dwight B., Jr. *Planters and the Making of a 'New South': Class, Politics, and Development in North Carolina, 1865–1900* (1979).

Ebert, Charles H. V. "Furniture Making in High Point." *North Carolina Historical Review* 36 (July 1959).

Escott, Paul D. *Many Excellent People: Power and Privilege in North Carolina, 1850–1900* (1985).

Gatton, T. Harry. *Banking in North Carolina: A Narrative History* (1987).

Glass, Brent D., ed. *North Carolina: An Inventory of Historic Engineering and Industrial Sites* (1975).

Griffin, Richard W. "Reconstruction of the North Carolina Textile Industry, 1865–1885." *North Carolina Historical Review* 42 (January 1964).

Hicks, John D. "The Farmers' Alliance in North Carolina." *North Carolina Historical Review* 2 (April 1925).

McMath, Robert C., Jr. *Populist Vanguard: A History of the Southern Farmers' Alliance* (1975).

Ratchford, B. U. "The Adjustment of the North Carolina Public Debt, 1879–1883." *North Carolina Historical Review* 10 (July 1933).

————. "The North Carolina Public Debt, 1870–1878." *North Carolina Historical Review* 10 (January 1933).

Sitterson, J. Carlyle. "Business Leaders in Post-Civil War North Carolina, 1865–1900." In J. Carlyle Sitterson, ed., *Studies in Southern History*, pp. 111–21. James Sprunt Studies in History and Political Science, vol. 39 (1957).

Watts, George B. *The Waldenses in the New World* (1941).

Chapter 22: A Time of Readjustment

Anderson, Eric. *Race and Politics in North Carolina, 1872–1901* (1981).

Bromberg, Alan B. " 'The Worst Muddle Ever Seen in North Carolina Politics': The

Farmers' Alliance, the Subtreasury, and Zeb Vance." *North Carolina Historical Review* 56 (January 1979).

Calhoon, Robert M. "An Agrarian and Evangelical Culture." In Lindley S. Butler and Alan D. Watson, eds., *The North Carolina Experience* (1984), pp. 171–91.

Crow, Jeffrey J. "Cracking the Solid South: Populism and the Fusionist Interlude." In Lindley S. Butler and Alan D. Watson, eds., *The North Carolina Experience* (1984), pp. 333–54.

———. "'Fusion, Confusion, and Negroism': Schisms among Negro Republicans in the North Carolina Election of 1896." *North Carolina Historical Review* 53 (October 1976).

———, and Robert F. Durden. *Maverick Republican in the Old North State: A Political Biography of Daniel L. Russell* (1977).

Davidson, Elizabeth H. "The Child-Labor Problem in North Carolina, 1883–1903." *North Carolina Historical Review* 13 (April 1936).

———. "Early Development of Public Opinion against Southern Child Labor." *North Carolina Historical Review* 14 (July 1937).

Durden, Robert F. "North Carolina in the New South." In Lindley S. Butler and Alan D. Watson, eds., *The North Carolina Experience* (1984), pp. 309–32.

Eller, Ron D. *Miners, Millhands, and Mountaineers: Industrialization of the Appalachian South, 1880–1930* (1982).

Faulkner, Ronnie W. "North Carolina Democrats and Silver Fusion Politics, 1892–1896." *North Carolina Historical Review* 59 (July 1982).

Gatewood, Willard B., Jr. "North Carolina and Federal Aid to Education: Public Reaction to the Blair Bill, 1881–1890." *North Carolina Historical Review* 40 (October 1963).

———. "North Carolina's Negro Regiment in the Spanish-American War." *North Carolina Historical Review* 48 (October 1971).

Hunt, James L. "The Making of a Populist: Marion Butler, 1863–1895." *North Carolina Historical Review* 62 (January, April, July 1985).

Jolley, Harley E. "The Labor Movement in North Carolina, 1880–1922." *North Carolina Historical Review* 30 (July 1953).

Logan, Frenise A. "The Movement of Negroes from North Carolina, 1876–1894." *North Carolina Historical Review* 33 (January 1956).

———. *The Negro in North Carolina, 1876–1894* (1964).

Noblin, Stuart. *Leonidas Lafayette Polk: Agrarian Crusader* (1949).

Palmer, Bruce. *"Man Over Money": The Southern Populist Critique of American Capitalism* (1980).

Pinkett, Harold T. "Gifford Pinchot at Biltmore." *North Carolina Historical Review* 34 (July 1957).

Prather, H. Leon, Sr. *We Have Taken a City: Wilmington Racial Massacre and Coup of 1898* (1984).

Sims, Anastatia. "'The Sword of the Spirit': The WCTU and Moral Reform in North Carolina, 1883–1933." *North Carolina Historical Review* 64 (October 1987).

Steelman, Joseph F. *North Carolina's Role in the Spanish-American War* (1975).

———. "Republican Party Strategists and the Issue of Fusion with Populists in North Carolina, 1893–1894." *North Carolina Historical Review* 47 (July 1970).

———. "Vicissitudes of Republican Party Politics: The Campaign of 1892 in North Carolina." *North Carolina Historical Review* 43 (October 1966).

Steelman, Lala Carr. "The Role of Elias Carr in the North Carolina Farmers' Alliance." *North Carolina Historical Review* 57 (April 1980).

Tilley, Nannie M. *The R. J. Reynolds Tobacco Company* (1985).

Trelease, Allen W. "The Fusion Legislature of 1895 and 1897: A Roll-Call Analysis of the North Carolina House of Representatives." *North Carolina Historical Review* 57 (July 1980).

Chapter 23: Great Anticipations for the Twentieth Century

Breen, William J. "The North Carolina Council of Defense during World War I, 1917–1918." *North Carolina Historical Review* 50 (January 1973).

———. "Southern Women in the War: The North Carolina Woman's Committee, 1917–1919." *North Carolina Historical Review* 55 (July 1978).

Brown, Cecil K. *The State Highway System of North Carolina: Its Evolution and Present Status* (1931).

Campbell, John C. *The Southern Highlander and His Homeland* (1921).

Claiborne, Jack. *The "Charlotte Observer": Its Time and Place, 1869–1986* (1986).

Cooper, John M., Jr. *Walter Hines Page: The Southerner as American, 1855–1918* (1977).

Davis, Burke. *The Southern Railway: Road of the Innovators* (1985).

Durden, Robert F. "Crisis in University Governance: The Launching of Duke University, 1925–1935." *North Carolina Historical Review* 64 (July, October 1987).

———. *The Dukes of Durham, 1865–1929* (1975).

———. "Governor Daniel L. Russell Explains His 'South Dakota Bond' Scheme." *North Carolina Historical Review* 38 (October 1961).

———. "The Origins of the Duke Endowment and the Launching of Duke University." *North Carolina Historical Review* 52 (April 1975).

———. *Reconstruction Bonds and Twentieth-Century Politics: South Dakota v. North Carolina (1904)* (1962).

Gatewood, Willard B., Jr. *Controversy in the Twenties: Fundamentalism, Modernism, and Evolution* (1969).

———. "Politics and Piety in North Carolina: The Fundamentalist Crusade at High Tide, 1925–1927." *North Carolina Historical Review* 42 (July 1965).

———. "Professors, Fundamentalists, and the Legislature." In Lindley S. Butler and Alan D. Watson, eds., *The North Carolina Experience* (1984), pp. 355–79.

Lemmon, Sarah M. *North Carolina's Role in the First World War* (1975).

Linder, Suzanne C. "William Louis Poteat and the Evolution Controversy." *North Carolina Historical Review* 40 (April 1963).

———. *William Louis Poteat: Prophet of Progress* (1966).

Loomis, Charles P. "Activities of the North Carolina Farmers' Union." *North Carolina Historical Review* 7 (October 1930).

———. "The Rise and Decline of the North Carolina Farmers' Union." *North Carolina Historical Review* 7 (July 1930).

McLaurin, Melton. "The Knights of Labor in North Carolina Politics." *North Carolina Historical Review* 49 (July 1972).

McMath, Robert C., Jr. "Agrarian Protest at the Forks of the Creek: Three Subordinate Farmers' Alliances in North Carolina." *North Carolina Historical Review* 51 (January 1974).

Mathews, Jane DeHart. "The Status of Women in North Carolina." In Lindley S. Butler and Alan D. Watson, eds., *The North Carolina Experience* (1984), pp. 427–51.

Morrison, Joseph L. *Josephus Daniels: The Small-d Democrat* (1966).

———. "The 'Tar Heel Editor' in North Carolina's Crisis, 1929–1932." *North Carolina Historical Review* 44 (July 1967).

———. *W. J. Cash: Southern Prophet* (1967).

Nathan, Sydney. *The Quest for Progress: The Way We Lived in North Carolina, 1870–1920* (1983).

Orr, Oliver H., Jr. *Charles Brantley Aycock* (1961).

Puryear, Elmer L. *Democratic Party Dissension in North Carolina, 1928–1936.* James Sprunt Studies in History and Political Science, vol. 44 (1962).

———. *Graham A. Barden: Conservative Carolina Congressman* (1979).

Roller, David C. "Republican Factionalism in North Carolina, 1904–1906." *North Carolina Historical Review* 41 (January 1964).

Taylor, A. Elizabeth. "The Woman Suffrage Movement in North Carolina." *North Carolina Historical Review* 38 (January, April 1961).

Watson, Richard L., Jr. "Furnifold M. Simmons: 'Jehovah of the Tar Heels'?" *North Carolina Historical Review* 44 (April 1967).

———. "Principle, Party, and Constituency: The North Carolina Congressional Delegation, 1917–1919." *North Carolina Historical Review* 56 (July 1979).

———. "A Southern Democratic Primary: Simmons vs. Bailey in 1930." *North Carolina Historical Review* 42 (January 1965).

Chapter 24: Down but Not Out: The State Survives the Great Depression

Abrams, Douglas Carl. *North Carolina and the New Deal, 1932–1940* (1981).

Badger, Anthony J. *North Carolina and the New Deal* (1981).

———. *Prosperity Road: The New Deal, Tobacco, and North Carolina* (1980).

Bell, John L. *Hard Times: Beginnings of the Great Depression in North Carolina, 1929–1933* (1982).

Betters, Paul B. *State Centralization in North Carolina* (1932).

Brown, D. Clayton. "North Carolina Rural Electrification: Precedent of the REA." *North Carolina Historical Review* 59 (April 1982).

Buston, Barry M., and Steven M. Beatty, eds. *Blue Ridge Parkway: Agent of Transition* (1986).

Claiborne, Jack. *The Charlotte Observer: Its Time and Place, 1869–1986* (1986).

Hoey, Clyde R. *Addresses, Letters and Papers of Governor Clyde Roark Hoey* (1944).

Morgan, Thomas S., Jr. "A 'folly . . . manifest to everyone': The Movement to Enact Unemployment Insurance Legislation in North Carolina, 1935–1936." *North Carolina Historical Review* 52 (July 1975).

Morrison, Joseph L. *Governor O. Max Gardner: A Power in North Carolina and New Deal Washington* (1971).

North Carolina Emergency Relief Administration. *Emergency Relief in North Carolina* (1936).

Parramore, Thomas C. *Express Lanes and Country Roads: The Way We Lived in North Carolina, 1920–1970* (1983).

Report on a Survey of the Organization and Administration of the State Government of North Carolina Submitted to Governor O. Max Gardner (1930).

Stoesen, Alexander R. "From Ordeal to New Deal: North Carolina in the Great Depression." In Lindley S. Butler and Alan D. Watson, eds., *The North Carolina Experience* (1984), pp. 381–404.

Terrill, Tom E., and Jerrold Hirsch, eds. *Such As Us: Southern Voices of the Thirties* (1978).

Chapter 25: New Points to Ponder in a Restless World

Billinger, Robert D., Jr. "Behind the Wire: German Prisoners at Camp Sutton, 1944–1946." *North Carolina Historical Review* 61 (October 1984).

Black, Earl. *Southern Governors and Civil Rights* (1976).

Burns, Augustus M., III. "Graduate Education for Blacks in North Carolina, 1930–1951." *Journal of Southern History* 46 (May 1980).

Eagles, Charles E. "Two 'Double V's': Jonathan Daniels, FDR, and Race Relations during World War II." *North Carolina Historical Review* 59 (July 1982).

Foushee, Ola Maie. *Art in North Carolina: Episodes and Developments, 1585–1970* (1972).

Gatewood, Willard B., Jr. "North Carolina's Role in the Establishment of the Great Smoky Mountains National Park." *North Carolina Historical Review* 37 (April 1960).

Hodges, Luther H. *Addresses and Papers of Governor Luther Hartwell Hodges*. 3 vols. (1960, 1962, 1964).

———. *Businessman in the Statehouse: Six Years as Governor of North Carolina* (1962).

Jolley, Harley E. *The Blue Ridge Parkway* (1969).

King, Arnold K. *The Multicampus University of North Carolina Comes of Age, 1956–1986* (1987).

Lemmon, Sarah M. *North Carolina's Role in World War II* (1985).

Morris, Willie, ed. *The South Today: 100 Years After Appomattox* (1965).

Parramore, Thomas C. "Sit-Ins and Civil Rights." In Lindley S. Butler and Alan D. Watson, eds., *The North Carolina Experience* (1984), pp. 405–25.

Reagan, Alice Elizabeth. *North Carolina State University: A Narrative History* (1987).

Sanford, Terry. *Addresses and Papers of Governor Terry Sanford* (1966).

———. *But What About the People?* (1966).

Scales, Junius I., and Richard Nickson. *Cause at Heart: A Former Communist Remembers* (1987).

Scott, W. Kerr. *A Report to the People* (1952).

Spence, James R. *The Moore-Preyer-Lake Primaries of 1964: The Making of a Governor* (1968).

Waynick, Capus M., and others, eds. *North Carolina and the Negro* (1964).

Chapter 26: A New Face for the State

Bagwell, William. *School Desegregation in the Carolinas: Two Case Studies* (1972).

Barrows, Frank. "School Busing, Charlotte, N.C." *Atlantic Monthly* 230 (November 1972).

Bass, Jack, and Walter De Vries. *The Transformation of Southern Politics: Social Change and Political Consequence since 1944* (1976).

Beyle, Thad L., and Merle Black, eds. *Politics and Policy in North Carolina* (1975).

Chafe, William H. *Civilities and Civil Rights: Greensboro, N.C., and the Black Struggle for Freedom* (1981).

Daniels, Lee A. "In Defense of Busing." *New York Times Magazine*, 17 April 1983.

A Dynamic Concept for Research: The Research Triangle Park of North Carolina (1981).

Furguson, Ernest B. *Hard Right: The Rise of Jesse Helms* (1986).

Hamilton, William B. "The Research Triangle of North Carolina: A Study in Leadership for the Common Weal." *South Atlantic Quarterly* 65 (Spring 1966).

Herzik, Eric B., and Sallye B. Teater, comps. *North Carolina Focus* (1981).

Holshouser, James E., Jr. *Addresses and Papers of Governor James Eubert Holshouser, Jr.* (1978).

Hunt, James B., Jr. *Addresses and Public Papers of James Baxter Hunt, Jr., Governor of North Carolina.* 2 vols. (1982, 1988).

Moore, Dan K. *Addresses and Papers of Governor Dan K. Moore* (1971).

Myerson, Michael. *Nothing Could Be Finer* (1978).

Reed, John S. *Southerners: The Social Psychology of Sectionalism* (1983).

Roland, Charles P. *The Improbable Era: The South since World War II* (1975).

Scott, Robert W. *Addresses and Public Papers of Robert W. Scott, Governor of North Carolina* (1974).

Snider, William D. *Helms and Hunt: The North Carolina Senate Race, 1984* (1985).

Watters, Pat. *Charlotte, North Carolina: "A Little Child Shall Lead Them"* (1971).

Wolff, Miles. *Lunch at the Five and Ten: The Greensboro Sit-Ins* (1970).

Chapter 27: The State Looks to the Future

Commission on the Future of North Carolina. *The Future of North Carolina: Goals and Recommendations for the Year 2000* (n.d.).

Wicker, Warren Jake, ed. *North Carolina: Directions for the 1980s: 1980 Proceedings: The Second Annual Urban Affairs Conference of the University of North Carolina* (1980).

————. *Urban Growth and Urban Lives: 1981 Proceedings: The Third Annual Urban Affairs Conference of the University of North Carolina* (1981).

INDEX

Pages on which illustrations appear are indicated in italic type.

A

Abbot, Rev. Henry, 125

Abbot, Rev. John, 125

Abbott, Gen. Joseph C. (carpetbagger), 392, 395

Abercromby, James (agent), 145

Aberdeen, 3

Abolition, 331-34, 351; societies, 308-9

Academic freedom, 458-59

Academies, 215-16, 245-46, 317

Act of Pardon and Oblivion, 208, 211

Adams, Rev. James, 127-30

Adams, John, 172, 186

"Address to the People of Granville County" (George Sims), 151

Address . . . on the Evils of Slavery, An, 298

Adult education, 496-97

Ad valorem tax, 187-90, 251-52, 339-45, 347-48

Advancement School (Winston Salem), 590

Advisory Budget Commission, 472, 475

Africa, exploration of, 28

Agents for North Carolina, stationed abroad, 102-3, 145, 189-90. *See also* Abercromby, James; Barker, Thomas; McCulloh, Henry Eustace

Agricultural and Technical College for Negroes (Greensboro), 479, 507-8

Agricultural relief programs, 493

Agriculture, 131-34, 309-11; poor conditions and low prices, 416-18, 422, 486; diversification in, 496. *See also* individual crops

Agriculture, Board of, 496-97

Agriculture, Department of, 405

Aircraft plants (World War II), 502

Airmail service, 477

Airplane flight, first manned, 450-51

Air raid drills (World War II), 504

Alabama, 5, 25-26, 32-33; migration to, 249-50

Alamance, Battle of, 140, 157-59, 167

Alamance County, 122-27, 338, 398, 408

"Alamance plaids," 315-16

Albany Congress, 99-100, 217-18

Albemarle (ship), 362-63, 367

Albemarle County, 55-86, 123

Albemarle section: and Cape Fear section, 83-84, 93; government of, 93-94, 143-44; joins forces with west, 269

Albemarle Sound, 29-30, 52, 76, 143, 261; channel for trade, 140; fisheries along, 314

Albright, William, 285

Albright, William R. (mayor and Union League leader), 397

Alcoholic beverages, 118-19, 121, 122; consumed at funerals, 120-21; control of, 451-52. *See also* Ale; Liquor; Prohibition

Alcoholic Control, State Board of, 498

Alderson, Simon, 69-70

Ale, 39, 43

Alexander, Julia (antievolutionist), 466

Alexander, Nathaniel (governor), 260

Alexander, Sydenham B., 441

Alexander VI (pope), 28

Alexander brothers, 150

Alfalfa, 133-34

Algonquian language, 17, 20

Almanacs, 110, 309-10, 323

Amadas, Philip (explorer), 16, 37-40

Amadas and Barlowe expedition, 21-22

Ambulance planes (World War II), 504

American Association of Textile Chemists and Colorists (Research Triangle Park), 530-31

American Colonization Society, 297-99, 330-31

American Federation of Labor, 487

American party, 367-69

American Revolution. *See* Revolutionary War

American Tobacco Company, created by Dukes, 408-9

America's Four Hundredth Anniversary, 544

Andrews, Alexander B., 407

Andrews, Samuel (Loyalist), 211

Andrews, T. Wingate (school superintendent), 462

Anglican church, 122-27, 292-93. *See also* Church of England

Annapolis (Maryland) Convention, 221

Anne (queen of England), 72, 108

Annual Register, The, 129

Anson County, 108-9, 154, 311-12, 548-49

Anti-Communist sentiment. *See* Labor unrest

Anti-Evolution League of America, 465

Anti-Federalists, 224-25, 230-31